管理学原理

（汉英对照）

Principles of Management

刘治江 编著　卜国琴 译

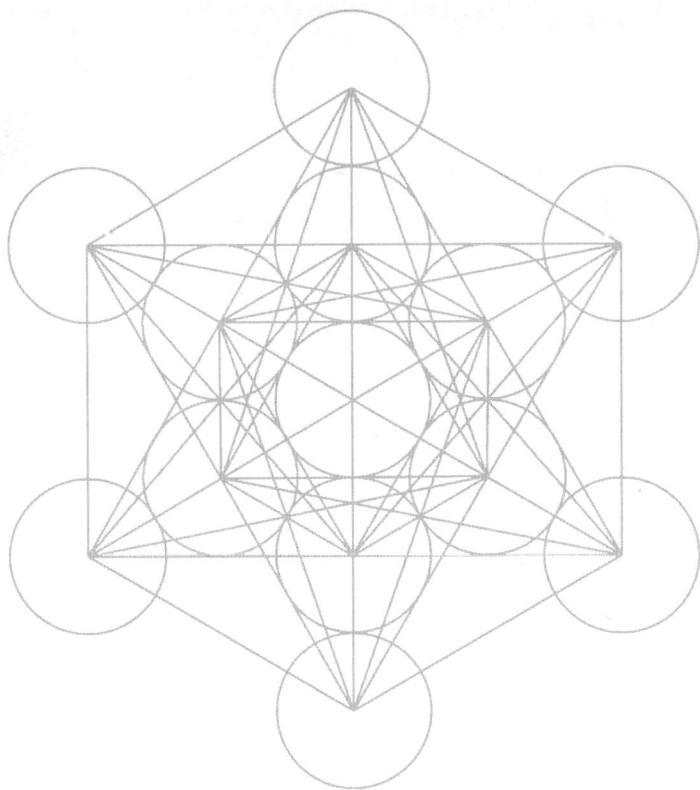

暨南大学出版社
JINAN UNIVERSITY PRESS

中国·广州

图书在版编目（CIP）数据

管理学原理：汉英对照/刘治江编著；卜国琴译. —广州：暨南大学出版社，2016.1

ISBN 978 - 7 - 5668 - 1584 - 2

Ⅰ. ①管…　Ⅱ. ①刘…②卜…　Ⅲ. ①管理学—成人高等教育—教材—汉英对照　Ⅳ. ①C93

中国版本图书馆 CIP 数据核字（2015）第 183785 号

出版发行：暨南大学出版社

地　址：中国广州暨南大学
电　话：总编室（8620）85221601
　　　　营销部（8620）85225284　85228291　85228292（邮购）
传　真：(8620) 85221583（办公室）　85223774（营销部）
邮　编：510630
网　址：http://www.jnupress.com　http://press.jnu.edu.cn
排　版：广州市科普电脑印务部
印　刷：广东广州日报传媒股份有限公司印务分公司
开　本：787mm×1092mm　1/16
印　张：27.25
字　数：750 千
版　次：2016 年 1 月第 1 版
印　次：2016 年 1 月第 1 次
定　价：68.00 元

（暨大版图书如有印装质量问题，请与出版社总编室联系调换）

前　言

　　早在人类文明的曙光初现，管理就已经与我们同行。管理是智慧、科学、能力和经验的完美结合。管理大师德鲁克指出：管理是一种实践，其本质不在于知，而在于行；其验证不在于逻辑，而在于成果。管理学融思想性、理论性、实践性和方法性于一体，不仅要传授管理的基本知识，更要培养和提升管理的基本技能。本书以培养高素质、创新型人才为目标，以传授管理知识为基础，以提升管理能力为本位，兼顾知识、技能与应用的统一，力求体系完整、内容简明、结构新颖、学用结合、注重应用、强化实践。

　　本书共分为五个部分：第一部分为管理概述，包括第一章、第二章；第二部分为计划，包括第三章、第四章、第五章；第三部分为组织，包括第六章、第七章、第八章；第四部分为领导，包括第九章、第十章、第十一章；第五部分为控制与创新，包括第十二章、第十三章。每章前有本章学习目标、小故事和引例作引导，章中适时插入新视角、小链接和阅读资料，章后有本章提要、关键词、复习与思考、研究与讨论、实践演练、管理模拟、本章案例和本章参考文献，丰富了学习资源，以便进一步深化学习内容、体验管理实践、提升管理能力。

　　本书内容为汉英对照，由刘治江编著，卜国琴主译，适用于准备或正在从事管理工作的人们，如经济、管理类本科生、专科生，各类管理人员等。本书在写作过程中，参阅和引用了许多管理学的教材和研究成果，在此谨向各位作者表示衷心的感谢，也感谢暨南大学国际商学院2012级国际商务专业参与文稿翻译的学生。同时，感谢暨南大学出版社对本书的大力支持和帮助。本书的出版得到了暨南大学相关经费支持。由于笔者水平有限，书中不妥之处在所难免，恳请广大读者不吝赐教。

刘治江

2015 年 10 月于暨南大学国际商学院

目　录

第一章　管理、管理者与管理系统

Chapter 1　Management, Manager and Management System

管理，从根本上说，意味着用智慧代替鲁莽，用知识代替习惯与传统，用合作代替强制。

彼得·F. 德鲁克

Management, fundamentally speaking, means substituting wisdom for reckless, substituting knowledge for habit and tradition, substituting cooperation for force.

Peter F. Drucker

管理是由心智所驱使的唯一无处不在的人类活动。

戴维·B. 赫尔茨

Management is driven by the mind and is the only ubiquitous human activity.

David B. Hertz

【本章学习目标】

知识目标：

管理的含义、特征和基本职能。

管理者的角色、心智模式及其能力结构。

管理系统的概念及其构成要素。

技能目标：

解释管理的基本概念。

认知管理者的角色与素质。

有意识地培养自己的管理能力。

学会分析管理案例。

【Learning Objectives of Chapter 1】

Objectives of Knowledge：

The definition, features and basic functions of management.

The role, mental model and ability structure of manager.

The definition and components of management system.

Objectives of Skill：

Explain the basic concepts of management.

Understand the role and qualities of manager.

Develop your own management ability consciously.

Learn to analyze management cases.

【小故事】

一把沉重的铁锁挂在门上，有人找来一根铁棒去敲打它，无论怎样用力也打不开。这时，另外一个人来了，他拿出一片小小的钥匙，往锁孔里一插，"咔嚓"一声，锁就开了。等别人都走了，迷惑不解的铁棒问小钥匙："为什么我用那么大的力气都打不开的锁，你轻轻一下就可以打开了呢？"小钥匙回答道："因为我懂得它的心。"是啊，管理永远与人打交道，如果能懂得人的心，就掌握了开启成功管理大门的钥匙。

【引例】

李先生和他的公司

李先生于 5 年前创建了一家服装公司，当时只有 6 个人的小公司，如今已发展到拥有 80 多名员工、年销售额达 500 万元的规模。

尽管企业的规模和利润水平发生了显著的变化，但李先生的行事方式却依然如故。他认为，自己是公司老板，最了解公司，自己能够对公司的所有决策负责。从公司成立开始，公司的大事小事全都由他一个人做主。当他出差到外地时，许多该做的事只好搁置下来，等他回来后再处理。他能叫出所有员工的名字，任何人都可以随时走进他的办公室。

随着公司的不断壮大，李先生觉得压力越来越大，日常事务花费了他大部分时间和精力，他没有时间坐下来考虑一下公司的将来。员工们碰到难题也很难找到他商量对策，士气大不如前，甚至有两名创业时的骨干也跳槽到了别的公司。

李先生自己也觉得不像以前那样得心应手了，过度的疲劳使他感到力不从心，他甚至想过卖掉公司以换回自己的健康和宁静。

（资料来源：刘治江：《管理学——知识、技能与应用》，北京：经济管理出版社 2008 年版）

思考问题：

1. 管理欲使工作复杂化还是简单化？

2. 该公司存在的主要问题是什么？

3. 如果你是李先生的管理顾问，你会给他提供什么样的建议？

第一节　什么是管理

管理活动自有人群出现便存在，管理思想也随之产生。管理是一种社会活动，由于人们在共同劳动中需要进行协作而产生，广泛适用于社会的各个领域。

一、管理的概念

究竟什么是管理，管理学界众说纷纭。由于管理实践的差异性，导致了人们对管理认识和理解的不同。

比较一致的观点是：①管理是为实现组织目标服务的，是一个有意识、有目的的活动过程。②管理工作由一系列相互关联、连续进行的活动（职能）构成。③管理要通过综合运用组织中的各种资源来实现组织的目标。④管理活动是在一定的环境条件下进行的，需要设计并维持一种环境，因而从时间的角度来看，管理是一个动态过程。

管理就是在特定的环境下，对组织所拥有的资源进行有效的计划、组织、领导和控制，以便达成既定的组织目标的活动过程。

【小链接】
管理的其他定义

马克思：一切规模较大的直接社会劳动或共同劳动都或多或少需要指挥以协调个人的活动，并执行生产总体的运动——不同于这一总体的独立器官的运动——所产生的各种一般职能。

泰　罗：管理就是"确切地知道你要别人去干什么，并使他用最好的方法去干。"

法约尔：管理是所有人类组织都有的人类活动，这种活动由五项要素组成——计划、组织、指挥、协调、控制。

西　蒙：管理就是决策。

梅　西：管理就是通过其他人来完成工作。

孔　茨：管理就是为在集体中工作的人员谋划和保持一个能使他们完成预定目标和任务的工作环境。

唐纳利：管理就是一个或更多的人来协调他人的活动，以便收到个人单独活动所不能收到的效果。

雷　恩：管理就是这样一种活动，即发挥某些职能，以便有效地获取、分配和利用人的努力和物资资源，来实现某种目标。

罗宾斯：管理是指同别人一起或通过别人使活动完成得更有效的过程。

德鲁克：管理是一种以绩效责任为基础的专业职能。

二、管理的特征

1. 动态性

动态性主要表现在管理活动需要在变动的环境与组织中进行，需要消除资源配置的各种不确定性。管理客体、管理对象、管理时空、管理工具和手段、管理结果等，均存在不确定性，因而管理是动态的、发展变化的。

2. 科学性

管理活动尽管是动态的，但还是可将其分成两大类，一是程序性的活动，二是非程序性的活动。这两类活动是可以转化的，这种转化过程就是人们对管理活动及其规律性的认识和科学总结，管理的科学性就体现在这里。

3. 艺术性

由于管理对象经常处在不同的环境、行业、产出要求、资源供给等状况下，这就导致对每一个具体管理对象没有一个唯一的、完全有效的模式，从而造成具体的管理活动与管理技巧的发挥有很大关系，这种管理技巧就是管理艺术性的体现。

4. 创造性

管理既然是一种动态活动，对具体管理对象没有唯一模式可参考，那么要想达到预期的目标就要发挥创造性，管理的创造性根植于动态性之中，与科学性和艺术性相关。"不创新即死亡"，就充分说明了这一点。

5. 经济性

资源配置是需要成本的，管理的经济性首先反映在资源配置的机会成本上；其次反映在管理方式、方法的成本比较上；再次还反映在对资源有效的整合过程中，选择不同的资源供给和配比，也有成本大小的问题。

三、管理的性质

从本质上看，管理具有二重性，一是与生产力相联系的自然属性；二是与生产关系、社会文化相联系的社会属性。

管理具有自然属性是因为管理过程就是对人力、财务、信息、时间等资源进行组合和利用的过程，管理揭示了这些规律，并创造了与之相适应的管理手段和方法。管理活动只有遵循这些规律，利用这些手段和方法才能取得成效。这为我们学习和借鉴发达国家先进管理经验和方法提供了理论依据。

管理具有社会属性是因为管理是人类活动，是在一定的生产关系和一定的社会文化中进行的。不同的生产关系和社会文化，都会使管理思想、管理目的、管理方式等呈现出一定的差别，从而使管理具有特殊性，它既是生产关系和社会文化的体现和反映，又反作用于生产关系和社会文化。这告诉我们管理必须从实际出发，建立有特色的管理模式。

四、管理的职能

管理的职能是指管理者为履行职责、完成任务所必须具备的基本功能，换句话说就是管理者在管理过程中所从事的各种活动或发挥的各种作用。关于管理的职能，人们的意见不一，但基本上可以概括为四项：计划、组织、领导、控制。

计划：是指管理者在实际行动之前，预先对应当追求的目标和应采取的行动方案，做出选择和具体的安排。它包括三项主要活动：一是确定目标，二是制定战略，三是编制并实施计划。

组织：是对实现组织目标的各种要素和人们在活动中的相互关系进行组合和配置，从而建立起一个有机整体。它包括四项主要活动：一是设计组织，二是配备人员，三是制定组织制度，四是监督运行。

领导：是指利用组织赋予的权力，通过信息沟通带领和指挥全体成员执行组织的计划，实现组织的目标，它包括三项主要活动：一是运用影响力，二是沟通，三是激励。

控制：是将计划的执行情况与计划、要求目标相对照，发现偏差并采取相应的管理行为，以确保计划目标的实现。它包括四项活动：一是确定控制标准，二是衡量实际成效，三是比较分析，四是采取管理行动。

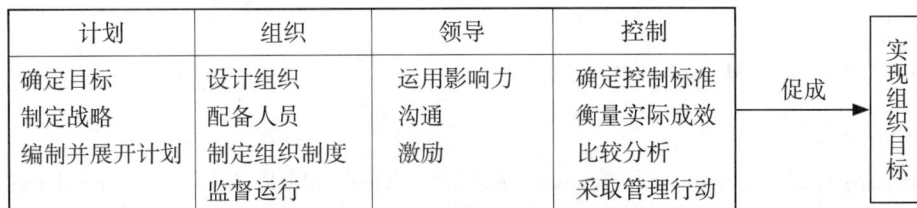

计划	组织	领导	控制		实现组织目标
确定目标 制定战略 编制并展开计划	设计组织 配备人员 制定组织制度 监督运行	运用影响力 沟通 激励	确定控制标准 衡量实际成效 比较分析 采取管理行动	促成	

图 1-1 管理的基本职能

在实际工作中，这四项职能从时间的逻辑关系看是按照计划—组织—领导—控制的顺序进行的，但实际上却是相互交叉的，在周而复始地循环，从而使管理过程不断推进和逐步提升。

越来越多的学者认为，创新是管理过程的重要环节，是重要的管理活动，贯穿于各种管理职能和各个组织层次，是管理职能的逻辑发展。

五、管理学

管理学是研究各类组织管理活动的基本规律和一般方法的科学。管理学的研究对象是管理活动中的各种现象及其内在的本质联系。管理学亦是发展中的一门科学，具有综合性、艺术性、不精确性和实践性的特点。

人们在整合管理知识时也有着不同的导向。我们认为，一般而论，这种导向分理论导向与应用导向两大类。仿照经济学的分类，我们可以把管理学分称为理论管理学和应用管理学。理论管理学侧重于对组织的活动进行描述、解释和预测，以发现管理的规律、原则及形成管理理论体系为主；应用管理学则侧重于对管理政策、管理方案进行研究，以总结经验、教训，以解决问题和运用管理理论中的规律与原则为主。

Section 1　What Is Management

Management activities appeared since human come into being, and the idea of management arose as well. Management is a kind of social activity generated because of the need of collaboration in collective labor, and widely used in every field of the society.

1.1.1　Concept of Management

Opinions vary greatly in the management academia about the concept of management. The differences in management practice lead to different cognitions and understandings of management.

The opinions that almost everyone agrees are: ①Management is a conscious and purposive activity process whose aim is to achieve the goal of an organization. ②Management consists of a series of correlative and ongoing activities (functions). ③To achieve the goals of the organization, management needs to comprehensively use various kinds of resources in the organization. ④Management activities are conducted under certain environmental conditions, it needs to design and maintain a certain kind of environment. So from the aspect of time, management is a dynamic process.

1.1.2　Features of Management

1. Dynamics

Dynamics is mainly embodied in management activities which should be carried out in the changing environments and organizations for eliminating various kinds of uncertainties in allocation of resources. Uncertainties exist in management object, management target, management time and space, management methods and means, management results, thus management is dynamic, developing and changing.

2. Scientificity

Although management activities are dynamic, they can be divided into two categories, one is procedural activities, and the other is non-procedural activities. These two types of activities can be reversed, the reversion process is the cognition and scientific summary of management activities and its regularity, and the science of management is reflected in it.

3. Artistry

Because the management target is often under different environments, industries, production requirements and resource supply, etc., there is no sole, completely effective mode for every specific management target. As a result, the specific management activities have much to do with the role of management skills, and this kind of management skills is the embodiment of management artistry.

4. Creativity

Since management is a kind of dynamic activities, and as there is no sole mode for a specific management target for reference, so if you want to achieve the prospective goal you have to develop creativity. The creativity of management is rooted in the dynamics relating to the scientificity and artistry. The saying "no innovation means death" fully illustrates this point.

5. Economy

Resource allocation needs cost, so firstly the economy of management is reflected in the opportunity cost of the allocation of resources. Secondly, the economy of management is reflected in the comparison of the costs of different management approaches, methods. Thirdly, the economy of management is also reflected in the effective integration process of resources which means the selection and proportioning of resource supplies which leads to different costs.

1.1.3　Nature of Management

In essence, management has duality, one is in natural quality which is associated with productivity, the other is in social attribute which is associated with productive relations and social culture.

Management has a natural quality because the management process is the process that combines and utilizes the personnel, finance, information, time and other resources. Management reveals these relative laws and creates corresponding management means and methods. Management activities have to follow these laws and use these means and methods in order to achieve certain effects. It provides a theoretical basis for us to study and draw lessons of advanced management experiences and methods from developed countries.

Management has social attribute because management is a human activity which is under certain production relations and certain social culture. Different production relationships and social culture will make the management idea, management purpose and management mode different, bringing forth particularity of management. It is the embodiment and reflection of production relations and social culture, and reacts upon production relationships and social culture. This tells us to establish distinctive management patterns practically.

1.1.4 Functions of Management

Functions of management mean the basic functions that managers must have to perform their duties to complete the tasks, in other words, they refer to various activities or roles the managers are engaged in during the management process. Opinions about the functions of management are different, but basically they can be summarized as four items: planning, organizing, leading, and controlling.

Planning: Planning means that the managers make choice and specific arrangement for the goals pursued and actions taken before the real actions. It consists of three major activities: the first is to determine the goal, the second is to formulate strategy, the third is to establish and execute the plan.

Organizing: Organizing is the combination and configuration of various elements to achieve organizational goals and the interrelationships of people's activities in order to establish an organic whole. It consists of four main activities: the first is to design organization, the second is to team it with staff, the third is to establish organizational institutions, the fourth is to supervise the operation.

Leading: Leading means guiding and commanding all the members to execute the organization's plan and achieve the goal of the organization by using the power given by the organization through information communication. It includes three main activities: the first is to use the influence, the second is to communicate, the third is to motivate.

Controlling: Controlling means comparing the implementation of a plan with the plan and the requiring goals to find out deviations and take corresponding managerial measures in order to ensure the realization of the target of the initial plan. It includes four activities: the first is to determine the control standards, the second is to measure the actual effects, the third is to compare and analyze, the fourth is to take managerial actions.

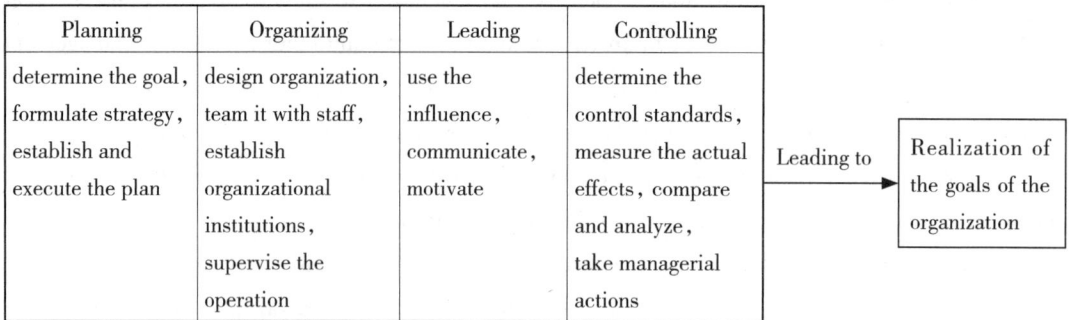

Planning	Organizing	Leading	Controlling		
determine the goal, formulate strategy, establish and execute the plan	design organization, team it with staff, establish organizational institutions, supervise the operation	use the influence, communicate, motivate	determine the control standards, measure the actual effects, compare and analyze, take managerial actions	Leading to	Realization of the goals of the organization

Diagram 1 – 1   Basic Functions of Management

In practice, these four functions are conducted in chronological order of planning, organization, leadership, and control. But they are employed alternatively, advancing in endless cycles, so that the managerial process can go ahead and upgrade.

A growing number of scholars believe that innovation is an important stage in the managerial process, and also an important managerial activity throughout various managerial functions and each level of the organization, what's more, it is the logical development of the managerial functions.

1. 1. 5   Management Science

Management is a science to study the basic rules and the general methods of managerial activities of various kinds of organizations. The research object of management science is the various phenomena in the managerial activities and their essential interrelationships. Management is also a science in development with the characteristics of comprehensiveness, artistry, inaccuracy and practicality.

People have different guidelines when trying to integrate managerial knowledge. Generally speaking, we think that there are two types of guidelines: the theoretical one and the applicable one. Following the classification of economics, we can divide management science into theoretic management and applicable management. Theoretic management focuses on describing, explaining and predicting activities of organizations to discover managerial laws, principles and develop the theoretical system of management. Applicable management mainly concentrates on the study of managerial policies, and schemes to sum up experience and lessons, solve problems and utilize the laws and principles of managerial theories.

【新视角】

管理是科学、艺术和哲学的统一

目前，认为管理既是科学又是艺术已成为神圣的信条，权威的教科书视之为公理。其实，管理不仅仅是科学、艺术，还是哲学。管理的科学性是指蕴藏在管理活动中的内在联系和客观规律，它表现为管理活动的一般原则及大量模型工具，这些不受时间、地域、行业、企业和管理者的制约。管理是艺术的主要是因为管理的主体和客体皆离不开人，管理活动会受到人的感情、意志、个性、能力等诸多无法用科学方法检测和度量的非理性因素的制约，管理活动因而千差万别。管理还是一种有目的的实践活动，会受到管理主体人生观、价值观、世界观的支配，这又与民族、地域、国家、文化、历史息息相关，主要表现在管理的理念、价值观等企业文化领域，属于哲学范畴。

第二节　管理者

一、谁是管理者

管理者就是在协作过程中，负责协调他人的活动，从而对组织完成预期任务做出贡献的人员。通常，管理者由两个部分构成：一是根据组织既定目标，将目标任务分解为各类管理活动、工作任务和负有最终督促完成既定目标任务的人，这类人是组织的核心人物，或高级领导人物；二是各方面具体执行诸如计划、组织、控制等管理活动的人，这类人通常是组织中的骨干人物。管理者是组织中的重要群体。

有效率的管理者既要完成任务，又要达到目标，在协调他人活动时要进行各种管理工作。所谓管理工作是指管理者在协调他人工作的过程中所从事的能够使他对组织完成预期任务做出贡献的各种活动。

二、管理者的类型

从纵向看或按管理者所处的层次划分，可把管理者分为基层管理者、中层管理者和高层管理者三种类型。管理者在每个层次的人数由基层到高层依次减少，形成一个金字塔。基层管理者负责指挥和协调非管理人员的活动，不指挥其他管理者。中层管理者负责指挥和协调下级管理者的活动，有时也直接指挥少数非管理人员。高层管理者通过指挥中层管理者来协调整个组织的活动，在一个组织内不受别人的指挥。

从横向看或按从事管理的领域来划分，可将管理者分为综合管理者和职能管理者两类。综合管理者一般是高层管理者，只负责管理组织中若干类乃至全部的管理者，如总经理；职能管理者仅仅负责某项管理职能活动，一般由中层或基层管理者担当，如人事、财务、营销等。

按不同的职务类型划分，可将管理者分为董事长、总经理、部门经理、项目经理等。

【阅读资料】

管理角色和任务的转变

	基层管理者	中层管理者	高层管理者
变化的角色	从运作执行者变成进取的企业家	从管理控制者变成支持性教练	从资源分配者变成机构领导者
基本价值观	在一线部门内通过专注于生产率、创新和成长实现业务绩效	通过支持和协调使大公司的优势体现到独立的一线部门中	在整个组织中创造一种方向感、投入精神和挑战的气氛
关键活动	创造和抓住新的业务成长机会； 吸引、开发资源和能力； 实行管理以使部门内的绩效不断改进	人员开发并提供支持； 将单位内分散的知识、技能和最佳经验联系起来； 协调短期绩效和长期战略间的矛盾	在确定扩张机遇范围和绩效标准时挑战已有假设； 建立一整套规范和价值观体系以支持合作与信任； 创立整个公司的目标和战略

（资料来源：C. Bartlett, S. Goshal. The Myth of the Generic Manager：New Personal Competencies for New Management Roles. *California Management Review*, Vol. 40, No. 1, 1977, pp. 92 – 116）

三、管理者的角色

管理学家亨利·明茨伯格通过研究发现：管理者通常扮演着十种不同的但又高度相关的角色。这十种角色又可以进一步归为三类：

（1）人际关系角色：指管理者与各种人发生各种联系时所担当的角色，这类角色以人为中心，以交往领导联络为手段，大致可分为三种不同的角色：①挂名领导；②领导者；③联络者。

（2）信息传递角色：指管理者在获取、处理、传递各种信息资源时所起的作用。这类角色以信息沟通为中心，以信息搜集、加工和传播为手段，大致可分为三种不同的角色：①监听者；②传播者；③发言人。

（3）决策制定角色：指管理者在管理过程中对一系列重大的或突发的问题做出决策并付诸实施，这类角色以角色为中心，以推动变革、排除故障、分配资源和谈判为手段，大致可分为四种角色：①企业家；②混乱驾驭者；③资源分配者；④谈判者。

在现实中，当组织类型不同，组织内所处不同层次的管理者所扮演的这十种角色的侧重点是不同的，这就是管理者角色的变动，如图1-2所示。

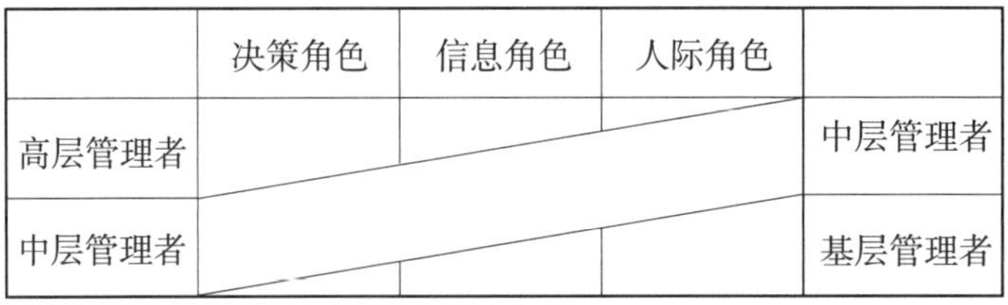

	决策角色	信息角色	人际角色	
高层管理者				中层管理者
中层管理者				基层管理者

图1-2 管理者角色与管理者层次

管理者的活动与花费的时间

费雷德·卢森斯认为管理者主要从事四种活动：①传统管理；②沟通；③人力资源管理；④网络联系。而且认为一般的管理者、成功的管理者、有效的管理者在这四种活动上所花费的时间是不同的。这三类管理者在传统管理上花费的时间分别为：32%、13%、19%；在沟通上花费的时间分别为：29%、28%、44%；在人力资源管理上花费的时间分别为：20%、11%、26%；在网络联系上花费的时间分别为：19%、48%、11%。

四、管理者的技能要求

一般来说，管理者应具备的技能包括：技术技能、人事技能、决策技能三种。

（1）技术技能：利用技术完成组织任务的能力，管理者要了解、掌握与其管理专业领域相关的基本技术知识，以便进行有效的管理。

（2）人事技能：管理人员必须具有识别人、任用人、团结人、组织人、调动人的积极性以实现组织目标的能力。

（3）决策技能：分析判断和做出决策的能力，管理者所处的层次越高，其面临的环境和问题就越复杂，就越需要决策技能。

上述三种技能，对于不同层次的管理人员其要求是不同的。处于较低层次的管理人员需要的主要是技术技能和人事技能；处于较高层次的管理人员，更强调人事技能和决策技能；对处于最高层次的管理人员来说，决策技能是最重要的。

五、管理者的心智模式

心智模式是指由过去的经历、知识素养、价值观形成的基本稳定的思维方式和行为习惯。心智模式一旦形成，人将自觉或不自觉地从某个固定的角度认识和思考出现的问题，并用习惯的方式加以解决。任何人都有自己特殊的心智模式，这既是受教育的结果，也是在特定的生活、工作环境下逐步形成的。

管理者的心智模式将在很大程度上决定管理者的思维和行为，最终直接影响管理活动的效率和效益。那么管理者尤其是优秀的管理者，其心智模式是怎样的呢？

（1）远见卓识：表现为：①及时掌握当代最新的管理科技知识和信息；②系统的思维方式；③奋发向上的价值取向。

（2）健全的心理：心理素质是指一个人的活动过程和个性方面表现出来的持久而稳定的基本特点，从众多的优秀个性心理来看，以下几种心理特征非常重要：①自知与自信；②情感与情绪；③智慧和胆识；④宽容和忍耐。

（3）优秀的品质：优秀的品质是一个人形成良好习惯的重要因素和基础，管理者良好心智模式的形成离不开其优秀品质的养成。这些品质包括：①勇于开拓；②使命感；③勤奋好学；④乐观热情；⑤诚实与机敏。

六、管理者的能力结构

管理者必须具备一定的能力，才能完成管理的过程，而这种能力是各种能力的集合。关键能力有以下几个方面：

（1）创新能力：它基于一个人的创新意识，是优秀管理者最重要的能力。富有创新能力的管理者，通常有如下一些主要特征：兴趣广泛，有敏锐的洞察力、系统思维和辩证思维，能独立思考，有自信心，敢于面对困境等。

（2）转化能力：指管理者将创意转化为可操作的具体工作方案的能力。所以，没有从事实际管理工作，就不能成为真正的管理者，转化能力表现为综合、移植、改造、创新的能力。

（3）应变能力：应变能力主要表现在能在变化中产生应对的创意和策略；能审时度势，随机应变，在变化中辨明方向，持之以恒。

（4）组织协调能力：在一个企业的投入—转化—产出过程中，组织协调能力显得尤为重要，没有组织协调就等于没有管理。管理的组织协调能力体现在能否培养出一种团队精神，使组织的各项工作优化运作，强化个体与整体的协调与反馈。

七、管理者的道德与社会责任

1. 四种不同的道德观

管理道德就是规定管理行为正确与否的原则或标准。在道德标准方面有四种不同的观点：

一是功利观，即完全按照成果或结果处理管理问题的一种观点。

二是权力观，这是与尊重和保护个人自由和特权有关的观点。

三是公正观，即管理者按公平或公正的原则行事。

四是社会契约观，即管理者要按各行业和各企业现有道德准则进行决策。

在实践中，大部分人采用功利观，因为这与效率、利润等目标相一致。功利主义为多数人的利益牺牲了少数人的利益，强调了社会的权利和社会公正的新趋势，意味着管理者需要以非公益标准为基础的道德组织，这对当今的管理者是一个挑战，因为依据个人权利和社会公正的标准来制定的决策，要比依据效率和利润等功利标准制定决策有更大的模糊性，因而导致管理面临道德管理的困境。

2. 影响管理道德的因素

一个管理者的行为是否合乎道德，是管理者道德管理发展阶段与个人特征、组织结构设计、组织文化及大多数问题的强度之间复杂的相互作用的结果。

【阅读资料】

不同的意见

商人有道德吗？下面的陈述摘自对美国总裁们颇有影响的杂志《跨越边界》最近的一篇文章：

● 商业"是一种游戏，其规则不同于社会中其他的规则"。

- "大部分大型企业……苦于道德规范太多。他们拥有高尚的道德……鼓吹的道德，但有时是实际中的道德。"
- MBA 的学生"在欺骗和说谎方面不一定比别人多，但他们……更容易接受他人的不道德行为，因为他们认为那是正常的"。
- "商业的实质是竞争。其实商业更是一种游戏，获胜比如何玩儿更重要。"
- "在大多数不出名的不光彩的案例中——Pinto 爆炸案是一个有名的例子——那不只是一个人做了错事，而通常是很多人都做了错事。"
- "所有的人都认为说谎是不道德的，但是在采购谈判过程中，很多人却认为误导不代表说谎，因为如果所有人都知道，每个人都在说谎，则既没有欺骗，也没有罪恶。"

另一方面，此文激起了许多读者的愤怒。他们在杂志接下来的一期中写道：

- "（我和其他人）强烈反对商业道德不同于日常道德的观念。"
- "有一个不讲道德或不分是非的经理，就至少有另一个讲道理和做好事的经理。"
- "人是可以有所不同的，他们可以为道德行为定调子……这很重要，对未来都有影响。虽然买卖成功终归是好事，然而未来毕竟是未来。"
- "当然也有许多很负责任的公司经理，即使面临激烈的竞争和很大的资金困难。有时这些行为实在令人鼓舞。"
- "企业将（必须）按市场规律去做，感谢当今社会市场对责任的要求和道德行为的检查。"
- "企业成功的核心……是消费者或顾客的信任和忠诚，这种信任和忠诚建立在产品的可靠性或服务的信誉之上，道德标准和行为则加强了商誉。任何想把商业利益与道德利益分开或对立的尝试都忽略了企业生存和发展的这一基本要素。"

（资料来源．J. Krohe Jr. Ethics Are Nice, But Business Is Business. *Across the Board*, April, 1997, pp. 16 - 22; D. Driscoll, M. Rion, M. Roth, D. Vogel, L. Pincus, and D. Orlov. Who Says Ethics Are "Nice"? *Across the Board*, June, 1997, pp. 47 - 50. Reprinted with permission of the Conference Board）

3. 如何改善道德行为

改善道德行为可以从以下几个方面着手：挑选道德素质高的员工；建立道德标准和决策规则；领导者倡导；工作目标规范；进行道德培训；综合绩效评价；进行社会审计；提供正式的保护机制。

【阅读资料】

强生公司的道德规范

我们信奉的原则是我们首先要向医生、护士、病人、母亲和其他使用我们产品与服务的人负责。为满足他们的需要，我们所做的一切都是高质量的。我们必须不断地降低成本以保持合理的价格。必须对每一份顾客订单给予迅速而准确无误的服务。我们必须向我们的供应商和分销商提供赚取应有的利润的机会。

我们必须对自己的雇员负责，向世界各地与我们一起工作的所有男士和女士负责。每个人都必须被视为独立的个体。我们必须尊重他们的人格，承认他们的优点，必须使他们在工作中有安全感。必须向雇员提供公正的、足够的补偿和清洁、有序、安全的工作环境。雇员有提意见和抱怨的自由。对于那些合格的人员，必须在雇用、发展和提升上为其提供均等的机会。

我们要对我们所生活和工作的社区负责，同时也向世界社区负责。

我们必须做好公民——支持有益的活动和捐助，缴纳足够的税金。我们必须提倡文明、改善健康和教育状况。

我们必须有序维护可使用的一切资产，保护环境和自然。

最终我们必须对我们的股东负责。企业必须赢利。我们必须敢于对新思想进行尝试，必须从事研究、开发创新项目、愿意为错误付出代价。必须采购新设备、提供新设施、投入新产品。创造储备以为困难时期提供后援。

在我们执行这些准则时，股东们能意识到他们将得到公正的回报。

（资料来源：贝特曼等著，王雪莉译：《管理学：新竞争格局》（第六版），北京：北京大学出版社 2007 年版）

4. 企业的社会责任

企业的社会责任就是一个企业追求有利于社会长远目标的义务。企业的社会责任已经成为管理者进行思考的一个重要因素。关于一个企业要不要承担社会责任，一直存在着两种观点：

赞成的观点：①社会大众的期望；②符合长期利益；③道德义务驱使；④建塑公众形象的要求；⑤创造更好的氛围；⑥解决与政府的冲突。⑦利于责任与权利的平衡；⑧股东利益的驱使；⑨合理占用和利用资源；⑩防止社会问题的发生。

反对的观点：①违反利润最大化原则；②淡化了企业的使命；③增加了企业成本；④扩大了企业的权力；⑤企业无法承担大量的责任；⑥没有广泛的社会授权；⑦缺乏社会大众的支持。

社会为企业的生存和发展提供了土壤，企业是基于社会而存在的。企业只有充分履行社会责任，才能最终获得社会的好评，建立起良好的形象，增强其竞争力。

5. 企业如何承担社会责任

企业承担的社会责任可分为两类：一类是企业对社会造成影响的责任；另一类是企业对社会问题的责任。对于前一种责任，企业必须予以承担，具体可采取三种办法：①通过消除不利影响的活动来承担社会责任；②把这些社会影响转化成企业发展的机会；③通过制定各种法律法规来限制企业对社会的影响。对于另一种责任，最有效的办法是通过社会创新，即把一项社会问题转化成一种新型的、有利可图的企业机会，使企业在解决社会问题、取得社会效益的同时，也能获得重大的经济效益。

6. 社会责任的具体体现

企业对环境的责任：企业既受环境的影响又影响着环境。因此，企业有承担保护环境的责任，主要体现在：企业要在保护环境方面发挥主导作用；企业要以绿色产品为研究和开发对象；企业还要推动环保技术的应用，治理环境。

企业对员工的责任：不歧视员工；培训员工；营造良好的工作环境；实施善待员工的其他举措。

企业对顾客的责任：提供安全的产品；提供正确的产品信息；提供售后服务；提供必要的技术指导；赋予顾客自主选择的权利。

企业对竞争者的责任：要形成有序竞争，处理好与对手的关系，既要在合作中竞争，又要在竞争中合作，不搞不正当竞争。

企业对投资者的责任：为投资者带来高回报；对投资者准确及时披露信息。

企业对所在社区的责任：提供就业机会；创造社会财富，为社区多做贡献。

Section 2 Manager

1.2.1 Who are the Managers

Managers are those individuals who are responsible for coordinating the activities of others so as to make contributions to the organization's accomplishment of its expected mission in the process of collaboration. Generally, managers consist of two parts: Firstly, there are persors who decompose the target task into many manageral activities, task and are responsible for the final push to complete the goal. This kind of person is the core of the organization or senior leaders. Secondly, there are organization's key members who execute all aspects of concrete managerial activities such as planning, organizing, controlling, etc. Managers are an important group in an organization.

The efficient managers devote themselves to completing the tasks, achieving the goals and coordinating activities of others with various managerial work. Managerial work refers to various activities that managers conduct to enable themselves to contribute to the completion of organization's expected tasks during the process of coordinating others' work.

1.2.2 Types of Managers

From the vertical angle or the different levels that managers belong to, the managers can be divided into three types: basic-level managers, middle-level managers and senior-level managers. The number of managers at every level decreases from base to top to form a pyramid. Basic-level managers are responsible for directing and coordinating the non-management employees' activities and never command other managers. The middle-level managers are responsible for directing and coordinating the activities of the subordinate managers, and sometimes command non-management personnel directly. Top or senior-level managers coordinate the activities of the entire organization through commanding middle-level managers, and they are not subject to the command of others within an organization.

From the horizontal angle or according to the different fields of management, managers can be divided into two types: comprehensive managers and functional managers. Comprehensive managers are generally senior managers who are responsible for the management of certain types or the whole in an organization such as the general manager. Functional managers are generally middle-level or basic-level managers who are only responsible for the activities of certain managerial functions such as personnel, finance, marketing and so on.

According to different types of positions, managers can be divided into chairman, general manager, department manager, project manager, etc.

1.2.3 Roles of Managers

The management expert Henry Mintzberg found out that managers usually play ten kinds of different but highly relevant roles through his study.

（1）Roles of interpersonal relationship: It refers to the roles the managers are playing when they bring about all kinds of contact with various people. This kind of role is people-centered by means of association, leadership and contact, which can be roughly divided into three different roles: ①Figurehead. ②Leader. ③Link man.

（2）Roles of information delivering: It refers to the managers' roles in acquisition, processing, transmission of various information resources. This kind of roles focuses on information communication by means of information gathering, processing and transmission, which can be roughly divided into three different roles: ①Listener. ②Spreader. ③Spokesman.

（3）Roles of decision-making: Roles of decision-making refer to the managers who make decisions and take measures toward a series of major or sudden problems in the managerial process. This type of roles takes decision-making as the center by means of promoting transformation, clearing troubles, allocating resources and negotiating, which can be roughly divided into four roles: ① Entrepreneur. ② Victor of chaos. ③ Distributor of resource. ④Negotiator.

In reality, the focuses of these ten types of roles that the managers play at different levels in the organizations are different because of different types of organizations. That is the conversion of roles of managers.

	Roles of Decision-Making	Roles of Information Passer	Roles of Interpersonal Relationship	
Senior-level Managers				Middle-level Managers
Middle-level Managers				Basic-level Managers

Diagram 1-2   Roles and Levels of Managers

1.2.4 Requirements of Managers' Skills

Generally speaking, managers should possess three kinds of skills: technical skills, personnel skills and decision-making skills.

（1）Technical skills: Technical skills are the ability to complete organization's missions by using technique. The managers need to understand and grasp the basic technical knowledge in the special fields of management in order to execute effective management.

（2）Personnel skills: The managers must be able to recognize each individual, give each individual a post, unite all the members, organize the members and arouse the enthusiasm of the members to achieve organizational goals.

（3）Decision-making skills: Decision-making skills are namely the ability of analyzing, judging and decision-making. The higher the level the manager belongs to, the more complicated the environment and the problems the manager is facing, and the more decision-making skills are needed.

The above three kinds of skills demand differently for different levels of managers. The managers at relatively lower levels mainly need technical skills and personnel skills. The managers at relatively higher levels mainly need personnel skills and decision-making skills. For the managers at the highest level, decision-making skills are the most important part.

1.2.5　Managers' Mental Models

Mental model is the basically stable thinking methods and behavioral habits which are shaped by one's past experiences, knowledge and values. A person will consciously or unconsciously understand and think about the problems that occur from a fixed angle, and use the customary manner to solve them once his/her mental models formed. Everyone has his or her own particular mental model as the result of education which is also formed in specific living and working environment.

Managers' mental models will decide in the large degree the thoughts and behaviors of themselves and eventually directly affect the efficiency and effectiveness of managerial activities. So what the mental models of the managers especially the excellent managers are?

（1）Foresight and sagacity: It includes: ①The ability of mastering the latest information about scientific and technological knowledge. ②Systematic method of thinking. ③Progressive values.

（2）Sound psychological quality: Psychological quality refers to the basic characteristics which are everlasting and stable manifested in the process of certain individual's activities and personality. Among a number of outstanding psychological qualities, the following characteristics are very important: ①Self-awareness and confidence. ②Emotions and feelings. ③Wisdom, courage and insight. ④Tolerance and patience.

（3）Excellent personal characters: Excellent personal characters are important elements and bases for a person to develop sound habits. Manager's mental model can not form without his/her excellent personal characters, which include: ①Bold and enterprising. ②A sense of mission. ③Hard-working and studious. ④Optimistic and enthusiastic. ⑤Honest and alert.

1.2.6　The Structure of Managers' Abilities

Managers must possess some abilities to complete the managerial process, and this kind of abilities is the assemble of various abilities. The key abilities include the following aspects：

（1）Innovative ability：It is based on a person's sense of innovation and is the most important ability of excellent managers. The managers with innovative ability usually have the following main features：broad interests, keen insights, systematic thinking, dialectical thinking, independent thinking, self-confidence, the courage to face difficulties and so on.

（2）Conversion ability：It refers to managers' abilities to transform the idea into workable and concrete work plan. No one can become a real manager without the experience of practical managerial working. Conversion ability often manifests as the abilities of integrating, transplanting, reforming and innovating.

（3）Adaptability：It mainly manifests as the abilities of innovating and scheming in coping with the changing situations. It means that the managers can consider the situations, adjust to the changing circumstances, discern the direction of the change and persevere.

（4）Organization and coordination ability：During the process of input – transformation – output of an enterprise, the ability of organization and coordination is particularly important. If there is no organization and coordination, there is no management. The managerial ability to organize and coordinate is concentrating on fostering team spirit to optimize the operation of the organization's work, and strengthening the coordination and feedback between the individual and the whole.

1.2.7 Managers' Ethics and Social Responsibilities

1. Four Different Moral Values

Administrative ethics are principles or standards for judging the managerial behaviors. With regard to moral standards there are four different points of view：

The first one is the utilitarian view. It is a point of view of processing managerial problems completely in accordance with the outcomes or results.

The second one is the view of power. It is the point of view relating to the respect for and protection of individual's freedoms and privileges.

The third one is the view of fairness. It means that the managers act according to the principles of fairness or justice.

The fourth one is the view of social contract. It means that the managers should make decisions according to various industries' and enterprises' existing standards of ethics.

In practice, most people adopt the utilitarian view, because it is consistent with the efficiency and profit targets. Utilitarianism takes it as the right thing to do for the majority by sacrificing the interests of the minority, emphasizes the new trend of social rights and social justice, so it means that managers need the rules of ethics based on the standard of non-charity. It is a challenge for today's managers because it is more ambiguous to make decisions according to the standards of the individual rights and social justice than to make decisions according to the utilitarian standards such as efficiency and profits. Thus it leads to moral managerial dilemma faced by the managers.

2. The Influencing Factors of Managerial Ethics

Whether a manager's behavior is ethical is the result of the complicated interactions among the developing stages of the managers' moral management and individual characteristics, the design of organizational structure, organizational culture, the intensity of most problems.

3. How to Improve Moral Behaviors

Moral behaviors can be improved from the following aspects: selecting the staff with higher moral qualities, building up moral standards and decision-making rules, advocating moral rules by the leaders, specifying work targets, doing moral training, evaluating comprehensive performance, doing social audit, providing a formal protection mechanism.

4. Social Responsibilities of Enterprises

Enterprises' social responsibilities are a kind of obligations to pursue a long-term beneficial target of the society. Enterprises' social responsibilities have become an important factor of managers' consideration. There have always been two viewpoints about whether an enterprise should bear the social responsibilities:

Favoring views include: ①Responsing to the public's expectation. ②Conforming to the long-term interests. ③Being driven by moral obligations. ④Meeting the requirements for building public images. ⑤Creating better atmosphere. ⑥Resolving the conflicts with the government. ⑦Good for favorable balance of responsibilities and rights. ⑧Being driven by the interests of shareholders. ⑨Meeting the needs of reasonable occupancy and resource utilization. ⑩Preventing social problems.

Opposing views include: ①Violating the principle of profit maximization. ②Undermining the company's mission. ③Increasing the cost of doing business. ④Expanding the power of the enterprise. ⑤Enterprises cannot take a lot of responsibilities. ⑥No broad social authorization. ⑦Lacking public support.

Society provides the soil for the survival and development of the enterprises, and the enterprises are existing by depending on the society. Only through full implementation of social responsibilities can the enterprise eventually win praise of the society, establish sound images and enhance its competitiveness.

5. How Do the Enterprises Take Social Responsibilities

Social responsibilities taken by enterprise can be divided into two categories: One is the enterprises' impacts on society, the other is enterprises' responsibilities toward social problems. For the former responsibilities that the enterprises must assume, specifically three approaches can be taken: ①To undertake the social responsibilities by taking actions to eliminate the adverse effects. ②To convert these social influences into enterprises' developing opportunities. ③To restrict the impact of enterprise on the society through the formulation of various laws and regulations. For the other kind of responsibilities, the most effective way is to take social innovation, namely to convert a social problem into a kind of new, profitable business opportunity, make the enterprise obtain social benefits in solving social problems and also get significant economic benefits at the same time.

6. The Embodiment of Social Responsibilities

The responsibility of the enterprises to the environment：Enterprises are influenced by the environment and are also affecting the environment. Therefore，enterprises shall take the responsibilities of protecting the environment：Enterprises should play a leading role in protecting the environment. Enterprises should take green products as the object of research and development. Enterprises should promote the application of environmentally friendly technology and the governance of environment.

The responsibility of the enterprises to the employees：Do not discriminate employees, organize staff training，create a good working environment，and take other measures to treat employees decent.

The responsibility of the enterprises to the customers：Provide safe products，give correct information of products，offer after-sales service and necessary technical guidance，give customers the right to choose.

The responsibility of the enterprise to the competitors：Form orderly competition，correctly deal with the relationship with the opponents，not only compete but also cooperate in competition, avoid unfair competition.

The responsibility of the enterprises to the investors：Bring high returns for investors，provide accurate and timely information to the investors.

The responsibility of the enterprises to the community：Provide employment opportunities, create social wealth，and make more contributions to the community.

第三节　管理系统

一、管理系统的含义

根据系统的观点，管理是一个完整的系统。管理系统是指由相互联系、相互作用的若干要素和子系统，按照管理的整体功能和目标结合而成的有机整体。这一概念包括以下具体含义：

（1）管理系统是由若干要素构成的，这些要素可以被看作管理系统的子系统，而且这些要素之间是相互联系、相互作用的。

（2）管理系统是一个多层次结构。对内，管理系统被划分成若干子系统，并组成有序结构；对外，任何管理系统又成为更大的社会管理系统的子系统。

（3）管理系统是整体的，发挥着整体功能。也就是说，其存在的价值在于其管理功效的大小，而任何一个子系统都必须是为实现管理的整体功能和目标服务的。

二、管理系统的构成

管理系统一般由以下要素构成：

（1）管理目标。管理目标是管理功能的集中体现。管理目标是管理系统建立与运行的出发点和归宿，管理系统必须围绕目标建立与运行。所有的管理行为都是为了有效实现目标。

（2）管理主体。管理主体即管理者，是管理系统中最核心、最关键的要素。配置资源、组织活动、推动整个系统运行、促进目标实现，所有这些管理行为都要靠管理者去实施。管理者是整个管理系统的驾驭者，是发挥系统功能、实现系统目标最关键的力量。作为管理的主体，管理者既表现为单个管理者，又表现为管理者群体及其构成的管理机构。

（3）管理对象。管理者对管理对象进行管理。管理对象作为管理行为的受作用一方，对管理成效以及目标的实现具有重要的影响。管理对象包括不同类型的组织，也包括各组织中的构成要素及职能活动。

（4）管理媒介。管理媒介主要指管理机制与方法。管理机制与方法是管理主体作用于管理对象过程中运用的一些原理与实施方式、手段。管理机制在管理系统中起着极为关键的作用，它是决定管理有效性最直接、最核心的因素；而管理方法是管理机制的实现形式，是管理的直接实施手段，具有过河所必需的"桥"与"船"的作用，也是十分重要的。

（5）管理环境。管理环境是指实施管理过程中的各种内外条件和因素的总和。管理行为存在于一定的环境中，并受到管理环境的重要影响。所以，管理环境是管理系统的有机组成部分。

三、管理机制

机制原意是指机器的构造及工作原理，引入管理领域后提出了管理机制的概念。所谓管理机制，是指管理系统的结构及运行机理。

1. 管理机制的特征

（1）内在性。管理机制是管理系统的内在结构与机理，其形成与运作是完全由自身决定的，是一种内运动过程。

（2）系统性。管理机制是一个完整的有机系统，具有保证其功能实现的结构与作用系统。

（3）客观性。任何组织，只要客观存在，内部结构、功能既定，则必然要产生与之相应的管理机制。这种机制的类型与功能是一种客观存在，是不以任何人的意志为转移的。

（4）自动性。管理机制一经形成，就会按一定的规律、秩序，自发地、能动地诱导和决定企业的行为。

（5）可调性。机制是由组织的基本结构决定的，只要改变组织的基本构成方式或结构，就会相应地改变管理机制的类型和作用效果。

2. 管理机制的构成

对于一般的管理系统，管理机制主要包括运行机制、动力机制和约束机制。

（1）运行机制。运行机制是组织中最基本的管理机制，是管理机制的主体，主要指组织基本职能的活动方式、系统功能和运行原理。运行机制具有普遍性。任何组织，大到一个国家，小到一个企业、单位、部门，都有其特定的运行机制。

（2）动力机制。动力机制是一种极为重要的管理机制，是为管理系统提供动力的机制，是指管理系统动力的产生与运行机理，主要由利益驱动、政令推动和社会心理推动三个方面构成。

（3）约束机制。约束机制是对管理系统行为进行修正的机制，其功能是保证管理系统正确运行，以实现管理目标。它是指对管理系统行为进行限定与修正的功能与机理，主要包括权力约束、利益约束、责任约束和社会心理约束等。

四、管理环境

环境是指存在于组织内部和外部并对组织的绩效产生影响的各种力量和条件因素的总和。环境是组织生存发展的基本条件。它存在于组织界限之外，并可能对管理当局的行为产生直接或间接的影响。按照组织与环境的关系，可将环境分为一般环境和具体环境，或者说间接环境和直接环境。

1. 一般环境

一般环境是指对某一特定社会中所有组织都产生影响的环境因素，包括以下几个方面：

（1）经济环境：主要指国民经济的发展情况，包括利率、通胀率、可支配收入、证券市场指数以及一般的经济周期等。这些宏观经济因素的变动，都将通过改变企业的供给环境和市场环境来影响企业的经营与决策。

（2）政治法律环境：主要指总的政治形势及立法和司法现状，包括政局稳定性、社会制度、党派关系、相关法律法规以及产业政策等。政治稳定是企业发展的前提条件，而法律则是企业公平竞争的基本保证。

（3）社会文化环境：主要包括社会价值观的变化，以及由此引起的社会成员行为态度的变化和人口数量及结构的变化等。社会价值观念的变化，对产业结构和规模会产生影响。

（4）技术环境：主要指目前社会技术总水平及其变化趋势。技术因素具有变化快、变化大和影响面广的特点。技术的突破将对企业产生极大的影响，有时某些新技术的产生能够引起一场社会性技术革命，创造一批新产业，同时迫使一批现有产业被淘汰。

（5）自然资源因素：主要包括地理位置、气候、资源、自然灾害、环境污染等因素。一个国家的自然资源和生态环境的变化会给企业带来发展机会或某种威胁和限制。

【小链接】

作为商业问题的全球变暖

全球气候变化是一个非常有争议的商业问题。气候变暖的证据到底有多大的可信度？一些人认为未来的冬季奥运会将可能被取消，因为可能就没有冬季了。其他人则认为讨论地球的厄运有些危言耸听，没有什么事实依据。

埃克森美孚石油公司（Exxon Mobil）就是一家主张全球气候变暖的证据并不可信的公司。这家公司能够推迟实施对于二氧化碳的排放限制吗？它能够保护的不过是其短期资产的价值罢了。它甚至能够使公众相信全球气候变暖的威胁要小于政府的管制所带来的威胁。但是对前景持有这种看法的公司的数量正在减少。绝大部分（并非所有）的科学家都在担心全球气候变暖所带来的可怕后果。根据在瑞士达沃斯举行的世界经济论坛（World Economic Forum）上商业领袖们的看法，全球气候变暖已经成为当今商业所面临的最紧迫的问题。

全球气候的变迁不仅是风险，也是商业机会。关注该问题的经理们将致力于影响政府管理，努力解决那些与气候变暖有关的问题，并且让公众知道他们的努力。

许多行业和公司都直接受天气的影响，因此现在就为将来可能的气候变化所带来的后果做打算是必需的。举个例子，保险公司必须修改它们关于财务损失的预测模型；房地产经纪人也必须熟知洪水的类型；旅游行业必须预先知道不同的风暴类型对该度假地区需求带来的影响（无论是热带地区还是滑雪胜地），农业公司有可能必须放弃在气候会变得更热的地区的投资，而将投资重点转移到那些由于气候的变化而更加适宜农业发展的地区；木材公司也可能要把更多的钱放在火灾防控方面。

环境变化也创造了商业机会。种子销售商能开发出在干旱环境下有更高产量的品种。ABB 和霍尼维尔（Honeywell）公司会投资更加复杂的空调设施和其他在能源成本增长时更加有利可图的产品。福特和通用汽车公司将全球气候变化看作是在与那些技术不太先进的对手的竞争中取得优势的机会。它们投资生产不排放二氧化碳的汽车，这将产生一个全新的市场。

英国石油公司在应对全球气候变暖方面是一个真正的领导者。在 1997 年，公司的 CEO John Brown 爵士成为第一个公开阐明全球气候变暖危险的石油界领导者，并且与业界其他人发生了冲突。他保证减少二氧化碳的排放，并且在业界引导了一种直面而非逃避环境问题的态度，包括废水处理问题。

（资料来源：K. O'Neill Packard, F. Reinhardt. What Every Executive Need to Know about Global Warming. *Harvard Business Review*, July-August, 2000, pp. 129－135；A Big-Oil Man Gets Religion. *Fortune*, March 6, 2000, pp. F87－F89；Defending Science. *The Economist*, February 2, 2002, pp. 15－16, R. C. Anderson and B. Mckibben. Winterless Olympics? *The Washington Post*, February 8, 2002, p. A31）

2. 具体环境

一个组织的具体环境，是指对某一特定组织构成影响的那些环境因素。与一般环境因素相比，具体环境因素能够更直接地给一个组织提供更为有用的信息，同时也更容易被组织人员识别。具体环境包括以下几个内容：

（1）客户：即向企业提供其所需求的环境因素，主要是市场需求，属于影响企业产出的环境因素。客户通过压低价格、要求较高的产品质量或索取更多的服务项目，并且从竞争者彼此对立的状态中获利。

（2）供应商：这是企业供应资源的环境因素，属于企业投入环境因素。供应商可能通过提价或降低所供产品或服务的质量来向某一企业施加压力，从而使该企业无法跟上成本控制的要求而失去利润。

（3）竞争者：包括同一产业中现存的竞争者、潜在进入者及替代产品的威胁。最明显的竞争方式是：竞争企业生产类似产品并卖到同一市场上，从而造成企业间激烈竞争。现有的竞争者通常以价格竞争、广告、产品引进、提高客户服务及维修等向某一企业施加压力；新的竞争对手引进了新的业务能力，带有获取市场份额的欲望，从而导致企业产品的价格压低或成本上升；替代产品限制了企业可获利润的上限，从而限制了企业的潜在收益。

（4）政府：政府部门是指为国家和社会利益而监督企业经营的各有关部门，如财政局、税务局、劳动局、质检局、工商局等。因此，企业的管理者也必须理顺同这些部门组织之间的关系，在它们的监督约束下进行生产经营活动。

（5）公众：公众通常是指所有实际上潜在地关注并影响着一个企业目标的达成的社区、组织、群众团体或居民。如金融公众、媒体公众、当地公众、内部公众等。在社会上，为了公众利益，也有很多组织，如消费者协会、绿色和平组织等也会对企业进行监督。

3. 环境的特征

环境的不确定性：任何组织的运行，都要受到一般环境和具体环境的影响，然而环境具有不确定性，不确定性增加了组织对环境反应失败的风险。组织环境的不确定性来自环境因素的变动性和复杂性。在某一特定时期内，如果组织的环境要素变化程度很大，称之为动态环境；如果变化程度很小，称之为稳定环境。稳定环境是一个相对的概念，随着时间的推移，稳定环境也可能转化为动态环境，环境的复杂程度是用于评估分析环境不确定性的另一要素，它是指环境要素的数目多少，以及这些企业对这些要素所需的知识范围。如：与组织打交道的顾客、供应商、政府、公众越少，其环境的复杂程度就越低，相应的不确定性也就越小。

环境不确定性的类型：环境的不确定性影响着组织的成败，因此，管理者要努力降低这种不确定性。将环境的稳定程度和复杂程度结合起来分析会出现以下四种类型：

（1）相对稳定和简单的环境。这种环境中的企业，面临的不确定性很低，可以通过纪律和规章制度以及标准化程序进行控制和管理。

（2）相对稳定但复杂的环境。处于这种情形的企业，面临许多不同的环境因素，这些因素可能发生变化，但变化只是渐进的，是可以预见的。

（3）不稳定但简单的环境。这种情况下的环境虽然只有少数几个不同质的因素，但往往在供求方面发生无常的变化，因而具有较高的不确定性。

（4）不稳定而且复杂的环境。组织有可能面对极度动荡且复杂的环境，这是一种极难对付的情况，具有高度的不确定性。

环境对企业的影响和限制是客观存在的，企业应付环境不外乎两种方式：一是面对环境的不确定性通过预测和不断调整内部结构，使其与环境相协调；一是可以通过对环境实施有效的控制，或者改善环境，以减小环境的制约。

4. 环境研究的意义

环境一方面为组织活动提供必要的条件，另一方面又对组织的活动起制约的作用。因此，把握住环境的现状及将来的变化趋势，利用有利于组织发展的机会，避开不利于组织发展的威胁，这是组织谋求生存和发展的首要任务。对企业来说，环境研究具有重要的意义。

（1）环境是企业生存和发展的土壤。

从宏观上讲，任何国家和政府为了解决本国的社会、政治、经济问题，总要制定一系列的路线、方针、政策，当国家形势发生变化时，其路线、方针、政策也会发生变化。企业如果不正确地预测、估计这些变化，就有可能面临十分被动的局面，如果企业对这些变化做了充分的准备，就能够抓住机遇，长足发展。

从微观上讲，企业经营的一切要素，都要从外部环境获取，企业生产出来的产品也要通过市场销售出去。因此企业的经济效益和社会效益，都要通过外部环境才能得以实现。

（2）外部环境影响企业内部的管理关系。

一个国家的社会制度、方针政策、经济计划、市场需求等，都会直接或间接地影响企业的结构，职工的想法以及利益的分配等。例如：企业的组织结构要随市场的竞争形式、科学技术发展等外部变化而做出调整，企业内部的分配制度也要根据市场上所实现并用以分配的总价值加以确定。

（3）外部环境影响企业经营管理的特色。

处于不同国家和地区的企业，都会形成自己的经营管理特色，这在很大程度上是由于环境的影响所致。例如，美国与日本的企业由于环境的不同，因而经营管理的特色也不同。

环境研究对管理之所以必要，根本原因就在于环境是在不断变化的，企业通过环境研究不仅能了解现在，而且能了解未来，这对企业的各项管理工作是必不可少的。

Section 3　Management System

1.3.1　The Definition of Management System

Based on the concept of system, management is a complete system. Management system is defined as the organic whole combined by a number of interrelating and interacting elements and subsystems according to the overall managerial functions and targets. This concept includes the following specific meanings:

（1）Management system is constituted by a number of elements, these elements can be seen as the managerial subsystems, and they are interrelating and interacting.

（2）Management system is a multi-layered structure. Internally, the management system is divided into a number of subsystems that form an orderly structure. Externally, each management system is also a subsystem in the greater social management system.

（3）Management system is comprehensive, playing the function of the whole organization. That is to say, its value of existence lies in its management effectiveness, and any subsystem must be subject to the realization of the overall managerial functions and targets.

1.3.2　The Composition of Management System

Management system generally consists of the following elements:

（1）The management goal. Management goal is a concentrated reflection of management functions. Management goal is the starting point and the ultimate aim of the establishment and operation of management system, management system must be set up and run around the target. All of the managerial behaviors aim to effectively achieve their goals.

（2）The management subject. Management subject is the managers who are the core and the key elements in a management system. All the management behaviors, including allocating resources, organizing activities, promoting the running of whole system, and the realization of target depend on the managers to implement. Managers are the driver of the whole management system and are the crucial power to play the system's functions and achieve the system's goals. As the subject of the management, the managers are represented by the individual manager and also by the managers' group and their constitutive management institutions.

（3）The management object. The managers supervise and control the management objects. As an affected part of management behaviors, the management objects have important influences on the management effectiveness and the realization of the goals. Management objects include not only different types of organizations, but also the components and functional activities in every organization.

（4）The management media. Media mainly refers to the management mechanisms and methods. Management mechanisms and methods are the applied executive methods and approaches that work on the management subjects. The management mechanisms play a crucial role in the management system, and they are the most direct and core factor that decides whether the management is effective or not. While management methods are the ways to realize management mechanisms, and are the directly implementing means of management having the necessary role of "bridge" and "ship" to cross the river which are also very important.

（5）The management environment. Management environment refers to the combination of all kinds of internal and external conditions and factors in the process of implementation of management. Management behavior exists in certain environment, and is considerably affected by the management environment. So the management environment is an organic part of the management system.

1. 3. 3 Management Mechanism

The original meaning of mechanism refers to the structure and working principles of the machine. After it was introduced into management field, the concept of management mechanisms was put forward. Management mechanism refers to the structure and operation mechanism of the management system.

1. The Characteristics of Management Mechanism

（1）Internality. Management mechanism is the inner structure and mechanism of management system. Its formation and operation are completely determined by itself, and it is a kind of inner movement.

（2）Systematicness. Management system is a complete organic system with the structure and the role of the system, guaranteeing the realization of its functions.

（3）Objectivity. Any organization, as long as it is existing objectively with established internal structure and functions, is bound to produce the corresponding management mechanisms.

The types and functions of this mechanism are objective reality that can not be changed by man's will.

（4）Automaticity. Once the management mechanism forms, it will spontaneously and dynamically induce and decide the enterprise's behaviors according to certain rules and orders.

（5）Adjustability. The management mechanism depends on the basic organizational structure, so if we change the organization's basic constitution or structure, the types and effects of the management mechanism will change accordingly.

2. The Composition of Management Mechanism

For a general management system, management mechanism mainly includes operating mechanism, dynamic mechanism and restraint mechanism as three sub-mechanisms.

（1）Operating mechanism. Operating mechanism is the most essential management mechanism in an organization and is the subject of management mechanism, which mainly refers to the operating methods, system's functions and operating principles of basic functions of an organization. Operating mechanism is universal. Any organization, big as a country or small as an enterprise, division or department, has its specific operation mechanism.

（2）Dynamic mechanism. Dynamic mechanism is a very important management mechanism. It is the mechanism of power generation for the operation of the management system and it refers to the mechanism of emerging and running of management system's power. It consists of three aspects, including interest-driven, government decree-promoted and social psychology-driven.

（3）Restraint mechanism. Restraint mechanism is the mechanism aiming to modify the behaviors of management system, it is to realize the management goals by guaranteeing correct running of the management system. It refers to the function and mechanism of constraining and correcting the management system's actions, which mainly includes the constraints on power, interests, responsibility and social psychology, etc.

1.3.4 Management Environment

Management environment refers to the combination of all kinds of forces and conditions that affect the organizational performance existing in the internal and external of organization. Environment is a basic condition for the survival and developing organization. It exists outside the boundaries of the organization and may affect the behaviors of the authorities directly or indirectly. According to the relationship between the organization and the environment, the management environment can be divided into general environment and specific environment, or indirect environment and direct environment.

1. General Environment

General environment refers to the environmental factors having impact on all the organizations in a particular society. It includes the following aspects：

（1）Economic environment：Economic environment mainly refers to the development of national economy, including interest rates, inflation rates, disposable income, stock market index and general economic cycles, etc. The changes in these macroeconomic factors will influence the enterprise's management and decision-making by changing the supply environment and market environment of the enterprise.

(2) Political and legal environment: Political and legal environment mainly refers to the overall political situation and the legislative and judicial status including political stability, social systems, party affiliation, the relevant laws and regulations and industrial policies, etc. Political stability is a prerequisite for the development of enterprises, and the law is the basic guarantee for fair competition among enterprises.

(3) Social cultural environment: Social cultural environment mainly includes the changes of social values, and the changes of social members, behavior and attitude and population's quantitative and structural changes, etc. The changes of social values will produce impact on industrial structure and scale.

(4) Technological environment: Technological environment mainly refers to the total level and changing trend of social technology. Technology has the characteristics of changing quickly and largely and effecting widely. Technological breakthroughs will have a great impact on enterprises, and sometimes the emerging of new technologies can cause a social technological revolution, create a series of new industries and force a number of existing industries to disappear.

(5) Natural resources factors: Natural resources factors mainly include the geographic locations, climate, resources, natural disasters, environmental pollutions and other factors. A country's natural resources and ecological environmental changes will bring the development opportunities or certain threat and restrictions to enterprises.

2. Specific Environment

An organization's specific environment refers to the environmental factors influencing a specific organization. Compared with the general environmental factors, specific environmental factors can directly provide more useful information to an organization. At the same time, it is more easily identified by organization's personnel. The specific environment includes the following contents:

(1) Client: Client is an environmental factor that satisfy the demand of an enterprise, mainly the market demand, and it can affect the enterprise's output. Customers benefit through lower prices, higher product quality or more services, and from the state that competitors opposite to each other.

(2) Supplier: It is the environmental factor relating to the enterprise's supplying resources, and belongs to enterprise's environmental factors of input. Suppliers can raise prices or reduce the quality of supplied products or services to place pressure on a particular enterprise, so that the enterprise can't keep up with the cost control and loose profit.

(3) Competitors: Competitors include the existing competitors in the same industry, potential new entrants and the threat of substitute products. The most obvious form of competition is: The enterprise produces and sells similar products in the same market resulting in the fierce

competition among enterprises. The existing competitors often increase pressures on an enterprise by price competition, advertising, product introduction, improving customer service and maintenance. By introducing new business capabilities, new competitors have a desire to gain market share leading to the lower price or higher costs of enterprise's products. Substitute products keep the upper bound of enterprise's profits which limits the potential benefits of the enterprise.

(4) Government: Governmental departments refer to various relative departments executing supervision on enterprises' business for the national and social interests such as financial bureau, tax bureau, labor bureau, bureau of quality supervision and inspection, industrial and commercial bureau, etc. Therefore, the enterprises' managers also need to deal well with the relationship between their enterprises and these organizations or departments, and execute the producing and business operating activities under their supervision and constraint.

(5) Public: The public generally refers to all the existing communities, organizations, mass organizations or residents that pay attention to and have impact on the realization of a company's goal. In the society, for the sake of public interests, there are also a lot of organizations such as consumers' association, greenpeace organization which will also supervise the enterprises.

3. The Characteristics of Environment

Uncertainty of environment: Any organization's operation will be affected by the general and specific environment. The feature of uncertainty of environment, however, increases the risks of the organizations' failure of responding to environmental uncertainty. The organizations' uncertainty of environment results from the environmental factors' volatility and complexity. In a certain period of time, it is called dynamic environment if the organizations' environmental elements are changing greatly. And it is called stable environment if there is a very small degree of change of environmental elements. Stable environment is a relative concept. With the passing of time, stable environment may also become dynamic environment. When the complexity of the environment is used as another element to evaluate and analyze the uncertainty of environment, it refers to the number of environmental factors and the scope of knowledge these enterprises are required for these elements. The less an organization deals with customers, suppliers, governments, the public, the lower the complexity of environments is, and correspondingly, the smaller the uncertainty is.

The types of uncertainties of environment: The uncertainty of environment threatens the organization's success, therefore, managers should devote themselves to reducing the uncertainty. Analyzing the environmental stability and complexity as a whole, there are following four types:

(1) Relatively stable and simple environment. The enterprises in this kind of environment are faced with low uncertainty, so managers can execute control and management by carrying out discipline, regulations and standardized procedures.

(2) Relatively stable but complex environment. Enterprises in this situation are faced with different environment. These factors may change, but the change is gradual and predictable.

(3) Unstable but simple environment. Although the environments in this case only have a

few different qualitative factors, the disordered changes often occur in supply and demand, so there is relatively high degree of uncertainty.

（4）Unstable and complex environment. Organizations may face the environment with extreme volatility and complexity. This is a very difficult situation with a high degree of uncertainty to deal with.

The influence and constraint of environment on the enterprises are objectively existing. There are only two ways for enterprises to cope with the environment. One is to make the enterprise in harmony with the environment while confronting the environmental uncertainty by predicting and constantly adjusting the internal structure. The other is to reduce the environmental constraints through the effective control on the environment, or improving the environment.

4. The Significance of Environmental Study

Environment on one hand provides the necessary conditions for organizations' activities, on the other hand, it plays a restricting role on organizations' activities. Therefore, it is a primary issue for the survival and development of the organization to grasp the present situation of environment and the changing trend of the future, utilize the opportunities and make them beneficial to organizational development, avoid the threats unfavorable to organizational development. For the enterprises, environmental study is of more vital significance.

（1）Environment is the soil for survival and development of enterprises.

From the macroscopic point of view, in order to solve the social, political, economic problems, every country and government always formulate a series of principles, policies which will change when the national situation changes. If an enterprise can't correctly predict and estimate these changes, it may face a very passive situation. If the enterprise make full preparation for these changes, it can seize the opportunity and realize the long-term development.

Speaking from the microscopic perspective, all the factors needed for enterprises' operation should be obtained from the external environment, and products produced by the enterprises are sold through the market. Thus, the enterprises' economic benefit and social benefit should be achieved through the external environment.

（2）External environment affects the internal management relations.

A country's social system, principles and policies, economic plans, as well as market demand, will directly or indirectly affect the structure of an enterprise, the workers' thought, and the distribution of interests, etc. For example, the enterprise's organizational structure should be adjusted in accordance with the external changes such as the model of market competition, scientific and technological development, etc. And the enterprise's internal distribution system should also be implemented according to the total value realized in the market for distribution.

（3）External environment affects the features of enterprise management.

Companies in different countries and regions will form their own management characteristics, and this is largely due to the influence of the environment. For example, due to the different environments, American and Japanese companies have different characteristics in management.

Environmental research is necessary for management and the fundamental cause is that the environment is in constant change. Through environment study the enterprise can understand not only now but also the future and it is essential for the various managerial works of enterprises.

【阅读资料】

韦尔奇：管理秘籍

杰克·韦尔奇在 GE（General Electric Co.，美国通用电气公司）的功过是非尚在争论之中，但人们对他在管理这个庞大帝国时的别出心裁仍然津津乐道。

1. 生产"人才"

杰克·韦尔奇在业界之所以重要，是因为他生产"人才"。在最近一次 GE 全球前 500 名经理人员会议上，杰克·韦尔奇透露他成功的重要秘诀之一时说：GE 成功的最重要原因是用人。与很多 CEO 不同，杰克·韦尔奇把 50% 以上的工作时间花在了人事上，他认为自己最大的成就是关心和培养人才。

杰克·韦尔奇至少能叫出 1 000 名通用电气高级管理人员（GE 约有员工 17 万名）的名字，知道他们的职责，知道他们在做什么。这对一名员工来说是莫大的鼓舞，杰克·韦尔奇自己曾说："我们所能做的是把赌注压在我们所选择的人身上。因此，我的全部工作就是选择适当的人。"杰克·韦尔奇亲自接见所有申请担任通用电气 500 个高级职位的人。他坚信只有了解他们才能信任他们。

他说："我不懂如何制造飞机引擎，我也不知道在 NBC 应播放什么节目，我们在英国有项有争议的保险业务，我不能做那项业务，但是那个给我提建议的人想干，我相信他，我相信他能干好。"在世界最令人钦佩的分公司中，很少有哪家公司的老板能这样做。

2. 非正式沟通

GE 最成功的地方是杰克·韦尔奇在通用电气建立起来的非正式沟通的企业文化。通过这种非正式沟通，杰克·韦尔奇不失时机地让人感到他的存在。

使公司变得"非正式"意味着打破发布命令的链条，促进不同层次之间的交流，改革付酬的方法，让员工们觉得他们是在为一个几乎人人都知之甚深的老板工作，而不是一个庞大的公司。杰克·韦尔奇比他人更知晓"意外"两字的价值。每个星期，他都会不事先通知地造访某些工厂的办公室；临时安排与下属经理人员共进午餐；工作人员还会从传真机上收到杰克·韦尔奇手书的便笺，上面是他干净利落的字体。所有这些的用意在于引导和影响一个机构庞大而复杂的公司，杰克·韦尔奇最擅长的非正式沟通方式就是写便笺。写这些便笺的目的就是为了鼓励、激发和要求行动。杰克·韦尔奇通过便笺表明他对员工的关怀，使员工感到他们之间已从单纯的主管与下属的关系转变为平等的关系。

3. 打破边界

杰克·韦尔奇还提出了一个"无边界行为"概念，并大力推广它。他坚信不论何时何地都会有一个拥有好想法的人存在，而当务之急是设法将他找出来，向他学习，并快速付诸行动。"无边界行为"的目的就是拆毁所有阻碍沟通、阻碍找出好想法的高墙。它是这些理念本身的价值。而非依照提出这些理念的人所在的层级来对其进行评价。杰克·韦尔奇这样做就是想铲除所有阻碍沟通的障碍。他有一个形象的比喻："一栋建筑物有墙壁和地板，墙壁分开了职务。地板则区分了层级，而我要将所有的人全都聚在一个打通的大房间里。"GE一直通过群策群力的方法大规模清除企业的界限。这一做法称为"Workout计划"。来自各个企业、各个层次的员工济济一堂，发泄他们的不满，提出各种建议，清除一个又一个不具有生产能力的工作，员工不必担心因为发表意见而受批评。群策群力的方法丰富了GE的企业文化，使之能够接受来自每一个人和每一个地方的创意。

【本章提要】

● 管理就是在特定的环境下，对组织所拥有的资源进行有效的计划、组织、领导和控制，以便达成既定的组织目标的活动过程。管理具有动态性、科学性、艺术性、创造性和经济性的特性。

● 管理的基本职能是：计划、组织、领导和控制。管理工作就是围绕这四项工作展开的。

● 管理者就是在协作过程中，负责协调他人的活动，从而对组织完成预期任务做出贡献的人员。管理者在协调他人活动时要进行各种管理工作。

● 管理者通常扮演处理人际关系、信息传递以及决策制定等角色，而且这些角色是变化的。

● 管理者良好的心智模式包括：远见卓识、健全的心理、优秀的品质。管理者应当具备创新能力、转化能力、应变能力、组织协调能力等关键能力。

● 管理是一个系统，由管理目标、管理主体、管理对象、管理媒介和管理环境构成。

● 管理机制本质上是管理系统的内在联系、功能及运行原理，包括运行机制、动力机制和约束机制。

● 环境是组织生存发展的基本条件。它存在于组织界限之外，并可能对管理当局的行为产生直接或间接的影响。按照组织与环境的关系，可将环境分为一般环境和具体环境，或者说间接环境和直接环境。

【关键词】

管理（Management）　　计划（Planning）　　组织（Organizing）　　领导（Leading）

控制（Controlling）　　管理者（Manager）　　管理职能（Management Function）

心智模式（Mental Model）　　管理系统（Management System）

管理机制（Management Mechanism）

【复习与思考】

1. 怎样全面理解管理的含义和特性？
2. 管理的性质和职能如何？
3. 管理者应当扮演什么角色？
4. 优秀的管理者应具有怎样的心智模式和管理能力？
5. 什么是管理系统和管理机制？
6. 管理环境的内容是怎样的？

【研究与讨论】

1. 学习管理学对于有志成为管理者的人来说有何意义？

2. 你认为管理的本质究竟是什么？为什么？

3. 并不是所有的人都认为他们所在的组织需要管理，还有许多人不想受人管理。你认为有可能吗？为什么？

4. 如果一个人在组织中没有下属人员，那他是不是管理者？为什么？

5. 有人认为"有权就会管理"，你认同这种观点吗？如果你想成为一名称职的管理者，你应当怎样塑造自己？

6. 管理能成为一种职业吗？

【实践演练】

1. 访问一位企业经理，了解他一天的工作并按时间顺序记录下来，然后按管理职能和管理角色对这些活动进行分类和比较，看看有什么发现。

2. 访问一位非企业组织的管理人员，了解他的工作与企业经理的工作有何不同。

3. 如果有一间餐馆让你去管理，你将怎样安排别人的工作和你自己的工作？

【管理模拟】

1. 学习组建一家小型公司。

2. 为该公司设计管理目标。

3. 为公司管理人员进行角色定位。

4. 由经理组织管理层研讨公司所处的环境。

【本章案例】

关于耐克的辩论

一位针对耐克公司的批评家说道："一个公司如果无视社会责任的话，那它就是在玩火。"还有人指责耐克公司所崇尚的是暴力和低劣的品位，在提高价值观方面无所作为，特别是对于那些容易受影响的青少年。国际足球巨商们怒斥耐克让美国足球染上了"金钱万能"的疾病。人权组织指责耐克的承包商经营着像监狱一样的工厂，雇用 13 岁的儿童，对待工人像对待奴隶一样。耐克公司虽否认这些指控，但也还是改变了其运营方式。

耐克一直为其激进、反叛、反定式的形象而骄傲。这种活跃的形象在美国获得了暴利。但是，耐克把未来寄予国际大市场。公司希望超过一半的收入来自海外市场。就在耐克努力向国际市场扩张时，有人指责公司的很多决策不负责任。

例如，在《美国足球》杂志上，耐克的一则广告是这样的："欧洲、亚洲和拉丁美洲关闭了运动馆，藏起了纪念章，把钱投向除臭剂。为此，亚洲不振、拉丁美洲不威、欧洲也将蹈此覆辙……世界的警钟已敲响。"除臭剂生产线并没有让人发笑，反而是一些视耐克为丑陋的美国人，正在破坏神圣的传统。

耐克的一个电视商业广告片刻画了一位曼联队队员正在怒斥一个球迷，并辱骂那位让他与耐克签约的教练。

亚特兰大奥林匹克运动会上，广告大战中的耐克采用了这样的标语："你不是赢得了银牌，而是失去了金牌。"来自几个国家的奥委会成员对此非常愤怒。据称该标语诋毁了奥林匹克的竞争精神，并贬低了未能获得金牌的所有运动员。

几年前，有报道称，在越南，耐克给当地雇员所发放的日工资还不够维持一天包括米饭、蔬菜和豆腐的三顿饭。美国商人 Thuyen Nguyen 采访了 35 位越南工人并做出如下总结：其中 32 人体重减轻，受到屈辱，其中包括冷酷的饮水量限制，一天只能喝两次水；8 小时换班时才有上厕所的机会；工作不好时头部被打，罚跪时两手朝上举并要求长达 25 分钟；嘴巴上贴胶条以禁止说话；在阳光下长时间罚站；一遍又一遍地罚写所犯的错误。为此，在 Doonesbury 杂志上，耐克因其越南工厂的条件而受到批评。尽管如此，耐克的批评家也承认耐克不是唯一的或最坏的违法公司。

许多人认为耐克越南工厂的条件是非常不道德的。但尼加拉瓜外长则认为反血汗工厂运动是以拉丁美洲最贫穷国家的就业和投资的损失为代价的，这些国家的失业率将近 50%。"公司离开，我们的就业就没有指望了……我们在最底层，关键是我们没有被踢开。"《财富》杂志上有一篇题为"血汗工厂案例"的文章，Hoover 研究所和纳瓦尔研究生院的大卫·R. 汉德森争辩道：批评家们一定不能无视这一个事实，即虽然这些童工的报酬低廉，但一旦失去了工作会发生什么？汉德森写道："如果你把他们不得已的选择中最好的东西抽走的话，你不会使他们过得更好……总之，血汗工厂是一条脱贫致富的道路。"

毛根是同意"耐克进入中国后，家庭生活好转了"这样的观点的。毛根在一家生产耐克和阿迪达斯的鞋厂工作，月收入 150 美元。他将绝大多数收入寄回家，为其父母的稻田添了新犁，盖了新房，买了 21 寸的彩电，还攒钱要与妻子开一个小商店。由于外资和出口的影响，中国农村人均收入自 1978 年以来增长了 10 倍。收入主要来自成千上万的鞋厂、服装厂、玩具厂和电器厂。

1997 年底，耐克在其股东大会上声称其将与印度尼西亚 4 家违反劳工标准的工厂断绝关系。其董事长说：这样的违法行为只是例外。1998 年年中，董事长菲尔·奈特公开承认这些违法行为有损公司形象，并声称将提高工人的最低工资，在其海外工厂中按美国空气质量标准运作。

现在，耐克宣布希望顾客监督生产工厂的情况，并邀请了 16 名学生监督其 32 个合作工厂，在网络发布其原始观察记录，同时发布一些其他审计报告。行业内其他厂家不想这样公开，而耐克则认为这样做一方面是针对反血汗工厂运动的计策，另一方面也能促使行业内的其他企业也这么做。

（资料来源：贝特曼等著，王雪莉译：《管理学：新竞争格局》（第六版），北京：北京大学出版社 2007 年版，第 167～169 页）

思考问题：

1. 耐克在美国的成功是无可争议的，其战略和战术是什么？你对上述行为的看法是什么？它们仅是美国商业决策所产生的不良后果吗？它们是不负责任的或不道德的吗？

2. 如果耐克的一些决定是不道德的，那么哪些是最严重的不道德行为？哪些是最不严重的？你是怎样得出这些判断的？

3. 你如何评价耐克对批评所做的反应？

4. 对于本案例提到的问题耐克还能做什么？

【本章参考文献】

[1]［美］小詹姆斯·H. 唐纳利等著，李柱流等译：《管理学基础——职能、行为、模型》，北京：中国人民大学出版社 1981 年版。

[2]［日］占部都美著，蒋道鼎译：《现代管理论》，北京：新华出版社 1984 年版。

[3] 芮明杰：《管理学》，上海：上海财经大学出版社 2005 年版。

[4]［美］斯蒂芬·P. 罗宾斯著，黄卫伟等译：《管理学》，北京：中国人民大学出版社 1997 年版。

[5] 吴照云：《管理学》，北京：中国社会科学出版社 2006 年版。

[6] 周三多：《管理学》，北京：中国高等教育出版社 2000 年版。

第二章　管理理论的发展

Chapter 2　Development of Management Theory

在人类历史上，还很少有什么事比管理的出现和发展更为迅猛，对人类具有重大和更为激烈的影响。

彼得·F. 德鲁克

In the history of mankind, there are few things developing more rapidly than the emergence and development of management, and having more significant and more intense impact on human beings.

Peter F. Drucker

管理是一种实践，其本质不在于"知"而在于"行"；其验证不在于逻辑，而在于成果；其唯一权威就是成就。

彼得·F. 德鲁克

Management is a kind of practice. Its essence is not "know" but "act". The validation is not logical, but in the results. The only authority is achievement.

Peter F. Drucker

【本章学习目标】

知识目标：

　　古典管理理论及其主要贡献。

　　行为科学理论及其主要贡献。

　　现代管理理论及其主要贡献。

技能目标：

　　掌握管理理论发展的基本过程。

　　了解管理理论的新发展。

　　提高管理的理论水平。

【Learning Objectives of Chapter 2】

Objectives of Knowledge：

　　Classical management theory and its main contribution.

　　Behavioral science theory and its main contribution.

　　Modern management theory and its main contribution.

Objectives of Skill:

Master the basic process of the development of management theory.

Get to know the new development of management theory.

Improve theoretical knowledge of management.

【小故事】

蛹看着美丽的蝴蝶在花丛中飞舞，非常美慕，就问："我能不能像你一样自由地飞翔？"蝴蝶告诉它："第一，你必须渴望飞翔；第二，你必须有脱离你那非常安全的、温暖的巢穴的勇气。"蛹又问："这是不是就意味着死亡？"蝴蝶意味深长地说："从蛹的生命意义上讲，你已经死亡了；从蝴蝶的生命意义上讲，你获得了新生。"

【引例】

戴姆勒—克莱斯勒的艰难步履

1998 年 5 月，戴姆勒—奔驰集团公司（Daimler Benz）和克莱斯勒汽车公司（Chrysler Corporation）宣布了一项惊人的 360 亿美元的合并计划。这场"联姻"注定会震动全球的汽车产业，并为大规模的国际合作描绘了宏伟的蓝图。但这个联盟并不是天作之合。戴姆勒的总裁 Jurgen E. Schrempp 执掌了戴姆勒—克莱斯勒的大权。与他合作的董事长，来自克莱斯勒的 Robert J. Eaton，占据次要位置。克莱斯勒的总裁 Thomas T. Stallkamp 占据两者之间的位置。

在全球管理团队的首次会议上，高级主管们有两天的时间在一起吃饭、喝酒、聚会。德国人加入美国人的小组讨论，由一名董事会的管理人员——公司的高级主管主持。在开场会议和午餐后，酒店就成了巨型的自由式鸡尾酒会。克莱斯勒的一名财务主管 Thomas F. Gilman 开始在酒吧弹琴，德国人和美国人以同样的方式一起唱歌。Schrempp 和那群人一首接一首地高歌到凌晨。德国联合董事长领唱了最后一曲合唱《再见，美国派小姐》。然后，Schrempp 眼中闪烁着狂热的激情，把他的常任助理 Lydia Deininger 扛在肩上。Schrempp 用空出的手掂起一瓶香槟，高举在空中，笑着喊道："伙计们，再见！""这很奇怪，"Stallkamp 说，"有人说这是欧洲大陆式的，但这是不恰当的商业行为。"

德国人和美国人的做事的方式不同。6 小时的时差并没有什么影响。美国人开始他们的一天时，德国人已经吃午餐了。德国管理部门的成员都有执行助理，为上司准备有关任何问题的详细文件。美国人不任命副手，通过与工程师或其他专家直接谈话来制定他们的政策。德国的决策为了得到最高层的最终批准要通过各层机构，然后才开始实施。美国人允许中层员工发挥他们的主观能动性，有时不必等待主管层的批准。

Eaton 慢慢地但毫不犹豫地退出了，不再出力了。Schrempp 并没有明确地威胁 Eaton，但却最终压倒了他。对 Eaton 来说，他把自己看作团队的组建者："我想我留给后人的是文化的变革和组建的强大的团队。如果我不在这里，这些不会发生。"但是他自己的一些主管人员不能越过他建立的障碍。Stallkamp 曾希望克莱斯勒方面能在关键的时期发射 Eaton 这枚"银弹"以扭转局势。但是如果 Eaton 不打算这样，这些就不会发生了。

将戴姆勒—克莱斯勒看作"强强联合"的公众观点已经破灭。美国的投资者已经抽资而逃，因为这个公司没有融入美国。克莱斯勒主管人员明显的缺点成为德国管理的典型。两位副总裁退出并加入了福特汽车公司。管理委员会从 17 人缩减到 13 人：8 名德国人和 5 名美国人。新的企业结构成型，由 3 种汽车作为支柱：奔驰汽车、克莱斯勒汽车和重型机车。

到 2000 年年底，Schrempp 告诉德国媒体，公司将用 2～4 年时间使克莱斯勒重生。他用 Dieter Zetsche 替换了 Eaton 短命的继承者 James P. Holden，Dieter Zetsche 47 岁，是个富有经验的戴姆勒高管人员，同时还任命了 Wolfgang Bernhard 为 COO，他曾负责旗舰品牌 S 级轿车的推广活动。至于其他团队成员，他主要仰仗克莱斯勒的人，那些在一连串的高官背信事件后的局面中被伤害的人。至少这些美国人不必等着将电话翻译过来才知道德国人是怎么想的。这么多美国人出现在团队中指向了另一件事：德国人还是承认了在管理类似克莱斯勒这样的规模化产品方面，还需要向美国人学习。

虽然 Zetsche 与团队其他成员公开交换信息，但一旦他做出决策，那就是最终决策。一名高官说："他可能这会儿非常可亲，但转眼你就可能希望上帝帮助你远离他。"此时，这个奇怪的拯救者和幸存者的组合，也是严格意义上的、公司历史上第一个真正的美—德组合，具有讽刺意义地成为克莱斯勒复苏的关键一环。

2002 年 7 月 18 日，戴姆勒—克莱斯勒的第二季度利润有了较大的增长，显示出复苏进入正轨。Schrempp 说："我们在正确的道路上。"这对他也是个好消息。第二季度的成绩在不景气的经济环境中更难能可贵。因为 2002 年汽车销售量在欧洲和美国都稍有减少，而且汽车厂商陷入了价格战，戴姆勒—克莱斯勒在其两大市场都面临压力。

（资料来源：Bill Vlasic，Bradley A. Stertz. Taken for a Ride. *Business Week Online*，June 5，2000；Joan Muller，Jeff Green and Christine Tierney. Chrysler's Rescue Team：Can it stop the Bleeding? *Business week Online*，January 15，2001；Christine N. Tierney. Daimler Chrysler Steps on the Gas. *Business Week*，July 19，2002）

思考问题：

1. 戴姆勒—克莱斯勒选择的依据是什么？
2. 为什么跨国管理让人欢喜让人愁？

第一节　古典管理理论

管理理论的发展是管理者和研究者在实践中不断对管理真谛、管理特性、管理规律认识与把握的过程。

管理实践由来已久，但管理理论的形成则是 20 世纪初的事情。古典管理理论主要包括科学管理理论、一般管理理论、行政组织理论三部分。

一、科学管理理论

科学管理理论由美国人泰罗（Frederick W. Taylor）及其追随者创立，创立的标志是 1911 年《科学管理原理》一书的出版。泰罗被誉为"科学管理之父"。

科学管理理论的主要内容：

（1）对工人工作的各个组成部分进行科学分析，以科学的操作方法代替不合理的操作方法。

（2）科学地挑选工人，对工人进行培训教育，以提高他们的技能和进取心。

（3）促进工人之间的相互协作，保证按科学的方法去完成任务。

（4）管理人员和工人都必须对各自的工作负责，计划与执行相分离。

为了实施上述理论，泰罗进一步提出了具体步骤：

（1）对工作环境进行分析。

（2）对工作任务进行分析。

（3）制定工作定额。

（4）安排好工人的工作，管理者要与工人密切合作，督促其完成任务。

泰罗科学管理理论的形成对当时美国社会经济的发展和企业管理水平的提高产生了极大的影响。其主要贡献是：

（1）进行时间和动作研究，规定了作业标准，提高了工作效率。

（2）通过标准化实行了激励工资和科学选培工人等，使任务管理科学化。

（3）作业人员和管理者相互分工和协作，完成各自的职能，提高了资源配置效益。

（4）完成了从管理经验到科学的转变，为管理理论奠定了基础。

二、一般管理理论

一般管理理论由法国人法约尔（Henri Fayol）创立，创立的标志是1916年《工业管理与一般管理》一书的出版。

一般管理理论的主要内容：

（1）企业经营的六项活动，即技术活动、商业活动、财务活动、安全活动、会计活动和管理活动。

（2）管理的五大职能，即计划、组织、指挥、协调和控制。

（3）管理的十四条原则，即劳动分工、权利与责任、纪律、统一指挥、统一领导、个人利益服从整体利益、合理的报酬、适当的集权和分权、等级链、秩序、公平、保持人员稳定、首创精神、团结精神。

法约尔的一般管理理论的主要贡献是：以整个企业为研究对象，认识到管理活动的普遍性，提出了管理的职能和原则。区分了经营与管理，奠定了组织管理理论的基础，至今仍具有指导意义。

三、行政组织理论

行政组织理论由德国人韦伯（Max Weber）创立，创立的标志是1947年《社会与经济组织理论》一书的出版。

行政组织理论的主要内容：

（1）韦伯认为等级、权威和行政是一切社会组织的基础。权威可分为三类：一是理性—合法权；二是传统权；三是个人崇拜权。只有理性—合法权能作为行政组织体系的基础。

（2）理想的行政组织体系：

①体现劳动分工原则：简单且清晰的任务。

②严格的权力等级和严密的规章制度：明确的等级；详细的规则；完整的工作流程。

③人与人之间的关系是非人格化：统一且不带个人偏好的运行机制。

④人员任用职业化和报酬薪金化。

这种高度结构化的、正式的、非人格化的理想的行政组织体系是强制控制的合理手段，是达到目标、提高效率的有效形式。这种组织在精确性、稳定性、纪律性和可靠性方面都优于其他形式，适用于各种政治、经济和社会组织。

古典管理理论的三位代表人物为管理学奠定了坚实的基础。泰罗率先在管理研究中采用近代科学方法，奠定了科学管理的基础；法约尔明确提出管理是企业的基本活动，管理的五职能为研究管理过程打下了基础；韦伯的行政组织理论为组织发展提供了理想的模型。

Section 1   Classical Management Theory

The development of management theory is a process in which managers and researchers constantly understand and grasp the essence, characteristics and principles of management.

Management practice is a long-standing issue, but the formation of management theory dates back to the beginning of twentieth century. Classical management theory mainly includes three parts: scientific management theory, general management theory, administrative organization theory.

2.1.1   Scientific Management Theory

It is founded by Frederick W. Taylor (America) and his followers, marked by the publishing of the book: *Principle of Scientific Management*. Taylor is known as "the father of scientific management".

The main contents of the scientific management theory:

(1) Scientifically analyze each part of workers' work, and replace the unreasonable operating method with scientific one.

(2) Scientifically select workers. Conduct training for workers to improve their skills and initiatives.

(3) Promote coordination among workers. Ensure that they complete the task with scientific methods.

(4) Both managers and workers must be responsible for their own work, planning and implementation are separated.

In order to implement the above theory, Taylor further puts forward the concrete steps:

(1) Analyze work environment.

(2) Analyze work tasks.

(3) Formulate work quota.

(4) Arrange workers' responsibility. Managers should cooperate closely with the workers, and urge them to complete the task.

Taylor's scientific management theory has a great impact on the development of America's social economy and the improvement of the level of business management. Its main contributions are:

(1) Study the time and action and make operation standards to improve work efficiency.

(2) Implement incentive salary, scientific selection of workers and so on, making the management become scientific.

(3) The workers and managers work independently and cooperatively to improve the efficiency of resource allocation.

(4) Accomplish the transformation from management experience to science, laying a foundation for management theory.

2.1.2 General Management Theory

It is founded by Henri Fayol (France), marked by the publishing of *Industrial Management and General Management* in 1916.

The main contents of the general management theory:

(1) Six activities of enterprise management: technical activities, commercial activities, financial activities, safety activities, accounting activities and management activities.

(2) The five functions of management: planning, organization, command, coordination and control.

(3) Fourteen principles of management: the division of labor, the right and responsibility, discipline, unity of command, unified leadership, personal interests submitting to the interests of the whole, reasonable compensation, appropriate centralization and decentralization, rank chain, orderliness, fairness, maintaining stability of the personnel, pioneering spirit, the spirit of solidarity.

The main contribution of Fayol's general theory of management is: Taking the whole enterprise as research object, understanding the universality of management activity, then putting up the functions and principles of management. Distinguishing between business and management, and laying the foundation of organization management theory, which still has guiding significance.

2.1.3 Administrative Organization Theory

It is founded by Max Weber (Germany), marked by the publishing of *Social and Economic Organization Theory* in 1947.

The main contents of the administrative organization theory:

(1) Weber thinks that the rank, authority and administration are the basis of all social organizations. Authority can be divided into three categories: First is the legitimate right of

rationality, second is tradition right, the third is individual right. Only the legitimate right of rationality can be the base of the administrative organization system.

（2）The ideal administrative organization system：

①Reflect the principle of division of labor：simple and clear task.

②A strict hierarchy of power and strict rules and regulations：explicit rating, detailed rules, complete work flow.

③The relationship between people is not of personality：unified, unbiased operation mechanism.

④Professional personnel appointment, pay the worker with salary.

This highly structured, formal, impersonal and ideal administrative organization system is a reasonable means of control, and it is an effective way to improve the efficiency and achieve the goal. This organization is better than other forms in accuracy, stability, discipline and reliability, and it can be applied to a variety of political, economic and social organizations.

The three representatives of the classical management theory lay a solid foundation for management. Taylor takes the lead in the use of modern scientific method in management research, laying the foundation for scientific management. Fayol claims that management is the basic activities of enterprises, the five functions of management lay a foundation for the research of the management process. Weber's theory of administrative organization provides an ideal model for organization development.

【新视角】

中国作为四大文明古国之一，在管理思想的发展史上也占有重要地位。《论语》《老子》《管子》《墨子》《韩非子》《孙子兵法》《贞观政要》《资治通鉴》《三国演义》等古代典籍都包含了极其丰富的管理思想。事实上，许多西方管理理论都可在中国古代管理思想中找到类似的论述。许多企业包括西方企业都在主动应用中国古代管理思想指导企业管理，日本、新加坡、韩国等亚洲国家和我国台湾地区的发展，与他们对中国古代管理思想的借鉴有密切的关系。

第二节　行为科学理论

正当科学管理理论为当时的企业界普遍接受的时候，新的管理思想和理论也在孕育之中，这就是美国人梅奥（Elton E. Mayo）于1924年到1932年所进行的"霍桑实验"。

【小链接】

霍桑试验是从1924年到1932年间在美国芝加哥郊外的西方电器公司的霍桑工厂中进行的。霍桑工厂具有完善的娱乐设施、医疗制度和养老金制度，但工人仍然有很强的不满情绪，生产效率很低。为探究原因，美国国家委员会组织了一个包括多方面专家的研究小组进驻霍桑工厂，开始进行试验。实验分为四个阶段：照明试验、继电器装配工人小组试验、大规模访问交谈和对接线板接线工作室的研究。

在照明试验中，专家们选择了两个工作小组，一个为试验组，一个为控制组。试验组照明度不断变化，控制组照明度始终不变。结果发现，照明度的改变不是效率变化的决定性因素。于是，他们继续进行继电器装配工人小组的实验。实验过程中，研究小组分期改善工人小组的工作条件，比如，增加工间休息时间、公司负责供应午餐和茶点、缩短工作时间、实行每周工作五天制、实行团体计件工资等，他们还允许装配小组的女工在工作时间自由交谈，观察人员对她们的态度也非常和蔼。经过研究，研究小组发现促使工人提高生产效率的原因可能是督导和指导方式以及工人工作态度的改善。为了研究工人的工作态度及可能影响工人工作态度的其他因素，研究小组决定进行大规模的访问交谈。他们共花了两年时间对两万名职工进行访问交谈。结果他们发现，影响生产力最重要的因素是工作中发展起来的人际关系，而不是待遇及工作环境。研究小组还了解到，每个工人工作效率的高低，不仅取决于他们的自身情况，而且与他所在小组中的其他同事有关，任何一个人的效率都要受到他的同事的影响。在试验的第四个阶段，研究小组花了 6 个月的时间观察接线板接线工作室的工人的生产效率和行为，结果又有许多发现，包括大部分成员都故意自行限制产量，工人对待他们不同层次的上级持不同态度，成员中存在一些小派系等。

一、人际关系理论

梅奥通过调查和实验发现管理中对人的假设有问题，因为工作环境和福利的好坏，与工人的生产效率没有明显的因果关系，相反，工人的心理因素和社会因素对生产积极性影响很大。这就是人际关系理论，该理论创立的标志是 1933 年《工业文明中的人类问题》一书的出版。

人际关系理论的主要内容：

（1）工人是社会人而不是经济人。以前的管理把人假设为经济人，认为金钱是刺激积极性的唯一动力；霍桑实验证明人是社会人，是复杂的人际关系中的成员。因此要调动人的积极性，还必须从社会、心理等方面努力。

（2）生产效率的提高，主要取决于职工的工作态度，以及和周围人的关系。以前的管理认为生产效率主要受工作方法和工作条件的制约，霍桑实验证明工作效率主要取决于工作的积极性、职工的家庭及社会、生活和组织中的人与人之间的关系。因此提高生产率的主要途径是提高职工的满足度。

（3）组织中存在着"非正式的组织"。以前的管理只注意组织的机构、职权化分、规章制度等，霍桑实验发现除了正式团体之外，还存在着非正式团体，这种无形的组织有它特殊的感情和倾向，左右成员的行为，对生产率的提高有着重要的影响。因此，管理者要充分认识到非正式组织的作用。

二、社会系统理论

社会系统理论是由美国人巴纳德（Chester I. Barnard）将社会学和系统论的思想应用于管理而创立的，其创立的标志是 1938 年《经理人员的职能》一书的出版。

社会系统理论的主要内容：

（1）强调组织的系统性，以前的管理总是把组织当成一种僵硬的结构，巴纳德认为组织应该成为一个系统。

（2）分析组织环境，组织所处的周围环境总是对组织施加多种压力、约束和限制。如自然的社会环境。

（3）组织中的个人，具有双重人格。即组织人格和个人人格。

（4）正式组织具备三个要素，即协作意愿、共同目标和信息沟通。

（5）经理人员的三项职能：①建立和维持一个信息联系的系统；②促使组织中的每个人都能做出重要贡献；③阐明并确定组织目标。

（6）组织平衡：组织内部的平衡；组织与环境的平衡；组织的动态平衡。

（7）组织效率和组织效能原则，组织效率是指组织实现目标的能力或实现目标的程度，而组织效能是指组织在实现目标的过程中满足其成员个人目标的能力和程度。这两方面是相互依存、相互促进的。

三、行为科学理论的主要贡献

将社会学、心理学等科学知识引进企业管理的研究领域，特别重视人的因素，强调通过调节组织中的人际关系以提高生产效率，这既是管理理论的发展又是管理实践的总结，它的产生和发展对管理理论及管理实践都有重大的贡献。

Section 2　Behavioral Science Theory

When scientific management theory is widely accepted in the business circle, a new management idea and theory are brewing. This is the subject of Mayo's Hawthorne Experiment conducted between 1924 and 1932.

2.2.1　Interpersonal Relationship Theory

Mayo found that there was a problem in previous management through investigation and experiment. Because whether the work environment and welfare is good or not, it has no obvious relationship with workers' production efficiency. On the contrary, psychological factors and social factors influence workers' production enthusiasm a lot. The mark of the founding of this theory was the publishing of *Human Problem of Industrial Civilization* in 1933.

The main contents of interpersonal relationship theory:

（1）The workers are social people rather than economic men. The previous management assumed person as economic man, supposing that money is the only motivation to stimulate enthusiasm. Hawthorne Experiment shows that person is social and is a member of the complex interpersonal relationship. Therefore, to mobilize the enthusiasm of people, we must work on the social and psychological aspects.

（2）The improvement of production efficiency mainly depends on the workers' working attitude and the relationships with the people around. The previous management holds that the production efficiency is mainly affected by the method of work and working conditions, while

Hawthorne Experiment proves that the production efficiency depends on enthusiasm, the relationship between people in family, society, life and organization. Therefore, the primary way to improve productivity is to improve employees' satisfaction.

(3) There is "informal organization" in an organization. The previous management only pays attention to organization, authority, rules and regulations. Hawthorne Experiment finds that in addition to the formal group, informal groups exist. This invisible organization has its special feelings and preferences to handle the behavior of members, and it has an important effect on the improvement of productivity. Therefore, managers should fully realize the importance of informal organization.

2.2.2　Social System Theory

This theory is found by the American Chester I. Barnard who applied the idea of sociology and system theory in management, The founding of this theory was marked by the publication of *The Function of the Executive* in 1938.

The main contents of social system theory:

(1) It emphasizes the systematicness of organization, the previous management always treated the organization as the structure of a stiff one, but Barnard thought that the organization should be a system.

(2) It analyzes organization environment. The surrounding environment of organization always brings pressure, constraints and limitations. Such as natural and social environment.

(3) The people in the organization has dual personality: organization personality and individual personality.

(4) Formal organization includes three key elements: the cooperation intention, common goals and information communication.

(5) The three functions of managers: ①To establish and maintain a information system. ②To encourage everyone in the organization to make contribution. ③To clarify and determine the organizational goals.

(6) Balance: balance inside the organization, balance between organization and environment, dynamic balance.

(7) Organizational efficiency and organizational effectiveness principle. Organizational efficiency refers to the organization's ability to achieve goals or the level it achieves its goals, and organizational effectiveness refers to the degree and ability it can meet its members' personal goals in the process of achieving its objectives. These two aspects are interdependent and promote each other.

2.2.3　The Main Contribution of Behavior Science Theory

It introduces sociology, psychology and other scientific knowledge into the field of enterprise management, pays special attention to the human factor, and emphasizes the importance of interpersonal relationship in the organization in improving the production efficiency. It is a summary of management theory and practice. Its emergence and development have a significant contribution to management theory and practice.

第三节　现代管理理论

第二次世界大战后，管理学广泛吸收了社会科学和自然科学的最新成果，使管理理论得到了迅速发展，形成了众多的学派，可称之为"管理理论的丛林"。

一、管理程序学派

该学派主要研究管理过程的职能，代表人物是美国的哈罗德·孔茨（Harold Koontz）和西里尔·奥唐奈（Cyril O. Donnell），代表作是《管理学》。该学派的主要研究方法是：把管理人员的工作划分为各种职能，然后对这些职能进行研究，并从丰富的管理实践中探求管理的基本规律，以便详细分析这些管理职能，并把管理职能分为：计划、组织、人事、领导、控制。

二、行为科学学派

该学派是在人际关系理论的基础上发展起来的，主要研究领导行为、群体动力学、需要动机和激励、人性假设、领导方式、组织变革等。强调探索人类行为的规律，个人目标和组织目标的一致性，引导职工自治。例如，马斯洛的需要层次理论、赫茨伯格的双因素理论、麦格雷戈的"X—Y"理论、布莱克和莫顿的管理方格理论等。

三、决策理论学派

该理论是由美国卡内基—梅隆大学教授赫伯特·西蒙（H. A. Simon）提出的，其代表作是《管理决策新科学》一书。它认为管理是一个复杂的过程，组织的任务就是建立一种制定决策的人机系统。

四、系统管理学派

该学派侧重于用系统的观点来考察组织结构及管理的基本职能，代表人物是卡斯特（F. E. Kast）等人，代表作是《系统理论和管理》。该学派认为组织是一个由若干相互联系的要素所组成的系统，它同时又是社会系统的分系统，它在与环境的相互影响中取得动态平衡。因此管理者必须从管理的整体出发，研究组织与环境之间的关系，使组织的各个部分之间以及组织和外界环境之间保持动态平衡。

五、权变理论学派

其代表人物是英国的伍德沃德（Joan Woodward）等人，代表作是《工业组织：理论和实践》。该学派认为组织与环境之间存在着一种函数关系，环境是自变量，组织是因变量。组织要随环境的变化而变化。如组织规模、工艺技术、环境的不确定程度等，被称为权变因素。

六、管理科学学派

其代表人物是美国的伯法（E. B. Buffa）等人，代表作是《生产管理基础》和《现代生产管理》。该学派认为要运用现代科学理论的方法和技术对管理进行系统分析，提供最优方案，追求最大的经济效益，并在管理中使用电子计算机。

七、经验主义学派

其代表人物有戴尔（Ernest Dale），代表作是《伟大的组织者》。另一位代表人物是德鲁克（Peter F. Drucker），代表作有《有效的管理者》《管理：任务责任和实践》。该学派主要从管理者的角度来研究管理经验，找出成功管理者的共同经验，然后使其系统化、理论化，为管理者提供借鉴。

综上所述，现代管理理论的发展可以概括为以下五个方面：①管理内涵进一步拓展；②管理组织多样化；③管理方法科学化；④管理手段自动化；⑤管理实践丰富化。

Section 3　Modern Management Theory

After the World War Ⅱ, management widely absorbs the latest achievements in social science and natural science, thus management theory which is called as "the management theory jungle" develops rapidly, and forms a large number of schools.

2.3.1　Management Program School

Their research mainly focuses on the process of management functions, its representatives are Harold Koontz and Cyril O. Donnell, and its representative work is *Management*. The main research method of this school is: divide the work of management staff into various functions, then study these functions, explore the basic rules of management from the rich management practice, so that they can analyze these management functions in detail, and the function of management is divided into: planning, organizing, human resource, leading and controlling.

2.3.2　Behavioral Science School

This school develops based on the theory of interpersonal relationship. They mainly research leadership, group dynamics, need motivation and incentive, the hypothesis of human nature, leadership style, organizational changes, etc. It emphasizes the exploration of human behavior, the consistency of individual goals and objectives for the organization, guidance and worker autonomy. For example, Maslow's hierarchy of needs theory, Hertzberg's two factor theory, Mc Gregor's "X-Y" theory, Blake and Mouton's theory of management grid, etc.

2.3.3　Decision Theory School

This theory was put forward by professor H. A. Simon from Carnegie-Mellon University in the

United States whose representative is *The New Science of Management Decision*. According to this theory, management is considered as a complex process and the task of organization is to set up a man-machine decision-making system.

2.3.4 System Management School

This school studies the basic function of organizational structure and management with the system point of view. F. E. Kast is the representative whose representative book is *System Theory and Management*. This school thinks that the organization is composed of elements of a number of interrelated systems, it is also a subsystem of the social system, it achieves dynamic balance by interacting with environment. So the manager must proceed from the management of the whole, and study the relationship between organization and environment to keep the dynamic balance between the various parts of the organization and between the organization and external environment.

2.3.5 Contingency Theory School

The representative is the British Joan Woodward whose representative work is *Industrial Organization: Theory and Practice*. This school thinks that there is a function relationship between organization and environment, the environment is the independent variable, organization is the dependent variable. Organization should change with the environment. The degree of uncertainty in the environment, the size of organization and technology are known as the contingency factors.

2.3.6 Management Science School

The representative is E. B. Buffa (American). His representative books are *Basic Production Management* and *Modern Production Management*. This school considers management should be analyzed systematically by using modern scientific managing method and technology, to provide the optimal solution, pursue the maximum economic benefit, and use electronic computer in management.

2.3.7 Empirical School

The representative are Ernest Dale whose representative book is *The Great Organizer*, and Peter F. Drucker, whose representative books include *Effective Management*, *Management: Tasks Responsibility and Practice*. This school mainly studies management experience from managers' view in practical aspects to find out the common points of successful management experience, and then make it systematic and theoretical for managers' reference.

In conclusion, the development of modern management theory can be summarized as: ①The concept develops. ②The management organization becomes varied. ③The management method becomes scientific. ④The management method becomes automatic. ⑤The management practice becomes plenty.

【新视角】

管理学者吴甘霖认为，现代管理学可以分为三个阶段：以美国为代表的物本管理阶段强调人是组织中的一个环节，是机器中的一个零件，管理重在对人的控制。以日本为代表的人本管理阶段重在对人的尊重，激发人的潜能，强调心灵的外在感动。以中国为代表的心本管理阶段由外在感动转为管理者和员工心灵的内在自觉，是人本管理的进一步升华。

第四节 管理理论的新发展

进入 20 世纪 90 年代以后，由于世界经济环境的发展变化，科学技术尤其是信息技术的突破性进展和广泛应用，市场竞争的日趋激烈和国际化，使得管理学在管理思想、方法、手段和组织等诸多方面都有重大发展。现简述如下：

一、战略管理步入了新的发展阶段

战略理论的发展大致可以划分为三个阶段：

第一个阶段是经典战略理论阶段。这是一个确定战略管理基本概念和理论框架的阶段。该阶段建立了对企业内部条件和外部环境进行系统分析的较完整的理论体系。这套体系内容涉及制定战略的科学程序、企业环境分析、战略目标确定、战略决策实施与评价等。

第二个阶段是波特开创的产业结构分析阶段。迈克尔·波特在其代表作《竞争战略》和《竞争优势》中，把传统的产业组织理论框架与企业战略问题研究结合，确立了"产业与竞争分析——一般竞争战略—获取和维持竞争优势"的企业与战略管理基本框架。波特的理论成为 20 世纪 80 年代企业战略管理的主流观点，对企业战略管理的理论和实践仍有巨大的影响。

第三个阶段是企业核心能力理论阶段。20 世纪 90 年代以后，由于企业经营环境的巨大变化，以及交易费用经济学的发展，以博弈论和信息经济学为基础的产业组织论的发展，尤其是以资源为基础的企业理论的发展和核心能力概念的提出，使人们对企业竞争优势的来源、企业战略的模式等都有了新的认识，企业战略管理理论步入了一个以核心能力理论为"核心"的新阶段。核心能力理论认为，企业战略管理的关键在于培育和发展能使企业在未来市场竞争中居于有利地位的核心能力。在战略管理过程中，企业应首先识别现有的资源和能力，并判断在一定的市场机会中这些资源和能力的价值，然后确定自己的能力和资源与未来可能的市场机会对企业资源和能力要求的差距，最后制定弥补这些差距的战略决策，包括自我培养和发展战略、战略联盟、企业兼并等。

二、"人本管理"的思想得到了极大的丰富和发展

传统的管理思想是把人作为和土地、资本一样重要的生产要素看待的，认为它们都能创造价值。泰勒的"科学管理"理论就是把人当作"经济人"对待的，因此，片面强调金钱的刺激作用，运用严厉的控制手段来管理工人，以达到高的生产率。随着科学技术的

发展，人类文明程度的提高、民主化的普及，企业家、专家、学者对人在生产经营活动中的地位和作用也有了新的认识，他们不再把企业职工看成生产要素和"经济人"，而是看成"社会人"和"文化人"，把他们看成企业的主体，于是提出了"人本管理"的新思想。

"人本管理"是与"以物为中心"的管理相对应的概念，它要求理解人、尊重人、充分发挥人的主动性和积极性。一般认为，"人本管理"可分为五个层次：情感管理、民主管理、自主管理、人才管理和文化管理，具体包括这样一些主要内容：运用行为科学，重新塑造人际关系；增加人力资本，提高劳动力质量；改善劳动管理，充分利用劳动力资源；推行民主管理，提高劳动者的参与意识；建设企业文化，培育企业精神，等等。

在国外具体管理实践中，企业文化建设和股权激励最能够体现人本管理的思想。因而，人本管理的思想极大地丰富了人力资源管理的理论和实践。

三、组织管理的变革更具革命性

近年来，组织管理发生了深刻的变革，出现了一些新的趋势，主要表现在以下几个方面：一是金字塔形的组织结构正在逐步被网络型的组织结构取代；二是由单一决策中心向多决策中心发展；三是企业组织结构形式向多样化发展；四是组织结构自我更新不断加快。特别是建立学习型的组织和流程再造代表了组织管理的两大创新方向。

所谓学习型组织，就是通过不断学习来改革的组织。善于不断地学习是它的本质特征。学习型组织的真谛就是全体成员全身心投入并有能力不断学习；能让成员在工作中体验到生命意义；成员能通过学习创造自我、扩展未来能量。学习型组织最早是由麻省理工学院教授彼得·圣吉（Peter M. Senge）在其著作《第五修炼——学习型组织的艺术与实务》中提出来的。他认为企业的领导者和全体职工都要进行五项修炼：①锻炼系统思考能力；②自我超越；③改善心智模式；④建立共同愿景；⑤开展团队学习。要进行这五项修炼，必须建立学习型组织。学习型组织是更适合人性的组织模式。组织由一些学习团队形成社群，它有崇高且正确的核心价值、信心和使命，具有强韧的生命力与实现共同目标的动力，不断创新，持续蜕变。在这种学习型组织中，人们胸怀大志，心手相连，相互反省求真，脚踏实地，勇于挑战极限及过去的成功模式，不为眼前近利益所诱惑，同时以令成员振奋的远大共同愿望，以及与整体动态搭配的政策与行动，充分发挥生命的潜能，创造超乎寻常的成果，从而在真正的学习中体悟工作的真义，追求心灵的满足与自我实现，并与周围的世界产生一体感。彼得·圣吉认为，判断一个组织是否是学习型组织，有以下四条基本标准：①人们能不能不断检验自己的经验；②人们有没有生产知识；③大家能否分享组织中的知识；④组织中的学习是否和组织的目标息息相关。

长期以来，人们对生产经营系统、管理组织结构的变革都持一种比较慎重的态度，主张用改良、完善的办法来改善和加强企业管理，对管理组织结构也是要求保持稳定性和灵活性的统一，避免出现大的震动，造成工作秩序的混乱。近年来，有的专家对传统思想提出了挑战，提出了"流程再造"的理论，主张对企业的生产工艺流程、管理组织系统进行重组、再造。

"流程再造"是美国麻省理工学院的电脑教授迈克尔·哈默（M. Hamer）提出来的。

他对再造工程下的定义是："对组织的作业流程做根本的重新思考与彻底翻新，以便在成本、品质、服务与速度上获得戏剧化的改善。"其中心思想是美国企业必须采取激烈的手段，彻底改变工作方法。因此，他强调企业流程要"一切重新开始"，摆脱以往陈旧的流程框架。迈克尔·哈默认为，流程再造工程必须组成团队来进行，要使信息在各个部门得到充分运用。再造工程一旦推行，就会带来以下一些根本性的变化：①工作单位的划分，从以职能基础变成以流程为基础；②工作内容从单一变成丰富；③人员从被控制变成有决策权；④获得工作能力的方法，从没有系统的训练，变成有全盘计划的教育；⑤绩效评估与奖励方面，从观察单一活动转变为观察整体活动的结果；⑥决定晋升的因素，由以绩效为主转变为兼顾绩效与技能；⑦在价值观方面，将为主观而工作变成为顾客而工作；⑧生产管理人员，由监督者变为教练；⑨组织结构由层级式变为扁平式；⑩高层主管由事后评分变为对员工主动引导。

四、管理信息化成为企业和社会普遍追求的目标

管理信息化的过程可以被划分为 20 世纪 50 年代初期到 60 年代中期的电子数据处理阶段；20 世纪 60 年代中期到 20 世纪 70 年代初期的综合数据处理阶段；20 世纪 70 年代初期以后的系统数据处理阶段等。进入 20 世纪 90 年代以后，管理信息化有了新的发展，尤其是朝着网络化、信息技术集成化方向迅速发展，管理信息化实现了从个人电脑到群组计算机工作网络、从孤立系统到联合系统以及从内部到跨企业计算机网络的飞跃。信息化给企业管理带来的变化是革命性的。正如著名学者莫顿（Morton M. Scott）所指出的，这种变化至少可以归纳为 6 个方面：①信息化给企业生产、管理活动的方式带来了根本性的变革；②信息技术将企业组织内外的各种经营管理职能、机制有机地结合起来；③信息化将在许多方面改变产业竞争格局和态势；④信息化给企业带来了新的、战略性的机遇，促使企业对其使命和活动进行反思；⑤为了成功地运用信息技术，必须进行组织结构和管理方法的变革；⑥企业面临的重大挑战是如何改造企业，使其有效地运用信息技术，适应信息社会，在全球竞争中立于不败之地。

随着 Internet 技术的发展，作为生产管理信息基础的管理信息系统发生了改变，使生产管理从封闭走向开放，还使生产管理系统更具有动态适应性，更能灵敏地对市场变化做出反应，更好地满足消费者需求，从而增强了企业的竞争力。现代科学技术的发展推动了市场需求的变化，进而为现代市场的营销理论与方法的创新提供了技术手段和基础。进入 20 世纪 80 年代以后，市场营销理论进入了分化和扩展时期，出现了大量的营销新概念，营销方法随着营销领域的生化和拓展，趋向多元化，如网络营销、关系营销、整合营销、绿色营销、文化营销、定制营销等。

五、知识管理将成为新时代管理的焦点

随着 21 世纪的到来，我们进入了一个全新的时代。在这个时代，知识成为推动社会发展和人类进步的最主要的因素，也是人类最可宝贵的资源。如何管理好智力资本，运用集体的智慧提高应变能力和创新能力，将成为未来竞争的关键。

知识经济是一种新的经济形态，具有如下特征：①知识成为发展经济的最重要和最关

键的资源；②高科技产业将成为经济的支柱，知识密集型产品的比例大大增加；③知识经济是一种全球一体化的经济，具有共享性；④知识经济是一种"低耗高效"型经济，具有可持续性和可再生性；⑤创新对知识经济有重要的推动作用；⑥学习具有特别重要的意义。

知识管理就是以知识为核心的管理，它通过有效获取和利用已有的知识，创造新的知识，并通过对知识的连续性管理，提高企业的创新能力和价值创造能力，从而获得核心竞争优势。因此，开展和加强知识管理，有利于企业有效地开发其知识资源，使知识资源在深度和广度上不断地得到扩展；有利于企业有效地利用其知识资源促进和强化企业的创新能力以适应经济的不断变化；有利于企业促使其知识资源与其他资源更好地结合从而提高创造价值的能力。

Section 4   New Development of Management Theory

After entering the 1990s, due to the change of the world economic environment, and the development and application of the science and technology especially the information technology breakthroughs, the market competition becomes increasingly fierce and international, which makes the management has a great development in the management idea, method, means, organization and so on. Summarized as follows:

2.4.1   Strategic Management Has Entered a New Stage of Development

The development of strategic management theory can be divided into three stages:

The first stage is the classical strategy theory. This is a stage that determines the basic concept and theoretical framework of strategic management. The stage establishes a theory system to analyze enterprise's internal conditions and external environment. The contents of the system involve science program of strategy formulation, business environment analysis, strategic objectives, strategic decision implementation and evaluation, etc.

The second stage is the industrial structure analysis, which is initiated by Potter. Michael Potter claimed in his masterpiece *Competitive Strategy* and *Competitive Advantage* by combining the frame work of traditional industrial organization theory with the enterprise strategic research and then established the basic frame of the enterprise and strategic management—industry and competitive analysis—the general competition strategy—to obtain and maintain competitive advantage. Potter's theory has become the mainstream view of strategic management of enterprises in the 1980s, which still has great influence on the theory and practice of strategic management of enterprises.

The third stage is the theory of the core competence of enterprises. After the 1990s, because of the great changes in business environment, and with the development of transaction cost economics, the development of industrial organization based on the game theory and information economics, especially the development of enterprise theory based on resource and the proposal of the concept of competence are made. People have a new awareness of the enterprise strategic management theory. Enterprise strategic management theory goes into a new stage with the theory of core competence as a "core". The theory of core competence holds that the key of enterprise strategy management is the core ability of cultivation and development which can make the enterprise occupy a favorable position in the future competition in the market. In the process of strategic management, the enterprise should firstly identify existing resources and capabilities, and judge the value of the resources and capabilities in market opportunities, and then determine the gap between their own ability and resources and the requirements of possible future market opportunities for the enterprise resources and capabilities, finally make strategic decisions to bridge the gap, including self-training and development strategy, strategic alliance, merger, etc.

2.4.2　The Thought of "Humanistic Management" Has Been Greatly Enriched and Developed

In the traditional management ideas, people are considered as important as factors of production such as capital and land, because they can create value. In Taylor's "scientific management" theory, people are treated as "economic men", so it one-sided emphasizes on the stimulus of money, using tough control as a method to manage workers in order to achieve high productivity. With the development of science and technology, the popularization of the degree of civilization and the improvement of democratization, entrepreneurs, experts and scholars have a new view on the role of the people in production and operation activities, they treat the enterprise workers not only as a factor of production and "economic men", but as "social men" and "cultural men", regard them as a main body of enterprises. So the new idea of "humanistic management" is put forward.

In opposition to "material-centered management", "humanistic management" is a concept which requires understanding and respecting people, and giving full play to the initiative and enthusiasm of people. Generally, "humanistic management" can be divided into five levels: emotional management, democratic management, independent management, personnel management and cultural management, including such contents: the use of behavioral science, reshaping of interpersonal relationship, increasing human capital, improving labor quality, improving labor management, making full use of labor resources, carrying out democratic management, improving workers' consciousness of participation, building enterprise culture, cultivating enterprise spirit, etc.

In some specific management in foreign countries' practice, the construction of enterprise culture and the stock ownership incentive can best embody the ideas of humanistic management. Therefore, humanistic management greatly enriches the theory and practice of human resource management.

2.4.3　Reform of Organization Management Is More Revolutionary

In recent years, profound revolutions have been taken in the organizational management.

There are some new trends mainly expressed in the following aspects: Firstly, the pyramid organizational structure has been gradually substituted by network organizational structure. Secondly, there is a development from single decision center to multiple decision centers. Thirdly, there is a development of the forms of enterprise organizational structures to diversity. Fourthly, the self-renewing of organizational structures unceasingly speeds up. Especially the establishment of learning organizations and process reengineering represent two innovational directions of organizational management.

The so-called learning organization reforms the organization itself through continuous learning. Being good at continuous learning is its essential characteristic. The essence of learning organization is that all members of organizations put their heart and soul into and have the ability of continuous learning. It's the organization that can let the members experience the meaning of life in the work. It's the organization that can make the members shape their identity through learning and boost their energy in the future. Professor Peter M. Senge from MIT proposed firstly learning organization in his work *The Fifth Discipline*. He believes that the enterprise leaders and all the staff have to practice five principles: ①Develop the ability to think systematically. ②Self-transcendence. ③Improve mental mode. ④Establishment of a common vision. ⑤To carry out team learning. To carry out the five disciplines, it is a must to establish the learning organization. Learning organization is the organization which is more suitable for human. In the organization, some learning teams form community which has noble and correct core values, faith and mission, keep innovating and disintegrating with strong vitality and motivation of realizing common targets. In such a learning organization, people aim high, work hand in hand, reflect on each other and pursue truth, stand on solid ground, have the courage to challenge the limits and the successful model of the past, not to be tempted by profit at present, at the same time, share common and ambitious wishes which make the members exciting and the policies and actions coordinated with the whole dynamically, give full play to the potential of life, to create extraordinary results which are composed of real learning experience of the true meaning of work, the pursuit of mental satisfaction and self-realization, and generate an oneness with the world around. Professor Peter M. Senge put forward four basic criteria to judge whether an organization is learning organization: ① Whether the people can continue to test their experience. ②Whether people produce knowledge. ③Whether they can share the knowledge of organizations. ④ Whether learning in the organization is closely related to the organization's target.

For a long time, people hold a relatively cautious attitude on the transformation of production and management system, managerial and organizational structure, claims to improve and strengthen enterprise management with perfect improvement measures, and unification of stability and flexibility of the management organization structure is also required to maintain to avoid the massive quake which would result in disorder of the work. In recent years, some experts challenge traditional thoughts and put forward the theory of "process reengineering", advocating restructuring and reengineering of enterprise production process and managerial organizational system.

"Process reengineering" was put forward by American computer professor Michael Hamer from Massachusetts Institute of Technology (MIT). He defines reengineering as: "Rethink and renovate the organization's work flow in order to obtain dramatic improvements in cost, quality, service and speed." The central idea is that American companies must take drastic measures to change the working methods thoroughly. Therefore, he stresses that the enterprise process "starts all over" and gets rid of the outdated working procedure. Michael Hamer believes that the process reengineering must be carried out by teams and make full use of the information in each department. Once the process reengineering is implemented, it will bring the following several fundamental changes: ①The base for division of working units changes from function to process. ②The work content becomes rich from single. ③The staff changes from being controlled into decision-maker. ④The method to obtain the ability to work changes from non-systematic training into the overall plan of education. ⑤The standards for performance evaluation and reward transforms from the observation of single activity to the observation of the activities of the whole results. ⑥The factor deciding the promotion changes from performance into performance and skills. ⑦In terms of the values, it changes from working for the employee into working for the customer. ⑧The production manager changes from a supervisor into a coach. ⑨The organizational structure changes from a hierarchical type into a flat one. ⑩Executives change from scoring afterwards to actively guiding the employees.

2.4.4　Management Informatization Becomes a Common Goal of Enterprise and Society

The process of management informatization can be divided into three stages. The first stage, called the electronic data processing stage, dates from the early 1950s to the mid-1960s. The second stage is from the mid-1960s to the early 1970s, called the integrated data processing stage. After the mid-1970s, there is third stage called system data processing stage. Since the 1990s, the management informatization technology has new advances, especially in the realization of the leap from personal network to integrated network, it has developed from an isolated system to a joint system, and from the intranet to the network that can be used across enterprises. The changes that the informatization brings to the enterprise management are revolutionary. As a famous scholar Morton pointed out that these changes can be summarized as six aspects at least: First, informatization brings fundamental changes to the way of enterprise production and management activities. Second, informatization integrates various management functions and mechanisms of both inside and outside the organization. Third, informatization will change the industry competition situation in many ways. Fourth, informatization brings new, strategic opportunities and prompts companies to review its mission and activities. Fifth, in order to use the informatization technology successfully, we should reform the organization structure and management principles. Sixth, the major challenge is how to transform the enterprise for the effective use of information technology and adapting to the information society to remaining invincible in global competition.

The development of Internet technology has changed the management information system, which is the basis for the production management. It makes production management change from closed to open and the production management system is more dynamic in adaptability, more sensitive to market changes, and better to meet consumer demand, thus enhances the enterprise's competitive ability. The development of modern science and technology promoted the change of market demand, and then provided technical means and basis to the innovation of the modern market marketing theory and method. After the 1980s, marketing theory went into the period of differentiation and extension, there were a lot of new marketing concepts. With biochemical and expansion of marketing, marketing method became diversified, such as network marketing, relationship marketing, integrated marketing, green marketing, cultural marketing, customized marketing and so on.

2.4.5　Knowledge Management Will Become the Focus of the New Era's Management

With the coming of the 21st century, we have entered a new era. In this era, knowledge has become the main factor to promote the social development and human progress, also it is the most precious resources for human beings. How to manage intellectual capital by using collective intelligence to improve adaptability and innovation ability become the key to the future competition.

Knowledge economy is a new economic form, it has the following characteristics: ①Knowledge has become one of the most important and critical resources of economic development. ②The high-tech industry will become the backbone of the economy, the ratio of knowledge-intensive product greatly increased. ③The knowledge economy is a kind of global integration economy which can be shared. ④The knowledge economy is a kind of "low consumption and high efficiency" economy, with sustainability and renewability. ⑤Innovation has an important impact on knowledge economy. ⑥Learning is of special importance.

Knowledge management is the management which takes the knowledge as the core. It creates new knowledge by effectively acquiring knowledge and making good use of them. Meanwhile, by continuous management, it improves enterprise's innovation ability and the ability to create value, thus obtaining the core competitive advantage. Therefore, to develop and strengthen the knowledge management, it is advantageous for the enterprise to effectively develop the knowledge resources, enriching knowledge resources in breadth and depth constantly. And it is beneficial for the enterprise to effectively use its knowledge resources to promote and strengthen the innovation capability of enterprises to adapt to economic changes, and is good for the combination of enterprise knowledge resources with other resources so as to improve the ability of creating value.

【新视角】

柔性管理

代表着新技术革命时代企业管理发展趋势的柔性管理日益成为企业管理的新特色。其主要特征有：①以对人的管理为核心。如注重感情投资，塑造企业文化，推行民主管理等。②强调组织的柔性化。如由集权向分权过渡，由金字塔形向大森林形组织发展，更注重弹性化等。③战略决策柔性化。如增强战略的灵活性，实行滚动计划等。④组织生产的柔性化。如采用柔性生产线，小批量、多品种生产等。⑤市场营销柔性化。如运用各种营销方式、多种营销组合等。⑥追求全方位优质。⑦利用高新技术进行管理。⑧重视视觉标识管理。

【本章提要】

- 管理理论的形成和管理的实践活动是紧密相连的，理论的形成基于实践。
- 泰罗的科学管理理论始于对劳动效率的研究，最终目的是寻求提高效率的最佳方式，第一次使管理从经验上升到科学。
- 法约尔的一般管理理论提出了管理的五大职能和十四条原则，奠定了一般管理理论的基础。
- 梅奥的人际关系理论提出了社会人的假设、调动积极性的主要因素和非正式组织等观点，为行为科学理论的进一步发展奠定了基础。
- 现代管理理论的发展形成了众多学派，这些学派在管理内涵、管理组织、管理方法、管理手段等方面，得到了进一步的拓展和丰富。
- 管理理论的发展是一个渐进的过程，新的管理理论不断涌现，代表了当代管理理论的新趋势。

【关键词】

科学管理（Scientific Management）　行为科学（Behavioral Science）

等级链（Rank Chain）　权变理论（Contingency Theory）

正式组织（Formal Organization）　非正式组织（Informal Organization）

学习型组织（Learning Organization）　知识管理（Knowledge Management）

【复习与思考】

1. 泰罗科学管理理论的主要内容是什么？对管理理论的发展有何贡献？
2. 法约尔一般管理理论的主要内容是什么？对管理理论的发展有何贡献？
3. 梅奥的霍桑实验和人际关系理论的主要内容是什么？对管理理论的发展有何贡献？
4. 现代管理理论的流派有哪些？
5. 现代管理理论的发展趋势是怎样的？

【研究与讨论】

1. 管理理论的发展过程对我们有何启示？
2. 何谓"管理理论的丛林"？谈谈你对这种现象的认识。
3. 为什么学习型组织备受企业界的青睐？
4. 说说"今天工作不努力，明天努力找工作"这句话包含的管理思想。

【实践演练】

1. 选择一种你熟悉的组织，如学校、企业、商店等，研究这些理论在该组织的应用情况。
2. 通过查阅资料，总结我国在管理理论研究方面的成就与存在的问题，试分析其原因。

【管理模拟】

1. 如何理解管理理论来源于管理实践，又可指导管理实践？
2. 行为科学理论有哪些新发展？对管理理论的发展有何贡献？
3. 知识管理能否成为 21 世纪管理的中心？
4. 将全班同学分成 4 组，每组一题，通过查阅资料，开展一次学术沙龙活动。

【本章案例】

管理理论真的能解决实际问题吗？

海伦、汉克、乔、萨利四个人都是美国西南金属制品公司的管理人员。海伦和乔负责产品销售，汉克和萨利负责生产。他们刚参加过在大学举办的为期两天的管理培训学习班。在培训班里主要学习了权变理论、社会系统理论和一些有关职工激励方面的内容。他们对所学的理论有不同的看法，现在展开了激烈的争论。

首先，乔说："我认为社会系统理论对于我们这样的公司是很有用的。例如，如果生产工人偷工减料或做手脚，如果原材料价格上涨，就会影响我们的产品销售。系统理论中讲的环境影响与我们公司的情况很相似。我的意思是，在目前这种经济环境中一个公司会受到环境的极大影响。在油价暴涨时期，我们当时还能控制自己的公司。现在呢？我们要想在营销方面每前进一步，都要经过艰苦的战斗。这方面的艰苦，你们大概都深有体会吧？"

萨利插话说："你的意思我已经知道了。我们的确有过艰苦的时期，但是我不认为这与社会系统理论之间有什么必然的内在联系。我们在这种经济系统中曾受到过伤害。当然，你可以认为这与系统理论是一致的。但是我并不认为我们就有采用社会系统理论的必要。我的意思是，如果每种事物都是一个系统，而所有的系统都能对某一个系统产生影响，我们又怎么能预见这些影响所带来的后果呢？所以，我认为权变理论更适用于我们。如果你说事物都是相互依存的话，系统理论又能帮我们什么呢？"

海伦对他们这样的讨论有不同的看法。她说："对社会系统理论我还没有很好地考虑。但是，我认为权变理论对我们是很有用的。虽然我们以前亦经常采用权变理论，但是我没有意识到自己是在运用权变理论。例如，我有一些家庭主妇顾客，听到她们经常讨论关于孩子和如何度过周末之类的问题，从她们的谈话中我就知道她们要采购什么东西了。顾客也不希望我们逼他们去买不需要的东西。我认为，如果我们花上一两个小时与他们自由交谈，那肯定会增加我们的销售量。但是，我也碰到一些截然不同的顾客，他们一定要我向他们推荐产品，要我替他们做主。这些人也经常到我这里来走走，但不是闲谈，而是做生意。因此，你们可以看到，我每天都在运用权变理论来应对不同的顾客。为了适应形势，我经常改变销售方式和风格，许多销售人员也都是这样做的。"

汉克显得有点激动，他插话说："我不懂这些被大肆宣传的理论是什么东西。但是，关于社会系统理论和权变理论问题，我同意萨利的观点。教授们都把自己的理论鼓吹得天花乱坠，他们的理论听起来很好，但是他们的理论却无助于我们的实际管理。对于培训班上讲的激励要素问题我也不同意。我认为泰罗在很久以前就对激励问题有了正确的论述。要激励工人，就是要根据他们所做的工作付给他们报酬。如果工人什么也没有做，就用不着付任何报酬。你们和我一样，都是为钱工作，钱就是最好的激励。"

思考问题：

1. 你同意哪一个人的意见？他们的观点有什么不同？
2. 如果你是海伦，你如何使萨利信服系统理论？

【**本章阅读与参考文献**】

［1］［美］泰罗著，胡隆昶译：《科学管理原理》，北京：中国社会科学出版社 1984 年版。

［2］［法］法约尔著，周安华等译：《工业管理与一般管理》，北京：中国社会科学出版社 1982 年版。

［3］［美］赫伯特·西蒙著，李柱流等译：《管理决策新科学》，北京：中国社会科学出版社 1982 年版。

［4］［美］彼得·圣吉著，郭进隆译：《第五项修炼——学习型组织的艺术与实务》，上海：上海三联书店 1995 年版。

［5］［美］彼得·F. 德鲁克著，孙耀君译：《管理——任务、责任、实践》，北京：中国社会科学出版社 1987 年版。

［6］侯贵松：《知识管理与创新》，北京：中国纺织出版社 2002 年版。

第三章　管理决策

Chapter 3　Management of Decision-making

知己知彼，百战不殆；不知彼而知己，一胜一负；不知彼，不知己，每战必殆。

孙子

Knowing the enemy and yourself, you can fight a hundred battles with no danger of being defeated. If you only know yourself, but not your enemy, you may win or lose. If you know neither yourself nor your enemy, you will always endanger yourself.

Sun Tzu

管理就是决策。

西蒙

Management is decision-making.

Simon

【本章学习目标】

知识目标：

了解决策的含义和要素。

掌握决策的类型。

熟悉决策的基本程序。

技能目标：

掌握科学决策的基本原则。

学会发现问题和分析问题。

能够运用决策的一般方法。

【Learning Objectives of Chapter 3】

Objectives of Knowledge：

Understand the definition and factors of decision-making.

Master the types of decision-making.

Be familiar with the basic procedures of decision-making.

Objectives of Skill：

Master the basic principles of scientific decision-making.

Learn to identify and analyze problems.

Be able to implement the general methods of decision-making.

【小故事】

1992 年 9 月，由于人人争购英镑，世界各地的货币市场都出现了混乱。狂潮达到高峰时，金融投资家乔治·索罗斯的同事对他说，他们敢打赌英镑价格下跌的时间到了，但是，第一个赌注不要下得太大。索罗斯不同意："如果连我们自己都没有信心，根本就不应该下注。"随即他命令在交易中采取强势手段。结果，这一决定让索罗斯赚了 16 亿美元。

【引例】

为什么企业会失败

为什么企业会失败呢？很可能是企业高层失败的决策导致的。企业家一旦决定开始做生意，他们就会全身心地投入进去，但是往往会在思考时发生错误。错误的思考方式包括：

"我需要自己决策。"早期，你要负责所有的事，但随着时间的推移，你要找些优秀的人，并适当地放手，尽管仍保持控制，但要让其他人有更多的责任，尽其所能。

"电子商务容易且便宜。"建立可以处理交易的网站容易，但多数在电子商务方面的努力失败了，许多大公司也是尝试了多次才步入正轨，战略、技术和组织问题不能被低估。

"我们不需要利润。"这明显是错误的，2000 年，许多人认识到新经济并不意味着老规则不适用了。

"我的预测是保守的。"虽然你认为你的计划是在非常谨慎的预计下做出的，但是你最好还是做一个预期无法实现的计划。因为经验告诉我们，真正开始实施一项计划所花费的时间和金钱往往是预想阶段的两到三倍。而销售预测几乎从未实现过。

"有这么多钱做保证，我们不会失败。"斤斤计较是不需要的，但是太多的钱会带来决策的不谨慎和成本失控的危险。

"太幸运了，我们最大的客户是通用汽车（或者 IBM）。"传统上，许多管理者都喜爱处于这种位置，现在你最好还是做好失去这种客户的准备——这种情况随时随地都会发生。

（资料来源：贝特曼等著，王雪莉译：《管理学：新竞争格局》（第六版），北京：北京大学出版社 2007 年版）

思考问题：

1. 企业决策为何会失败？
2. 如何避免企业决策的失败？

第一节　决策的含义和要素

决策是管理者的基本行为，是人类思维活动的一部分，是管理工作的重要环节之一。管理成功的关键是做出正确的决策。

一、决策的含义

所谓决策就是为解决问题或实现目标，在两个及以上的备选方案中，选择一个合理方案的分析判断过程。上述定义包括以下几点含义：

（1）任何决策都是为了实现一定的目标，无目标就无从决策。

（2）决策必须要有两个以上的备选方案，如果只有一个方案，那就不用选择，也不存在决策。

（3）决策是在特定的条件下，寻求优化目标和优化实现目标的途径和手段，是一个分析判断过程。

（4）决策是要付诸实施的，因此，决策方案必须是可行的。

二、决策的要素

决策是一个由决策对象、决策标准、决策信息、决策者和决策方法五个要素构成的系统，它们之间相互联系和相互制约。

（1）决策对象。决策对象指决策要解决的问题。不同的问题有不同的决策标准，需要不同的信息，由不同的决策者，采用不同的方法来进行决策。一般来说，战略性问题的决策者是高层管理者，决策标准是效益，信息主要来自宏观领域，决策方法多数是非程序化的，决策结果是影响全局的、长远的。如果决策问题是战术性的，决策者大多数是中层管理者，决策标准是效果，信息主要来自中观领域，决策方法都是半程序化的，影响面较大。如果决策问题是作业性的，决策者为基层主管，决策标准是效率，信息来自微观领域，决策方法是程序化的，影响面较小。

（2）决策标准。决策标准指决策的质量标准（成本与效益）、速度标准（时间）、运行标准（社会支持率）。不同的决策标准要求不同的决策者，决策的参考信息、决策方法等也是有区别的，决策标准主要由决策的性质决定，组织文化和决策者的价值观也有很大的影响。

（3）决策信息。决策实际上是一个信息处理过程。因此，决策信息状况对决策者、决策方法、决策结果有着重要的影响。决策的信息占有情况决定或影响决策者的定论，也影响决策方法的选择。决策信息越丰富准确，决策的失误率越低。

（4）决策者。决策者是整个决策的核心，其价值观、知识、能力、风格和权力等对决策的标准和方法甚至对决策问题的选择都有直接的影响。决策者可以是集体也可以是个人，各有其利弊，集体决策比个体决策质量高，个体决策比集体决策效率高，可在不同的条件下灵活运用。

（5）决策方法。决策方法直接影响决策的结果，科学的决策方法是决策科学化的重要因素。

Section 1　Definition and Elements of Decision-making

Decision-making is the daily behavior of a manger, which is a part of human thinking, and one of the significant parts of management activities. To make an accurate decision is the key to successful management.

3.1.1　The Definition of Decision-making

Decision-making is the process to select a reasonable plan from two or more alternative offers through analyzing and evaluating in order to solve the problems or achieve the goals. The definition above includes:

(1) Decision-making aims at achieving a certain goal. There is no decision-making without a goal.

(2) Decision-making must have two or more alternative offers, if there is only one offer, then the selection is not necessary, and decision-making will not exist.

(3) Decision-making means to find out the approaches and methods to optimize and achieve the goal under given conditions. It is a process of analyzing and judging.

(4) Decision-making is to implement, therefore, the plan must be feasible.

3.1.2　The Elements of Decision-making

Decision-making is a system comprised of five elements: object, standard, information, decision-maker and methods, which are inter-related and inter-constraint.

(1) Decision-making object. It refers to the problems which needed to be solved by decision-making. Different problems have different decision-making standards and information is undertaken by different decision-makers with different methods to make decision. Generally speaking, strategic problems are undertaken by top managers. The decision-making standard is about efficiency, the information comes from macroscopic level, the decision-making methods are mostly non-procedural, and the outcome is overall effective and long-term. If the decision-making problems are tactical, then the decision-makers are mostly middle managers, the decision-making standard is about effectiveness, the information mainly comes from the medium level, the decision-making methods are mostly semi-procedural, and the influence is widespread. If the decision-making problems are operative, the decision-makers are first-line managers, the decision-making standard is about efficiency, the information comes from microscopic level, the decision-making methods are procedural, and the influence is limited.

(2) Decision-making standard. It refers to the quality standard (cost and efficiency), the speed standard (time), and the operative standard (social supportive rate). Different standards require different decision-makers, the reference information of decision-making and decision-making methods are also distinctive. Decision-making standard is mainly determined by the nature of decision-making. Organizational culture and decision-makers' values also have a great impact on it.

(3) Decision-making information. Decision-making is actually a process that deals with information. Therefore, the situation of decision-making information has a great impact on

decision-maker, methods and results. The occupancy of decision-making information not only determines or affects decision-maker's final conclusion, but also influences the selection of decision-making methods. The more abundant the information is, the lower the error rate is.

（4）Decision-maker. Decision-maker is the core of decision-making, whose values, knowledge, ability, style and power have direct influence on decision-making standard and methods and even the selection of decision-making problems. Decision-maker can be either a group or individual, which has pros and cons. Collective decision-making has higher quality than individual, while individual decision-making is more efficient. Both of them can be used flexibly under different situations.

（5）Decision-making methods. Decision-making methods directly influence the consequence of decision-making. Scientific decision-making methods are the important factor of scientific decision-making.

【新视角】

对国内失败企业的研究发现，80%的国企失败源于决策失误，而几乎所有失败的民营企业在自我反思时无一例外地检讨自己的决策失误。决策失误已经成为企业家失败和企业失败的首要原因。决策问题牵动着每个企业的神经。然而在寻找决策失误的原因时，人们往往归咎于信息不对称、信息不准确以及决策本身是否成熟的问题。而很少有人意识到，模仿、克隆、盲目跟进是决策失误的一个重要原因。因此，决策也需要创新。

第二节　决策的类型

决策涉及各个方面的工作。依据不同的标准，决策可以分为多种类型。了解不同类型决策的特点有助于管理者合理决策。

一、战略决策、战术决策和业务决策

这是根据决策的重要程度划分的。

战略决策是解决时间较长、范围较广、性质比较重大的全局性问题的决策。战略决策正确与否决定着组织的发展发向和成败。

战术决策是为实现战略决策目标的分阶段决策，或是实现战略决策过程中解决面临问题的决策。战术决策是战略决策的重要组成部分，是实现战略决策的重大步骤。

业务决策是在日常工作中为提高工作效率、生产效率而做出的决策，涉及范围较窄，只对局部有影响，如工作任务的日常分配、责任制的落实以及库存控制等。

二、程序化决策和非程序化决策

这是根据决策问题的重复性划分的。

程序化决策是指经常发生，结构清晰，能按原规定的程序、处理方案和标准进行的决策，如采购、配送、服务等。

非程序化决策不经常出现，具有极大的偶然性和随机性，无先例可循，只能在问题出现时进行非常规处理。如新产品开发、新项目投资等。

三、确定型决策、不确定型决策和风险型决策

这是根据决策所依据的条件划分的。

确定型决策是指决策问题的未来情况已有完整的信息，没有不确定性因素，备选方案只有一种确定的执行结果，只要根据决策目标做出选择就可以了。

不确定型决策是指决策面临的条件是完全未知的，只能估计各种条件出现的概率，依据不同的条件进行决策，其结果也难以确切估计。

风险型决策是指影响决策的主要因素在客观上存在几种可能的情况，这些可能情况事先虽可知道，但决策后会出现什么样的结果，决策者事先却不能完全了解。

四、集体决策和个人决策

这是根据决策的主体划分的。

集体决策是指多个人一起做出的决策，其优点是：能集思广益，能拟订更多的备选方案，能得到更多的认同与沟通，决策的质量高。个人决策是指单个人做出的决策，与集体决策相比，具有较高的决策效率。

【小链接】

个性影响决策

个体之间在如何决策上是不同的。众所周知，用来评价人们决策的方法就是 Myers-Briggs 类型指示（MBTI），它包含对个人和集体的评价。

MBTI 评价的基础是认为人们在做事情时都有自己的偏好，这个偏好不是能力或技巧，而是在自由进行选择时实现的真正做什么和如何做的偏好。如果完成 MBTI 检验，你就会发现你的偏好有四个基本选择：

（1）内视还是外视：外视（E）聚焦于行动、任务、活动、事件等外部因素；内视（I）聚焦于反应、思想、主意、构思等内部因素。

（2）理性还是直觉：理性（S）指获取通过直接体验和所有感官得到的详细的、实际的信息；直觉（N）着眼于大处，通过阅读、讨论、理解来学习。

（3）思考还是感觉：思考（T）指在理性、经济逻辑、客观、数量分析等基础上的决策；感觉（F）指虽然也用逻辑方法进行决策，但是包含了个人价值和对他人的影响。

（4）判断还是理解：判断（J）指在一个结构化、周密的组织里为了达到结果而迅速地决策；理解（P）具有灵活性和适应性，对随意的、延期决策也没有不舒适感并对新选择保持开放的态度。

思考一下你的偏好属于以上哪个维度。这些不同类型在决策中意味着什么？特别是 S 对 N，T 对 F。对于群体决策来说，这有什么启发？例如，所有人都是 E，或者都是 I，都是 T，都是 F。

（资料来源：S. K Hirsh, J. M. Kummerow. *Introduction to Type in Organizations*. Oxford：Oxford Psychologists Press,

1994；D. Leonard, S. Straus. Putting Your Company's Whole Brain to Work. *Harvard Business Review*, July-August, 1977, pp. 110 – 121）

五、高层决策、中层决策和基层决策

这是根据决策者所处的管理层次划分的。

高层决策指企业高层领导者所做的有关企业全局和重大问题的决策。

中层决策指中层管理者所做的业务性决策。

基层决策指基层管理者在解决日常管理问题的所做的决策。

六、定性决策和定量决策

这是根据决策目标、变量和条件能否量化来划分的。

定性决策是依靠决策者过去的经验和对未来的直觉进行的，主要靠决策者的主观判断和价值观。

定量决策是用数学方法、电子计算机等现代科学方法确定决策目标、方案、数量，进而分析判断的方法。

Section 2　Types of Decision-making

Decision-making involves various aspects. According to different standards, decision-making can be divided into different types. Understanding the features of different types of decision-making helps managers to make rational decisions.

3.2.1　Strategic Decision-making, Tactical Decision-making, Business Decision-making

This is divided according to the degree of importance of decision-making.

Strategic decision-making concerns overall problem with long time, wide scope and great importance. The accuracy of decision-making determines the development direction and success of an organization.

Tactical decision-making is phased decision-making in order to achieve the strategic decision-making, or to deal with the problems encountered in the process of strategic decision-making. Tactical decision-making is an important component of strategic decision-making, is a big step to achieve the strategic decision-making.

Business decision-making is to increase the efficiency and productivity in daily work, which involves in a narrow scope and partial influence. Such as the daily allocation of work tasks, the implementation of responsibility and control of the stock, etc.

3.2.2　Procedural Decision-making and Non-procedural Decision-making

This is divided according to the repeatability of decision problems.

Procedural decision-making refers to decisions with clear structure that recur and can be implemented according to the original regulated procedure, plan and standard, such as procurement, distribution, service, etc.

Non-procedural decision-making rarely occurs, which has great contingency and randomness with no precedent to refer, and can only be unconventional handled when the problems arise, such as new product development, new investment project, etc.

3.2.3　Certainty Decision-making, Uncertainty Decision-making and Risk Decision-making

This is divided according to the conditions decision-making depends on.

Certainty decision-making means that the future situation of the decision problem has complete information without any uncertainty. The selected proposal only has one certain result, so that selection is made according to the decision goal.

Uncertainty decision-making refers to conditions faced by the decision are totally unknown and we can merely estimate the probability. Decision-making depends on different conditions, and the consequences can't be exactly evaluated.

Risk decision-making means the major elements affecting the decision objectively have several possibilities, though the probable situations can be foresaw, the possible outcome remains unknown to decision-makers.

3.2.4　Collective Decision-making and Individual Decision-making

This is divided according to the subject of decision-making.

Collective decision-making means more than one person making decisions together. The advantages are as follow: more alternative options due to brainstorming; more agreements and communication; improved quality of decision-making. Individual decision-making refers to decisions made by one person. Compared with collective decision-making, it has relatively high efficiency.

3.2.5　High Level Decision-making, Middle Level Decision-making and Basic Level Decision-making

This is divided according to the management level that the decision-maker is in.

High level decision-making refers to the decisions about overall and significant issues of the enterprise, which are made by the top managers.

Middle level decision-making is the business decision made by middle-level managers.

Basic level decision-making is the decisions made by basic-level managers to solve the daily management problems.

3.2.6　Qualitative Decision-making and Quantitative Decision-making

This is divided by considering whether the decision objectives, variables and conditions could be quantified.

Qualitative decision-making is based on the experience and intuition of decision-makers, which mainly depends on decision-makers' intuitive judgment and values.

Quantitative decision-making utilizes modern science such as mathematical methods, electronic computers to determine decision objectives, plans, quantities so as to analyze and judge.

【阅读资料】

选定管理决策：规范模式

美国学者弗鲁姆在《管理决策新探》一文中，从决策的合理性、可接受性和时效性这三种不同的效能要求角度，将管理决策的过程分为五种规范模式，即第一类专断式（AI）、第二类专断式（AII）、第一类协商式（CI）、第二类协商式（CII）和群体参与式（GII）。这五种决策模式或风格的界定如下：

AI：管理者利用当时可得到的信息自己解决问题或做出决策。

AII：管理者从下属那里得到必要信息，自己决定解决问题的方案。

CI：管理者和有关下属个别地讨论问题，他做出的决策可以反映出下属的影响，也可以不反映。

CII：管理者和作为一个群体的下属讨论问题，集体地征求他们的意见和建议。

GII：管理者和作为一个群体的下属讨论问题，共同制订和评价解决问题的备选方案，并力求就解决方案达成一致意见。

弗鲁姆认为，每一种决策模式的有效性取决于其应用的情境特性。可以从如下七个方面的属性来明确所要决策问题的类型：

A：决策是否有某种质量上的要求，从而使某一解决方案可能比另一方案更为合理？

B：是否已经掌握了做出高质量决策的足够信息？

C：所做决策是否属于结构性问题？

D：下属对决策的认可是否对有效执行决策具有重要作用？

E：如果由个人做出决策，是否有适当的把握能得到下属的接受？

F：下属是否愿意参加所要解决问题的决策，以便实现既定的组织目标？

G：下属之间是否可能在偏好方案方面产生冲突？

请运用弗鲁姆提出的这一理论来为如下四个案例分别确定一种最合适的决策模式。

案例 1

你是一家大电子厂的制造经理。该公司的管理部门最近安装了一些新机器，实行了一种简化的工作系统，使每一个人感到惊讶的是，提高生产率的期望并未实现。实际上，生产开始下降，质量降低，离职的雇员数目增加。

你认为机器没有任何故障。你有使用这种机器的其他公司的报告，这些报告坚定了你的想法。你也曾要求制造这种机器的公司的一些代表对机器进行过仔细检查，他们报告，机器运转正处于最高效率。你怀疑，问题可能出在新的工作系统上。但是，你的直接下属并非都持有这种看法，他们是四个基层主管人，每人负责一个科组，还有一个是你的物资供应经理。他们对生产率下降的原因看法不同，他们认为是操作工训练差、缺乏适当的经济刺激体制和士气低落。显然，这种问题说明各人各有想法，你的下属中存在着分歧。

这天早晨，你接到分部经理的一个电话，他刚刚得到你近 6 个月的生产数据，打电话表示他的关切。他指示，你应以你认为的最好方式解决这一问题，他很想在一周内知道你计划采取什么步骤。你和部门经理同样关心生产率下降的原因，并且你知道，你的下属也同样关心。问题在于采取什么步骤扭转这种情况。

案例 2

你是总工长，负责一个铺设石油管道的大队，你必须估计工程的进展，以便安排把材料运送到下一个作业地点。你了解当地的地形特点，并且有计算该地形铺设速率的平均数及方差所需要的历史数据。在给定了这两个变量时，就很容易计算出把材料和设备运到下一地点所需要的最快时间和最慢时间。重要的是，你的计算要有适当的准确性，估计过低，会使工长和工人闲着无事；估计过高，会使材料在使用前有一段时间闲置无用。

如果铺设管道进展顺利，提前完成计划，你的 5 名工长和大队的其他成员可以得到很多奖金。

案例 3

你正在监督 12 名工程师的工作。他们受过同样的正规训练，工作经验也很类似，你可以在工程项目上调换他们的岗位。经理在昨天通知你，国外的分支机构要求 4 名工程师出国工作 6 至 8 个月。由于某些原因，他提出通过群体方式考虑这一要求，你也表示同意。

不管是从现在的工程项目，还是从未来的工程项目来看，你管理的所有工程师都有能力完成这些任务，没有任何理由说明某个人比其他人更强。一般认为，此次出国的任务是不受人欢迎的，这种实际情况使问题变得多少有点复杂。

案例 4

你是分部经理所管的工作人员，工作涉及管理、技术等各种各样的问题。分配给你的任务是制定出一种分部所辖的 5 个工厂通用的标准方法，用于人工查看设备计数器、记录读数，并把评分传递到集中设置的信息系统。

到目前为止，查看和（或）传递数据的错误率很高。某些工厂的错误率明显比其他工厂高，各个工厂之间用于记录和传递数据的方法出入很大。因此，有一部分错误率最可能是由具体的地方条件造成的，这给建立各厂通用的系统带来了困难。你有错误率方面的信息，但是没有各地产生这些错误的实际工作情况的信息，也没有必然造成实际工作差别的地方条件方面的信息。

提高数据质量可以使每一个人都得到好处。某些重要决策要运用这些数据，你通过质量检察员和各个工厂保持联系，他们负责收集数据。他们诚心诚意地想把自己的工作做好，但是对高层管理部门的干预很敏感，任何解决方案，如果得不到各厂检查员的积极支持，都不可能明显地降低错误率。

（资料来源：王凤彬、朱克强：《管理学教学案例精选》，上海：复旦大学出版社 1998 年版）

第三节　决策的程序

决策的一般程序包括八个步骤：①提出问题；②确定目标；③科学预测；④拟订方案；⑤评价方案；⑥选定方案；⑦检验决策；⑧实施决策（见图3-1）。

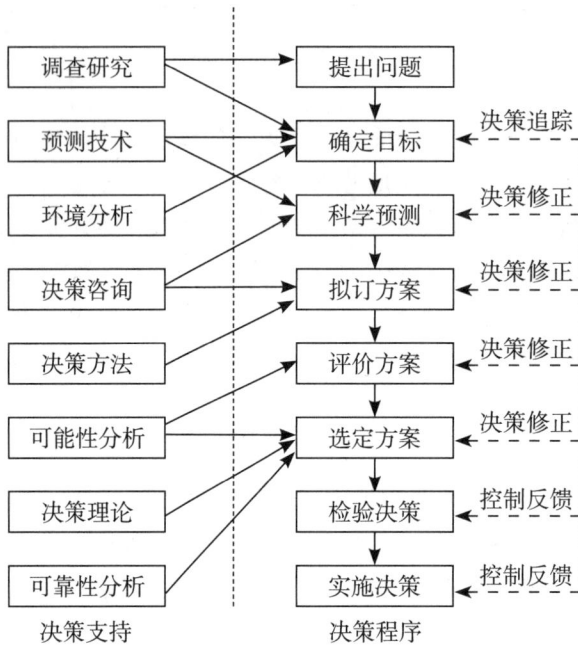

图3-1　决策的程序

1. 提出问题

问题是决策的起点，所有决策都是针对决策者要解决的问题而展开的。因此，决策者在决策之前必须根据调查研究，提出需要解决的问题，没有需要解决的问题，也就不需要进行决策了，这里所说的问题是指应有现象与实际现象之间存在的差距。为了确保决策目标正确合理，必须深入分析存在问题的原因，包括横向分析和纵向分析。横向分析是从许多错综复杂的原因中找出主要原因；纵向分析是从各层次原因中，找出根本原因。

2. 确定目标

决策目标是决策者对未来一段时期内要达到的目的和结果的判断。决策目标的正确与否对决策的成败关系极大，决策目标选择不准确，势必导致决策的失误。目标是决策的方向，没有目标的决策是盲目的决策。在确定决策目标时，要注意以下问题：

（1）决策目标要明确具体。一般来说，越是近期的目标，就越要求明确具体，远期目标则允许有一定的模糊性。

（2）目标要切合实际。这就是说，要防止目标偏高或偏低。目标偏高，按现有条件很难达成目标的要求；目标偏低，按现有条件即使不经过努力也可以达到目标。这两种情况都不利于充分发挥组织的潜能。

（3）多目标应有主次之分。在多目标决策的情况下，应尽可能剔除那些从属性的或不太重要的目标，减少决策目标的数量，从而更有效地把握主要目标。为此，首先要弄清目标间的相互关系，分清主次。

3. 科学预测

决策是针对未来行动的，因此，在决策之前，必须对决策对象及其所处的外部条件可能发生的变化进行预测。在此基础上，才能根据决策的目标和现实条件及未来可能发生的变化，合理地制订决策方案。

决策过程中所需要的信息和所要进行的预测，随决策内容和决策对象的不同而有所不同。一般而言，任何决策都需要了解以下几个方面的信息和预测：决策对象的现状、决策对象的发展规律、决策对象的外部发展变化。

4. 拟订方案

决策的本质是选择，而选择就必须有多个备选方案，没有选择也就没有决策，因此，在决策过程中拟订多个备选方案是一个非常重要的阶段，它直接决定了决策的质量。

决策方案的拟订应满足整体上的齐全性和个体间的排斥性这两个条件。整体上的齐全性是指应把所有可能的备选方案都找出来，不使其有任何遗漏（当然这是很难甚至不可能达到的）；个体间的排斥，指的是各个方案之间应有原则的差异且互相排斥，执行了方案甲就不能同时执行方案乙。

拟订方案的步骤，基本上可以分为条件分析、措施分析和行动阶段分析三大步骤。条件分析应从多方面入手，主要包括约束条件分析、边界条件分析、现有条件分析和可能条件分析等，其中，边界条件分析是指目标一般都是有伸缩性的，最高限度的目标和最低限度的目标所对应的条件就是边界条件。措施分析即分析如何使可能条件变为现实条件，它包括直接促进目标实现的措施的分析和应变措施的分析。行动阶段分析即要分析如何分步骤一步步地实现目标。

5. 评价方案

为了从多个备选方案中选出最佳的方案，需要对这些方案进行比较和评价，对方案的评估不能凭个人的主观好恶，而应采取科学的态度、依据科学的标准来进行，要研究各个方案的限制因素，综合评价各个方案的技术合理性、措施可操作性、经济时效性、环境适应性以及它对社会和生态的影响，分析各个方案可能出现的问题、困难、障碍、风险，并制定相应的防范、应变措施。

经过以上分析评价，就可对每个方案的利弊有一个结论，并可据此来进行选择。

6. 选定方案

这是决策过程中最关键的一步，在这一步中，有以下问题应予以强调：

（1）在实际决策过程中，由于受主客观条件的限制，很难找到最优方案，一般地，只要找到决策者认为满意的方案就行了。

（2）选定方案不是简单地挑选一个，而丢弃其他方案。因为不同的决策方案往往是不同专业的人、不同的业务人员或同组织人员从不同角度出发来拟订的，它受决策方案拟订者主观意识的限制。对一个问题的看法不一致，并不等于他们的看法就是错误的，或是一点也不可取的。往往是各种不同方案各有利弊。决策者要把这些方案都放在一起，综合考察它们的利弊得失，尽量发挥各方案的长处，克服其短处，把不同方案综合成更优且可行的方案。这实际上是在原有方案基础上的再创造过程。

（3）要综合考虑各种指标，防止片面注重经济效益指标。

（4）决策者要准确地权衡不同方案的利弊并做出正确的选择。要注意以下问题：①要正确处理与专家的关系。现代决策必须有专家参与。决策者应该尊重专家的意见，但也不能被专家的意见左右，从而放弃自己在决策过程中的责任。②决策者要有战略的系统观点，要依靠当初确定的目标来审查方案，并且对不同的方案要有不同的考虑。③要敢于承担风险。这是对一个决策者的开拓意识与进取精神的考验。

7. 检验决策

决策方案选定之后，应在对全局具有典型意义的地方，严格按照选定的决策方案进行试点，既不能随便找一个地方试点，也不能给试点单位提供特殊条件。同时，这种试点不能只在一处进行，而必须有相同条件下的一般"对照组"（对照点），以便能够进行比较鉴别，得出科学的结论，从而保证方案的可靠性。

如果试点成功，即决策方案被试验证实，选定的决策方案就可以进行普遍实施；如果试点失败，即决策方案被试验证伪，则应及时反馈，进行跟踪检查和决策修正。

8. 实施决策

制定、检验决策的完成，并不意味着决策过程的结束，只有把它们和实施、执行决策结合起来，才能构成科学决策的完整过程。在决策实施的过程中，即使决策方案事先经过了细致周密的考虑，也会由于各种因素的不断变化而出现偏离目标的情况，这就要在决策执行的过程中，实施控制反馈，进行追踪检查。追踪检查应该从三个方面入手：①制定规章制度；②用规章制度衡量执行情况；③随时纠正偏差。如果主客观条件发生重大变化，以致必须重新确定目标，就必须果断决定，进行追踪决策。

所谓追踪决策，是指当原定决策方案的执行表明决策目标将难以实现时，而对目标或决策方案所进行的一种根本性的修正。发生这种情况有两种可能：一是执行过程表明原决策方案有错误，二是原决策方案是正确的，但主客观条件发生了重大变化。在这两种情况下，原决策方案都不能继续执行下去而必须重新进行决策，即追踪决策。

追踪决策是一种战略转移，但并不意味着原决策的崩溃。决策者要对此保持清醒的认识。只有在实践证明原决策方案是错误的，决策者又坚持错误而拒不修正，或者不顾主客观条件的变化，盲目地执行原决策时，才会导致原决策的崩溃。

以上是决策的一般程序，并不是说所有决策都必须包含以上所有步骤，对于较简单的决策，其中有的步骤是可以省略的。决策又是一个复杂的过程，受到环境、过去的决策、个人或组织的态度、文化以及时间等因素的影响。

Section 3 Procedures of Decision-making

The procedures of decision-making generally includes eight step：① Propose questions. ②Determine target. ③Make scientific prediction. ④Formulate schemes. ⑤Evaluate schemes. ⑥Select schemes. ⑦Examine decision. ⑧Implement decision （in reference to Diagram 3 – 1）.

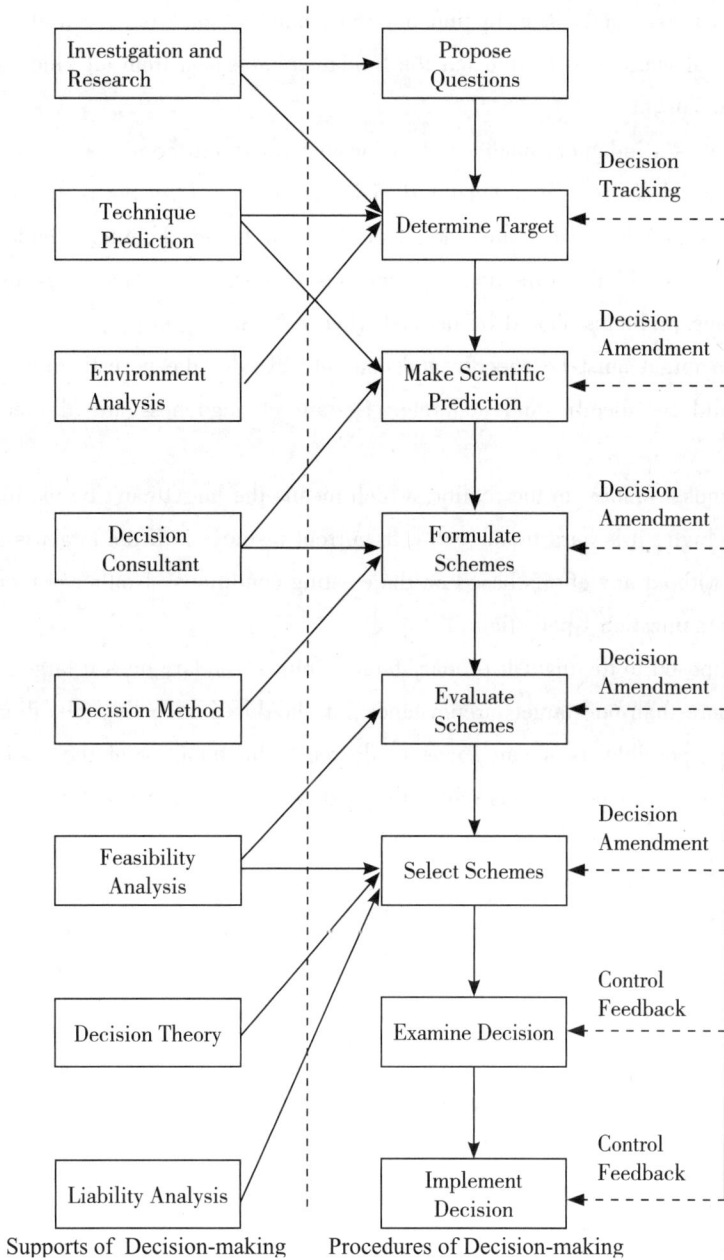

Diagram 3 – 1　Procedures of Decision-making

1. Propose Questions

Questions are the beginning of decision-making. All the decision-making is unfolded according to the questions needed to be solved by decision-makers. As a result, decision-makers have to propose the questions needed to be solved according to the research conducted before making a decision. There is no decision-making without questions, and the questions mentioned here refer to the distance between the ideal and reality. In order to assure the accuracy and rationality of the decision objective, deep analysis from both horizontal and vertical angles is indispensable. Horizontal analysis is to find out the prime reason from a variety of complicated reasons while vertical analysis is to find out the fundamental reason from all kinds of levels.

2. Determine Target

Decision target is a judgment made by decision-makers about the aim and outcome needed to reach in a future period of time. Whether the decision target is right or not is closely related to the success of decision-making, inaccurate choice of decision target definitely render the lapse of decision-making. Target is the direction of decision-making, and decision is blind without a target. The following problems should be noticed when determining target:

(1) Decision target must be specific and concrete. Under the normal circumstance, short-term targets, should be specific and concrete. Certain of vagueness are allowed in long-term target.

(2) Target must conform to the reality, which means the target can't be too high or too low. If the target is too high, it is hard to achieve with current resources. If the target is too low, it can be easily reached without any efforts based on the existing conditions. Neither of them is beneficial to fully exert the organization's potentials.

(3) It is supposed to distinguish primary targets from secondary ones if targets are more than one. Under the more-than-one-target circumstance, it should exclude the subordinate and not so important targets as possible as it can so as to decrease the quantity of the decision targets to effectively grasp the prime target. Thereby, the first step is to figure out the interrelationship between the targets.

3. Scientific Prediction

Decision-making aims at future actions, hence, before the decision, we must predict the probable variation of decision objective and its external environment. Only under such situation, can we rationally formulate decision plans according to decision targets and realistic conditions and future change.

The necessary information and ongoing prediction in the process of decision vary from the contents and objectives of decision-making. Generally speaking, decision-making needs to understand the following aspects: the current situation of objectives, the development law of decision objectives, and the external change of the objectives.

4. Formulate Schemes

The instinct of decision-making is to make choices, which must have more than one alternative offers. Therefore, formulating several alternative offers is a very important phase in the process of decision-making. It directly determines the quality of decision.

Formulating schemes must satisfy two principles: First, integrity and elimination between individuals. Integrity means to find out all the alternative offers without any omission (of course it is hard and even impossible). Second, mutual exclusion between individuals, which means each scheme should differentiate in principle and mutually repel. Implementing A means no implementation of B.

The steps of formulating schemes can be basically divided into conditions analysis, measurement analysis and action phase analysis. Conditions analysis should start with diverse aspects, mainly includes restraint conditions analysis, marginal conditions analysis, current conditions analysis and probable conditions analysis. Among them, marginal conditions analysis means the target is flexible, the counterparts of maximum conditions and minimum conditions are marginal conditions. Measurement analysis is to analyze how to transform the probable conditions into realistic conditions, which includes the analysis of measurement about directly prompting the goal to come true and analysis of contingency measurement. Action phase analysis means to achieve the goals step by step.

5. Evaluate Schemes

In order to pick out the optimal schemes form plenty alternative schemes, we need to compare and evaluate each scheme. Evaluating schemes cannot base on personal preferences, but adopt scientific attitude and standard to proceed. We should research the restraint elements of each scheme, comprehensively evaluate the rationality of technology, availability of measurement, time-effect of economy, adaptability of environment of every schemes and the influence it has on society and ecology, and analyze the possible problems, difficulties, obstacles, risks and formulate corresponding prevention and contingency measurements.

Through the analysis above, we can draw a conclusion on the advantages and disadvantages of every scheme, and make a choice accordingly.

6. Select Schemes

This is the most critical step of decision, in this step, the following questions need to be emphasized:

(1) In the process of decision-making, it is hard to find out the optimal schemes due to the restriction of subjectivity. Generally, it suffices to find out the plan satisfying the decision-maker.

(2) Schemes selection is not simply pick out one and give up the others because different schemes are mostly formulated by staff from different fields and business or members of the same organization form different angles, which are restricted to the subjectivity of the decision-makers. Having different opinions on one issue doesn't mean their perspectives are wrong, or are not feasible at all. Different schemes have their pros and cons most of the time. Decision-makers should place them together to comprehensively consider their advantages and disadvantages to exert each scheme's advantages as much as possible, and overcome their shortages so as to integrate a better and more feasible plan. This is actual a recreation process on the basis of the original plan.

(3) Consider all kinds of index to avoid partially focusing on the economic index.

(4) Decision-makers have to accurately trade off the pros and cons of different schemes to make a correct selection, and they should pay attention to following issues. First, correctly handle the relationship with the experts. Modern decision-making must involve the participation of experts. Decision-makers should respect the experts' opinions, but they can't be totally influenced by that and give up their responsibility in the process of decision-making. Second, decision-

makers should have strategic and systematic opinions, should base on the initial target to examine the plan, and have different considerations on different plans. Third, decision-makers should dare to deal with the risks. This is a challenge to their awareness of exploration and aggressive spirit.

7. Examine Decision

After the decision plan is selected, it should strictly make experiments in the places that are typical in the whole situation according to selected plan, which means we cannot randomly find a place or provide any special conditions. Meanwhile, such an experiment can't be conducted just in one place. We must set up a reference group (reference point) under the same condition so as to make comparison. Draw a scientific conclusion to assure the liability of the scheme.

If the trial is successful, which means the decision scheme is confirmed by the experiment, then the scheme can be universally implemented. If the trial fails, which means the scheme is proved to be unavailable, we should feedback in time and do a follow-up inspection and revise the decision.

8. Implement Decision

The accomplishment of plan's formulation and examination doesn't mean the end of the decision-making process. Only after combing them with decision execution and implementation, can we constitute a scientific and complete decision-making process. During the implementation of decision, even if the schemes are meticulously and prudently taken into account, there can be situation deviating from the goal because of the constant variation of all kinds of elements. This requires us to implement and control feedback, do follow-up inspection in the process of decision implementation. Follow-up inspection should be done from three aspects: ①Formulate regulation. ②Use regulations to measure the implementation. ③Rectify the deviation anytime. If the subjective conditions have considerable changes, rendering us to redetermine the target, we must be decisive and tract the decision.

The so-called tracking decision refers to the radical revision of the goal or the decision scheme when the implementation of original scheme shows that the goal is hard to achieve. The situation happens in two conditions: The first is that the process of implementation shows the initial plan is incorrect. The second is the initial plan is accurate, but the subjective conditions change a lot. The original scheme cannot proceed under either of them, and this is the tracking decision.

Tracking decision is kind of strategic shift, but it doesn't mean the initial decision collapsed. Decision-makers are supposed to keep a clear mind on this. Only after the initial plan is practically proved to be wrong, and the decision-makers insist on the mistakes and refuse to revise, or regardless of the change of subjective conditions to blindly implement the initial decision, can the decision collapse.

Above are the general decision-making procedures, but it doesn't mean these steps are indispensable in all decisions. For the simple decisions, several of the steps can be omitted. Decision-making is a complicated process that is prone to be influenced by factors like environment, the past decisions, personal or organizational attitude, culture and time.

第四节 决策的方法

决策的方法很多，概括起来主要有两大类：一类是定性决策方法，另一类是定量决策方法。随着决策理论和实践的不断发展，人们在决策中所采用的方法也不断地得到充实和完善。

一、定性决策方法

常用的定性决策方法有以下几种：

（1）案例法，又称借鉴法。采用以往被证明行之有效的解决方案，如：按规章制度奖惩员工，按惯例支付报酬等。

（2）专家意见法，又分为头脑风暴法、德尔菲法和专家会议法。

头脑风暴法：这是一种产生新思想、拟订备选方案的方法。其做法是把一些人集中在一起，由主持人点明问题，所有人围绕问题自由发言、畅所欲言，在发言过程中须遵守以下规则：①不许批评。无论发言多么荒诞离奇、不合理，所有人均不允许发表批评意见。②多多益善。鼓励参与者海阔天空尽情发挥，想法、方案越多越好。③允许补充。发言者可以在别人想法的基础上进行补充和改进，从而形成新的设想和方案。

主持人在此过程中主要有两项任务：一是不断地对发言者给予表扬和鼓励，从而激励他们说出更多的想法来；二是要负责记录所有的方案，最好能写在黑板上，让所有人都看见。

德尔菲法：这是一种对方案进行评估和选择的方法，其目标是通过综合专家们各自的意见来对方案做出评估和选择。专家既可以是来自一线的管理人员，也可以是高层经理；既可以是组织内的专家，也可以是请来的专家。必须避免专家们面对面地集体讨论，因为专家组织的成员之间存在着身份或地位差别，这样会使一些人因不愿批评其他人而放弃自己合理的主张。德尔菲法的方法是使用一个中间人（或中间组织），由中间人把在第一轮调查过程中专家们各自单独提出的意见集中起来并加以归纳后反馈给他们，然后重复这一过程，使专家们有机会修改他们的观点并说明修改的原因，一般重复 3～5 次之后，专家们的意见便趋于一致。

德尔菲法主要有三个特点：①匿名性。调查过程中不透露专家的名字，也不清楚有多少专家参加，这就使专家们能够客观地发表意见。②集中反馈。专家可从中间人的反馈中得知集体的主要意见并据此做出新的判断，从而减少了干扰。③对回答进行统计学处理。德尔菲法比较费时间，对时间敏感性决策通常行不通。另外，要物色到合适的专家也有一定难度。

专家会议法：是根据决策问题的目的和要求，邀请有关方面的专家，通过会议形式，提出有关问题，展开讨论分析，做出判断。最后综合专家们的意见，做出决策。这种方法的优点是：通过座谈讨论能够相互启发、集思广益、取长补短，能较快、较全面地集中各方面的意见，得出决策结论。缺点是：由于参加的人数有限，代表很容易受到权威的影响，往往不能畅所欲言。因此，采用这种方法时一定要注意：①参加的人数不易太多；②要召开讨论式的会议，尽抒己见；③决策者要虚心听取专家们的意见。

（3）简化法。在决策实践中有时会面临复杂的问题，很难用上面的方法直接解决，这时就可以将问题层层分解，以寻求答案。例如，某种商品在市场上销路差，怎么解决这个问题？就可采用以下简化程序（如图3-2所示）。

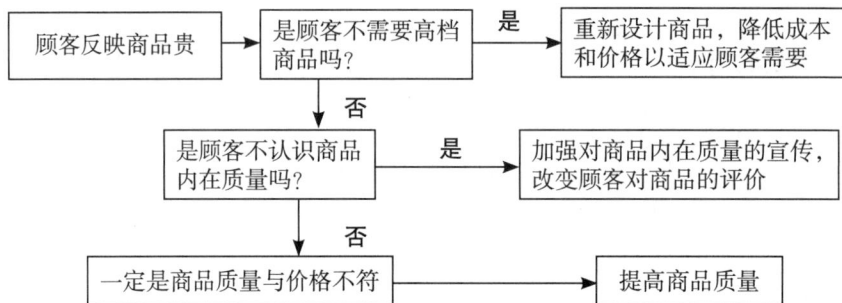

图3-2　决策的简化法

【小链接】

在一次研讨会上，一位企业家讲述了他成功的经验。有人问他："你在管理上取得了巨大的成功，我想请问，对你来说，最重要的是什么？"

企业家没有直接回答，而是拿起粉笔，在黑板上画了一个圈，只是没有画圆满，留下了一个缺口。他反问道："这是什么？"人们异口同声地回答："圈！"

他带笑摇摇头，对这个答案未置可否，而是顺着自己的思路说："实际上，这只是一个未画完整的句号。你们问我为什么会取得辉煌的业绩，道理很简单：我会事先留缺口。我不仅会在大街上留下缺口作为运输通道，而且做出任何决策都不是画个圆满的句号，而是一定要留个缺口，让我的下属去填满它。只有这样，下属才能在事情完成后，有一种自豪感和成就感。"

二、定量决策方法

经常根据决策过程中信息的完备程度来讨论定量决策方法，从这个角度来分析，主要有确定型决策、风险型决策和不确定型决策三种。

1. 确定型决策

常用的确定型决策方法有线性规划法和盈亏平衡分析法。

（1）线性规划法。线性规划是在一些线性等式或不等式的约束条件下，求出线性目标函数的最大值或最小值的方法。其步骤是：第一，确定影响目标大小的变量；第二，列出目标函数的方程；第三，找出实现目标的约束条件；第四，找出实现目标函数达到最优的可行解。

【例3.1】某企业生产桌子和椅子两种产品，它们需要经过制造和装配两道工序，有关资料见表3-1。假设生产的桌椅都能销售出去，何种产品组合才能使企业的利润最大？

表 3 - 1 某企业的有关资料

	桌子	椅子	工序可利用的时间
在制造工序上的时间（小时）	2	4	48
在装配工序上的时间（小时）	4	2	60
单位产品利润（元）	8	6	—

第一步，确定影响目标大小的变量。在本例中，目标是利润 P，影响利润的变量是桌子的数量 T 和椅子的数量 C。

第二步，列出目标函数方程：$P = 8T + 6C$。

第三步，找出约束条件。本例中，工序可利用的时间为约束条件，即：

制造工序：$2T + 4C \leqslant 48$；

装配工序：$4T + 2C \leqslant 60$，$T \geqslant 0$，$C \geqslant 0$。

第四步，求出最优解——最优产品组合。通过图解法（如图 3 - 3 所示）求出解为：$T = 12$，$C = 6$，即生产 12 张桌子和 6 把椅子时企业的利润最大，最大利润为 132 元。

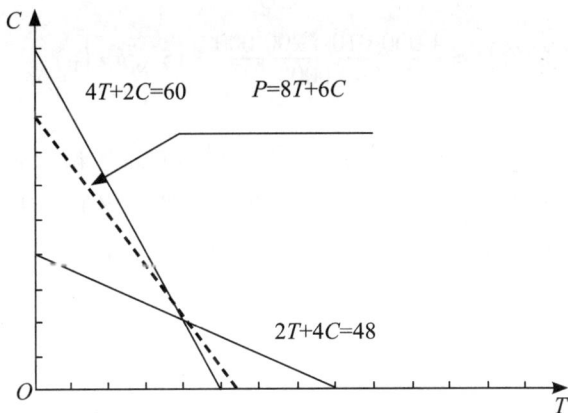

图 3 - 3 线性规划图解法

（2）盈亏平衡分析法。盈亏平衡分析法是研究生产、经营一种产品达到不盈不亏时的产量或收入的决策方法。这个不盈也不亏的平衡点就是盈亏平衡点。显然，当生产量低于这个产量时，发生亏损；超过这个产量时，则获得盈利。如图 3 - 4 所示，随着产量的增加，总成本与销售额随之增加，当达到平衡点 A 时，总成本等于销售额，此时不盈也不亏，正对应此点的产量 Q 为平衡点产量；销售额 R 为平衡点销售额。同时，以 A 点为分界，形成亏损与盈利两个区域。此模型中的总成本是由固定成本和变动成本构成的。

根据图 3 - 4，盈亏平衡点产量的计算公式为：

$\because PQ = F + VQ$ $\therefore Q = F/(P - V)$

【例 3.2】某企业生产一种产品，其总固定成本为 200 000 元，单位产品变动成本和价格分别为 10 元和 15 元，企业达到盈亏平衡点的销量是多少？

$$Q = 200\,000/(15 - 10) = 40\,000（件）$$

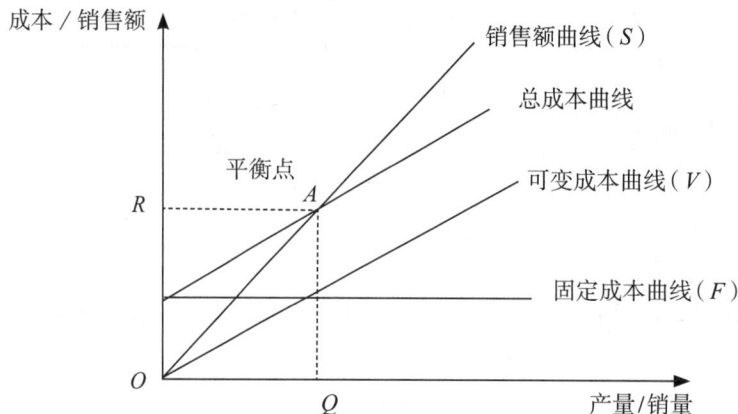

图 3 - 4　盈亏平衡分析基本模型

【例 3.3】某企业生产一种产品，其总固定成本为 200 000 元，单位产品变动成本为 10 元，若产品销售达到盈亏平衡点，该种产品应定价多少？

根据盈亏平衡点产量计算公式，可以得出盈亏产量平衡点的价格应该为：

$$P = \frac{QV + C}{Q}$$

所以，达到平衡点的价格 $= \dfrac{4\,000\,010 + 200\,000}{40\,000} = 15$（元/件）。

2. 风险型决策

常用的风险型决策方法是决策树法。决策树法就是借助于树形分析图，根据各种自然状态出现的概率及方案的预期损益，计算比较各方案的期望值，从而选择最优方案的方法。其决策的步骤是：第一步，绘制决策树。实际上这是拟订各种决策方案的过程，也是对未来可能发生的各种状况进行周密思考和预测的过程。第二步，计算期望损益值。根据图中有关数据，计算不同的备选方案在不同的自然状态下的损益期望值及其综合值，将综合值填写在相应的方案枝末端的机会点上方，表示该方案的经济效果。第三步，剪枝决策。比较各方案的期望收益值，从中选择收益值最大的作为最佳方案，其余的方案枝一律剪掉，最终剩下一条贯穿始终的方案枝，即决策方案。

【例 3.4】某公司计划未来 3 年生产某产品，需要确定产品批量。根据预估，这种产品的市场状况的概率是：畅销为 0.2，一般为 0.5，滞销为 0.3。现提出大、中、小三种批量的生产方案，求能取得最大经济效益的方案。有关数据如表 3 - 2 所示。

表 3 - 2　某企业的有关资料　　　　　　　　　　　　单位：万元

	畅销（0.2）	一般（0.5）	滞销（0.3）
大批量	40	30	-10
中批量	30	20	8
小批量	20	18	14

第一步，绘制决策树。首先从左端决策点（用"□"表示）出发，按备选方案引出相应的方案枝（用"——"表示），每条方案枝上注明所代表的方案；然后，每条方案枝到

达一个方案的结点（用"○"表示），再由各方案结点引出各个状态枝（也称概率枝，用"——"表示），并在每个状态枝上注明状态内容及其概率；最后，在状态枝末端（用"△"表示）注明不同状态下的损益值。决策树完成后，再在下面注明时间长度，如图3-5所示。

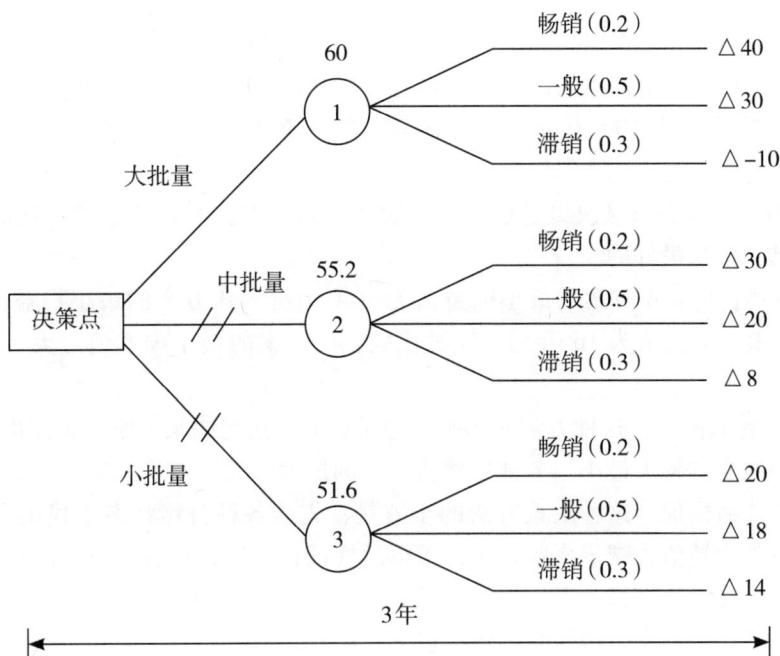

图3-5 决策树图

第二步，计算期望损益值。根据决策树资料，计算如下：

大批量生产期望值 = ［40×0.2 +30×0.5 + （－10）×0.3］×3 =60（万元）

中批量生产期望值 = （30×0.2 +20×0.5 +8×0.3）×3 =55.2（万元）

小批量生产期望值 = （20×0.2 +18×0.5 +14×0.3）×3 =51.6（万元）

第三步，剪枝决策。将各方案的期望值标在各个方案的结点上；然后比较各方案的期望值，从中选择期望值最大的作为最佳方案，并把最佳方案的期望值写在决策点方框的上边，同时剪去（用"∥"表示）其他方案枝。此例中，大批量生产期望值最大，所以选择该方案。

3．不确定型决策

常用的不确定型决策方法有乐观法、悲观法和最小后悔值法。

（1）乐观法。这种决策方法是建立在决策者对未来形势的估计非常乐观的基础之上的，即认为极有可能出现最好的自然状态，于是争取好中取好。

【例3.5】某公司计划生产一种新产品。该产品在市场上的销售情况有三种可能：销路好、销路一般和销路差。对每种情况出现的概率均无法预测。现有三种方案：A方案是自己动手改造原有设备；B方案是全部更新，购进新设备；C方案是购进关键设备，其余自己制造。该产品计划生产5年。据测算，各个方案在各种自然状态下的预期损益如表3-3所示。

表 3 - 3　各方案在不同情况下的损益值　　　　　单位：万元

	销路好	销路一般	销路差
A 方案	180	120	-40
B 方案	240	100	-80
C 方案	100	70	16

在【例3.5】中，A 方案的最大损益值为180万元，B 方案的最大损益值为240万元，C 方案的最大损益值为100万元。经过比较，B 方案的最大损益值最大，所以选择 B 方案。

（2）悲观法。这种方法决策是建立在决策者对未来形势的估计非常悲观的基础上的，故从最坏的结果中选最好的。

在【例3.5】中，A 方案的最小损益值为 -40万元，B 方案的最小损益值为 -80万元，C 方案的最小损益值为16万元。经过比较，C 方案的最小损益值最大，所以选择 C 方案。

（3）最小后悔值法。这种方法的基本思想是如何使选定决策方案后可能出现的后悔值达到最小，即蒙受的损失最小。各种自然状态下的最大收益值与实际采用方案的收益值之间的差额，叫作后悔值。这种决策方法的步骤是：先从各种自然状态下找出最大收益值；再用各个方案的收益值去减最大收益值，求得后悔值；然后，从各个方案的后悔值中找出最大后悔值，并从中选择最大后悔值最小的方案为决策方案。

在【例3.5】中，在销路好的自然状态下，B 方案的收益最大，为240万元。在将来发生的自然状态是销路好的情况下，如果管理者恰好选择了这一方案，他就不会后悔，即后悔值为0。如果他选择的不是 B 方案，而是其他方案，他就会后悔（后悔没有选择 B 方案）。比如，他选择的是 C 方案，该方案在销路好时带来的收益是100万元，比选择 B 方案少了140万元的收益，即后悔值为140万元。各个后悔值的计算结果如表3 - 4所示。

表 3 - 4　各方案在不同情况下的后悔值　　　　　单位：万元

	销路好	销路一般	销路差
A 方案	60	0	56
B 方案	0	20	96
C 方案	140	50	0

由表3 - 4可以看出，A 方案的最大后悔值为60万元，B 方案的最大后悔值为96万元，C 方案的最大后悔值为140万元，经过比较，A 方案的最大后悔值最小，所以选择 A 方案。

Section 4　Methods of Decision-making

There are many decision-making methods, which can be concluded into two major categories: one is qualitative decision-making method, and the other is quantitative decision-making method.

With the constant development of decision theories and practices, the decision-making methods adopted are constantly enriched and improved.

3.4.1 Qualitative Decision-making Method

Regular decision-making methods include several following types:

(1) Case study method, also called reference method. Use the solution scheme that was proved to be available in the past, for example, rewarding and punishing staff according to the regulations, paying the reward conventionally, etc.

(2) Experts' suggestions method, which is divided into brainstorming method, Delphi method and expert conference method.

Brainstorming method: Brainstorming method is a method that generates the new ideas and formulate alternative offers. This method is to gather some volunteers who will be asked brief questions by a host and then they will speak out their minds about the questions. Here are some rules needed to be observed during the speaking: ①No criticism, no matter how ridiculous and unreasonable the speaking is, none of them is allowed to make a critical comment. ②The more the better. The participants are encouraged to speak out freely and dramatically, the more ideas and plans they put forward, the better it will be. ③Supplementation is allowed. Spokesmen are allowed to supplement and improve on the basis of others' opinions, so as to form new assumptions and schemes.

The host mainly has two assignments during the process: The first is to encourage and praise the speakers in order to motivate more opinions. The second is to record all the schemes. It is better to write down the schemes on the blackboard so that they are visible for everyone.

Delphi method: Delphi method is to evaluate and select the schemes by integrating the opinions from each expert. The experts may be first-line managers or top managers. They can also come from the interior or be invited. It is necessary to restrain the experts from discussing face to face, because there are identity or status differences among experts, which will render some of them to abandon their reasonable opinions because they are not willing to criticize. The Delphi method is to use a middle man (or middle organization) to collect and conclude the opinions given by experts respectively as feedback to them, and then circulate the step allowing the experts to amend their opinions and give reasons. Generally, it will repeat for 3 to 5 times, and then the opinions of experts may verge to consensus.

Delphi method has three features: ①Anonymity. Survey doesn't reveal the names of experts, and there is no idea how many experts have taken part in the discussion, so that the experts can speak out their opinions objectively. ②Collective feedback. Experts can realize the overall opinions from the middle man's feedback and make a new judgment, which can decrease the obstruction. ③Deal with the response with statistics. Delphic method takes time, so it is unavailable to sensitive decision-making. In addition, it is quite difficult to seek out the suitable experts.

Expert conference method: Expert conference method is based on the purpose and requirement of the decision-making problem. It needs to invite the relative experts to propose questions, start discussion and analysis and make a judgment through a conference. Advantages of such a method are: Through the conference, it is able to illuminate each other, to draw on the wisdom of the mass and to learn from the strong points to offset the weakness, and it is able to collect opinions from all aspects to draw a conclusion quickly and completely. Disadvantages are: Due to the limitation of participating number, the representatives are prone to be influenced by the authority, and often cannot speak out their minds. Therefore, the following aspects must be paid attention to: ①The participants are limited. ②We have to hold a discussing conference to speak out everybody's thoughts. ③Decision-makers are supposed to listen to the experts modestly.

(3) Simplicity method. It is hard to directly solve the complicated problems emerged in the decision-making practice using the methods above, but we can divide the questions little by little to find out the answer. For example, the sales of a certain commodity in the market is bad, so how to solve this problem? The following simplified procedure is the answer:

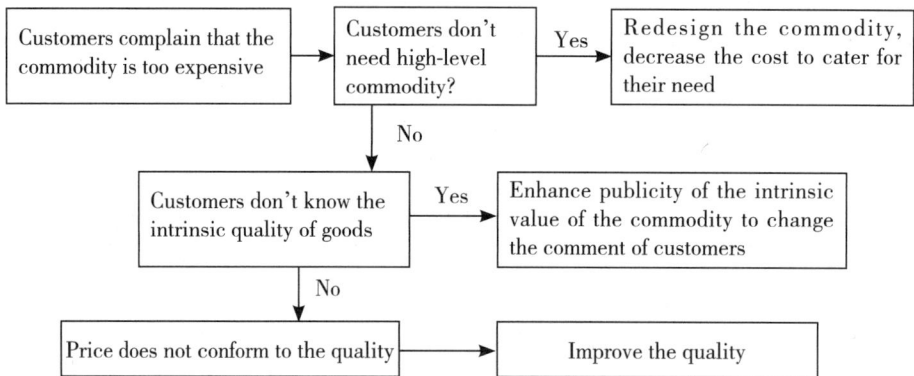

Diagram 3 - 2   Simplicity Method of Decision-making

3.4.2　Quantitative Decision-making Method

Usually, we discuss quantitative decision-making method based on the complete degree of the information in the process of decision-making. From this aspect, it mainly includes certainty decision-making method, risk decision-making method and uncertainty decision-making method.

1. Certainty Decision-making Method

Common certainty decision-making methods involve linear programming method and break-even analysis method.

(1) Linear programming method. Liner programming is to work out the maximum or minimum of the linear target under the restraint of linear equality or inequality. The steps are: Firstly, determine the variables affecting the numerical value of the target. Secondly, formulate the equation of objective function. Thirdly, find out the restraints to achieve the target. Fourthly, find out the feasible solution to optimize the objective function.

（2）Break-even analysis method. Break-even analysis method is a kind of decision-making method to figure out the balance point that a product keeps balance between profit and loss, which is known as break-event point. Apparently, when the output is lower than the point, the company has loss, when exceeds the point, the company gain profit. Shown as Diagram 3 – 4, the total cost and turnover increase as the outputs increase, when it reaches the break-even point A, the total cost equals the turnover, which means there is no profit and no loss at this moment, the corresponding output point Q is the break-even output, point R is the break-even turnover. In the meantime, demarcation point A forms two areas: loss and profit. The total cost of this model is comprised of fixed costs and variable costs.

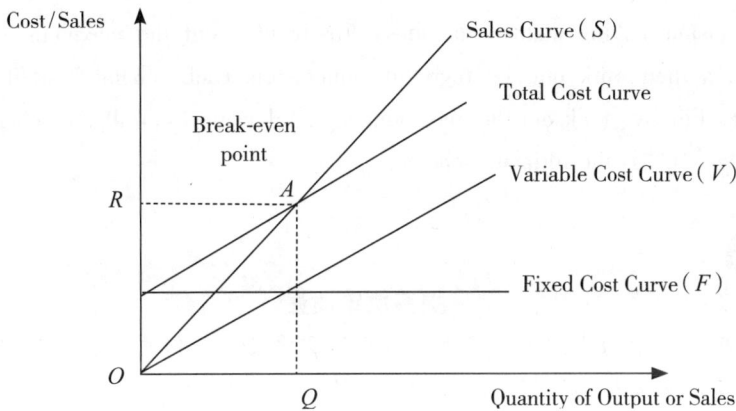

Diagram 3 – 4　Break-even Analysis Method

According to Diagram 3 – 4, the output of break-even point is calculated as:

$\because PQ = F + VQ \qquad \therefore Q = F/ (P - V)$

2. Risk Decision-making Method

Commonly-used risk decision-making method is decision tree method. Decision tree method resorts to the tree diagram to calculate and compare the expected values of each scheme based on the probability of each natural state and expected profit or loss of each scheme, thus, to pick out the optimal one. The steps are: Firstly, portray the decision tree. Actually it is a process to formulate all the decision plans, while meticulously to consider and predict all the future probable situations as well. Secondly, calculate the expected loss and profit. According to the relevant data from the diagram, calculate the expected profit and loss value and comprehensive value under the different natural states of different schemes. And then write down the comprehensive value above the opportunity point of corresponding end of branch to represent the economic effectiveness of the scheme. Thirdly, cut the branches to make decision, compare the expected profit of each scheme to pick out the optimal one with maximum value, and cut off the rest, and the decision scheme is the remaining one.

3. Uncertainty Decision-making Method

Frequently-used uncertainty decision-making method are optimistic method, pessimistic method and the least regretful method.

（1）Optimistic method. Optimistic method is built on the basis that decision-makers have optimistic estimation for the future situation, namely to consider the best natural state to take place, therefore strive to sort out the best from the good.

（2）Pessimistic method. Pessimistic method is based on the badly pessimistic estimation that the decision-makers have made toward the future situation, so that pick out the best from the worse.

（3）The least regretful method. The main idea of this method is how to reach the least regretful value after picking out the decision scheme, namely undertake the least loss. The balance between the maximum value of each natural state and that of the actual scheme calls regretful value. Such decision-making method includes：Firstly pick out the maximum value from each natural state, and then work out the regretful value using each schemes' profit to subtract the maximum value. Finally, pick out the maximum regretful value from all the schemes, and select the relatively least one as the ultimate scheme.

【阅读资料】

提高决策质量

决策在管理过程中的地位决定了决策质量的重要性。如何决策、决策的效果如何，是检验领导者水平的重要标志。提高决策质量必须做到以下几点。

1. 确立科学的决策观

科学决策是指企业领导者在决定方针、政策、方案等重大活动中，要始终遵循一定的科学程序，依靠专家，运用现代科学方法和先进的科学技术手段，在科学预测的前提下，切实把握决策对象的变化规律和条件。科学决策观的确立，并不排斥个人的阅历、知识、智慧和胆略，但是日益复杂的现代生活已经超出个人能力的范围而不得不求助于一套科学的体系。

2. 加强防范分析

防范分析的一般方法和步骤有：①估计决策执行后会出现哪些副作用或不良后果；②对每一项可能发生的问题的危险性进行估计；③分析每个问题的可能原因；④制定相应的应急措施。

3. 采用智能化决策

智能化决策包括三个系统：①电子数据处理系统；②管理信息系统；③决策支持系统。

4. 利用群体决策的优势

为了提高决策的科学性，应当更多地实行群体决策。群体决策的优势是与个人决策相比较而言的：①群体决策的精确性高于个人决策；②群体决策的创造性在一定条件下高于个人决策；③群体对逻辑性问题的决策也可能优于个人决策。

5. 克服群体决策的小集团意识

通过群体决策有利于改善决策的效果，但群体决策也有不足之处，小集团意识就是其中之一。所谓小集团意识，是指群体表面一致的压力和群体成员追求一致的期望，阻碍了人们对智慧的运用和对现实的思考，不能对问题和解决问题的办法做符合实际的评价和分析，从而做出错误的决策。

为了充分发挥群体决策的优势，必须克服小集团意识的干扰，为此，可采取的措施有：①领导人不要在群体讨论之前表明个人偏好，否则会阻碍有价值的不同意见的表达；②指派若干个人专门扮演反对派，专门挑毛病；③不要匆忙决定，应有意给大家一个深思熟虑的"第二次机会"；④保证反对意见的"匿名性"，安排群体成员在会后单独陈述不同的意见；⑤加强与外界的联系更多地吸收外部信息，以避免小集团意识所造成的"坐井观天"。

6. 借助智囊团的作用

现代管理决策目标多样，因素众多，变化迅速。在这种条件下，要做出科学决策，单靠决策者和组织内部的力量是难以做到的，因而必须借助组织外部的智囊团，主要有以下几种：①政府研究机构；②社会咨询服务公司；③工程总体设计机构；④项目型的临时性智囊机构。

有效地借助智囊团的作用，应注意两点：第一，必须充分尊重智囊团的独立性；第二，必须正确处理"谋"与"断"的关系。

【本章提要】

　●决策是为实现一定的目标从两个以上的备选方案中选择一个合理方案的分析判断过程。决策是一个管理者的基本行为，是计划的核心环节。

　●决策是一个系统，一般由决策对象、决策标准、决策信息、决策者以及决策方法五个要素构成。

　●决策按照不同的标准可以划分为不同的类型，科学地划分决策类型，能够为采用科学的决策方法和进行科学决策奠定基础。

　●决策是一个提出问题、分析问题和解决问题的动态过程，一般分为八个步骤：提出问题、确定目标、科学预测、拟订方案、评价方案、选定方案、检验决策、实施决策。

　●定性决策方法主要有头脑风暴法、德尔菲法、专家会议法和简化法。定量决策方法主要有盈亏平衡分析法、决策树法、最小后悔值法、线性规划法。

【关键词】

决策（Decision-making）　程序化决策（Procedural Decision-making）

非程序化决策（Non-Procedural Decision-making）　风险型决策（Risk Decision-making）

不确定型决策（Uncertainty Decision-making）　德尔菲法（Delphi Method）

决策树法（Decision Tree Method）　盈亏平衡分析法（Break-even Analysis Method）

【复习与思考】

1. 什么是决策？其构成要素有哪些？

2. 决策的基本类型有哪些？

3. 决策的一般程序包括哪些步骤？

4. 确定决策目标时应注意哪些问题？拟订方案有哪些基本步骤？

5. 定性决策方法主要有哪些？正确运用各种定量决策方法。

【研究与讨论】

1. 如何正确理解"管理的重心在经营，经营的重心在决策"这句话的含义？

2. 有人曾向一些公司的经理人员做过调查，提出三个问题：你每天花时间最多的是什么？你每天最重要的事情是什么？你在履行职责时感到最困难的是什么？绝大多数人的回答是决策。这说明了什么？

3. 在战略、政策、程序、规则、规划、预算和目标等计划要素中，哪些属于程序性决策？哪些属于非程序性决策？

4. 辨析集体决策与个人决策优缺点。

【实践演练】

1. 描述你在生活或事业中的一次重要决策，你是如何做出决策的？有哪些因素影响你的决策？

2. 在就业和创业两者之间，你将做出何种选择？为什么？

3. 有一家拥有四层楼的百货公司，在安装了两部电梯后仍然听到顾客的抱怨声："等电梯时间太长。"公司不想再减少营业面积来增加电梯。请你为该公司设计出五种新的解决方案。

【管理模拟】

1. 模拟麦当劳公司的一项决策：要不要增加果蔬饮料？

2. 对大学生究竟是先就业还是先创业做出选择？要求：个人写出决策方案，分小组进行讨论，并做出总结。

【本章案例】

贝尔电话公司的决策

费尔在20世纪初曾担任过美国贝尔电话公司将近20年的总裁。在这个时期，费尔创造了一个世界上最大的民营企业。这在美国乃至全球均传为佳话。

电话系统可以民营，这在今天的美国被认为是理所当然的，然而在当时世界上已开发地区的电话系统中，只有贝尔公司经营的北美大部分地区（美国和加拿大的魁北克和安大略两省）不是由政府经营。同时，一个公用事业能够经得起风险并在风险中迅速成长，是不多见的。贝尔公司之所以能有这样的成就，主要是因为费尔在20年中做出的四大决策：

第一大决策：在20世纪初，贝尔电话公司已预测到社会大众的服务要求，并打算满足这些要求。于是便提出了"本公司以服务为目的"的口号。当初，费尔看清了一个民营企业能站得住脚，不被政府收回国有，必须比其他任何企业更加考虑社会利益，积极为社会服务。费尔还认为，应有一个判断管理人员及其作业的尺度，用以衡量服务的程度。把服务成果视作管理人员的一种责任，从而成为公司高层的职责，旨在组织调整资源，提供最佳服务，并获得适当的收益。

第二大决策：费尔认为，作为一个全国性的电信事业，绝不能以传统的"自由企业"无拘束地经营，必须服从"公众管制"。因此，费尔把有效的"公众管制"作为公司的目标。这样，在保证公众利益的同时又能使贝尔公司顺利经营。

第三大决策：公司建立了贝尔研究所，使其成为业界最成功的科研机构之一。费尔的这一决策是以一个独立性民营企业必须自强不息才能保持活力的观念为出发点的。他认为一个企业，没有竞争力便不能成长。电信业的技术最为重要。

第四大决策：费尔在20世纪20年代，为保证公司所需资金，发行了一种美国电话电报公司的普通股，直到今天这只股票仍然是美国和加拿大中产阶级投资的对象，从而使贝尔公司获得了大量的社会资金。这也是不被政府接管的重要原因。

思考问题：

1. 你认为费尔所做的四大决策的正确性表现在哪里？
2. 你从费尔的决策中学到了什么？
3. 你认为中国电信业的发展态势如何？民营企业有无进入电信业的可能？

【本章参考文献】

［1］［美］赫伯特·西蒙著，杨砾等译：《管理行为——管理组织决策过程的研究》，北京：北京经济学院出版社1988年版。

［2］［美］赫伯特·西蒙著，杨砾、徐立译：《现代决策理论的基石——有限理性说》，北京：北京经济学院出版社1989年版。

［3］［美］C. I. 巴纳德著，孙耀君等译：《经理人员的职能》，北京：中国社会科学出版社1997年版。

［4］周三多：《管理学》，北京：中国高等教育出版社2000年版。

［5］王风彬、李东：《管理学》，北京：中国人民大学2003年版。

第四章　计划工作

Chapter 4　Planning Work

凡事预则立，不预则废。

《礼记·中庸》

Preparedness ensures success, unpreparedness spells failure.

The doctrine of the Mean, The Book of Rites

不先将大的目标放进计划中，也许以后永远没有机会把它再放进去了。

苏格拉底

Don't put big goals into plans and might never have a chance to put it back in.

Socrates

【本章学习目标】

知识目标：

> 了解计划的含义和特征。
>
> 掌握计划的类型。
>
> 掌握目标及目标管理的含义。
>
> 掌握时间管理的法则。

技能目标：

> 理解计划的结构体系。
>
> 熟悉计划工作的流程。
>
> 能够运用计划工作的方法。
>
> 掌握目标管理的实施步骤。

【Learning Objectives of Chapter 4】

Objectives of Knowledge：

> Understand the meaning and characteristics of plan.
>
> Master the types of plan.
>
> Grasp the meaning of objective and objective management.
>
> Grasp principles of time management.

Objectives of Skill：

> Understand the structure system of plan.
>
> Be familiar with procedures of planning work.

Be able to utilize the methods of planning work.

Grasp steps of objective management.

【小故事】

有一位父亲带着三个孩子去沙漠猎杀骆驼。他们到达了目的地。父亲问老大："你看到了什么？"老大回答："我看到了猎枪、骆驼，还有一望无际的沙漠。"父亲摇摇头说："不对。"父亲问老二相同的问题。老二回答："我看到了爸爸、大哥、弟弟、猎枪、骆驼，还有一望无际的沙漠。"父亲又摇摇头说："不对。"父亲又问老三相同的问题。老三回答："我只看到了骆驼。"父亲高兴地点点头说："答对了。"

【引例】

预言未来

今天你能否预测到，21世纪哪个行业注定兴旺？哪个行业又会衰亡？如果你能预测到的话，十年前你应该可以想象到互联网的影响了。五年前你应该已预见今天的劳动力市场和激增的保健成本。那样的话也许你可以挂出预言家的招牌，向公司或联邦政府收取大笔费用，来帮助他们为多变的未来做准备。

即使拥有统计数据和其他历史数据，任何人也无法预测2001年的"9·11"恐怖袭击，以及其随后对国内社会和经济产生的影响。虽然下面的预测并没有将恐怖袭击的影响纳入考虑范围，它们还是代表了战略计划使用者的前瞻性思考模式。下面就是袭击后的预测。

预言1：劳动力

预测：如果你在等待失业率上升来缓解你的劳动力压力，那你将会等很长时间。还要经历更长时间的劳动力供应紧张时期，预言家Roger E. Herman这样预测。在那之后也不要期望过高，曼哈顿区的Weiner Edrich Brown Inc.的总裁Edie Weiner警告道。由于Y世代人的成熟，在今后几年进入职场的人才会越来越多，但高级管理人员的储备几年内都不会增加。7 600万生育高峰时出生的人正在涌入劳动力市场，但只有4 400万X世代的人，即第一批在2004年达到40岁的人。

建议：在招聘和留用员工方面的努力比以往任何时候都要重要，特别是在高级管理人员方面。"如果你没有稳定的员工队伍，你将处于竞争劣势"，Herman提醒道。看到你的竞争对手和你一样承受很大的压力，也许你会很宽心。但那其实意味着他们将会打你员工的注意。你想尽量安全地保持自己的成功策略，你的对手当然也想。

预言2：房地产

预测：今后十年，小公司的数目将会有所变化，因为受到两大压力的胁迫——供不应求的劳动力市场和上涨的租金，房地产预言家Roulac这样预测。今后五年，二三十岁的员工会很紧俏，更换工作的速度是年纪较大的人的两倍。

为了吸引这些流动劳动力，小公司被迫为自己创造强大的形象，要花费更多的时间和金钱推销自己。Roulac说，正确的地点很关键。他进行了一个整合文化、经济和其他帮助企业确定最好的经营地点的因素的"地理战略"分析。

建议：你希望选择你的目标员工也想要那种基地——一个生活质量高、教育力量强、交通运输和娱乐设施都令人满意的地点。Roulac 说："如果你处在一个人们并不选择的地方，你将不能吸引员工。"由于越来越多的公司寻找新的本部，这种需求推动房租不断上涨，越来越多的公司也就试图购买自己的办公场所。它们也可能缩小现有空间，或把一些员工送到公共交通可以到达的较便宜的偏远地区，Chrisopher Ireland 这样认为。她是 Cheskin 研究中心的 CEO，Cheskin 是一个位于红木海岸（加利福尼亚州）的预测公司（事实上，今年年初她自己的公司就是这么做的）。那意味着小公司将失去在同一地点工作时具备的灵活、富有凝聚力的典型优势。它们将面临多地点的员工管理问题，这需要后勤管理的协调和技巧，以使大家能够共同工作。Ireland 说她现在管理着五个地方的员工，沟通和办公室文化问题比以往更为凸显。

预言 3：顾客关系

预测：目前的公司并购步伐在今后十年还将继续。所以，当可靠的大客户消失时，小企业就举步维艰了。总部设在华盛顿的 Coates & Jarratt 公司的预言家 Jennifer Jarratt 做了以上预测。他说："你不再有像几年前那样的连贯性了。"

建议：为了应付客户的剧烈变动，越来越多的小企业不得不重视营销并重新审视它们的企业战略。它们不再过于把精力放在大客户身上，而是寻求更稳定的小到中规模的客户群，Jarratt 这样预测。公司也可以尝试集中精力服务于一个经过严格挑选的客户群，向他们提供优质的服务。这种策略可以帮助小企业保持住它们已经合并或被购买的客户。

虽然随着合并的升级，拥有良好业务的小企业无疑会被吞并，不过 Weiner 并没有预测说未来将没有小企业。相反，巨型合并发生时，大集团会舍弃一些小市场，从而留给小企业新的机会，她说："当合并的企业试图寻找效率时，它们就创造了外包的需求，这将刺激中小型企业的成长。"

预言 4：财富转移

预测：在"什么将会是历史上最大的财富转移之一"这个问题上，语言家 Johnson 说，今后 20 年，生育高峰时出生的孩子将会从他们的父母那里继承成千上万美元的家族企业和数十亿美元的资金。

建议：有些小企业将会从新鲜血液和新领导那里获得利润，这有助于它们的成长，另一些小企业将会被收购，把钱留给继承人去投资其他企业。Weiner 说，生育高峰期出生的人在工作中将开始面对年龄上的歧视，也会用他们的遗产开办新的公司或收购销售额上涨的公司。

Weiner 说，由于小公司成长的刺激，商业咨询机会将大量涌现，它们为新诞生的企业提供从成功计划到金融服务的一切咨询。例如，Weiner 已经研究了这种趋势并为她自己的公司展望了未来。她说她已经计划扩展未来的咨询服务业务，从而为更多的小公司服务。其他公司也有类似的动向。

预言 5：技术

预测：今后 50 年将会看到如 Technology Futures 公司的 David Smith 所称的"生物科学时代"的变革。生物科学将会应用于生产、信息处理和其他领域。到 2040 年，计算机的力量将会超过人脑的能力，人工智能将会成为现实。

建议："生物信息学"领域将蓬勃发展。也许有一天，你会把你的计算机监督程序换成"视网膜显示器"或 DNA 计算机。Smith 说："为了得到专业化的化学药品，我们不必再在地下挖掘而可以自己培养。"这些变化将带来新的商机。所有这些新技术都需要更多的能源。但是石油价格上涨和自然资源的减少将会刺激所谓绿色产业（使用替代能源）的成长，Jarratt 说。企业经营也会变得容易。人工智能会让你把持续增长的成批任务转交给计算机来处理，Smith 说。但因为计算机仍然没有感觉，因此将需要更多的咨询人员处理工作中出现的人的问题。

当企业害怕停滞

"新千年"是从 2001 年 9 月 11 日开始的。美国的经济和世界其他地方一样，在恐怖分子袭击世贸中心和五角大楼后的几周内开始表现出对衰退的担心。这一事件挫败了美国对自身领导地位的一贯认识——其对自身安全的过分自信。这一事件将世界带到了一个不确定的新时代。当冷战成为历史，许多国家投向自由市场的怀抱时，世界似乎被共同的机会联合了起来，而现在，则被对风险的恐惧联合在一起。

当时的美国人有理由恐惧。我们知道恐怖分子想要摧毁这个国家。人们可能因打开装有炭疽病毒的信封而死去。而在企业界，一些受人尊敬的企业高管变成了无耻的骗子。股票市场比多数人想象的还不可靠，熊市既是恐惧的信号，也是恐惧的原因。但是也许人们反应过度了，因谨慎陷入了无理由的恐惧，这可能让美国倒退，使经济增长停滞。

投资者对风险的规避可能有更广泛的影响。从基础设施说起。减少对资本市场的关注，电话和有线供电被迫缩小其可能带来的巨大收益的宽带通信网络的规模。许多新产品可能永远没有机会获得成功，因为公司没有足够的资本进行规模化生产并将其推向市场。对风险的规避可能使企业减少对研发的投入，使一些领域内（从软件、生物技术到燃料电池）很好的新产品推迟诞生。

这不仅是钱的问题。创新企业很难获得和保留员工，"三年前，许多人排队等着加入新企业，因为他们认为这里很有前途"，波士顿 Russell Reynolds Associates 的高管招聘人员 Steve Maxwell 这样说。现在季节性管理者更看紧位子，"现在比过去几年更为注重规避风险。"加利福尼亚风险投资商 Accel Partners 的 James W. Breyer 如是评价。

繁荣时代最没有得到认可的发展就是金融创新，而现在这种看法正受到攻击。过去，投资银行为企业对冲或投资寻找新办法。现在，可以理解的是，许多 CEO 不希望创造性和融资挨得过紧，但拘泥于规矩的金融工具使企业效率更为低下，而且更加不稳定。

（资料来源：Alison Stein Wellner. What Comes Next. *Business Week*, December 4, 2000；Peter Coy. When Business Is Scared Stagnant. *Business Week*, August 26, 2002）

思考问题：

1. 既然计划赶不上变化，那还要不要计划？
2. 如何增强计划的适应性、减少其盲目性？

第一节　计划的含义、特征和作用

计划是管理活动的起点，是一项重要的管理职能，组织中的各项活动都离不开计划，计划工作的质量也集中体现了组织管理的水平。

一、计划的含义

为了使集体活动卓有成效，就必须首先明确追求的目标，明确为了实现这些目标所必须经过的路径和行动方案。计划有静态和动态之分，静态意义上的计划是指用文字和指标等形式所表述的组织在未来一定时期内有关行动方向、内容和方式等安排的管理文件；动态意义上的计划是指组织根据环境的需要和自身的特点，确定组织在一定时期内的目标，并通过计划的编制、执行和控制来协调、组织各类资源以实现预期目标的过程。这一过程可归纳为"5W1H"，即做什么（what）、为什么做（why）、何时做（when）、在哪里做（where）、谁来做（who）和怎么做（how）。

二、计划的特征

（1）目的性。任何组织和个人制订计划都是为了有效地达到某种目标，目标是计划的核心内容，实现目标是计划的出发点和归宿，没有目标就没有计划。计划是为组织目标服务的。

（2）先行性。计划是对未来活动的预先安排。计划相对于其他管理职能来说，处于首位。组织、领导、控制等职能，只有在计划确定了目标以后才能进行，计划是实施其他管理职能的基础。

（3）普遍性。不管什么组织，也不管组织中的哪个层次的管理者，要想实施有效管理，就必须做好计划工作。组织的任何管理活动都必须要进行计划，计划也是所有管理者应具有的能力。

（4）效率性。计划工作就是要更有效地配置资源以实现目标，因此，计划必须讲效率，即以更小的投入获得更大的产出。

（5）创造性。计划总是要针对所要解决的新问题、新变化、新机会做出设计，因而是一个创新过程。计划也称为面向未来的管理。

三、计划的作用

（1）指引方向，指导工作。计划能使组织置身于复杂多变和充满不确定性因素的环境中而始终把其主要的注意力集中在一定的目标上，使组织所有的行动保持同一方向；管理者可以根据计划来组织人员、分派任务，使组织的各项工作得到落实，从而保证组织目标的实现。

（2）降低风险，掌握主动。计划是面向未来的，能使组织较早地预见未来的变化，早做准备，掌握主动权，从而降低乃至消除不确定性，把风险减少到最低限度。

（3）减少浪费，提高效益。计划能从多条实现目标的途径中，通过技术经济论证和可行性分析，选择最适当、最有效的方案，从而减少浪费，以最低的费用或最高的效率实现既定的目标。计划能使组织未来的各项活动均衡发展，使组织中各成员的努力合成一种组织效应，从而大大提高工作效率并带来经济效益。

（4）提供控制标准。计划工作建立的目标和指标是控制的依据和尺度。组织的各个部门、各种人员、各项工作都需靠计划来协调。

Section 1   Meaning, Characteristics and Functions of Plan

Making plan is the starting point for management activities, and it is an important management function. Organization's activities are inseparable from planning. The quality of planning work also embodies the level of organization and management.

4.1.1   Meaning of Plan

In order to make collective activity effective, we must first be clear of paths and action plans to achieve these goals. Plans can be divided into static and dynamic. A static plan is the management document that expressed by text and targets, which is related to arrangements about action, content and methods in a certain period in the future. Dynamic plan is the process that an organization sets a goal based on the requirement of environment or itself, coordinates and organizes all kinds of resources by setting, carrying and controlling the plan to achieve the expected goal. This process can be concluded as "5W1H", which are what, why, when, where, who and how.

4.1.2   Characteristics of Plan

(1) Finality. The aim of any organization or individual setting up a plan is to reach a certain goal effectively. The goal is the core content of a plan. To achieve the goal is the starting point and destination of a plan. Plan cannot be a plan without a goal. Plan serves the organization's goal.

(2) Antecedence. Plan is the pre-arrangement for future activities. Compared with other management functions, plan is in the first place. Organizing, leading, controlling and other functions can only be carried out after the goal is determined in a plan. Plan is the basis of the implementation of other management functions.

(3) Universality. No matter what organization it is, no matter which level managers are in the organization, they must do planning work if they want to implement effective management. Every organization's management activity needs plan. Planning is also the basic function required for all managers.

(4) Efficiency. Planning means to allocate resources more effectively to achieve the goal, therefore, the plan must be efficient—make the greater output with the smaller input.

(5) Innovation. Plan always aims at the new question, the new change, the new opportunity which have to be solved. Thus it is an innovation process. Plan is also called the management that faces the future.

4.1.3   Functions of Plan

(1) Give direction and guidance. Plan can make the organization always focus on a certain

target in a complicated and uncertain environment and take all actions to keep the same direction. Managers can organize employees and distribute tasks according to the plan while implementing the work, so as to ensure the realization of organizational goals.

(2) Reduce risk and grasp the initiative. Plan is for the future, it can enable the organization to foresee the future changes at an early time. Preparing early, grasping the initiative can help reduce and even eliminate uncertainties so as to reduce the risk to the minimum.

(3) Reduce waste and improve efficiency. Plan can help select the most appropriate and effective programs from multiple ways to achieve goals through technical and economic feasibility and feasibility analysis, reduce waste and achieve the established goals with the lowest cost or highest efficiency. Plan can make the activities develop in balance, and make the efforts of the members of the organization synthesized, thus greatly improve the efficiency and economic benefits.

(4) Provide control standard. Goals and indicators established in plans are the basis and measure of control. All departments of an organization, all kinds of personnel and work also need to be coordinated by plan.

【小链接】

计划工作就是根据社会需要和组织的自身能力，在科学预测未来的基础上确定组织在一定时期内的奋斗目标，通过计划的编制、执行和检查，协调和合理安排组织中各方面的经营和管理活动，有效地利用组织的人力、物力和财力资源，以取得最佳的经济效益和社会效益的组织活动过程。计划工作与未来密切相关，要想取得预期的效果，必须正确地预测未来。因此也就要求管理者要对过去的信息情报加以科学地分析，根据分析结果和现在的现实条件设立组织的未来目标，确定达到目标的一系列政策和方法，最后才能形成一个完整的计划。

第二节　计划体系

一、计划的类型

依照不同的标准，可将计划分为不同的类型，各种类型的计划不是彼此割裂的，而是由分别适用于不同条件下的计划组成的一个计划体系。

（1）按期限划分：短期计划、中期计划、长期计划。

（2）按综合程度划分：战略计划、战术计划。

（3）按明确程度划分：指导性计划、具体计划。

（4）按组织层次划分：高层计划、中层计划、基层计划。

（5）按组织职能划分：生产计划、营销计划、财务计划。

（6）按对象划分：综合计划、局部计划、单项计划。

二、计划的结构体系

一般来说，一项完整的计划应当包括以下结构要素，如图 4-1 所示：

（1）组织的宗旨或使命。宗旨或使命，指明一定的组织在社会上应起的作用和所处的地位，也是一个组织何以存在的基本理由。服务社会，发展自己，是一般企业的目的和使命。

（2）组织的目标。组织的使命说明了组织要从事的事业，而组织的目标更加具体地说明了组织从事这项事业的预期结果。目标是组织行动的出发点和归宿。

（3）组织的战略。为了实现组织的目标，组织就需要选择一个关于发展方向、行动方针，以及各类资源分配方案的总纲，这就是组织的战略。

图 4-1 计划的层次体系

（4）组织的政策。政策是管理者考虑问题的指南，制定政策是为了规定组织行为的方向和界限，使管理人员的工作有了重要的依据。

（5）组织的程序。程序规定了某些经常发生问题的解决方法和步骤，程序是一种经过优化的计划，是通过总结大量经验而形成的、规范化的日常工作过程和方法，往往能够较好地体现政策的内容。

（6）组织的规章。规章是一个最简单的计划，它规定了某种情况下采取或不采取某种具体行动，规则只是对具体情况下的单个行动的规定。

（7）组织的规划。规划方案是一个综合性的计划，它包括为实施既定方针所必需的目标、政策、程序、规则、任务分派、资源安排以及其他要素。

（8）组织的预算。预算是一种数字化的计划，把预期的结果用数字化的方式表示出来，就形成了预算。预算不仅表现在财务指标上，还是一种主要的控制指标。

Section 2　Plan System

4.2.1　Types of Plan

According to different standards, plan can be divided into different types. Different types of plan are not separated from each other, but are suitable for different conditions, which make up a plan system.

（1）According to the deadline: short-term plan, medium-term plan, long-term plan.

（2）According to the comprehensive degree: strategic plan, tactical plan.

（3）According to the degree of certainty: directional plan, specific plan.

（4）According to the organization's structure: high-level plan, middle-level plan, basic plan.

（5）According to the function of an organization: productive plan, marketing plan, financial plan.

（6）According to the objective: integrated plan, partial plan, single plan.

4.2.2 Structure System of Plan

Generally speaking, a complete plan shall include the following structural elements shown in Diagram 4 – 1:

（1）The purpose or mission of an organization. Purpose or mission, indicating the role and position that a certain organization should play, is also a fundamental reason why an organization exists. Serving the society and developing itself are the general purpose and mission of an enterprise.

（2）The objective of an organization. An organization's mission shows the business that organization must be engaged in, but its goal more specifically shows the anticipated result that an organization is engaged in this enterprise. The goal is the starting point and the destination of an organization.

Diagram 4 – 1   The Level of the Plan System

（3）The strategy of an organization. In order to achieve organization's goal, the organization needs to choose one outline about the development direction, the program of action, as well as every kind of resource's distribution, this is organization's strategy.

（4）The policy of an organization. Policy is the guidance that the managers consider the question. The formulation of policy is also aim to stipulate the direction and the boundary of the organization's behavior, which enable administrative personnel's work to have the important basis.

（5）The procedure of an organization. Procedure specifies some frequent problems' solving methods and steps. Procedure is a kind of optimized plan which is the standardization of daily work process and method formed by a large amount of experience, can better reflect the content of policy.

（6）The rule of an organization. Rule is one of the simplest plans. It provides some specific actions taken or not taken in some cases. Rule only make the provisions of the specific case of a single action.

（7）The plan of an organization. It is a comprehensive plan, including objectives, policies, procedures, rules, tasks, resources arrangement, and other factors that are necessary for the implementation of the policies.

（8）The budget of an organization. Budget is a kind of digitized plan, expressing the anticipated result in the digitized way to form the budget. Budget not only displays in the financial index, but also is a kind of major control index.

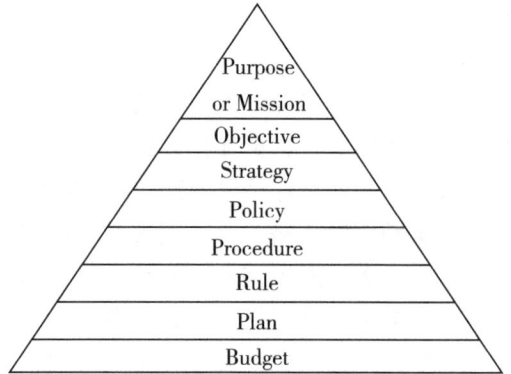

【新视角】

在组织的各个发展阶段上，计划的类型同样随着组织的成长具有不同的性质，即计划在各个阶段上其时间长度与目标特性都要进行相应调整。

一般来说，处于形成期的组织规模小、人心齐、关系简单，一切由创业者决策、指挥，组织需要极大的灵活性。这阶段的目标是尝试性的，资源的获取也带有不确定性，要确认谁是真正的用户和顾客也比较困难，所以，此阶段导向计划（指导性计划）更适用。

当组织处于成长期时，目标变得明确，资源也更容易获取，顾客的忠诚度较高，因而，计划也就更具体了，常表现为短期的、更具体的计划。

当组织处于成熟期时，可预见性最大，目标更为明确，这时具体计划也更为适用，同时计划的时间跨度也变长了。

当组织进入衰退期时，计划模式也随之改变，计划从具体性转入指导性，这时目标要重新考虑，资源将被重新分配，在其他方面也要做出相的调整，管理者应制订短期的、更具指导性的计划。

第三节　计划工作的流程与方法

一、计划工作的原则

管理者要想出色地做好计划工作，提交满意的切合实际的计划方案，就应当熟练地掌握和运用计划的原则。

（1）限制因素原则。限制因素是指妨碍组织目标实现的因素，也就是说，在其他因素不变的情况下，只改变这些因素，就可以影响组织目标的实现程度。限制因素原则是指在优选方案时，人们越准确地识别并解决那些妨碍既定目标实现的限定性因素或关键性因素，也就越容易和越准确地选定最有利的方案。

（2）许诺原则。任何一项计划都是对完成各项工作所做出的许诺，因而，许诺越大，实现许诺的时间就越长，实现许诺的可能性就越小。这一原则主要涉及计划的期限问题。因此，这一原则要求：①计划必须有明确的时间要求；②必须合理地确定计划的期限，避免随意性；③每项计划的许诺不能太多，因为许诺（任务）越多，计划时间就越长。

（3）灵活性原则。在计划中加进灵活性会减少突发事件带来的危险，也就是说，计划要留有余地。这是一项非常重要的原则。但灵活性是有限度的：①未来更多难以预料的不确定因素使我们不能总是以推迟决策的时间来确保计划的灵活性；②确保计划有灵活性是要付出代价的，而代价过高的灵活性计划又是缺乏效率的；③有时现有的客观条件和现实情况会影响甚至完全扼制计划的灵活性。

（4）导向变化原则。计划赶不上变化，是说在计划执行过程中，会发生各种各样的变化，这时就要根据实际情况的变化对计划进行检查和修订，甚至重新制订，使计划能够跟上变化，以便最终实现计划目标。

二、计划工作的流程

计划工作的流程，主要有以下九个步骤。这九个步骤又可归纳为三个环节，即预测、决策和部署。计划的一般流程如图4-2所示。图中1、2构成预测环节；3、4、5、6构成决策环节；7、8构成部署环节；至于计划的反馈可认为是计划和控制职能共有的内容。

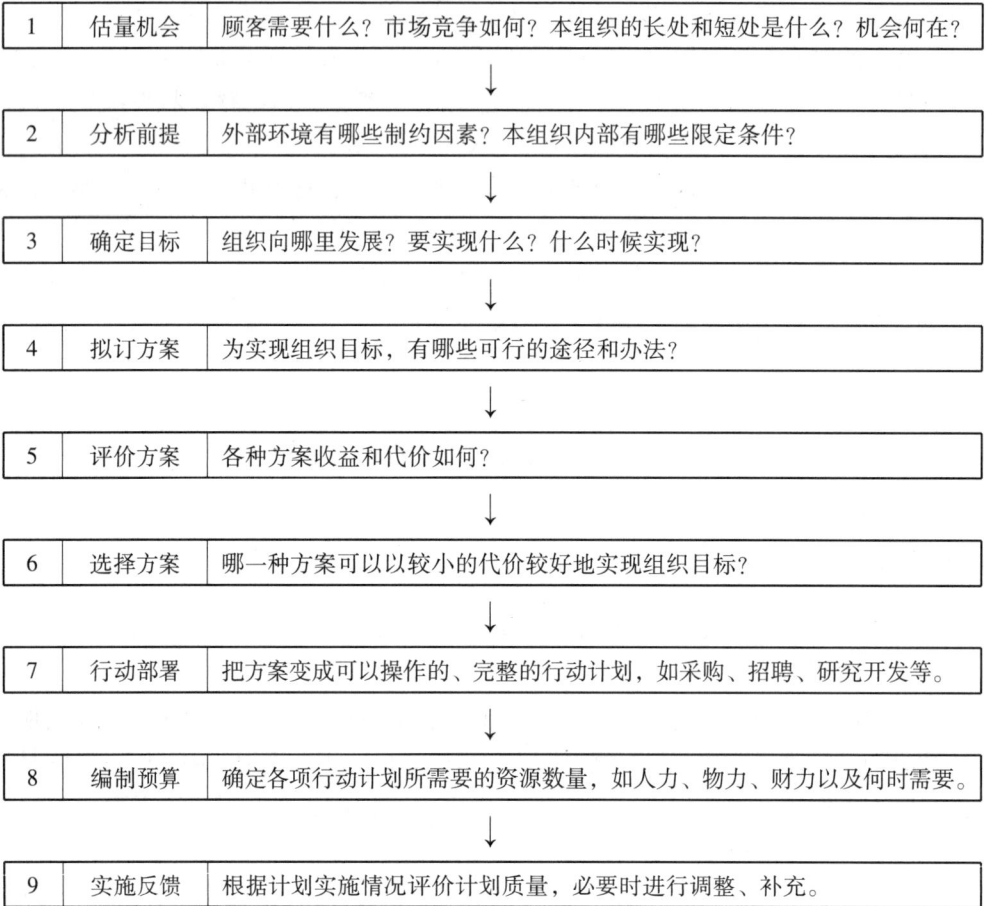

1	估量机会	顾客需要什么？市场竞争如何？本组织的长处和短处是什么？机会何在？
2	分析前提	外部环境有哪些制约因素？本组织内部有哪些限定条件？
3	确定目标	组织向哪里发展？要实现什么？什么时候实现？
4	拟订方案	为实现组织目标，有哪些可行的途径和办法？
5	评价方案	各种方案收益和代价如何？
6	选择方案	哪一种方案可以以较小的代价较好地实现组织目标？
7	行动部署	把方案变成可以操作的、完整的行动计划，如采购、招聘、研究开发等。
8	编制预算	确定各项行动计划所需要的资源数量，如人力、物力、财力以及何时需要。
9	实施反馈	根据计划实施情况评价计划质量，必要时进行调整、补充。

图4-2　计划工作的流程

【阅读资料】

计划的综合平衡

首先，综合平衡要研究任务之间的平衡。为此要分析由目标结构决定或与目标结构对应的组织各部分在各时期的任务是否能相互衔接和协调，因此这里也就包括任务的时间平衡和空间平衡。时间平衡是要分析组织在各时段的任务是否有机地衔接起来，从而确保组织的长远目标在各个时期的任务逐步完成中自然而然地得到顺利实现；空间平衡则要研究组织的各个部分的任务是否保持相应的比例关系，从而能保证组织的整体活动协调地进行。在平衡过程中，如果发现较低层次的某个具体任务不能充分实现，则应考虑能否采取有关补救措施，否则就应调整较高层次的目标要求，而此时可能就会导致整个组织的决策需要做出修订。

其次，综合平衡还要研究组织活动的进行与资源供应的关系，分析组织能否在适当的时间筹集到适当品种、数量和质量的资源，从而保证组织活动能连续、稳定地进行。

最后，综合平衡还要分析不同环节在不同时间的任务与能力之间是否平衡，即研究组织的各个部分是否能够保证在任何时间都有足够的能力去完成规定的任务。由于组织的外环境和活动条件经常发生变化，从而导致任务可能需要调整，因此，在任务与能力平衡的同时，还须留有一定的余地，以保证这种将会产生的调整在必要时有可能进行。

三、计划工作的方法

计划的方法很多，计划工作的效率高低、质量好坏在很大程度上取决于采用的计划方法。在此我们仅介绍其中几种典型的计划方法。

1. 滚动计划法

这是一种定期修订未来计划的方法。这种方法采用"远粗近细"的方法，即把近期的详细计划和远期的粗略计划结合在一起。在近期计划完成后，再根据执行结果的情况和新的环境变化逐步细化并修正远期计划，每次修正都向前滚动一个时段，这就是滚动计划，如图4-3所示。

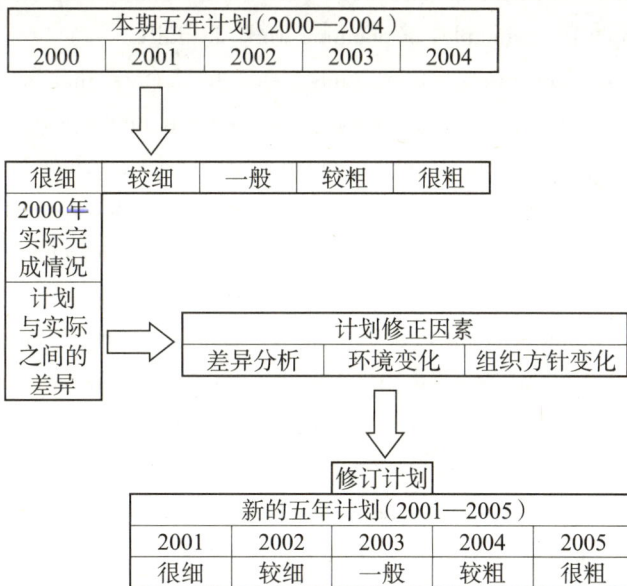

图4-3 滚动计划

这种方法的缺点在于加大了计划的工作量，优点是：①增加了计划的准确性，提高了工作的质量；②保证了长期计划的指导作用，使得各期计划基本上保持一致；③保证计划具有基本弹性，有助于提高组织的应变能力。

2. 网络计划技术

网络计划技术，是利用网络计划对任务的工作进度进行安排和控制，以保证实现预定目标的科学的计划管理技术。网络计划是在网络图上加注工作的时间参数而编制成的进度计划。因此，网络计划由两部分组成，即网络图和网络参数。网络图是由箭线和结点组成的用来表示工作流程的有向、有序的网状图形。网络参数是根据计划中各项工作的延续时间和网络图所计算的工作、节点、线路等要素的各种时间参数。

网络计划的基本形式是关键线路法（CPM）和计划评审技术（PERT）。两者的区别在于：关键线路法可以确定各项工作最早、最迟开始和结束的时间，通过最早、最迟时间的差额可以分析每一项工作相对的时间紧迫程度及工作的重要程度，这种时间差额称为机动时间，机动时间最小的工作称为关键工作。关键线路法的主要目的就是确保计划项目中的关键工作，在实施过程中能够被重点关照，保证按期完成计划。

网络计划技术既是一种科学的计划方法，又是一种有效的科学管理方法。这种方法不仅能完整地揭示一个项目所包含的全部工作以及它们之间的关系，还能根据数学原理，应用最优化技术，揭示整个项目的关键工作并合理安排计划中的各项工作。

Section 3　Procedures and Methods of Planning Work

4.3.1　Principles of Planning Work

If managers want to do planning work well, submitting a satisfactory and realistic plan, they should master and apply the principles of planning work skillfully.

（1）Principle of constraints. Constraints refer to factors that prevent achieving the organization's objectives, that is, if the other factors remain unchanged, only changing these factors can affect the degree of achievement of organizational goals. Principle of constraints means when selecting the best program, if people can identify and resolve those constrains and key factors that hinder the achievement of given goals, the solution will be easier and more accurately to be picked out.

（2）Principle of promise. Plan is a promise to finish the work, therefore, the greater the promise is, the longer the time needed to achieve promise, and the less likely to achieve the promise. This principle is mainly related to duration of the plan. Therefore, this principle requires：①The plan must have a clear time table. ②Reasonable duration of the program must be determined to avoid randomness. ③We can not promise too much thing in one program, because the more the promises（tasks）are, the longer the plan takes.

（3）Principle of flexibility. Adding flexibility to the plan will reduce the risk that incident brings. That is to say plans have to leave room. This is an very important principle. But there is a limit to flexibility：①In the future, there are more unpredictable factors so that we can't always delay decisions to ensure the flexibility of the plan. ②Ensure program flexibility comes with a price, and the high flexibility costs too much and lacks of efficiency. ③Sometimes the existing objective conditions and the reality will affect or even completely stem plan flexibility.

（4）Principle of orientation change. Plan cannot catch up with changes, that is, in the process of plan implementation, all kinds of changes might happen, at this time, we have to check and revise, or even redesign the plan according to actual conditions to keep up with changes and achieve goals.

4.3.2 Procedures of Planning Work

Procedures of planning work mainly have the following nine steps. These nine steps can be summarized as three links, namely, forecasting, decision-making and arranging. The following Diagram 4 – 2 is the general process. The following figure 1, 2—forecasting link; 3, 4, 5, 6—decision-making link, 7, 8—arranging link. As for the feedback of the plan, it can be regarded as a mutual content of the planning and control functions.

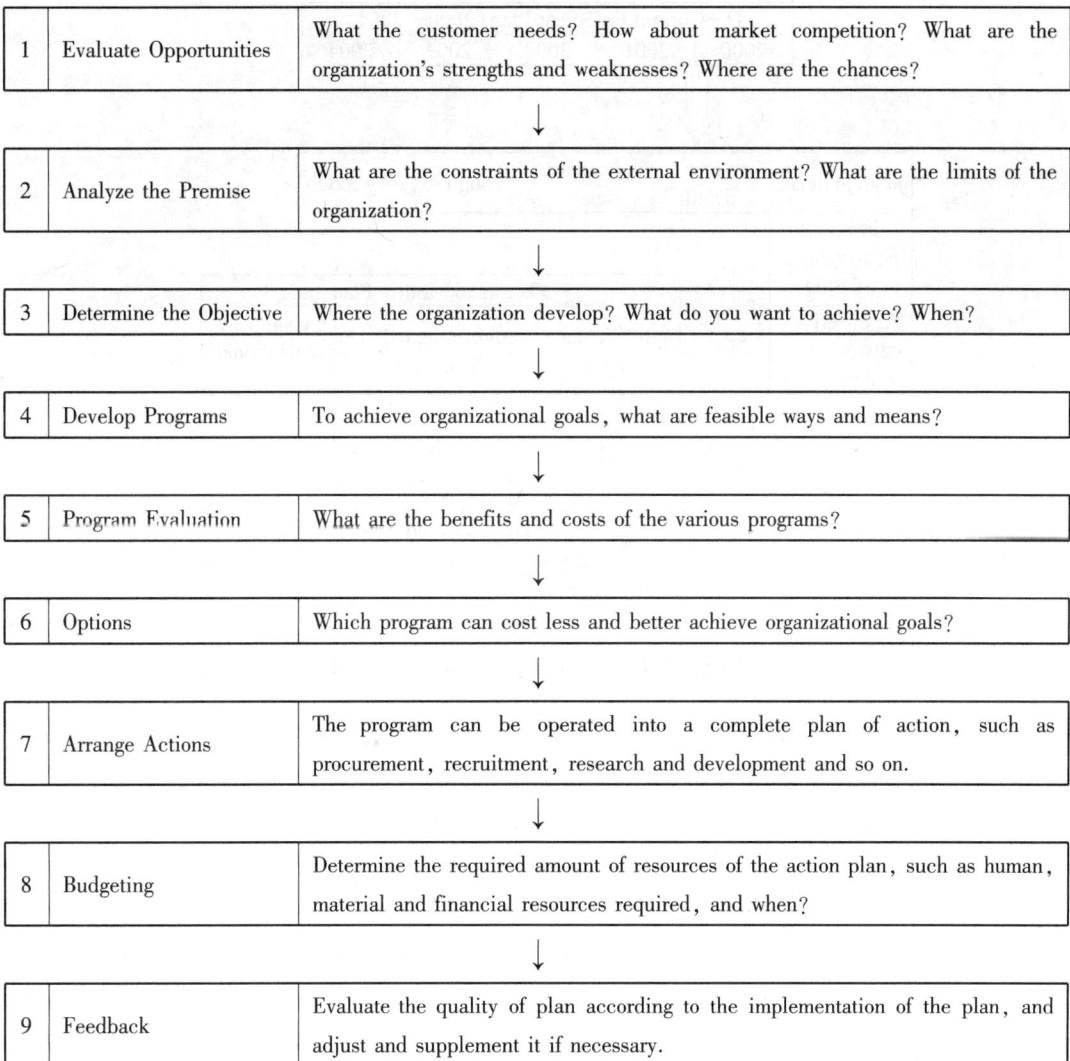

1	Evaluate Opportunities	What the customer needs? How about market competition? What are the organization's strengths and weaknesses? Where are the chances?

↓

2	Analyze the Premise	What are the constraints of the external environment? What are the limits of the organization?

↓

3	Determine the Objective	Where the organization develop? What do you want to achieve? When?

↓

4	Develop Programs	To achieve organizational goals, what are feasible ways and means?

↓

5	Program Evaluation	What are the benefits and costs of the various programs?

↓

6	Options	Which program can cost less and better achieve organizational goals?

↓

7	Arrange Actions	The program can be operated into a complete plan of action, such as procurement, recruitment, research and development and so on.

↓

8	Budgeting	Determine the required amount of resources of the action plan, such as human, material and financial resources required, and when?

↓

9	Feedback	Evaluate the quality of plan according to the implementation of the plan, and adjust and supplement it if necessary.

Diagram 4 – 2 Nine Steps of Planning Process

4.3.3 Methods of Planning Work

There are so many methods of planning work. Whether high or low the planning work efficiency and quality highly depends on the planning methods. Here we only introduce several typical planning methods.

1. Rolling Planning Method

This is a revised method of future plan on a regular basis. This method combines the general long-term plan and detailed short-term plan. After the completion of the short-term plan, according to the results of situation and new environmental changes, decision-makers gradually refine and fix the long-term plan, rolling forward by a period of time after revision every time. This is rolling planning method.

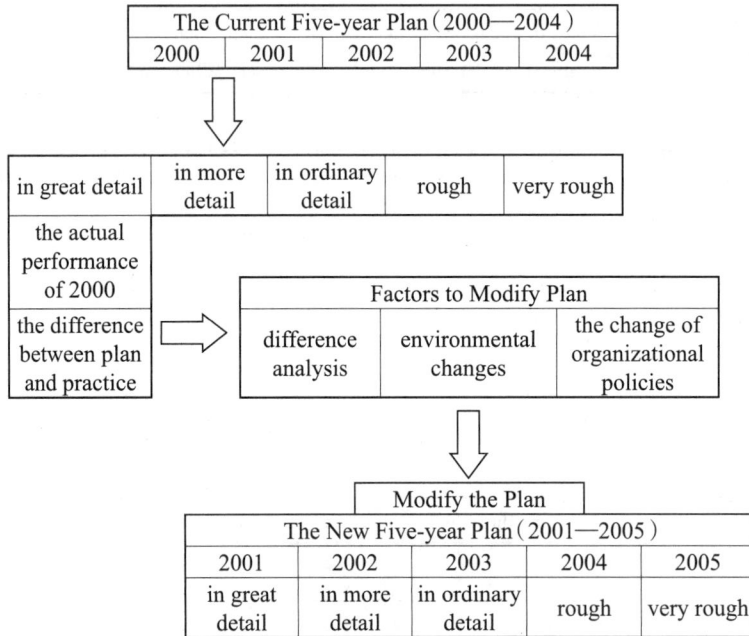

Diagram 4 – 3   Rolling Planning Method

The disadvantage of this method is that it increases the workload of plan, the advantages are: ①Increase the accuracy of the plan and improve the quality of the work. ②Ensure the guidance of long-term plan, so that each phase of the project is basically consistent. ③Assure that the plan has the basic elasticity and can help to improve the strain capacity of the organization

2. Network Planning Technique

Network planning technique is the scientific planning management technique to arrange and control the working schedules of tasks by using the network plans to ensure the realization of the intended target. Network planning is the progressing planning drawn up by compiling time parameters into the network map. Therefore, the network plan consists of two parts—network map and network parameters. Network map consists of lines, arrows and nodes is used to indicate the workflow with directions and orders. Network parameters are the various time parameters of work, nodes, lines and other elements calculated based on the durations of the various works and network diagrams.

The basic forms of network planning are the Critical Path Method (CPM) and the Planning Evaluation and Review Technique (PERT). There are two differences between them: The CPM can determine the earliest and latest starting and ending times of each work. By calculating the difference between the earliest and latest time, the manager can analyze the extent of time urgency and importance of each task. This time difference is called the flexible time. The work with the shortest flexible time is called critical work. The main purpose of the CPM is to focus on critical works in the implementation process to ensure them and the whole project completed according to schedule.

Network planning technology is both a scientific planning method and an effective and scientific management method. This approach can not only completely reveal all the works of a project and the relationships among them, but also reveal the key work of the entire project and arrange all the works reasonably through the application of optimization techniques based on mathematical principles.

第四节　目标和目标管理

一、目标的含义和特征

确定目标是计划首要的、核心的内容。目标是目的或宗旨的具体化，是指个人或组织根据自身的情况而提出的在一定的时期内经过努力要达到的预期成果。每一个组织都有自己的目标，目标是一个组织各项管理活动所指向的终点。

组织目标的特征：

（1）层次性。组织的目标从上到下可分为多个层次。在这个多层次的目标体系中，最上层是组织的总体目标，最下层是组织成员的个人目标，中间是组织中各部门、各分支机构等的目标。下层目标是由上层目标派生出来的，是实现上层目标的手段，越是上层的目标就越模糊和不可控，越是下层的目标就越具体而可控。

（2）系统性。组织的各种目标之间通常会构成一种比较复杂的相互影响、相互促进的网络系统，不同的目标之间都有直接或间接的联系，形成一种相辅相成的关系。如目标与目标之间、目标和手段之间、手段和手段之间均会形成一定的联系，只有相互协调才能实现目标。

（3）多样性。组织追求的目标往往是多方面的，可以从不同的侧面用不同的指标加以反映。例如，某企业的总目标是争取某种产品在市场上占有绝对地位，那么这一目标就可以从不同的侧面来表示：获得一定的利润率；获得一定的市场占有率；达到行业中的优势地位等。

组织目标的作用：①为组织工作指明方向。②激励组织成员实现目标。③凝聚组织成员的力量。④是考核工作绩效的标准。

二、目标的分类

由于目标具有不同的属性，因而使得目标表现出不同的对应类型，它们是：

1. 主要目标和次要目标

主要目标是关系组织生存和发展方向的目标，也就是组织的总目标。一般要在以下主要方面设立目标：①市场地位；②技术创新；③生产率；④资源状况；⑤利润率；⑥个人效率及发展；⑦积极性；⑧社会责任。

次要目标是有助于实现主要目标的目标。它与主要目标是一致的，也是主要目标所必需的。如人事目标作为次要目标，追求的是创造良好的工作环境。每一个次要目标都要贯穿于组织的活动当中，并有助于组织目标的实现。但次要目标的数量应尽可能少，以突出主要目标。

2. 控制性目标和突破性目标

所谓控制性目标是指组织有意识地让其活动维持在现有水平。如可口可乐公司在20世纪60年代以前，一直以单一的口味、单一的瓶装和统一的广告作为其营销的目标。

突破性目标是指组织的某些活动有重大突破，达到一个新的水平，如企业的销售增长率从5%提高到10%。

3. 长期目标和短期目标

一般来说五年以上的目标可称为长期目标。因为时间跨度长，期间不确定因素较多，所以长期目标在实施过程中要不断进行调整。

短期目标是长期目标的体现，长期目标和短期目标必须相互协调和相互促进。一年以下的目标一般称为短期目标。此外还有中期目标。

4. 明确目标和模糊目标

从管理的角度讲，目标越明确越好，这样便于计划与控制。如成本、销售额、利润额。

有些管理工作或经营活动很难规定明确的目标，只能提出一个模糊的目标。如要使每个员工充分发挥其聪明才智，这就是一个模糊的目标。

5. 定量目标和定性目标

组织中的目标可以用数量表示，我们称为定量目标。如销售量、劳动生产率等。

组织中也有些目标不易或不能用数量表示，我们称为定性目标，可以用详细说明或完成的时间来加以考核，如企业形象、员工积极性等。

【新视角】

两类目标扭曲现象

目标是制订行动方案的基础，这句话并不表明只要有了被称为"目标"的东西，组织就一定会产生正确的行动。事实上，组织中制定的各式各样的目标常常有不合理、不真实的成分。以下两类目标扭曲现象就是现实中普遍存在和需要管理者特别注意的。

第一，脱离实际的目标。目标是对组织想要达到的状态的描述，它反映了人们的一种向往，但这种向往要成为指导人们行动的准则，所制定的目标就应该具有可行性，不应脱离客观实际，尤其是组织当前的实际情况。但由于对组织现实状况的反思有时不免令人沮丧，这使得许多管理人员在考虑目标问题时会有意无意地回避这一点，从而导致了许多目标的扭曲，这又给组织的资源配置和相应的工作安排造成了许多问题。

第二，不真实的目标。组织对外宣称的目标与它实际追求的目标不一致，是另一类常见的目标扭曲现象。在许多场合，组织宣称的目标被当成了改善和提升自身形象的手段。企业为了迎合投资者、顾客、协作者、一般公众以及政府的偏好，会宣布一些经过选择和修饰的目标，而企业真正追求的目标可能是另一些东西。了解这类目标扭曲现象是有意义的，它可以帮助我们理解企业"言行不一"背后的原因。

三、目标管理的概念及优缺点

1. 目标管理的概念

目标管理是组织内部各部门及每个人为实现组织目标，自上而下地制定各自的目标，并自主地确定行动方针、工作进度、有效实施和对成果严格考核的系统管理方式。具体来说，它是一个组织中上级管理人员同下级管理人员以及员工一起共同制定组织目标，并把其具体化，展开至每个部门、每个层次、每个员工，使责任和成果密切联系，明确规定各部门、各层次和各成员的职责范围，通过保证措施和层层落实，有效地实现组织目标。

2. 目标管理的特点

（1）明确目标。组织各部门、各层次、各环节、各成员都要明确目标。

（2）参与决策。每个人既是目标的制定者，又是目标的实施者，既自上而下，又自下而上。

（3）规定时限。每个目标都要有明确的时间期限要求。

（4）评价绩效。目标管理寻求不断地将目标实施的进展情况反馈给个人，以便调整其行为。

（5）系统管理。目标管理必须建立目标锁链与目标体系，从而使目标管理系统化。

3. 目标管理的优点与不足

（1）优点。

①形成激励。当目标有可能变成现实时，就会产生内在的激励作用。

②有效管理。目标管理可以切实提高管理组织的效率。

③明确任务。目标管理通过制定目标、落实目标，使每个成员都明确各自的任务。

④自我管理。目标管理实际上是自我管理的一种方式。

⑤控制有效。目标管理也是一种控制方式，即通来目标分解和落实，最终保证总目标的实现。

（2）不足。

①强调短期目标。

②目标设置困难。

③缺乏灵活性。

四、目标管理的实施步骤

目标管理的实施大致可分为：目标的制定、目标的实施和成果评价三个阶段。

1．目标的制定

实现目标管理，首先要制定合理、明确的目标。该阶段可细分为三个步骤：

（1）设定总目标。总目标是组织共同愿景、宗旨和使命的某一阶段欲达到的某一状态或结果。总目标设定的关键是：①如何能够确切地分析和判断组织的实际实力、可调动资源的多少、组织中存在的问题和相对优势所在，从而判断组织有无核心专长。②如何能够透彻了解组织的外部环境以及环境因素的未来变化。③总目标一旦设定，就成了组织计划工作的前提，也成了组织未来行为或成果的标志。因此，总目标应该是可以度量的。④组织上下共同商量决定组织的总目标。

（2）进行目标展开。建立目标体系，将已设定的总目标按照组织结构进行纵向与横向的分解，是目标管理过程中最关键的一步。具体来说：①将组织总目标按组织体系层次、部门逐步展开，直至组织的每一个成员，是一个自上而下层层展开的过程。②组织体系中的每个层次、每个部门、每个成员可根据自己的部门、层次、岗位、分工和职责要求，结合上级下达的目标进行思考和分析，提出自己的目标，这是一个自下而上的过程。③组织将自下而上的目标与下达的目标比较，分析差异再进行分析修订后下达。经过一个上下多次反复，最终将总目标分解成一个目标体系，下达到各层次、各部门和组织成员。

（3）明确责任。目标展开完成后，上一级根据目标的要求，遵循权责相称的原则，授予下属部门以及个人相应的权力，明确他们的责任，使接受目标的每个层次、每个部门和每个成员，都有明确的工作方向、责任和行为特点，实行自主管理。

2．目标的实施

目标的实施过程，主要依靠目标的执行者进行自主管理，并由执行人组织具有创造性的工作，并以目标为依据，不断检查对比，分析实施中的问题，采取有效措施，减少偏差，实施自我控制。同时，领导者的管理多体现在指导、协作、提供信息情报，以及创造良好的工作环境方面。

3．成果评价

这是目标管理过程的最后一环，该阶段主要应做好两方面的工作：①对目标执行者的工作成果进行考评，并决定奖惩。考评的方式有两种：一是组织各层次、各部门、各成员的自我考评；二是上级部门对下级部门和组织成员的考评。考评过程是对照目标和所取得的成果进行分析和评判。②总结经验教训，把成功的经验、好的作法固定下来，并加以完善，使之科学化、系统化、标准化、制度化。对不足之处要分析原因，及时反馈给目标执行者，以便采取有效措施加以改进，从而为下一循环打好基础。

Section 4　Objective and Objective Management

4.4.1　Meaning and Characteristics of Objective

Identifying the objective （goal） is the prior and core part of planning. Goal is the specific of purpose and objective, which means that individual and organization put forward their expected results after a certain period based on their situation. Every organization has its objective, and an objective is the end of the management activities of an organization.

The characteristics of the organizational objectives:

(1) Hierarchy. Organization's objectives can be divided into multiple hierarchies from top to bottom. In this multi-level objective system, on the top is the overall objectives of the organization, at the bottom is the personal objective of organization's members and in the middle is the objectives of various departments, branches. The lower objective is derived from the top objective and is the tool to achieve the top one. The upper objective is more vague and uncontrollable, and the lower objective is more specific and manageable.

(2) Systematic. Various objectives of an organization often constitute a complex network system. They influence each other and promote each other. Different objectives have direct or indirect contact forming a complementary relationship. For example, between objectives and objectives, objectives and means, means and means, there can form a certain connection and only through coordination can an organization achieve objectives.

(3) Diversity. Objective of an organization is often various, and it can be reflected differently by using different indicators from different sides. For example, an enterprise's overall objective is an absolute position for a product in the market and this objective can be interpret into different sides: to obtain a certain profit margin, to obtain a certain market share, to achieve the dominant position in the industry, and so on.

The roles of organizational objectives: ① Indicate the direction for organizational work. ② Motivate members to achieve their objectives. ③ Agglomerate organization's members. ④ Is the standard for examing the work performance.

4.4.2 The Classification of the Objectives

Objective has different properties, so it can be divided into different types. They are:

1. Primary and Secondary Objectives

Primary objective is about the survival and development of an organization. It is the overall objective of the organization. Generally, we set objectives from the following aspects: ① Market position; ② Technology innovation; ③ Productivity; ④ Resources; ⑤ The profit margin; ⑥ Individual efficiency and development; ⑦ Enthusiasm; ⑧ Social responsibility.

Secondary objective is to help achieve primary objective. It is consistent with primary objective, and it is also necessary for the primary one. For example, personnel objective is a secondary objective which pursuits to create a good working environment. Each secondary objective is to contribute to the realization of organizational objectives. But the number of the secondary objective should be reduced as many as possible in order to highlight the primary objective.

2. Controllable and Breakthrough Objectives

Controllable objective means that an organization consciously makes its activities remain at current levels. Such as the Coca-Cola made the single taste, single bottled and unified advertising as its marketing objectives before the 1960s.

Breakthrough objective refers to some activities that make a major breakthrough to reach a new level. For example, sales growth rate increases from 5% to 10%.

3. Long-term and Short-term Objectives

Generally, an objective for more than 5 years' time can be called a long-term objective. Because of long time span, there are many uncertain factors, so in the implementation of the long-term objective, we have to adjust our objectives accordingly.

Short-term objective is a reflection of the long-term objective, long-term and short-term objectives must coordinate with each other and promote each other. An objective for less than one year's time generally referred to as short-term objective, in addition there is medium-term objective.

4. Clear and Fuzzy Objectives

From the perspective of management, the more clear the objective, the better it is, because it is easy to plan and control. Such as cost, sales and profits.

Some management work or business activities are hard to define clear objectives, so they can only put forward a fuzzy objective. For example, to make each staff give full play to their talents, is a fuzzy objective.

5. Quantitative and Qualitative Objectives

The objective in an organization can be expressed by number, and we call them quantitative objective, such as sales and productivity.

Some objectives cannot be expressed by number, we call it qualitative objectives, which can be assessed by details or implementation time, such as corporate image and motivation.

4.4.3 The Concept of Objective Management and Its Advantages and Disadvantages

1. The Concept of Objective Management

Objective management is a systemic management method that every department and member set up their objectives from the top to bottom and determine the action, work progress and effective implementation and strict appraisal system for achieving the organization's objectives. In particular, it is an organizational objective made by the superior managers in an organization and the subordinate employees, and each department, each level, each employee are involved to make the responsibility matches the result, defines the clear area of responsibility of each department, each level, and each member through the guarantee measures and layers of implementation for the implementation of effective organizational objectives.

2. The Characteristics of Objective Management

(1) Clear objectives. Each department, each level, each link, each member should be clear about objectives.

(2) Participation in decision-making. Everyone is both the objective setters, and executors of the objective, both top-down and bottom-up.

（3）Prescribed time limit. Every objective must have a clear time limit requirements.

（4）Performance evaluation. Objective management is to seek constantly the process of achieving the objective and give feedback to individuals, in order to adjust their behavior.

（5）System management. Objective chains and system must be established, so that the objective management is systematical.

3. Advantages and Disadvantages of Objective Management

（1）Advantages.

①Formation of incentive. When the target is likely to become reality, it can produce internal incentive.

②Effective management. Objective management can effectively improve the efficiency of the management of an organization.

③Clear mission. Objective management makes every member clear about his or her tasks by setting up the objectives, and carrying out the objectives.

④Self-management. Objective management is actually a way of self-management.

⑤Effective control. Objective management is a way of control, namely access to carry out the target.

（2）Disadvantages.

①Emphasis on short-term objectives.

②Hard to set up a objective.

③Lack of flexibility.

4.4.4　Steps of Objective Management

Objective management can be divided into three stages: Formulation of objectives, implementation of objectives and evaluation of the results.

1. Formulation of Objectives

In order to achieve objective management, the first stage is to formulate reasonable and clear objectives. This stage can be subdivided into three steps.

（1）Set up an overall objective. Overall objective is a particular state or results that an organization wants to achieve at a certain stage based on a common vision, purpose and mission. The keys when setting up the overall objective are: ①How can we exactly analyze and judge the organization's actual strength, the available resources, the problems and relative advantages of an organization, so as to determine the presence of the core expertise. ②How can we thoroughly understand the organization's external environment and the change of environmental factors of the future. ③Once the overall objective is set, it is the premise of organizational planning, and it will also become the sign of future actions or achievement, so the overall objective should be measurable. ④The overall objective of the organization is decided by all the members.

（2）Objective deploying. Establishing the objective system and decomposing the overall objective according to the organizational structure of longitudinal and transverse are the most crucial step in the process of objective management. Specifically：①To carry out gradually the overall objective according to the organization's system level, the department, every member of the organization is a top-down unfolding process. ② Each level of organization system, each department and each member can put forward his or her own objective according to his or her own department, level, position, roles and responsibilities by thinking and analyzing the objective that the superior put forward. This is a bottom-up process. ③An organization compares the issued objective with the bottom-up objective, analyzes the differences and issues the objective after revision. After repeated revisions, the objective will be divided into a system and issued to members at all levels, departments and organizations.

（3）Clear responsibilities. After the completion of the objective, the superior will grant the power of subordinate departments and individual, clear their responsibilities according to the requirement of the target and follow the principle of accurate proportion to make sure that each level, each department and each member can have a clear direction of work, responsibility and behavior characteristics to achieve independent management.

2. Implementation of Objectives

The process of implementation highly depends on the independent management and the creative work that the executors organize, meanwhile, they have to constantly check, analyze the problems in the implementation, taking effective measures to reduce the deviation, implement self-control based on the objective.

3. Evaluation of the Results

This is the last step in the process of objective management. This step should contain two main aspects：①Evaluate the work of objective done by the executors and decide the rewards and punishments. There are two ways to evaluate：one is the self-evaluation of all levels, departments, and members; the other is that the departments at lower levels are evaluated by higher ones. The evaluation process is the analysis and evaluation between objectives and achievements. ②Learn from the experience and lessons, fix the successful experience, good practice and make it perfect, scientific, systematic, standardized and institutionalized. For deficiencies, we should analyze reasons, give timely feedback to the executors in order to take effective measures to improve, so as to lay a good foundation for the next cycle.

第五节　时间管理

我们经常会听到管理者们发出的一个共同声音："太忙了""没时间"。或许有些管理者真的不知道时间是什么，如何才能有效地利用时间、发挥时间的价值。因此，一个现实的管理问题——时间管理被忽视了。德鲁克认为："有效的管理者不是从他们的任务开始的，而是从掌握时间开始的。"

一、时间是什么

法国思想家伏尔泰在他的小说《查第格》中，用一段谜语来描述时间："世界上最长最短的东西是什么？最快最慢的东西是什么？最平凡而又最珍贵的东西是什么？最容易被忽视而又最令人后悔的东西是什么？"答案告诉我们：世界上最长的是时间，因为它永无止境；最短的莫过于时间，因为它让所有的计划都来不及完成；在作乐的人，时间是最快的；在等待的人，时间是最慢的；它可以扩展到无限大，也可以分割到无穷小；开始谁都无视它，过后又都后悔不已；没有它，什么事都做不成；不值得纪念的，它都令人忘怀；伟大的，它都使他们永垂不朽。

时间是世界赋予我们每个人最珍贵、最公平的财富。任何财富都是时间与行动结合后的成果。"一寸光阴一寸金、寸金难买寸光阴"这句古训也道出了时间的珍贵。

时间是不能再生和不可替代的宝贵资源。金钱可以赚取，人才可以培养，道路可以修建。可时间却租不到、借不来、买不到，也无法生产。时间不等人，过去了就不再回来。

时间最公平，也最吝啬。不管你是谁，都会给你，但每天只有 24 个小时，8.64 万秒，一秒也不多给。时间既不能贮存，不用就白白浪费了，不能去做交易，又没有弹性，不管你需要多长时间，供给绝不会增加。

所以，时间是生命，时间是金钱，时间是速度，时间是力量，时间是最特殊的资源。

二、时间是需要管理的

在现实生活中，人们往往忽视对时间的管理和有效利用。这是因为时间太公平，每天都是 24 小时，今天过后是明天，今年过了有明年。因而人们对时间没有紧迫感，很容易导向"明日复明日"的轨道。时间是有价值的资源，每个人都不能无限期地拥有时间，只要你稍有疏忽，它就毫不留情地从你的身边流逝，带走你的金钱和事业，带走你的青春和梦想。因此，时间是需要管理的。正如马克思所说："一切节约归根到底是时间的节约"。

时间对每个人的含金量是不同的。智者利用时间来创造机会，庸者将时间拿来把握机会，愚者以浪费时间来错过机会。

时间是成功者的阶梯，是成功者的资本，成功与失败的分界线就在于能否合理分配和利用时间。因此，我们可以通过有效的管理来减少无效时间（浪费时间）和增加有效时间，从而实现时间资源价值的最大化。

美国麻省理工学院曾经对 3 000 名经理做过一项调查，发现凡是优秀的经理都能做到精于安排时间，使浪费的时间减少到最低限度。管理大师德鲁克认为："认识你的时间是每个人只要肯做就能做到的。这是一个人走向成功的有效的自由之路。"

三、如何有效地管理时间

时间不仅需要管理，而且是可以管理的。有效管理时间的方法和技巧就在于如何减少浪费时间和提高时间利用效率，使其产生更多的价值。

时间管理需要遵循以下法则：

1. 明确目标

目标是指人们经过努力所要达到的预期成果。确立明确的目标，就是要将梦想、理想、工作具体化。

没有目标，我们就不会努力，因为我们不知道为什么要努力。没有目标，我们很难抓住机会和管好用好自己的时间，因为我们不知道自己到底要什么。

有了明确的目标，我们才能把握有利时机。时机是事物转折的关键，抓住有利时机就是充分利用时间，让时间的价值倍增，促进事物向好的方向转化，推动事物向前发展。

有了明确的目标，我们才会主动寻找解决问题的途径。管理是解决一连串问题的过程，围绕目标主动解决问题，是为了以后少花时间。例如，提高产品质量和服务质量，就是为了减少顾客投诉。

有了明确的目标，可以将有限的时间用在关键目标的实现上，提高时间利用的效率。

2．分清轻重缓急

人的时间和精力是有限的。有效的管理者要把主要精力放在可以实现目标并获得最大回报的事情上，而不能将时间花费在对成功无益或有很少益处的事情上。

因此，为了有效利用时间，在开始做事之前，就要认真考虑，分清轻重缓急，安排好做事先后顺序。一般来说，工作可分为几个层次：

（1）重要且紧急的工作，如确定工作目标、会见重要客户等，必须先做。

（2）重要但不紧急的工作，如参加专业技术培训等，可以放在第二位。

（3）紧急但不重要的工作，如主持或参加一次会议，或有人向你请示工作等，可以放在第三位。

（4）繁忙的工作，有不少工作只有一点价值，既不紧急也不重要，但占用了大量时间，比如应酬，可以放在第四位。

（5）浪费时间的消极娱乐，如看电视连续剧、打牌等，应杜绝。

总之，有效的管理者要用20%的时间获得80%的绩效，而不是用80%的时间获得20%的绩效。

3．制订计划

有了目标，就要设法去实现；要实现目标，就需要有一套工作（行动）计划。成功的管理者总是从认识自己的时间开始，从计划自己的时间起步。制订工作计划是有效利用时间的重要方法。有关研究证实：用更多的时间为一项工作做事前计划，会减少做这项工作的总时间。不要让繁忙的工作把你的计划时间从工作时间表中挤出去。

管理者应当有60%的工作时间是计划好的，大约20%的工作时间未纳入计划，还有20%的时间用来应对突发状况。通过加强计划，合理统筹时间，可减少用于操作的时间，从而赢得更多的时间。

还要根据目标分解的结果，制订出年度、季度、月、周、日的工作计划。特别是"每日工作计划表"，前一天晚上找出明天必须完成的几项工作，第二天早晨检查这些工作是否确实要办，确定这些工作的优先次序并做出时间安排。还要将工作计划表放在最容易看到的地方。

4．立即行动

当目标和计划确定之后，就要立即行动。只有积极行动，才会让目标变为现实；只有积极行动，才会让我们有效地利用时间，抓住机遇，超越自我。人生最昂贵的代价之一就是凡事等待明天。今日事，今日毕。今天的事必须今天做完，最好是多做一件。克服拖延恶习，定出完成期限。

时间包括过去的时间、现在的时间和未来的时间，现在连接过去和未来，是最宝贵、最重要时间。如果每个人都能抓住今天，那他一定能抓住成功。

立即行动需要热忱，需要永葆进取心，需要学会专注，需要发挥创造力。

记录每天完成的事项，每天下班前要列出工作清单，对"已办事项"和"待办事项"的原因进行分析，找出成功的地方和失败的地方以及需要改进的地方。

管理者有效运筹时间，还应活用以下技巧：

（1）集中时间办大事。切忌平均分配时间。管理者要善于把有限的时间集中用于处理那些"牵一发而动全身"的事情上，增加一些自由时间，减少一些可做可不做的事情。每天要从工作计划表中找出三项非完成不可的重要工作，并一件一件加以落实。

（2）黄金时间办要事。在大脑清静、思维活跃的时候去做那些重要的事，把那些例行的、不重要的工作安排在其他时间去做。管理者应当总结自己的工作规律和生物节律，学会思考，学会掌握工作节奏，以提高工作效率。

（3）有效利用零散时间。零散时间是指不构成连续时间的空余时间，如上下班的过渡时间，吃饭前后的时间等。这些时间很容易被人们忽视。珍惜和充分利用零散时间，既可以减少浪费时间，又可以增加有效工作时间。

（4）充分利用每一天。昨天是一张已兑付的支票，明天是一张未付的期票，只有今天才是你手上真正的现金。管理者要树立"今天"观念，认真做好每一天的工作并养成习惯。控制你的会议，不要让会占据你太多时间。

（5）找出"时间杀手"。管理者的时间很容易被分解，也很容易被浪费掉。因此，要找出浪费你时间最多的人和事，设法抵制这些人和事，如学会说"不"，学会暗示和快速结束。因为浪费时间就等于浪费生命。

（6）学会暂停和休息。学会暂停和休息，也是赢得时间的秘诀之一。做事不偷懒，要做正确的事，但也应适时知难而退、见好就收。埋头苦干不一定有效率，为保持工作效率而积极休息也是必要的。

（7）借用"外脑"。管理者不可能成为所有工作的内行，借用别人的智慧为我所用，也是节约时间和有效利用时间的重要途径。

（8）善于委派。不论你如何有能力，你不可能做完所有的事情，一定要学会委派别人去完成工作。有时候，有些工作你不想做或耗时太多，不妨委托给一个更合适、更乐于做的人，节省下时间做你擅长的、更有价值的事。

时间管理是一个很容易被人们忽视的管理问题。安东尼·罗宾曾说过一句话："时间和金钱对于每一个人都很重要。然而，只有智者才知道如何去安排它们。"时间是常数，只要管理得当，就能让时间为企业创造更多的价值。

Section 5　Time Management

We often hear a saying from managers："so busy""no time". Maybe some managers don't really know what time is and how to efficiently make the best use of time and its value. Therefore, a realistic management problem—time management has been ignored. Drucker said："The efficient managers do not start from their tasks, but start from mastering time. "

4.5.1 What is Time

The French thinker Voltaire described time with a riddle in his novel *Chadig*: "What is the longest and shortest thing in the world? What is the fastest and slowest thing? What is the most ordinary while the most valuable thing? What is the most easily overlooked and most regretted thing?" The answer is: The world's longest thing is time, because it has no end; the shortest is time, because it doesn't make all the plans complete timely; for the enjoyed, time is the fastest; for the waiting people, time is the slowest; it can be extended to infinite, also can be partitioned into infinitesimal. Everyone ignores it at first, but later regret; without it, nothing could be done; not memorable, it makes them be forgotten; great, it makes them stay forever.

Time is the most precious, most fair wealth that the world gives to everybody. Any wealth is a combination of time and action. "An inch of time equals an inch of gold, an inch of gold will not buy an inch of time." The old adage also reveals the preciousness of time.

Time is non-renewable and irreplaceable resources. Money can be earned, talents can be cultivated, road can be built. But you can't rent, borrow, buy, produce time. Time waits for no man and it no longer comes back after passing.

Time is the most fair and also the most miserly thing. No matter who you are, you've got only 24 hours a day, 86,400 seconds, no more one second. Time cannot be stored. You waste time if you can't make best use of it. You can't make a deal with time. There is no flexibility in time. No matter how much you need, the supply of time will not increase.

So time is life, time is money, time is speed, time is strength, time is the most special resource.

4.5.2 Time Needs to Be Managed

In real life, people tend to neglect the management and effective use of time. This is because time is fair. Every day has 24 hours, after today, there is tomorrow, this year is followed by the next year. And therefore there is no sense of urgency of time. It is easy to guide the orbit of "tomorrow after tomorrow". Time is a valuable resource, each of us can't indefinitely possess time. As long as you slightly neglect, it relentlessly slides away from your side, taking your money and career, taking away your youth and dreams. Therefore, time needs to be managed. As Marx said: "All saving in the final analysis is saving time. "

The value of time for everyone is different. The wise will use time to create opportunity. The loser will use time to grasp the opportunity. A fool who wastes time will miss the opportunity.

Time is the ladder of success, and the capital of success. The border between success and failure is whether one can appropriately allocate and use time. Therefore, we can reduce inefficient time (wasted time) and add efficient time through effective management in order to maximize the value of time resource.

A survey of 3,000 managers conducted by Massachusetts Institute of Technology（MIT）found that a good manager can allocate time successfully, and reduce the waste of time to a minimum. Drucker, the master of management said: "Everyone can know his time as long as he is willing to. This is one of effective, free path to success."

4.5.3 How to Manage Time Effectively

Time not only needs to be managed but also can be managed. Methods and skills of effective time management is how to reduce the waste of time and improve the efficiency of using time to make it produce more value.

Time management needs observing the following rules:

1. Clear the Objective

Objective refers to expected results through people's efforts. Establishing distinguished objective is to specify the dream, ideal and work.

Without an objective, we would not work hard, because we don't know why. Without an objective, it is difficult to seize the opportunities and manage and use our time well, because we don't know what we want.

With a clear objective, we grasp the favorable opportunity. Opportunity is the key to make a difference. Seizing the favorable opportunity is to make full use of time, so that we can multiply the value of time, promote the transformation of things for the better, and push things forward.

With a clear objective, we will take the initiative to find the method to solve the problem. Management is the process to solve a series of problems. Solving the problem actively by focusing on the objective is to spend less time later. For example, improving product quality and service quality is to reduce complaints from customers.

With a clear objective, we can spend limited time on the implementation of key objectives by increasing the efficiency of using time.

2. Distinguish the Priority

People's time and energy is limited. Effective managers can focus on the things to realize the objective and get the maximum return from them with major energy and can't spend their time on those things useless or rarely benefit to success.

Therefore, in order to use time effectively, before starting work, we must consider seriously, clear the priority, arrange the work order well. In general, the work can be divided into several levels:

（1）Important and urgent work. Such as setting up the objective, meeting with an important client, must be done first.

（2）Important but not urgent work. Such as taking part in professional and technical training can be put in the second place.

（3）Urgent but not important work. Such as hosting or attending a meeting, or someone asking for instructions of work from you can be placed thirdly.

（4）Busy work. Lots of works only have little value, they are neither urgent nor important, but take up a lot of time, such as entertainment, etc., can be placed in the fourth position.

（5）The work that wastes time. Like watching TV series, playing cards, should be avoided.

In short, effective managers get 80% of the performance with 20% of the time, rather than with the 80% of the time to get 20% of the performance.

3. Make Plan

Having a objective, we need to try to achieve; to achieve the objective, we need to have a working（action）plan. Successful managers always start from the realizing of their own time, from planning their time. Making plan is an important way to the use their time effectively. Relevant research has proved that spending more time on making plan before starting the work will reduce the total time for the work. Don't let busy job squeeze your plan-making time out from your work schedule.

Managers should have 60% of the work time planned, about 20% of working time are not included in the plan, another 20% of the time is for sudden events. By strengthening planning, reasonably planning the time as a whole, the managers can reduce the time for operation so as to win more time.

What's more, according to the results of objective decomposition, the managers should make annual, quarterly, monthly, weekly, daily working plans. Especially in the daily work schedule, the manager should list the tasks needed to be completed tomorrow the night before, check whether these tasks are really needed to be conducted next morning, and determine the priority of these tasks and make out a schedule. And put the schedule in the place where it is easiest to see.

4. Take Action Immediately

After the objective and plan are determined, we have to take actions immediately. Only positive action can make objectives come true; only positive action can make effective use of our time, seize the opportunity, surpass ourselves. One of the most expensive cost of life is delaying everything to tomorrow. Today's work must be finished today, it is best to do one more. The manager should overcome procrastination and set deadlines.

Time includes the past, present and future. Now is the most important and the most precious time connecting the past and the future. If everyone can seize today, he or she will be able to seize the success.

Immediate action needs enthusiasm, aggressiveness, needs people to learn how to focus, and to be creative.

The manager should record what have been done every day. He should make a working list at the end of each day to analyze the reasons of items done and to be done, find out the failure and the success and what need to be improved.

If managers want to use time effectively, they should use the following tips:

（1）Concentrate time on important tasks. Averaging time must be avoided by all means. Managers must be good at spending limited time on the single point relating the whole, increasing some free time and reducing time of social activities. He must find out three important tasks needed be completed from the work schedule and implement it one by one.

（2）Spend the prime time on urgent tasks. Do those important things when the brain is quiet, and in active thinking. Those routine, unimportant works can be finished in other time. Managers should summarize their work patterns and biological rhythms, learn to think, master the pace of work in order to improve efficiency.

（3）Use fragmented time effectively. Fragmented time is the spare time which does not constitute continuous time such as time around working, eating, etc. This kind of time is easily overlooked. Cherishing and making full use of fragmented time can reduce waste of time and increase the effective working hours.

（4）Make full use of every day. Yesterday is an already cashed check, tomorrow is an unpaid promissory note, today is your only real cash on hand. Managers should establish the "today" concept, work hard every day and form good habits. Managers should reduce meetings and do not let too much time be occupied by meetings.

（5）Find out the "time killer". For managers, time can easily be broken, and is likely to be wasted. Therefore, try to identify the people and things wasting most time, try to resist these people and things such as learning to say "no", giving hints and ending quickly. Because waste of time is waste of life.

（6）Learn to pause and rest. Learning to pause and rest is also one of the secrets to win time. Don't be lazy, do the right thing, but also quit timely with awareness of difficulties or just leave right after obtaining good results. Working hard is not necessarily efficient. Rest is necessary in order to maintain efficiency.

（7）Borrow the "brain". Managers cannot become as experts in all fields. Borrowing someone else's wisdom is also an important way to effectively use and save time.

（8）Be good at delegating. Whatever your ability is, you cannot finish all the things, so that you must learn to delegate someone else to complete the work. Sometimes, you don't want to do some work or to waste time, it may be better to delegate a more appropriate person who is more willing to do so that you can save the time to be spent on the things you are good at and more valuable.

Time management is an easily overlooked management issue. Anthony Robin once said: "Time and money are important for everyone, however, only the wise know how to arrange them." Time is a constant, as long as it is managed properly, the manager can make time create more values for enterprises.

【本章提要】

• 计划是最基本的管理职能之一，它是一个确定目标和评估实现目标最佳方式的过程。计划具有目的性、先行性、普遍性、效率性和创造性的特点。计划对管理工作具有重要意义。

● 计划的种类有很多，可按不同的标准加以划分。计划的结构要素包括组织的宗旨或使命、目标、战略、政策、程序、规则、规划和预算这九项。

● 计划工作的流程一般分为三个阶段、九个步骤，即估量机会、分析前提、确定目标、拟订方案、评价方案、选择方案、部署行动、编制预算和实施反馈。

● 计划工作应遵循的主要原则有：限制因素原则、许诺原则、灵活性原则和导向变化性原则。计划的方法很多，主要有滚动计划法和网络计划技术。

● 目标是组织欲达成的状态或结果，既可引导组织发展的方向，又是激励组织成员努力奋斗的手段。目标具有层次性、系统性、多样性的特点。

● 目标管理是一种自我管理方式，具有形成激励、有效管理、明确任务、自我管理、控制有效的优点，也存在强调短期目标、目标设置困难、缺乏灵活性的不足。目标管理的实施过程大致可分为目标的制定、目标的实施、成果评价三个阶段。

● 时间是成功者的阶梯，是成功者的资本，成功与失败的分界线就在于能否合理分配和利用时间。因此，我们可以通过有效的管理来减少无效时间（浪费时间）和增加有效时间，从而实现时间资源价值的最大化。

【关键词】

计划（Plan）　　目标（Objective）

目标管理（Objective Management）　　目标展开（Objective Deploying）

限制因素原则（Principle of Constraints）　　滚动计划法（Rolling Planning Method）

网络计划技术（Network Planning Technique）

【复习与思考】

1. 计划的性质是什么？它有哪些作用？

2. 计划大体分为哪几类？

3. 计划的结构要素有哪些？它们之间的关系是怎样的？

4. 计划的流程分为哪几个主要步骤？

5. 什么是目标和目标管理？

6. 目标管理的实施步骤是怎样的？组织总目标设定过程中的关键环节是什么？

7. 何为滚动计划法？其优缺点是什么？

【研究与讨论】

1. 有不少管理人员不喜欢在工作中制订计划，有各种各样的理由，最常听到的是"计划赶不上变化"。这种认识正确吗？为什么？

2. 计划在管理中的地位是怎样的？它与其他管理职能的关系又是怎样的？

3. 格力只生产空调，格兰仕只发展微波炉。这既可以看作一种战略，也可以看作一项政策。战略与政策之间到底有什么区别和联系？

4. 管理大师德鲁克说："企业的目的必须在企业本身之外""企业的目的和任务必须

转化为目标"。谈谈你对这两句话的理解。

5. 如何正确理解目标的多样性和目标体系?

6. 如何提高时间的利用效率?

【实践演练】

1. 请列出今后 5 年内你想实现的 5 个主要目标。

2. 访问一名企业经理,了解他是如何做计划工作的。并尽力用图来描述。

3. 3 个同学分为一组,模拟一家快餐公司。分别负责采购、销售和财会。请分别制定各自的目标,找到实现目标的方法,并使目标之间相互协调。

【管理模拟】

1. 分组撰写一份计划书。

2. 分析编制此计划的难点。

3. 估计实施中可能遇到的主要障碍。

【本章案例】

进入 12 月以来,宏远公司老总顾军一直想着两件事:一是年终了,该好好总结一下一年来的工作。这一年来外部环境变化很大,使公司步履艰难,虽经苦苦挣扎,总算摇摇晃晃走过来了,但应该清醒地认识到问题确实存在。二是要好好谋划一下明年的工作怎么做,以后 5 年、10 年该怎么走。

宏远公司是一家民营企业,是改革开放的春风为宏远公司的建立和发展创造了条件。15 年前,顾军带领两位兄弟和 800 元积蓄进城打工,开始收破烂、打短工,后来贩卖沙石,与建筑打上交道。过了一段时间,他们发现建筑用的水泥很紧俏,就开始贩运水泥,顾军在贩运水泥过程中又干起了工程队,用两条腿走路。后来成立了自己的公司,现已拥有几千万资产。公司由一家贸易公司、一家建筑装饰公司和一家房地产公司组成,员工 300 多人。老大顾军当总经理,老二、老三做副总经理,并分兼任下属 3 个公司的经理,公司里的主要职位都由家族成员担任。

公司成立至今,已有十多个年头,取得了很大的成绩,靠运气、靠机遇,当然也靠大家的努力。细细想来,公司的管理全靠顾军自己的经验,遇事都由顾军拍板,从来没有通盘的目标与计划,因而常常是走到哪儿算哪儿。顾军每想到这些,晚上总睡不好觉,公司到底该怎样制定发展目标和计划呢?对于初中还没有毕业的顾总来说,这确实是一件伤脑筋的事。顾军心里明白,公司这几年的日子不太好过,特别是今年。建筑公司任务还可以,但由于成本上升,获利已不能与前几年同日而语了,只能维持现状,前景不容乐观。贸易公司能勉强维持生计,库存商品很多,难以出手。房地产公司更是一年不如一年,市场疲软,生意更加难做,至今还有几十套商品房压得公司喘不过气来。

面对这些困难,顾总一直想着摆脱困难的办法。发展的机会不是没有,顾军认识的一位国有大企业老总曾经向他透露,他们公司的当家产品——小型柴油机在非洲,据说销路不错，当地的代理商很想与宏远合作，利用民营企业的优势，去抢占非洲市场。顾总深感是个机会，但不知该如何把握。最近还有一位市建委的处长跟他说，市里规划从明年开始江海路要拓宽，这是商业旺地，想借此机会建几座商业大厦，但苦于资金不足。这位处长有意为顾军牵线搭桥。这一机会也很诱人，但投入也不会少，该怎么办？随着改革开放的深入，福利分房将结束，房地产市场将会转暖，宏远公司感到机会不久就会到来。

总之，摆在顾军面前的既有机会，也有困难。公司向何处去？顾军真得动点脑筋了。

思考问题：

1. 你怎样评价宏远公司和顾军？

2. 宏远公司应该制订什么计划才能推动公司进一步发展？

【本章阅读与参考文献】

［1］［美］哈罗德·孔茨、海因茨·韦里克著，郝国华等译：《管理学》（第9版），北京：经济科学出版社1993年版。

［2］［美］彼得·F. 德鲁克著，张耀君等译：《管理——任务、责任、实践》，北京：中国社会科学出版社1987年版。

［3］［美］W. E. 纽曼、小 C. E. 萨默著，李柱流等泽：《管理过程：概念、行为、实践》，北京：中国社会科学出版社1995年版。

［4］杨文士、张雁：《管理学原理》，北京：中国人民大学出版社1994年版。

［5］［美］迈克尔·哈默著，赵学凯等译：《企业行动纲领》，北京：中信出版社2002年版。

第五章　战略管理

Chapter 5　Strategic Management

人无远虑，必有近忧。

孔子

A man without distant care must have near sorrow.

Confucius

战略是影响和决定企业的基本长期目标与目的，选择达到既定目标所遵循的路径，并为实现这些目标和路径对企业已有资源进行优化配置。

钱德勒

Strategy is a path to follow, which influences and determines the basic long-term goals and objectives of the enterprise. For the realization of those goals, you should optimize the allocation of the enterprise's existing resource.

Chandler

【本章学习目标】

知识目标：
　　掌握战略和战略管理的含义。
　　了解企业战略的构成要素与类型。
　　熟悉组织的共同愿景及其构成。

技能目标：
　　深刻领会战略管理的理论与现实意义。
　　学会分析和构建组织的共同愿景。
　　掌握和运用战略管理过程。

【Learning Objectives of Chapter 5】

Objectives of Knowledge：
　　Grasp the meaning of strategy and strategic management.
　　Understand enterprise's strategic elements and types.
　　Be familiar with the organization's shared vision and its components.

Objectives of Skill：
　　Understand the strategic management theory and practical significance.
　　Learn to analyze and build the organization's shared vision.
　　Master and apply the strategic management process.

【小故事】

老鹰是世界上寿命最长的鸟类。

当老鹰活到 40 岁时，它的爪子开始老化，无法有力地抓住猎物。老鹰的寿命可达 70 岁。要活那么长的寿命，它在 40 岁时必须做出困难却重要的决定。

渐渐地，老鹰的喙会变得又长又弯，几乎碰到胸膛。它的翅膀变得十分沉重，因为它的羽毛长得又浓又厚，使得飞翔变得十分吃力。它只有两种选择：一是等死。二是经过一个十分痛苦的更新过程：150 天漫长的操练。它必须很努力地飞到山顶，在悬崖上筑巢。停留在那里，不得飞翔。老鹰首先用它的喙击打岩石，直到完全脱落。它会用新长出的喙把老化的爪子一根一根地拔出来。然后静静地等候新的爪子长出来。然后再把羽毛一根一根地拔掉。

5 个月以后，新的羽毛长出来了。老鹰重新开始飞翔，可再过 30 年的岁月！

【引例】

海尔的战略历程

中国最大的综合家电企业海尔集团的前身是青岛冰箱总厂，创立于 1984 年，当时年销售收入 348 万元，赤字 147 万元。2007 年海尔的全球营业额已超过 1 000 亿元，成为全球第四大白色家电制造商。自 1984 年至今，海尔的战略经历了以下四个主要阶段。

第一个阶段，品牌战略阶段（1984—1991 年）。该阶段只生产冰箱一种产品，探索并积累了企业管理的经验，为今后的发展奠定了坚实的基础，总结出一套可移植的管理模式。

第二个阶段，多元化战略阶段（1992—1998 年）。该阶段从一种产品向多个产品发展（1984 年只有冰箱，1998 年时已有几十种产品），从白色家电领域进入黑色家电领域，以"吃休克鱼"的方式进行资本运营，以无形资产盘活有形资产，在最短的时间里以最低的成本把规模做大，把企业做强。

第三个阶段，国际化战略阶段（1999—2005 年）。该阶段产品批量销往全球主要经济区域市场，有自己的海外经销商网络与售后服务网络，海尔品牌已经有了一定的知名度、信誉度与美誉度。

第四个阶段，全球化品牌战略阶段（2006 年至今）。为了适应全球经济一体化的形势，在全球范围内运作海尔品牌，从 2006 年开始，海尔集团继品牌战略阶段、多元化战略阶段、国际化战略阶段之后进入第四个发展战略创新阶段——全球化品牌战略阶段，即要在每一个国家的市场上创造出本土化的海尔品牌。

思考问题：

1. 海尔的战略历程说明了什么？
2. 海尔未来的战略应该是什么样的？

第一节　战略管理及其意义

当组织的生存环境变化莫测，组织的生存和发展受到严重的挑战时，战略管理便至关重要。

一、战略和战略管理

1. 战略的含义

战略一词出自军事术语，意指打仗用兵的艺术，对战争全局的谋划，泛指对重大问题所做的带有全局性、方向性的谋划。现代社会常把战略用于社会、政治、经济、科技等领域，当把战略用于企业的经营管理当中，就出现了企业战略或企业战略管理。在欧美，企业战略的产生和发展经历了一个漫长的时期。在20世纪初，管理的重点是偏差控制与复杂管理，管理的形式是预算控制。20世纪50年代，管理的重点是预测和决策，管理的形式是长期计划。20世纪60年代，管理的重点是战略推进和能力变革，管理的形式是战略计划。从20世纪70年代中期开始，管理的重点转向战略的突变与适时反应，管理的形式也转向了战略管理。

2. 战略管理的定义

自安索夫1972年正式提出"战略管理"的概念以来，对战略管理的研究在不断深入和发展，主要有以下几种观点：

作为确定组织使命的手段，战略管理要明确组织的长期目标、活动程序和资源配置的优先次序。

战略管理是一种事先的计划，是对未来行动方案的说明和要求。

战略管理的主旨在于限定企业的竞争范围。

战略管理是为获得持续竞争优势而对外部的机会与威胁以及内部的优势与劣势的辨识和积极反应。

战略管理是一种连续一致的决策模式。

战略管理是一种定位。

战略管理是企业获得竞争优势的手段。

战略管理是一种观念或意图。

综合以上观点，应当从以下几个方面来理解战略管理的概念：一是应把企业未来的生存和发展作为战略管理的出发点和归宿；二是应为企业确定一个简单的、一致的、长远的目标或远景；三是应主动地迎接和适应环境变化带来的挑战；四是帮助企业建立和维持一种长久的竞争优势。

因此，我们把战略管理定义为：面对变化激烈、挑战严峻的环境，企业为求得长期生存和不断发展而进行的总体性谋划。

具体地说，战略管理是在符合和保证实现企业使命的条件下，在充分利用环境中存在的各种机会或创造新机会的基础上，确定企业同环境的关系，规定企业的经营范围、成长方向和竞争对策，合理地调动企业结构和分配企业资源，从而使企业获得某种竞争优势的动态管理过程。从企业制定战略的要素来看，战略就是充分利用企业的机会和威胁来评价企业现在和未来的环境，用优势和劣势来评价企业的内部条件，进而选择和确定企业的总体目标，制订和选择实现目标的行动方案。

这个定义说明：

（1）战略是有形的，不仅是一种指导思想或原则，而且是一种具体设计或规划。

（2）要根据对环境和条件的分析，为企业设计长期发展的目标。

（3）重点是选择实现企业成长目标的途径和指导方针。

（4）实现企业成长目标的途径和方针的选择，必须以扬长避短、发挥企业竞争优势为基点。

二、战略管理的特征

（1）目的性。战略管理服务于一个目的，那就是引导企业在竞争的环境里生存和发展。

（2）长期性。战略管理不是着眼于解决企业当前遇到的困难，而是着眼于迎接未来的挑战。

（3）对策性。对策性有两重含义：一是面对环境变化的挑战，设计走向未来的对策；二是根据同行业竞争者的战略，设计企业的战略以保持企业的竞争优势。

（4）系统性。其一，战略是指导企业的对策与谋划，是为系统解决各种问题而制定的行动纲领；其二，战略本身是一个系统，既有战略目标，又有实现这一目标的途径和方针，还有落实这个方针的政策和措施；其三，战略是分层次的，既有总战略，又有分战略，可形成一个战略体系。

策略是形成战略的手段，是战略的补充，具有战术性、短期性、局部性和灵活性的特点。

【新视角】

普拉哈拉德和哈梅尔认为竞争就是竞争预见能力、竞争未来，企业的核心能力辨识并不能顺理成章地导致竞争优势，许多企业的成功不是完全依靠已有的实力，而是依靠"野心"，他们认为在复杂与变革的年代，企业需要建立战略远景。

（1）战略意图：这是一个口号式的词汇，它是指"我们用以催人奋进的理想的代名词。……战略意图意味着公司要有长远的眼光和奋力拼搏的决心。战略意图还包含着情感因素，员工们从内心把它看作值得追求的目标。"两位学者认为方向感、探索感和使命感是战略意图的特征。

（2）战略使命：战略使命是战略意图的外在焦点，是公司对特定目标在产品以及市场方面运作范围的描述。战略使命基本确立了公司是怎样的公司、公司的基本方向等问题。

（3）战略发展框架：普拉哈拉德和哈梅尔认为公司间的竞争可以归结为管理框架之争，构建战略发展框架从根本上说"是关于新功能的调配、新专长的获取（或现有专长的转移）以及客户界面的重新设计等一系列问题的高级蓝图"。

三、战略管理的必然性

如果说，20 世纪 50 年代以前管理的重心是生产，20 世纪 50 年代管理的重心是质量，20 世纪 60 年代管理的重心是市场，20 世纪 70 年代管理的重心是财务，那么 20 世纪 80 年代管理的重心就是战略，这种管理重心的转移是不以人们的意志而转移的，是社会生产力发展和社会经济发展的必然结果。具体表现在：

（1）科学技术飞速发展。现代科学技术的突飞猛进，使得产品的生命周期缩短，附加价值提高，从而使生产的技术和产品更新换代的技术大大加快。这就促使管理者必须高瞻远瞩，具有战略思想，探索和遇见未来科学技术发展带来的挑战和机遇，做出正确的战略决策。

（2）市场需求结构发生变化。通过工业时代的生产发展，基本消费品的需求已经得到满足。随着社会经济的发展和消费者的收入水平的不断提高，人们需求的结构正在向多层次、多样化、高水平转变。消费需求的不断变化和发展，迫使企业要满足潜在的和未来的需求。

（3）全球性竞争日益激烈。竞争是世界市场的本质特征之一，各国企业为了生存和发展，必须进行激烈的竞争，企业如何面对激烈的竞争对手，找出适合于本企业自下而上的发展道路，就成了企业领导者的一项重要任务。

（4）社会政治经济形势复杂多变。这种变化是客观存在的，时刻给企业的生存和发展带来生存的机会和新的威胁，企业必须随时能够做出反应，否则就会陷入被动地位。

（5）资源短缺，突发事件不断出现。这些特点使企业外部形成一种复杂的、不确定的环境。这就给企业的生存造成了压力，企业要想求得生存和发展，必须对环境进行深入分析，并通过创造性的管理来应对环境的变化。

四、战略管理的意义

对企业来说，战略管理的成功是最大的成功，战略管理的失败也是最大的失败。战略管理的核心问题是使企业自身条件与环境相适应，以实现预期的目标，求得企业的生存和发展。因此，企业实行战略管理意义重大。

（1）战略管理是面向未来的管理，能够明确企业的发展方向，增强企业对环境的适应性。

（2）战略管理是企业全部管理活动的总纲领，能够加强对管理的指导作用，提升企业管理水平。

（3）战略管理是一种整合性的管理，有利于充分利用各种企业资源，提高协同作用。

（4）战略管理是企业高层管理者最重要的活动和技能，能够促进企业和企业管理的创新。

因此，战略管理将成为越来越多的企业在激烈的环境里取得长期发展的锐利武器。

五、战略计划

战略计划是根据企业战略所制订的计划。它与长期计划的区别在于：

（1）战略计划是可以改变企业性质的重点计划，如投资新事业、开发新产品等；而长期计划则是全面性的计划，包括企业的各项主要工作。

（2）战略计划是一个长远规划，是非程序性的；而长期计划的编制时间是例行化的、是程序性的。

（3）战略计划由企业高层领导者参与制订；而长期计划则由各层管理人员制订。

（4）战略计划着眼于外部环境的变化，以寻求发展的机会；而长期计划着眼于如何使企业本身与企业的目标保持长期协调和配合。

Section 1　Strategic Management and Its Significance

Strategic management becomes crucial when the living environment of organization becomes changeable and the survival and development of organization is faced with serious challenges.

5.1.1　Strategy and Strategic Management

1. The Meaning of Strategy

The word "strategy" comes from military term. It means the art of war fight and the whole planning over combat. In general, it refers to the overall and directional scheme on important issues. In modern life, strategic is often applied to society, politics, economy and technology. When strategy is applied to corporate management, the according corporation strategy and corporation strategic management come into being. In Europe and America, the generation and development of corporation management has experienced a very long process. During the early 20th century, the focus on management is the deviation control and complicated management and the management takes the from of budget control. While in the 1950s, the emphasis on management lays on prediction and decision, and the form of management turns to long-term plan. Later in the 1960s, the key point of management is the strategy advance and ability innovation whereas the form is strategy plan. From the middle 1970s, the key point turns into strategy mutation and timely response while the form turns into strategic management.

2. The Definition of Strategic Management

Since Ansoff formally puts forward the notion of "strategic management" in 1972, studies on it have been unceasingly deepening and advancing. The following are some opinions about it:

Serving as a method to determine organization's mission, strategic management has to confirm the organization's long-term project, activity procedures and priorities in resources allocation.

Strategic management is a prepared plan, including specific illustration and requirements of future program.

The purpose of strategy management is to limit corporation's competition range.

Strategic management is the identification and positive reaction of external opportunities and threats plus internal advantages and disadvantages, aiming to achieve continuous competition superiority.

Strategic management is a consistent decisive model.

Strategic management is positioning.

Strategic management is an approach for companies to achieve competitive edge.

Strategic management is a viewpoint or motivation.

Overall, it is reasonable to understand the notion of strategic management from the following perspectives. Firstly, the starting point and end-result should be the future existence and development of a corporation. Secondly, it's necessary to make a simple, consistent and long-term goal or prospect for corporation. Thirdly, corporation should actively embrace and adapt to challenges caused by environment changes. Fourthly, we should help corporation establish and maintain enduring competition superiority.

Hence, strategic management is defined as the overall conducted plan aiming to fulfill lasting existence and continuous development when facing with violent changes and severely challenging environment.

Specifically, under the conditions of being consistent with the enterprise's mission and on the basis of fully utilizing the existing opportunities or orgenerating new ones in the environment, strategic management is a dynamic management process with competitive advantages included by confirming the connection between the enterprise and the environment, setting the business scope, developing direction and competitive strategy, adjusting reasonable enterprise structure and distributing enterprise resources. As the elements on which corporation make strategy reveal, strategy is to fully utilize the chances and weakness of corporation in order to comment on its current and future circumstance, evaluate its internal conditions according to advantages and disadvantages, furthermore, to select and determine overall corporate target and accordingly make action plan to achieve it.

This definition shows:

(1) Strategy is visible, and it's not only a guiding theory or principle but also a specific design or plan.

(2) The plan or design need to make long-term development target for corporation according to environment and condition analysis.

(3) The key point is to select method and guiding policy to achieve corporation's growth target.

(4) To achieve corporation's growth target, policy choice must be based on playing corporation's strengths and making use of corporation's competitive advantages.

5.1.2 The Features of Strategic Management

(1) Motivational. Strategic management serves one purpose, which is to lead corporation survive and develop in competitive environment.

(2) Long-term. Strategic management not only concentrates on challenges that the corporation currently encounter, but also focuses on future challenges.

(3) Measurable. Measures include two meanings: one is working out solution to future path when faced with challenges brought by environment changes, and the other is working out corporate strategy to maintain company's competitive advantage according to fellow competitors' strategies.

(4) Systematic. Firstly, strategy is the solution and planning to guide corporation, and it is the action guideline made to solve various problems for the system. Secondly, strategy itself is a system, which includes strategic target and the solution along with policy to fulfill it, and the

method to carry out the policy. Thirdly, strategy is hierarchical, including the whole strategy and branch strategy, which amount to the strategy system.

Policy, which is tactic, short-term, partial and flexible, is a method to form strategy and supplement to strategy.

5.1.3 The Necessity of Strategic Management

If the key point of management before the 1950s was manufacture, and quality in the 1950s and market in the 1960s, while finance in the 1970s, then the focus on management in the 1980s was strategy. The shift of management focus was not due to people's will, but the result of the development of social productivity and economy, which was specifically revealed in the following aspects:

(1) Rapidly developing science and technology. The impressive advancement of modern technology greatly shortens product life circle and elevated its added value. Consequently, the speed of technology update increases rapidly. Then managers are pushed to look in the long run and think in strategic way to explore and encounter challenges and opportunities brought by technology advancement. In this way, managers can make right decisions.

(2) Changed market demand structure. Through the manufacturing development in industrial era, basic consumption needs have been fulfilled. As economy continuously develops and living standards improve, people's demand structure is switching to be multi-level, diverse and high-level. The constant advancement and changes push the corporation to achieve its potential and future needs.

(3) The intensifying global competition. Competition is one of the essential characteristics of the global market, thus severe competition is inevitable because corporations around the world have to survive and develop. How can corporation find a developing path suitable to the whole staff when facing with strong competitors becomes a primary task for the company's leaders.

(4) Complicated social and economic situations. These changes are objective and it continuously bring both development opportunities and new threats. Corporation must react and respond at any time. Otherwise it will end up in a passive situation.

(5) Resources scarcity and constant emergencies. These characteristics add complicated and unstable elements to corporation's external environment, posing stress to corporations. In order to survive and develop, corporation must make deep analysis about the environment and cope with environment changes through innovative management.

5.1.4 The Significance of Strategic Management

As for corporation, the biggest success is the strategic success while the biggest failure is the strategic failure. The core issue of strategic management rests with adjusting corporation's specific conditions to the environment for achieving expected target and pursuing corporation's survival and development. Hence, that the corporation adopting strategic management is full of significance.

（1）Strategic management focuses on the future, which is able to determine the corporation's development direction and enhance its adaptation to the environment.

（2）Strategic management is an overall policy that guides the corporation's whole management. The strategic management can reinforce the guidance over management and improve corporation's management level.

（3）Strategic management is a combined management, which can fully utilize various corporate resources and improve collaboration.

（4）Strategic management is the most important activity and skill for top managers in the corporation.

Hence, strategic management will become a powerful weapon for more and more corporations in obtaining the long-term development in competitive environment.

5.1.5　Strategic Plan

Strategic plan is produced according to corporate strategies. It differs from long-term plan in the following aspects:

（1）Strategic plan is a key plan which can change a corporation's nature, for example, investing in new businesses, developing new products, etc., while long-term plan is a comprehensive plan including corporation's various main tools.

（2）Strategic plan is a non-programmed long-term plan, while a long-term plan's authorized time is routinized and programmed.

（3）Top leaders in corporation are in charge of making the strategic plan while administrators from different levels are in charge of the long-term plan.

（4）Strategic plan focuses on external environment changes in order to seek development opportunities while long-term plan aims at keeping a long term coordination and cooperation between the enterprise itself and its goal's structure.

【阅读资料】

通用电气：战略计划

通用电气是美国最大的电气公司。该公司拥有职工近 40 万人，制造、销售和维修的产品约 13 万种，其中包括飞机引擎、核子反应堆、医疗器械、塑料和家用电器等，业务范围遍及 144 个国家和地区。1978 年，公司的销售额约达 200 亿美元，利润超过了 10 亿美元，其中 40% 来自国际市场。

1．战略计划的由来

由于通用电气的规模越来越大，产品的种类越来越多样化，公司在经营管理上，面临着以下几个关键问题：第一，是冒一定的风险使利润迅速增长，还是使利润持续不断低速增长；第二，是需要一个分权式的组织机构以保持组织上的灵活性，还是建立一个集权式的组织机构以加强对整个公司的控制；第三，如何应对环境、技术和国际等方面的新挑战。经过研究，公司选择了利润高速增长的经营战略，这意味着即使在经济下降时期，也要使利润持续不断地增长。为了做到这一点，该公司在业务上保持了多种经营的方式，以应对经济危机对某些业务的影响。为此又需要一个分权的组织机构以促使下属各单位不断地改进经营管理并使利润增长。但是，怎样管理这样一个机构，并应对来自环境、政治、经济、技术和国际上的各种挑战？通用电气的答案是制订战略性计划。

2. 制订战略计划的机构、程序和原则

（1）建立一种制订计划的机构。从组织机构上说，通用电气在传统的事业部和大组的机构上，又建立了一种制订计划的机构——战略（计划）经营单位。战略经营单位的规模不一，大组、部、部门都可成为战略经营单位。从定义上来说，一个战略（计划）经营单位，必须有一致的业务、相同的竞争对象，有市场重点以及所有的主要业务职能（制造、设计、财务和经销），所有这些都由战略（计划）经营单位的经理负责。在建立了战略（计划）经营单位之后，新建的战略（计划）经营单位是计划机构，其职责是制定战略，原有的组织机构的任务是执行战略。

例如，公司的大型蒸汽轮机部是一个庞大的组织，其年销售额近10亿美元，此外，公司还有一个燃气轮机部，其规模为前者的一半。虽然这两个部都很庞大，但都不是计划部门或战略（计划）经营单位。计划的制订工作是在统辖这两个部（以及其他部）的轮机业务大组一级进行，也就是说，这个轮机业务大组是个战略（计划）经营单位。这个大组的战略思想是向全世界的工业和公用事业用户提供发电设备。大型蒸汽轮机的功率高，而燃气轮机的特点是灵活，将二者包括在一个战略（计划）经营单位之内，就可使它们相辅相成，而不是相互竞争。

又如，通用电气用两种牌子（通用电气和热点）销售包括电冰箱、洗衣机设备在内的全套家用电器设备。为了有效地进行生产，这些家用电器被分别组织在一些不同的部门之内。但是，为了制订战略性计划，所有生产家用电器的部门，被集中到一个单独的主要家用电器业务大组内。这个大组便成为一个战略（计划）经营单位。这既可使公司对顾客有一个内外一致的战略，又可使公司具有业务上的敏感性。

（2）制订战略计划的程序可简化为如下图所示的过程。

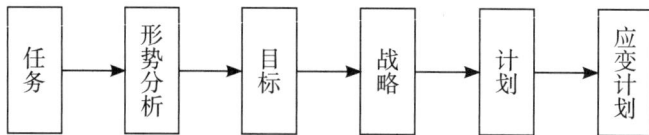

$$\boxed{任务} \rightarrow \boxed{形势分析} \rightarrow \boxed{目标} \rightarrow \boxed{战略} \rightarrow \boxed{计划} \rightarrow \boxed{应变计划}$$

制度战略计划的程序

制订战略计划的程序，主要是一步一步地进行分析。例如，当观察外界环境时，应考虑社会、经济、政治和技术的发展趋势将如何影响市场、顾客、竞争对手和供应厂商，由此可找出发展机会和对公司的威胁；当分析本公司的资源时，应考虑本公司酝酿、设计、生产、销售和管理等方面的能力，以找出本公司的强点和弱点；当分析企业目标时，应考虑公司股东、贷方、顾客、雇员、供应厂商、政府和社会的期望，并辨别出每一个因素将如何指导或限制企业的发展。总之，这个过程所强调的是进行全面的分析，在分析时将一切因素都考虑进去。通用电气公司认为，经过这种分析，就会出现非常有效的战略。

制订战略计划过程中的各个分析步骤，也使通用电气找到了发展业务和进行多样化生产的机会。通用电气下属的战略计划经营单位下决心兼并考克斯广播公司，这使得通用电气在广播和可视电报方面有了新的市场。公司之所以如此快地进行这次兼并，是由于通过战略性的分析，预计到在这方面有发展机会。

同样，对其他国际公司的兼并，也是出自战略上的考虑。兼并使得通用电气加强了自己在能源和工业原料供应方面的地位。

（3）规定一些共同遵守的原则，以保证计划的制订。这些原则可以从以下几个方面加以说明：

①所有管理人员都要参加战略计划的制订和学习。通用电气的300多名高级管理人员，要集中4天时间研究和制订战略计划。100多名未来的计划人员，要集中2周时间全部完成战略计划的制订工作。全公司1万多名各级经理人员，要接受1天了解战略计划的视听训练。公司认为，这种做法的时间代价虽然大，却是成功的关键。

②制订计划时间表以便对各种战略计划进行检查，并通过预算对不同的发展机会分配公司的资源。对战略计划的审查是为了使其付诸实施，通过预算对不同的发展机会分配资源，是为了从物质上保证战略性计划的实施。

③用投资矩阵图（又称业务屏幕）来表明投资的轻重缓急。每年通用电气公司都用矩阵安排自己的投资。战略计划经营单位用横轴估计工业的吸引力，用纵轴估计自己的企业在该行业中的竞争力量。对投资增长类的企业在投资时予以优先照顾，对选择增长类的企业（即还有一定发展前途的企业）在投资时排在第二位。而对选择营利性的企业则要求它们在投资同利润之间保持平衡。对业务萎缩类的企业，则逐渐撤回投资。

公司认为，关键的问题是如何衡量工业的吸引力和企业本身的力量。为了解决这个问题，公司应用了多种因素估计表。

在对与外界各种因素和本企业本身的力量有了精确的估计后，战略计划经营单位的经理就有了做出决策的信心。

④对战略计划经营单位的经理人员实行奖励制度。对战略计划经营单位经理人员的考核，主要是看这些经理人员对通用电气公司的全面贡献如何。对投资增长类企业的经理人员来说，当他们的行动和计划能为全公司带来长远利益时，他们会得到更多的奖励。对业务萎缩企业的经理人员来说，奖励的多少主要是看这些经理人员能否在短期内为公司赚到更多的利润。把奖励与战略性的任务联系起来，有助于克服那种不顾企业本身的实际潜力而使业务盲目增长的倾向。

通用电气认为，从20世纪60年代的分权管理发展到20世纪70年代的战略性计划的制订，又发展到20世纪80年代的战略性经营管理，由于这种管理制度的演变，适应了公司规模和经营多样化的发展，因而给公司带来了巨大利益。为了管理像通用电气这样规模巨大的多样化的企业，公司还在继续研究新的管理方法。但公司认为，管理程序、管理结构和管理制度固然重要，但同样重要的是，还需要一批经理人员，这些处于各阶层的经理人员必须能够从战略上去思考问题。

（资料来源：杨明刚：《现代实用管理学——知识·技能·案例·实训》，上海：华东理工大学出版社2005年版）

第二节　战略的构成要素与类型

一、战略的构成要素

一般来讲，战略由以下四个要素构成：

（1）经营范围：指企业从事生产经营活动的领域。经营范围是企业生存发展的空间，反映出企业目前与外部环境相互作用的程度。经营范围的大小，在某种程度上取决于企业与环境的适应性，取决于市场和顾客的需求。对于大多数的企业来说，应该根据所处的行业、市场、产品来确定经营范围。经营范围既可以为企业提供发展机会，也可能会给企业发展造成压力。

（2）资源配置：指企业过去和目前资源和技能的配置水平和模式。资源配置的好坏，会极大地影响企业实现目标的程度。因此，资源配置又称企业的特殊能力。企业资源是企业从事经营生产活动的支持点，资源配置差，支持力度就小，经营范围也因而受到制约。

（3）竞争优势：指企业通过其资源配置与经营范围的决策，在市场上所形成的与竞争对手不同的竞争地位。实际上，竞争优势既可来自企业在产品和市场上的地位，也可来自企业对特殊资源的正确利用。

（4）协同作用：指企业从资源配置和经营的范围中，所能寻求的各种共同努力的效果。包括投资协同作用、作业协同作用、销售协同作用和管理协同作用等。协同作用是决定企业效率的首要因素，并在各种特殊能力与产品和市场之间形成和发展。

探讨战略构成要素的意义有二：一是认识构成要素对企业效能和效率的影响：效能是指企业实际产出达到希望产出的程度；效率是指产出与投入的比率。战略构成要素中，经营范围、资源配置和经营优势决定着企业效能的发挥程度，协同作用则决定着企业效率的高低。二是构成要素存在于企业各个层次的战略中，在不同层次的战略中，这四个要素的相对重要程度也不同。

二、战略的类型

人们按照不同的标准对企业战略进行不同的分类，说明战略的多样性和复杂性，也为企业选择战略提供了广阔途径。

（1）按照战略的目的，可把战略分为成长战略和竞争战略。

成长战略：指企业内部适应外部环境的变化，有效地利用企业资源，研究以成长为目标的企业如何选择成长基点、成长指向等成长机会，及为保证实现成长机会而采取的战略。对大多数企业来说，成长问题是首要问题，因而多采用成长战略。成长战略的重点是产品战略、市场战略、投资战略。

竞争战略：指企业在特定的时空范围内，为了取得差别优势，维持和扩大这些优势所采取的战略。竞争战略要从企业所处的竞争地位出发，处于优势地位的企业要通过战略来维持这种优势并伺机扩大。处于劣势地位的企业，要以竞争战略来改变这种劣势，或缩小这种同优势企业的差距，常用的竞争战略有成本领先战略、差别化战略、目标集中战略。

①成本领先战略，就是企业力争企业的总成本取得行业的领先地位，并按照这一基本目标采取相应的方针和政策，从而使企业在竞争中占据有利的地位；②差别化战略，就是与其他企业相比，在某个方面和某些方面形成显著差别，并具有独特性；③目标集中战略，就是企业将所拥有的开发、设计、制造等能力，集中在某个特定的、较小的目标市场上以取得更高的效率，从而获得竞争优势。

（2）按照成长方向，可把战略分为产品战略、市场战略和投资战略。

产品战略：主要包括产品扩展战略、产品维持战略、产品收缩战略、更新换代战略、多样化战略以及名牌战略等。

市场战略：主要包括市场渗透战略、市场开拓战略、新产品市场战略、混合市场战略、市场细分战略、市场营销组合战略等。

投资战略：它是一种资源分配战略，主要包括产品投资战略、市场投资战略、技术投资战略、规模化投资战略。

（3）按照竞争态势，可把战略分为进攻战略、防守战略和撤退战略。

进攻战略：指不断地开发新产品和新市场，掌握市场主动权，不断提高市场占有率的一种战略，具体内容包括：①技术开发战略，即大量投入技术开发，占领技术制高点；②产品发展战略，即以比同行业更高的投资去开发新产品，占领产品制高点；③市场扩展战略，即增加投资以提高进入市场和市场占有率的能力，占领市场占有率的制高点；④生产扩展战略。即扩大生产规模、联合兼并扩散生产等等。

防守战略：也称维持战略：这种战略并不是消极防守，而是以守为攻，后发制人。其具体内容包括：①在战略方针上采取避实就虚，乘虚而入，不与强手正面竞争；②在技术上奉行拿来主义，不搞风险性开发投资；③在产品开发方面，实行跟随主义，后发制人；④在生产方面不盲目追求生产规模的扩大，而是着眼于实际效率，降低成本的节约方式。

撤退战略：也称收缩战略：这是一种战略性的撤退，一般有四种情况：①环境的突变，对企业产生了严重的冲击，原定的战略失去了作用；②战略转移，环境发生了变化，出现了更好的机会；③局部撤退，积蓄优势力量，以保证重点进攻方向取得胜利；④先退后进，审时度势，进行战略调整，暂时退却，再突然进去。

（4）按照战略的层次可把战略分为公司战略、事业战略和职能战略。

公司战略：这是企业最高层次的战略，它需要根据企业的目标，选择企业可以竞争的经营范围，合理配置企业经营所必需的资源，使各项经营业务相互支持与协调。它要回答以下问题：①公司的使命与方针是什么？②公司的总体战略目标是什么？③公司应采取怎样的战略态势？④应该有怎样的事业组合？⑤各项事业如何相互发展和相互协调？

事业战略：这是在公司战略的指导下，各经营单位、事业部或子公司所制定的战略，属于支持性战略。主要回答为完成公司总目标本单位应该采取什么行动。

职能战略：这是企业内部各职能部门为支持事业性战略而制定的本部门战略，从而使职能部门的管理人员更加清楚地认识到本职能部门在实施总体战略的过程中的责任和要求，有效地运用开发、生产、营销、财务、人力资源等方面的营销职能，保证企业目标的实现。

Section 2　Elements and Types of Strategy

5.2.1　Elements of Strategy

Generally speaking, strategy consists of four elements:

(1) Business scope: It refers to the area that enterprises engage in during production and operation activities, is the space of the enterprises' survival and development. It reflects how the enterprises interact with the external environment and how large the business scope is, which depends on the adaptability between the enterprises and the external environment and the demand from the market and consumers. For most of the enterprises, they should determine the business scope according to the industries, markets and products they are in. Business scope can not only provide development chance for the enterprises but also lay stress on their development.

(2) Resource allocation: It refers to the enterprises' past and current configuration levels and patterns of the resources and skills. The stand or fall of resource allocation, will greatly affect the achievement of enterprise goals. Therefore, the resource allocation is also called the special ability of an enterprise. Enterprises' resources are the supportive point of production and operation activities. Being weak in the resource allocation may result in the low in the support and thus limits the business scope.

(3) Competitive advantage: It refers to the competitive position of the enterprise which is different from the rivals in the market through the decision of resource allocation and business scope.

(4) Synergistic effect: It refers to the joint efforts made by the enterprise from resource allocation and business scope, including investment synergistic effect, operation synergistic effect, sales synergistic effect and management synergistic effect etc. Synergistic effect is the dominating factor which determines the efficiency of the enterprise, forming and developing in various special abilities and products and markets.

There are two meanings of exploring the elements of strategy: First, understand how do the consisting elements influence the enterprises' effectiveness and efficiency. Effectiveness refers to the level that the enterprises' actual output by comparing with the wanted output. Efficiency refers to the ratio of output to input. In the consisting elements of strategy, business scope, resource allocation and competitive advantage determine the degree of business effectiveness, and synergistic effect determines whether the enterprise's efficiency is high or low. Second, the consisting elements exist in different layers of strategy and in different layer, the degree of importance of the four elements are different.

5.2.2　Types of Strategy

According to different standards, people classify the enterprise strategy to illustrate the complexity and the diversity of the strategy and at the same time to provide a broad way for enterprises to choose strategies.

(1) According to the strategic purpose, the strategy can be divided into growth strategy and competition strategy.

Growth strategy: It refers to the strategy adopted by the enterprises in adapting to the changes of external environment, for the purpose of efficient using of business resource. It discusses how the enterprises aim at choosing the growth points, growth base and other growth chances and ensure accomplishing growth chance. For most of the enterprises, the growth problem is the dominate problem, so they adopt growth strategy whose key point is product strategy, market strategy and investment strategy.

Competition strategy: It refers to the strategy that aims at obtaining differential advantages, maintaining and expanding the advantages within the scope of the specific time and space. Competition strategy starts from the competitive position the enterprises in, and it means that enterprises in the dominant position should maintain and expand the advantages through this strategy while the weaker one should change the inferior position or lessen the gap by taking this method. The usual strategy includes cost leadership strategy, differentiation strategy and target concentration strategy. ①Cost leadership strategy: The enterprises strive for the total cost of the industry's leading position, and take the corresponding principles and policies according to the basic goal so that the enterprises can occupy a favorable position in competition. ②Differentiation strategy: Compared with other companies, the enterprises form some prominent differences and get peculiarity in some way. ③Target concentration strategy: Enterprises concentrate their abilities of developing, designing and manufacturing on a specific and smaller target market, they can get higher efficiency, so as to gain competitive advantage.

(2) According to the expectation of development, the strategy can be divided into product strategy, marketing strategy and investment strategy.

Product strategy: It mainly includes the strategies of market expansion, maintenance and constriction as well as the innovation, diversity and reputation of the products.

Marketing strategy: It mainly consists of market penetration, market expansion, new product marketing, complex marketing, market subdivision and integrated marketing strategies.

Investment strategy: It is a kind of resource division that mainly includes the investment strategies in products, market, technology and scale.

(3) According to the situation of competition, the strategy can be divided into offensive strategies, defensive strategy and exit strategy.

Offensive strategy: It refers to the constant development of new products and market and the control of the initiative to enhance the market share. In detail, it includes: ① Technology development, which means to invest heavily in technology research and command advanced technology. ②Product development, which refers to more investment in products and manufacture best goods. ③Market expansion. It means to increase investment to improve the capability of entering market and market share; ④Production expansion. It means to expand the scale of production and develop the production by conglomeration and merger.

Defensive strategy: Named maintenance strategy as well. It is not passive defense, but transforms defense into offense and gains mastery by striking only after the enemy has struck. In details, it includes: ①On strategic guideline, keep clear of the enemy's main force and strike at his weak points, and then swoop in avoiding direct competition with powerful competitors. ②Take advantage of others' technologies, avoid investing in risky development. ③Follow others' development of new products and let the opponent start hitting and then get the better of it. ④Don't pursue enlargement of production scale but pay attention to real efficiency and economical method of reducing cost.

Exit strategy: Named constriction strategy as well. It is a strategic withdrawal mainly occurs in four situations. ①The sudden change of environment makes the previous strategy out of effect. ②The strategic shift, which means better opportunities turn up after the environment change. ③Partial retreat to retain strength so as to guarantee the success in major offense. ④Temporary withdrawal after evaluating the environment, withdraw temporarily to expect better chances.

（4）According to the hierarchy of the strategy, it can be divided into corporation strategy, enterprise strategy and function strategy.

Corporation strategy: It is the highest level of strategy. It is on the basis of the target of the enterprise to choose the operate range that the enterprise can compete with and to allocate the resources the enterprise need in operation reasonably. And then make the business support and harmonize with each other. It has to answer the following questions: ①What is the mission and policy of the enterprise? ②What is the overall strategic target of the enterprise? ③What kind of strategic state should the enterprise adopt? ④What kind of business combination should it have? ⑤How does each business support and harmonize with others?

Enterprise strategy: It is a kind of supporting strategy made by the business branch, division and the subsidiary under the guidance of the corporation strategy. It is the answer to what action should this division take to fulfill the overall target of the corporation.

Function strategy: It is the strategy that every department or inner enterprise makes to support the enterprise strategy. Through this way, managers and administrative staff can clearly realize the duties and requests of their own department in the implement of the overall strategy, effectively use the resources in exploiting, manufacturing, marketing, financing and manpower to guarantee the achievement of the corporation target.

第三节　组织的共同愿景

无论是新建组织还是已经存在的组织，都必须对自己未来的发展方向做出描述，以便正确地制定、选择和实施战略。

一、何谓共同愿景

共同愿景的英文为 shared vision，意指大家共同分享、共同愿望的景象。那么，组织的共同愿景就是全体成员共同的愿望和追求的景象。企业战略、企业精神、创意等是不是共同愿景呢？准确地说，这些都不是。组织的共同愿景与组织的性质有关，它由组织的职能决定。它包括两个部分：核心信仰和未来景象。前者包括使命和核心价值观，用以说明组织存在的原因和基本价值观，是企业长久不变的东西；后者包括组织在未来一段时期努力实现的远景目标和对它鲜活的描述，是企业通过努力想象、创造才能获得的东西，其作用是激发变革和进步。战略是硬件，而共同愿景是软件，是组织的梦。

二、共同愿景的构成

（1）使命。使命是组织的一种本质属性，是组织未来基本的社会责任和期望在某些方面对社会的贡献。使命代表了组织存在的根本理由。例如，索尼公司的使命就是为包括股东、顾客、员工乃至商业伙伴在内的所有人提供创造和实现他们美好梦想的机会。组织成员有了使命感才可能产生持续的内在动力。

（2）核心价值观。核心价值观是组织对社会和组织的总看法，它是组织最基本和最持久的信念，具有内在性。例如，索尼公司的核心价值观可概括为：弘扬日本文化，提高国家地位；勇作开拓者，不模仿别人；尊重和鼓励每个人的才能和创造力。

（3）景象。景象是未来组织所能达到的一种状态及描述这种状态的蓝图。例如，某公司的未来景象是在 2020 年进入世界 500 强。显然，景象应具有一定的气魄和诱人特性，它应给人以希望、激动，催人奋进，但不是空想。只有这样，景象才能成为全员发自内心的共同愿望。

（4）目标。目标指组织在努力实现共同愿望或景象过程中的短期目标，如产出或市场目标。这些目标不仅从组织未来发展的角度出发，而且也从员工个人的目标中产生，员工在追求自己目标的同时实现了组织的目标。短期目标的不断实现与不断向共同愿景靠拢引导了成员持续地努力。

上述四个部分是相互关联、有机结合的。核心价值观和使命支撑了景象本身，也就是说，景象具体是什么很大程度上受到价值观和使命的约束；宏伟的景象决定了阶段性的目标，但价值观和使命也对目标的构成和实现有重大影响；良好的价值观与崇高的使命是互动的；共同愿景也是一定文化背景下的产物。

三、构建共同愿景的意义

组织的共同愿景孕育着无限的创造力、驱动力和发展机会。

（1）共同愿景是战略决策的前提。组织有了共同愿景，就给定了一个长远的、经得起推敲的未来，它为企业确定战略目标、为实现战略目标而进行哪些活动和以什么方式进行这些活动指明了方向、提供了依据。

（2）共同愿景是组织发展的核心动力。共同愿景通常建立一个高远但又可逐步实现的目标，它引导人们一步一步排除干扰，沿着正确的方向到达成功的彼岸。好的共同愿景能够促使成员产生追求愿景的内在动力。

（3）共同愿景能够帮助组织树立区别于其他组织的形象。共同愿景中关于组织使命和核心价值观的陈述，有利于组织树立独特的、不同于竞争对手或其他组织的形象。

四、构建共同愿景的基本途径

（1）培养共同语言。共同愿景应用组织全员的共同语言来表示，是所有人一致使用的或特定使用的语言，反映员工的共同价值观、共同兴趣等。共同语言是可以培养的，包括归纳组织内小团体的共同语言和组织制定官方语言推广给员工等方法。

（2）开展团队学习。共同语言的形成与团队学习是分不开的。团队学习是一个群体沟通的过程，在此过程中更容易形成共同语言。为了取得良好的学习效果，应防止学习中出现消极因素，在学习中反复练习，让不同团队的学习成果相互交流。

（3）进行深度会谈。深度会谈可以敞开每个参与者的内心，从而挖掘个人愿景的闪光点，形成真正的共同语言，进而为建立共同愿景奠定基础。

（4）实现自我超越。自我超越是指不断突破自己的成就、目标、愿望，这对构建共同愿景是非常重要的，只有成员都有一种不断超越自我的欲望，才有动力去追寻产生于个人愿景之中的共同愿景。

Section 3　Shared Vision of Organization

Both an infant or established organization has to elaborate on its future direction for accurate strategic developing, determining and implementing.

5.3.1　Definition of Shared Vision

Shared vision, which means a mutually shared and desired vision. For organization, it means the mutual wish and pursuing vision shared by the staff. Enterprise's strategies, the spirit of the enterprise and innovation seem to be related to the shared vision, while actually, they are not exactly the same. The shared vision of an organization is relevant to the nature of the organization thus should be determined by the function of it. The function of an organization includes core belief and the scene of the future. The former includes missions and core values which are permanent and are used for illustrating why the organization exists and what its fundamental value is. The latter includes the long-term target and vivid description of it. It can only be reached through the aspiration and creation of the enterprise. The function of the future scene is to provoke revolution and make progress. Strategy is hardware while shared vision is software and the dream of the organization.

5.3.2　Components of Shared Vision

（1）Mission. Mission is an essential attribute of an organization. It is the fundamental social responsibility, expectation and distribution of an organization which represents the essential reason of its existence. For example, the mission of Sony is to provide opportunities for its investors, customers, employees and even its business partners to realize their dreams. Only when the staff members have cultivated a sense of mission could they develop persistent internal impetus.

(2) Core value. Core value is a general idea about the society and organization. It is permanent and inherent and is the most essential belief of an organization. The core value of Sony is to promote Japanese culture, elevate the position of the country to be a pioneer, respect talents and encourage creations.

(3) Vision. Vision is a blueprint for the state in the future of an organization and its description. For example, the vision of a company is to edge itself into the Top 500 in the world by 2020. It's quite obvious that vision is tempting and requires ambitions. It is supposed to make people hopeful, excited and inspired without daydreaming and thus to become the interior mutual vision of the staff.

(4) Goal. Goals, such as output or marketing target, are short-term targets in the process of attempting to achieve organization's shared vision. These goals are generated not only from the development of the organization, but also from the personal goals of the staff. Staff members pursue their own goals, and simultaneously, promote the achievement of the organization's goal. Continuous achievements of the short-term goals and the gradual proximity to the shared vision spur the staff on persistent effort.

The four parts above are connected with each other. Core value and mission support the vision itself, which means what does the vision like is greatly restricted by them. Magnificent vision determines the stage goal while the value and mission also have great influence on composing and achieving the goal. Good value and noble mission are closely related. Shared vision is the product of for development.

5.3.3　Significance of Establishing Shared Vision

Shared vision of an organization contains infinite creativity, driving force and opportunities for develepment.

(1) Shared vision is the premise of strategic decision. If an organization has a shared vision, it confirms a long-term future that can stack up to scrutiny. It ensures the enterprise's strategic goal, what activities which aim at realizing the strategic goal, and by providing it a direction and basis about what and how to do for achieving goals.

(2) Shared vision is the core driving force of organization development. Shared vision establishes a lofty and gradually implemented goal. It leads people to eliminate the interference step by step, achieve success through the right direction. A good shared vision can drive members to produce the inherent power of pursuing the vision.

(3) Shared vision can help the organization establish an image different from other organizations. The statements on the organizational mission and core values stated in shared vision are conducive to the organization and establish an unique image that is different from the

competitors or other organizations.

5.3.4　Basic Approaches to Establish Shared Vision

（1）Cultivate common language. Shared vision can be expressed in common language among organization members. Common language is a kind of language that all members use or the language used in a specific circumstance. It reflects members' common values and interests, etc. Common language can be cultivated through the method of organizing small group's common language and formulating the official language to introduce among the employees.

（2）Carry out team learning. Creating a common language and team learning is inseparable. Team learning is a process of group communication, during which it can easily create common language. In order to achieve good learning effects, the negative factors should be prevented. During the process of study we should practice more in learning and develop mutual exchange of learning outcomes among teams.

（3）Conduct in-depth conversation. In-depth conversation can open each participant's heart, thus dig out the flash point of personal vision, form a common language, and lay the foundation for the establishment of a common vision.

（4）Realize self-transcendence. Self transcendence refers to the accomplishments of self-transcendence of achievements, goals, desires, which is very important for building a common vision. Only if members have a desire to beyond themselves constantly, can shared vision produced in the personal vision possess an incentive power.

第四节　战略管理过程

战略管理是一个动态的过程，基本思路是：企业高层管理者根据企业的使命和目标即共同愿景，分析企业的外部环境，确定存在的经营机会和威胁；评估企业的内部条件，认清企业的优势和劣势；在此基础上形成战略计划。根据战略计划的要求，分配企业的资源，调整企业的结构，并通过计划、预算等形式落实战略计划。在实施战略过程中，要将实施中的各种信息，反映到战略管理系统中来，以便对战略活动加以有效地控制。

战略管理过程一般包括战略分析、战略选择和战略实施三个阶段。

一、战略分析

战略分析是指对影响企业现在和未来生存和发展的一些关键因素进行分析，并预测这些因素未来的发展趋势，以及这些趋势可能对企业造成的影响及影响方法，这是战略管理的基础。战略分析涉及三个方面：

（1）利益相关者的期望分析：就是在重新确立或审视企业共同愿景的基础上，估计与企业有利益关系的人和组织对企业未来的期望，这直接关系到企业战略目标的设定。

（2）环境分析：环境影响和制约着企业的生存和发展，同时，企业通过自己出色的工作也影响着环境。环境分析的目的是发现外部环境变化对企业所产生的某些机会和可能的威胁，这是企业战略形成的重要前提，也是战略成功实施的基础。环境分析的主要内容包括：①一般环境分析，如国家的政治、经济、技术、社会、文化等环境；②具体环境分析，如行业性质、目标市场、竞争力量等环境。

（3）资源分析：主要通过对企业的资产状况、财务力量、组织结构、管理水平、产品结构、企业文化等企业能力和条件的分析，来认识企业的优势和劣势以便发挥优势，克服劣势，建立企业的优势地位。

二、战略选择

按照战略管理过程的逻辑，战略分析为战略选择提供了前提。战略选择涉及三个部分：

（1）确定战略目标，形成战略方案。战略目标是指企业在完成其基本使命的过程中，所追求的最终结果，具体包括：①成长性目标，指表明企业成长发展程度的目标，如提高市场占有率、扩张资本等；②收益性目标，指表明企业获利程度的目标，如利润额、利润率等；③社会性目标，指表明企业对社会的贡献程度或企业形象等方面的目标，如环境保护、知名度等。

战略方案的形成是一个完整的系统分析过程，包括：①确定企业的经营领域，即经营范围。这个领域应该是对企业有吸引力的，如市场潜力巨大，投资回报率大，而风险较小，能有效利用企业资源等。②寻求企业在竞争领域里的优势。优势既可以是现实存在的，也可以是创造出来的，寻求优势就是要扬长避短。③明确企业的经营重点，即在一定时期内企业根据自己的经营范围确定资源的重点投向。④设计企业从现有地位走向既定目标的战略方案。战略方案要从客观环境和创造性出发，达到发挥优势、保持优势和弥补劣势的目的，以保证战略目标得以实现。

（2）战略方案的评价。战略方案的评价是在战略分析的基础上，论证战略方案的可行性。由于企业可供选择的战略方案不止一种，所以，战略选择是要选择方案中最适合企业特点的方案。为了保证战略方案选择的准确性，战略方案评价应符合以下原则：①整体优势最大化。通过方案的比较和方案同外部环境、企业经营情况的比较，使得战略方案的整体功能达到最大化。②竞争优势最大化。一个较好的竞争方案，应符合三项要求：卓越的资源、卓越的技术和卓越的位置。③长远优势最大化。在战略方案评价中，应重点强调纵向评价，就是将一项方案实施后所形成的行业优势，同方案实施前该企业在特定行业或相关行业的优势进行比较，做出评价。行业优势是一种竞争优势，也是一种整体优势，它是由产品优势、技术优势、人才优势、市场优势组成的。

战略评价常用的方法有三种：①常规定性分析，即主要通过个人的创造力、判断力、直觉力和经验等分析、评价战略方案，如头脑风暴法、德尔菲法等；②常规定量分析法，即主要运用传统的定量分析技术来分析、评价战略方案的可行性，如盈亏平衡分析、相关分析、投入产出分析等；③波士顿矩阵法，这是一种用于分析评价公司所属的战略经营单位的战略方案，从而为公司的总战略方案提供依据的一种战略方法。

（3）战略的选择。综合判定各方案的优劣之后，就可以选择满意的战略方案，战略管理过程从而进入战略实施阶段。

三、战略实施

战略实施就是将战略方案转化为战略行动，通过编制各种计划，采取各种战略措施，将战略方案具体化。具体包括以下几方面：

（1）资源配置。这是实施战略的重要手段，资源配置得当，就会有利于战略的顺利实施，资源配置不当，可能会形成瓶颈，抑制战略的实施。战略组织的功能就是要充分利用现有资源和挖掘一切资源，为战略实施服务。

（2）组织结构设计。这是战略实施的保证，组织要适应战略，战略要通过有效的组织结构去实施。战略是随环境的变化而变化的，组织也随环境的变化而变化，一般有三种战略组织形态可供选择：防御型、开拓型、反应型。此外，还要进行人员配备，要使领导者的素质和能力与所执行的战略相匹配。

（3）制定政策。战略实施的全部细节，要有指导战略实施的政策来进一步阐明。因此，政策可视为实施战略的细则，其作用有三：①通过政策的制定来审议战略的各个环节是否有可操作性；②确保战略的意义被正确理解变成公司各层次、各部门的行动纲领；③帮助建立正常可控的行为模式。

（4）战略控制。为确保战略实施过程的顺利进行、实现战略目标，需要对战略实施过程中的情况进行信息反馈。如果发生意外的环境变化，则要重新制定战略，进行新一轮的战略管理过程。有效的战略控制取决于三个条件：①根据战略目标制定绩效评价标准；②建立有效的信息系统，监控外部环境的变化和内部组织的功能与效率；③及时有效地采取纠偏措施。

Section 4　Process of Strategic Management

Strategic managers is a dynamic process. The basic idea is that the enterprise's top managers analyze enterprise's external environment, determine the opportunities and threats; assess the enterprise's internal conditions, clearly understand their advantages and disadvantages; form strategic plan on these basics. According to the requirements of strategic plan, top managers need to allocate enterprise's resources, adjust the structure of enterprise and implement the strategic plan through planning, budget and other forms. During the process of the implementation of the strategy, they need feedback all kinds of information to the strategic management system, in order to control the strategic activities effectively.

The process of strategic management generally includes strategy analysis, strategy selection and the implementation of the strategy.

5.4.1　Strategy Analysis

Strategy analysis refers to the analysis of some key factors that will affect the enterprise of their now and future survival and development. It forecasts the future development trend of these factors, as well as the influence of these trends may be caused to the enterprise, and it is the foundation of strategic management. Strategic analysis involves three aspects:

(1) The analysis of stakeholders' expectations: On the foundation of re-examining and re-establishing the shared vision of an enterprise, estimate the future expectation by people and organizations related to the enterprise's benefit, which is directly related to the setting of enterprise's strategic target.

(2) The environmental analysis: Environment influences and restricts the survival and development of enterprises. At the same time, enterprises have an impact on the environment through enterprises' excellent work. Environmental analysis is supposed to find some opportunities and possible threats of the enterprise produced from the changes in the external environment, which is an important prerequisite for the formation of corporate strategy, and it is also the foundation of successful implementation of strategy. The main contents of environmental analysis include: analysis of general environment, such as the national politics, economy, technology, society, culture and other areas of environment; analysis of specific environment, such as the nature of the industry, the target market, competitive power.

(3) The analysis of resources: It mainly analyzes the enterprise's abilities and conditions such as the enterprise's assets, financial strength, organization structure, management level, product structure, enterprise culture in order to understand the advantages and disadvantages of the enterprise for exerting the advantages and overcoming the disadvantages as well as establishing the advantage position.

5.4.2　Strategy Selection

According to the logic of the process of strategic management, strategy analysis provides the precondition for strategy selection. Strategy selection involves three parts:

(1) Determine the strategic target, conform the formation of strategic plan. The strategic goal refers to the final result the enterprise pursues in the process of the completion of its fundamental mission, which specifically includes: ①Growth target. It shows the target of the development degree of the enterprise's growth, such as higher market share, capital expansion. ②Revenue objective. It indicates the enterprise's profitability goal, such as profit, profit rate. ③Social target. It refers to the degree on the contribution for the society of the enterprise, or the enterprise's image, such as environmental protection, reputation, etc.

The formation of strategic plan is a complete process of system analysis. It includes: ①Determining business areas, namely, the scope of business. This field may be attractive to enterprises, for example, advantages are: the great potential of the market; high rate of return on investment with low cost; an effective use of enterprises' resources and so on. ②Seeking for advantages in the field of competition. Advantages may be an existing one, but it can also be created. To seek advantages is to avoid weaknesses, play to the advantages. ③Clearifing business focus. The enterprises determine their key investment in a certain period according to their own business scope. ④Designing enterprise's strategic plan, which is to target from the existing status. The strategic plan should proceed from objective environment and creativity, to play the advantages, maintain the advantages and make up the weaknesses, in order to ensure the realization of strategic target.

(2) Evaluate strategic plan. Strategy evaluation is on the basis of strategy analysis to demonstrate the feasibility of strategic plan. Due to the strategic plan of enterprises can be chosen from more than one, the strategic selection is to choose the most suited one according to the characteristics of the enterprises. In order to ensure the accuracy of strategic selection, strategy evaluation shall comply with the following principles: ①The maximum overall advantage. Through the comparison of strategies and the comparison with external environment and business conditions, the overall function of the strategic plan can be achieved to the maximization. ②The maximum competitive advantage. A strong competitive solution should meet three requirements: excellent resources, excellent technology and the outstanding position. ③The maximum long-term advantage. In strategy evaluation, the focus should be put on longitudinal evaluation, which is to compare the advantages of the industry formed after a scheme implementation with the advantages of the enterprise in a particular industry or related industry before a scheme implementation. The advantage of the industry is a competitive advantage, which is also a kind of overall superiority. It is composed of the product superiority, technical superiority, talent advantages, and market advantages.

The three commonly used methods of strategy evaluation's are: ①Conventional qualitative analysis. It analyses and evaluates strategy mainly through individual creativity, judgment, intuition and experience, such as brainstorming and Delphy method. ②Conventional quantitative analysis namely, the feasibility of strategy evaluation is mainly used traditional quantitative, such as profit and loss balance analysis, correlation analysis, input-output analysis. ③The Boston matrix method. This is a strategic plan for evaluating the company's strategic business unit, so as to provide the basis for the general strategic plan of the company.

(3) Select the strategy. After the comprehensive judgment of all schemes, the strategic plan can be chosen, then the process of strategic management enters the implementation stage.

5.4.3 The Implementation of the Strategy

The implementation of the strategy transforms the strategic plan into strategic action through the establishment of various plans and adoption of various strategy measures to specify the strategic plan. It includes the following aspects:

(1) The allocation of resources. This is an important means of implementation of the strategy. The proper allocation of resources will be conducive to the smooth implementation of the strategy. An improper allocation of resources may cause a bottleneck, or provide inhibition of strategy implementation. Strategic organization's function is to make full use of existing resources, mining all the resources to implement the service strategy.

(2) The organization structure design. This is the guarantee of the implementation of the

strategy. Organization should adapt to the strategy, while strategy can be conducted through effective organization structure. The strategy changes with the environment, and the organization also varies because of the environment. There are generally three kinds of strategic organizational forms: defensive strategy organization, development strategy organization and reactive strategy organization. The staffing is also needed to make the leader's quality and ability match with the implementation of the strategy.

(3) The policy making. Full details of the implementation of the strategy, should be further clarified by the polity which guides the implementation of the strategy. Therefore, the policy can be regarded as the rules for the implementation of the strategy, and it has three functions: ①Through policy formulation, consider whether each link of the strategy can be operated. ②To ensure the strategic significance can be well understood and become the action rules of the company among different levels and departments. ③To help establish the normal controllable behavior pattern.

(4) The strategic control. To ensure the smooth implementation of the strategy and realize the strategic target, the information feedback in the process of the implementation of the strategy is needed. If an unexpected environmental change happens, we should reformulate the strategy and implement a new round of strategic management process. Effective strategic control depends on three conditions: ①Develop performance evaluation standard according to the strategic objectives. ②To establish an effective information system, to monitor the changes of the external environment and the function and efficiency of the internal organization. ③Timely and effectively conduct corrective measures.

【阅读资料】

战略管理理论的演进

战略管理理论自 20 世纪 60 年代起，经历了一个兴起、上升、回落、重振的过程，战略管理理论的研究从零散到系统、从静态到动态、从企业内部到企业外部，再到内外结合，不断丰富和发展，形成了战略管理的"丛林"。战略管理理论大致分为以下四个发展阶段：

1. 基于环境分析的战略管理阶段

1962 年，美国著名管理学家钱德勒（A. D. Chandler）的《战略与结构》一书的出版，揭开了企业战略问题研究的序幕。他从案例研究入手，分析了环境、战略与组织结构，从而揭示了成长方式与结构变革的关系，指出企业战略应适应环境变化，而组织结构又必须适应企业战略。从而形成了环境—战略—组织相互影响的战略思想。其后，就战略结构问题的研究，形成了两个主要学派，一个是设计学派，另一个是计划学派。

设计学派以哈佛商学院的安德鲁斯（K. Andrews）等为代表，安德鲁斯在 1971 年出版的《公司战略思想》一书中认为，企业战略使企业组织自身的条件与遇到的机会相适应，他将战略结构分为制定和实施两大部分，提出了 SWOT 战略分析模型，全面分析了 S、W、O、T 四个因素，设计出了内在能力与外部机会的最佳契合点，通过选择适应的战略加以实施，以期形成竞争优势。设计学派为战略管理理论提供了许多有价值的概念。

计划学派以安索夫（I. H. Asoff）于1965年出版的《公司战略论》一书为标志。他在1972年发表的《战略管理思想》一文和1975年出版的《战略管理》一书中，正式提出了战略管理的概念，并系统阐述了战略管理的基本框架。他认为，战略管理行为是企业对自身环境的适应过程以及由此带来的企业内部结构化的过程，战略管理的出发点是追求企业自身的生存和发展。安索夫的观点为战略管理理论的发展奠定了基础。

20世纪70年代，战略管理理论得到了进一步发展，极大地推动了企业战略管理的实践。美国最大的500家公司中，85%的企业建立了战略规划部门。就在这一时期，由于世界经济形势的剧烈动荡，很多美国企业在追求多元化增长的过程中遇到挫折，战略管理理论也由"热"逐渐"冷"了下来。

2. 基于产业分析的战略管理阶段

20世纪80年代初，美国著名管理学家麦克尔·波特（Michael E. Porter）在对美国30多家多元化经营的企业做了调查研究后发现，多数企业对战略的应用不够得当，他认为竞争是企业成败的关键。1980年，他出版了《竞争战略》一书，1985年又出版了《竞争优势》一书，将产业组织理论中的结构（S）—行为（C）—绩效（P）这一分析方法引入企业战略管理的研究，提出了以产业分析开始的产业竞争战略。波特认为，竞争战略受制于该企业所属产业结构的现状，制定战略应从产业分析开始。产业结构强烈地影响着竞争规则的确立以及可供企业选择的竞争战略，企业成败的关键在于选择何种竞争战略，而竞争战略的选择应基于两点：①选择有吸引力、高潜在利润的产业。②在已选择的产业中确立自己的优势地位。他提出了由五种竞争力量合成的模型、企业赢得竞争优势的三种基本战略（即成本领先战略、差异化战略和目标集聚战略），以及企业价值链分析模型。从竞争定位到基本战略再到价值链，波特提出了企业获取竞争优势的较为完整的体系，不仅开创了战略管理理论研究的崭新领域，而且为企业制定竞争战略提供了基本方法。

3. 基于资源和能力的战略管理阶段

20世纪80年代中期，以鲁梅尔特（Rumelt，1984）、沃尔纳菲特（Wernerfelt，1984）为代表的一些学者认为，企业是一个资源集合体，而能力是资源的组合；这些资源依附于企业内的组织，具有无形性和知识性，难于模仿，为企业专有；企业战略要以资源为基础。企业保持持续竞争的优势就在于不断形成和利用这些独特的资源和能力。他们还指出企业获取资源的主要途径有两个：一是从外部市场获取；二是内部积累和培养。科利斯（D. J. Collis）和蒙哥马利（C. A. Mongomery）进一步指出：资源是一个企业所拥有的资产和能力的总和。因此，企业要获得佳绩，必须发展出一系列独特的具有竞争力的资源并将其配置到拟定的竞争战略中去，并通过评估资源价值的五项标准，判明一个企业资源的总体状况，从而为制定和选择战略提供可靠坚实的基础。

4. 基于核心能力的战略管理阶段

1990年，美国密执安大学的普拉哈拉德（C. K. Prhalad）和伦敦学院的哈麦尔（G. Hamel）在《哈佛商业评论》上发表了《企业核心能力》一文，认为企业战略上的成功来源于它们在发展过程中的核心能力，核心能力是企业持续竞争优势之源，是通向未来之路，而核心能力的形成经历了企业内部资源、知识、技能等的积累和整合过程。从此，以核心能力为基础的战略管理理论得到了很大发展。之后，学者们做了进一步的分析和研究，还提出动力能力的观点，为基于核心能力的战略管理提供了分析方法。也有学者认为战略管理要整合与重组公司内外的组织、技能、资源和职能能力，并通过组织和管理过程、现有地位和发展路径来建立战略管理的框架。核心能力理论概括起来有四个方面：①企业是一个能力的集合体，是一个开放的动态的能力系统；②企业能力可以从各个角度进行计量和评价；③核心能力才是企业长期竞争优势之源；④积累、保持、运用核心能力是企业生存和发展的根本性战略。一套强有力的核心能力的存在决定了企业有效的战略活动领域，也就是说产生了企业特有的生命线。如果置身于企业能力能够发挥价值的状态中，就构成了企业的优势。基于核心能力的战略管理不仅是企业战略管理理论的创新发展，也是当今战略管理发展的最高层次。正如福斯、克努森在其《企业万能：面向企业能力理论》一书中指出的那样："时至今日，战略研究专家仍然热衷于把企业拥有的特殊资源和能力作为影响企业长期竞争优势的关键因素，因而，这种理论也就成为企业战略管理研究的时代主旋律。"

【本章提要】

- 当企业面临的生存环境变得纷繁复杂、动荡迷离时，战略管理就显得至关重要了。当今世界的企业已进入战略制胜的时代。
- 战略管理就是企业面对激烈变化、严峻挑战的环境，为求得长期生存和不断发展而进行的总体性谋划，它是企业战略思想的集中体现，是企业经营范围的科学规定，又是企业制订各种计划的基础。
- 战略管理的产生是科学技术的发展、需求结构的变化、全球竞争性的加剧、社会政治经济形势复杂多变、资源短缺、突发事件不断等原因所致。加强战略管理对企业的生存和发展意义重大。
- 企业战略的构成要素主要包括：经营范围、资源配置、竞争优势和协同作用。战略可以划分为若干类型，划分战略类型有助于企业选择合理的战略。
- 共同愿景是组织全体成员共同发自内心的愿望和追求的景象，是战略管理的重要前提。共同愿景由使命、核心价值观、景象和目标四个部分构成。它对组织管理与发展具有重要意义。
- 战略分析是指对影响企业现在和未来生存和发展的一些关键因素进行分析，主要包括：利益相关者的期望分析、环境分析、资源分析。
- 战略选择，就是要把企业有限的资源集中在关键的领域，形成竞争优势，从而选择满意方案的过程。主要包括：确定战略目标、形成战略方案；战略方案的评价；战略的选择。
- 战略实施，就是将战略方案转化为战略行动，主要包括：资源配置；组织结构设计；制定政策；战略控制。

【关键词】

战略管理（Strategic Management） 经营范围（Business Scope）

竞争优势（Competitive Advantage） 共同愿景（Shared Vision）

核心价值观（Core Value） 战略分析（Strategy Analysis）

战略目标（Strategic Objective） 战略控制（Strategic Control）

【复习与思考】

1. 什么是战略管理？它有哪些特点？

2. 战略计划与长期计划有何区别？

3. 战略的构成要素有哪些？

4. 解析不同类型的战略。

5. 什么是共同愿景？为什么要构建共同愿景？

6. 战略管理过程包括哪几个阶段？每个阶段又包括哪些内容？

【研究与讨论】

1. 为什么说当今的企业管理已进入战略制胜的时代？

2. 以海尔公司为例，描述企业战略管理过程。

3. 如何正确认识战略四要素及其相互关系？

4. 企业构建共同愿景的目的是什么？难点在哪里？

5. 共同愿景与战略管理有何关系？

【实践演练】

1. 访问 3 家公司，调查它们是否实施了战略管理？为什么？

2. 试帮助一家没有实施战略管理的企业建立战略管理的框架。

3. 为你所在的组织构建一个共同愿景。

【管理模拟】

1. 全班分组展开辩论：企业的成功是不是"七分靠战略，三分靠战术"？

2. 假设你要创业，想成立一家小公司。请为你的公司提出一个初步的战略构想。

【本章案例】

在 20 世纪 50 年代，当医生们把香烟与癌症联系在一起时，烟草公司就立即意识到，如果他们要想生存下去，就必须采用新的战略。由于消费者的抵制和广告的限制，大多数著名烟草商开始寻求多种经营的途径，进入新的市场领域。

菲利普·莫里斯公司是规模最大、获利最丰的烟草公司之一。它的主要产品——万宝路牌香烟风靡全世界，它拥有的强大财力促使它购买其他企业。

1959 年，菲利普·莫里斯公司用 1.3 亿美元收购了米勒啤酒公司。过去，啤酒行业都采用保守和陈旧的方法来开发市场。菲利普·莫里斯公司用了与之不同的新方法，并附以庞大的市场开发预算。还对原先米勒公司的产品结构进行了改造，淘汰老产品，主要生产低度的高级啤酒和高度的低级啤酒，并加强广告宣传。结果米勒啤酒大获成功，在美国销量位居第二。接着，以米勒啤酒为基础，又生产出迎合不同顾客需求的莱特啤酒，这样就使菲利普·莫里斯公司的销量和利润都大幅上升。

1978 年，菲利普·莫里斯公司又收购了七喜饮料公司，并把原来含咖啡因的饮料改为无咖啡因的饮料。随后又发展了一种无咖啡因的可乐饮料，并大力宣传这两种饮料，使销量迅速上升。

菲利普·莫里斯公司后来又购买了国际第四大烟草公司——罗思曼斯，使菲利普·莫里斯公司成为全方位的国际公司，使其不但能保持原产品线和市场，而且把万宝路牌香烟推向了国际市场。

思考问题：

1. 菲利普·莫里斯公司采取了怎样的战略来赢得主动权？
2. 是哪些因素促使菲利普·莫里斯公司进行战略转移的？
3. 你能为该公司提出哪些新战略以促使其大发展？

【本章参考文献】

［1］［美］迈克尔·波特著，陈小悦译：《竞争战略》，北京：华夏出版社 2004 年版。

［2］杨锡怀等：《企业战略管理理论与案例》（第二版），北京：高等教育出版社 2004 年版。

［3］刘冀生：《企业战略管理理论与案例》，北京：清华大学出版社 2003 年版。

［4］干方华、吕魏等：《战略管理理论与案例》，北京：机械工业出版社 2011 年版。

第六章 组织设计

Chapter 6 Organizational Design

为了使组织能够存续，需要谋求个人价值与组织价值的平衡。

占部都美

In order to survive, it is necessary for the organization to seek the balance of personal value and organizational value.

Urabe Kuniyoshi

提高管理效率取决于组织结构。

谢尔登

The improvement of the efficiency of management depends on the organization structure.

Sheldon

【本章学习目标】

知识目标：

了解组织的含义和要素。

理解组织设计的影响因素和原则。

掌握组织结构设计的程序。

熟悉组织结构的基本类型。

技能目标：

学会设计组织系统图和职务说明书。

掌握部门设计的方法。

掌握层级设计的方法。

【Learning Objectives of Chapter 6】

Objectives of Knowledge：

Understand the meaning and elements of organization.

Understand the influence factors and principles of organizational design.

Master the procedure of organizational structure design.

Be familiar with the basic types of organization structure.

Objectives of Skill：

Learn to design organization chart and job description.

Master the methods of department design.

Master the methods of hierarchical design.

【小故事】

有七个人组成了一个小团体共同生活，其中每个人都是平凡而平等的，没有什么凶险祸害之心，但不免自私自利。他们想用非暴力的方式，通过制定制度来解决每天的吃饭问题：分食一锅粥。但并没有称量用具和有刻度的容器。大家试验了不同的方法，发挥了聪明才智，多次博弈形成了日益完善的制度。大体说来主要有以下几种：

方案一：拟定一个人负责分粥事宜。很快大家就发现，这个人为自己分的粥最多，于是又换了一个人，但是总是主持分粥的人碗里的粥最多。由此我们可以看到：权力导致腐败，绝对的权力导致绝对腐败。

方案二：大家轮流主持分粥，每人一天。这样等于承认了个人有为自己多分粥的权力，同时给予了每个人为自己多分的机会。虽然看起来平等了，但是每个人在一周中只有一天吃得饱而且有剩余，其余六天都饥饿难挨。于是我们又可得到结论：绝对权力导致了资源浪费。

方案三：大家选举一个信得过的人主持分粥。开始这品德尚属上乘的人还能基本公平，但不久他就开始为自己和溜须拍马的人多分。不能放任其堕落和败坏风气，还得寻找新思路。

方案四：选举一个分粥委员会和一个监督委员会，形成监督和制约。基本上做到了公平，可是由于监督委员会常提出多种议案，分粥委员会又据理力争，等分粥完毕时，粥早就凉了。

方案五：每个人轮流值日分粥，但是分粥的那个人要最后一个领粥。令人惊奇的是，在这个制度下，七只碗里的粥每次都是一样多，就像用科学仪器量过一样。因为，每个主持分粥的人都意识到，如果七只碗里的粥不相同，他尤疑将享有那份最少的。

【引例】

某跨国制药公司国际业务的组织调整

一、公司组织结构的现状

这家公司是总部设在美国的一家跨国制药公司，它是通过"国际部"和三个"地区分部"对设立在36个国家和地区的分公司（或子公司）的国际业务进行管理。其管理机构设置和工作人员配备情况如下：设在美国本土的国际部共有250名职员；在它下面按地理区域设有三个地区分部，其中设在法国的欧洲分部有150名职员（从销售额看它也是最大的一个分部），设在巴西的拉丁美洲分部有30名职员，设在新加坡的亚洲分部有20名职员。这些分部负责对所属地区的分（子）公司进行控制和协调（但亚洲分部下属的日本子公司，由于其规模较大、业务特殊，实际上拥有与地区分部相同的地位。）这样，介于分（子）公司和总公司之间的管理层次就有两层，共有450名职员。

二、面临的挑战和问题

上述跨国制药公司借以管理国际业务的组织结构曾在过去一段时间内运行得相当良好。但是现在，公司的国际经营环境发生了很大变化，其竞争对手以大幅度精减管理人员和强有力的新产品开发逐渐赢得了竞争优势。相比之下，这家跨国制药公司却因为商标影响力减弱、产品更新换代慢以及人工成本在整个公司总收入中占据30%的比例等原因导致公司盈利水平逐年下降。面对这种严峻的形势，总公司决定对国际业务的管理机构进行调整。其考虑的中心有两个方面：①在不影响管理效能的前提下，是否能使国际部和地区分部的管理人员获得较大幅度的精减？②从长远来看，是取消分部管理机构或转变分部职能（也即集权）好，还是取消国际部管理机构（也即分权）好？

围绕这两个问题，总公司成立专门班子对各层次的150名管理人员进行了调查访问，了解他们对国际业务现行管理方式和各管理层次职能划分的意见和看法。总的说来，国际部有关人员认为，国际部的职能应是全面计划和控制，地区分部的职能是贯彻落实，分（子）公司的职能是具体执行；地区分部的人员认为，国际部应该负责总括性、一般性的计划和控制，地区分部负责详细的计划和控制，分（子）公司负责具体执行。两方面似乎都在强调各自层次职能的重要性。比较客观地看待问题的人士则认为，目前国际业务管理上存在的主要弊端是过多的控制、多余的信息中转和没有考虑各地条件的差异。对于他们所认识的问题，各层次人员建议采取的解决办法分别是：国际部人员建议借助现代化的通信手段取消地区分部设置，地区分部人员建议着眼于避免职能重复，其他人员则建议突出控制的重点。根据收集、了解到的各种意见和建议，总公司负责组织结构调整的专门班子拟订了五种改组方案。

三、可供选择的改组方案

专门班子通过讨论认识到，对公司国际业务的管理不存在任何一种"完全理想"的组织结构方案。他们提出了如下五种备选方案：①保持原组织结构形式不变；②精减国际部和地区分部的管理人员；③集权，即撤销地区分部，由国际部直接对分（子）公司进行控制；④分权，即加强地区分部，削减国际部的职能和人员；⑤转变职能，即通过简化各种行动计划，变控制为支持和服务。基于专门班子提出的这些方案，公司召开了董事会会议，进行决策。那么，究竟哪个方案更为可取呢？

四、决策方案的实施及其效果

组织结构改组的决策既取决于客观因素，如有利于改善经营绩效，同时也考虑个人或群体的需要，尤其是与现任人员工作安全和权力威望方面的需要有关。但面临严峻的成本竞争形势和新产品开发任务的这家跨国制药公司，在激烈的辩论和利益冲突中最终还是做出了改组现行组织结构的决策。其选定的改组方案是这样的：在转变地区分部组建方式和职能性质的基础上实现权力调整与人员精减。这一方案可以说是综合了以上各种改组方案后形成的。具体地说，就是将原来三个按地理区域设立的分部改组为两个按市场类型划分的分部，即发展中国家分部和发达国家分部，前者设在美国本土的国际部大楼内，后者设立于欧洲，这样设立分部是为了考虑不同国家和地区在药品消费层次上的差别，以便更好地组织新产品开发（发展中国家分部侧重于儿童药品和抗"传染病"药，发达国家分部侧重于老年人保健药品和抗"富贵病"药）。另外，鉴于日本子公司的原有特殊地位，现将其从分部中独立出来，直接向国际部报告工作及接受控制。而在分部组建方式改变的同时，分部的管理职能从以控制为主转变为以参谋和服务为主。配合这种职能转变，分部的管理机构只配备制造、营销、财务、研究开发、人力资源和税务等方面的一些专家、经理和秘书人员。

为实施上述国际业务管理的组织结构改组方案，这家跨国制药公司共投资了800万美元，并花费了相当长的一段时间来修改原工作程序及培养管理人员树立新观念、学习新技能，并对被解雇人员加以安置。该方案实施的结果，使分（子）公司拥有了较大的经营自主权，增加了其经理人员的管理能力，并促进了他们的创新精神。实践证明，以这种方式改组组织结构，有效解决了这家公司当时存在的两大问题：管理人员（主要是分部一级的）精减28%，使国际业务管理费用大大降低，从而提高了公司的成本竞争力；按市场类型和消费层次组织新产品开发，不仅有利于保持新产品开发中的规模经济，还可以提高公司的整体研究开发能力。值得一提的是，这家公司投入组织结构改组的800万美元费用，在不到2年的时间内就全部收回了。

（资料来源：王凤彬、朱克强：《管理学教学案例精选》，上海：复旦大学出版社1998年版）

思考问题：

1. 该企业国际业务组织面临的挑战和问题是什么？
2. 该企业是如何选择改组方案的？

第一节　组织的含义和要素

一、组织的含义

组织可以从不同的角度去解释和理解：

（1）从静态角度看，组织是一种实体。组织是为了达到某些特定目标，经由分工与合作及不同层次的权力和责任制度而构成的集合，有四层含义：①组织必须有共同的目标；②组织必须有分工与合作；③组织必须有不同层次的权力和责任制度；④组织必须适应环境。

作为一种实体，任何组织都有一定的结构，即组织结构。它是组织全体成员为实现组织目标而进行分工协作，在职务范围、责任、权力方面所形成的结构体系。

（2）从动态角度看，组织就是组织工作。它是指在特定环境中为了有效地实现组织的目标和任务，确定组织成员、组织任务以及组织各层次、各部门、各项活动之间的关系，对资源进行合理的配置的过程。其目的就是要建立一个适于组织成员相互合作、发挥组织成员才能的良好环境，来消除工作或职责方面所引起的各种冲突，使组织成员都能在各自的岗位上为组织目标的实现做出应有的贡献。主要内容包括：①组织设计；②组织运行；③组织变革。

（3）正式组织和非正式组织。正式组织是为了实现组织目标而设计的组织结构，具有明确的目标、任务、结构和职能，其特征是目的性、正规性和稳定性，例如，企业设立的生产部门、营销部门、财务部门等。非正式组织是因价值观、爱好、兴趣、习惯等一致而自发形成的组织，其特征是自发性、内聚性和不稳定性。它在满足个人心理和情感需要上比正式组织更具优越性。但是，非正式组织的作用具有两面性。

二、组织的要素

为了深入地研究组织系统的构成、联系及功能，有必要搞清楚组织的要素。组织的要素包括有形要素和无形要素两类。

1. 组织的有形要素

（1）实现预期目标所需完成的工作。

（2）确定完成工作的人员。

（3）提供必备的物质条件。

（4）确定权责结构。

2. 组织的无形要素

（1）共同的目标。

（2）工作的主动性和积极性。

（3）良好的沟通网络和制度。

（4）和谐的人际关系。

（5）有效配合和通力合作。

三、组织的功能

（1）组织力量的汇聚作用。把分散的个体汇集成集体，用"拧成一股绳"的力量去完成任务，这就是组织力量的汇聚。1＋1＝2。

（2）组织力量的放大作用。一个有效的组织，不仅要汇聚力量，更要放大力量，实现"整体大于部分之和"的功能。1＋1＞2。

（3）个人与机构之间的交换作用。从个人角度讲，之所以加入某一机构并投入一定的时间、技能，目的是想从机构中得到益处，满足个人的要求。只有个人借助组织活动的合成效应的发挥，使个人集合成的整体在总体力量上大于所有组成人员的个体力量的简单相加，才能使个人与机构之间的关系建立在一种相辅相成、平等交换的基础上，形成双方都感到满意的关系。如果不满意，就有冲突，要通过组织变革加以解决。

Section 1 Definition and Elements of Organization

6. 1. 1 Definition of Organization

We can explain and understand organization from different perspectives：

（1）From static point of view，organization is an entity. An organization is to achieve certain goals collected by the division of labor and cooperation，and the different levels of authority and accountability system. It has four meanings：①An organization should have a common goal. ②An organization should have a division of labor and cooperation. ③An organization should have different levels of authority and accountability. ④An organization should adapt to the environment.

As an entity, an organization has a certain structure, named organizational structure. It is a structural system in duties, responsibilities and power formed by the division of labor and cooperation of all the members of the organization to achieve organizational goals.

(2) From dynamic point of view, organization is to organize the work. It refers to the effective achievement of the organizations goals and tasks in specific environment, and it is a process to determine the relationship among the members of the organization, the organization's tasks as well as all levels, departments and activities for the rational allocation of resources. The purpose is to establish an environment that organization members can cooperate with each other and exploit talent to eliminate all aspects of conflict arising from work or duties that organization members can in their respective positions to achieve organizational goal to make due contributions. The main contents include: ①Organizational design. ②Organizational operation. ③Organizational change.

(3) Formal organization and informal organization. Formal organization is designed to achieve the organization's goals with clear objectives, tasks, structures and functions, which is characterized by purpose, normality and stability. For example, there are production department, marketing department, financial department and so on in a company. Informal organization is spontaneously formed for the same values, hobbies, interests and customs and so on. It is characterized by spontaneity, cohesion and instability. It is more advantageous than the formal organization in meeting individual psychological and emotional needs. However, the function of the informal organization is two-fold.

6.1.2　Elements of Organization

In order to carry out in-depth research on the formation, connection and function of an organization, it is necessary to figure out the elements of organization. The elements of organization can be divided into two sections: tangible elements and intangible elements.

1. Tangible Elements of Organization

(1) Works needed to achieve the desired goals.

(2) Determine personnel to complete the work.

(3) Provide the necessary material conditions.

(4) Determine responsibility structure.

2. Intangible Elements of Organization

(1) A common goal.

(2) Initiative and enthusiasm to work.

(3) Good communication networks and systems.

(4) Harmonious interpersonal relationships.

(5) Effective coordination and cooperation.

6.1.3　Organizational Functions

(1) Gathering strength. Scattered individuals are pooled into a collective completing the task

with an "united" strength, which is the convergence of organization forces. $1+1=2$.

(2) Amplify organization's power. An effective organization is not only to join hands, but also to enlarge the power and achieve the effect of "the whole is greater than the sum of its parts". $1+1>2$.

(3) Exchange interaction between individuals and institutions. From a personal perspective, the reason for joining an organization and putting certain time and skills in it is to get benefit from the organization to meet individual requirements. With the individual activities of the organization to play a synthesis effects, the synthesis of individual strengths is greater than the simple addition of individual strengths. Thus, the relationship between individual and organization which can be said to be based on a complementary and equal exchange, based on the satisfaction of both sides to form a relationship. If not, there will be conflicts and it should be addressed through organizational change.

第二节　组织设计的任务和原则

组织设计是一种以结构安排为核心的组织系统的整体设计工作，是一项实践性很强的工作，组织设计有静态和动态之分。静态组织设计就是组织结构的设计；动态组织设计除组织结构设计外，还包括保证组织正确运行所需的各项制度和方法的设计。

一、组织设计的目的和意义

组织设计是执行组织职能的基础工作，目的是通过创建柔性灵活的组织，动态地反映环境变化的要求，并在组织演化成长过程中，有效集聚组织资源要素，同时协调好组织中部门与部门之间、人员与任务之间的关系，使成员明确在组织中的权利与责任，有效地保证组织活动的开展，最终实现组织目标。其意义在于：

（1）符合组织活动的目的，能够为组织活动提供明确的指令。

（2）有助于组织成员之间的相互合作，使能力得以最大限度地发挥。

（3）有助于及时总结组织活动的经验与教训，从而形成合理的组织结构。

（4）有助于提高成员的归宿感，提高组织效率。

（5）有助于保持组织活动的连续性，并促使其不断地发展。

二、组织设计的任务

组织设计的任务是设计清晰的组织结构，规划和设计组织中各部门的职能和职权，确定组织中职能职权、参谋职权和直线职权的活动范围，即提供组织结构系统图和编制职务说明书。

（1）组织结构系统图。它是用图形方式表示组织内的职权关系和重要职能，图中的方框表示各种管理职务或相应的部门，其垂直排列的位置表示在组织中的等级地位；直线表示权力的流向；直线与方框的连接则表明了各种管理职务或部门在组织结构中的地位，以及它们之间的相互关系。

（2）职务说明书。职务说明书应能够简明地指出各项管理职务的工作内容、职责与权力，与组织中其他部门和其他职务的关系。担任该职务者所必须具备的条件，包括基本素质、技术知识、工作经验、工作能力及学历等。

为提供以上两种组织设计的最终成果，组织设计需要完成以下几项工作：

（1）确定组织设计的基本方针和原则。这就是要根据组织的目标及内外部环境，确定组织设计的基本思路，规定一些设计的主要原则和参数。

（2）职能分析和设计。这包括确定为了完成组织目标而需要设置的各项管理职能，明确其中的关键性职能；不仅要确定组织总的管理职能及其结构，还要分解为各项具体的管理业务和工作；在确定具体的管理业务时，还要进行初步的管理流程总体设计，以优化流程，提高管理工作效率。这是组织设计首要和最基础的工作。

（3）职务分析和设计。即在职能分析和设计的基础上，设计和确定组织内从事具体管理工作所需要的职务类别和数量，分析担任每个职务的人员应负的责任、应有的权力以及应具备的条件。

（4）部门设计。部门设计实际上就是进行管理业务的组合，即要根据组织内各个职务所从事的工作内容性质及职务间的相互联系，在理清关系的基础上，依据一定的原则，将各个职务组合成"部门"这种管理单位。

（5）结构形成。在上述工作的基础上，根据组织内外现有的以及能获取的人力资源，对初步设计的部门和职务进行调整，并平衡各部门、各职务的工作量，以使组织结构设计更为合理。

三、组织设计的影响因素

每一组织内外的各种变化因素，都会对其组织设计产生重大的影响。影响组织设计的因素主要有：

1. 战略因素

一个组织的战略就是它的总目标，它决定着本组织在一定时期内的活动方向和水平。战略与组织设计具有强相关性。组织结构是帮助管理当局实现其目标的手段，如果管理当局对组织的战略做了重大调整，那么组织设计也要随之进行调整，使组织结构适应和支持战略。

2. 规模因素

企业规模对组织设计具有明显的作用。大型组织的结构比小型组织的结构要复杂得多。因为：①组织规模越大，工作就越专业化；②组织规模越大，标准操作化程序和制度就越健全；③组织规模越大，分权的程度就越高。因此组织结构与规模呈正相关。

3. 技术因素

组织的活动需要利用一定技术水平的物质手段来进行。越是常规的技术，越需要高度结构化的组织；反之非常规的技术，则要求更大的结构灵活性。例如，信息处理的计算机化，必将改变组织中的会计、文书、统计等部门的操作形式和性质。

4. 环境因素

任何组织都存在于一定的社会环境之中，任何环境因素的变化都会对组织发生着不同程度的作用。一般说来，环境对组织设计的影响主要有：①对职务和部门设计的影响；②对各部门关系的影响；③对组织结构总体特征的影响。需要特别指出的是，人类环境对组织设计的影响日益重要。

5. 权力控制因素

S. Robbings 在长期研究的基础上总结到：规模、战略、技术和环境等因素，会对组织结构产生较大的影响。但即使这些因素组合起来，也只能对组织结构产生 50% 的影响作用。而对组织结构产生决定性作用的是权力控制。因为从若干备选方案中挑选哪一个，最终由权力控制者决定。

四、组织设计的原则

在进行组织设计的过程中，有一些最基本的组织原则是必须遵循的。

1. 目标明确化原则

任何一个组织的存在，都是由它的特定目标决定的。目标是组织的出发点和归宿。因此，组织结构设计必须有利于组织目标的实现，并且要明确这个组织每一部分的目标。

2. 分工协作原则

分工与协作是社会化大生产的产物，分工越细密，协作越复杂，而且越必要。分工就是按照管理专业化程度和提高工作效率的要求，把单位的任务、目标分解成各级、各部门的任务和目标，明确干什么、怎么干。协作就是要明确部门之间和部门内部成员之间的协调关系与配合方法。只有分工没有协作，分工就失去了意义；而没有分工更谈不上协作。

3. 权责相称原则

职权是指在一定的职位上，在某人职务范围内，完成其责任应具有的权力；职责是指职位的责任和义务。在组织设计时，既要明确规定每一管理层次和职能机构的职责范围，又要赋予其完成职责所必需的管理权限，职责与权限必须协调一致。有责无权就会束缚主动性；有权无责就会导致滥用职权。

4. 统一指挥原则

各级管理组织必须服从它的上级管理机构的命令和指挥，而且特别强调任何一个下级只能接受一个上级的指挥。这将有助于减少冲突，保证组织目标的实现和绩效的提高。在强调集权的同时，也可以适当分权。

5. 管理幅度原则

管理幅度是指一名上级领导者所能直接有效地领导下级的人数，也称为管理跨度。这是因为个人的能力和精力都是有限的，所以一个上级领导人能够直接有效地指挥下级的人数也是有限的。管理幅度与管理层次有关。管理层次就是组织层次，它是描述组织纵向特征的一个概念，是指从企业最高一级的管理组织到最低一级的管理组织的各个等级，每一个组织等级，即为一个管理层次。

管理幅度与管理层次成反比例关系，即管理幅度如要加大，管理层次则应减少；管理层次越多，管理幅度应该越小。管理幅度的大小，取决于管理者的时间、经历、偏好及素质等。一般来说有四类影响因素：①管理素质。管理者的素质状况会直接影响管理幅度的大小。②管理内容。管理工作的复杂性、相似性以及计划与控制的明确性、非管理性事务的多少，都会影响管理幅度的大小。③管理条件。助手的配备情况、信息手段的使用情况、下级人员工作地点的相近性也会影响管理幅度。④管理环境。组织环境是否稳定，会在很大程度上影响组织活动的内容和政策的调整频率与幅度，环境变化越快，变化程度越大，组织中遇到的新问题就越多，请示就越有必要。因此，环境越不稳定，管理幅度就越受到限制。

6. 部门化原则

组织设计的很大一部分工作是将管理职能部门化。部门是组织的细胞，部门设置直接关系着组织的健康和运作绩效。部门化就是将整个管理系统分解成若干个相互依存的基本单位。一般来说，组织设计中的部门化有：

（1）职能部门化——根据业务活动的相似性来设立管理部门。

（2）产品部门化——根据企业产品的不同类别来设立管理部门。

（3）过程部门化——根据提供产品或服务的过程来设立管理部门。

（4）地区部门化——根据地理位置来设立管理部门。

（5）顾客部门化——根据顾客类别的不同来设立管理部门。

7. 集权与分权相结合原则

集权与分权指的是组织决策权的集中化与分散化。集中化就是趋向把较多的和较大的决策权集中到组织高层，组织的中下层则处于决策权少而且小的地位；反之，如果把较多或较大的决策权授予组织的中下层，组织高层只保留少数较重要的决策权，则称为决策权的分散化。影响一个企业集权与分权程度的因素主要有：①产品结构及生产技术特点；②企业的规模与组织形式；③决策的重要性；④环境条件；⑤人员素质；⑥工作性质。一个组织是集权程度高一些好，还是分权程度高一些好，并没有统一的结论，必须综合考虑各种相关因素而定，基本出发点是保证决策的迅速性、正确性。

8. 精干高效原则

任何组织结构形式，都必须把精干、高效放在重要位置。所谓精干就是在保证完成目标，达到高效和高质量的前提下，设置最少的机构，用最少的人完成组织管理工作。所谓高效就是在组织结构中的每个部门、每个环节甚至每个人，为了一个统一的目标，组成最合理的组织结构形式，进行最有效的内部协调，提高办事效率。

9. 稳定性与适应性相结合原则

管理的组织结构既要有相对的稳定性，又必须根据组织内外环境的变化及长远目标做出相应的调整。

Section 2　Missions and Principles of Organizational Design

Organizational design is a structural arrangement being considered as the core of the overall design of the system of work organization. It is a very practical work. Organizational design can be divided into static and dynamic. Static organizational design is the design of the organizational structure. Dynamic organizational design includes not only the organizational structure of the design, but also the design of system and methods that are needed to ensure the correct operation of the organization.

6.2.1 Purpose and Significance of Organizational Design

Organizational design is the basic work to perform functions of the organization. Its purpose is to create a soft and flexible organization by dynamically reflecting the requirements of environmental changes, and in the growth process of the organization, it can effectively concentrate the elements of organizational resources and coordinate the inter-relationship among departments, people and tasks. Meanwhile, it enables members to clarify the rights and responsibilities in the organization, effectively ensure the conduct of organizational activities, and it can ultimately achieve organizational goals. Its significance lies in:

(1) Being in line with the purpose of the activities in the organization and providing clear instructions for the organizational activities.

(2) Contributing to cooperation between members of the organization and giving full play to members' ability.

(3) Helping to sum up the experience and lessons of organized activities to form rational organizational structure.

(4) Helping to improve members' sense of belonging and enhance organizational efficiency.

(5) Helping to maintain the continuity of organizational activities and promoting its continuous development.

6.2.2 Task of Organizational Design

Organizational design is to design a clear organizational structure, plan and design the functions and powers of each apartment in the organization. It helps determine the scope of activities of the functional authority, staff authority and line authority that provides organizational structure chart of the system and job description.

(1) Organizational structure chart of the system. It is a graphical representation of the relationship between competence and important functions within the organization. The figure in the box represents a variety of management positions or the appropriate department, and its vertically ranked position represents the position in the organization, the line represents the flow of power, the straight connection box indicates the status of various management positions or departments and the relationship between them in the organizational structure.

(2) Job description. It should point out a concise content of the management duties, responsibilities and authority as well as the relationship with other departments and other duties. Those who are assigned a job must have the capabilities including the basic qualities, technical knowledge, work experience, work ability, educational background and so on.

In order to provide the two results above of organizational design, organizational design should complete the following tasks:

（1）Determination of the basic guidelines and principles of organizational design. According to the organization's goals and the internal and external environment, we should determine the basic idea of organizational design providing some key principles and design parameters.

（2）Functional analysis and design. This includes identifying of the various management functions in order to achieve organizational goals, and clarifying critical functions. It is not only to determine the organization's overall management function structure, but also to classify the specific management business and work. When determining specific management business, it is necessary to design the overall management process to optimize the process and improve management efficiency. This is the first and most basic work of organizational design.

（3）Job analysis and design. Based on functional analysis and design, design and determine the necessary categories and number of positions involved in specific management works in the organization and analyze each person's responsibility, authority and indispensable qualities in each position.

（4）The design department. It is actually a combination of management business, which is to work according to the interrelated nature of the content and duty of each position within the organization. On the basis of sorting the relationship, combine various positions into "apartment" management unit according to certain principles.

（5）Structure formation. It is based on the work above, according to the existing human resources both inside and outside the organization, adjust the preliminary design of departments and positions and balance the various departments and the workload of each job in order to make more rational organizational structure design.

6. 2. 3　Influence Factors in Organizational Design

A variety of internal and external variables of each organization will have a significant impact on organizational design. The influence factors in organizational design include:

1. Strategic Factors

An organization's strategy is its overall goal, which determines the direction of the organization and the level of activity in a given period. Strategy and organizational design are closely related. Organizational structure is to help the authorities to achieve its goals, if the management authorities of the strategic organizations make a huge adjustment, it needs to be adjusted along with organizational design, making organizational structure suitable and supporting adaptation strategies.

2. Scale Factors

Business scale plays a significant role in the structure of organizational design. Large organizations are much more complex than small organizations. ①The larger scale the organization is, the more specialized it is. ②The larger scale the organization is, the more sound of standard operating procedures and systems it processes. ③The larger scale of the organization is, the higher the degree of decentralization is. Organizational structure and scale are positively correlated.

3. Technical Factors

The activities of an organization need to take the material means of certain level of technology. The more conventional techniques are, the higher structured organization it need, Otherwise, unconventional techniques require greater structural flexibility. For example, computerized information processing operation will change the form and nature of the organization's accounting, documents, statistics and other departments.

4. Environmental Factors

Any organization exists in a certain social environment, any environmental factor will influence the organization in different levels. In general, the impacts of the environment on the organizational design include: ①Impact on job and sector design. ②Impact on the relationship between the various departments. ③Impact on the overall characteristics of the structure of the organization. In particular, human's environment has become increasingly important to organization design.

5. Power Control Factors

S. Robbings concludes on the basis of long-term research: The scale, strategic, technical and environmental factors together will have a great impact on the organizational structure. But even being combined, they can only produce 50% of the influence on organizational structure. Power control have a decisive influence, because it is the power controller who determines which alternative plan to be chosen.

6.2.4　Principles of Organizational Design

There are some basic organizational principles that we must follow during the process of organizational design.

1. The Principle of Clear Objective

The existence of any organization is determined by its specific objective. Organizational objectives are the starting point and destination for an organization. Therefore, the design of organizational structure must be in favor of the achievement of the goals of the organization. Furthermore, it is necessary to clear objectives for each part of the organization.

2. The Principle of Division and Collaboration

The division and collaboration of labor is a product of the social mass production, the more detailed it is divided into, and the more complex collaboration it is, the more necessary the division is. The division of labor is making the task units, goals transform down into levels, and each department's missions and goals in accordance with the degree of management specialization and work efficiency, and then clear what to do and how to do it. Collaboration is the methods to clear the way of coordination between the departments and the members within the department. If there is no collaboration but division of labor, the division of labor will be meaningless; of course if there is no division of labor, let alone collaboration.

3. The Principle of Equal Rights and Responsibilities

Authority refers to the power someone should have to complete his or her responsibilities in a certain position and within the scope of their duties. Responsibilities mean the duties and obligations for the position. In organizational design, it is necessary to clearly define the range of responsibilities for each management level institutions, and also give complete administrative privileges for their duties. Responsibilities and authorities must be coordinated. Having responsibility but no right, the initiative will be undermined; having right but no responsibility may lead to the abuse of power.

4. The Principle of Unity of Command

Each level of management organizations must obey its senior organization's command and control, and it should be particularly emphasized that any subordinate only accept one higher level of command, which will help to reduce conflicts and improve performance to ensure the realization of organizational goals. While emphasizing centralization, the decentralization should also be appropriately used.

5. The Principle of Management Range

Management range refers to the number of subordinates that a superior can exert directly and effectively, which is also known as management span. Because the individual's ability and energy are limited, the number of subordinates a superior can directly and effectively lead is limited. Management range is related to management levels. Management level is the organizational level, it is a concept that describes the characteristics of vertical organization, it refers to the number of organizational levels from the company's highest level to the lowest level, and a level of an organization is a level of management.

Management range is inversely proportional with management level. It means if the range of management is increased, the management level will reduce; the higher level of management is, the smaller management range will be. Management range's width is largely depending on manager's time, experiences, preferences, quality and so on. In general, there are four factors: ①Management quality. Qualities of a manager will directly affect the width of management range. ②Management content. The management's complexity, similarity, the clarity of planning and controlling, and the number of non-administrative affairs will affect the size of the management range. ③Management conditions. The placement of assistants, the use of information tools and proximity of subordinate workplace will affect management range as well. ④ Management environment. The stability of organizational environment will affect the frequency and the magnitude of the adjustment of policies and contents for activities of the organization. The faster the environment changes, the greater the degree changes, and the more new problems will the organization encounter, so the more necessary it is to ask for instructions. Therefore, the more unstable environment will be, the more restricted management range will be.

6. The Principle of Departmentalization

The main work of organizational design is the departmentalization of management functions. Departments are organization's cells. A united setting is directly related to the health and operational performance of the organization. Departmentalization is to decompose the entire management system into several interdependent basic units.

In general, the departments of the organizational design include：

（1）Functional departmentalization—Setting up management departments according to the similarity of business activities.

（2）Product departmentalization—Setting up management departments according to the different types of products.

（3）Process departmentalization—Setting up management departments according to the process of providing products or services.

（4）Geographical departmentalization—Setting up management departments according to the different allocations.

（5）Customer departmentalization—Setting up management departments according to the different types of customers.

7. The Principle of Combining Centralization and Decentralization

Centralization and decentralization means that the decision-making of the organization is centralized or decentralized. Centralization is a tendency to concentrate more and greater decision-making power to the upper levels of the organization, while the organization's middle and lower classes are in fewer and smaller decision-making power. On the other hand, if more or larger decision-making power is granted to the lower of the organization and leaving only a small part of power for some important decision-making to the high-level of the organization, then it is known as the decentralization of decision-making power. Factors affecting the degree of centralization and decentralization mainly include：①Product structure and production technical characteristics. ②Scale and organization of the enterprise. ③Importance of the decision. ④Environmental conditions. ⑤Quality of personnel. ⑥Nature of the work. There is no agreement on if an organization is better with a high degree of centralization or a high degree of decentralization, we must consider all relevant factors, the basic starting point is to ensure speedy and correctly decision-making.

8. The Principle of Elite and Efficiency

Elite and efficiency should be put in an important position in any form of organizational structure. Elite is to ensure the objectives achieved under the premise of efficiency. It refers to high-quality setting of institutions with a minimum of organization and management. Efficiency is that each department in the organizational structure, all aspects and even each person form into the most rational organizational structure for a unified purpose to conduct the most effective forms of internal coordination to improve efficiency.

9. The Principle of Combining Stability and Adaptability

The organizational structure of management should have relatively stability as well as changeability, and adjust itself according to internal and external environment as well as the long-term goal.

第三节　组织结构设计

一、组织结构

组织结构是指描述组织的框架体系，是对完成组织目标的人员、工作、技术和信息所做的制度性安排。由于组织是不断发展的，因而组织的结构不是一成不变的。一是当新建组织时，需要设计组织系统；二是当原有组织结构出现较大问题或整个组织的目标发生变化时，需要对组织系统重新设计；三是对组织系统的局部进行增减或完善。

二、组织结构的特性

（1）复杂性：是指组织内部的专业化分工程度、组织层级、管理幅度以及人员之间、部门之间所存在着的差别。一个组织分工越细、层级越多、管理幅度越大，组织的复杂性就越高；组织单位的地理分布越广泛、部门越多，则协调人员及其活动就越困难。

（2）规范性：是指组织依靠规则和程序引导员工行为的程度。有些组织的规范准则和规章条例较少，那么这些组织的规范化的程度较小；有些组织的规范准则和规章条例较多，那么这些组织的规范化程度较高。

（3）集权性：是指决策制定权力的集中程度。在一些组织中，决策是高度集中的，问题自下而上传递给高层管理人员，由他们来制订行动方案，说明组织的集权化程度较高；而另外一些组织，其决策权责则予下层管理人员，说明组织的集权化程度较低。

三、组织结构设计的程序

1. 确定组织目标

组织目标是进行组织设计的出发点，是管理组织设计的第一步，就是在综合分析组织外部环境和内部条件的基础上，合理确定组织的总目标及各种具体的派生目标。

2. 确定业务内容

根据组织目标的要求，确定为实现组织目标所进行的业务管理工作项目，并按其性质适当分类，如市场研究、产品开发、营销管理等。明确各类活动的范围和大概的工作量，进行业务流程的总体设计，使总体业务流程优化。

3. 确定组织结构

根据组织规模、技术特点、业务工作量的大小，确定应采取什么样的管理组织形式，需要设计哪些单位和部门，并把性质相同或相近的管理业务工作分归适当的单位和部门负责，形成层次化、部门化的结构。

4. 配备职务人员

根据各单位和部门所分管业务工作的性质，以及对人员素质的要求，挑选和配备称职的人员及其负责人，并明确其职务。

5. 规定职责权限

根据组织目标的要求，明确规定各单位和部门及其负责人对管理业务工作应负的责任以及评价工作成绩的标准。同时，还要根据搞好业务工作的实际需要，授予各单位和部门及其负责人适当的权力。

6. 连成一体

这是组织设计的最后一步，即通过明确规定各单位、各部门之间的相互关系，吸收它们之间在信息沟通和相互协调方面的原则和方法，把各组织实体上下左右联结起来，形成一个能够协调运作、有效地实现组织目标的管理组织系统。

四、组织结构的选择

组织结构是随着社会发展而发展的，在现代社会，组织结构有多种类型。这里我们介绍八种常见的基本的组织结构形式。

1. 直线结构

直线结构又称简单结构，这是最早、最简单的一种组织结构形式。其特点是：组织中各种职务按垂直系统直线排列，全部管理职能由各级行政领导人负责，不设职能或参谋机构；命令从最高层管理者经过各级管理人员，直至组织末端（工人），是直线式的流动；组织中每个成员只受最近的一个上级指挥，仅对该上级负责，并汇报工作；一个人一个上级，彻底贯彻统一指挥原则。其结构如图6-1所示。

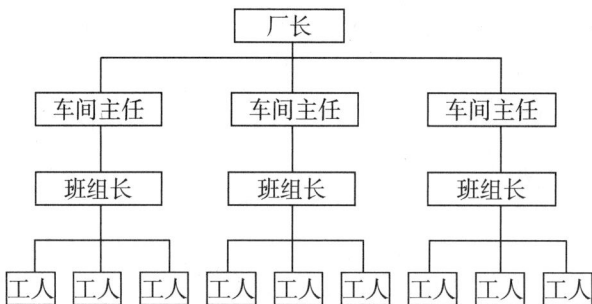

图6-1 直线结构

直线结构的长处都来源于其简单性：①指挥命令系统单纯，决策迅速，命令统一，容易贯彻到底；②每个组织成员的责任和权限非常明确，不易产生目标不清的情况，每个人对实现组织目标的贡献也较易评价；③容易维持组织纪律，确保组织秩序；④灵活；⑤管理费用低。

直线结构的缺点：①每个人只注意听上级批示，每个部门只关心本部门工作，横向协调差；②权力完全集中于一人，对最高领导者的依赖性大，容易发生失误。

这种结构一般适用于那些没有必要按职能实行专业化管理的小型组织，以及处于初建阶段、所处环境较简单且易变或突然面临困难甚至处于敌对环境的组织。

2. 职能结构

职能结构的特点是，组织内除直线主管外，还设立一些职能部门，各职能部门有权在自己的业务范围内向下级下达命令和指示。下级直线主管除了接受上级直线主管的领导外，还必须接受上级职能部门的指挥。其结构如图6-2所示。

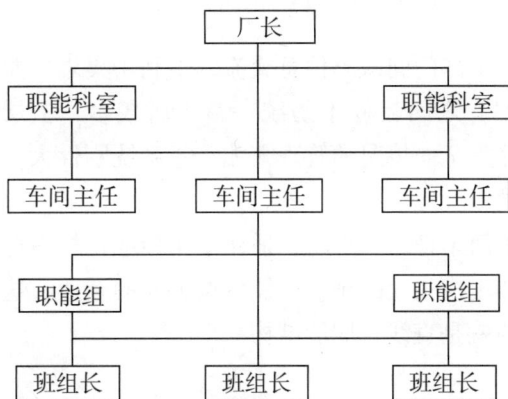

图 6-2　职能结构

职能结构的主要优点有：①能发挥职能机构的专业管理作用，对下级指导得更细；②减轻了直线主管的负担；③管理者职能分工，使对管理者的选用和培养变得容易。

职能结构的缺点也比较明显：①妨碍了组织必要的集中领导和统一指挥，形成多头领导，容易出现命令的重复或矛盾，从而造成管理的混乱；②不利于明确划分直线人员与职能部门的职责权限，容易出现争夺权力、推卸责任的情况。

这种组织结构多见于医院、高等院校、设计院、图书馆、会计事务所等组织。

3. 直线—职能结构

这种结构的特点是以直线结构为基础，在各级直线主管之下设置相应的职能部门，即在保持直线组织的统一指挥的原则下，增加了参谋机构。其结构如图 6-3 所示。

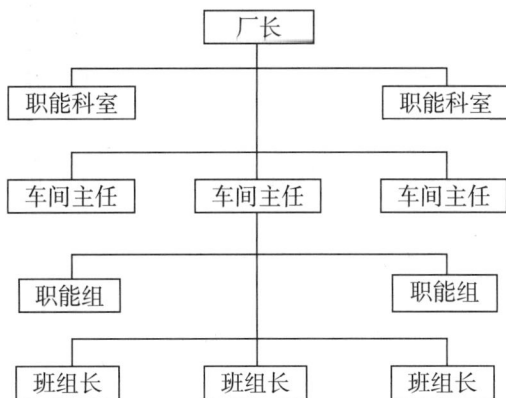

图 6-3　直线—职能结构

在这种组织形式下，直线部门是骨干，原则上担负着实现组织目标所需要完成的直线业务，如生产销售；而职能部门只是同级直线主管的参谋与助手，可以对下级职能机构进行业务指导，但无权对下级直线主管发号施令，除非上级直线主管授予他们某种权力。

直线—职能结构的优点是：①把直线结构和职能结构的优点结合起来，既能保持指挥的统一，又能发挥参谋人员的作用；②分工细密，职责清楚，各部门仅对自己应做的工作负责，效率较高；③组织的稳定性较高，在外部环境变化不大的情况下，易于发挥组织的集团效率。

这种结构的缺点是：①部门间缺乏信息交流，不利于集思广益地做出决策；②直线部门与职能部门（参谋部门）之间目标不易统一，矛盾较多，上层主管的协调工作量大；③难以从组织内部培养熟悉全面情况的管理人才；④系统刚性大，适应性差，容易因循守旧，对新情况不易及时做出反应。

这种结构主要适用于简单稳定的环境，适用于用标准化技术进行常规性大批量生产的场合。对于多品种生产和规模很大的企业以及强调创新的企业，这种结构就不适宜了。目前，我国企业采用最多的就是直线—职能结构。

4．事业部结构

事业部结构又称联邦分权结构，是一种分权制的企业组织形式。这种组织结构是由美国通用汽车公司前副总经理斯隆创立的，所以又称为"斯隆模型"。它是一个企业内对于具有独立的产品和市场、独立的责任和利益的部门实行分权管理的一种组织形态，这样的部门就是事业部。它必须具备三个要素：第一，具备独立的产品和市场，是产品责任或市场责任单位。第二，具有独立的利益，实行独立核算，是一个利益责任单位，即利润中心。第三，是一个分权单位，具有足够的权力，能自主经营。其结构如图 6-4 所示。

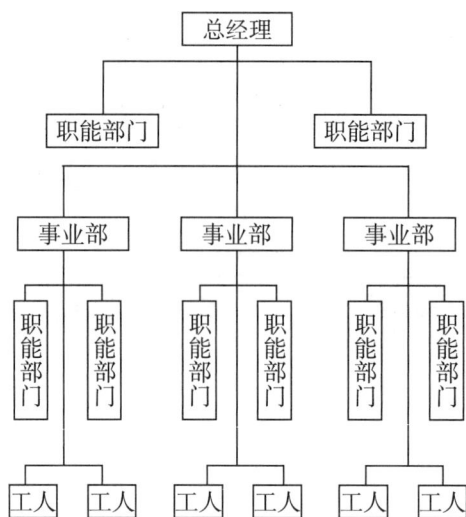

图 6-4　事业部结构

事业部结构的特点是最高管理当局保留资金分配、重要人事任免和战略方针等重大问题的决策权力，其他权力尽量下放，事业部成为日常经营活动的决策中心，是完全自主的经营单位。

事业部结构的优点：①使最高管理部门摆脱了日常行政事务，成为坚强有力的决策机构，并使各个事业部充分发挥经营管理的主动性、灵活性，因而，这种结构既有较高的稳定性，又有较强的适应性；②能够锻炼事业部经理，是培养全面管理人才的最好组织形式之一；③扩大了有效控制的幅度，增加了上级领导直接控制下层单位的数目；④可以在各事业部之间展开比较和竞争，有助于克服组织的僵化和官僚化。

　　事业部结构也有缺点：①需要的管理人员多，管理成本较高，管理经济性较差；②对总公司和事业部管理人员的水平要求高；③集权和分权关系比较敏感，一旦处理不当，可能会削弱整个组织的协调一致；④容易产生本位主义，控制难度大；⑤对公司的全部资源的利用不是很有效。

　　事业部结构不适合于规模较小的企业。当企业规模比较大，而且其下层单位能够成为一个"完整的企业机构"（具有独立的产品、独立的市场，成为利润中心）时，才适宜采用这种组织结构。

　　如果在最高管理层与各个事业部之间增加一级管理机构，来负责统辖和协调所属各个事业部的活动，则事业部结构就发展成为一种新的结构形式——超事业部结构，从而能够增强组织的灵活性。

　　5．模拟分权结构

　　这是一种介于直线—职能结构和事业部结构之间的组织结构。它模仿事业部结构的形式进行分权，但与事业部结构有重要差别。这种结构的组成单元并不是真正的事业部，实际上只是生产阶段，这些生产阶段有自己的管理层和利润指标，但这种指标是按企业内部价格确定的，并不来源于市场；这些生产阶段都没有独立的外部市场，并且生产阶段之间关系相当密切，一个生产阶段出现障碍，可能导致其他生产阶段也出现障碍。该结构如图6-5所示。

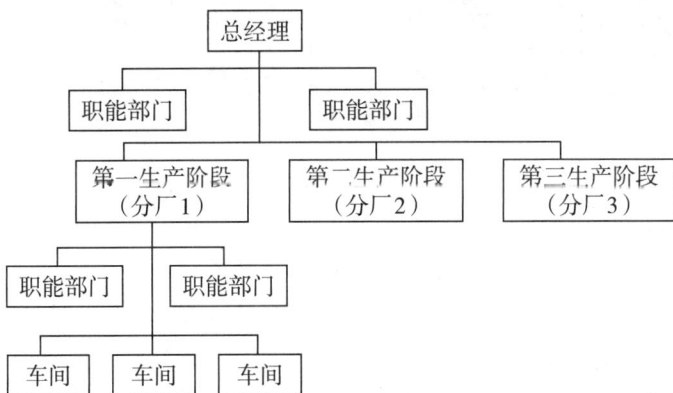

图6-5　模拟分权结构

　　模拟分权结构最大的优点在于它解决了企业规模过大、不易管理的问题。在这种结构下，高层管理人员可以在可能的范围内把权力分给生产阶段一级的管理人员，减少自己的行政工作，从而把精力集中到战略性问题上来。同时，生产阶段一级单位的权力得到了扩大。

　　模拟分权结构的缺点是：①分权不彻底，分厂领导权力不够，但责任较大，决策上受到较大限制；②沟通效率低，部门领导人不易了解企业的全貌；③对干部素质要求高。

　　这种结构适用于那些规模很大，但由于产品品种或生产过程所限，根本无法分解成独立的事业部的企业。

　　6．矩阵结构

　　矩阵结构是从专门从事某项工作的工作小组发展而来的一种组织结构。所谓工作小组一般是由一群不同背景、不同技能、不同知识、分别来自不同部门的人员组成的。其结构特点是根据任务的需要把各种人才集合起来，任务完成后小组就解散。如果一个企业中同时组织几个工作小组，而且这种工作小组长期存在，结果就会形成一种新的组织结构——矩阵结构，又称规划—目标结构。

矩阵结构主要是在直线—职能结构垂直形态组织系统的基础上，再增加一种横向的领导系统，即工作小组。工作小组的成员，一般都要接受两个方面的领导，即在工作业务方面接受原单位或部门的垂直领导，而在执行具体任务方面，接受工作小组领导人或项目负责人的领导。其结构如图6-6所示。

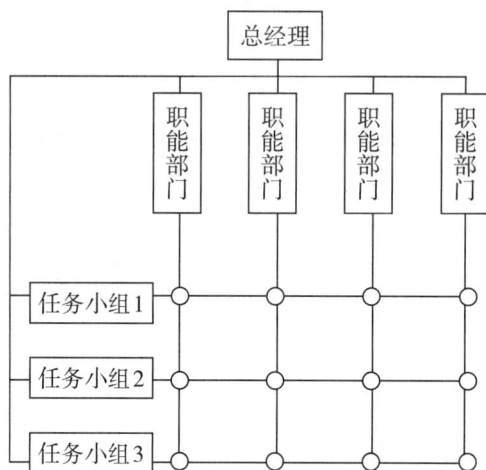

图6-6　矩阵结构

矩阵结构的优点是：①加强了不同部门之间的配合和信息交流，能集中各部门专业人员的智慧，加强组织的协调性和整体性；②机动灵活，适应能力强；③可加快工作进度；④可避免各部门的重复劳动，一个人可同时参加几个工作小组，提高了人员的利用率，可缩减成本开支；⑤管理方法和管理技术可以更加专业化；⑥工作小组领导人对项目最终效益负责，从而增强了整个组织的效益性。

矩阵结构的缺点是：①造成了双重领导；②组织关系复杂，对工作小组领导人的要求较高；③具有一定的临时性，容易导致人心不稳。

矩阵结构适用于大型协作项目和以开发与实验项目为主的单位，如大型运动会组委会、电影制片厂、应用研究单位等。

7. 委员会组织

为达到某种特定的管理目的，还常常设立各种委员会组织。委员会组织多数是为了补充和加强直线组织，是和直线组织结合起来建立的。其行动特点是集体行动，这和其他组织形式有明显的不同。

委员会组织有以下几种：有的执行管理职能，有的不执行管理职能；有的要做出决策，有的只讨论而不做出决策；有的是正式的，有的是非正式的，有的是常设的，有的是临时的。

委员会组织作为经营管理的一种手段而设立，其目的是：①集思广益；②作为制约或限制的手段，防止个人或部门权限过大；③反映和听取不同利益集团的要求；④协调计划和执行的矛盾；⑤作为信息沟通和交换意见的机构；⑥激发执行决定的积极性，让有关人员参加讨论。

委员会组织的优点是：①集思广益，能产生解决问题的理想方案，提高决策的质量。②可防止个人滥用权力，也可以避免忽视某个层次、某个方面人士的意见和利益。③有助于部门间及有关人员间的沟通和协调。④使基层干部和职工有可能参与决策的制定，从而更好地执行决策。

委员会组织的缺点是：①决策迟缓。做出决定往往需要很长时间，费时费钱。②折中调和。当意见不一致时，往往采取折中的办法解决，富有新意的主张和方案因而容易被封杀。③责任不清。委员会的责任不明确，责任感往往不强。

8. 网络结构

网络结构是最新出现的组织形式，这种结构只有很小的中心组织，要依靠其他组织以合同为基础进行制造、分销、营销或其他关键业务的经营活动（如图 6－7 所示）。中心组织的小型化使得采用这种结构的企业能够大大减少管理层次；由于其大部分职能都是"外购"的，中心组织就具有了高度的灵活性，并能集中精力做自己最擅长的事。在实际中，采用网络结构的企业大部分将自己的职能集中于设计或营销。

网络结构的缺点是：①中心组织难以对制造活动实施严密的控制，因而在产品质量上存在风险；②网络组织所取得的设计上的创新很容易被窃取，因为产品一旦交予其他企业生产，要对创新加以严密控制，就算不是不可能的，至少也是困难的。

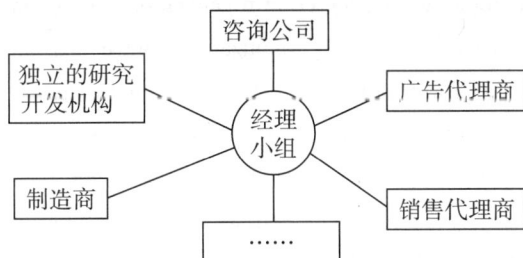

图 6－7　网络结构

网络结构既适用于小型组织，也适用于大型组织。例如著名的耐克公司、卡西欧公司都采用了网络结构，IBM 公司、美国电话电报公司、美孚石油公司也部分采用了网络结构。但是，网络结构并不是对所有企业都适用。一般来说，它比较适合于玩具和服装制造业，因为这两个行业都需要很高的灵活性以对时尚变化做出迅速反应。网络结构也适合那些制造活动需要低廉劳动力的公司，这也是发达国家和地区的大公司较多采用网络结构的主要原因之一。

网络结构是在地区乃至全球经济一体化、企业间的联系和协作增强的大背景下出现并发展起来的。信息技术的快速发展，为这种组织形式的进一步普及创造了有利的条件。

Section 3　Organizational Structure Design

6.3.1　Organizational Structure

Organizational structure is the framework that describes the organization and the institutional arrangements for personnel, work, technology and information, which are needed to achieve organization's goals. The organization is growing, so the organization's structure is not always the same. First, when start a new organization, we need to design organizational systems. Second, when serious problems occurs in the original, or the target of the entire organization changes, the organizational structure needs to be redesigned. Third, the organization's system needs partly increase, decrease or complete.

6.3.2　Characteristics of Organizational Structure

(1) Complexity: It refers to the differences of the degree of specialization among the organization, the organizational level, management range and the relationship of personnel departments. The more detailed and ranged division of an organization it is, the more complicated the organization is. And the more geographic distribution of organizational units it involves, the more difficult the coordination department and activities will be.

(2) Normalization: It refers to the degree of organization relying on the rules and procedures to guide the employees' behavior. Some organizations have less normative guidelines and regulations, so they have a lower degree of standardization; some organizations have more normative guidelines and regulations, so they have a higher degree of standardization.

(3) Centralization: It refers to the concentration degree of the power of decision-making. In some organizations, decision-making is highly centralized that the problems will be passed to the senior management to develop an action plan for them, indicating a higher degree of centralization; while some organizations, whose decision-making powers and responsibilities are granted to lower management personnel, indicating a lower degree of centralization.

6.3.3　The Procedure of Organizational Structure Design

1. Determine Organizational Objectives

An organizational objective is the starting point of organizational design and the first step in the management of organizational design. It is to analyze the organization on a consolidated basis in the external environment and internal conditions to determine reasonably the overall objectives of the organization and a variety of derived specific targets.

2. Determine Business Contents

According to the requirements of the organization's objectives, the managers determine the management programs for achieving organizational goals and properly classify various works according to their nature, such as market research, product development, marketing and management. The managers should clear the scope and range of activities of the workload, conduct the overall design of business process, so that the overall business process will be optimized.

3. Determine the Organizational Structure

According to the scale of the organization, the technical characteristics and the operational workload, the managers need to determine what kind of form of the management organization should be taken, which units and departments need to be designed, and allocate the same or similar work to the appropriate sub-units and departments to form a hierarchical and departmentalized structure.

4. Equip Personnel

According to the natures of works of the various units and departments and the requirements of qualities of personnel, the qualified staff and their leader should be selected and equipped, and their duties and responsibilities should be clarified.

5. Specify Duty and Power

According to the requirements of the organization's objectives, we should clearly define units' and departments' responsibilities for the management work and performance evaluation criteria. At the same time, according to the actual needs of the work, the manager should grant the responsible persons from each unit and department some appropriate authorities.

6. Join Together

This is the final step in organizational design. That is to clearly define the relationship among the various departments to absorb the principles and methods of communication and coordination between them and join together in terms of the vertical and horizontal organizational entities to form a coordinated and effective management system of organization.

6.3.4 Selection of Organizational Structure

With the social development, in modern society, the organization's structure has many types. Here we introduce eight basic forms of regular organizational structure.

1. Linear Structure

Linear structure, also known as simple structure, is the earliest and the simplest form of organizational structure. It is characterized by a variety of positions in the organization aligned by vertical system, all management functions are conducted by executive leaders at all levels of responsibility. There is no functional or counseling agency and command passes from top managers down to the workers. It is a linear flow. Each member in the organization will only accept the nearest superior's command, only take responsibilities from and report to the superior. A person has only a superior and thoroughly implements the principle of unity of command. Its structure is shown in Diagram 6 – 1.

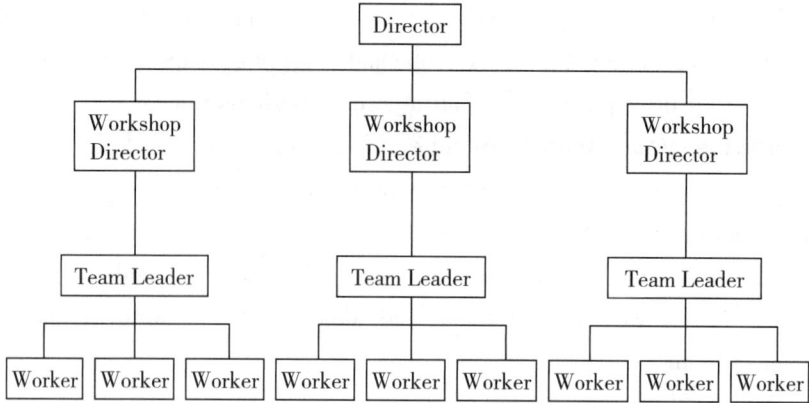

Diagram 6 – 1   Linear Structure

Strengths of the linear structure derive from its simplicity：①The command system is simple, decision-making is rapid, unified command is easy to carry out in the end. ②The attribution of responsibility and authority of each member in the organization is very clear, so it is less likely for the situation of unclear target to occur, everyone's contribution to the achievement of organizational goals will be easily evaluated. ③It is easy to maintain organizational discipline and ensure the organizational order. ④It is flexible. ⑤It takes a low management cost.

Disadvantages of linear structure are：①Everyone just follows to the superior's instructions, and each department is concerned only with its own sector, so it has poor horizontal coordination. ②The power entirely is concentrated on one person, so there is high dependency for the leader and mistakes easily occur.

This structure is generally applicable to small organizations which do not need to carry out the functions of professional management and those in the early stages of construction, and when the organizational environment is relatively simple and variable, or the organization is suddenly faced with difficult situations and even a hostile environment.

2. Functional Structure

In addition to linear managers within the organization, there are in the functional structure a number of functional departments with the rights within the scope of their business to make orders and instructions to the subordinate. In addition to receiving the lead of the higher linear superior, the lower linear superior must also accept the command of the higher functional departments. Its structure is shown in Diagram 6 – 2.

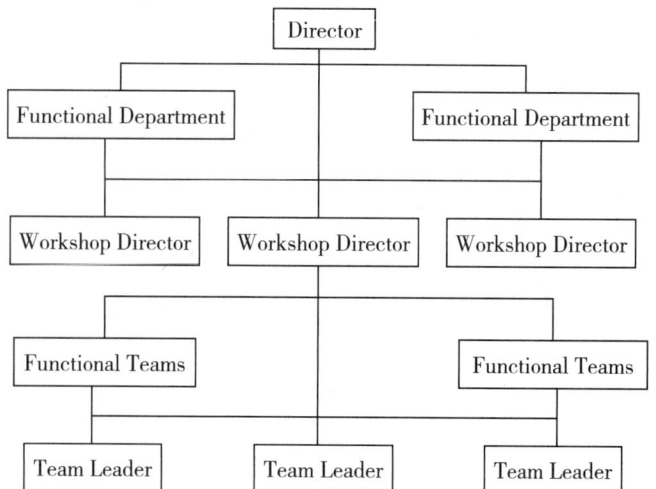

Diagram 6 – 2   Functional Structure

The main advantages of the functional structure are: ① The functional departments are playing their roles in professional management, and the guidance to the subordinates is more detailed. ②It can reduce the burden of linear managers. ③The manager's division of functions make the selection and training of managers easier.

Disadvantages of the functional structure are very obvious: ①It hinders the organization's necessary centralized leadership and unity of command and the formation of leadership of many leaders is prone to duplication or contradiction of command that results in management confusion. ②It is not conducive to a clear division of responsibility and authority of the straight linear personnel and departments, and likely to cause competition for power, shirking responsibility.

This organizational structure is common in hospitals, universities, design institutes, libraries, accounting firms and other organizations.

3. Linear-functional Structure

This structure is characterized by a linear system as the basis for setting the appropriate departments under the straight-line managers at all levels, that is, when maintaining the principle of unity of command of a straight linear organization, the counseling agency is added. Its structure is shown in Diagram 6 – 3.

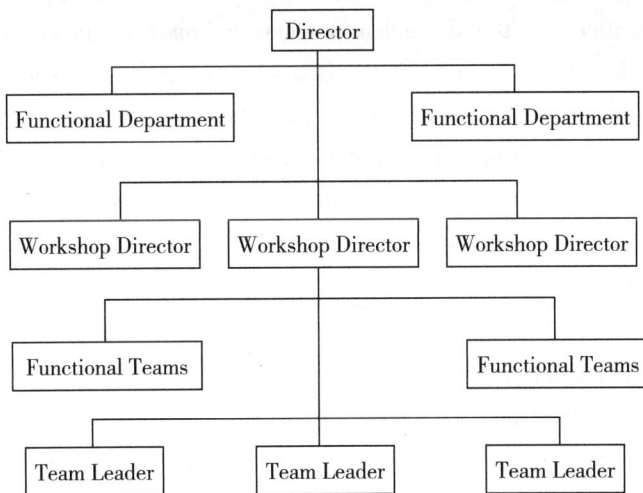

Diagram 6 – 3　Linear-functional Structure

In this form of organization, linear departments are the backbone, responsible for the implementation of the organizational objectives, such as production and sales. And functional departments are just the assistants of the managers at the same level and only can give guidance to the lower functional departments, but can't give orders to subordinate linear managers unless they have been granted the power from the higher linear superior.

Linear-functional structure's advantages are: ①It combines the advantages of linear structure and functional structure, so it can maintain unity of command and also make the use of counseling agency. ② It has fine division, clear responsibilities and each department only runs for its responsibility with high efficiency and stability. ③It has high stability of the organization and in the cases of small changes it is easy to play the efficiency role of organizational team.

Disadvantages of this structure are: ①The lack of information exchange between departments is not conducive to brainstorming to make decisions. ②The targets of linear departments and functional departments are difficult to be unified and there are many contradictions. This results in large coordinating work of higher superior. ③It is difficult to cultivate management elite who are familiar with the overall situation within the organization. ④It is of large system rigidity, poor adaptability, easy conservative and it is not easy to react timely for the new situations.

This structure is mainly for simple and stable environment and for conventional large-volume production by using standardized techniques. For the diverse production and very large enterprises as well as the enterprises emphasizing innovation, this structure will be not so appropriate. At present, most enterprises in China use linear-functional structure.

4. Division Structure

Division structure, also known as the federal decentralized structure, is a form of decentralized system of enterprises' organization. This organizational structure was founded by the former deputy general manager of General Motors Corporation named Sloan, so it is also called Sloan Model. It is an organizational form of decentralized management implemented in an enterprise for the departments with independent products and markets, independent responsibilities and interests. Such department is a division. It must have three elements: Firstly, it should possess separate products and markets, and it should be a unit of product liability or market responsibility. Secondly, it should possess independent interests and independent accounting as well. It should be a unit of the benefit liability which is the profit center. Thirdly, it is a decentralized unit with sufficient power to be able to operate independently. Its stucture is shown in Diagram 6 – 4.

The characteristics of division structure is that the highest authorities only have the decision-making power of important things, such as the allocation of funds, appointment of major personnel and removal and strategic approach, and other powers are decentralized. Divisions become as daily decision-making centers for business activities, and each division is a completely independent business unit.

Advantages of division structure include: ①The top management can get rid of the daily administrative affairs to become a strong and effective decision-making body and to give full play of each business unit's management initiative, flexibility, and therefore, this structure has both higher stability and strong adaptability. ②Division manager can get great exercise so division is one of the best forms to develop overall management personnel. ③It can expand the effective control of the amplitude, so the number of subordinate the higher-ups can direct control in the unit will increase. ④It can expand comparison and competition among divisions, which helps to overcome the ossification and bureaucratization in the organization.

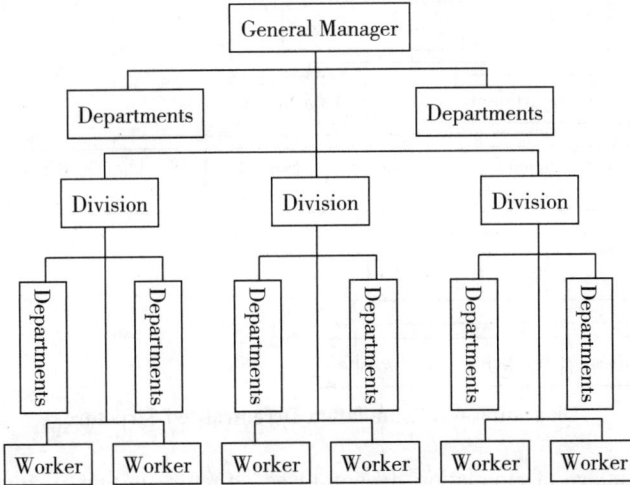

Diagram 6 – 4　Division Structure

Division structure also has disadvantages, including: ①More managers, high administrative costs, poor management economy. ②It needs higher qualities of managers from both headquarters and divisions. ③The relationship between centralization and decentralization is more sensitive, if handled improperly, it could weaken the coherence throughout the organization. ④Selfishness may occur and it is difficulty to control. ⑤The use of all the resources of the company is not very effective.

Division structure is not suitable for smaller businesses. It is appropriate to adopt this organizational structure for large-scale enterprise or when its lower units become a "complete enterprise agency" (An agency that has independent products, independent markets and has become a profit center).

If a level of administration is added between the top management and the divisions to control and coordinate the activities of various divisions, the division structure will develop into a new structure—super division structure, within which the organizational flexibility will be enhanced.

5. Simulation Decentralized Structure

This is an organizational structure between linear-functional structure and division structure. It mimics the decentralized form of division structure, but there are differences between them. Constituent elements of this structure are not real divisions, in fact, it just happen in production stages, the production stages have their own management and profit targets, but these targets are determined by the internal price of the company which does not come from market. These production stages do not have independent external market, and there are very close relationships among the production stages. One production stage's obstacles might hinder other stages of production. Its structure is shown in Diagram 6 – 5.

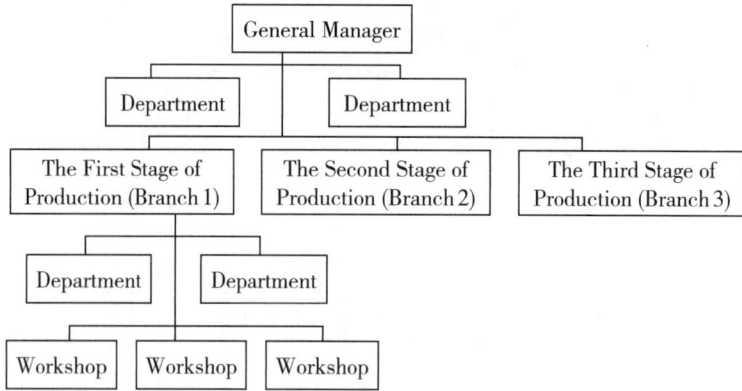

Diagram 6 – 5　Simulation Decentralized Structure

The biggest advantage of simulation decentralized structure is that it solves problem like the firm is too large to manage. In this structure, senior managers can give the power to managers of the production stage to the possible extent, reducing their administrative work, thus they are able to concentrate on strategic issues. Meanwhile, the power of the unit of production stage has been expanded.

Disadvantages of simulation decentralized structure are: ①Decentralization is not complete, and the sub-factory's leader has not enough leadership. Meanwhile he will take a great responsibility and be subjected to greater restrictions on the decision-making. ②Sector leaders are not easy to understand the whole picture of the enterprise because of low efficiency of communication. ③It has high requirements for the quality of leadership.

This structure is applicable to the large-scale enterprise that can't be decomposed into independent business units due to the product variety or limited production process.

6. Matrix Structure

Matrix structure is a form of organizational structure developing from the working group that specializes in a particular job. The working group is normally provided by a group of personnel from different backgrounds, skills, knowledge and departments. Its structure is characterized by joining the personnel together according to the tasks' requirements, and the group will be disbanded after the tasks are completed. If there were several working groups in a business organization at the same time in the form of long-term existence, it would form a new organizational structure—matrix structure, also known as plan-target structure.

Matrix structure is built on the basis in vertical form of organizational system of linear-functional structure with an extra horizontal leadership system, namely the working groups. Members in the working group are generally required to accept the leader from two aspects, the first one is under the vertical lead of the original unit or department at work business, and the second one is in the implementation of specific tasks, accepting the lead of working group's leader or project leader. As shown in Diagram 6 – 6.

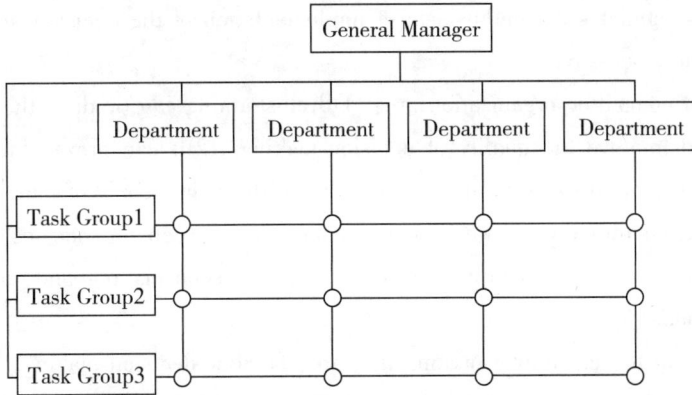

Diagram 6 – 6　Matrix Structure

Advantages of matrix structure are: ①It strengthens cooperation and communication for information between different departments, each department can focus on intelligence professionals and it can strengthen coordination and organizational integrity. ②It is flexible and adaptable. ③It can accelerate the progress of work. ④It can avoid duplication of work of various departments. A person can also participate in several working groups to improve the utilization of personnel which can reduce costs. ⑤Management methods and techniques can be more specialized. ⑥The working group's leader is responsible for the projects' ultimately benefits, thus it can improve the efficiency of the entire organization.

Disadvantages of matrix structure are: ①It results in dual leadership. ②It results in complex organizational relationships, so it has higher requirements for the working group's leader. ③It will easily cause worries among people because of temporality.

Matrix structure is suitable for organizations focusing on large-scale cooperative project including developing and experimental projects, such as large-scale games organizing committee, film studios, and applied research units and so on.

7. Committee Organization

In order to achieve specific management purposes, various committee organizations are often set up. The majority of the committee organizations are to complement and strengthen the linear organization. They are established by combining with linear organizations. Their actions are characterized by collective action, which are significantly different from other forms of organization.

The committee may have a variety of forms: some perform administrative function, and some do not perform management functions; some want to make decisions, some only make discussion without decision-making; some are formal, some are informal; some are permanent, some are temporary.

The purposes of commission organization which is established as a means of management are: ①Brainstorming. ②Prevent excessive power of person or departments as a means to restrict or limit. ③Reflect and listen to the demands of different interest groups. ④Promote contradictions between planning and execution. ⑤ Promote communication and exchange of views in an organization. ⑥It stimulates the enthusiasm of implementation of the decision and allows its staff to participate in the discussion.

Advantages of committee organization are：①Brainstorming can produce the ideal solution to solve problems and improve the quality of decision-making. ②It can prevent abuse of power by individuals and also avoid neglecting the views and interests of the people of some level. ③It helps communication and coordination between departments and between the persons concerned. ④It can involve the grassroots level cadres and workers in decision-making and thus ensure better execution of decisions.

Disadvantages of the committee organization are：①Slow decision-making. Decision-making often takes a long time and much money. ② Compromise to reconcile. When there is a disagreement, a compromise solution is often adopted, so the innovative ideas and solutions can easily be blocked. ③Everybody's responsibilities are unclear. Responsibilities of committee are not clear, and sense of responsibility is often poor.

8. Network Structure

Network structure is the latest form of organization. This structure only has a small central organization, and it relies on other organizations for manufacturing, distribution, marketing or other critical business activities based on contracts (Diagram 6－7). The miniaturization of central organizations makes this structure can greatly reduce the management levels. Since most of its functions are "outsourcing", the central organization has a high degree of flexibility, and it can concentrate on doing what it is good at. In practice, the enterprises taking the form of a network structure mostly focus on the design or marketing.

The drawbacks of the network structure are：① It is difficult for central organization to implement strict control on manufacturing activities, thus there is a risk in product quality. ②Innovative design made by the network organization can easily be stolen. If it is not impossible, at least it is very difficult to have a close control on innovation once the product is produced by other enterprises.

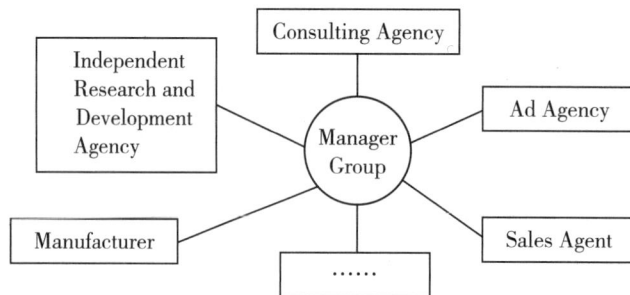

Diagram 6－7   Network Structure

Network structure suits both for small organizations and large organizations. For example, the famous Nike, Casio have adopted the network structure. IBM, American Telephone and Telegraph Company, Mobil Oil also partly takes the form of network structure. However, the network structure is not suitable for all businesses. In general, it is more suitable for toys and clothing manufacturers, because high flexibility is required in these two industries to respond quickly to the change of fashion. Network structure is also suitable for companies which need cheap labor for manufacturing. This is the main reason for large companies in developed countries and regions often to adopt the network structure.

Network structure appeared and developed under the background of regional and global economic integration, and the enhancement of inter-firm linkages and collaboration. The rapid development of information technology has created favorable conditions to further popularize this form of organization.

第四节　组织的部门设计

组织设计任务的实质是按照劳动分工的原则将组织中的活动专业化，而劳动分工又要求组织活动保持高度的协调一致性。协调的有效方法就是组织的部门设计，也称部门化，即按照职能相似性、任务活动相似性或关系紧密性的原则把组织中的专业技术人员分类集合在一个部门，然后配以专职的管理人员来协调领导，统一指挥。

部门设计可以依据多种不同的标准进行选择安排，例如业务的职能、所提供的产品和服务、目标顾客、地区、流程等。在不同时期、不同环境条件下，组织所依据的选择标准可以是不同的，但这种选择安排应当遵循部门化的一些基本原则，并以组织目标的容易实现为基准。

一、部门设计的基本原则

要想有效、合理地集合组织资源，安排好组织内全部的业务活动，必须提供一些基本的指导原则，使组织的部门设计能够具备科学性和可操作性。

1. 因事设职和因人设职相结合的原则

为了保证组织目标的实现，必须使组织活动落实到每一个具体的部门和岗位上去，确保"事事有人做"。另外，组织中的每一项活动终究要由人去完成，组织部门设计就必须考虑人员的配置情况，使得人尽其能、人尽其用。特别是，当组织需要根据外部环境的变化进一步调整和再设计组织部门结构时，必须贯彻因事设职和因人设职相结合的原则，及时调整与组织环境不相适应的部门和人员，使组织内的人力资源能够得到有效的整合和优化。

2. 分工和协作相结合的原则

分工和协作是社会化大生产的必然结果。古典的管理理论强调分工是效率的基础。在组织的部门设计中，必须对每一个部门、每一个岗位进行必要的工作分析和关系分析，并按照分工与协作的要求进行业务活动的组合。部门设计者可以依据技能相似性的归类方法来集合相关的业务活动，以期提高专业化分工的水平。但是，过分强调专业化分工也会造成管理机构增多、部门之间难以协调等问题，这反而会使管理效率下降。这时，可以依据关系紧密性的归类方法，按照业务流程管理的逻辑顺序来集合业务活动，以期达到紧凑、连续、利于协作的工作效果。

3. 精简高效的部门设计原则

部门精简高效是每一个部门设计者所追求的理想效果，作为一项基本的原则，其应当贯彻在部门设计的每一个阶段和每一项活动过程中。按照这一原则，部门设计应当体现局部利益服从组织整体利益的思想，并将单个部门效率目标与组织整体效率目标有机地结合起来。另外，部门设计应在保证组织目标能够实现的前提条件下，力求人员配置和部门设置精简合理，不仅要做到"事事有人做"，而且要"人人有事做"，工作任务充实饱满，部门活动精密有序。

二、部门设计的基本形式与特征

组织的部门有多种不同的划分方式，依据不同的划分标准，可以形成以下几种不同的部门化形式。其中，职能部门化和流程部门化是按工作的过程标准来划分的，而其余几种则是按工作的结果标准来划分的。

1. 职能部门化

职能部门化是一种传统而基本的组织形式。职能部门化就是按照生产、财务、营销、人事、研发等基本活动相似或技能相似的要求，分类设立专门的管理部门。

职能部门化的优点主要是：能够突出业务活动的重点，确保高层主管的权威并使之有效地管理组织的基本活动；符合活动专业化的分工要求，能够充分有效地发挥员工的才能，调动员工学习的积极性，并且简化了培训，强化了控制，避免了重叠，最终有利于管理目标的实现。

职能部门化的缺点主要是：由于人、财、物等资源的过分集中，不利于开拓远区市场或按照目标顾客的需求组织分工。同时，这种分法也有可能会助长部门主义风气，使得部门之间难以协调配合。部门利益高于企业整体利益的后果是可能会影响到组织总目标的实现。另外，由于职权过分集中，部门主管虽容易得到锻炼，却不能像高级管理人员那样得到全面培养和提高，也不利于"多面手"式人才的成长。图6-8是一个典型的按职能划分的部门化组织图。

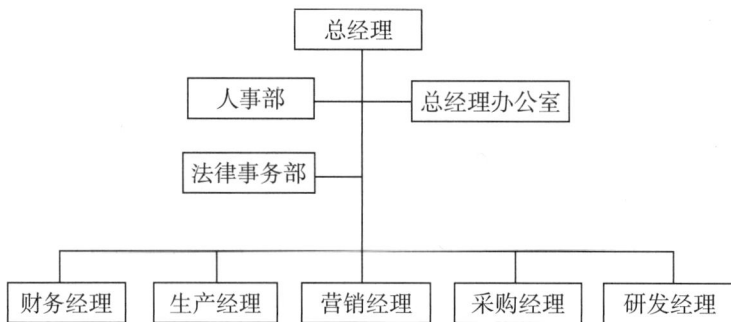

图6-8　按职能划分的部门化组织图

2. 产品或服务部门化

在品种单一、规模较小的企业，按职能进行组织分工是理想的部门化划分形式。然而，随着企业的进一步成长与发展，企业面临着增加产品线和扩大生产规模以获得规模经济和范围经济的经营压力，管理组织的工作也将变得日益复杂。这时，就有必要以业务活动的结果为标准来重新划分企业的活动，产品或服务部门化，就是一种典型的结果划分法。

产品或服务部门化的优点是：各部门会专注于产品的经营，并且充分合理地利用专有资产，提高专业化经营的效率水平，这不仅有利于促进不同产品和服务项目间的合理竞争，而且有助于比较不同部门对企业的贡献，有助于决策部门加强对企业产品与服务的指导和调整，另外，这种分工方式也为"多面手"式的管理人才提供了较好的成长条件。

产品或服务部门化的缺点是：企业需要更多的"多面手"式的人才去管理各个产品部门；各个部门同样有可能存在本位主义倾向，这势必会影响到企业总目标的实现；另外，部门中某些职能管理机构的重整会导致管理费用的增加，同时也增加了总部对"多面手"式人才的监督成本。图6-9是一个典型的按产品划分的部门化组织图。

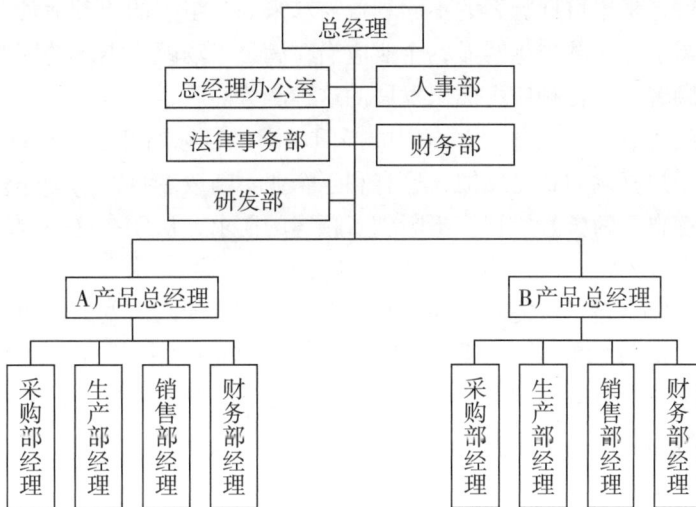

图6-9 按产品划分的部门化组织图

3. 地域部门化

地域部门化就是按照地域的分散化程度划分企业的业务活动，继而设置管理部门管理其业务活动。随着经济活动范围的日趋广阔，企业特别是大型企业越来越需要跨越地域的限制去开拓外部的市场。而不同的文化环境，造就出不同的劳动价值观，企业根据地域的不同划设管理部门，为的是更好地针对各地的特殊环境条件组织业务活动的开展。

地域部门化的优点是：可以把责权下放到地方，鼓励地方参与决策和经营；地区管理者还可以直接对本地市场的需求灵活决策；通过在当地招募职能部门人员，既可以缓解当地的就业压力，争取宽松的经营环境，又可以充分利用当地有效的资源进行市场开拓，同时减少了许多外派成本，以及许多不确定性风险。

地域部门化的缺点是：企业所需的能够派赴各个区域的地区主管比较稀缺，且比较难控制；另外，各地区可能会存在因职能机构设置重叠而导致管理成本过高的问题。图6-10是一个典型的按地域划分的部门化组织图。

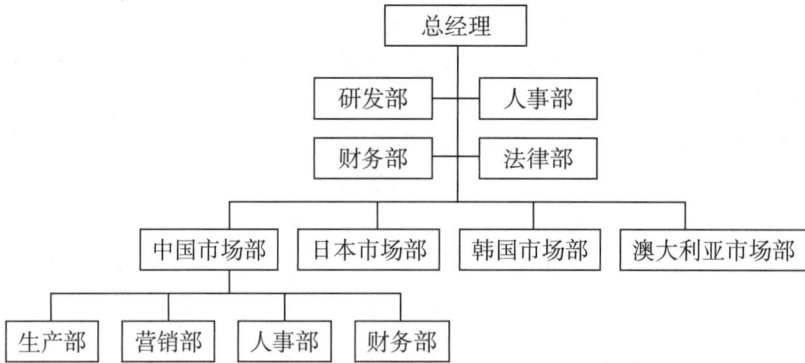

图 6 - 10　按地域划分的部门化组织图

4. 顾客部门化

顾客部门化就是根据目标顾客的不同利益需求来划分组织的业务活动，在激烈的市场竞争中，顾客的需求导向越来越明显，企业应当在满足市场顾客需求的同时，努力创造顾客的未来需求，顾客部门化顺应了需求发展的这种趋势。

顾客部门化的优点是：通过设立不同的部门以满足目标顾客各种特殊而广泛的需求，企业能有效获得用户真诚的意见反馈，这有利于企业不断改变自己的工作；另外，企业能够持续有效地发挥自己的核心专长，不断创新顾客的需求，从而在这一领域内建立持久的竞争优势。

顾客部门化的缺点是：可能会增加因与顾客需求不匹配而引发的矛盾和冲突；需要更多能妥善协调和处理与顾客关系问题的管理人员和一般人员；另外，顾客需求偏好的转移，可能使企业无法时时刻刻都能明确顾客的需求分类，结果会造成产品或服务结构的不合理，影响对顾客需求的满足。图 6 - 11 是一个典型的按顾客划分的部门化组织图。

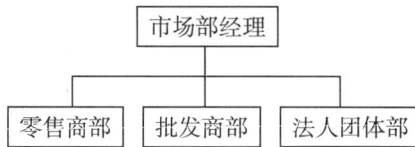

图 6 - 11　按顾客划分的部门化组织图

5. 流程部门化

流程部门化就是按照工作或业务流程来组织业务活动。人员、材料、设备比较集中或业务流程比较连续精密是流程部门化的实现基础。例如，一家发电厂的生产流程会经过燃煤输送、锅炉燃烧、汽轮机冲动、电力输出、电力配送等几个主要过程。

流程部门化的优点是：组织能够充分发挥人员集中的技术优势，易于协调管理，对市场需求的变动也能够快速敏捷地做出反应，容易取得较明显的集中优势；另外，简化了培训，容易在组织内部形成良好的互相学习氛围，会产生较为明显的学习经验曲线效应。

流程部门化的缺点是：部门之间的精密协作有可能得不到贯彻，也会产生部门间的利益冲突；另外，权责相对集中，不利于培养出"多面手"式的管理人才。图 6 - 12 是一个典型的按流程划分的部门化组织图。

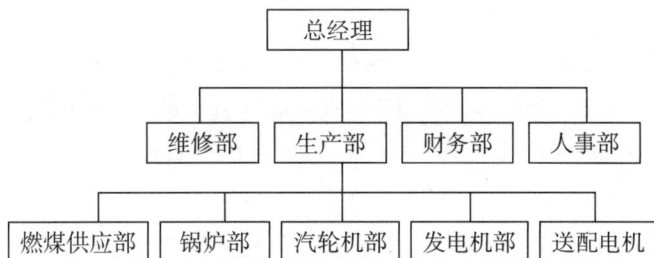

图 6 - 12 按流程划分的部门化组织图

Section 4　Department Design of Organization

The essence of the tasks of organizational design is to specialize the activities of organization according to the principle of division of labor, while division of labor requires the organization's activities to retain a high consensus. The effective way for coordination is to design the organization's departments, which is also called departmentalization. That means gathering the professional technical personnel within one department in the organization according to the principles of function similarity, assignment similarity and relationship tightness. Then a specialized manager can be allocated to take charge in coordination, leading and unified command.

Departmentalization can be designed according to different criteria, such as the function of business, products and services provided, target customers, areas, flow, etc. Under different periods and different environment, organization can choose different standards, but the selection is supposed to observe some basic principles and based on the easy achievement of organizational goals.

6.4.1　Basic Principles of Department Design

If you want to effectively and rationally gather the organizational resources and to arrange all the business activities within the organization, some necessary principles are needed to endow the departmentalization with science and availability.

1. The Principle in Combination of Setting Positions for Works and Persons

In order to guarantee the achievement of organizational goals, we must make sure that the organizational activities are allocated to every position so that to ensure everyone gets his business. In addition, every job in the organization must be done by someone, and the allocation of staff must be taken into consideration during the design of departmentalization as to make everybody do his best. Particularly, when the organization needs to further adjust and reconstruct the structure of department according to the change of external environment, it must conform to the principle in combination of setting positions for works and persons to adjust the departments and staff that are not suitable to the organization environment in time and enable the interior humane resources to be effectively integrated and optimized.

2. The Principle of Combining Division of Labor and Cooperation

Division of labor and cooperation is the necessary result of socialized production. Classical management theories emphasize that division of labor is the foundation of efficiency. During the process of department design of organization, we must evaluate every department and position with job analysis and relationship analysis, and combine business activities according to the requirement of division of labor and cooperation. Department designer can assemble the relative business activities according to the function similarity so as to enhance the level of professional division. However, unduly emphasizing the professional division can lead to problems like the increase of management institutions or hard coordination among departments, which lower the management efficiency. By now, we can integrate business activities based on the logical sequence of business flow management by using the method of classifying the relationship tightness, so as to reach a compact, successive and cooperative effectiveness.

3. The Principle of Simplified and High Efficient Department

Simplified and high efficient department is the ideal for department designer, and it should be run through every stage and activity of department design as a basic principle. According to the requirement of this principle, department design should embody the idea that partial benefit should comply with the overall benefit, and organically combine the efficient goal of single department with the overall efficient goal. In addition, department design should strive to concisely and rationally allocate staff and set departments on the premise that the organizational goal is guaranteed to come true. Not only shall every job be done, but also every employee shall be delegated, and the job assignments are ample, the department activities are precise and sequential.

6.4.2 Basic Patterns and Features of Department Design

Organizational departments have more than one dividing method, according to different standards, which can be divided into several following departmentalization patterns. Among them, functional departmentalization and process departmentalization are divided according to the standard of working process, and the rest are divided based on the standard of outcome.

1. Functional Departmentalization

Functional departmentalization is a traditional and basic organizational form, which sets up specialized management departments based on the similar activities or similar skills like production, finance, marketing, personnel, research and development, etc.

The advantages of functional departmentalization are: It able to highlight the key point of business activities, meanwhile, it assures the authority of top managers and enables them to manage the basic organizational activities effectively. In accordance with the division requirement of activity specialization, it enables the staff to exert their ability effectively and motivates their enthusiasm to learn. In the meantime, it simplifies the training, strengthens control, avoids overlap, which are ultimately beneficial to achieving the management goal.

The disadvantages of functional departmentalization are: Due to the over gathering of people, money and materials, it is not good to exploit the remote market or divide the job according to the requirement of target customers. Meanwhile, this division may foster the atmosphere of centering on the department, leading to difficult cooperation among sectors. The consequence that departmental benefit is over the overall may influence the achievement of organizational goals. In addition, because of the undue centralization of power, though the director is prone to get exercise, he or she is not able to gain the overall cultivation and improvement as a top manager, and it is against the training of a "comprehensive" employee. Diagram 6 – 8 is a typical departmentalization chart divided by function.

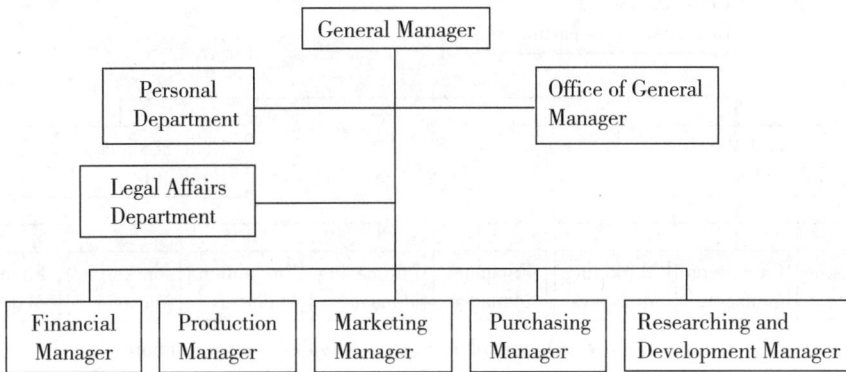

Diagram 6 – 8   Departmentalization Divided by Function

2. Product or Service Departmentalization

If the venture is of small scale with simplex production, then dividing the organization according to the function is an ideal departmentalization. However, as the company further develops, it has to face the running pressure to increase production lines and enlarge the scale for economics of scale and economics of scope, and the management job will become complicated. At this moment, it is necessary to subdivide the corporate activities based on the consequence of operations activities, which is product or service departmentalization, and it is a typical division method.

The advantages of product or service departmentalization are: Each department will focus on the management of products, and seize the assets fully and sensibly to improve the efficient level of specialized management. It is not only good to prompt the sensible competition among different products and services, but also contributes to the comparison of the contributions different departments have made for the company, which helps the decision sector to enhance the guidance and adjustment to corporate products and services. In addition, such dividing method provides better conditions for the development of "comprehensive" employees.

The disadvantages of product or service departmentalization are: Corporations might need more "comprehensive" employees to manage each department, and each department is also likely to have the tendency of selfishness, which may definitely influence the achievement of overall goals. Besides, the reform of some management institutions might lead to the increase of management costs, and also raise the supervision costs of "comprehensive" employees. Diagram 6 – 9 is a typical departmentalization chart divided by production.

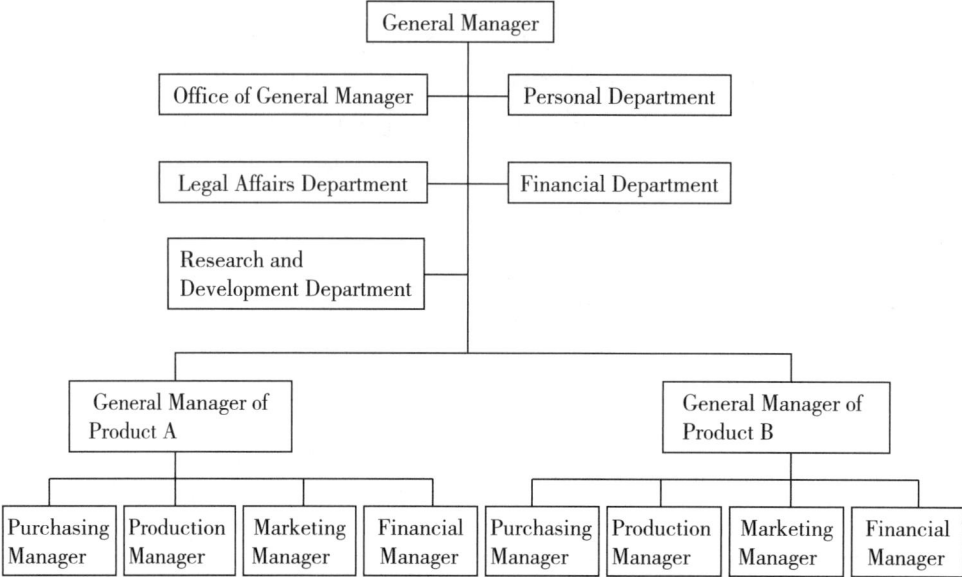

Diagram 6 – 9　Departmentalization Divided by Production

3. Area Departmentalization

Area departmentalization divides the corporate activities based on the decentralized degree of areas, and then arranges management sectors to manage their operation activities. As the scope of economic activities became larger, enterprises, especially large-scale enterprises, need to cross the restriction of areas to explore external market. As different cultural environment might foster different labor values, the reason why the corporation sets departments according to different areas is to carry out the business suitable to special environment.

Advantages of area departmentalization are: It allocates power to local places, encourages them to participate in decision-making and management, and local managers can flexibly make decision directly responding to the demand of local market. By recruiting local employees for functional departments, it not only helps to relieve the pressure of employment and strive for loose management environment, but also makes a fully use of local resources to enlarge market. In the meantime, it helps to reduce the assignment costs, decrease the risk of uncertainty.

Disadvantages of area departmentalization are: The corporation is lack of directors to be delegated to each area, and it is hard to control as well. In addition, the likelihood that the overlap of functional institutions may increase the management cost. Diagram 6 – 10 is a typical departmentalization chart divided by area.

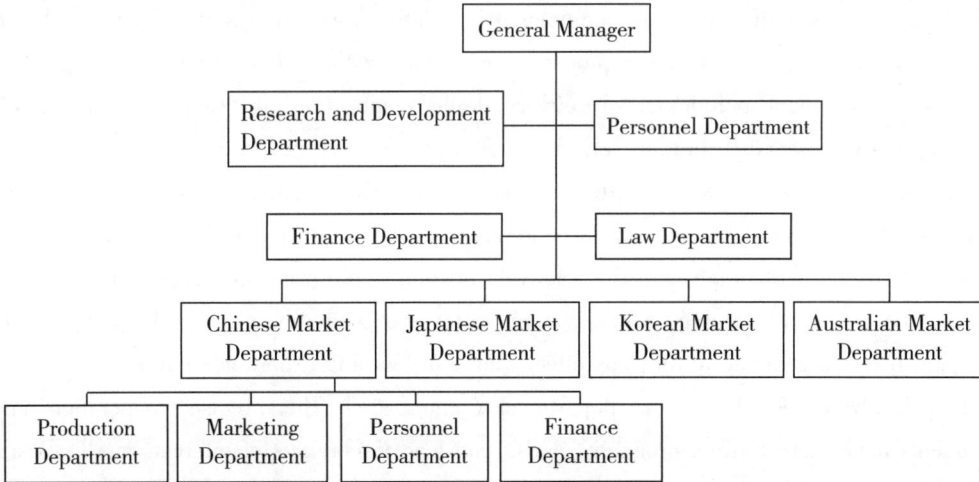

Diagram 6 – 10   Departmentalization Divided by Area

4. Customer Departmentalization

Customer departmentalization divides organizational business activities according to the different beneficial requirements of target customer. In the fierce market competition, the requirement orientation of customers becomes more and more clearly. Companies are supposed to satisfy customer need as well as to create the future demand. Customer departmentalization complies for this trend.

The advantages of customer departmentalization are: Enterprises can satisfy customers' special and extensive requirements by setting up different divisions, meanwhile, a faithful feedback from the customers can be effectively received, which benefits the companies to improve their work constantly. In addition, companies are able to constantly exert its major strength and renew the requirements of customers, so that they can build up a lasting competitive advantage in the field.

The disadvantages of customer departmentalization are: It is likely to increase the conflicts and contradictions because of the discrepancy with the need of customers. It needs more management staff and ordinary staff who are able to coordinate and handle the relationship with customers; in addition, it is unlikely for the company to analyze the shift of customer's preference, and the consequence might lead to the unreasonable structure of products or services, which influences the satisfaction of customer need. Diagram 6 – 11 is a typical departmentalization chart divided by customer.

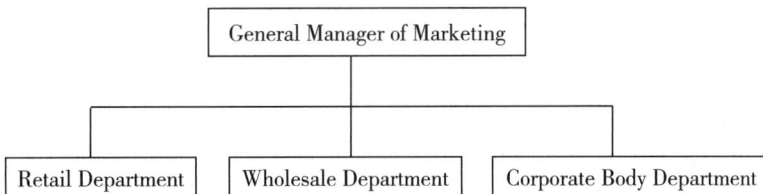

Diagram 6 – 11   Departmentalization Divided by Customer

5. Process Departmentalization

Process departmentalization is to organize the operations by work or business process.

Relative gathering of staff, materials, equipment or relative succession and precision of business process is the foundation to achieve process departmentalization. For example, the production process of a power plant includes: coal delivery, boiler combustion, the steam turbine operation, power output and power distribution, etc.

The advantages of process departmentalization are: The organization is able to exert the centralized advantage of staff and easy to coordinate. Also, it can react to the change of market requirement swiftly, which can gain the relatively obvious centralized advantages. In addition, it simplifies the process of training, which is prone to foster a good atmosphere of learning from each other, and this will generate an obvious effectiveness of learning experience curve.

The disadvantages of process departmentalization are: The precise cooperation among departments might not be run thoroughly, and it can lead to conflicts of interestas well. Besides, the power is relatively centralized, which is not good to cultivate "comprehensive" employees. Diagram 6 – 12 is a typical departmentalization chart divided by process.

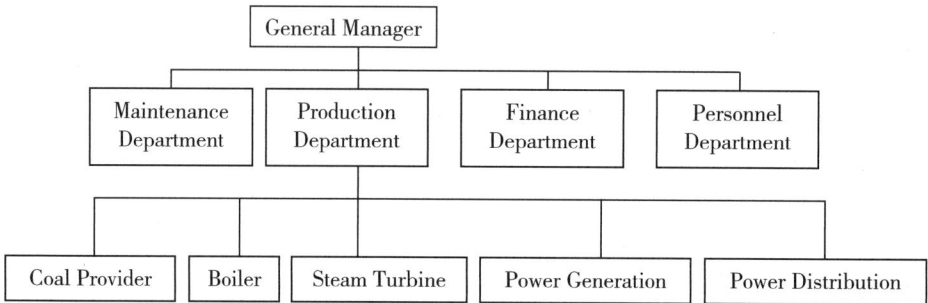

Diagram 6 – 12   Departmentalization Divided by Process

【新视角】

　　有研究表明，部门划分受以下一些因素的影响：①组织目标。目标是部门存在的前提，它是部门划分的首要因素。②业务量大小。业务量增加则分立部门；否则应考虑合并部门。③专业性与独立性。专业性强、独立性强则分立部门；否则应合并部门。④业务前景。业务前景好则需要加强，可以独立为一个部门。⑤监督与控制。某些业务存在明显的制约关系，合并容易掩盖矛盾时应考虑分立部门。

第五节　组织的层级设计

　　组织的层级设计，也称层级化，是指组织在纵向结构设计中需要确定层级数目和有效的管理幅度，需要根据组织集权化的程度，规定纵向各层级之间的权责关系，最终形成一个能够对内外环境要求做出动态反应的有效的组织结构形式。

一、组织的层级设计与管理幅度

　　组织层级化设计的核心任务是确定完成任务需要设定的层级数目，而有效的管理幅度是决定组织中层级数目的最基本因素。所谓管理幅度，也称组织幅度，是指组织中上级主管能够直接有效地指挥和领导下属的数量。

由于组织任务存在递减性，在最高的直接主管到最低的基层具体工作人员之间就形成了一定的层次，这种层次便称为组织层级。组织层级受到组织规模和组织幅度的影响，它与组织规模呈正比，规模越大，包括的人员越多，组织工作也越复杂，则层级也就越多；在组织规模已确定的条件下，组织层级与组织幅度具有互动性，它与组织幅度呈反比，即上级直接领导的下属越多，组织层级也就越少，反之则越多。

组织层级与组织幅度的互动关系决定了两种基本的组织结构形态：一种是扁平式组织结构形态；另一种是锥形式组织结构形态。图6-13显示了这两种组织结构形态的幅度与层级的差别。

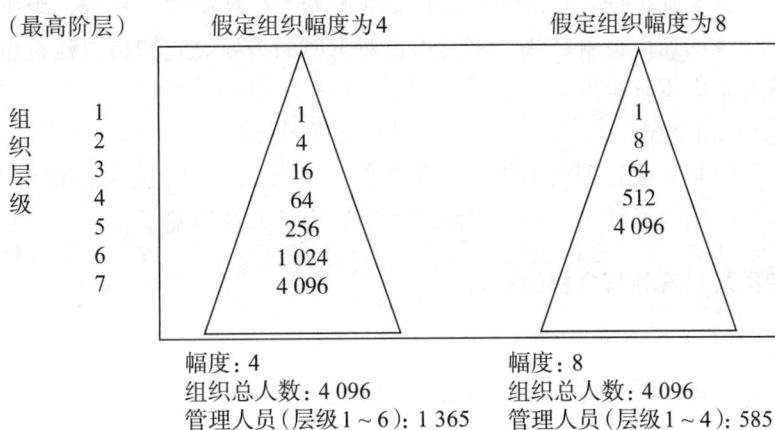

图6-13　组织幅度与组织层级比较图

扁平式组织结构形态的优点是：由于管理的层级比较少，信息的沟通和传递速度比较快，因而信息的失真度也比较低，同时，上级主管对下属的控制也不会太呆板，这有利于发挥下属人员的积极性和创造性。其缺点是：过大的管理幅度增加了主管对下属的监督和协调控制难度，同时，下属也缺少了更多的提升机会。

锥形式组织结构形态的优点是：由于管理的层级比较多，管理幅度比较小，每一管理层级上的主管都能对下属进行及时的指导和控制；另外，层级之间的关系也比较紧密，这有利于工作任务的衔接，同时也为下属提供了更多的提升机会。其缺点是：过多的管理层级往往会影响信息的传递速度，因而信息的失真度可能会比较高，这又增加了高层主管与基层之间的沟通和协调成本，增加了管理工作的复杂性。

二、管理幅度设计的影响因素

有效的管理幅度设计应考虑以下诸多因素的影响：

（1）管理工作的内容和性质。

管理工作内容越多，上下左右之间的联系就越多，需要花费的工作时间也就越多；管理工作越是复杂多变，管理人员需要耗费的时间和精力就越多，组织就越是需要缩小控制幅度。另外，下属人员工作的相似性越大，管理的指挥和监督工作就越容易，扩大管理幅度就越有可能。

（2）管理人员的工作能力情况。

如果管理人员和下属都具有较强的工作能力，管理人员就能准确而迅速地把握问题的关键，及时提出指导性的建议和方法，而下属也同样能够准确领会上级的命令和意图，从而减少协调和沟通的频率，有效扩大管理幅度。

（3）下属人员的空间分布状况。

如果下属人员在空间上的分布比较分散，就会增加上下左右之间协调和沟通的困难，尽管现代通信手段提供了较为便捷的联系渠道，但是这多少会影响上级主管增加管理幅度的主动性。

（4）组织变革的速度。

每一个组织都必须根据环境的变化进行及时的调整，环境变化越快，组织遇到的问题就越多，组织变革的速度也就越快，主管人员对下属的指导时间和精力耗费也就越多，组织也就越不容易扩大管理幅度。

（5）信息沟通的情况。

信息充分及时是有效管理的前提，如果组织上下级之间的信息交流能够充分、快捷，并且具有较高的横向沟通效果，那么组织就可以适当扩大管理幅度。

三、组织的层级设计与集权和分权

1. 职权的来源及其形式

职权是指组织内部授予的指导下属活动及其行为的决定权，这些决定一旦下达，下属必须服从。职权跟组织层级化设计中的职权紧密相关，跟个人特质无关。

职权分为三种形式：直接职权、参谋职权、职能职权。

所谓直接职权是指管理者直接指导下属工作的职权。所谓参谋职权是指管理者拥有某种特定的建议权或审核权，可以评价直线组织的活动情况，进而提出建议或提供服务。所谓职能职权则是一种权益职权，是由直线管理者向自己辖属以外的个人或职能部门授权，允许他们按照一定的制度，在一定的职能范围内行使的某种职权。传统观念认为职权来源于组织的顶层，即职权的发展是由上至下，然后贯穿整个组织的。

由此可见，管理中的职权来源于三个方面：

（1）在层级组织中居于某一特殊职位所拥有的命令指挥权。

（2）由于个人具备某些核心专长或高级技术知识而拥有的技术能力职权。

（3）由于个人能够有效地激励、领导和影响他人而拥有的管理能力职权。

2. 组织层级设计中的集权与分权

集权和分权是组织层级化设计中的两种相反的权力分配方式。集权是指决策指挥权在组织层级系统中较高层次上的集中，也就是说下级部门和机构只能依据上级的决定、命令和指示办事，一切行动必须服从上级指挥。

分权是指决策权在组织层级系统中较低管理层次上的分散。在组织层级化设计中，影响组织分权程度的主要因素有：组织规模的大小；政策的统一性；员工的数量和基本素质；组织的可控性；组织所处的成长阶段。

3. 组织层级设计中的有效授权

（1）授权的含义及其有效性。

所谓授权就是组织为了共享内部权力，使员工努力工作，而把某种权力或职权授予下级。授权的含义有：①分派任务。向被托付人交代所要委派的任务。②授予权力或职权。授予被托付人相应的权力或职权，使之能有权履行原本无权处理的事务。③明确责任。要求被托付人对托付的工作负全责。所负责任不仅包括需要完成的指定任务，也包括向上级汇报任务的具体情况和成果。

（2）授权的过程。

认识到授权的重要性之后，组织设计者就必须针对授权中的一些障碍，制订科学合理的实施计划。授权的过程大致可以分为以下几个基本阶段。

第一个阶段是授权诊断阶段。在这一阶段，组织设计者要分析是哪一些因素导致了权力的不平衡和分配的不合理，进而识别在授权阶段所必须变革的基本要素。

第二个阶段是授权实施阶段。在这一阶段，组织设计者首先要对诊断阶段所出现的不合理要素进行变革，然后努力创造和提供有效授权所必须具备的一些要素条件，如信息共享、知识与技能、权力和奖励制度等。组织高层主管需要进一步明确组织的目标和远景，使组织中的成员充分理解授权的基本要求。

第三个阶段是授权反馈阶段。在这一阶段，组织设计者应将重点放在授权实施之后对员工绩效的考核上，使贡献卓越的员工能够得到及时的回报反馈，这样，就可以对授权的效果进行巩固，并对偏差进行及时的反馈和调整。

（3）授权的原则。

①重要性原则。组织授权必须建立在相互信任的基础上，所授权限不能只是一些无关紧要的部分，要敢于把一些重要的权力或职权放下去，使下级充分认识到上级的信任和管理工作的重要性，把具体任务落到实处。

②适度原则。组织授权还必须建立在效率的基础上。授权过少往往造成主管工作量过大，授权过多又会造成工作杂乱无序，甚至失控，所以不能无原则地放权。

③权责一致原则。组织在授权的同时，必须向被托付人明确所授任务的目标、责任及权力范围，权责必须一致，否则，被托付人要么可能会滥用职权并导致形式主义，要么会对任务无所适从，造成工作失误。

④级差授权原则。组织只能在工作关系紧密的层级上进行级差授权。越级授权可能造成中间层次在工作上的混乱和被动，伤害他们的负责精神，并导致管理机构的失衡，进而破坏管理的秩序。

Section 5　Hierarchy Design of Organization

The hierarchy design of organization refers to the number of hierarchy and effective span of management that organizations need to identify in the longitudinal structure. It clarifies the relation between responsibility and power at all levels in the longitudinal according to the degree of centralization, and finally form effective organization structure which can make dynamic response to internal and external environmental requirements.

6.5.1 Hierarchy Design of Organization and Span of Management

The core task of the organizational hierarchy design is to determine the number of levels to complete the task, and effective management span is the most basic factor that determines the number of hierarchies. Management span, also known as management amplitude, refers to the number of subordinates the supervisor of the organization can direct and effective command.

Due to the regression of the organization's mission, it forms a certain levels from the highest immediate supervisor to the lowest grassroots staff. This level is called hierarchy. Organizational level is affected by organization's scale and span, which is proportional to the size of the organization, the larger the scale is, the more people it needs, thus the more complex the work is, and so is the levels. Under the condition of organizational scale is identified, the organization hierarchy and organizational scope are interactive, but it is inversely proportional with organizational scope, namely, the more direct subordinates, the less the hierarchy is, the more if on opposite side.

The interaction between the organizational span and the organizational hierarchy determines two basic forms of organizational structure: one is flat organizational structure, the other is cone organizational structure. Diagram 6 − 13 shows the differences between them.

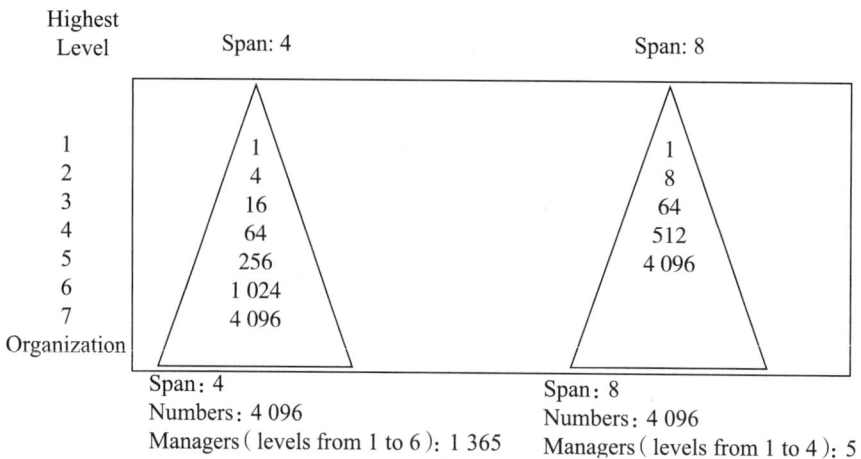

Diagram 6 − 13 Comparison Chart Between Organization Level and Span

Advantages of flat organizational structure are: Due to the less number of levels of management, communication and information transfer very fast, and thus the distortion of information is relatively low. At the same time, the control of the supervisor will not be too rigid, which is conducive to develop the enthusiasm and creativity of subordinate staff. Its disadvantages are: the extension management increases the difficulty to supervise and coordinate subordinate, while subordinates are lack of many promotion opportunities.

Advantages of cone organizational structure are: As many layers of management, management scope is relatively small, superiors can guide and control subordinate timely. Besides, hierarchy relationship is very close, which contributes to the cohesion of task, but it also provides more promotion opportunities for subordinates. The disadvantages are: Too many layers of management tends to affect the speed of information transfer, thus distortion of information may be relatively large, which in return increases the cost of communication and coordination between the executives and the grassroots, that increases the complexity of management.

6.5.2 Factors that Influence the Design of Management Span

Effective design of management span should consider the following factors:

(1) The content and quality of management.

The more contents the management has, the more connections in the organization and the more time it will take. The more complex and changing conditions the management work face, the more time and energy managers need to take, and the more we need to reduce the control range. In addition, the greater the similarity of subordinate staff, the easier command and supervision work, and more likelihood to expand the range.

(2) The working ability of managers.

If the managers and subordinates have a strong ability to work, the managers will be able to accurately and quickly grasp the problems, and provide timely advices and methods, and the subordinates are also able to accurately understand the superiors' command and intent. Thereby the frequency of coordination and communication can be reduced and the management scope can be effectively expanded.

(3) The space distribution of subordinates.

If the subordinates are more dispersed in space distribution, it will increase the difficulty of coordination and communication between all levels. Although modern communications links provide a more convenient way, this will affect the initiative of the superiors to enlarge management scope more or less.

(4) The speed of adjustment of organization.

Every organization must carry on prompt adjustment according to changes in the environment, the faster the environmental changes, the more problems organization will confront, the faster organizational changing, and the executives have to spend more time and energy on guiding subordinates and the organization becomes less easy to expand management span.

(5) The situation of information communication.

Adequate and timely information is the precondition of effective management, if the information communication between superiors and subordinates in the organization can be full and quick, and has high lateral communication affect, management span can be expanded in the organization appropriately.

6.5.3 Hierarchy Design of Organization: Centralization and Decentralization

1. The Source and Form of Authority

Authority refers to the decision-making power entitled by the organization to guide the activities and behavior, once the decision is issued, subordinate must obey. Functions and powers are closely related with authority in hierarchy design of organization, but not with personal traits.

Authority is divided into three types: direct authority, staff authority and functional authority.

Direct authority refers to the authority that managers have to directly guide the work. Staff authority refers to the right that managers suggest or audit, which can evaluate the linear organizations activities, and then put forward the proposal or provide services. Functional authority is a kind of rights and powers of the individual or department that authorized by the linear managers outside their management span allowing them to act some authority according to certain rules. Conventional ideas suggest authority comes from the top of the organization, that is, the development of the functions and powers is from top to bottom, and then throughout the entire organization.

Therefore, authority comes from three aspects:

(1) The commanding power is owned by a special position in the organization.

(2) Technical capability is owned by individual who has core competence or advanced technical knowledge.

(3) Management authority is owned by individual who can motivate, lead and influence others effectively.

2. Centralization and Decentralization in the Hierarchy Design of Organization

Centralization and decentralization are two opposite ways for distribution of power in the hierarchy design of organization. Centralization refers to the decision-making authority held on the higher level in the organization hierarchy system. It means all actions of subordinates departments should only follow the decisions, orders and instructions determined by the higher command of the superiors.

Decentralization refers to the authority of decision-making is decentralized in lower management levels in the organization system. In the design of organizational hierarchy, the main factors affecting the degree of decentralization of the organization are: the size of the organization, the unity of policies, the number of employees and their basic qualities, the controllability of the organization, and the growth stage the organization is located in.

3. The Effective Authorization in the Hierarchy Design of Organization

(1) The meaning and effectiveness of the authorization.

The authorization means that organization grants some kind of power or authority to subordinates in order to share the internal power, motivate staff to work hard. The meanings of the authorization are: ① Assigning tasks. Assign tasks to mandataries. ② Granting the power or authority. It means to grant the equal power or authority to mandataries, enable them to handle affairs which they have no right to handle before. ③ Clearing responsibility. Ask mandataries to be full responsible for the work. Responsibility not only include the specified task needs to be completed, but also the report to the superior about tasks and results.

（2）The process of authorization.

After realizing the importance of authorization, it is necessary for the designers to make up appropriate plans based on the obstacles during the process. The process can be roughly divided into the following stages.

The first stage is the diagnosis stage. At this stage, the organization designers analyze what factors lead to the imbalance of power and unreasonable distribution, and then identify the basic elements which must be changed in implement stage.

The second stage is the implement stage. At this stage, the organization designers must firstly change the unreasonable elements in the diagnosis stage, and then strive to create and provide some elements of conditions, such as information sharing, knowledge and skills, the power and the reward system and so on, which are necessary for effective authorization. Organization executives need to make clear about the organization's goals and vision, make the organization members to fully understand the basic requirement of authorization.

The third stage is the feedback stage. At this stage, the organization designers should focus on the evaluation of employees after the practice of authorization, make sure that the outstanding employees can get timely feedback, so as to enable us to consolidate the effect of the authorization, and timely adjust the deviation.

（3）Principles of authorization.

① Principle of importance. Organization authorization must be established on the basis of mutual trust. The power authorized can not just on some irrelevant parts, but also some important power or authority in order to make the subordinate fully understand the trust from the higher level and the importance of management work, to implement the specific task.

②Principle of moderation. Organization authorization must also be based on efficiency. The lack of authorization tends to cause too much work for directors, while too much authorization tends to cause chaos, even out of control, so we can't delegate powers to lower levels without principles.

③Principle of consistence between power and responsibility. When organization authorizes the power, it must clear the goal, scope of responsibility and authority to the mandataries, and power and responsibility must be consistent, otherwise, mandataries may either abuse their power which leads to formalism or make mistakes.

④Principle of differential authorization. Organizations can only authorize powers on the levels that have close relationship with each other. Skip-authorization may cause the confusion and passivity in the work of intermediate level that damage their spirit of responsibility, and lead to imbalance of management mechanism, thereby destroy the order of management.

【阅读资料】

直接职权与参谋的七种基本关系

在实际管理工作中，直接职权与参谋的关系是复杂微妙的，概括起来有七种基本类型：

（1）提供个人性质的服务。例如，经理助理在经理的指派下，协助经理本人处理某些问题，他是为经理本人提供专门服务的。

（2）提供对上级的咨询服务。例如，经理助理仅负责为经理提供咨询性意见，是否采纳则由经理来决定，这是一种纯粹的服务。

（3）按规定要求提供服务。直接主管对服务的内容、方式、时间等做出具体要求和规定，然后要求参谋机构和参谋人员按质、按量、按时提供相应的服务。这种服务往往具有专门活动的性质。

（4）提供全方位的咨询服务。参谋机构人员既要为上级提供意见、建议与咨询服务并代为制定政策与计划，又要为下级直接人员提供咨询服务并为下级参谋机构或人员提供帮助与指导。

（5）提供专门技术服务。参谋人员提供常规性的、专业性很强的、专门领域内的技术服务。他们在行政隶属管理上接受参谋部门的领导，被服务部门无权直接指挥参谋人员的工作但可以对其工作提出自己的建议与要求，若对服务不满，可以向上一级直接主管或参谋主管反映，以督促参谋人员改进工作。

（6）参谋行使职能职权。当直接主管授予参谋机构或人员某些权力处理直线主管的一些工作时，参谋机构或人员不仅为其上级提供咨询、代拟计划和政策服务，还可以在授权范围内直接指挥下级单位，享有部分的直线指挥权力，甚至当直接主管因事外出时，参谋还可以代行全部指挥权。

（7）提供独立的监督服务。例如，大型组织设立监事会、审计科等独立的监督服务机构，负责对包括各级直接人员在内的所有机构和人员行使独立的审计、监督和检察权。此时的直接—参谋关系就变成了一种监督与被监督的关系，这是一种特殊的直接—参谋关系。

【本章提要】

● 组织是一个复杂的、开放的社会系统，可以从静态和动态两个方面来考察。组织由有形要素和无形要素构成。组织一般具有力量汇聚、力量放大、相互交换等作用。

● 组织设计是一种以结构安排为核心的组织系统的整体设计工作，对组织管理意义重大，组织设计相关因素包括战略、规模、技术、环境、权力控制五个因素。组织设计的任务是提供组织结构系统图和编制职务说明书。

● 组织设计应遵循以下一些原则：目标明确化原则、分工协作原则、权责相称原则、统一指挥原则、管理幅度原则、部门化原则、集权与分权相结合原则、精干高效原则、稳定性与适应性相结合原则。

● 组织结构是描述组织的框架体系，具有复杂性、规范性、集权性的特性。组织结构是随社会生产力的发展而不断发展的，其形式也在不断地发生变化。一般有八种常用的基本组织结构形式。

● 组织结构设计的一般程序包括：确定组织目标、确定业务内容、确定组织结构、配备职务人员、规定职责权限、连成一体。

● 组织的部门设计，也称部门化，即按照职能相似性、任务活动相似性或关系紧密性的原则把组织中的专业技术人员分类集合在一个部门内，然后配以专职的管理人员来协调领导，统一指挥。部门设计有五种基本形式。

● 组织的层级设计，也称层级化，是指组织在纵向结构设计中需要确定层级数目和有效的管理幅度，需要根据组织集权化的程度，规定纵向各层级之间的权责关系，最终形成一个能够对内外环境要求做出动态反应的有效组织结构形式。

【关键词】

组织结构（Organizational Structure）　组织设计（Organizational Design）

职能分析（Function Analysis）　职务分析（Job Analysis）

管理幅度（Management Span）　部门化（Departmentalization）

集权（Centralization）　分权（Decentralization）

授权（Authorization）　事业部结构（Division Structure）

矩阵结构（Matrix Structure）　网络结构（Network Structure）

【复习与思考】

1. 组织的含义是什么？它有哪些功能？

2. 影响组织设计的因素有哪些？

3. 组织设计应遵循哪些原则？

4. 组织结构设计的程序是怎样的？

5. 组织结构形式主要有哪些？其特点、优缺点和适用范围是怎样的？

6. 五种部门形式各有哪些优劣势？

7. 什么是集权、分权和授权？

【研究与讨论】

1. 钱德勒认为战略决定结构。也有人主张战略追随结构，认为先战略后结构会使结构调整永远滞后，影响战略的实施；而先结构后战略的顺序能缩短结构与战略相适应的时间。你怎样看待战略与结构的关系？

2. 影响集权与分权程度的主要因素有哪些？为什么？

3. 如何正确处理组织结构中的集权与分权的关系？

4. 为什么要划分部门？如何有效地划分部门？

5. 你认为哪一种组织结构形式更能适应企业发展的要求？为什么？

6. 在现实中存在两种似乎相对立的主张：一是组织应当尽可能减少层次以增进协调，二是组织应当压缩幅度以加强控制。你认为这两种主张能调和吗？

【实践演练】

1. 调查或收集一个公司或机构的组织系统图，运用所学知识加以描述和评析。

2. 实地调查一家企业，了解这家企业组织机构的设置及相互关系，并弄清主要部门管理人员的职责与权限。根据了解的情况和存在的问题为其重新设计组织结构。

【管理模拟】

1. 模拟一家公司或机构，为其绘制组织系统图并编制出职务说明书。
2. 为你所在的组织设计基本的组织结构框架。

【本章案例】

朗讯：破旧立新

朗讯在 1996 年脱离 AT&T 后的最初三年表面上没有做错什么，但在 2000 年，它已经严重迷失了方向。最糟的是，它的光导电话转换器的关键市场已经被主要竞争对手北电网络公司彻底击败了。

与北电网络公司的对比深深刺痛了朗讯的主管人员。在几年以前，北电网络公司还处在这个行业的尾部。但是今天，它已经占据了正在扩张的光导通信转换器市场 45% 的份额。与之相比，朗讯只占了 15% 的市场份额。1996 年它决定开发一种比较慢的转换器，这是因为顾客并没有要求比较快的东西。而现在朗讯很后悔当初满足于低传输速度的决策。总裁 Henry Schacht 承认他与前 CEO Richard Mcginn 一样失败。Schacht 说，他计划与朗讯的顾客进行一对一的会面，并审查所有现在的流程以考虑简化朗讯复杂的结构。

在 Schacht 的领导下，2000 年 9 月，朗讯开始着手革新组织。为了领导关键部门，他任命了一些积极进取的、没有陷入企业官僚作风的局外人。CFO Deborah C. Hopkins 就是其中之一。他推行使用了按产品利润评价的新标准，用来替代以前使用的按业务部门划分的单一的标准，公司还砍掉了管理层级，将报酬与业绩更紧密地联系起来，尝试更好地整合贝尔实验室和产品研发队伍。但是，实际上它有更重要的任务：它必须把自己改造成能够快速响应需求、快速应用新技术、不官僚的企业。所有这些都要在 20% 的人员更换率和流失顶尖人才的情况下完成。

这一革新是对一切笨拙的旧经济的庞然大物开出的药方。朗讯决定要快速跟上市场的步伐。它有一个秘密武器：朗讯任命了 Jeong Kim 领导它的光导网络业务。Kim 与他周围的人明显不同，他对这个团体进行了重组，根据产品线将其划分为 17 个部门，管理人员与顾客紧密匹配，报酬和业绩挂钩。他的目标是使交货时间减少 30%。他说："我有一个百日计划。"

朗讯非常需要 Kim 的企业家精神。Kim 确信他对员工士气已经有了积极的影响。最近他参观了在麻省北安多佛的一个工厂，发现那里的总经理非常关注能够改善运作的建议。"他们真正掌握了工作的主动性，员工的士气很高，我很受鼓舞。"

1999 年 10 月 1 日，在主管人员有限认购股权被实现后，人才流失开始了。如果朗讯想阻止人才流失，必须重新取得员工的信任。那些由于大量并购而加入朗讯的员工还没好转。朗讯的员工经常抱怨自己被多层管理机构压抑着。一个猎头说："有许多高层人员设法立刻离开朗讯。"

朗讯的主管人员正在全方位地听取正确的意见。负责公司战略和业务发展的副总裁 William T. O'Shea. 正在负责用 2000 年的一个夏天的时间来精简朗讯的业务。其目标是鼓励企业家精神。他说："我们正在让新人负责和组织团队,把他们的精力集中在小团队上,而不是把公司构建成大的、不沟通的部门。同时公司把贝尔实验室的研究员囊括在团队中,以确保他们的发明得到推广。我们把企业内部更多的人带到了决策桌前。"

新 CEO Patricia Russo 正在尽力使朗讯回到正轨。2001 年 11 月,在伊士曼柯达担任 COO 8 个月后,她被任命为伊士曼柯达的 CEO。她是有扭转乾坤的经验的,她在朗讯时以将通信业务卖给现在的一家独立公司 Avaya 提高了利润而出名。她说:"对于那些离开再回来的人来说,这里已经很不同了,有了非常巨大的发展。"

毫无异议,在总裁 Henry Schacht 的裁员政策下,运营成本减少了 20 亿美元。资本费用从 2000 年的 19 亿美元减少为 2001 年的 14 亿美元。公司减少了 20 亿美元的运营成本,还开发了新产品,从而重新得到了市场。

Russo 认为转折仍将继续,即使整个通信设备行业依然不那么景气。她说:"我们可以有很多办法。"Russo、D'Amelio 和产品组织的副总裁 Robert C. Holder 以及其他朗讯的管理者开会讨论 2003 年的业务规划。将在本周结束的会议里,他们可能决定要继续裁减 5 000 个工作岗位,以减少资本支出以及运营费用,而且可能出售更多的资产。他们估计这些做法可以将利润率大约提高 35%。

（资料来源：Catherine Arnst, Roger O. Crockett, Andy Reinhardt and John Shinal. Lucent: Clean Break, Clean State? *Business Week Online*, October 26, 2000; Steve Rosenbush. Lucent: One Step Forward, Two Steps Back, *Business Week*, April 8, 2002）

思考问题：
1. 你如何描述朗讯垂直和水平结构的变化?
2. 这些变化后面的战略原因是什么?
3. 在这个案例中你看到了哪些其他的管理问题? 它们如何与结构问题相结合?

【本章参考文献】

[1]［美］费里蒙特·E. 卡斯特,詹姆斯·E. 罗森茨韦克著,李柱流等译:《组织与管理——系统方法与权变理论》,北京:中国社会科学出版社 1985 年版。

[2] 芮明杰:《管理学》,上海:上海财经大学出版社 2005 年版。

[3]［美］斯蒂芬·P. 罗宾斯著,黄卫伟等译:《管理学》,北京:中国人民大学出版社 1997 年版。

[4] 周三多:《管理学》,北京:中国高等教育出版社 2000 年版。

[5] 吴照云:《管理学》,北京:中国社会科学出版社 2006 年版。

第七章　组织运行

Chapter 7　Organizational Operation

如果你希望某个人工作出色，那么就要给他一份出色的工作。

赫茨伯格

If you want someone to do a good job, then you are supposed to give him a good job.

Hertzberg

组织的生存，其实就是价值观的维系，以及大家对价值观的认同。

赛尔兹尼克

The organization's survival is actually the maintenance as well as the identification of the values.

Selznick

【本章学习目标】

知识目标：

了解人员配备的任务、原则与内容。

了解组织制度的含义和类型。

熟悉组织文化的结构与功能。

技能目标：

掌握人员招聘、培训、考核的程序和方法。

掌握组织制度的内容与制定方法。

学会分析和塑造组织文化。

【Learning Objectives of Chapter 7】

Objectives of Knowledge：

Learn about missions, principles and contents of staffing.

Learn about definition and types of organizational system.

Be familiar with organizational culture's structure and function.

Objectives of skills：

Master procedures and methods of recruitment, training and evaluation.

Master contents and establishing method of organizational system.

Learn to analyze and shape the organizational culture.

【小故事】

美国福特公司的老板福特刚从大学毕业，到一家汽车公司应聘，一同应聘的几个人的学历都比他高，在其他人面试时，福特感到几乎没有希望了。

当他敲门走进董事长办公室时，发现门口的地上有一张纸，很自然地弯腰把它捡了起来，看了看，原来是一张废纸，就顺手把它扔进了垃圾桶。董事长把这一切都看在眼里。福特刚说了一句"我是来应聘的福特"，董事长就发出了邀请："很好，很好，福特先生，你已经被我们录用了。"这个让福特感到惊讶的决定，实际上源于董事长对他品德的信任。事实上，福特也确实没有让董事长失望，以自己的品行和能力一次次使公司转危为安。

【引例】

韩国企业：共同体式的企业文化

韩国的成功企业非常重视企业中的人和团结精神，积极致力于创立能够反映员工创造性建议和意见的企业文化，提倡每个员工承担责任，并培养其主人翁精神，从而形成了共同体式的企业文化。东洋制果公司的"好丽友家族会议"、东洋证券公司的"青年理事会制度"等都是由企业的最高经营者直接听取员工意见和建议而定的制度，而东洋水泥公司的"一起向前运动"，则是由工会组织的经营革新运动。

此外，韩国大多数成功企业在"公司的成长与健康的劳资关系是同步的"这样一种信念的指导下，积极培育"劳资共同体意识"和"劳资和解"气氛，从而使企业的经营活动能够在稳定的劳资关系中顺利进行。韩国众多的优秀企业都制定了诸如"修订福利制度""员工持股制度""对员工采取家庭成员式待遇""通过提供经营情报诱导员工参与企业经营""终生员工"等一系列制度，特别是许多优秀的中小企业常常将企业的经营状况向自己的员工公开，通过经营者与员工之间坚实的人际关系实现劳资和解。正因为有了劳资间的相互信任，企业才克服了许许多多意想不到的经营危机。

鲜京集团把在劳资协商中能够提及的事项（工资、福利等）和不能提及的事项（经营决策权、人事权等）严格区分，分别采取不同的政策；同时公司还将经营状况向员工公开，培育了让工会自己判断企业经营能力的土壤，其结果是遏制了因劳资纠纷而导致的经营损失。锦湖电器公司则规定，每月召开一次的经营计划会议必须有工会代表参加，将公司所有的经营情况向员工全部公开，以消除劳资不信任的阴影，建立良好的相互信任关系；工会方面也会分析公司每周的生产情况，并向会员说明企业的现状。"劳资不疑"的精神深深植根于企业内部，正是这种劳资和解的氛围有力地推动了韩国企业的发展。

同时，韩国的优秀企业大都以"人才第一"为基点，通过建立企业内部的研修院或利用产业教育机构培育了大量优秀的人才。现在韩国主要的企业集团都已采用了科学的人力资源管理制度。一些专业性比较强的大企业和中小企业为了拥有自己的专业技术人才，还建立了相应的人才储备系统，或是从销售额中提取一定的比例持续进行教育投资。此外，韩国的优势企业还普遍重视员工的海外研修工作，以促进员工的自我开发。

三星集团的创始人李秉哲会长生前就信奉"疑则不用，用则不疑"的信条，主张对三星的员工实行"国内最高待遇"。为此，三星公司采用了公开招聘录用制度，新员工一旦被公司录用就要接受三星公司彻底的培训，目的是使之成为"三星之星"，以实现公司成为超一流企业的目标。三星公司在"企业即人"的创业精神的指引下，彻底贯彻了"能力主义""适才适用""赏罚分明"等原则。为了挖掘企业员工的潜在能力，总公司建立了三星集团综合研修院，除此之外，各分公司分别建立了自己的研修院，并通过海外研修等形式对员工进行有效的教育培训。LG集团则通过建立"社长评价委员会""人事咨询委员会""人才开发委员会"等机构，对高级管理人员进行系统的培育。

韩国通过任用有能力的职业经理（专门经营者），从而创立了经营责任体制，并营造了责任经营的风气，其主要的企业集团都建立了事业本部制，根据经营活动多元化的要求采用具备专门经营能力的经营者这一制度，有力地推动了企业的良性发展；专门行业的大企业则通过按产品组建事业部，将经营者分为管理主管和经营主管，按事业部实施独立资产等方式确立了经营责任体制。伴随着企业经营的多元化，鲜京集团迎来了一批职业经理人，公司将经营权委托给他们，同时要求他们对自己的经营决策负责，这一措施使公司的市场分析和经营预测能力得到了明显的提高。

思考问题：
1. 什么是共同体式的企业文化？
2. 如何提高组织运行的效率？

第一节　人员配备

组织设计为组织系统的运行提供了基本框架，为使组织系统有效运行，还必须为组织配置合适的人力资源。因为，所有的管理活动都需要通过人来进行。人员配备是组织设计的延续，也是组织运行的保证。

一、人员配备的任务

人员配备是通过对人员的招聘、选拔、培训、任用和考核，为每个岗位配备适当的人员，以保证组织活动的进行和组织目标的实现。人员配备的任务可以从组织和个人两个不同的角度去考察。

（1）从组织需要的角度去考察，其任务是：①要通过人员配备使组织系统有效运转；②为组织发展准备人力资源；③维持成员对组织的忠诚。

（2）从组织成员需要的角度去考察，其任务是：①通过人员配备，使每个人的知识和能力得到公正的评价、运用；②通过人员配备，使每个人的知识和能力不断发展，素质不断提高。

二、人员配备的原则

（1）因事择人原则：指应根据职位和工作的实际要求来选拔具有相应知识和能力的各类人员，以使工作卓有成效地完成。

（2）因材使用原则：指根据每个人的特点、能力和素质的不同，去安排不同要求的工作。

（3）用人所长原则：指在用人时应发挥其长处，不能求全责备，以使人的潜能得到最充分的发挥。

（4）不断培养原则：组织应通过各种形式进行人才开发和培养，鼓励和支持员工终身学习。

（5）动态平衡原则：指人与事的配合需要进行不断的协调平衡，以实现人与工作的动态平衡和最佳配合。

三、人员配备的内容与程序

为了完成上述任务，人员配备过程中要进行以下工作：

1. 确定人员需要量

人员配备是在组织设计的基础上进行的。人员需要量的确定要以设计出的职务数量和类型为依据。职务类型提出了需要什么样的人，职务数量则告诉我们每种类型的职务需要多少。构成组织机构基础的职务可以分成许多类型。比如：全体职务可分成管理人员与生产作业人员；管理人员可分成高层、中层、基层管理人员；每一层次的管理人员又可分成直接主管与参谋或管理研究人员；生产操作人员可分成技术工人与专业工人，基本生产工人与辅助生产工人，等等。

2. 人员招聘与选用

职务设计和分析指出了组织中需要具备哪些素质的人。为了保证担任职务的人员具备职务要求的知识和技能，必须对组织内外的候选人进行筛选，做出最恰当的选择。这些人员可能来自企业内部，也可能来自外部社会。

3. 人员培训

人员培训，既是为了适应组织技术变革、规模扩大的需要，也是为了适应成员个人发展的需要，是人员配备中的一项重要工作。

4. 人员考核

人员考核是组织与员工之间的一种互动关系，在人员配备中意义重大。

四、人员招聘

人员招聘是指组织及时寻找、吸引并鼓励符合要求的人到本组织中任职和工作的过程。

1. 人员招聘的标准

人员招聘必须依据一定的标准慎重决策。

职位的要求：组织设计中给出的职务（或职位）说明书对各职位的责任、任职人员的能力和素质，都做出了具体的要求。在选聘之前，首先要明确：组织中有哪些职位需要配备人员？需要多少？这些职位的具体要求是什么？这是人员招聘的出发点，也是招聘的重要标准。

人员应具备的素质和能力：这是对招聘人员的一般要求而言的，所招聘的人既要具备所担任职务要求的特殊知识和技能，又要具备合格员工都应具备的共同的素质和能力，包括强烈的事业心和责任感、诚实和正直的品质、决策能力、沟通能力、团队精神、创新精神、冒险精神等。

2. 人员招聘的来源与方法

（1）人员招聘的来源。

人员招聘的来源，不外乎两种：从组织内部选聘和从组织外部招聘。

从组织内部选聘是指从组织内部聘用或提拔那些能够胜任的人员来充实组织中的各种空缺职位。这种做法的优点是：①有利于对选聘对象的全面了解，更好地保证选聘工作的准确性；②有利于鼓舞士气，激励组织成员上进，调动组织成员的积极性；③有利于被聘者迅速开展工作和胜任工作；④可使组织对其成员的培训投资得到回报，有利于吸引外部人才。内部选聘的缺点有：①人员来源有较大的局限性，有时会妨碍获得一流人才；②容易造成"近亲繁殖"，不利于创新；③会引起一些人的不满，造成内部矛盾。

从组织外部招聘是根据一定的标准和程序，从组织外部的众多候选人中选拔出符合空缺职位要求的人员。外部招聘的好处是：①人员来源广泛，有利于聘到一流的员工；②能给组织带来新思想、新方法，防止组织的僵化和停滞；③可缓和内部竞争者之间的紧张关系；④外聘人才是"现成的"，可节省培训时间和费用。其缺点有：①外聘人员不熟悉组织内部情况，缺乏人事基础，需要有一个了解和适应的过程；②组织对应聘者的情况无法深入了解；③内部员工的积极性会受到影响。

（2）人员招聘的方法。

不论是内部选聘还是外部招聘，为了保证招聘的员工符合工作的要求，使招聘工作有效和可行，需要按照一定的程序并引入竞争机制来组织招聘工作。通过竞争方式选聘管理人员的程序和方法如下：

①制订并落实招聘计划，公开招聘。

②对应聘者进行初选。

③对初选合格者进行知识与能力的考核。

④选定录用人员。

⑤评价和反馈。

在招聘员工的过程中需要借助一些方法，如招聘表、面试、书面或口头测试、能力测试、情景模拟、背景调查、体检等。

五、人员培训

人员培训是指组织通过对员工有计划、有针对性的教育和训练，使其能够改进目前的知识和能力的一项连续而有效的工作。一个组织的命运，归根结底取决于组织的成员，特别是管理人员素质的高低。个人的素质的提高，一方面要靠个人在工作中的学习、钻研，另一方面要靠组织有计划的培训。

1. 人员培训的目标

培训旨在提高员工队伍的素质，促进组织的发展，实现以下具体目标：更新知识，提炼技能；发展能力，提高素质；转变观念，稳定队伍；交流信息，加强协作。

2. 人员培训的方法

依据所在职位的不同，培训可分为新员工培训、在职员工培训和离职员工培训三种形式；依据不同的培训目标和内容，可分为以下几种形式：①专业知识和技能培训；②职务轮换培训；③提升培训；④助理职务培训；⑤临时职务培训。

培训的一些具体方式包括：讨论会、角色扮演、案例分析、商业游戏、讲座等。

3．人员培训的原则

（1）理论联系实际、学用一致

（2）专业知识技能培训与组织文化培训兼顾。

（3）全员培训与重点提高相结合。

（4）严格考核、择优奖励。

六、人员考核

人员考核是指组织定期对员工在工作岗位上的行为表现和业绩进行考察、评估和测度的过程，大体分为正式和非正式两种。

1．人员考核的作用

人员考核是为了了解企业员工队伍的基本情况，包括基本素质和实际工作情况等，并在此基础上实现以下目的和作用：为确定员工的工作报酬提供依据；为员工的提拔、调整提供依据；为员工的培训提供依据；促进组织内部的沟通和协调，为组织发展提供支持；为组织目标的实现提供支持。

2．人员考核的内容

人员考核包括贡献考核和能力考核两方面。贡献考核是指考核和评估员工在一定时期内担任某项职务的过程中对实现企业目标的贡献程度，在这方面，尽可能把员工的个人努力与部门的成就区别开来。能力考核是指通过考察员工在一定时间内的工作来评估他们的现实能力和发展潜力，即分析他们是否符合现任职务的要求，任现职后素质和能力是否有所提高等。贡献考核可以成为决定员工报酬的主要依据，能力考核则可用来指导组织人事调整以及制订人员培训计划。

3．人员考核的程序与方法

对员工进行考核的具体方法有很多。在此，我们不去一一介绍这些方法，只就一般的考核程序和方法说明如下：

（1）确定考核内容。考核内容要根据考核目的、不同岗位的工作性质以及对人员的不同要求来确定，一般涉及德、能、勤、绩等方面，并要尽可能具体化，以便于考察，只有这样，才能保证考核工作的效果。

（2）确定考核方法。人员考核的具体方法有很多，每种方法都各有其优点和缺点，要根据考核的目的、对象等具体情况选择适宜的方法。

（3）选择考核者，实施考核。考核工作往往被视为人事部门的任务，实际上，人事部门的主要职责是组织考核工作，组织各部门有关人员有序地参加考核。在考核工作中常常用到的考核表应该交给与被考评对象在业务上有联系的相关部门的人员去填写，这些人员主要有三类：上级、关系部门、下属。其他的考核方式，也都需要选择人事部门以外的人员参加。

（4）公布考核的结果，辨识误差。首先要剔除那些不符合要求的无效考核材料；然后对有效材料进行综合分析，得出考核结论。同时，要检查和分析考核中有无不符合事实、不负责任的评价，检查考核结论的可信程度。

（5）分析考核结果，交流考核意见。考核结果应及时反馈给有关当事人。反馈的形式可以是上级主管与被考核对象直接单独面谈，也可以用书面形式通知，有效的方法则是把这两种形式结合起来。

（6）根据考核结果，建立企业的人才档案，为企业制定人事政策、对人员进行培训和管理提供依据。

Section 1　Staffing

Organization design provides a basic framework for the operation of organizational system. We must also configure the appropriate human resources for the organization in order to make the system run efficiently. Because all management activities need to be carried out by staffs. Staffing is a continuation of organization design, and the ensurance of the operation of the organization.

7.1.1　Missions of Staffing

Through recruitment, selection, training, using and assessment, staffing will provide appropriate staff for each job to ensure both the activities of organization and the realization of organization's goals. In addition, missions of staffing can be examined from two different views of organization and individual.

（1）View of organization：① Make organization system run efficiently by personnel allocation. ②Prepare human resources for organization development. ③Maintain members' loyalty to the organization.

（2）View of individual：①Through personnel allocation, each individual's knowledge and ability can get a fair evaluation and usage. ②Through personnel allocation, each staff's knowledge and ability continue to develop, and his quality can be improved.

7.1.2　Principles of Staffing

（1）Selection：Select staffs who have appropriate knowledge and ability based on actual requirements of the job positions so as to make effective completion of work.

（2）Fitness：Arrange the work with different requirements according to each staff's characteristics, capability and quality.

（3）Strength：Play staffs' strengths, do not demand perfection in order to get the full play of one's potential.

（4）Cultivation：Develop and cultivate talents with various forms, encourage and support staffs' lifelong learning.

（5）Equilibrium. Staffs and works need to be constantly coordinated in order to achieve dynamic balance and best fit of both sides.

7.1.3　Contents and Procedures of Staffing

The following works should be carried out in order to accomplish the above missions:

1. Determining Requirement

Staffing is based on organization design. It's necessary for staff requirement designed to be on the basis of position numbers and types which are designed. Types put forward what kind of staffs is needed of while numbers reveal the need of various types of positions. Fundamental positions of organization can be divided into many types, for instances: all positions can be divided into manager and production personnel. Managers can be divided into the top, middle and basic levels, each level of managers can be divided into line managers and staff or management researchers. Production personnel can be divided into technical, professional, basic and auxiliary types.

2. Recruitment and Selection

Position design and analysis have pointed that what kind of quality is necessary for organization. In order to ensure knowledge and skills that positions need, it's required to select candidates and make an optimal choice. Those personnel come from both enterprises and society.

3. Training

Training is an important work of staffing because it is a job for the need to both adapt to technological change and scale expansion, as well as personnel development.

4. Evaluation

Evaluation is an interactive relationship between organization and staff. It also plays a significant role in personnel allocation.

7.1.4　Staff Recruitment

Staff recruitment refers to the process that an organization finds, attracts and encourages suitable people to undertake the position.

1. Standards of Staff Recruitment

Staff recruitment is decided based on specific standards.

Requirements of position: Job specification makes specific requirements to the responsibilities of various positions, abilities as well as the quality of staff. Before recruitment, we must first define: Which positions need staff? How many do we need? What are the specific requirements of these positions? It's the starting point and an important criterion for recruitment.

Qualities and abilities: It is the general requirement for recruitment. Employees must not only have special knowledge and skills that the job requires, but also the common qualities, and abilities that qualified employees should have, including a strong sense of professionalism and responsibility, honesty and integrity quality, decision-making skills, communication skills, teamwork, innovation, risk-taking, etc.

2. Sources and Methods of Staff Recruitment

（1）Sources.

There are two sources for recruitment: internal recruitment and external recruitment.

Internal recruitment means to hire or promote staffs who are able to enrich the various vacancies from organization. Advantages of internal recruitment: ①Conducive to a comprehensive understanding of the candidates and better ensurance of the accuracy of hiring work. ②Conducive to motivate members to make progress and arouse enthusiasm of them. ③Conducive to carry out work quickly. ④Enable to return on investment of training staffs and will help attract talents from outside of the organization. Disadvantages of internal recruitment: ①There is a big limitation in personnel source and sometimes interfere with top-class talent. ②Easy to cause "inbreeding", and is not conducive to innovation. ③May cause internal contradictions.

External recruitment is to hire candidates who meet the requirements of the open positions outside the organization according to certain standards and procedures. Advantages of external recruitment: ①Wide variety of sources and conducive to recruit top-class staffs. ②Bring new ideas and methods to prevent rigidity and stagnation for the organization. ③Ease internal tensions between competitors. ④Save training time and costs. Disadvantages of external recruitment: ①External personnel are not familiar with the organization's internal situation, they are lack of basic personnel information, so an understanding and adaptation process is need. ②Organization cannot know the candidates in detail. ③The enthusiasm of staffs would be affected.

（2）Procedures and Methods.

Both internal and external recruitment need to follow certain procedures and introduce competition mechanism to organize recruitment in order to ensure compliance with the requirements of the work as well as make recruitment effective and feasible.

Procedures and methods are as follows:

①Develop and implement recruitment plan, recruit openly;

②Pick candidates;

③Assess the knowledge and ability of the primary qualifier;

④Hire staffs;

⑤Evaluation and feedback.

Employers need to use some methods during recruiting, For example, issuing applying form, interviewing, holding written or spoken test, holding capacity test, making scenario simulation, conducting background investigation, conducting physical examination, etc.

7.1.5　Staff Training

Staff training refers to the continous and effective work which aims to improve the current knowledge and ability of the employees by offering planned, targeted education and training. An organization's fate ultimately depends on its members, in particular the level of management quality. The improvement of the quality of staffs, on one hand, relies on individuals learning at work, on the other hand, relies on planned training provided by organization.

1. Objectives of Staff Training

Training aims at improving the quality of workforce, promoting the development of organization, and achieving the following specific objectives: update knowledge and refine skills, develop ability and improve quality, change concepts and stabilize the team, exchange information and strengthen collaboration.

2. Methods of Staff Training

According to different positions, training can be divided into new employee training, in-service staff training and former employee training. According to different objectives and contents, training can be divided into the following forms: ①Professional knowledge and skills training. ②Job rotation training. ③Improve training. ④Assistant job training. ⑤Temporary job training.

Some specific methods for training include discussion, role playing, case analysis, business games, lectures, etc.

3. Principles

(1) Integrate theory and reality.

(2) Take into account both training of professional knowledge and skills and organizational culture.

(3) Full training combined with emphasis on improving training.

(4) Strict appraisal and merit awards.

7.1.6 Staff Evaluation

Staff evaluation refers to the process of examination, evaluation and measurement of employees' regular work behavior and performance. It is divided into formal evaluation and informal evaluation.

1. Functions

Staff evaluation is to understand the basic situation of staffs, including their basic quality and actual working conditions, on this basis it aims at achieving the following objectives and functions: Provide the basis for determine the employee's work remuneration, provide the basis for staff promotion and adjustment, provide the basis for staff training, promote the organization's internal communication and coordination and support the development of the organization and the realization of the organizational goals.

2. Contents

Staff evaluation focuses on both contribution and ability. Contribution evaluation refers to the evaluation and assessment on the degree of contribution made by staffs in a certain period of time. In this respect, we should separate individual abilities and department achievements as far as possible. Ability evaluation refers to the evaluation of employees' actual ability and development potential by investigating their work in a certain period of time, namely to analyze whether they meet the requirements of current positions and whether their qualities and abilities are improved during their work, etc. Contribution evaluation can be the main basis which decides employees' compensation while ability evaluation is available to guide the personnel adjustment and personnel training plan.

3. Procedures and Methods

The general evaluation procedures and methods are stated below:

（1）Determine content of examination. Evaluation content is determined according to the appraisal purpose, different job nature of different positions and requirements for personnel, and generally relates to morality, ability, work, performance, etc. It should be as specific as possible in order to facilitate inspection, only in this way, can we ensure the effect.

（2）Determine methods of examination. There are many methods for evaluating, and each method has its advantages and disadvantages. We should choose the suitable method according to the appraisal purpose, object and other specific situation.

（3）Select examiner and carry out examination. The primary responsibility of personnel department is to organize the examination and assign relevant personnel. Employee evaluation forms should be filled out by staffs from relevant departments who are closed with the appraisal object in the business contact. There are mainly three categories: subordinates, superiors and relationship department. If other ways of appraisal are chosen, personnel outside of the department also need to participate in.

（4）Declare results and identify error. We should weed out invalid evaluation materials which do not meet the requirements, then make comprehensive analysis of effective materials and obtain results and check whether there is any inconsistent facts and irresponsible evaluation on examination, inspect the credibility degree of results.

（5）Analyze results and exchange advices. The assessment results should be timely fed back to the relevant parties. Feedback can be in the form that supervisor and appraisal object make a direct interview alone, and the other form is to use the written notice. Combining these two forms is an effective method.

（6）Establish the personnel file according to the result of evaluation. We should provide the basis for the enterprise's personnel policy, personnel training and management.

【新视角】

GE 前任首席执行官杰克·韦尔奇绘制出了著名的"活力曲线"。他按照业绩以及潜力，将员工分为 A、B、C 三类，比例为：A 类 20%；B 类 70%；C 类 10%。对 A 类这 20% 的员工采用的是"奖励、奖励、再奖励"的方法，提高工资、股票期权以及晋升职务。A 类员工所得到的工资是 B 类员工的两至三倍；对于 B 类员工，也根据情况，确认其贡献，并提高工资。但是，对于 C 类员工，不仅没有奖励，还要从企业中淘汰。

第二节　组织制度

组织作为一个实体，在投入运行之前还需要建立规范，以明确组织结构内部的具体权限职责、联系方式及行动原则。制度是将组织中比较重要的而且稳定的东西加以概括而形成的行动规则。它规定着组织管理的基本程式、联系以及工作的标准程序、要求、方式等，强制性地指导人们怎样正确行事，约束人们按照规定的标准有序地进行工作。

一、组织制度的含义和特点

1. 组织制度的含义

组织制度是指组织管理过程中借以约束全体组织成员行为、确定办事方法、规定工作程序的各种章程、条例、守则、规程、程序、标准、办法等的总称，是对组织本身所做的各项规定。组织制度可以从广义和狭义两个层面予以分析说明。广义的组织制度包括组织管理中具有稳定性和约束力的、体系化的标准和规程，如组织结构、计划与控制规范等都具有制约和规范作用。狭义的组织制度指组织结构认识问题、分析问题、解决问题的能力和在计划与控制的基础上用来约束和协调组织全体员工行为、规定活动程序和方法的规范。我们主要研究的是狭义的组织制度。

2. 组织制度的特点

（1）权威性。组织制度是由组织或其上级制定颁布的，具有明确的是非分明的特征，一旦通过，所有组织成员都必须执行，违反规定要受到必要的惩罚。组织制度是组织内部的"法律"。

（2）科学性。组织制度建立在科学合理的基础上，是事物的技术规律要求或客观规律的充分体现，反映了组织管理科学、成熟、合理的一面。

（3）系统性。健全的组织制度是对组织内部各层次的部门、岗位人员的制度规范，它们之间具有内在的一致性、相互衔接和补充，形成了一套严密完整的制度规范体系。

（4）强制性。组织制度是组织中的法律，它作为约束和规定组织活动和行为的管理手段，是一套理性的、非人格化的体系，强制性地要求组织成员去执行和遵守。在制度规范约束范围内，组织制度对任何人都一视同仁，没有变通的余地，违反规定者将视情况不同受到降职降薪、开除等处罚。

（5）稳定性。组织制度往往是在长期的管理实践基础上经过分析、研究、总结、提炼形成的理性准则，它在很大程度上反映了组织活动和管理过程的内在要求，具有较强的稳定性。在条件未发生较大变化的前提下，通常不会发生变动。频繁变动的制度不易贯彻，更难以巩固。

二、组织制度的类型

（1）基本制度。组织基本制度是组织的"宪法"，它是规定组织形式和决定组织性质的根本制度。它制约着组织活动的范围和性质，是涉及组织所有层次、决定组织行为方向的根本制度，如企业的产权制度、公司治理制度、企业章程等。

（2）管理制度。管理制度是对组织各领域、各层次的管理工作所制定的指导与约束规范体系。管理制度比组织基本制度层次略低，它是用来约束集体行为的成体系的活动和行为规范，主要针对集体而非个人。组织管理体系中，有相当一部分就是管理制度，它是以单独分散的个人行为整合为目的的集体化行为的必要环节，是管理赖以依托的基本手段。

（3）技术与业务规范。技术与业务规范是指组织中的各种关于技术标准、技术规程以及业务活动的工作标准与处理程序的规定。它反映生产和流通过程中客观事物的内在技术和业务活动要求，是经济活动中必须尊重的。技术规范约束的主要是业务活动，业务规范多是定性的，程序性强，大都有技术背景，以经验为基础，如企业的技术规程、业务流程、技术标准等。

（4）个人行为规范。个人行为规范是对组织成员的个人行为进行引导与约束的规范。个人行为规范是所有对个人行为起制约作用的制度规范的统称，它是企业组织中层次最低、约束范围最宽但也最具基础性的制度规范。个人行为规范是组织中对行为和活动进行约束的第一个层次，其效果好坏、程度如何往往是更高层次约束能否有效实现的先决条件，如员工职业道德规范、劳动纪律规范、仪态仪表规范等。

三、组织制度的设计

1. 组织制度设计的原则

（1）法制性原则。组织制定的一切规章制度都要符合国家的政策法规，并同本组织的章程等基本制度相一致。

（2）目标性原则。必须根据组织的目标来制定组织的规章制度，所有制度都必须服从、服务于组织的目标。一些专业性的制度规范还应紧密服务于具体的经营管理目标。

（3）科学性原则。组织制定规章制度，一是必须体现客观规律，特别是管理规律的要求；二是必须从实际出发，充分考虑本组织实际；三是必须将先进性与可行性结合起来。

（4）系统性原则。组织制定规章制度必须考虑各种制度的衔接与统一，并形成配套体系。

2. 组织制度设计的步骤

（1）调研与确定目标。要根据组织总目标的需要，在充分调查研究的基础上，提出制度与规范的具体目标。

（2）制定草案。在大量分析的基础上，制定制度与规范草案。

（3）讨论与审定。制度草案提出后，要广泛征求意见，反复讨论修改。最后完善定稿，报制度审定部门审批。

（4）试行。将制度在组织内试行，经进一步修改、检验使之完善。

（5）正式执行。以正式的、具有法律效果的文件形式颁布实施。

3. 组织制度设计的内容

（1）基本制度设计。基本制度设计中最重要的是组织领导制度的设计，领导制度的中心问题，其实质是组织领导层的职权划分问题，其实质是决策权、指挥权、监督权三种基本的管理职权的划分。划分的依据是组织生产关系的性质和所反映的生产力的性质和水平。

（2）管理制度设计。它主要包括专项管理制度和部门（岗位）责任制度的设计。专项管理制度通常采用条例或规定的形式，其内容一般包括：①该项管理工作的目的、意义及地位；②做好该项管理工作的指导方针与原则；③开展该项管理工作的依据和采集信息的渠道；④该项管理工作的范围与内容；⑤该项管理工作的具体程序、方法与手段；⑥该项管理工作完成的时限与达到的标准；⑦该项管理工作的主管部门、承担者与相关部门；⑧该项管理工作与其他专项管理工作之间的关系与联系方式等。部门（岗位）责任制度主要包括的内容有：各部门或工作岗位（个人）工作范围、工作目标、职责与职权、工作标准、工作绩效与奖惩等。责任制度可分为部门责任制度和岗位责任制度。

（3）技术与业务规范设计。企业的技术与业务规范主要有生产技术标准、生产技术规程和生产定额等。生产技术标准是对企业产品或工程等在质量、技术、规格等方面所做的规定，这主要体现为质量与水平性质的标准。根据制定的单位与使用的范围，我国企业执行的技术标准分为国家标准、地方标准、行业标准和企业标准。生产技术规程是对企业的产品设计、生产制造、服务运作、设备使用与维护等生产技术活动的程序、方法所做的规定，其主要内容是生产经营活动的基本流程与要求。

4. 组织制度的执行与调整

（1）组织制度在执行过程中应注意以下几方面：

①加强宣传教育。要利用各种有效途径与方式，将组织的规章制度向全体成员进行宣传，做到"人人皆知"，并教育组织成员认真贯彻实施。

②明确责任，严格执行。组织制度的生命就在于执行。再好的制度，如果束之高阁，也是毫无意义的。贯彻执行组织制度，必须有严格的责任制度作保证，并狠抓落实，严格执行。

③坚持原则性与灵活性的统一。在具体工作实践过程中，必须依法办事，保证规章制度的严肃性；同时，一定要结合具体情况，灵活而创造性地执行制度，注重规章制度的实效。

④加强考核与监督。制度工作的重点在落实，而落实的关键在于考核与监督。执行组织制度只停留在号召与要求上是远远不够的，最关键是要做好制度贯彻情况的监控，进行科学的考核，实行严格的监督。

⑤加大奖惩力度。制度的执行总是会遇到这样或那样的困难，特别是可能会涉及利益冲突。因此，必须有较大力度的奖惩来加以推进与保证。对制度执行好的予以奖励，执行不好的坚决处罚。通过加大奖惩力度来保证制度的实施，并加大组织制度规范的作用。

⑥跟踪控制，在适当时机进行调整与进一步完善。

（2）组织制度的调整。

组织制度应当保持较强的稳定性，但当制度赖以存在的前提条件发生变化时，组织制度也要做相应调整。组织制度的调整包括现行组织制度的修改、废除和新制度的制定。组织制度的修改，通常在出现以下三种情况之一的条件下进行：①与组织制度有关的法令、政策有变化；②组织决策有重大改变；③实施过程中暴露出制度本身不合理、不完善。制度修改的内容、程度取决于具体情况，有时可能是个别条款，有时可能是某一类规定，有时可能是制度约束的程度。

组织制度的废除发生在下述情况下：①组织破产倒闭；②某些基本法令、制度的废除使组织有关制度失去依托，失去意义；③制度约束的事项已告结束；④同一事项有了新的制度规范。

组织制度调整的主要工作是修改，其中一个需要注意的问题是要把"破"和"立"结合起来。认识到原制度不合理时，应积极调整和修改。还需要注意制度的调整不宜太频繁，局部的、小的不合理出现时，不宜轻易修改制度，要维护组织制度的严肃性和稳定性。

Section 2 Organizational System

As an entity, before putting into operation, the organization needs to establish standards in order to make clear of the specific jurisdiction of internal responsibilities, contact information and action principles. System is the operation rules generalized and formed from the important and stable work of organization. It provides a basic program of management, correlation and the standard working procedure, requirements, methods, etc. And it is mandatory to instruct people how to do things right, constraining people to work in accordance with standards.

7.2.1 Definition and Feature of Organizational System

1. Definition of Organizational System

Organizational system is the general terms of restraining members determining methods and work procedures, and it is the provision made to the organization itself. Organizational system can be divided into generalized and narrow level. Generalized system includes stable and systematic standards or procedures of organization management, such as organization structure, planning and control standards which have restriction and specification. Narrow system refers to organizational structure's understanding ability, analysis ability and problem-solving skills and the standards with constraints and coordination of staff behavior and activity procedures and methods on the basis of planning and constraining. We mainly study the narrow organizational system.

2. Feature of Organizational System

(1) Authoritative. Organizational system is set by organization or its superior with distinct characteristics. Once it is formed and settled, all members must carry out and people who violates it will be punished. Organizational system is the law of an organization.

(2) Scientific. Organizational system is established on the scientific and reasonable basis. It is the fully reflection of the technical rules of things or the objective law. It reflects the mature and reasonable side of management.

(3) Systemic. A perfect organizational system is the system specification for the personnel and departments of all levels within the organization. There is intrinsic consistency, cohesion and complement among them, which formed a set of strict and complete system specification.

(4) Mandatory. As a law of organization and a realistic constraint, organizational system is rational and impersonal. It is mandatory organizing the activities and behavior of the management, and asking members to follow and observe. It is equal for everyone in the system of organization, there is no room for flexibility. Offenders will receive demotion, pay cuts, fire and other penalties.

(5) Stable. Organizational system is often based on the long-term management practice through analysing, studying, summing up experience to form rational criterion. It largely reflects the organizational activities and the inherent requirement of the management process with strong

stability. Usually it can't be changed until great changes take place. Frequent changes of system are not easy to implement, and it is difficult to consolidate as well.

7.2.2 Types of Organizational System

(1) Basic system. Basic system is the "constitution". It is the basic system of organization which sets organization form and determines organization nature. It is the basic system which involves all levels and determines the orientation of organization as well as the restriction scope and nature of activities. Basic system includes enterprise's property right system, corporate governance system and articles of association of the enterprise, etc.

(2) Management system. Management system is the guidance and constraint system of the organization in all areas and at all levels. It is slightly lower than basic system and used to restrict the activities of collective behavior and code of conduct, which is mainly for the collective rather than individual. Management system is the necessary link in the collective behavior which aims at combining individuals, and it is also the basic approach for management.

(3) Technology and business standards. They include various technical standards, technological processes, job standards of operational actions and processing procedures in an organization. It reflects requirements, scientificity and regularity of internal skills and business activities of objective things during production and circulation, and they must be respected in the economic activities. Technology standards mainly restrict operation actions, while business standards usually are qualitative and followed by strong procedures, they have technical backgrounds and are based on experiences, such as enterprise's technical procedures, business processes, technical standards, etc.

(4) Personal conduct. Personal conduct aims at guiding and restricting individual behavior of organization members. Individual behavior norms are a joint name of personal conduct of all kinds of constrains. It is in the lowest level, but is of the widest range and also the most basic system specification of organization. Personal conduct puts behavior and activity in the first level with constraints. Its effect is the prerequisites vital to determine whether higher level constraints can be effectively realized. It includes staff ethics, labor discipline, and manners, etc.

7.2.3 Design of Organizational System

1. Principles of Organizational Design

(1) Legal. All rules and regulations should be made in accordance with national policies and regulations, and consistent with the basic system such as the articles of association.

(2) Targeted. All systems must be made according to the organization's goals and must obey in the service of the organization's goals. Some professional regulations should also be closely in service of the specific operation and management goals.

(3) Scientific. The system must firstly reflect the objective law, especially the laws of management. We must base on the reality and give full consideration to the actuality of the

organization, and we must combine advancement with feasibility.

(4) Systematic. To set up rules and regulations, we must consider cohesion and unity of all kinds of system and form the supporting system.

2. Procedures of Organizational System Design

(1) Research and objectives. According to the needs of the organizations overall goal, on the basis of full investigation and study, we should point out specific target of the system and norms.

(2) Draft. Draft out system and standards after analyzing massive materials.

(3) Discussion and determination. The draft system should be discussed repeatedly and modified. We should improve the finalized script and submit it to the examination department for approval.

(4) Trial. Try out the system in organization, test and modify in order to perfect it.

(5) Implement. Declare to carry out the system with formal and legal files.

3. Contents of Organizational System Design

(1) Basic system design. The most important thing in basic system design is the design of system's leadership system, and its essence is the power division of the leadership. That is the division of three basic functions and powers: command, decision-making and supervision. Division is based on nature of productive relations of organization and productivity's nature and level.

(2) Management system design. It mainly includes the design of special management system and department (jobs) responsibility system. It usually takes the form of regulation or special system, and its contents generally include: ① Objectives, meaning and status of current management. ②Guidelines and principles for working well. ③The reasons of the task and the gathering channel to carryout the management. ④Scope and contents of current management. ⑤Specific procedures and methods of the management. ⑥The finish time and the standard of the management. ⑦Departments, stakeholders and the related departments of the management. ⑧The relationship and information between the management and other special management, etc. Department responsibility system mainly includes: scope of each department or work (person), work goal, duties and authorities, work standards, work performance and rewards and punishments, etc. Responsibility system can be divided into the department and job responsibility system.

(3) Technology and operation standards design. Technology and operation standards contain production technical standard, production technical regulation and production quota, etc. Production technical standard is the regulation on the enterprise's product or project in terms of quality, technology and specification, it mainly embodies the standards of the quality and level. According to departments and scope of usage, our country's enterprise standards for execution are divided into state standards and local standards, industry standards and enterprise standards. Production technical regulation is the regulation of procedures, methods of enterprise's product design, manufacturing, services, operation, usage and maintenance of equipment, and other

production technical activities. Its main content is the basic process and requirement of business operation activities.

4. Execution and Adjustment of Organizational System

（1）Execution of organizational system.

①Strengthen education. Use a variety of effective ways and methods, show organization's rules and regulations to all members, and seriously lead members to implement.

②Refine the responsibility and strictly execution. It's essential to execute. To carry out the system, there must be a strict liability system as a guarantee, and do substantial work and strict enforcement.

③Stick to the unite principle and flexibility. In the process of specific work practice, we must handle affairs according to law, ensure the autority of the rules and regulations. At the same time, we must combine with the specific circumstances, executing the system flexibly and creatively and paying attention to the effective rules and regulations

④Strengthen inspection and supervision. Inspection and supervision is the key to execution. The most important thing is to monitor the implement situation by carrying on the scientific assessment and exercising strict supervision.

⑤Increase the intensity of rewards and punishments. We must have a large strength of rewards and punishments to promote and guarantee execution. We should make greater efforts to guarantee the execution of system by strengthening the realization of rewards and punishments and increase the role of organizational system.

⑥Track and control. Adjust and perfect the system at proper time.

（2）Adjustment of organizational system.

Organizational system should remain strong stability, but when preconditions on which systems relied change, the organizational system should also be adjusted correspondingly. The adjustment includes modification and abolishment of current systems, establishment of new systems. Modification is carried out in one of following three situations：①Changes in laws and policies related to organizational system. ②Significant changes in organizational decisions. ③The system is not reasonable and perfect in the process of implementing. Contents and extends of modification depend on specific circumstances, sometimes may be some terms, sometimes may be one type of regulation or the degree of institutional constraints.

Conditions for abolishment：①The organization goes bankrupt. ②The abolition of some basic laws makes the organizational system lose its meaning. ③Matters constricted by organization system have come to an end. ④The same item has new system specification.

Modification is the main work of adjustment. So we should pay attention to both abolishment and establishment. We should actively adjust and modify when realizing the original system is not reasonable, but the system can not be adjusted too often. We should not easily modify organizational system, in order to maintain the seriousness and stability of organizational system.

第三节　组织文化

组织是按照一定的目的和形式构建起来的社会集合体。为了满足自身发展的要求，组织必须要有共同的目标、共同的理想、共同的行为准则以及相适应的机构和制度，这都是在一定的文化氛围中存活的，否则组织就难以有效运行。

一、组织文化的概念与特征

组织文化是20世纪80年代初由经济高度发达的美国首先提出的，是一种文化和经济相结合的产物。组织文化指组织在长期实践活动中所形成的并为组织成员普遍认同和遵循的、具有本组织特色的价值观念、团体意识、工作作风、行为规范和思维方式的总和。一个组织的文化，通常由其创始人和领导者倡导，把特定的理念和价值观表达出来，并贯彻于活动之中，为全体成员所认同。不同的组织会有不同的组织文化，组织文化影响着组织成员的思想和意识，并约束组织成员的行为。组织文化的主要特征有：

（1）客观性。组织文化是一种客观存在的文化现象。作为人类文化系统的一个重要组成部分，组织文化如同其他文化一样是与其载体共生的，即有赖于组织的存在，直接来源于组织的活动。尽管不同的组织由于规模、结构、内容、组织形式、成员素质的不同而具有不同特点的组织文化，尽管在同一组织的不同发展阶段，其组织文化的鲜明、系统、成熟程度会存在明显差异，但组织文化必然与组织相伴而生。

（2）个异性。组织文化是社会文化与民族文化的现实反映。组织作为社会成员，存在于一定的社会文化环境之中，会受到民族文化的熏陶，具社会性和民族性的特征。不仅如此，每个组织由于其使命不同，所拥有的资源和所处的环境不同，其组织文化也具有明显的个性，而且强弱也不同。例如，美国的组织文化强调个人能力、独立精神；而日本的组织文化则强调团队合作、家族精神。

（3）人本性。人是一切文化的缔造者，也是组织的物质、制度及精神文化的创造者，在构成组织文化的诸要素中，人始终处于主体地位。组织文化的主旨与核心就是以人为本，关心人、尊重人，为人的全面发展和价值实现创造条件。

（4）稳定性。组织文化是在长期的实践中逐渐积累而成的，具有较强的稳定性，不会因组织结构的改变、战略的转移或产品与服务的调整而变化。但是，组织文化会随着历史的积累、社会的进步、环境的变迁和组织革新而逐步提升和发展。

组织文化可以通过判断一个组织具有的十个特征的程度来加以识别，这十个特征是：成员的同一性；团体的重要性；对人的关注；单位的一体化；控制；风险承受能力；报酬标准；冲突的宽容度；手段—结果倾向性；系统的开放性。组织文化是这十个特征的复合，这些特征是相对稳定和持久的，通过对其进行分析，可把握某个组织的文化。

二、组织文化的结构与内容

1. 组织文化的结构

组织文化一般有三个层次结构，即潜层、表层和显现层。

（1）潜层的精神活动。这是组织文化的核心和主体，是组织成员共同而潜在的意识形态，包括管理哲学、敬业精神、价值观念、道德规范等。

（2）表层的制度系统。这是体现某个具体组织的文化特色的各种规章制度、行为准则、伦理规范以及组织内分工协作的组织结构。它是组织文化核心层（内隐部分）与显现层的中间层，是虚体文化向实体文化转化的中介。

（3）显现层的文化载体。显现层的文化载体又称物质层文化，是凝聚着组织文化抽象内容的物质体的外在显现，它既包括了组织整个物质和精神的活动过程、组织行为、产出等外在表现形式，又包括了组织实体性的文化设施，如图书馆。它是组织文化最直观、最易感知的部分。

2．组织文化的内容

组织文化的主要内容有：

（1）组织的价值观。这是组织内管理层和全体员工对该组织的生产、经营、服务等活动的一般看法和基本观点。它包括组织存在的意义和目的、组织各项规章制度的价值和作用、组织中各种行为与组织利益的关系等。价值观念是组织文化的重要组成部分，为组织的生存和发展提供基本方法和行动指南，为组织成员形成共同的行为准则奠定基础。

（2）组织精神。这是指组织群体的共同心理定式和价值取向，是一个组织的精神支柱，是组织文化的核心，它反映了组织成员对组织的特征、形象、地位等的理解和认同，也包含了对组织未来发展和命运所抱有的理想和希望。

（3）道德规范。这是指所有组织成员自觉遵守的行为准则、道德标准和风俗，它包括是非界限、善恶标准和荣辱观念等。道德规范的形成主要取决于价值观念和组织精神的作用。良好的道德规范主要表现为尊重知识、尊重人才、友好相处、勤奋工作、与组织共命运等。

（4）组织素养。这是指组织中全体成员的思想素养、科技文化水平、工作能力以及健康状况等。其中，组织的基本思想素养水平越高，其价值观念、精神风貌、道德修养的基础越深厚，组织文化的内容也就越丰富。

三、组织文化的功能与塑造

1．组织文化的功能

组织文化作为一种自组织系统，具有如下主要功能：

（1）凝聚功能。这指通过培育组织成员的认同感和归属感，建立起成员与组织之间的相互依存和信任的关系，使个人的思想、感情、行为、习惯、信念等与整个组织有机地整合在一起，形成相对稳固的文化氛围，凝聚成一种无形的合力，激发人们的积极性、智慧和创造力。

（2）导向功能。这指通过组织的共同价值观不断向个人价值观渗透和内化，使组织自动生成一套自我调控机制，从而引导组织及其成员的行为和活动。

（3）适应功能。这指组织文化能从根本上改变旧的价值观念，建立起新的价值观，使之适应组织外部环境变化的要求。组织文化本身也会随着实践的发展而不断地更新与优化，从而得到提升。

（4）规范功能。这指组织文化一经形成，就会通过制度系统从整体上规范组织的行为，并对成员个体的心理、性格、行为等起规范作用，引导成员不断趋近目标，起到行政命令无法替代的作用。

2. 组织文化的塑造

组织文化的塑造是一个长期的过程，也是组织发展过程中的一项艰巨、细致的系统工程。从路径上讲，组织文化的塑造需要经过以下几个过程：

（1）选择合适的组织价值观标准。一是要根据组织自身的目的、环境要求和组成方式等特点选择适合自身发展的文化模式，二是要协调好组织价值观与组织文化各要素之间的关系，三是要符合组织的战略发展方向。

（2）强化成员的认同感。一是要通过宣传等强化方法使其深入人心，二是通过培养和树立典型来感召和影响成员，三是加强培训和教育使成员系统地接受组织的价值观并强化成员的认同感。

（3）提炼定格。组织文化的塑造不可能一蹴而就，必须经过认真分析、全面归纳、提炼，方能定格。

（4）巩固落实。一是通过建立制度来保证，二是领导者要率先垂范。

（5）不断丰富和完善。这也是一个不断淘汰旧文化和生成新文化的过程，也是一个认识与实践不断深化的过程。

四、组织文化对组织管理的影响

1. 组织文化对管理职能的影响

当组织文化形成并加强时，它会渗透到管理人员的一切活动中，并产生重大影响。在任何组织中，其计划、组织、领导、控制等各项管理职能肯定带有一定的文化色彩，脱离文化的管理是不存在的。组织文化之所以能对管理职能产生影响，是因为它建立了在这个组织中可以做什么和不可以做什么的规范。如迪斯尼公司"让千百万人快乐"的价值观一直左右着公司的决策。

2. 组织文化对组织成员的影响

组织文化具有整合组织成员思想和行为的功能。它通过精神的力量，帮助组织成员发展出一种集体认同感，并知道该如何相互合作以有效地工作。组织文化能使员工对组织的目标和利益达成共识，从而调整全体员工的行为使其趋于一致，以实现企业的目标。例如，一些企业提出"今天的质量就是企业明天的下场"的理念，以促使企业员工在经营活动中必须做到向消费者提供优质产品和卓越服务。

3. 组织文化对企业业绩的影响

美国哈佛商学院著名教授约翰·科特等人在对美国实业界许多大公司进行了长期的实证研究后，得出如下结论：某些特定的企业文化肯定会促进企业经营业绩的长期增长，而另一些类型的企业文化会减弱企业经营业绩的长期增长。他进一步指出：良好的企业文化会有助于企业经营业绩的长期增长，但这种情形的出现，必须要求一个条件——企业的行为与企业经营策略相一致，并能够帮助企业适应不断变化的市场环境。如果企业员工的共同行为或行为方式无法适应相应的市场环境，企业经营业绩就不会增长。

4. 组织文化对组织变革的影响

组织文化通常是一系列相互依存的价值观念和行为方式的总和。这些价值观念、行为方式往往是一个组织全体员工共有的，往往是通过较长时间的积淀存留下来的。一套构建牢固的组织文化一旦形成，它对企业固有模式上的转变是怀有敌意的。在企业中，员工们相信他们自己在企业里的生存是建立在"公司拥护什么"或按"正确的方式做事"的基础上的。因此，组织文化对一个组织的变革起着重要的推动作用。

Section 3　Organizational Culture

Organization is social group built up according to a certain purpose. In order to meet the requirements of their own development, it's necessary to have common goals, ideals and codes of conduct as well as suitable agencies and institutions. The above are all existing in a certain culture atmosphere, otherwise, an organization can be difficult to run efficiently.

7.3.1　Definition and Feature of Organizational Culture

Organizational culture was put forward by the United States in the early 1980s. It's the result of combination of culture and economy. Organizational culture, which is approved and followed by people refers to the sum of values, group consciousness, working style, behavior norms and the way of thinking that formed in the long-term practice. Founder and leader usually advocate the culture, showing their expression to specific ideas and values, implementing in the activities and accepted by all members. Different organizations have different organizational cultures. This culture affects members' thought and values. Main features of organizational culture are as following:

(1) Objective. Organizational culture is an objective existence in cultural phenomenon. As an important part of human culture system, organizational culture is symbiotic with carrier like other cultures, which depends on the organization, directly rooting in the organizational activities. Organizational culture must be accompanied by organization though different organizations owe different cultures because of different scales, structures, contents, forms and member qualities that cause differences in culture's level in different stages of development.

(2) Unique. Organizational culture is a real reflection of social culture and national culture. Organization exists in certain social cultural environment and will be affected by the culture, so organization has the feature of localization and nationality. Furthermore, different organizations have different missions, different resources and environment, so their organizational cultures also have distinct personality and different strength. For example, organizational culture of the United States emphasizes on personal ability and independent spirt, While Japan's organizational culture emphasizes on team spirit and family spirit.

(3) Humanistic. Human is the founder of all culture, also it is the creator of the material, institutional and spiritual culture of organization. In various elements that make up the

organizational culture, people always be in the subject position. The subject and the core of organizational culture are people-oriented that care about people, respect people, create conditions for people's comprehensive development and value realization.

(4) Stable. Organizational culture is formed in the long-term practice and of strong stability. It will not change with the adjustment of the organizational structure, strategic shift or products and services. However, organizational culture will gradually improve and develop with historical accumulation, the progress of the society, the change of environment and organization innovation.

Organizational culture can be identified by 10 features of organization as following: the identity of members, the importance of the group, the focus on people, unit integration, control, risk tolerance, compensation standard, tolerance of conflict, method-result orientation, openness of the system. Organizational culture is the collection of these 10 features, which are stable and lasting. We can understand the organizational culture by analyzing these features.

7.3.2　Structures and Contents of Organizational Culture

1. Structures of Organizational Culture

There are three layers of organizational culture: the hidden layer, the surface layer and the visible layer.

(1) Hidden layer of mental activity. This is the core and main body of organizational culture, and it is the potential ideology of members. It includes management philosophy, professional spirit, values, ethics, etc.

(2) Surface layer of regulation system. This reflects the culture characteristics of a particular organization of various rules and regulations, code of conduct, ethics, and the structure of the collaboration in the organization. It's the intermediate layer between the hidden layer of organizational culture and visible layer and the mediation from virtual culture to actual culture.

(3) Visible layer of culture carrier. It is also known as the physical culture. It is the external show of the organizational culture of abstract content. It includes the external form of both the whole process of material and spiritual activities, organizational behavior, output, and the substantive cultural facilities, such as library, etc. It is the most intuitive and perceived part of organizational culture.

2. Contents of Organizational Culture

(1) Values of organizationan. It is the general and basic view of the organization's managers and all employees on production, management, service and other activities. It includes the meaning and purpose of the existence of organization, the various values and function of the regulation, organization behavior and the relationship between organizational interests, etc. Value is an important part of organizational culture that provides the basic methods and guidelines for survival and development and lays the foundation for members to form a common code of conduct.

(2) Spirit of organization. It refers to the common mental set and value orientation of an organization, and it is the spiritual pillar of the organization and the core of organizational culture.

It reflects the understanding and recognition about the organization's features, image status, and so on from members and the ideals of the organization's future and destiny.

(3) Code of ethics. It refers to the code of conduct, moral standards and customs abided by all members. It includes the concept between right and wrong, good and evil, and the credit standards etc. Code of ethics depends on the effect of values and spirit of organization. Good ethics mainly include respect knowledge, respect talented person, be good with others, hard working, and organization casting and so on.

(4) Organizational quality. It refers to members' thoughts quality, level of technology and culture, working ability and health condition, etc. The higher the basic literacy level is, the deeper the basis of its value idea, spirit and moral cultivation are, and the richer the content of the organizational culture will be.

7.3.3　Function and Shaping of Organizational Culture

1. Function of Organizational Culture

The organizational culture conducts as a self-organizing system, and it has the following main functions:

(1) Cohesion. It sets up the relationship of interdependence and trust between organization and members by cultivating the sense of identity and belonging in order to combine the individual's thoughts, feelings, behavior, habits, belief with organization, forming a relatively stable cultural atmosphere and condensing them into a kind of invisible force, and finally to stimulate people's enthusiasm, wisdom and creativity.

(2) Guide. It means that permeating and internalizing individual values gradually by the organization's shared value, and automatically generating a set of self-regulatory mechanism for the organization so as to guide behaviors and activities of the organization and its members.

(3) Adaptation. Organizational culture can fundamentally change the old values and establish new values in order to meet the needs for external environment change of the organization. Organizational culture will renew and optimize with the development of practice, so it can be advanced.

(4) Standard. Once organizational culture is formed, it can standardize the organizational behavior by system as a whole and standardize individual psychology, personality, behavior, etc. It will lead members to approach the objectives and play the role which executive orders cannot replace.

2. Shaping of Organizational Culture

The shaping of organizational culture is a long-term process, and is also a difficult and detailed systematic job in the process of organizational development. To tell from the stages, shaping organizational culture needs to go through the following process:

(1) Select the appropriate organization value standard. Firstly, choose the suitable cultural pattern for organization development according to their own purposes, environmental requirements

and composition. Secondly, keep the coordination between organizational values and elements of organizational culture. Thirdly, conform to the strategic direction of organization.

（2）Strengthen the identity of members. ①Be deeply rooted in the hearts of staffs by improving methods such as publicity. ②Cultivate and shape model to inspire and affect members. ③Strengthen training in order to make members accept values and strengthen identity.

（3）Refine and confirm. Shaping organizational culture can't accomplish within a short period of time, it can be achieved after careful analysis, comprehensive induction, and refining.

（4）Consolidate and practice. ①Consolidate the culture by establishing policies. ②Leaders need to set an example.

（5）Constantly enrich and perfect itself. This is a process of phasing out old culture and generating new culture gradually, and a process of deepening understanding and practice.

7. 3. 4　Impacts of Organizational Culture on Organizational Management

1. Impacts on Management

When the organizational culture comes to form and strengthen, it will permeate all the activities of managers and make significant impacts. In any organization, its planning, organizing, leading, and controlling function must be in a certain culture. No management exists without culture. The reason why organizational culture can affect the management function is that it establishes standards by telling us what can do and what can not do. For example, the Walt Disney Company's value of "let ten million people happy" has affected the company's decision-making all the time.

2. Impacts on Members

Organizational culture integrates members' thoughts and behaviors. Through the power of spirit, it helps members to develop a collective identity and know how to cooperate to work effectively. Organizational culture can make employees reach a consensus to the organization's goals and interests so as to adjust the behavior of all the staffs to make it consistent in order to achieve the goals of the enterprise. For example, some enterprises put forward the concept of "today's quality is tomorrow's destiny" to promote enterprise's employees provide high-quality products and services for customers.

3. Impacts on Results

Professor John Kotter in Harvard business school, after doing empirical research of many large companies in the United States for a long period of time, has drawn the following conclusions: Certain corporate culture will certainly promote the growth of the long-term business, while other types of corporate culture will weak long-term business growth. He also points out that good corporate culture will contribute to enterpriser's long-term growth, but this situation depends on a specific condition—the behavior is consistent with management strategy, and it can help enterprises to adapt to the changing market environment. If staffs' joint conducts or conducting ways cannot adapt to the corresponding market environment, business will not grow.

4. Impacts on Organizational Reform

Organizational culture usually is the sum of a series of interdependent values and behavior. These values and behavior are often common to all staffs and survive through a long time of accumulation. Once a set of strong organizational culture is formed, it is hostile to the transition of the inherent mode. In the enterprise, the employees believe that their own survival is based on "what company upholds" or "in accordance with the right way". Therefore, the organizational culture plays an important role in promoting organizational reform.

【阅读资料】

日本和美国的企业文化

1. 日本

日本企业文化具有鲜明的民族特色，强调团队意识、家族精神。日本企业文化的表现形式是多种多样的，如"社风""社训""社魂""组织风土""经营原则""企业使命感"等。

日本的资本主义是在封建家族制的基础上发展起来的，封建家庭和村社的群体意识深深植根于日本传统文化之中。日本的企业又是由武士阶层首先发展起来的，武士阶层强烈的民族意识对日本文化有深远的影响。日本的企业依靠传统的风土观念，在长期经营实践过程中，建立起独特的思考和行为方式。它以重视群体为特征，倡导个体对群体的归属，强调群体的和谐统一的价值观。以此为基础，建立起民族主义的、家长式的和反个人主义的企业文化。

与其他国家相比，日本企业文化的主要特点有：

（1）现代文化同日本传统文化相结合。日本通过解散财阀等改革，以及引进欧美的先进思想和体制，抛弃了封建糟粕，在建立的企业文化中保留了民族的特点。在日本企业文化中，体现了组织上的集团意识和思想上的"和""忍""信"等观念。

（2）企业家族化。在日本，强调企业是一个大家庭，员工、管理人员之间有一种亲属式的团结感。在企业决策方面采取集体决策的稟议制（即非正式协商的务虚活动），征求各级管理人员的意见，以保持群体的亲和感。

（3）重视培养员工忠于企业的观念。企业除了对员工进行技术、业务培训外，还十分重视对员工的精神培养，树立荣辱共存的集团主义精神，使员工把忠于企业作为自身行为的基本准则。

（4）加强企业内部的凝聚力。采用各种制度，加强员工的群体观念。例如在用工制度方面实行终身雇用制，注重人的品质、忠诚和长期为公司服务的愿望，以实现企业群体长期稳定的发展；在分配制度方面采取年功序列制，以工龄长短作为衡量员工对企业贡献大小的重要标志，力求使员工的需要在企业内得到满足，增强员工对企业的归属感，增强群体的凝聚力。

（5）充分发挥群体的优势。提倡企业内部员工之间的竞争是一种竞相为企业出力的竞争。鼓励员工积极参与企业之间的竞争，提倡一致对外。

对日本企业文化形成的主要原因，学者们有如下看法：

（1）日本民族的单一性和社会结构的同质性，使日本国民的意识和行为趋向统一，具有相同的民族习惯。

（2）日本战后的改革为日本企业文化的发展创造了适宜的环境。

（3）日本社会文化的荣辱观，强化了从业人员同所属集团的"一体感"，成为孕育日本企业文化的土壤。

（4）善于吸取外来文化。将外来文化与本国文化相结合，熔人性精神与无情效率为一炉，形成既有"原则"，又有"信条"和"原则"的企业文化。

（5）依靠企业自身的努力，依赖于宣传、教育、灌输、渗透、身体力行、潜移默化等一系列有效手段，经历了漫长的实践过程，而逐步形成。

2. 美国

美国的企业文化具有其明显的特色。各国移民所带来的民族、种族文化在美国企业文化中得到了体现，资本主义所提倡的个人至上、个人奋斗的个人主义在企业文化中得到充分发展。

美国企业文化与美国的社会文化有着天然的联系。美国是一个只有两百多年历史的多民族国家，它的社会文化流派甚多，十分复杂，其文化源头主要是基督教文化。这种社会文化背景决定了美国企业文化的最大特点是：提倡自由贸易、自由经营，鼓励个人凭才智和工作致富。美国企业文化与美国管理理论的发展也密切相关。长期以来，美国是世界上管理科学最发达的国家，从科学管理到行为科学以及第二次世界大战后出现的"管理理论丛林"这几个阶段来看，美国都出现过十分著名的、对世界管理理论做出重大贡献的管理专家，各种学派的理论对美国企业文化的形成和发展也产生了重大的影响。

美国的企业文化从总体上讲具有以下主要特点：

（1）强烈的竞争意识。鼓励发明创造，制定高水平的工作规范、生产计划和经营战略，强调个人竞争。

（2）强烈的个人奋斗意识和进取精神。它是美国企业文化的基本价值观。美国人认为，凭个人成绩和个人能力去工作、奋斗，是培养企业优秀人才的最好方法。

（3）强烈的自我驾驭生活的意识。强调个人决策，领导者身体力行。

（4）明显的雇佣观念。由于个人有权选择自己的生活道路，使美国从业人员流动迅速，形成企业管理中的短期雇佣和对员工迅速评估及升级的特点。

（5）人际关系淡漠。由于不干涉个人私事，企业和员工之间、员工和员工之间的关系成为单纯的工作关系，造成美国企业文化中人际关系淡漠。同时，也形成重视利润、市场占有率和技术革新等实际价值的特点。

美国企业文化的发展迄今大体经历了三个阶段：

（1）美日比较管理学阶段。这是20世纪70年代美国管理界兴起的一股热潮，它的基本特征是寻求美日两国在管理方面的文化差异，而企业文化理论的诞生则奠定了理论基础。

（2）公司文化阶段。进入20世纪80年代后，从对美日管理比较的研究转移到对美国自身管理模式的研究上，确立了立足于美国国情，寻求自身优势，创建具有美国特色的企业文化。同时，把美国企业文化的理论和概念传到国外。

（3）组织文化阶段。美学者 E. 谢思于 1985 年出版了《组织文化与领导》一书，标志着美国企业文化的研究由经验阶段发展到理论研究阶段。研究的内容和方向明显带有学术色彩，不再是经验的罗列和事例的陈述，形成一支以学者为主，有广泛的企业文化理论研究人员参加的队伍，使企业文化成为一种理论。

美国企业文化理论的研究，从管理哲学和文化哲学的高度，开拓了管理学研究的新视野，把管理科学的研究推向了一个新的阶段。然而，美国传统的个人主义文化的超然独立的态度，又影响着他们对国外先进文化的吸收，阻碍了美国企业文化的发展。20 世纪 80 年代以来，美国在全国进行了一场对企业文化进行研究与重塑的实践运动，强调研究和探索企业文化对企业生产率、企业效率以及企业市场地位等各方面的影响，寻求适应新经济形势的企业价值准则，重塑和发展美国企业文化。

【本章提要】

• 人员配备是组织设计的延续，也是组织运行的保证。它包括了确定人员需要量、人员招聘与选用、人员培训、人员考核等环节的工作。

• 人员招聘是人员配备的一个重要步骤，可以从外部和内部招聘，并且要按一定的程序和方法来进行，旨在获得组织所需要的人力资源。

• 对员工进行培训的目的就是要提高员工的素质，增强竞争力。培训的方法与方式多种多样。

• 组织制度是组织运行的重要条件，通常有基本制度、管理制度、技术与业务规范、个人行为规范等。

• 组织文化是一个组织共有的价值体系，包括价值观念、道德观念、行为准则等，组织文化影响着组织成员的思想和意识，并约束其行为。组织文化具有客观性、个异性、人本性和稳定性等特征。

• 组织文化有其自身的结构和内容体系，具有凝聚、导向、适应、规范等功能。塑造组织文化是一个长期的过程，需要做出艰苦的探索。

• 组织文化对组织和管理有重要影响，主要表现在对管理职能、组织成员、企业业绩和组织变革的影响。

【关键词】

人员配备（Staffing） 人员招聘（Staff Recruitment） 职务轮换（Job Rotation）
人员考核（Staff Evaluation） 组织制度（Organizational System）
组织文化（Organizational Culture） 组织精神（Spirit of Organization）
价值观念（Value）

【复习与思考】

1. 人员配备的任务有哪些？
2. 人员配备的内容与程序如何？

3. 人员招聘的程序和方法是怎样的？

4. 培训员工的目的何在？

5. 人员考核的作用与内容各有哪些？

6. 组织运行需要哪些制度来保证？

7. 组织文化的结构和内容体系如何？

【研究与讨论】

1. 你认为人员配备在组织运行中处于什么位置？

2. 如何才能留住人才是人力资源管理中最难也是最迫切需要解决的问题，有人提出"靠事业、用感情、给待遇可以留住人"。你怎么看？

3. 企业花钱培训员工，是为了增强企业的竞争力，但很有可能得不偿失。因为受过良好训练的员工更容易跳槽。你认为如何解决此类矛盾？

4. 组织文化究竟应该怎样塑造？

【实践演练】

1. 访问一位人事经理，向他了解所在企业评价管理人员的标准是什么？这些标准是否可以考核以及如何考核？他认为绩效考评的结果怎样？

2. 以招聘者和被招聘者的身份参加一些人才招聘会，谈一谈感想。

3. 通过网上或书店，调查研究中国知名企业文化与国外知名企业文化的共性与差异。

【管理模拟】

请你关注周围的某一项工作，并为其设计职务说明和职务规范。

【本章案例】

韩国的鲜京集团株式会社设有鲜京研修院，集团每年投入 500 万美元的经费，用于集团员工的培训。鲜京研修院为形成从最高经营者到普通职员都统一的意愿和工作方法，以现有的经营管理体系和"最优"的目标为基础，设置了基本课程、专业课程、特殊课程等多种教育课程。鲜京研修院作为实践教育机关，正在通过这些课程履行着造就鲜京人面貌、提高其管理能力的使命，他们的目标是培训优秀的各层次专门人才。所有进入鲜京集团的职员都要先在研修院学习两周，之后平均每人每三年要接受考试培训一次，并且职位越高受培训的机会和时间越多。研修采取住校学习的方式，由研修院自己编写教材；教师基本上为兼职，请本社内部和特聘的社外（高等院校、研究院所）专家教授担任；其考核方式除学习结束时需交一份报告并要接受实践的检验外，还采取相互评价的方式，即教师—学员、学员—学员之间进行考核。其成绩直接关系学员日后的工作安排、职务升迁等。鲜京集团的研修则分为 EMD、一般课程、特殊课程三种类型。EMD 为集团理事、董事等参加的培训，主要内容为作为经营者所应具备的知识；一般课程为公司职员晋升前后所进行的培训，包括新入社员课程、社员能力课程、新任课长课程、课长能力向上课程、新任部长课程等，主要内容为基本素质的培训；特殊课程为特殊信息的提供、身心修炼、经营技法训练等，如对驻海外人员进行所在地区地理环境、风俗习惯、市场状况的介绍，对女性员工进行"资质向上"的教育，另外还进行气功训练，等等。

韩国企业的员工一般不轻易调离原企业，除了进公司第一天起就受到公司文化的教育、熏陶并得到全面系统的培训等原因外，更与其合理的职员晋升制度有密切的关系。

鲜京公司的职员从3～12级，共分为10个档次。高中毕业的职员一进入公司即为3级；大学毕业生进入公司为5级，属于普通职员；6～7级为代理；8～9级为课长；10～11级为次长、部长；12级以上叫任员，实际上已是理事、董事层。一般来说，工作努力，有一定成绩，平均每三年晋升一级；有特殊贡献、才干超群的，经过特别选拔，一年便可升级，但数量很少。级别越高，晋级所需时间越长，要求也越严格。如此算来，一个大学生从进公司到升到课长、次长等中层干部一般已是人到中年。在这种晋级制度下，在本企业工作的工龄是晋升的主要条件之一。公司职员如想换一家企业工作，无疑要从头干起，一年一年重新攀登职务阶梯。而与职务紧密挂钩的工资、奖金，相差一级，其收入是相当高的。这样，如没有特殊原因，企业职工跳槽现象几乎是不可能出现的。

思考问题：
1. 你认为这家公司的人力资源管理有什么特色？
2. 公司的培训与晋升制度如何？

【本章参考文献】

［1］［美］唐·黑尔里格尔等著，张燕等译：《管理学：能力培养取向》，北京：中信出版社2005年版。

［2］芮明杰：《管理学——现代的观点》（第二版），上海：上海人民出版社2005年版。

［3］［美］查尔斯·萨维著，谢强华等译：《第五代管理》，珠海：珠海出版社1998年版。

［4］戴钢书：《现代企业文化新论》，武汉：武汉大学出版社2002年版。

［5］［美］德斯勒著，吴雯芳、刘昕译：《人力资源管理》，北京：中国人民大学出版社2005版。

第八章　组织变革

Chapter 8　Organizational Reform

一个组织不是一台静止的机器，而是一个演变着的社会系统。

卡那

An organization is not a static machine, but a social system in evolution.

N. D. Kana

变革包括两个步骤：首先达到一种新的精神境界，然后转变为行动或转变为物质形式。

哈根

Reform includes two steps: first of all to reach a new level of mental state, and then to change it into action or into physical form.

Hagen

【本章学习目标】

知识目标：

掌握组织的生命周期理论。

了解组织变革的动力、内容和目标。

熟悉组织变革的过程和程序。

了解组织变革的途径。

技能目标：

掌握组织变革的方式。

理解组织再造的过程。

学会创建学习型组织。

【Learning Objectives of Chapter 8】

Objectives of Knowledge：

Have a command of the organizational life cycle theory.

Get to know the motive power, content and objective of organizational reform.

Be familiar with the process and procedure of organizational reform.

Get to know the method of organizational reform.

Objectives of Skill：

Have a command of the method of organizational reform.

Understand the process of reorganization.

Learn to construct learning organization.

【小故事】

　　森林里住着三只蜥蜴。其中一只看见自己的身体和周围的环境大不相同，便对另外两只蜥蜴说："我们住在这里实在太不安全了，要想办法改变环境才可以。"说完，这只蜥蜴便开始大兴土木。另一只蜥蜴看了说："这样太麻烦了，环境有时不是我们能改变的，不如我们另外找一个地方生活。"说完，它便拎起包袱走了。第三只蜥蜴，也看了看四周，问道："为什么一定要改变环境来适应我们，为什么不改变自己来适应环境呢？"说完，它便借着阳光和阴影，慢慢改变自己的肤色，不一会儿，它就渐渐地在树干上隐没了。

【引例】

奥尼尔的变革

　　在匹兹堡市区最近的一个夏日里，美国炼铝公司的首席执行官保罗·奥尼尔公布了这个原料"巨人"的宏伟规划，该规划要对这个横跨 22 个国家、拥有 63 000 多名员工的公司进行一次全面彻底的革新。

　　奥尼尔提出了一个新结构，它集中于美国炼铝公司的主顾和业务单位："不是匹兹堡，不是为他们服务的副总经理们，也不是董事长，而是业务单位。"为了这个目标，公司集中所有的资源，并联系和支持着公司的 22 个业务单位。

　　与变革有关的不仅仅是公司结构一个因素。通过引进公司的新战略，奥尼尔向众人皆知的持续改进的变革观点提出挑战。他声称，这种方法对那些已经成为市场领导者的公司或许奏效，但是，"如果你落后于世界领先水平，这是个糟糕的方法；如果你远远落后于世界水平，这可能是一个灾难性的方法。"

　　对美国炼铝公司来说，他们似乎是个落伍者。奥尼尔认为公司需要做出迅速的巨大改进，而不是缓慢的渐进变革。奥尼尔对员工提出的挑战是：两年内要消除公司和世界先进水平之间的 80% 差距。

　　"等外部事件来迫使组织进行变革，这是最佳的反应式管理办法，但也是最胆小的管理做法。"他告诉员工，领导并不是"那种组织绩效一团糟，以至于股东强烈要求改变现状的强迫变革者"。

思考问题：

1. 组织要跟着战略走还是跟着领导走？
2. 为什么要进行组织变革？

第一节　组织的生命周期理论

　　组织与任何有机体一样有生命周期。格林纳（Greiner）认为一个组织的成长大致可分为：创业、聚合、规范化、成熟、成熟后五个阶段。每个阶段的组织结构、领导方式、管理体制和职工心态都各有特点。每个阶段最后都面临着某种危机和管理问题，都需要采用一定的管理策略加以解决，以达成组织成长的目的。

第一阶段——创业。这是组织的幼年期。规模小、人心齐、关系简单，一切由创业者指挥。组织的生存与成长完全取决于创业者的素质与创造力。这些创业者一般属于技术业务型，不重视管理。随着组织的发展，管理问题日趋复杂，创业者感到无法以个人非正式沟通来解决问题，特别是到了创业阶段的后期，组织内部的管理问题层出不穷，从而产生了"领导危机"。

第二阶段——聚合。这是组织的青年时期。企业在市场上取得了成功，人员迅速地增多，组织不断地扩大。创业者经过锤炼成了管理者或引进了专门的管理人才。为了整顿正陷入混乱状态的组织，必须重新确立发展目标，并用铁腕作风、集权的管理方式来指挥各级管理者。在这种管理方式下，中基层管理者由于事事必须请示、听命于上级而逐渐感到不满，要求获得一定的自主权。但是高层管理者已经习惯于集权管理，一时很难改变，从而产生了"自主性危机"。

第三阶段——规范化。这是组织的中年时期。这时，企业已有相当规模，增加了许多生产经营单位，甚至形成了跨地区经营和多元化发展。如果组织要继续成长，就要采取授权的管理方式，采用分权式组织结构，允许各级管理者有较大的决策权力，但是时间长了又使高层主管感到由于过度分权与自由管理，企业业务发展分散，各阶层、各部门各自为政，本位主义盛行，使整个组织产生了"失控危机"。

第四阶段——成熟。为了防止"失控危机"，组织又有采取集权管理的必要，将许多原属中基层管理者的决策权重新收归总公司或高层管理者。但由于组织采取过分权的办法，不可能恢复第二阶段的命令式管理。解决问题的办法是在加强高层主管监督的同时，加强各部门之间的协调、配合，加强整体规划，建立管理信息系统，成立委员会组织，或实行矩阵式组织。一方面使各部门有所作为，另一方面使高层主管能够掌握、控制整个公司的活动与发展。为此就必须拟定许多规章制度、工作程序和守则。随着业务的发展，这些规定、制度成了妨碍效率提高的因素，文牍主义盛行，产生了"官僚主义危机"或"硬化危机"。

第五阶段——成熟后。此阶段组织的发展前景既可以通过组织变革与创新获得再发展，也可以更趋向成熟、稳定，也可能由于不适应环境的变化而走向衰退。为了避免过分依赖正式规章制度和刻板程序的文牍主义，必须培养管理者和各部门之间的合作精神，通过团队合作与自我控制达到协调配合的目的。另外要进一步增加组织的弹性，采取新的变革措施，如精简机构、划小核算单位、开拓新的经营项目、更换高级管理人员等。

一个组织并不一定都按上述的阶段顺序发展，但组织生命周期理论却说明了组织在不同的时期会面临不同的问题，需要采用不同的管理方式。任何组织要生存和发展都需要变革。

Section 1　Organizational Life Cycle Theory

The organization has its own life cycle just like any other organisms. Greiner held that the growth of an organization can be roughly divided into five stages. They are business start-up, aggregation, standardization, maturity and after-maturity. There are different characteristics in organizational structure, leading method, management system and mentality of employees of different stages. All stages have to face crises or management problems, which would be solved with appropriate management tactics to achieve the growth of an organization.

The first stage—business start-up. This is the infancy of an organization in which the scale is small, all the staff have the same goal, the relationship is simple and the entrepreneur conducts everything. The survival and the growth of an organization rely on the entrepreneur's quality and creativity who is generally technical and business person and ignores management. With the development of the organization, managerial problems become so complicated that the entrepreneur finds it difficult to solve problems with personal and informal communication. Especially at the later stage, problems inside the organization emerge one after another, so that the "leadership crisis" arises.

The second stage—aggregation. This is the youth of an organization in which the enterprise gets a great success, employees increase rapidly and the organization expands unceasingly. Entrepreneurs make themselves good managers through practice or import specialized management talents. It is necessary to establish a new developmental objective to readjust the chaotic organization and arrange managers at all levels with iron-fisted style and centralized management. In this stage, middle and first-line level managers are becoming increasingly disgruntled with having less rights to make their own decisions while the senior managers have been too accustomed to centralized management to change it immediately. Thus "autonomy crisis" arises.

The third stage—standardization. This is the midlife of an organization when the enterprise has set up fairly scope, increased production and business units and even formed a trans-regional operation or developed in all aspects. In order to keep going, the organization needs to adopt decentralized management and organization structure to allow managers at all levels to have more decision-making rights. However, excessive separation of powers and uncontrolled management in long time will result in the fragmented development of business, the independent management of all strata and all departments, and even the fashion of selfish departmentalism. Thus "uncontrolled crisis" appears.

The fourth stage—maturity. In order to prevent the "uncontrolled crisis", it is necessary to adopt centralized management to take back the decision-making power from the middle and first-line level managers. However, it is impossible to return to command management in the second stage again due to the condition that decentralized management has been adopted. The way to solve the problem is to strengthen the control of top-level managers, enhance the cooperation of different departments, reinforce comprehensive planning, set up management information system and found the council at the same time or try to put matrix organization into practice. In this case, on the one hand all departments can amount to something, on the other hand the top-level managers can control the activities and development of the whole organization. Therefore varieties of regulatory framework, working routine and procedure come into effect. With the development of business, these rules become obstacles of the improvement of efficiency and bureaucracy prevails. Thus "bureaucratic crisis" or "ossified crisis" emerges.

The fifth stage—after-maturity. The development prospect of organization in this stage can be more mature and stable, the organization can get the chance of redevelopment through organizational reform and innovation, what is more, it may even fall into recession because of maladjustment to the change of environment. In order to avoid the bureaucracy that all the staff rely on official regulatory framework or inflexible procedure, it is necessary to cultivate the team spirit among the managers and all the departments, to reach the objective of coordination through teamwork and self-control. In addition, managers also need to strengthen the flexibility of the organization and adopt revolution such as downsizing, minifying accounting unit, developing new operating project and changing senior managers.

An organization does not always develop in the above sequence, but the theory of organizational life cycle explains that the problems of an organization in different periods need to be solved with different methods. The survival and development of every organization need revolution.

第二节 组织变革的动力与方式

组织变革就是组织为适应内外环境的变化，对组织的目标、结构及组成要素等适时而有效地进行各种调整和修正。一个组织要生存和发展，就必须依据外部环境和内部条件的变化做出调整。因此，组织变革是组织保持活力的一种手段。

一、组织变革的动力

组织变革的动力分为外部动力和内部动力两类。

1. 外部动力

市场变化：包括顾客的收入、价值观念、偏好等的变化；竞争者推出了新产品或给产品增添新功能，加强广告宣传、降低价格、改进服务，从而使本企业的产品不再具有吸引力。

资源变化：包括人力资源，能源，资金，原材料供应的质量、数量以及价格的变化。例如，劳动力素质的提高使得传统的"权力—服从"式管理越来越不适应新的组织环境，组织必须寻找符合现代员工需要的新的管理制度和办法，包括实行参与管理、自由选择工作岗位、职务丰富化等。

技术变化：包括新工艺、新材料、新技术、新设备等的出现。技术变化不仅会影响到产品，而且会带来新的职业和部门，引起管理方式、责权分工以及人与人关系的变化。

一般社会环境变化：包括政治形势、经济形势、制度、投资、贸易、税收、产业政策与企业政策的变化。例如，我国从计划经济体制向社会主义市场经济体制的转变，就给企业的组织形式带来了深刻的变革。按现代化企业制度改革或建立起来的企业组织，与传统的企业组织是完全不同的。

2．内部动力

人的变化：这主要是指领导者的变化。新的领导者上任或原有领导人接受了新的管理思想、采用了新的管理方法，都可能引起组织的变革。职工参与意识的增强、对现状的不满也会使他们产生变革的要求，从而促使组织进行变革。

组织运行、成长中遇到的矛盾和问题：对此，我们前面在介绍组织生命周期理论时已经介绍过了。组织在其成长的每个阶段都会遇到各种各样的矛盾，这些都促使管理者采取变革措施，以保证组织的生存和发展。

二、组织变革的方式

针对现存的问题和面临的内外环境的变化，以及所选定的组织变革方向、目标和变革内容，组织需要采取适当的方式对现有组织进行切实的改造和变革。组织在选择变革方式时，需要本着权变与适用的原则进行。一般来说，有以下几种变革方式：

1．量变式和质变式——按照变革的程度划分

量变式是以改变组织机构和人员的数量为主的一种变革方式。其变革的重点在于增设或撤销部门单位，增加或减少管理人员等。这种变革较简单易行，适合于在组织关系结构、责权体制和行为规范等方面都基本适宜的情况下，解决机构臃肿、人员过多、管理费用过大等问题。但这种变革只涉及组织中的表层问题，因而是一种以控制管理组织规模为主要目的的变革。

质变式以解决组织的深层次问题为重点，是使组织效能和内部关系发生根本变化的一种变革方式。根据质变的广度来分，质变可以是局部的，也可以是全局的。局部质变会对全局质变产生影响。再从质变的深度来看，质变可以发生于组织中较浅的层次，也可能发生于深层次，越是深层的变革越重要，它涉及基本价值观念和制度体系的变革。

2．正式关系式、非正式关系式和人员式——按照变革的对象划分

正式关系式以组织中经过正式筹划的、为实现组织目标而围绕着工作任务展开的人与人或人与机之间的关系作为变革对象。其主要是通过管理机构和管理体制的设计和再设计实现的，具体包括职位和部门组合、工作程序设计、等级层次划分、横向联系手段设置以及职责权限分配等。

非正式关系式以组织中未经正式筹划而产生的相互影响和相互作用的关系为变革对象，具体技巧和方法包括相互交往分析、敏感性训练、群体发展、组织会议和人事调解等。

人员式以改变组织成员的知识、技能、态度和价值观等为对象，具体变革策略包括各种管理发展和教育培训计划等。

3．主动思变式和被动应变式——按照变革的力量来源划分

主动思变式的动力来源于组织内部，而且是在事先预见的基础上做变革的决策，属于居安思危、高瞻远瞩、防患于未然。

被动应变式是在迫于外部压力的情况下产生的，如来自内部的不协调或宏观经济压力等，为了应付这些变化企业不得不变革组织。

4．突变式和分段发展式——按照变革的进程划分

突变式是在短时间内一次性地变革组织。这种变革方式雷厉风行、一次到位，解决问

题迅速。但由于涉及面广、速度快，容易引起组织成员心理振荡，甚至产生抵触情绪。因而需要在组织成员心理承受力和政策允许的基础上进行。

分段发展式是在对组织现状和内外条件的全面论证及组合分析的基础上，有计划、有步骤地逐个实现变革的分阶段目标，最终促成变革总目标的实现。

5. 强制式、民主式和参与式——按照变革方案的形式过程划分

强制式，指变革涉及者不参加变革方案的制订过程，这样形成的变革方案往往需要通过强制命令来付诸实施。

民主式与强制式相反，指在变革的有关人员相互协调的基础上形成变革方案。

参与式，亦称民主集中式，既广泛地动员各层次人员参与，又对人们的思想观念有意识地加以引导，以便尽快地形成统一的方案。

6. 自上而下式、自下而上式和上下结合式——按照变革的起始点划分

自上而下式，即从变革上层管理组织入手，再扩展到整个组织。这一方式便于对总体组织做出调整，但其涉及面大、范围广，需要进行周密计划，从而减少阻力。

自下而上式，即从基层组织的变革入手，再考虑上层组织的变革。有时会拖延变革的进程。

上下结合式，即对组织的上下各方面同时进行变革。

7. 战略性变革、结构性变革、流程主导性变革和以人为中心的变革——按照变革的侧重点划分

战略性变革是指组织对其长期发展战略或使命所做的变革。如果组织决定进行业务收缩，就必须考虑如何剥离非关联业务；如果组织决定进行战略扩张，就必须考虑并购的对象和方式，以及组织文化重构等问题。

结构性变革是指组织需要根据环境的变化适时地对组织的结构进行变革，并重新在组织中进行权力和责任的分配，使组织变得更为柔性灵活、易于合作。

流程主导性变革是指组织紧密围绕其关键和核心能力，充分应用现代信息技术对业务流程进行重新构造。这种变革会使组织结构、组织文化、用户服务、质量、成本等各个方面发生重大的改变。

以人为中心的变革是指组织必须通过对员工的培训、教育等引导，使他们能够在理念、态度和行为方面与组织保持一致。组织中人的因素最为重要，若不能转变人的观念和态度，组织变革就无从谈起。

以上各种变革方式在实际中往往相互交叉，应根据实际情况灵活运用各种方式，充分发挥各自的功效，取长补短，以取得整体效果。

Section 2　Motive Power and Methods of Organizational Reform

Organizational reform is a variety of seasonable and effective adjustments and corrections of organizational objectives, structure and other composing factors for adapting the changes of the inner and outer environments. An organization cannot survive and develop without the adjustment to the variety of external environment and internal condition. Thus organizational reform is a means to keep the organization alive.

8.2.1 The Motive Power of Organizational Reform

The motive power of organizational reform can be divided into external power and internal power.

1. External Power

The change of market: It includes the changes of customer's income, value, preference and so on. The product of the enterprise will become less attractive when the competitors launch new products, add new functions, enhance advertizing, decrease the price or improve service.

The change of resources: It includes the changes of human resources, energy, capital, the quality and the quantity of raw material supply as well as the price. For example, the increase of the quality of the labor force out dates the traditional management of "right-compliance". Therefore the organization needs to search for a new system or method which suits modern employees, including putting individual-participated management, free choice of job and work enrichment into practice.

The change of technology: It includes the appearance of new craft, new material, new technique and new equipment. The changes of technology will not only influence the product, but also create new vocations and new departments, and cause the change of the way of management, division of rights and responsibilities and the relationship of staff.

The change of social environment: It includes the changes of political situation, economic situation, system, investment, trade, revenue, industrial policy and business policy. For example, China's reform from planned economy to market economy brings a great influence on organizational form of enterprise. There are enormous differences between the enterprise which is transformed or set up on the basis of modernized enterprise system and the traditional enterprise.

2. Internal Power

Change of staff: It mainly refers to the change of the leader. The appointment of new leader or the adoption of new management theory or management method by the original leader may lead to organizational reform. What is more, the increase of the sense of participation and the dissatisfaction with the status quo of the workers will require organizational reform as well.

The contradictions and problems when the organization runs and grows: Just as we introduced, the organization will face varieties of contradiction in every stage of growth. All of these force the managers to adopt measures to ensure the survival and the development of the organization.

8.2.2 The Method of Organizational Reform

Aiming at the existing problems, the changes of internal and external environment as well as the designated orientation, goals, and content of organizational reform, it is necessary to adopt an appropriate method to change and reform the organization practically. And the principle of adaptability and applicability should be followed. Generally speaking, there are several forms of reform:

1. Quantitative Reform and Qualitative Reforms—Divided by the Degree of Reform

The quantitative reform is a revolutionary method that focuses on the change of the number of the organization and staff. The key point of it is to increase or decrease business units, add or cut back managers, etc. This is a simple and practicable way to solve the problems such as over staffing in organizations and superabundant administration cost especially when the relationship of administrative structure, the system of rights and liabilities as well as the code of conduction are suitable. However, the quantitative reform only involves the surface problems, therefore, the fundamental purpose of it is to control the scope of an organization.

The qualitative reform is a revolutionary method that focuses on solving the deeper problems of the organization. It is able to make radical reforms between organization effect and internal relationship. Divided by the breadth of the reform, it can be local or global. The local reform may have effect on the global reform. Then divided by the depth, the reform may occur on the junior level, or on the senior level. The more senior the reform occurs, the more important the reform is, because it refers to the reform of the fundamental conception of value and the institutional system.

2. Official Relationship Reform, Unofficial Relationship Reform and Individual Reform—Divided by the Objects of Reform

The official relationship reform makes the relationship of employees or between the human and the machine, which is designed formally and focuses on the mission in order to achieve the organizational goals, as the revolutionary object. Designing or redesigning the regulatory agency and management system is the main method to achieve it. To be specific, it includes the combination of jobs or departments, the design of the working routine, the partition of the ranks and levels, the means of transverse connection and the distribution of the rights and responsibility and so on.

The unofficial relationship reform makes the mutual relationship, which is not designed formally, as the revolutionary object. The specific skill and method include the analysis of interaction, the training of sensitivity, the development of the group, the arrangement of meetings as well as the conciliation of personnel and so on.

The individual reform makes the changes of organizational members' knowledge, skill, attitude and value as the revolutionary objects. The specific tactics include various management development plans and educational training plans.

3. Active Reform and Passive Reform—Divided by the Source of Revolutionary Power

The active reform means its power source is inside the organization. And managers made the decision to reform on the basis of seeing things in advance and preparing for war in time of peace.

The passive reform occurs under outside pressure, such as the internal maladjustment, macro-economy's pressure and so on. And the enterprise has to reform itself to handle these changes.

4. Immediate Reform and Gradual Reform—Divided by the Course of Reform

The immediate reforming means reform the organization in a short period of time. It is a rapid method to solve the problems but often results in the unrest of human psyche and even the conflicts due to its wide cover and blistering speed. Therefore the precondition of it is the allowance of psychological endurance capability and policies.

The gradual reform means achieving the objectives of every stage step by step on the basis of having good command of the organization's status quo and the internal and external condition and finally making the general objective a reality.

5. Compulsive Reform, Democratic Reform and Participant Reform—Divided by Reform Scheme-making Process

The compulsive reform means the employees who are influenced by the reform cannot take part in the reform scheme-making process. Therefore the managers often put the scheme into effect through mandatory order.

On the contrary, the democratic reform means all the staff that are related to the reform cooperate to draft reform scheme.

The participant reform also is known as the reform of democratic centralism. On the one hand, it encourages the staff at all levels to take part in the reform; on the other hand, it tries to correct employees' ideological ideas consciously, so that the agreed scheme can be made as soon as possible.

6. Top-down Reform, Bottom-up Reform and Below-on Combining Reform—Divided by the Starting Point of Reform

The top-down reform means starting from the top management, then expanding to the whole organization. It is convenient to adjust the general organization, but due to the wide cover and range, managers should plan carefully to reduce the resistance.

The bottom-up reform means starting from the basic level, then taking the reform of top management into account. Sometimes it may slow the progress of reform.

The below-on combining reform means reforming all aspects of the organization at the same time.

7. Strategic Reform, Structural Reform, Reform Dominated by the Process and Human-centered Reform—Divided by the Emphasis of Reform

The strategic reform is the reform of the long-term development strategy or missions conducted by the organization. If the managers decide to pull back business, then it is necessary to give up irrelevant business. If the managers want to implement the expansion strategy, the object and method of merger as well as reconstitution of organizational culture should be taken into account.

The structural reform refers to the reform of organizational structure according to the change of environment and reallocating the rights and responsibilities in order to make the organization more flexible and easier to cooperate with.

The reform dominated by the process means the organization reconfigures the business process with the full advantage of modern information technology around its key and core ability closely. This reform will change organizational structure, organizational culture, customer service, quality, cost and many other aspects significantly.

The human-centered reform means the organization has to make the employees' concept, attitude and behavior keep pace with the organization through guiding the staff by training, educating and so on. The staff is the most important factor. Organizational reform cannot succeed without the transformation of people's concept or attitude.

The reforms said above often cross each other in practice, managers should use various means flexibly according to the reality, and give full play to their respective functions to complement each other, in order to get the overall effect.

第三节　组织变革的目标与内容

一、组织变革的目标

总的来看，组织变革的基本目标包括以下三个方面：

1. 使组织更具环境适应性

环境因素具有不可控性，组织要想在动荡的环境中生存并得以发展，就必须顺势变革自己的任务目标、组织结构、决策程序、人员配备、管理制度等，只有这样，组织才能有效地把握各种机会，识别并应对各种威胁。

2. 使管理者更具环境适应性

在组织变革中，作为决策的制定者和组织资源的分配人，管理者必须清醒地认识到自己是否具备足够的决策、组织和领导能力来应对未来的挑战。因此，管理者既需要调整过去的领导风格和决策程序，使组织更具有灵活性和柔性，同时也要根据环境的变化要求重构层级之间、工作团队之间的各种关系，使组织变革的实施更具有针对性和可操作性。

3. 使员工更具环境适应性

组织的员工是组织变革的最直接感受者。组织只有使员工充分认识到变革的重要性，顺势改变员工对变革的观念、态度、行为方式等，才能使组织变革措施得到员工的认同、支持和贯彻执行。而要改变员工的观念、态度和行为是非常困难的，组织要使人员更具有环境适应性，就必须不断地进行再教育和再培训、重视员工的参与管理、改造和更新组织文化。

二、组织变革的内容

由于组织所面对的环境情况各不相同，因此，组织变革的内容和侧重点也有所不同。美国管理学家李维特（Harold J. Leavitt）认为，组织是一个多变量系统，在此系统中，至少包含三个最重要的变量，那就是任务、技术、结构。因此，组织变革的内容也包括三个方面：

1. 任务的变革

任务的变革是指组织在运行目标和方向上的变革。当组织对运行目标和方向进行调整时，组织结构要随之进行变革。在复杂的组织系统内，尚有许多亚层次任务存在，它们是为总任务服务的。这些亚层次任务实际上就是各个部门的具体工作任务和目标，这是决定各级部门机构设置的重要因素。

2. 技术的变革

技术的变革是指对作业流程与方法的重新设计、修正和组合，包括更换机械设备，采用新工艺、新技术和新方法等。组织系统中的技术因素包括设备、建筑物、工作方法、新技术、新材料、新的质量标准和新的管理技术控制手段等。技术因素的变革，可以间接地促进组织任务的改变，或直接促进组织技术条件与制造方法的改进，从而影响组织人员与组织结构。

3. 结构的变革

结构的变革是指组织权力关系、协调机制、集权程度、职务与工作再设计等结构参数的变化。管理者的任务就是要对如何选择组织设计模式、如何制订工作计划、如何授予权力以及授权程度等一系列行动做出决策。现实中，固化式的结构设计往往不具有可操作性，需要随着环境条件的变化而变化，管理者应该根据实际情况灵活改变其中的某些组成要素。

Section 3　The Objectives and Contents of Organizational Reform

8.3.1　The Objectives of Organizational Reform

In general, the objectives of organizational reform include the following three aspects:

1. Make the Organization Better-adapted

Environmental factors are not controllable, in order to survive and develop in such turbulent environment, the organization has to change their objectives, organizational structure, decision procedures, personnel, management system, etc., only in this way, the organization can effectively grasp the opportunities, identify and deal with all kinds of risks.

2. Make the Managers Better-adapted

In organizational reform, as the decision-makers and the allocators of organizational resources, managers must know clearly that whether they have enough ability of decision-making, organizing and leadership to cope with the challenges of the future. Managers, therefore, not only need to adjust the style of leading and decision-making procedure to make the organization more flexible, but also need to reconstruct the relationships between the levels, between the work teams according to the requirements of the environmental changes to make the implementation of organizational reform more targeted and operable.

3. Make the Employees Better-adapted

The employees of organization have the most direct experience of organizational reform. Only if the organization makes employees fully understand the importance of change, and then change the staff's ideas, attitudes, behaviors and so on, can the organization get the employees' recognition, support and implementing of the measures of reform. But it is very difficult to change the employees' ideas, attitudes and behavior. In order to make the employees better-adapted, the organization has to continue the education and retraining of employees, attach great importance to the employees' participation in management, as well as renovate and update the organizational culture.

8.3.2　The Contents of Organizational Reform

Because the organization faces different environmental conditions, the contents and the emphasis of organizational reform are also different. The American management expert Harold J. Leavitt believes that the organization is a multi-variable system, and it includes at least three important variables: task, technology and structure. Therefore, the organizational reform also includes these three aspects:

1. The Reform of Task

The reform of task means the reform of running target and direction in an organization. The organizational structure of the organization will change accordingly when running target and direction of the organization are adjusted. There are many subordinate tasks in a complicated organization system, which are serving for the general assignment. These subordinate tasks are actually the specific work tasks and goals of each department and they are the important factors deciding institutions' setting at all levels.

2. The Reform of Technology

The reform of technology refers to redesign, modification and combination of the process and methods, including the replacement of mechanical equipment, using new techniques, new technology and new methods and so on. The technology factors of organizational system include equipment, buildings, work methods, new technology, new materials, new quality standards and new management control measures, etc. The reform of technology factors can indirectly promote the change of the organizational mission, or directly promote the improvement of organization's technology conditions and methods, thus affect the organizational personnel and organizational structure.

3. The Reform of Structure

It refers to the changes of the organizational power relations, coordination mechanism, the degree of centralization, the redesign of positions and jobs as well as the changes of other structural parameters. The tasks of a manager are to make decisions on a series of actions such as how to choose the organizational design mode, how to make the work plan, how to grant authority and the degree of authorization. In reality, the fixed structure designs are often not operable and need to be adjusted to the change of environment conditions, the managers should change some of these components flexibly according to actual condition.

第四节　组织变革的实施与管理

一、组织变革的过程

组织变革的一般过程：

（1）解冻阶段。这是改革前的心理准备阶段。本阶段的中心任务是改变员工原有的观念和态度，组织必须通过积极的引导，激励员工更新观念、接受改革并参与其中。

（2）变革阶段。这是变革过程中的行为转换阶段。此时组织已对变革做好了充分的准备，变革措施就此开始。组织要把激发起来的改革热情转化为改革的行为，关键是要能运用一些策略和技巧减少对变革的抵制，进一步调动员工参与变革的积极性，使变革成为全体员工的共同事业。

（3）再冻结阶段。这是变革后的行为强化阶段，其目的是通过对变革驱动力和约束力的平衡，使新的组织状态保持相对稳定。人的传统习惯、价值观念、行为模式、心理特征等都是在长期的社会生活中逐渐形成的，并非一次变革所能彻底改变的，因此，改革措施顺利实施后，还应采取种种手段对员工的心理状态、行为规范和行为方式等不断地巩固和强化；否则，稍遇挫折便会反复，使改革的成果无法巩固。

二、组织变革的程序

组织变革的基本程序：

（1）进行组织诊断，发现变革征兆。组织变革的第一步就是对现有的组织进行全面的诊断。这种诊断必须有针对性，要通过搜集资料，对组织的职能系统、工作流程系统、决策系统以及内在关系等进行全面的诊断。组织除了要从外部信息中发现对自有利或不利的因素之外，更主要的是要从各种内在征兆中找出导致组织或部门绩效差的具体原因，并确定需要进行整改的具体部门和人员。

（2）分析变革因素，制订改革方案。组织诊断任务完成之后，就要对组织变革的具体因素进行分析，如职能设置是否合理、决策中的分权程度如何、员工参与改革的积极性怎样、流程中的业务衔接是否紧密、各管理层级间或职能机构间的关系是否易于协调等。在此基础上制订几个可行的变革方案，以供选择。

（3）选择正确方案，实施变革计划。制订改革方案的任务完成之后，组织需要选择正确的改革方案，然后制订具体的改革计划并贯彻实施。推进改革的方式有多种，组织在选择具体方案时要充分考虑改革的深度和难度、改革的影响程度、变革速度以及员工的可接受程度和参与程度等，做到有计划、有步骤、有控制地进行，当改革出现某些偏差时要有各种纠偏措施及时纠正。

（4）评价变革效果，及时进行反馈。组织变革是一个包括众多复杂变量的转换过程，再好的改革计划也不能保证取得完全理想的效果。因此，变革结束之后，管理者必须对改革的结果进行总结和评价，及时反馈新的信息。对于没有取得理想效果的改革措施，应当给予必要的分析和评价，然后再做取舍。

三、组织变革的管理

1. 组织变革的阻力

组织在其变革当中，总会遭到部门和成员的抵制。从某种意义上说，这是积极的，有助于变革方案的优化。这些阻力主要来自个体、群体、组织与领导者三个方面。

（1）来自个体方面的阻力。变革的实施最终是要通过组织中的个体来完成，它必然要给个体带来影响，因而必然要遭到来自组织中的个体的阻力。主要包括：经济利益、安全、习惯、求稳心理、求全心理、保守心理以及对未知的恐惧等。

（2）来自群体方面的阻力。组织中的个人往往是组合群体，而组织变革会与群体原有的规范产生冲突，会威胁群体原有的关系，从而对组织变革产生阻力。主要包括群体规范冲突产生的阻力和人际关系变革产生的阻力。

（3）来自组织与领导者方面的阻力。一是结构惯性：组织有其固有的结构和机制来保持其稳定性，这种维持稳定组织的惯性，在组织变革时会在一定程度上形成阻碍变革的反作用力。二是变革范围的有限性：组织是由一系列相互依赖的子系统组成的，子系统中的有限变革很可能因为更大系统的问题而变得无效。三是对已有权力关系的威胁：组织变革常常涉及机构精简、权力的重新分配等，从而威胁到组织已有的权力关系。四是已有的资源分配问题：组织中控制一定数量资源的领导，常常视变革为威胁，他们担心变革会使自己控制的资源减少。

2. 组织变革阻力的排除

在组织变革中，要讲艺术性，积极创造条件，采取有效措施，消除阻力，以保证组织变革的顺利进行，消除的具体对策主要有：客观分析变革阻力与动力的强弱，采取有效措施增强支持因素，削弱反对因素，推动变革的深入进行；创新组织文化并使之渗透到每个员工的行为之中，使变革具有稳固的发展基础；创新策略方法与手段，使周密可行的变革方案由点到面地铺开，调动管理层变革的积极性，坚定人们变革成功的信心。

因此在变革前，应详细分析可能发生的各种问题，预先采取防范措施，从而为组织创造最佳的变革环境与气氛，当组织变革的大致方针确定以后，策略和艺术就成为保证变革成功的生命所在。

3. 组织变革的压力、冲突与管理

压力是指在动态的环境条件下个人面对种种机遇、规定以及追求的不确定性所形成的一种心理负担。压力可以带来正面的激励效果，也可以造成负面影响。压力往往与组织的各种规定、对目标的追求相关联，只有当目标结果具有不确定性和重要性时，组织中的潜在压力才会变成真实的压力。产生压力的原因有很多，概括起来有组织因素和个人因素两类。

并非所有的压力都是不良的。对组织而言，如何对待变革压力是很重要的，而如何减轻和消除不适的压力更为重要，因为这种压力不仅会危害身心健康、削弱工作能力，而且会降低组织绩效。对个体来说，积极处理压力的途径主要有减轻过重的压力感、适应工作变化、保持积极的工作态度、加强时间管理、处理好工作与生活的矛盾、加强锻炼、劳逸结合；而组织可以从识别、改变或消除压力源，减轻压力带来的不良后果等方面减轻压力的消极影响。

组织冲突是指组织内部成员之间、不同部门之间由于在工作方式、利益、性格、文化价值观等方面的不一致所导致的彼此相抵触、争执甚至攻击等行为。常见的组织冲突来源于组织目标不相容、资源相对稀缺、层级结构关系差异、信息沟通失真等。组织冲突会对组织造成很大的影响。研究表明，竞争是导致团体内部或团体之间发生冲突的最直接因素，组织变革的一个主要目标就是要在效率目标的前提下通过有效的竞争来降低组织的交易成本。因此，团体内部或团体之间的竞争是不可避免的，组织冲突可以说是这种竞争的一种表现形式。

无论是竞争胜利还是竞争失败，组织冲突都会存在两种截然不同的结果，即建设性冲突和破坏性冲突。所谓建设性冲突是指组织成员从组织利益角度出发，对组织中存在的不合理之处提出意见。它可以使组织中存在的不良功能和问题充分暴露出来，防止事态的进一步恶化，也可以促进不同组织交流和探讨自身弱点，有力地促进良性竞争。所谓破坏性冲突是指由于认识上的不一致、组织资源和利益分配方面的矛盾，员工发生相互抵触、争执甚至攻击等行为，从而导致组织效率下降，并最终影响到组织发展的冲突。它会造成组织资源的极大浪费和破坏，种种内耗影响员工的工作热情，导致组织凝聚力严重下降，从根本上妨碍组织任务的顺利完成。

组织冲突会在不同的层次上产生，如个体内部的心理冲突、组织内个人之间的冲突、各种不同部门之间的冲突等，而其中组织内的非正式组织与正式组织之间、直线与参谋之间以及委员会内部之间的冲突最为典型。

Section 4　The Implementation and Management of Organizational Reform

8.4.1　The Process of Organizational Reform

The general process of organizational reform:

(1) The thawing phase. This is the stage of psychological preparation before the reform. A central task of this stage is to change the employee's original ideas and attitudes. Organizations must motivate staff to update ideas, accept and take part in the reform through positive guidance.

(2) The revolutionary phase. This is the stage of behavior transforming in the process of change. After the organization has fully prepared for the reform, the changes begin. The key of turning the enthusiasm inspired into the behavior of reform is to be able to use some strategies and techniques to reduce the resistance to the reform, and further arouse the enthusiasm of employees to take part in the reform and make the reform become the career of the whole staff.

(3) The refreezing phase. This is the stage of behavior reinforcement after the reform. Its purpose is to make the new organizational state remain relatively stable through the balance of

driving force and binding force. Because people's habits, values, behavior patterns and psychological characteristics are gradually formed in long-term social life and cannot be changed by a reform, therefore the managers should also take a variety of measures to consolidate and strengthen the employees' mental state, behavior norms and behaviors constantly after the reform was implemented smoothly. Otherwise, the reform results cannot be consolidated due to a slip-up.

8.4.2 The Procedure of Organizational Reform

The basic procedure of organizational reform:

（1）Making the structure diagnosis and finding signs for reform. The first step of organizational reform is to conduct a comprehensive judgement for the existing organization. This diagnosis must be a comprehensive diagnosis that targets at the functional system of the organization, work procedure system, decision-making system and internal relations, etc., made through the way of data collection. Besides finding out the advantageous or disadvantageous factors from the external information, what is more important for an organization is to find out the specific cause of the poor performance of the organization or the department from various of internal signs, and decide the specific departments and personnel that need to be improved.

（2）Analyzing the revolutionary factors, and making the revolutionary plan. After the task of structure diagnosis is completed, the organization needs to analyze the specific factors of organizational reform, such as whether the function is set reasonably, what separated degree should be, how is the enthusiasm of employees to participate in the reform, whether the process of business is closely linked, whether the relations of the management level or functional institutions are easy to coordinate, etc. On this basis, making a few feasible reform schemes from which managers can choose.

（3）Choosing the right scheme and implementing the reform plan. After the completion of making the reform schemes, the organization needs to select a correct one, and then formulate a specific reform plan and implement it. There are multiple ways of reform, the organization should fully consider the depth and difficulties of reform, the degree of influence of reform, the speed of change and acceptable and participating degree of employees and so on when choosing concrete plans to reform. Do it step by step and make it under control. When there are some deviations in the reform, managers need to correct it with corrective measures timely.

（4）Evaluating the efficacy of reform, and giving feedback timely. Organizational reform is a transformation process including many complex variables, so a good plan cannot guarantee to completely achieve the ideal effect. After reform, therefore, managers must summarize and evaluate the results of reform, feedback the new information in time. For the reform measures that cannot obtain the expected effect, necessary analysis and evaluation should be done to decide remain it or not.

8. 4. 3　Management of Organizational Reform

1. The Resistance of Organizational Reform

The organizational reform is always rejected by departments and some members. In a sense, this is positive, and will lead to optimization of the scheme. The resistance mainly comes from three aspects: individual, group, organization and leaders.

(1) The resistance from the individual. The implementation of reform is ultimately to be done through individuals in the organization, and it is bound to affect the individuals, therefore it has to face the resistance from individuals in the organization. It mainly includes: economic interests, security, habits, stable mentality, defending mentality, conservative mentality and the fear of the unknown.

(2) The resistance from the group. The individuals in the organization often act as the combination group, and organizational reform will conflict with the original specification of the group, threaten the original relations of the group, so as to produce resistance to organizational reform. The conflict mainly includes the resistance produced by the conflict of group norms and the resistance produced by the change of interpersonal relationship.

(3) The resistance from the organization and leaders. The first one is structural inertia. The organization has its inherent structure and mechanism to maintain its stability. When organizational reform occurs, inertia that can keep the organization stable will form counterforce to change in some extent. The second one is the limitations of reform range. The organization is composed of a series of interdependent subsystems, and the limited change in the subsystem is likely to become invalid because of the larger systemic problem. The third one is the threat to the relationship between the existing powers. The organizational reform often involves the streamline, the redistribution of power and so on, which affects and threatens the relationship between the existing powers. The forth one is the problem of the allocation of existing resources. The departments that control a certain number of resources, often treat the reform as a threat, they worry that the reform will reduce the resources controlled by them.

2. The Removal of the Resistance of Organizational Reform

In the organizational reform, the managers should lay stress on artistry, create the condition actively and take effective measures to eliminate the resistance and ensure the smooth progress of the organizational reform. The countermeasures mainly include: Analyzing the strength of the resistance to reform and the motive power of reform objectively, then taking effective measures to strengthen the supporting factors, weakening negative factors to guarantee the running of reform. Innovating the organizational culture and making it penetrate into each employee's behavior, so that the solid developmental foundation of reform can be set. Innovating strategy and means, making the feasible scheme of reform to spread out, arousing the enthusiasm of reform of management, and strengthening people's faith in the success of reform.

Before the change, therefore, managers should analyze all kinds of possible problems specifically. Take precautions beforehand, so that the best environment and atmosphere of reform for an organization can be created. After the policy of organizational reform is roughly confirmed, strategy and artistry have become the key to ensure a successful reform.

3. Stress, Conflict and Management of Organizational Reform

Stress refers to the psychological burden formed when the individual faces opportunities, rules and the uncertainty of the pursuit in the dynamic environment. Stress can have a positive incentive effect, and also can have a negative impact. Pressure is often closely related to various provisions of the organization, the pursuit of goals. Only when the results of target are uncertain and important, will the potential pressure of the organization become true. There are many causes of stress, in summary, they are organizational factors and personal factors.

Not all stress is harmful. For an organization, how to deal with revolutionary pressure is very important, and how to reduce and eliminate the uncomfortable pressure is more important, because this kind of pressure will not only do harm to the mental and physical health, weaken work ability, but also can reduce the organization's performance. For individuals, the positive ways to handle stress mainly include relieving the pressure, adapting to the changes of work, maintaining a positive attitude towards work, strengthening time management, dealing with the contradiction between work and life, strengthening exercise, combining exertion and rest. And organizations can reduce the negative effects of stress through recognizing, changing or eliminating stress source, minimizing the bad consequences of stress and so on.

Organizational conflict refers to the contradiction, arguments and even attacking behavior existing in the members of the organization or different departments due to differences in manner of working, interests, personality and cultural values. Common organizational conflicts come from the incompatible goals of the organization, the relatively scarce resources, the differences between the hierarchical relationships, the distortion on information communication and so on. Organizational conflict will have a big impact on the organization. Research shows that the competition is the most direct cause of conflicts within the team or between the groups. One of the major goals of organizational reform is to reduce the transaction costs of the organization through the effective competition under the premise of efficiency aim. Therefore, the competition within the team or between the groups is inevitable, organizational conflict can be treated as a manifestation of this competition.

Whether wins or be defeated, there will be two completely different results of organizational conflict, one is constructive conflict and the other is destructive conflict. In a constructive conflict, the members of the organization point out the faultiness and put forward the suggestion for the benefit of group interests. It can make the poor functions and problems of an organization fully exposed, to prevent the situation from worsening, also can promote the communication of different organizations and the discussion of their own weakness. In a word, it is beneficial to healthy competition. Destructive conflict refers to the competing, disputes and even attacking behavior of employees because of different understandings, the conflict of organizational resources and the distribution of interests lead to the drop of organizational efficiency, and ultimately affect the organizational development. It can cause enormous waste and destruction of organizational resources, the terrible influence of staff's working enthusiasm, leads to serious decrease of organizational cohesive force and fundamentally hinders the smooth completion of organizational task.

Organizational conflict may happen on different hierarchical levels, such as the psychological conflict of individuals, the conflict between individuals in organizations, the conflict between various departments, etc., of which the most typical ones are the conflict between the formal organization and informal organization within the organization, and between lines and advisers as well as the conflict of the internal committee.

【阅读资料】

组织冲突的类型

（1）正式组织与非正式组织之间的冲突。

这种冲突主要源于两者成员交叉混合，感性因素、非理性因素的作用，会对正式组织的工作产生负面影响，特别是在强调竞争的情况下，非正式组织可能会因为竞争成员间的不和而抵制竞争。非正式组织还要求成员行动保持一致，这不仅会束缚成员的个人发展，使个人才智受到压抑，而且影响组织工作的效率，严重时还可能演化成组织变革的一种反对势力。

（2）直线与参谋之间的冲突。

直线关系是一种指挥和命令的关系，具有决策和行动的权力，而参谋关系则应当是一种服务和协调关系，具有思考、筹划和建议的权力。实践中，保证命令的统一性往往会忽视参谋发挥的作用，参谋作用发挥失当，又会破坏统一指挥的原则。这将使直线和参谋有可能相互指责、推诿，导致组织缺乏效率。

（3）委员会内部之间的冲突。

委员会是集体工作的一种形式，委员代表了不同的利益集团、部门、个人的行为目标。在资源一定的条件下，成员之间的利益很难取得一致。一旦某个利益代表未能得到支持，他将会被动执行或拒绝执行委员会的统一行动，导致组织效率的下降；而委员会充分考虑各方利益所达成的各方势力妥协、折中的结果，势必会影响决策的质量和效率。

第五节 组织变革的途径

一、组织变革的趋势

动态性和灵活性将成为组织未来发展的主要趋势。因为未来的组织面对的将是一个比现在更为复杂多变的环境，组织只能以变应变，只有主动应变，才能求得生存和发展，如果组织不能保持相应的动态性和灵活性，是不可能适应未来的环境的。

组织变革的总趋势有以下几个方面：

1. 扁平化

组织结构的扁平化是管理层次的减少和管理幅度的扩大。扁平化的结果是现代组织在规模一定的情况下，往往采取扁平的组织结构，它与传统的高耸型组织结构不同。高耸型的组织结构管理幅度较小，管理层次较多，也就是传统所谓的"金字塔"式的结构。

2. 柔性化

组织结构的柔性化，是指在组织结构中不设置固定的和正式的组织机构，而代之以一些临时的以任务为导向的团队式组织。柔性化突破了传统层级制组织等级分明、层级较多和官僚主义等缺陷，从而能够增强组织对环境动态变化的适应能力。柔性化的组织是以组织结构的灵活性和可塑性为基础的。在组织内部，它能够不断地对其拥有的人力资源进行灵活地调配，组建各种跨业务单位的内部联系网络。在组织外部，则表现为企业同外部其他企业建立起的战略联盟，联盟组织之间通过优势互补，创造竞争优势。

3. 分立化

分立化是在产权关系上对组织进行的变革，公司分立化是指从一个大公司里分离出几个小的公司，总公司以一种市场关系来联结总部与所属各个分公司和子公司之间的关系，总部对所分立的各个分公司和子公司通过股权投资和股东管理等手段进行控制，从而把公司部门与下属单位之间内部型的上下级关系变为类似外部型的公司与公司之间的关系。分公司是母公司的分支机构，但在法律上和经济上均无独立性；子公司是受集团公司或母公司控制但在法律上独立的法人企业，母公司通过股权对子公司的经营方向和主要负责人的任免进行控制。分公司和子公司集中在母公司周围，共同构成企业集团的紧密层组织。

4. 网络化

现代网络技术对组织结构变革的直接影响是网络化。在组织内部，通过网络技术对组织结构进行重新构造，突破了传统层级制组织结构的纵向一体化的特点，组建了由小型、自主和创新的经营单元构成的以横向一体化为特征的网络化组织形式。网络化在组织结构方面最显著的变化是大量裁员、精简机构。在组织外部，通过联合与兼并组成企业集团，各种企业集团和经济联合体以网络制的形式把若干命运休戚相关的企业紧密联结在一起。

5. 虚拟化

虚拟化是组织网络化的极端形式。虚拟化使组织的边界变得模糊，出现了所谓的"空壳组织"，即由于组织内部的高度网络化，使企业组织把尽可能多的实体转变成数字信息，减少实体空间，而更多地依赖电子空间，最终使企业组织本身成为"主壳型组织"。虚拟化的另一种表现是组织之间虚拟的联盟关系。与传统的联盟关系相比较，它更多地表现出短暂性和临时性的特点，往往是由于一个特定的市场机会、一个特定的业务项目使得不同的企业之间建立起合作。

二、组织变革的途径

组织变革和创新有两个主要途径：一是从组织内部着手，通过企业再造、团队建设、组织学习等来完成；二是从改变与其他企业之间的关系着手，通过如前所述的网络化和虚拟化来实现。网络化和虚拟化就目前来说，主要表现在外包生产、精益生产、新的战略联盟和虚拟运作等。

（一）企业再造

1. 企业再造的含义

企业再造是对企业业务流程进行根本的再思考和彻底的再设计，以显著提高企业的效率。企业再造是企业内部的一场革命，企业再造的对象是企业流程。企业的流程是指完成某一目标或任务而进行的一系列跨越时间和空间的相关活动的有序集合。

所谓根本性再思考，是指企业流程再造并不限于考虑如何改进现有机制，而是对现有机制批判性地吸收和革命性地创新。所谓彻底性再设计，不是指表面改进或小修小改现有的系统，而是以提高顾客满意度为主要方向，从根本上抛弃旧的运行机制，重新设计组织结构和运行机制。

企业组织是由目标、技术、制度和活动四个要素构成的整体。企业再造以企业运作的基础流程为对象，把被职能单位割裂开来的活动进行整合，使流程完整，并对有关制度进行相应的调整，以确保流程能更好地运作。活动是构成流程的最基本单位，原本一个人完成的活动交由不同的人去执行，就形成一个流程。企业再造就是对活动流程进行再设计，即对活动进行重新安排，包括活动的内容、顺序、实现方式和活动的承担者。

2. 企业再造的原则

一般来讲，企业再造的原则有：横向集成活动，实行团队工作方式；纵向压缩组织，使组织扁平化；推行并行工程；应用信息技术。

（1）横向集成活动：对活动的整合、分散和废除。

企业再造的一个原则是通过横向集成活动，对活动进行整合、分散和废除。活动的整合就是对复杂的流程进行活动归并，使复杂流程简单化，从而提高流程运作的整体效率。活动的分散与活动的整合相反，它通过将某一专业职能工作分散到相关专业中，并取消原有专业活动，来提高流程效率。活动的废除，即尽可能精简企业流程中不创造价值的活动，而将企业集中到创造价值的活动上来。

（2）纵向压缩组织：活动承担者充分授权。

企业再造在组织结构方面，需要减少管理层次，建立扁平化的组织结构。组织结构必然随着运行机制的变化而变化，包括运行流程、约束机制和激励机制。

（3）推行并行工程：改变活动的顺序。

推行并行工程，旨在突破活动间的关系。改变活动的顺序，将串行的活动变成并行的活动，从而提高流程的运作效率。

（4）应用信息技术：活动方式的突破。

信息技术为企业再造提供了强有力的手段。信息技术突破了活动的实现方式。企业再造是一项系统工程，它是人力、技术和组织的重新组合，是社会技术系统的重新设计。信息技术可以协调分散与集中的矛盾，它可以使统一过程中活动之间的连接方式发生变化，使各个活动并行执行。创造性地利用信息技术是企业流程再造的关键之一。

3. 企业再造的变化

企业再造给企业组织带来了以下变化：组织结构的变化；企业流程及其运行方式的变化；企业管理观念的变化。

4. 企业再造的过程

（1）组织与发动阶段：一是组建再造队伍。企业再造的关键一步就是选择并组建再造队伍。领导者、流程负责人、再造团队、指导委员会、再造总监，是进行再造的五种角色。二是企业再造的发动。如树立危机意识、勾画公司远景等，既要有危机感，又要有明确的方向。

（2）识别与选择阶段：流程识别——企业流程有特定的输入和输出，其跨部门而且与顾客及其需要相关，要对流程做出界定和识别。流程选择——企业应选择那些问题严重、功能失调、举足轻重、影响巨大、切实可行、便于操作的流程来进行再造。

（3）创新与设计阶段：这是一项创造性的工作。其主要策略有：废除，对于产品增值无效的环节要予以彻底废除；合并，把分散在不同部门、由多人完成的几项活动进行必要的整合；分散，把一些独立的活动进行分散并将其融入系统，这可以减少流程，提高效率；改变，通过改变活动间的顺序和逻辑关系以重新设计流程；自动化，在流程再造中更为有效地采用信息技术。

（4）实施与运转阶段：一是进行新流程的试运转；二是克服新流程实施的阻力；三是培养复合型人才。

（二）构建学习型组织

从 20 世纪 80 年代开始，在企业界和管理界，出现了推广和研究学习型组织的热潮，并逐渐风靡全球。美国的杜邦、英特尔、苹果、联邦快递等世界一流企业，纷纷建立学习型组织。初步统计，美国排名前 25 名的企业中，已有 20 家按照学习型组织的模式改造自己。已经成为时代标志的著名的微软公司，其成功的秘诀就是着力建设学习型组织。在我国，建立学习型组织也是管理界和企业界共同认识和关注的热点。

1. 学习型组织理论概述

（1）从个人学习到学习型组织。

学习有三个层次，首先是个人学习，其次是组织学习，最后是学习型组织。对个人学习而言，主要是指认知学习、技能学习和情感学习，而组织学习是将组织作为学习的主体看待的。适应性学习和创造性学习是组织学习的两个阶段，对应而言，学习型组织是一种组织管理模式，组织学习是一个组织成为学习型组织的必要条件。

（2）知识视野的学习型组织。

在知识经济时代，工作的性质是以知识和学习为标志的，学习型组织充分体现了知识经济时代对组织管理模式变化的要求。传统方式的组织与学习型组织有非常明显的不同之处：①传统的基于命令—执行的工作方式：在投入阶段，利用各种资源，以下达命令为具体活动内容；在中间阶段，工作形式是生产经营过程，以执行命令为具体活动方式；在产出阶段，工作形式主要转向商品和服务，活动形式是完成命令。②知识经济时代的知识流动及工作方式：知识类型分为环境知识、公司知识和内部知识。环境知识包括市场情报、技术、政治因素、供应商关系、客户关系，由环境流向组织；公司知识包括声望、品牌形象、广告和促销等，由组织流向环境；内部知识包括公司文化、风气、数据、雇员等，由组织流向组织。

从以上对比可以看出，在知识经济时代，知识经济的企业是以上述第二种情形中的三个知识流动来促使企业运作的。从知识角度理解学习型组织，组织学习包括知识的获得（技能、观察力、关系的发展创造）、共享（知识的传播）和利用（如何使知识产生效益）三个阶段。

（3）圣吉对学习型组织的研究。

麻省理工学院教授圣吉是从另一个角度论述学习型组织的，他认为：学习型组织不在于描述组织如何获得和利用知识，而在于告诉人们如何才能塑造一个学习型组织。他说："学习型组织的战略目标是提高学习的速度、能力和才能，通过建立愿景和能够发现、尝试和改进组织的思维模式并因此而改变它们的行为，这才是最成功的学习型组织。"圣吉提出了建立学习型组织的"五项修炼"模型：

自我超越（personal mastery）：能够不断理清个人的真实愿望，集中精力和培养耐心，实现自我超越。

改善心智模式（improving mental models）：心智模式是看待旧事物形成的特定的思维定式。在知识经济时代，这会影响对待新事物的观点。

建立共同愿景（building shared vision）：共同愿景就是组织中人们所共同持有的愿望，简单地说，就是我们想要创造什么。

团队学习（team learning）：是发展成员整体配合与实现共同目标的能力的过程。

系统思考（system thinking）：要求人们用系统的观点对待组织的发展。

根据上述内容可知，学习型组织具有五个特征：有一个人人赞同的共同构想；在工作中抛弃旧的思维方式和常规程序；作为相互关系系统的一部分，成员对所有的组织过程、活动、功能和环境的相互作用进行思考；人们之间坦率地相互沟通；人们抛弃个人利益和部门利益，为实现组织的共同构想一起工作。所谓学习型组织，就是充分发挥每个员工的创造性的能力，努力形成一种弥漫于群体与组织的学习气氛，凭借着学习，个体价值得到体现，组织绩效得以大幅度提高。

（4）实现学习和工作的组合。

工业时代的许多组织不能称为学习型组织，是因为存在两种分离：从组织角度看，工作与学习分离；从个人角度看，是工作与知识分离。前者导致组织绩效中没有学习带来的改善，后者则妨碍了个人成长。而整合学习、工作与知识的方法，就是创建学习型组织。在成熟的学习型组织中，学习和工作是融为一体的，员工要成为学习型组织的一员，而管理者则要千方百计地提高组织的学习能力。这一方面要求有高素质、自我超越的员工，另一方面在于管理者的认识。

2. 激活学习型组织的细胞

（1）"自我超越的人"的假设。

员工是组织的细胞，如何看待员工，即对人性有何种假设，是进一步讨论的出发点，同时"激活组织细胞"也是建立学习型组织的关键。

理性经济人：人的一切行为都是为了最大限度地满足自己的利益，人是由经济诱因引发工作动机的，人的行为通常是合乎理性、精打细算的。

X 理论：人性是懒惰的、缺乏雄心、没有责任感，以自我为中心，反对改革。

Y 理论：基本上与 X 理论相反，认为激发人的潜力和责任心是管理者的工作。

超 Y 理论：人的需求和动机是不同的，因此在管理上就不存在对一切人都适用的人性假设。

学习型组织的人性观：理性经济人、X 理论的经济人、Y 理论的社会人以及超 Y 理论的复杂人，反映了对人性认识的不断深化。在学习型组织中，人被看作不断成长的人。

（2）自我超越的修炼。

个人美梦通过组织才能实现，组织的发展必须以个人发展为基础。在学习型组织中，个人的自我超越是必不可少的条件，而只有在学习型组织中才有自我超越的环境。

组织中个体的自我超越需要把握以下几个方面：①建立个人愿景：一种期望的未来景象或愿望。②保持创造性张力：愿景与现实的差距是创造力的源泉。③看清结构性冲突：愿景和现实的差距带给人们心理影响，即人性的意志力能否战胜阻力。④诚实地面对真相：要义是根除看清真实状况的障碍。⑤运用潜意识：使内心真正关注的目标清晰地展现在人们的脑海中。

（3）管理者与员工关系的新格局。

将员工视为自我超越的个体，意味着员工和企业的关系发生了根本的变化。自我超越这项修炼，使得员工成为积极主动的具有创造性的知识工作者，不仅被赋予权力，而且直接获得工作的内在热情。

3. 构建学习型组织的团队

（1）工作群体和团队。

团队是从工作群体发展起来的，是学习型组织的基本工作单位和学习单位。团队学习在学习型组织中的作用体现在：是学习型组织的基本构建单位，是学习型组织的基本学习方式，是构建学习型组织的基本过程。从另一个角度看，学习型组织是团队思想的一种引申，或者说它是以团队运行为基石的。

团队的形成：工作群体的形成—震荡阶段—规范化—修整。

团队的绩效：有效的自我管理团队具有比工作群体更高的绩效，这为许多企业所证实。

（2）团队学习的方式。

信息交换会议：是团队通常采用的学习方式。

特别会议制度：是对信息交换会议的有效改造。

深度会谈和讨论：是团队学习的两项基本技术。在此列出典型的中国会议方式，它和团队学习精神差别很大。

团队学习的过程可以描述为：事件带来混乱—面对冲突的根源—大容器中探询—激发共同创造力。

（3）团队学习与群体决策技术的比较。

群体决策的若干方法：

脑力风暴法：创造一种进行决策的程序，克服互动群体中妨碍创造性方案的从众压力。

名义群体法：在决策过程中，对群体成员的讨论或沟通加以限制。

德尔菲法：除不需要群体成员见面外，与名义群体法相似。

电子会议法：借助计算机技术发展起来的一种群体决策技术。

团体学习与群体决策技术相比具有本质上的进步性，表现在：团体学习可以提炼出高于个人的团体智力；可以促使组织在具有创造性的同时又产生协调一致的行动；成果随着成员扩散到其他团体中去，进而在组织中形成学习的气氛。

（4）团队学习的典范——微软。

分析微软的经验，可以对团队的学习形成更加直接的认识。从微软的"事后共同分析""过程审计""休假会"中，可以看出这些团队学习设计都符合悬念假设，参加者互相视为工作伙伴，有一个好的"过程顾问"。此外，博览会议、自带食物午餐会等提供了员工之间面对面的交流方式。

4. 检视学习型组织的心智

（1）组织的心智模式。

心智模式指那些深深固结于人们心中，影响人们如何认识周围世界，以及如何采取行动的许多假设和印象。心智模式影响人们看待问题和采取行动。在组织中，心智模式具有多方面的体现。组织行为理论认为，组织中也存在拟人化的集体思维或组织的心智模式。组织的心智模式的主要特点是：一方面它是个人心智模式；另一方面它存在于群体之中，影响着群体的成员。

（2）检视组织的心智模式。

检视组织的心智模式，是完善组织心智模式的重要基础。例如，检视就是要把隐藏在企业重要问题背后的假设找出来。应该认识到，检视具有难度，因为这种假设是牢牢地植根于组织背后的，反过来又影响着组织的成员。

检视的技术：促进观点多元化，培养探询和辩护的精神。

检视心智模式的工作机制：内部董事会（由 2 ~ 3 名资深经理组成，可以在各个组织层次产生）；改进企划工作（现在的企划工作是建立在旧的心智模式之上的，遵循新的心智模式建立企划工作，如"情景企划"等）。

一般经过多年发展已经占领统治地位的大企业，常常会滋生一种特有的思维模式：3C模式，即自满（complacency）、保守（conservatism）、自大（conceit）。由于 3C 模式的存在，企业的心智模式大大强化，心智模式得以改善的途径被割断，企业的发展将会遇到难题。因此，从心智模式的角度分析大公司病，就成为一个新的视角。检视心智模式对于企业的长期发展至关重要，而知识经济时代要求我们把检视心智模式提到更高的层次加以认识，从一定意义上讲，知识经济时代就是加速检视心智模式的新时代。

5. 确定学习型组织的共同愿景

（1）共同愿景及其描述。

建立共同愿景是学习型组织的一项修炼，共同愿景对于企业的转型和维持现状都有重要的意义。共同愿景的简单说法就是："我们想要创造什么?"它是组织中人们共同持有的愿望，它创造出众人一体的感觉，并遍布组织活动的全部，使组织的各种不同的活动融为一体。共同愿景的培养要有一个过程。

共同愿景的描述：根据奋斗目标描述愿景；依据"共同敌人"描述愿景；依据"角色榜样"描述愿景；依据内部转型的构想描述愿景。

（2）建立共同愿景的意义。

没有共同愿景，就没有学习型组织。无论是转型企业还是维持现状型企业，共同愿景都起着重要的作用。

转型企业的愿景分析：产生急迫感；识别和讨论危机和机遇；建立强有力的领导联盟；群体成员协同作战，发挥高阶层的核心作用；构建愿景规划，设计实现愿望的战略；沟通愿景规划；授权他人实施愿景规划；计划并实现短期目标；巩固已有成果，深化改革；使新的工作制度化。

维持现状企业的愿望分析：斯坦福大学的教授们，通过观察许多企业的成长情况，得出结论——当前核心价值和长远愿景规划的统一是维持现状企业愿景的核心。

（3）共同愿景的修炼。

鼓励个人愿望：通过会聚个人愿望，共同愿望才能获得能量。必须不断地鼓励成员发展自己的个人愿望，然后把拥有强烈目标感的成员结合起来，可以创造强大的综合效果。

改进高层做法：抛弃原有的从高层开始的做法，要从告知、推销、测试、协商和共同创造五个阶段，建立组织的共同愿望。

学习聆听他人：善于建立共同愿望的管理者，需要在日常工作中谈论这个过程，并与日常生活联系在一起，这样突出的特点就是具有互动性。

融入企业理念：建立共同愿望是企业基本理念的一项，其他理念还包括：目的、使命、价值观。企业的基本理念要回答三个基本问题：追寻什么、为何追寻、如何追寻。追寻什么：一个大家共同创造的未来景象；为何追寻：企业的目标和使命，组织存在的根源；如何追寻：在达成愿望的过程中，核心价值观是一切行动、任务的最高依据和准则。

（4）共同愿景夭折的原因。

缺乏协调的能力；创造性张力消失；专注的时间不够；对新的愿景产生分歧。

6. 把握学习型组织的核心

（1）系统思考的管理观念。

锻炼系统思考工作是创造学习型组织的核心。系统本质上是处于一定的相互关系中并与环境发生关系的各组成部分（要素）的总体（集）。概括地讲，系统思考的管理观念是指管理主体自觉地运用系统理论和系统方法，对管理要素、管理组织、管理过程进行系统分析，旨在优化管理的整体功能，取得较好的管理效果。

（2）学习型组织的系统思考。

学习型组织系统思考的基础是系统动力学。系统动力学强调的是相互作用，作为系统动力学研究对象的社会经济系统本身处于千变万化的运动过程中，其构成要素（生产力、人力、物力、财力、技术等）都表现出系统动力学的相互作用的本质。

学习型组织系统思考的层次有三个：①事件层次的思考：采取反应式的行为，结果是专注于个别的事件、局限思考、归罪于外等；②行为变化层次的思考：能顺应变动中的趋势，但容易造成学习障碍，如从经验中学习等；③系统结构层次的思考：能改造行为的变化形态，超越了事件层次和行为层次的局限，专注于解释是什么造成行为变化的形态。例如：对于集制造和销售于一体的企业，系统结构层次的思考必须显示出发出的订单、出货、库存如何变动，从互动中寻找货物不稳定与扩大的效应。由结构触及行为背后的原因，进而进行行为改造。

（3）学习型组织系统思考的工具。

学习型组织系统思考的要义就是看清复杂事物背后结构的形态。由于这种形态结构一再出现，圣吉给出了它们的基本模型，称为系统基模。不断增强的反馈、反复调节的反馈、时间的滞延是系统基模三个主要方面。不断增强的反馈是成长的引擎，包括经常听到的词语，如滚雪球效应、连锁反应、恶性循环。反复调节的反馈是系统追求稳定和平衡的一种力量，一个调节的系统会自我修正，以维持这种状态。时间的滞延是行动和结果的时间差。学习型组织系统思考就是这样一个过程，是通过增加循环、调节循环与时间的滞延进行的。圣吉根据这些基本的过程，建立了反应迟缓的调节环路、舍本逐末、目标侵蚀、恶性竞争、成长上限、共同悲剧等模型。

（4）系统思考在学习型组织中的作用。

系统思考的核心作用：①系统思考和自我超越的修炼：用系统思考的语言和方式指导自我超越的修炼，在系统思考的指引下，个人修炼将彰显自我超越的几个方面，如对环境的认同感、对整体的使命感。②系统思考与团队学习：系统思考的工具对于团队学习是至关重要的。在团队学习中，要让讨论和深度会谈持续下去，必须克服许多障碍。系统思考的方法帮助我们从组织发展的整体认识出现障碍的原因，从而跳出个人的圈子。③系统思考与改善心智模式：管理者必须学习如何反思他们现有的心智模式，直到习以为常地假设公开接受检验。根深蒂固的心智模式将阻碍系统思考的产生，反过来，系统思考对于有效改进心智模式至关重要。④系统思考与建立共同愿望：系统思考是建立共同愿望的沃土。共同愿望描述的是未来的状况，而系统思考则揭示了通向未来的必经之路。有了系统思考，组织中的人们可以清楚地了解现有的政策和行为如何创造或改变现状，找到启动现实的杠杆，信心的来源就建立起来了，适合建立共同愿望的沃土就开发出来了。

（5）学习型组织的整合。

个人的自我超越是整个学习型组织的基础。它为学习型组织提供了宝贵的人力资源，团队的学习都依赖于个人的努力，比如改进心智模式、建立共同愿望、系统思考等。

团队学习是一种组织内部的学习，团队学习既是团队的活动内容，同时又是检视心智模式、建立共同愿望的载体和手段。

检视心智模式和建立共同愿望，从时间上看，前者针对业已形成的"组织记忆"，是组织从记忆中学习的体现，后者则是对未来生动的描述，对组织的成长起牵动作用。

系统思考是学习型组织的灵魂。它提供了一种完善的思维方式，个人学习、团体学习、检视心智模式、建立愿望，都因为系统思考的存在而连在一起，共同达到组织的目标。

7. 描摹学习型组织的结构

（1）学习型组织结构的演进。

组织的行为和组织的结构是组织的统一体，学习型组织不同于以往的横向或纵向的组织结构。典型的学习型组织表现为网状结构、以地方为主的扁平结构，且在实践中不断变化，将运作和学习融为一体。

基本的组织结构：纵向层级的结构（职能式、事业部式、矩阵式结构）。在横向联系上取得突破的是矩阵式结构，但是，矩阵式结构并没有从本质上改变权力支配的作用，许多公司发现，矩阵结构的建立和维持很困难。

学习型组织的网状结构：学习型组织对组织结构的突破就是雇员为公司战略做出以往不能达到的贡献，组织的网状结构中的不同部分在独立地调整和变革的同时，也在为组织的整体使命做出贡献。

（2）以地方为主的扁平式结构。

以地方为主是学习型组织网状结构的主要特点。学习型组织日益成为以地方为主的扁平式组织，这种组织会尽最大可能将决策权延至离高层最远的地方。"以地方为主"的意思是：决策权往组织结构的下层移动，尽可能地让当地决策者面对所有的课题。

采取以地方为主的网络结构是知识经济对组织结构的本质要求。因为当我们对自己的行动有真正的责任感时，学习的速度最快。在知识经济时代，知识就是一种主要资源，知识的分布影响着组织结构。以地方为主的扁平式结构代表着组织结构的方向。与此对应，一些官僚色彩浓厚、"高耸"型的传统结构目前都遇到了一些困难。例如，美国的 GE 具有光荣的历史，但是从 20 世纪 70 年代以来，陷入了困境，GE 总裁韦尔齐认为 GE 的突破点就是组织结构变革，主要包括三个方面的内容：精简（削减比例达 30%）、扁平化（等级层次平均减少 4 个）、有弹性（适应外部变化、有弹性的灵活组织）。GE 恢复生机，而韦尔齐本人也被称为"管理奇才"。

以地方为主的扁平化结构，对传统的领导观念是个极大的冲击。这是因为，在知识经济时代，首先，变革仅从高层领导开始，组织很难发生实质性的变革；其次，没有员工参与的领导行为，造成只有服从而没有参与；再次，高层的判断经常失败。而在未来的学习型组织中，将会出现自上而下、自下而上、平行交流的全方位变革模式，最终目的就是形成平等交流的网络。

（3）不断变动的有机结构。

创建学习型组织是要比竞争对手学习得更好、变化得更快。然而组织问题的根本解决方式就是学习型组织能够形成不断变动的有机结构。不断变动包括：变化、稳定；集权、分权；单一性和多样性等一系列倾向相反，同时又能保持连贯的内聚作用。

对不断变动的必要性的描述，虽然着力点不同，但是主要特点都是寻找两个不同方向（全球化与地区化、稳定与变化、集权与分权、常规与创造等）之间微妙的平衡。这些不同方向的管理观点本身并没有绝对的好与坏，问题就在于它们与什么样的环境相匹配，同时是否超过了必要的限度。总之，学习型组织的有效管理，表明组织始终是在寻找最佳效益状态的微妙平衡。

（4）运作与学习融为一体。

与以往所有的组织形态不同的是，学习型组织代表着一种随时间、环境而不断变化的形态。学习型组织体现为一个过程，一旦过程的动态特征消失，学习型组织将演变为一个僵硬的"运作型组织"。学习型组织意味着变化正在进行着。因此要防范学习型组织转向"运作型组织"。在知识经济时代，由于环境的急剧变化，组织必须及时调整结构，因为昨天的成功不能预示明天继续成功。

8. 探索学习型组织的活力

（1）组织活力的直观验证。

学习型组织受到人们关注的主要原因就是它本身具有活力。从员工和组织的关系来看，创建学习型组织就是提高员工与组织相互忠诚度的过程。从组织适应社会环境的角度来看，学习型组织强调将组织与周围的关系看成一个系统。这些极大地提高了学习型组织的活力。

学习型组织能够带来活力的主要原因就是学习曲线。学习曲线就是随着累计产量的提高单位成本下降的趋势。出现学习曲线的主要原因有：劳动技能不断提高、管理者发现更好的制造方法、设计方法简化、引进新的制造技术等。实际上，学习型组织中有许多学习以及由此得来的改进，它们是每时每刻都在发生的。

（2）对学习型组织的经济分析。

学习型组织与较高的经济绩效相联系，从直观上看，是因为学习曲线的存在。但是，只有在学习型组织中，这种获利相比较传统企业才越发明显。学习型组织的获利体现在：从降低成本中获利，从灵活性上获利。相应地，学习型组织中，不断改进的变化是没有成本的。传统的观点认为，学习型组织必然存在成本（时间延长、培训费用等），事实上因为学习和问题的解决是生产运作过程中不可分割的一部分，改进是连续的、生产力持续提高。如果学习型组织以生产为中心而停止考虑改进，才会产生巨大的成本。例如：员工的建议很快得到反馈、评价和实施，使得节约成本等。

（3）新的测评办法。

学习型组织的创建和发展，要求对新的绩效测评体系做出修正。一种新的把学习和创新列入测评体系的平衡计分测评法，就是针对学习型组织的。平衡计分测评法从四个方面来观察企业，它向经理们提出四个问题：顾客如何看我们（顾客角度）？我们必须擅长什么（内部角度）？我们能否继续提高并创造价值（创新和学习角度）？我们怎样满足股东（财务角度）？从创新和学习角度进行测评，要求经理们在一段时间内有所改进，而不能躺在荣誉上睡觉！

9．拓展学习型组织的空间

（1）企业内部层次的创建。

虽然组织的规模不同，但是都可以向学习型组织迈进。甚至有人说，我们的社会是正在迈向学习型组织的社会。从实际运用的角度，把企业拓展学习型组织空间的做法看作一个连续不断的过程，在这个步骤中，包括三个层次的空间：企业内部的学习型组织、作为学习型组织的企业和学习型组织的联盟。

企业在创建学习型组织的过程中，应从内部高层团队开始，一步一步拓展学习型组织的空间，最终建立一个学习型组织的企业。从企业内部进行学习型组织的拓展的主要形式有：从高层团队突破、从职能部门突破、建立学习型组织的实验室。

（2）作为学习型组织的企业。

在企业的层次上，学习型组织主要有两种体现形式，一种是校办企业，另一种就是作为学习实验室的企业。作为学习型组织的企业与传统企业明显不同，一个完整的学习型组织的企业表现为一个完整的系统。

（3）在联盟中学习。

企业的实践表明，随着企业关系的改变，一种联盟形态的学习型组织正在逐步兴起。

表现为：企业关系的改变：从单纯竞争到合作中的竞争；在联盟中学习：两极学习型组织，例如公司 A 与 B，两极学习包括 A 加 B、A 乘以 B 两种情况。联盟中学习的目的是通过学习扩展能力、通过学习转换能力。

构建联盟形态的学习型组织必须具备以下条件：联盟的合作者必须相互信任、鼓励员工为联盟学习、确立联盟的共同愿望、提高跨文化的理解能力等许多方面。

10. 开展学习型组织的演练

（1）学习型组织在国内的发展现状。

学习型组织发起于西方管理学界和企业界，近年来，我国不少企业也对创建学习型组织充满兴趣。但是，真正开始学习型组织演练的企业并不太多，不过有望在不远的将来形成一个热潮。总的来说，对学习型组织前期的研究和推广，基本上还停留在较小的范围，值得一提的是，我国台湾的企业界掀起了改造学习型组织的热潮。

（2）对待学习型组织的正确观念。

企业的经验表明，开展学习型组织的演练是提高企业活力的有效办法，是应对知识经济的必然选择。虽然企业的具体环境不同、基础条件有差异，但是在迈向学习型组织的过程中，许多共性的东西是值得相互借鉴的。其中，树立对学习型组织的正确观念是主要因素，主要包括：广泛适用的观念、重点突破的观念（自我超越和提高员工素质、建立共同愿望和提高组织向心力、系统思考与提高组织的思维水平等）、不断进步的观念、综合运用的观念。

（3）联想——创建学习型组织的典范。

联想集团创建于 1984 年，诞生以来一直健康、迅速发展，成为行业的优秀企业和成功的典范。联想的成功是有多方面的原因的，但不可忽视的是联想极富特色的组织学习实践，使得联想能够顺应环境的变化，及时调整组织结构管理方式，从而健康成长。联想具有以下几种组织学习方式：从合作中学习（与惠普、英特尔、微软、东芝等保持良好的合作关系）、向他人学习（"前车之鉴、后事之师""它山之石、可以攻玉"，以及向顾客学习等）、从自己过去的经验中学习。联想的学习机制有：会议、教育和培训、领导议事机制、委员会和工作小组。联想的组织学习保证和促进机制有："鸵鸟理论"（只有具有非常明显的优势时，才具有竞争优势）、建立共同愿望（把联想建设成长久的、有规模的高技术企业）、企业文化认同、领导以身作则、及时调整组织结构、人员合理流动、建立健全管理制度、合理的知识收集和利用。

Section 5　The Ways of Organizational Reform

8.5.1　The Trend of Organizational Reform

Dynamic and flexibility will become the main trend of future development of organizations. Because the future organization will face a much more complex and changeful world, the organization has to change to deal with changes. Only when the changes are handled with initiative, can the organization survive and develop. If the organization cannot keep the corresponding dynamic and flexibility, it is impossible to adapt to the environment in the future.

The general trend of organizational change has the following several aspects:

1. Flattening

The flattening of the organization structure means the decrease of the management levels and the amplitude of the management. The result of flattening is that the modern organization often adopts the flat organization structure under the condition of a certain scale. It is different from traditional towering structure. Management range of the towering type is small, and its levels of management are plentiful, which is called "pyramid" type of structure traditionally.

2. Flexibility

The flexibility of the organization structure means not to set fixed and formal institutions in the organization structure, and replace it with some temporary and task-oriented team organizations. Flexibility breaks through the shortcomings of traditional hierarchical organization, such as clear-cut hierarchies, multiple levels and the bureaucracy, so it can enhance the organization's ability to adapt to dynamic changes of environment. Flexibility of the organization is based on the flexibility and plasticity of organization structure. Within the organization, it can allocate human resources of its own constantly and flexibly as well as form a variety of internal networks across business units. At the outside of the organization, it helps the enterprise set up strategic alliance with other enterprises, and alliance will create the competitive advantages through complementing each other's advantages.

3. Division

Division is the organizational reform on relations of the property right, the division of a company is isolated several small companies from a big company, and the head office connects headquarters with branch companies and subsidiary companies in market relations. Through equity investment and managing shareholders, the head office realizes the control of each branch of company and subsidiary company, thus turning the company's internal type of parent-child relationships between departments and subordinate units into a similar external type of relationship between the companies. Branch is the parent company's branch, but is not legally or economically independent. The subsidiary is controlled by the group company or parent company but is legally independent, and the parent company controls the direction of management and the appointment and removal of the leaders of the subsidiaries through the stock equity. Branches and subsidiaries gather around the parent company, constitute the fixed layer of enterprise group organization.

4. Networking

The direct impact that modern network technology has on the reform of the organization structure is networking. Within the organization, it breaks through the traditional hierarchical organization structure that is characterized by vertical integration through the reconstruction of the organization structure conducted by the network technology, and forms networked organization that is characterized by the horizontal integration and consists of small, independent and innovative business units. The most significant impact network has on the organization structure is a large number of layoffs, streamline institutions. On the outside of the organization, all kinds of enterprise group and economic union tie a number of related enterprises together tightly through joint and merger of enterprise groups.

5. Virtualization

Virtualization is the extreme form of organization network. Virtualization enables the organization's boundaries become blurred, and the so-called "shell" appears. That is to say the highly networked organization makes the enterprise organization turn the entities into digital information as much as possible, reduce the physical space, and rely more on electronic space, eventually makes the enterprise organization itself as the "main shell mold organization". Another manifestation of virtualization is virtual alliance between organizations. Compared with the traditional alliance, it appears to be more transient and temporary. A specific market opportunity or a specific business project often sets up cooperation between different enterprises.

8.5.2　The Approach of Organizational Reform

There are two main ways to reform or innovate the organization. One is to start from the inside of the organization, and reach it through reengineering enterprise, team building, organization learning and so on. Another is to start with changing the relationship with other enterprises, and reach it through networking and virtualization as described above. And for now, networking and virtualization mainly display in outsourcing production, lean production, new strategic alliances and virtual operation, etc.

8.5.2.1　Reorganization

1. The Meaning of Reorganization

Reorganization is the fundamental rethinking and radical redesign of business processes, in order to improve the efficiency of enterprises. Reorganization is a revolution of the internal enterprise, and the object of reorganization is enterprise process. Enterprise process refers to an ordered set of activities across space and time in order to accomplish a goal or a task.

Fundamental rethinking refers to that reengineering enterprise process is not limited to consider how to improve the existing mechanism, but critically absorb and revolutionarily innovate the existing mechanism. As for radical redesign, it is not minor repairs or small changes on the surface of the existing system, but to abandon the old operation mechanism fundamentally to redesign organization structure and operation mechanism with the main direction of improvement of the customer satisfaction.

Enterprise organization is consisted of four key elements: goal, technology, system and activity. Reorganization sets the basic process of enterprise operation as the object, integrates the activities separated by functional units to make the process integral, and adjusts the relevant system, to ensure that the process can work better. Activity is the most basic unit of process, sending the activity completed by a person to different persons to perform forms a process. The redesign of business process of reorganization refers to rescheduling activities, including the content, order, implementation mode and the undertaker of activities.

2. The Principle of Reorganization

Generally speaking, the principles of reorganization are as follows: horizontal integration of activities, practice of team work; longitudinal compression of organizations, flattening of organization; implementation of concurrent engineering; the application of information technology.

(1) Horizontal integration of activities: the integration, dispersion and abolishment of the activities.

One of principles of reorganization is to integrate, disperse and abolish the activities through horizontal integration. Integration means merging and simplifying complex process, so as to improve the overall efficiency of operation of the process. The dispersion of the activities is contrary to the integration of activities, it improves the efficiency of the process through dispersing a professional work into relevant professions and canceling the original professional activities. The abolishment of the activities means that compacting the activities that do not create profit in the enterprise process as more as possible and focusing on the activities that can create profit.

(2) Longitudinal compression of organizations: licensing to the undertaker of the activities fully.

In terms of organization structure, reorganization needs to reduce the levels of management, to establish a flat organization structure. The change of the organization structure must be accompanied by the change of the operating mechanism, including operation process, restraining mechanism and incentive mechanism.

(3) Implementation of concurrent engineering: changing the order of the activities.

Implementation of concurrent engineering aims to break the relationship between activities. The managers should change the order of the activities, and turn the serial activities into parallel activities, so as to improve the operational efficiency of the process.

(4) The application of information technology: breaking the mode of the activities.

Information technology provides powerful means for reorganization. And it breaks through the implementation model of activities. Reorganization is a system engineering that is the recombination of people, technology and organization, is the redesign of social technology system. Information technology can coordinate the contradiction between dispersion and centralization, it can also change connection between the activities in the unified process, make each activity being executed in parallel. The creative use of information technology is one of the keys to rebuild the enterprise process.

3. The Change of Reorganization

Reorganization has brought about the following changes to the enterprise organization: the change of organization structure, the change of enterprise process and its operation mode, and the change in the enterprise management concepts.

4. The Process of Reorganization

（1）Organizing and launching phase: One is the formation of reengineering team. The key step of reorganization is to choose and form a team. Leader, process owner, reengineering team, steering committee and director of reengineering are the five roles of reorganization. Another is the onset of reorganization, such as fostering a sense of crisis, constructing the company vision. In a word, the reorganization not only needs a sense of crisis, but also needs a clear direction.

（2）Identifying and selecting phase: The identification process—Business process has a specific input and output, and is related to the customers and their needs as well as inter-departmental. The reengineering team should define and identify the process, to make namely, process selection. The selection of process—Enterprise should choose the feasible and easy-operating process to reengineer, whose problems are terrible, function is poor and impact is great.

（3）Innovating and designing phase: This is a creative work. Its main strategies are: Abolishment, to abolish the links which are not useful for adding product value. Merger, to make the necessary integration with several activities dispersed by people in different departments. Dispersion, to spread out some of the independent activities into the system to reduce the process and improve efficiency. Change, to redesign process by changing the sequence and logical relation between the activities. Automation, to adopt information technology more effectively in the process of reengineering.

（4）Implementing and operating phase: One is the commissioning of a new process; the second is the overcoming of the resistance in the implementation of the new process; and the third is the cultivating of inter-disciplinary talents.

8.5.2.2　Create a Learning Organization

Starting in the 1980s, in the business world and the management world, the promotion and research of the learning organization appeared, and gradually became popular in the world. Dupont, Intel, Apple, Fedex and other world-class enterprises, have been setting up learning organization. According to the preliminary statistics, 20 companies of the top 25 companies in the United States have transformed themselves according to the learning organization model. The secret of success of Microsoft who has become a famous company of era is to establish learning organization. To establish learning organization in our country is also the common understanding focused issue of business world.

1. Introduction to the Theory of the Learning Organization

（1）From individual learning to learning organization.

There are three levels in learning, the first is individual learning, followed by organizational learning, and the last is learning organization. For individual learning, it mainly refers to the cognitive learning, skill learning and emotional learning, and organizational learning means treating the organization as the main body of learning. Adaptive learning and creative learning are two stages of organizational learning, correspondingly the learning organization is a kind of management mode, and organizational learning is necessary for an organization to become a learning organization.

（2）Knowledge learning organization.

In the era of knowledge economy, the nature of the work is symbolized by knowledge and learning, the learning organization fully reflects the requirements of the knowledge economy era to the change of organizational management mode. There are very obvious differences between the traditional organization and the learning organization: ① The traditional working style based on command-execution: In the input stage, using various resources, and setting the following of command as the specific content. In the middle stage, the working form is the process of production and management, executing the command becomes the specific mode of activity. In the output stage, the working form mainly turns to goods and services and activity form is to complete orders. ② The knowledge flow and manner of work of the knowledge economy era: Knowledge is classified into environmental knowledge, company knowledge and internal knowledge. Environmental knowledge such as market information, technology, political factors, the relationship with the suppliers and customers, flows from the environment to the organization. Company knowledge such as reputation, brand image, advertising and promotion flows from the organization to the environment. Internal knowledge such as company culture, atmosphere, data, employees flows from the organization to the organization.

It can be seen from the above comparison, that in the knowledge economy era, enterprise of the knowledge economy operates by the promotion of the three knowledge flows in the second circumstance described above. To understand the learning organization from the perspective of knowledge, organizational learning includes three stages: acquiring knowledge (the development and creation of skills, observation and relationship), sharing knowledge (the spread of knowledge) and the use of knowledge (how to make knowledge productive).

（3）Senge's study of the learning organization.

Senge, a professor of the Massachusetts Institute of Technology, discusses the learning organization from another angle, he thinks: The point of the learning organization is not to describe how to obtain and make use of knowledge, but to tell people how to build a learning organization. He said: "Learning organization's strategic goal is to improve the speed, ability and talent of learning, to change their behaviors through the establishment of a vision and the thinking mode that is capable of finding, trying, and improving the organization, this is one of the most successful learning organizations." Senge proposed the "five disciplines" model of establishing learning organization:

Personal mastery: To clarify the real ambition of individual, concentrate and cultivate patience, and achieve self-transcendence.

Improving mental models: Mental model is the specific mind-set formed by looking at the old form. In the knowledge economy era, it will affect the viewpoint about new things.

Building shared vision: It is the ambition by people in the organization, in simple terms, is what we want to create.

Team learning: It is the process of integral collocation of members and the achievement of shared goals.

Systems thinking: It requires people to treat the development of the organization with a view of system.

On the basis of the above model, there are five characteristics in the learning organization: a common idea shared by everyone; when solving the problems and working, abandoning the old ways of thinking and routine procedures; as a part of the correlated system, members should have a consideration on all organizational processes, activities, functions and the interaction of environment; the frank communication between people; abandoning personal interests and departmental interests, working together to achieve the shared vision of the organization. A learning organization gives a full play to each employee's creativity and forms a climate of learning in groups and organizations. With learning, individual value is reflected, organizational performance is improved.

(4) To realize the combination of work and study.

Many organizations cannot be called learning organizations during the industrial age, because there are two kinds of separation: From the perspective of the organization, it is the separation of work and study. From a personal point of view, it is the separation of work and knowledge. The former leads to no learning to improve the organizational performance, while the latter hinders the growth of individual. And the method of integrating study, work and knowledge, is to create a learning organization. In a mature learning organization, learning and working are in harmony as an organic. Employees need to be members of the learning organization, while managers try to improve the learning ability of organization by all means. On the one hand it requires employees of self-surpassing with high quality, on the other hand it relies on the understanding of the managers.

2. To Activate Cells of the Learning Organization

(1) The hypothesis of self-surpassing.

Employees are the cells of an organization. How to treat employees, namely what assumptions about human nature are set, is the starting point of further discussion, at the same time "activating cells" is the key for establishing the learning organization.

Rational economic man: All human actions are in order to satisfy their own interests furthest. People's work motivation is caused by economic incentives. People's behavior is always rational and economical.

Theory X: Human is lazy and self-centered by nature, lacks of ambition, does not have the sense of responsibility, and opposes reform.

Theory Y: Basically contrary to theory X, it holds that the job of the manager is to stimulate people's potential and sense of responsibility.

Super Y theory: The person's needs and motives are different, so there is no hypothesis to apply to all humanity in management.

Humanity of learning organization: From the rational economic man, economic person of theory X social person of theory Y to complicated person of super Y theory, it reflects the deepening of understanding of human nature. In a learning organization, man can be thought of as growing man.

(2) Cultivation of self-surpassing.

Personal dream can be achieved only through the organization, and the organization's development must be based on personal development. In the learning organization, the individual self-surpassing is essential, and only in a learning organization, can the person have the environment of self-surpassing.

The self-surpassing of individuals in the organization needs to grasp the following aspects: ①To establish personal vision: a future expectations or desire. ②To hold the creative tension: The gap between vision and reality is the source of creativity. ③To recognize the structural conflict: The gap between vision and reality gives people psychological effects, namely whether the willpower can overcome resistance or not. ④To be honest about truth: The essence is to eradicate the obstacle to see the reality. ⑤To apply the subconsciousness: Make the goal which is inner concerned clearly show in people's mind.

(3) The new pattern of the relationship between managers and employees.

Seeing employees as individuals of self-surpassing, means that fundamental changes have taken place in the relationship between employees and enterprises. Through the exercise of self-surpassing, employees become actively engaged in creative work, not only have power, but also have direct access to the inner passion to work.

3. To Construct a Learning Organization Team

(1) Work groups and teams.

Team develops form work group, and is the basic working unit and learning unit of the learning organization. The role of team learning in the learning organization is reflected in: It is the basic building unit of the learning organization, the basic approach to learning, the basic process of building the learning organization. In another point of view, the learning organization is a kind of extension of the thought of a team, or it is based on team operation.

The formation of the team: the formation of the working group – shocking stage – standardization – finishing.

The performance of the team: Effective self-management team has better performance than work group, which is proved by many enterprises.

(2) The method of team learning.

Information exchange meeting: It is a learning method that is always adopted by the team.

The special meeting system: It is the effective transformation of information exchange meeting.

In-depth talks and discussion: They are the two basic techniques of team learning. Listed the typical Chinese ways of meeting, it is different from the spirit of team learning greatly.

The process of group learning can be described as: Events bring about chaos – face the source of conflicts – explore in a large container – stimulate creativity together.

(3) The comparison of group learning and the skill of group decision-making.

There are several methods of group decision making:

Brainstorming: Creating a kind of decision-making process to overcome the conformity pressure which can obstruct the creative solutions in interactive group.

Nominal group technique: To limit the discussion or communication of group members in the decision-making process.

Delphi method: It is similar to the nominal group technique except that the group members have no need of meeting.

Electronic conference method: It is a kind of group decision-making techniques developed by using computer technology.

Compared with group technology, group learning has the essential progressiveness, for example: Group learning can extract group intelligence which is higher than personal intelligence, can make organization be creative and at the same time produce concerted actions, and the results can spread to other groups with members, therefore form the learning atmosphere in the organization.

(4) A model of group learning—Microsoft.

Through the analysis of Microsoft's experience, managers will have more intuitive understanding of the team learning. From Microsoft's "the common analysis afterwards" "auditing of process" "the meeting of vacation", you can see that the design of the team learning fits with hypotheses, participants work as partners to each other, having a good "adviser of process". In addition, the exhibition meeting and bringing their own food to have lunch meeting provide employees a face-to-face communication.

4. To Review the Mind of the Learning Organization

(1) The mental model of the organization.

Mental model refers to the assumptions and impression that consolidated deeply in people's minds, which influence people how to learn the world, and how to take action. Mental model affects people's way of perceiving problems and taking actions. In the organization, there are various embodiment of mental models. Organizational behavior theory believes that, there is also anthropopathic and collective mind or mental model in the organization. The main features of organizational mental model: On the one hand it is the mental model of the individuals; on the other hand, it exists in groups, and affects the members of the group.

(2) The examination of the mental model of the organization.

The examination of the mental model of the organization is the important foundation to perfect organizational mental model. For example, the examination is to find the assumption hides behind the important problems of the enterprise out. We should realize that examination is not easy, because the assumption is firmly rooted in the organization, which in turn influences the members of the organization.

The skill of examination: to promote diversification of views, to cultivate the spirit of exploration and defense.

The working mechanisms of examing mental model: the internal board of directors (composed of 2 – 3 senior managers, which can be selected from all levels of the organization), improving the work of layout (the present work of layout is based on the old mental model, managers should establish the work of layout according to the new mental model, such as "scenario planning").

The large enterprises which have already taken dominance after years of development, often develop a kind of thinking mode: 3C model, namely, complacency, conservatism and conceit. Because of 3C model, the enterprise's mental model is greatly strengthened, and the way to improve the mental model is cut out, the development of the enterprise will encounter problems. Therefore, analyzing the disease of large corporations from the perspective of mental model has become a new perspective. The examination of the mental model is vital for the long-term development of the enterprise, and the knowledge economy era requires us to understand the examination of mental model at a higher level, in a sense, the knowledge economy age is a new era of accelerating the examination of mental model.

5. To Determine the Shared Vision of the Learning Organization

(1) The shared vision and its description.

Establishing a shared vision is a kind of training of the learning organization. Shared vision has the important meaning for the transformed enterprises and enterprises keeping the status quo. The simple words of shared vision are: "What we want to create?" The shared vision is the expectation shared by the people in the organization. It creates the sense of integration, and throughout all of the organization's activities, makes a variety of different activities of organization into an organic whole. The cultivation of shared vision requires a process.

The description of the shared vision: According to the goals to describe the vision, according to the "common enemy" to describe the vision, according to the "role model" to describe vision, and according to the idea of internal transformation to describe the vision.

(2) The meaning of establishing a shared vision.

Without the shared vision, there is no learning organization. Whether the transformed enterprises or enterprises keeping the status quo, shared vision plays an important role.

The analysis of the transformed enterprise's vision: to produce urgency, to identify and discuss the crisis and opportunities, to set up a strong leadership alliance, to fight together and give play to the role of the core of the high class, to build the planning of vision, to design strategy to realize the ambition, to communicate about the design of vision, to authorize others to implement the plan of vision, to plan and realize the short-term goals, to consolidate achievements, to deepen the reform, to make new task institutionalized.

The analysis of enterprise's vision which wants to maintain the status quo: The professors from Stanford University, draw a conclusion by observing the growth of many enterprises—The unification of the current core value and long-term vision planning is the core to maintain the status quo.

（3）The practice of the shared vision.

To encourage personal desire: Only through convergence of personal desire, can common desire gain energy. The managers must constantly encourage members to develop their own personal desires, and then combine the members who have a strong sense of purpose to create a powerful comprehensive effect.

To improve the practice of the high-level: To abandon the original practice started from the top, go through the five stages of informing, marketing, testing, consulting and creating together to establish the shared vision of the enterprise.

To learn to listen to others: Managers, who are good at building shared vision, need to talk about the process in daily work, and link it with the daily life, whose outstanding characteristic is interactive.

To integrate into the enterprise concepts: The shared vision is a basic idea of the enterprise concepts, other ideas include: purpose, mission and values. The basic idea of enterprise is to answer three basic questions: What, why and how to pursue. What to pursue: A future vision created by the all. Why to pursue: The goals and mission of the enterprise, the root of an organization. How to pursue: In the process of reaching the desire, core values are the highest basis and principles of all action and tasks.

（4）The cause of the abortion of shared vision.

The lack of coordinating ability, the disappearance of creative tension, short of focused time, the divergence of new vision.

6. To Grasp the Core of the Learning Organization

（1）The management concept of system thinking.

The exercising work of system thinking is the core of creating learning organization. System essentially is overall set of components in a certain relationship and produces the relationship with the environment. In summary, the management concept of system thinking refers to the main body of management uses system theory and method consciously to analyze the factors of management system, management organization and management process, aiming at optimizing integrated function of the management and obtaining the good management effect.

（2）The system thinking of learning organization.

The basis of the system thinking of learning organization is system dynamics. System dynamics emphasizes the interaction, as the researching object of system dynamics—the social economic system itself is in a an ever-changing process, its components (productivity, manpower, material resources, financial resources, technology, etc.) are shown the nature of the interaction of system dynamics.

There are three levels of the system thinking of learning organization: ①The thinking in the level of events: To take reactive action, the result is focusing on individual event, limited thinking, blaming on outside factors, etc. ②The thinking in the level of behavior change: Be able to adapt to the trend of changes, but it is easy to cause learning disabilities, such as learning from experience, etc. ③The thinking in the level of system structure: Be able to change the alternate form of behavior, and beyond the limitations of the level of event and the level of behavior and focus on explaining what leads to the alternate form of behavior, for example, for the enterprise that integrated the manufacture and sales, the thinking in the level of system structure must display the change of order, delivery, inventory, looking for the instability and expansion effect of the goods from the interaction. Only the structure touches the reasons behind the behavior, can we modify behavior.

(3) The tools of system thinking of learning organization.

The core of system thinking of learning organization lies in seeing the form of structure behind the complex things. This type of structure appeared again and again, so Senge gave the basic model, referred to as the basic model of system. Increasing feedback, repeatedly-adjusted feedback and the lag of time are the three main aspects of the basic model of system. Increasing feedback is the engine of growth, includes words heard frequently, like snowball effect, a chain reaction and vicious circle. The repeatedly-adjusted feedback is a kind of power of going for stability and balance by the system, a regulating system will correct itself to maintain this status. The lag of time is mistiming between actions and results. The system thinking of learning organization is such a process, running by increasing circulation, adjusting circulation and time lag. Senge, according to the basic process, established some models such as regulating loop with slow reaction, attending to trifles and neglecting the essentials, target eroded, vicious competition, limited growth, and common tragedy.

(4) The role of system thinking in learning organization.

The essential role of system thinking: ①The practice of system thinking and self-surpassing: Using the language and method of system thinking to guide the practice of self-surpassing, under the guidance of system thinking, personal cultivation will reveal some aspects of self-surpassing, such as the sense of identity on the environment and the sense of mission on the whole. ②The system thinking and team learning: The tools of system thinking is very important for group learning. In team learning, the continuation of discussion and in-depth talks require the solution many problems. The approaches of system thinking help us to jump out of the individual circles to understand the problems of organizational development from the overall. ③The models of system thinking and improving mental: Managers must learn to introspect their existing mental models, until adapting to be tested in public hypothetically. Deep-rooted mental models will hinder the generation of system thinking, in turn, system thinking is very important to effectively improve mental models. ④The system thinking and establishing the shared vision: System thinking is the fertile soil of establishing the shared vision. The shared vision is the description of future condition, while the system thinking points out the road to future. With system thinking, the people in the organization can understand how the existing policies and actions create or change the status quo clearly, find the leverage to start the reality, thus a source of confidence is established, the fertile soil fitting for building the shared vision is developed.

(5) The integration of the learning organization.

Self-surpassing is the foundation of the learning organization. It provides valuable human resources for the learning organization. Team learning depends on individual effort, such as improving mental models, establishing a shared vision, system thinking, etc.

Team learning is a kind of internal learning. It is not only the content of team's activities, but also the carrier and means of examining the mental models, setting up the shared vision.

From the time, the review of mental models in the view of the "memory" already formed, is the embodiment of learning from memory, while establishing the shared vision is a vivid description about the future, affects the growth of the organization.

System thinking is the soul of the learning organization. It provides a perfect way of thinking, individual learning, team learning, mental model inspection and shared vision construction connect together because of the existence of system thinking, to achieve organizational goals together.

7. To Depict the Structure of the Learning Organization

(1) The evolution of the learning organization structure.

The organizational behavior and organizational structure are the unity of organization. A learning group has a different structure which is neither horizontal nor vertical. Typical learning organization shows the network structure or the flat structure which gives priority to the local, and changes in practice, connects work and study as one.

The basic organization structure: The structure of longitudinal hierarchy (functional, divisional, matrix structure). In horizontal connection, the matrix structure gets a breakthrough, however, the matrix structure does not fundamentally change the role of power control, many companies have found that the building and maintaining of matrix structure are difficult.

Network structure of learning organization: The breakthrough a learning organization has on the organization structure is that employees contribute to the company's strategy, which is impossible in the past, in the network structure of organization, its different parts adjust and change themselves independently, at the same time contributing to the organization's overall mission.

(2) The flat structure which gives priority to the local.

Local orientation is the main characteristic of the network structure of learning organization. Learning organization has been becoming a flat organization which gives priority to the local. The organization will extend the decision-making power from the top as much as possible. "Local-orientated" means: decision-making power moves to the lower of organization structure, lets local decision makers face all the subjects as much as possible.

Taking the network structure which gives priority to local is the basic requirement of knowledge economy on the organization structure. Because when we have a real sense of responsibility for our actions, we can learn at the highest speed. In the era of knowledge economy, knowledge is a main resource. The distribution of knowledge influences the organization structure. The flat structure which gives priority to the local represents the direction of the organization structure. Correspondingly, some traditional structures that are "high" and bureaucratic have met some difficulties at present. GE, for example, which has the glorious history, has been in trouble since the 1970s. Since the president, Verzy, believes that the breakthrough point of GE is organizational reform, which mainly includes three aspects: lean (the percentage of cuts-up is 30%), flatten (reducing the hierarchy by an average of four), being flexible (adapting to external changes, elastic and flexible organization). GE comes back to life, and Verzy himself is known as the "management wizard".

The flat structure which gives priority to the local is a great shock for the traditional concept of leadership. Because in the knowledge economy era, first of all, the reform starts from top leaders, organization is hard to change substantively. Secondly, the leadership behavior without employees; involvement, only causes obedience but no involvement. Thirdly, the tops' judgment often fails. In the future learning organization, there will be a top-down, bottom-up, parallel communication mode of comprehensive reform, and the ultimate purpose is to form equal communication network.

(3) The constantly-changing organic structure.

Creating a learning organization means to study better and change faster than competitors. However, the fundamental solution of organization problems lies in that the learning organization can form constantly-changing organic structure. The constant changes include a series of contrary tendency such as change and stability, centralization and decentralization, oneness and diversity, and at the same time the structure is able to maintain a coherent function of cohesion.

Though the focuses of the descriptions of the necessity of changing are different, the main features are looking for a subtle balance between two different directions (globalization and localization, stability and change, centralization and decentralization, regulation and creation, etc.). The management ideas of these different directions themselves are not absolutely good or bad. The problem is that what kind of environment they match, and whether they surpass limits of necessity. In short, the effective management of the learning organization indicates that organization is always looking for the subtle balance of the optimal conditions.

(4) To connect work and study as one.

What is different from all the traditional organization forms is that the learning organization represents a form changing with the changes of time and environment. Learning organization is shown by a process, once the dynamic characteristics of the process disappear, the learning organization will develop into stiff "operation organization". The learning organization means that the change is happening. So we need to prevent the learning organization from becoming "operation organization". In the knowledge economy era, because of the dramatic change of environment, organizations must adjust structure in time, because yesterday's success does not represent tomorrow's success.

8. To Explore the Vitality of the Learning Organization

（1）The visual verification of the organizational vitality.

The main reason why learning organization is focused is the vigor it has. From the point of the relationship between employees and the organization, to create a learning organization is the process of improving the loyalty between employees and the organization. From the perspective of organization adapting to the social environment, the learning organization emphasizes the seeing of the relationship between the organization and the surrounding as a system. These aspects greatly enhance the vitality of the learning organization.

The main factor that makes learning organization bring vitality is its learning curve. Learning curve is a trend that the cost of per unit falls with the improvement of cumulative production. The main reasons causing the learning curve are: the improvement of skills, better manufacturing methods found by managers, simplified design methods and the introduction of new manufacturing technology, etc. In fact, there are much learning and thus gaining improvement in the learning organization, and they happen in every moment.

（2）The economic analysis of the learning organization.

The learning organization is associated with higher economic performance, resulting from the existence of the learning curve. But only in a learning organization can the profit increases clearly compared to the traditional enterprise. Profit of the learning organization is embodied in: Benefit from lowering costs, profits from the flexibility. Comparatively, there is no cost of continuous improvement in the learning organization. In the traditional view, it is inevitable that the learning organization costs (time extension, training expenses, etc.) exist. In fact because learning and problem-solving are an integral part in the process of production operation, and improvement is the continuous improvement of productivity, if learning organization only centers on production to stop considering improvements, it will produce a great costs. For example, the employee's suggestions get feedback, evaluation and implementation soon, so that the cost can be saved, etc.

（3）A new method of evaluation.

The creation and development of learning organization requires correction of the new performance evaluation system. The balanced scoring system, which includes learning and innovation in assessment system, is designed for learning organization. Balanced scoring system observes the enterprise from four aspects. It puts forwards four questions to managers: How customers think of us (from the customer's perspective)? What we must be good at (from the internal perspective)? Whether we can continue to increase and create profit (from the perspective of innovation and learning)? How do we satisfy shareholders (from the financial perspective)? Here, evaluating from the viewpoint of innovation and learning, it requires managers to improve in a period, instead of sleeping on the honor.

9. To Expand the Space of the Learning Organization

（1）The creation of internal levels of enterprise.

The sizes of the organizations are different, but all the organizations can get closer to the learning organization. Some people even say that our society is heading for the learning society. From the perspective of practical application, we can treat the practice of the enterprise expanding the space of learning organization as a continuous process. In this process, it includes three levels of space: Learning organization inside the enterprise, the enterprise as a learning organization and the alliance of learning organizations.

When creating learning organization, the enterprises should start form internal high-level team, then expand the space of learning organization step by step, finally establish a learning organization. The main forms of expanding the learning organization from the internal enterprise include: making breakthrough from the senior team, from laboratory functions, and establishing the laboratory for learning organization.

(2) The enterprise as a learning organization.

At the level of the enterprise, there are two main types of learning organization form. One is school-run enterprises. The other is the enterprise as a learning lab. And the enterprise as a learning organization is obviously different from the traditional enterprise, the enterprise as a complete learning organization performs as a complete system.

(3) Learning in the alliance.

Enterprise's practice shows that with the change of the business relationship, the learning organization in the form of alliance is gradually rising. Its performances include: The change of the business relationship—from pure competition to competition in cooperation; learning in the alliance—learning organization of the poles, for example, company A and company B, learning of the poles includes A adding B, A by B two cases. The purpose of learning in the alliance is expanding ability by learning, transforming ability by learning.

Building a learning organization in the form of alliance must meet the following conditions: Alliance partners must trust each other, encourage the staff to study for the alliance, establish the shared vision of alliance and improve cross-cultural understanding and many other aspects.

10. To Carry out the Practice of the Learning Organization

(1) Development status of the learning organization in China.

Learning organization launched in western management and business world, in recent years, many enterprises in China are also interested in creating a learning organization. The enterprises that really start the practice of learning organization are not too much, but it is possible to form a boom in the near future. Overall, the preliminary study and the promotion of the learning organization, basically still stay in a smaller range. It is worth mentioning that there is a wave of learning organization in the corporate world of Taiwan.

(2) The right concept of treating learning organization.

Experience has shown that the practice of the learning organization is an effective way to improve the vitality of enterprise, and is the inevitable choice to cope with the knowledge economy. Although the specific environment is different, there are differences between the basic conditions, in the process towards treating learning organizations, many common things are worth learning from each other. Among them, setting up the correct view of treating learning organization is the main factor, mainly includes: the concept used widely, the breakthrough of the key ideas (beyond ourselves and improving the quality of employees, establishing the shared vision and improving the organizational centripetal force, systems thinking and improving the level of the organization's thinking, etc.), the concept of constant perfection, the concept used synthetically.

(3) Lenovo: The model of creating learning organization.

Lenovo group, founded in 1984, since its birth, has been developing healthily and rapidly, and becomes an outstanding enterprise of industry and a model of success. Lenovo's success lies in all sorts of reasons, but what cannot be ignored is the characteristic practice of organizational learning, which enables Lenovo to conform to the changes of environment, timely adjust the management of organization structure, and grow healthily. Lenovo has the following several approaches of organizational learning: learning from cooperation (maintain good relations of cooperation with HP, Intel, Microsoft, Toshiba, etc.), learning from others (lessons, using and learning from the customers, etc.), and learning from the past experience. Lenovo's learning mechanisms are: meeting, educating and training, the leadership mechanism, the committee and working groups. The guaranteeing and promoting mechanism of Lenovo's organizational learning are: "ostrich theory" (only with very obvious advantages than others, can a company have the competitive edge), establishing the shared vision (building Lenovo into a longevous successful high technology enterprise), the identity of organizational culture, leaders leading by example, adjusting the organizational structure in time, the rational flow of personnel, establishing a sound management system, reasonable collection and utilization of knowledge.

【本章提要】

● 组织的生命周期，大致可分为创业、聚合、规范化、成熟、成熟后五个阶段。每一阶段都会面临不同的问题，需要采取不同的管理方式。

● 任何组织的生存和发展都需要变革，组织变革的动力分为内部动力和外部动力。

● 组织变革有不同的方式，组织应该根据实际情况加以灵活地综合运用，并采取相应的策略，以便取得组织变革的整体效果。

● 组织变革的阻力，主要来自个体、群体和领导者三个方面，其中有的是公开的，有的是潜在的，有的是直接的，也有的是滞后的。必须采取有效措施予以排除。

● 组织变革是手段，组织发展才是目的。动态性和灵活性，将成为组织发展变化的首要趋势。

● 企业再造是对企业业务流程进行根本的再思考和彻底的再设计，以显著提高企业的效率。企业再造是企业内部的一场革命，企业再造的对象是企业流程。

● 构建学习型组织是一项复杂的系统工程，但基本思路是进行五项修炼：自我超越、改善心智模式、建立共同远景、团队学习、系统思考。

【关键词】

组织生命周期（Organizational Life Cycle）　　组织变革（Organizational Reform）

组织冲突（Organizational Conflict）　　　　　组织再造（Reorganization）

学习型组织（Learning Organization）　　　　深度会谈（In-depth Talk）

团队学习（Group Learning）　　　　　　　　系统思考（System Thinking）

【复习与思考】

1. 组织变革的动力是什么？

2. 组织变革有哪些不同的方式？

3. 组织变革的阻力是什么？如何排除？

4. 组织再造的过程是怎样的？

5. 学习型组织的五项修炼是什么？

【研究与讨论】

1. 为什么要变革组织？举例说明。

2. 所有的管理者都是变革的推动者吗？为什么？

3. 举例说明如何建设学习型组织。

4. 什么是组织再造？如何实施组织再造工程？

5. 我国国有企业（如银行）变革的阻力是什么？为什么？

【实践演练】

1. 通过学习和研究，列举出两个以上组织变革成功和失败的例子，并加以说明。

2. 找一个你熟悉的组织，试探讨建设学习型组织的具体方案。

3. 通过调查，请列举一两个行业中进行企业再造的实际例子。

【管理模拟】

1. 选一家经营不景气企业的资料进行分析，提出再造的基本思路。

2. 学校能否构建学习型组织？为什么？如何构建？

【本章案例】

通用电气的改革

杰克·韦尔奇1981年4月成为通用电气的董事长和CEO。最近，他宣布退休。他在通用电气的工作以持续的战略和组织变革为特点。其中与韦尔奇有关的变革主要包括：

1. 改变业务组合

韦尔奇确定了在通用电气决定业务组合的两套标准。第一个是宣布："我们只从事在全球市场上占第一或第二位置的业务，如果是服务，也要占相当的份额，而且规模在500亿美元左右。"第二就是韦尔奇明确了通用电气的三大业务领域：核心、高技术和服务业。这些标准实行的结果就是20世纪80年代，通用电器卖掉了价值100亿美元的资产，收购了180亿美元的资产。不再投资的包括犹他国际、家庭用具和小的装备、消费电子和半导体，买入的是RCA、雇主再保险、Kidder Peabody Group、Navistar Financial和几个新塑料企业、汤姆森的医疗电子，与Fanuc的合资企业（工厂自动化）、Robert Bosch（电动摩托）、GEC（主要设备和电子装备）以及Ericsson（移动通信）。

2. 改变战略规划

韦尔奇对通用电气采用了数十年的高度复杂的战略规划体系进行了大胆的改革。大量减少了文件，而且计划检查过程更加非正式。其主要部分是韦尔奇和两个副董事长以及每一战略业务单位（SBU）的负责人举行会议，集中明确和讨论几个关键议题。到1984年，200多名战略规划员工被裁员了，它的目标是"让总经理与总经理，而不是计划员与计划员"讨论战略。

（1）层次减少。计划的变化是一个更大的变革项目的一部分，这一变化就是使总部员工从"检查者、询问者和权利代表转到提供便利者、支持者和协助者"。这个变革带来了文山会海的大量减少和个人决策权力的增加。这些变化使管理跨度显著增大，管理层级有所减少。在通用电气的多数地方，管理层人数从九个减少到四个。

（2）裁员。撤资压力、管理层级减少、总部员工减少和持续改进带来了生产力的提高。在1980—1990年的十年时间，通用电气的销售量增加了一倍，而员工总数从40.2万人减少到29.8万人。

（3）价值观。韦尔奇领导的持续的主题就是坚持价值观。韦尔奇总是强调公司的"软件"（价值观、激励和投入）而不是"硬件"（业务和管理结构）。韦尔奇的哲学为以下十个原则和价值观：在每项业务中数一数二；成为并保持精益；所有权——个体承担决策和行动的责任；效率——个体确保通用电气的资源得到充分的利用；企业家精神；卓越——个人的最高目标；现实；率直；开放沟通——内部与外部；财务支持——获得支持成功需要的回报。这种对价值观的重视以强调沟通和在公司内传播价值观的领导方式表现出来。韦尔奇花了大量的时间在通用电气位于克罗顿维尔的管理开发学院的员工和管理研讨会上发表演讲。

3. 新文化，新体系

在他上任的前五年里，韦尔奇主要考虑战略和结构。通用电气的业务组合逐步转变。在主要业务中，通用电气将战略重点放在了全球成功和对新技术的开发和应用上。在组织和结构方面，韦尔奇对过多的成本、自满和无效管理的憎恨导致了组织层级的大量减少和更扁平的组织。

作为"新文化"的基础，韦尔奇要在通用电气重新定义通用电气和员工的关系合约：

像美国、欧洲和日本的许多大公司一样，通用电气有基于终身雇佣的隐含的心理合约……这导致了一种家长式统治的、封建的、模糊的忠诚。你投入时间、努力工作，公司就会照顾你一辈子。这种忠诚使员工内向……心理合约不得不改变，所有层次的人都要有风险意识。我的忠诚概念不是"贡献时间"给某个公司，并换得保护。忠诚是人们要抓住外部世界并取胜的心态……新的心理合约，如果有的话，就是在通用电气工作对那些想要竞争的人来讲是最好的工作。我们最好的培训和开发资源的承诺提供个人和职业成长的环境。

创造新态度要求从内部导向转变成外部导向：

决定你命运的不是你的手，而是如何运用它。最好的办法是面对现实，尊重世界本来的面目并采取相应的行动……我的想法是不要一点点，而是要大跨步。多数官僚机构仍想一步步来，而不是根本的变革，我们也不例外。它们想渐进是因为它们的内部导向——使它向大的改变开放意味着不断问自己，我与外界比做得多好快，而不是与一年或两年前比，自己做得多好多快。

建立新文化和改掉通用电气的"老做法"的障碍不仅仅是官僚主义，还包括由官僚主义所产生的习惯和态度："上百年的大公司的内部高墙不会因为进行了组织变革或管理层发表了演讲就倒塌，还有许多支撑它的积习。那些本位主义、地位、斗争、功能主义，更为重要的就是关注自身和内部的官僚主义，它们总是兴风作浪。"

4. 群策群力——总览

通用电气的群策群力是为了加快在通用电气进行的组织变革。韦尔奇在 1988 年 9 月提出了这个计划。韦尔奇在通用电气的管理者在克罗顿维尔的管理开发学院的每周六管理开发课上负责一个部分。他被课上管理者的精力、激情和众多的创意所打动，同时，他也被通用电气的官僚主义和管理者将个人想法付诸行动的困难所困扰。在一次克罗顿维尔的特别积极的课程之后，韦尔奇和通用电气的教育主任 James Braughman 讨论如何引起公司对这些问题的重视，以使公司的所有员工都能参与并在通用电气产生更快的变革。在从克罗顿维尔飞回总部的直升机上，他们俩提出了群策群力的基本概念和框架。

通用电气群策群力的典型代表是新英格兰小镇会议。居民们一起讨论问题、想法，最后就采取的行动达成一致。韦尔奇认为："群策群力有实践和智慧双重目标。实践的目标是去除通用电气创建以来的所有坏习惯……第二件事就是智慧的部分，就是让每个业务的领导者每年 8—10 月在此 100 名左右的员工面前，倾听他们的想法。群策群力将管理者暴露在不同意见、感受、情绪和不满面前，而不是管理和组织的抽象的理论。"

群策群力的总结显示了三个互相联系的目的：激发持续变革和改善的过程，激发以信任、授权、去除不必要工作和无边界组织为特点的文化变革，提高业务绩效。

5. 群策群力的结构

群策群力的核心是创建一个论坛，使同一业务部门不同部分的人能够聚集在一起开诚布公地说出对业务管理的想法。因为经常是最好的员工提出改进工作的建议，这样的行动被视作去除不必要的工作和改善业务流程的第一步。1989 年 1 月，韦尔奇在通用电气 500 名高层主管的年度会议上宣布了群策群力，并将基本的框架发给通用电气的 14 个核心业务负责人。但是，如何具体实施还是相当灵活的。群策群力的主要要素包括：

（1）离岗会议：群策群力是一个论坛，而且要远离公司环境。2～3天的群策群力活动通常在公司外举行。

（2）集中与问题和关键流程：对行动导向的部分总有很强的偏见。最早的群策群力集中于去除不必要的工作，这就是Braughman所说的"低处的果实"。随着计划的进展，群策群力更集中于复杂的业务流程。例如，在通用电气照明、集团范围的会议讨论如何加快新产品的开发、降低次品率和提高部件生产装配的整合。在塑料业务部门，优先考虑质量改进、低回收时间和提高跨职能的协调。

（3）跨部门参与：群策群力通常有50～100个不同层次和不同职务的员工参加。过程的关键是特殊业务的高层领导的参与。

（4）小群体和市民会议：群策群力活动通常由一些小群体会议组成。开始是头脑风暴部分，然后是自由讨论，得出的建议交给高层管理者，然后公开辩论。在每次讨论结束时，领导者要马上做出决策，即采用、拒绝还是进一步研究。

（5）跟进：群策群力的关键一步是跟进的过程，以确保做出的决策能够得到实施。

6. 群策群力的结果

群策群力的结果是显著的。在头四年，通用电气开展了3 000多次群策群力活动，结果是许多"垃圾工作"的消失和组织结构与管理流程的复杂和深远的改变。"响尾蛇"和"蟒蛇"被分别用来形容两种问题。"响尾蛇"是简单的问题，必须马上解决。"蟒蛇"则是更复杂的问题，需要进一步理出头绪。

除了有形的结构变化和业绩增长外，最重要的影响是组织文化的改变。在通用电气资本——一个最集权和官僚的业务部门，一位员工这样描述这种变革："我们被压抑在这里很久了，现在管理层终于开始听我们的意见了，那感觉就像柏林墙倒了一样。"

五年内，超过30万名员工、顾客和供应商参加了群策群力的活动。在通用电气的内部文件上，在有关群策群力的介绍之后，记录了更重大和更有意义的业绩和效率改善。例如，在纽约的Gas Engine Turbines建造时间减少了80%，航空发动机则将生产时间从30周减少为4周。通用电气的金融服务部门的票据成本从5.10美元减少为4.55美元。人均票据额增加了34%，人工成本降低了19%，员工生产效率提高了32%。航天工厂则报告说，除了100%符合环保规定外，工厂将有害物排放从1990年的759吨减少为1992年的275吨。

7. 管理群策群力

群策群力作为一个基本的过程是让：①每个业务的员工都可以自由挑战其领导者。②管理者保证计划的长久性并保证做出的决策得到实施。但群策群力不是公司内的行动，它需要指向通用电气在20世纪90年代想要成为的公司的方向。杰克·韦尔奇认为他的角色就是沟通和传播能够使通用电气持续成功的原则、价值观和主题。

1989年，韦尔奇提出通用电气的管理围绕三个主题：速度、简化和自信。

在20世纪80年代，我们发现简化与速度是相关的，我们拥有上万名员工的企业不会对带有更多文字和脚注的愿景有反应，如果我们不简化，就无法快速……而如果我们不快，就无法赢。

对工程师来讲，简化意味着干净、有用和先进的设计，不烦琐。对营销人员来讲，简化就是尽量明确地表达自己并清晰地提出建议。对制造部门来讲，就是使生产线上的每个人都明白逻辑流程。他们与自己周围的人分享信息，倾听他们的意见并大胆地前进。

但公司不能分销自信。我们要做的而且必须做的是给他们机会去赢、去贡献，并因此获得自信。没有这样的机会，他们就无法体会胜利，而会在官僚体系中沉沦下来。

速度……简化……自信。我们增加了衡量标准，我们知道它从哪里来……而且我们计划在20世纪90年代提高他们。

8. 最佳做法

群策群力的众多醒目结果之一就是它成为新改进业务的催化剂。其中一个新项目是"最佳做法"，目标是提高生产力。通用电气的业务发展员工集中于200家比通用电气获得更佳生产并至少持续10年的公司中选出的24家企业。其中12家公司同意通用电气派员工到它们公司学习成功的秘密。作为交换，通用电气与它们分享研究的结果和成功的故事。参与这个计划的公司有福特、惠普、施乐和Chaparral钢铁和三家日本企业。

与公司的实际工作相比，通用电气更关心管理实践和员工的态度。"最佳做法"与一般基准化的不同在于前者不用记录成绩，关键是确认学习成功的管理经验和流程是长期生产力改善的最重要部分。基本的假设是通过其他管理实践，管理者和员工可以受到激励去持续改进自己的做法，继续指导计划。"最佳做法"成为一个正式的培训课程，每个业务单位每月至少有12名员工和管理者参加该培训。

（资料来源：贝特曼等著，王雪莉译：《管理学：新竞争格局》（第六版），北京：北京大学出版社2007年版，第630~634页）

思考问题：

1. 根据提供的信息，描述韦尔奇领导的变革方式和阶段。

2. 明确并简要描述群策群力的主要特征。

3. 讨论组织文化是如何变革的。是什么引起了变革？文化变革对人的行为和组织绩效的影响是什么？

【本章参考文献】

[1][美]理查德·L.达夫特著，李维安等译：《组织理论与设计精要》，北京：机械工业出版社1999年版。

[2][美]彼得·圣吉著，郭进隆译：《第五项修炼——学习型组织的艺术与实务》，上海：上海三联书店1994年版。

[3][美]迈克尔·哈默、詹姆斯·钱皮著，胡毓源等译：《改革公司》，上海：上海译文出版社1998年版。

[4]黄速建：《现代企业管理：变革的观点》，北京：经济管理出版社2001年版。

[5]俞文钊：《管理的革命：创建学习型组织的理论与方法》，上海：上海教育出版社2003年版。

第九章 领 导

Chapter 9　Leadership

将者，智、信、仁、勇、严也。

孙子

The general needs the wisdom, faith, benevolence, braveness, and strictness.

Sun Tzu

最有效的领导方式是领导者去设计一种环境，使群体成员潜在地或明显地受到动机的激励，并能对它做出有效的响应。

豪斯

The most effective style of leadership is that the leader designs a kind of environment to make the group members potentially or obviously motivated by the motivation and make effective response to it.

House

【本章学习目标】

知识目标：

了解领导的基本含义和领导权力。

熟悉领导方式。

掌握领导素质与艺术。

认识领导的发展趋势。

技能目标：

能够识别领导者和管理者。

掌握主要领导理论，提升领导能力。

【Learning Objectives of Chapter 9】

Objectives of Knowledge：

Get to know the definition and authority of leadership.

Be familiar with the style of leadership.

Master the quality and art of leadership.

Acknowledge the development tendency of leadership.

Objectives of Skill：

Be able to distinguish leaders and managers.

Master the main theories of leadership, improve the leading ability.

【小故事】

20世纪80年代末，金宝汤公司（Campbell Soup）被利润下降、市场份额减少、领导无方所困扰。1990年戴卫·约翰逊接任首席执行官后，公司利润大幅提高，新产品不断问世，销量急剧增加。这些业绩的取得，是因为约翰逊出色地领导分布在全球各地的44 000多名公司员工。约翰逊的领导方式是非正式的，他和所有员工打成一片。他定期和员工一起就餐、谈论新产品的开发和工作中遇到的问题。每当员工提出一项开发新产品的建议时，约翰逊就授权员工组成一个工作团队来开发该项新产品。成功后，约翰逊会和他一起庆祝。为了让公司成为全球食品行业的领导者，约翰逊让员工把注意力集中在数字上，即利润额比竞争对手（如雀巢公司）增长得更快。相应地，员工工资的增长是建立在公司利润额增长的基础上的。同时，员工被鼓励以公司股东的身份来工作与思考，例如，约翰逊要求300名高级主管拥有超过年薪3倍的公司股票，公司董事不拿工资，只分红利。

【引例】

乔布斯：无穷魅力

这里充满着青春的活力，这些年轻人正是一种中坚力量，是他们研制了苹果计算机，并将公司发展成与IBM具有同等竞争力的电脑公司。1976年斯蒂夫·沃兹尼亚克和史蒂夫·乔布斯设计出个人用的计算机，并于一年之后以苹果II型的商标投放市场，仅仅3年之后的1980年，苹果电脑公司已迅速发展成拥有1.18亿美元的企业。尽管第二年IBM也推出了自己制造的个人计算机，但当年28岁的董事长史蒂夫·乔布斯并没有打算让路。

他和他的同事亲密无间，像一群海盗一样大胆。乔布斯在充当教练、一个班子的领导和冠军栽培人的新型经理方面是一个完美的典型。他是一个既狂热又明察秋毫的天才，他的工作就是专门出各种新点子，他是传统观念的活跃剂，他不会把什么事情丢在一边，他容不得无能与迁就的存在。

这些年轻人也纷纷对董事长乔布斯表述了自己的看法，他们希望在从事的工作中做出伟大的成绩。他们说："我们不是什么临时工，而是兢兢业业的技术人员。"他们要对技术有最新的理解，知道如何运用这些技术并用来造福于人。所以最简便的办法就是网罗十分出色的人物组成一个核心，让他们自觉地监督自己。苹果电脑公司招聘的办法是面谈。一个新来的人要和公司至少谈一次，也许要谈两三次，之后再来谈第二轮。当对录用做出最后决定时，就把苹果电脑公司的个人电脑产品——麦肯塔式拿给他/她看，让他/她坐在机器跟前，如果他/她没有显示出不耐烦，面试官就说这可是一部挺棒的计算机来刺激一下，目的是让他/她的眼睛一下子亮起来，真正激动起来，这样就知道他/她和苹果电脑公司是否志同道合了。

现在公司人人都愿意工作，并不是因为有工作非干不可，而是因为他们满怀信心、目标一致。员工们一致认为苹果电脑公司将成为一个大企业。

公司现在正在扩展事业的版图，四处奔走招聘专业经理人才。许多人是外行，只懂管理，不懂干活儿，但是他们懂得什么是兴趣、什么是最好的经理，他们是最伟大的献身者，所以他们上任，肯定能够干出别人干不出的杰出成绩来，苹果电脑公司的决策者一直是这样认为的。

苹果电脑公司在1984年1月24日推出麦肯塔式计算机，在头100天里销售了75 000台，而且销量还在持续上升，这种个人用的计算机粗略计算占到公司全年15亿美元销售额的一半。

在苹果电脑公司中，如今一切都要看麦肯塔式的经验，并且加以证明，他们可以得到许多这类概念来应用，在某些方面做些改进，然后形成模式，在所有的工厂中他们都在采用麦肯塔式市场的模式，每个制造新产品的小组都是按照麦肯塔式的模式干的。麦肯塔式的例子表明，当一个发明班子组成以后，能够多么有效地完成任务。其办法是分工负责、各尽其职，在人们意识到要为之做出贡献时，一个项目能否成功就是一次考验。在麦肯塔式外壳中不为顾客所见的部分是全组的签名，苹果电脑公司这一特殊做法的目的就是给每一个最新发明的创造者本人而不是给公司树碑立传。

苹果电脑公司的董事长史蒂夫·乔布斯是一位优秀的领导者。优秀的领导者的最主要特征就是，具有洞察市场的慧眼和难以抗拒的感召力，在他周围集结着与他志同道合的崇拜者。为什么领导者具有感召力，关键是他和他的企业的价值观具有无穷的魅力。

（资料来源：杨明刚：《现代实用管理学——知识·技能·案例·实训》（第二版），上海：华东理工大学出版社2005年版）

思考问题：
1. 史蒂夫·乔布斯是不是一个优秀的经理？
2. 史蒂夫·乔布斯的魅力在哪里？

第一节　领导的基本含义

领导是重要的管理职能之一，组织的目标要靠领导者的指引来实现。但在现实中，有的企业成功了，有的企业则失败了，其中一个重要原因就是领导能力问题。因此，领导水平的高低，常常决定组织的生死存亡。

一、领导的含义

领导一词，通常有两种含义。

一是指组织的领导者，即组织中确定和实现组织目标的指挥者。他在组织中起着十分重要的作用：①在组织的管理体系中，领导者发挥着核心作用；②在组织的决策方面，领导者起着指挥和决断作用；③在组织行为方面，领导者发挥着激励和协调作用。

二是指一种管理职能，即领导者通过与被领导者之间的交往过程，来影响、激励和引导组织成员，执行某些任务，以实现组织目标的一种行为。这一概念包含了以下四个方面的含义：①领导一定要与群体或组织中的其他人发生交往，这些人就是领导的对象；②领导者与其下属可以相互影响，但两方面的影响力是不同的，领导者对下属的影响力要远远大于其下属对领导者的影响力；③领导要有目标，即一切领导行为必须指向组织或群体目标；④领导的本质其实是一种影响力，领导者通过组织的活动施加影响，并造成组织成员的追随和服从。

领导者与管理者一样吗？有时我们很难区分，因为他们的关系太密切，但并不完全相同。管理者是被任命的或是被选举的，他们拥有合法的权力，其影响力来自他们所在的职位、被赋予的正式权力。而领导者可以是任命的，也可以是从一个群体自发产生的，领导更多的是建立在个人影响力和专长权以及模范作用的基础之上的。因此，一个人只有他在行使法定权的时候，更多地依靠自身的影响力来指挥下属，才可能既是领导者又是管理者，否则，两者就可能是分离的。

【新视角】

领导与管理在类似活动上的侧重点各不相同。管理意味着操纵事情、维持秩序、控制偏差，领导意味着指挥、带领跟随者探索新领域。管理者通过计划与预算处理复杂问题，他们设置目标，确定完成目标的方法，分配资源以实现目标。而领导者首先规划组织的愿景以引导下属的行为，然后开发创新战略去实现愿景。有效的领导者通过组织与人员配置去完成目标，他们创造组织结构、设计工作职位、配备合格员工、沟通相关信息以保证目标实现。领导者招聘、留住那些认同组织愿景的员工，让员工组成工作团队，自主决定如何达成组织愿景。管理者通过控制员工行为来保证员工完成目标。他们运用各种形式的报告和会议监控员工的工作绩效，时刻注意工作偏差。有效的领导者需要激励和鼓舞员工团队，帮助他们克服各种困难，支持他们出色地完成各项任务。

二、领导权力

领导权力是指领导者有目的地影响下属的心理和行为的能力。权力是领导的基础，也是领导者发挥基本效能的条件。领导权力一般可分为五类：

（1）法定权。这是由组织中等级制度所规定的正式权力，这通常因职位而产生，并被法律规章、传统习惯甚至常识所认可，法定权就是职权，它的作用基础就是职权的权威性。

（2）奖赏权。这是给予或取消报酬的一种权力，此权力建立在利益性遵从的基础之上，来自下级追求满足的欲望。如对员工进行提升、表扬、奖励等。

（3）强制权。这是一种对下属在精神或物质上进行威胁强迫，使其服从的权力，这种权力建立在惧怕处罚的基础上，实质上是一种处罚性权力。

（4）表率权。这是因领导者特殊品格、个人魅力而形成的权力，这种权力建立在下属对领导的感性认同，甚至崇拜的基础之上。

（5）专长权。这是由于领导者具有某种专门知识和技能而获得的权力，这种权力以敬佩和理性崇拜为基础。

上述各种权力中，法定权、奖赏权和强制权主要源于组织中的职位，他们是职位和责任结合在一起的制度化权力。组织的各级领导为履行所在职位的职责，就必须拥有相应的权力。当领导者不在其位时，其权力也随之减除，因此，这些权力是一种外在性权力。表率权和专长权，无须外界授予，来自领导者本身的因素，是一种内在性的权力。这种权力对权力的施受双方均没有强制性的约束力。外在性权力构成领导权力的基础，内在性权力则是提高领导效能的重要方面。

三、领导的作用和效果

1. 领导的作用

指挥：指挥的基础是职位权力，即某个人具有的可以施加给别人的控制力，这是一种靠行政权力施加影响的活动。

激励：领导者要设法去了解下属在不同时间、不同情况的需求因素及其强烈程度，设计出满足这些需求的方法，并加以实施。

协调：组织由于内外因素的干扰，需要领导者来协调组织成员之间的关系和活动，使其朝着共同的目标前进。

感召：感召就是要激发和鼓舞追随者全力以赴地进行工作，这种感召力量主要来自领导者以其人格魅力而引发的下属的忠诚、热忱、献身精神。

造势：造势就是要营造和维持一个良好的工作环境和文化氛围，来影响组织成员的行为。

2. 领导的效果

领导的效果主要表现在：下级的支持、相互关系、员工的评价、激励程度、沟通效果、工作效率、目标的实现。

四、领导的任务

一般来说，领导者的任务有两项：一是实现组织或群体目标，即完成上级或组织下达的任务。二是尽可能满足组织或群体成员的具体需要。这两项任务是相辅相成的，只有满足组织或群体成员的需要，才能调动其积极性，保持其旺盛的士气，并维护领导的影响力，从而保证第一项任务的完成；只有实现群体或组织的目标，才能更好地满足个体的需要。群体或组织目标实现不了，成员个体需要必然得不到满足。具体地说，领导者应该做好以下几项工作：

（1）主持确立组织或群体的目标。

（2）组织与协调下级的工作。

（3）协调本组织或群体与外部的关系。

（4）激励下级为实现目标而努力工作，并控制和评定下级的工作。

（5）发现人才、培养人才、起用人才。使人尽其才，才尽其用。

Section 1　Basic Meaning of Leadership

Leadership is one of the important functions of management. The achievement of the organizational goals depends on leaders' guidance. But in reality, some enterprises succeed, while others fail. One of the important reasons is leadership. As a result, the level of leadership often determines the organization's survival.

9.1.1 Meaning of Leadership

There are usually two meanings of leadership.

One refers to the leader of the organization, namely commander in the organization to identify and achieve organizational goals. He plays a very important role in the organization: ①In the management system of an organization, a leader plays a central role. ② In the aspect of organizational decision-making, a leader plays a commanding and deciding role. ③In the aspect of organizational behavior, a leader plays an incentive and coordinating role.

The other refers to the management function, namely a kind of behavior that leaders influence, motivate and guide the members of the organization throughout interpersonal process with those who are under leadership, to perform certain tasks to achieve organizational goals. This concept includes the meaning of the following four aspects: ①Leaders must associate with other members in the group or organization, who are the objects under leadership. ②Leaders and their subordinates can influence each other, but the two types of influence are different, the influence of leaders on subordinate is far greater than their subordinates on leaders. ③Leaders must have goals, that is to say, the leadership behavior must point to the organization's or group's goal. ④ The essence of leadership is an influence, leaders influence members through the activities of the organization, which cause them to follow and obey.

Are leaders the same as managers? Sometimes it is difficult to distinguish, because they are similar, but they are not exactly the same. Managers are appointed or elected so they have legitimate power. Their influence comes from their positions and their legitimate power. The leader can be appointed or be elected from a group. Leadership is more built on personal influence, expertise power and exemplary role. Therefore, it is when a person exercises his legal rights more relying on his influence to command subordinates that could both be leaders and managers, otherwise, they could be separated.

9.1.2 Power of Leadership

Power of leadership refers to the leaders' ability that purposely influences subordinates' psychology and behavior. Power is the basis of leadership, and also the conditions for leaders to give play to basic efficiency. Leadership power generally can be divided into five categories as follows:

(1) Legitimate power. It is the formal power stipulated by the organization hierarchy, and usually is caused by position and is approved by laws and regulations of traditional habits and even common sense. Legitimate power is authority. Its function is the power of authority.

(2) Reward power. It is a kind of power that leaders determine to award or cancel the reward. This power is based on the interests of compliance, and comes from the desire of the subordinates to pursue satisfaction, such as staff promotion, praise, and so on.

(3) Coercive power. It is a kind of power which threats the subordinates on their mental or

physical coercion to obey authority, such authority established on the basis of fear of punishment. It is essentially a punitive power.

(4) Model power. It is a leading power due to the leader's special character, charisma, and the formation of such power is built under the leadership of emotional recognition, even on the basis of worship.

(5) Expert power. It is a kind of power acquired by leaders with certain specialized knowledge and skills, and the formation of such power is built on admiration and rational worship.

These above various powers, the legitimate power, the reward power and the coercive power mainly stem from the positions in the organization, which are institutional powers combined positions with responsibilities. Leaders at all levels of the organization to fulfill the responsibilities of the post must have the appropriate authority. When the leader is not in his place, his power will be undermined. Therefore, these kinds of power are external power. Model power and expert power, without external grant but from the leader's own factors, are internal powers. These kinds of power applied by both parties have no mandatory binding. External power constitutes the basis of the power of leadership, while inherent power is an important aspect of improving leadership effectiveness.

9.1.3 The Function and Effectiveness of Leadership

1. The Function of Leadership

Command: Position power is the basis of command that someone has the controlling power over others, which is an activity to influence by the executive power.

Motive: Leaders should try to understand the subordinates' demand factors and intensity in different times and cases, thus devise a method to meet these needs, and implement them.

Coordinate: Due to the interference of the internal and the external factors, organizations need leaders to coordinate the relationship between the members and the activities of the organization towards a common goal.

Inspire: It is to motivate and inspire subordinates to devote themselves to working, which is mainly form the loyalty, strength, dedication of subordinates inspired by the charisma of their leader.

. Campaign: A campaign is to create and maintain a good working environment and culture, in order to influence the behavior of members of the organization.

2. The Effectiveness of Leadership

Leadership effectiveness mainly reflects on: the support from the subordinates, relationships, evaluation of employees, incentives degree, communication effectiveness, efficiency and the realization of goals.

9.1.4 Tasks of Leaders

Generally speaking, the leaders have two tasks: First, to achieve goals of the organization and group, namely to complete the tasks assigned by superiors or organization. Second, meet the specific needs of organization or group members as much as possible. The two tasks are complementary. Only when the needs of organization or group are met can it mobilizes their enthusiasm to maintain its strong potential, and maintain influence of leadership to ensure the completion of the first task. Only by achieving the goals of the group or organization, can it meet the needs of individuals better. If the goals of group or organization are not achieved, it is impossible to meet individual needs. Specifically, leaders should do the following work:

(1) Preside over the establishment of the goals of the organization or group.

(2) Organize and coordinate the subordinates' work.

(3) Coordinate the relationship between the organization or group and the external.

(4) Motivate subordinates to work hard to achieve the goals, control and assess the subordinates' work.

(5) Find talents, train and make best use of them.

【阅读资料】

亚科卡：传奇领导者

亚科卡是美国汽车行业著名的企业家，曾任美国两大汽车公司的总裁。1984年《亚科卡自传》的出版轰动了美国，引起世界瞩目。该书一出版就以每周出售10万册的纪录发行，1985年底已再版16次。1982年美国《华尔街日报》和《时代》周刊都曾刊登过关于亚科卡可能被提名担任总统候选人的新闻，一时其成为美国人民心目中的民族英雄。亚科卡的一生充满传奇色彩：

(1) 一个意大利移民的后裔居然能一步步地当上福特汽车公司总裁，他凭的是什么本领？

(2) 连任福特汽车公司八年总裁的亚科卡，为什么正当他立下了汗马功劳，大展宏图时，却突然被解雇，用他的话说，"从珠穆朗玛峰顶被一脚踢到谷底"，这是为什么？

(3) 临危受命，出任美国第三大汽车公司克莱斯勒公司总裁。当时，该公司濒于崩溃。从1978至1981年，克莱斯勒公司共亏损36亿美元，创下了美国历史上亏损的最高纪录。人们普遍认为，该公司马上就要倒闭。然而，事情发展并不如人们所料，在亚科卡的领导下，经过几年的惨淡经营后，克莱斯勒公司竟奇迹般地从死亡线上活过来了。那么，亚科卡是如何挣扎、奋斗、战胜险恶，使企业扭亏为盈的？

亚科卡的传奇经历充分说明了领导的重要性。领导是一种重要的管理职能，也是人类社会活动的重要因素。任何一个组织都离不开领导和领导者。

（资料来源：杨明刚：《现代实用管理学——知识·技能·案例·实训》（第二版），上海：华东理工大学出版社2005年版）

第二节　领导方式

领导方式是领导者对其下属施加影响，以使他们去完成组织目标的行为方式。

一、领导的影响方式

在领导活动中，领导者运用权力的目的是对被领导者施加影响，使其心理和行为发生预期的改变。因此，权力是影响的基础，影响则是权力的核心和实施过程，根据权力的不同，以权力为基础的影响也分为两类：

（1）外在影响。即以领导的外在性权力为基础，对被领导者的影响具有强迫性和不可违抗性。被领导者的心理和行为表现为消极的、被动的服从。这种服从具有表面性和暂时性的特点。具体作用方式有：①传统观念的影响；②利益满足的影响；③恐惧心理的影响。

（2）内在影响。即建立在内在性的权力基础之上，主要着眼于以领导的良好素质和行为，来吸引和感化被领导者，通过激发内在的动力，对员工心理和行为发生影响。内在影响不带有任何强制、压服性因素，而是以潜移默化、循序渐进的方式发生作用。具体方式有：①理性崇拜的影响；②感情的影响。

二、领导方式的类型

领导方式可以从不同的角度将其划分为不同的类型。

（1）从职权运用的角度，可以把领导方式分为：专制型、民主型和放任型三种基本类型。

专制型领导方式的特点：领导者独断专行，喜欢命令别人，让别人无条件地服从，完全靠奖惩来控制其下属。这种领导方式有时在短期内可以生效，但无法为连续不断地取得成功奠定坚实的基础，因为它不能使被领导的人长期感到满意。

民主型领导方式的特点：领导不仅依靠他们自己的才能，而且还善于听取其下属们的意见，并鼓励和允许他们参与管理。这种领导方式会促成一种合作的精神，并使下属的创造性和才能得到施展。

放任型领导方式的特点：领导者很少使用自己的权力，在活动中给予下属高度的独立性和自由。这种领导方式由于成员可以自行其是，因而很容易各自为政。

（2）从领导行为的偏好角度可以把领导方式划分为以任务为中心的领导方式和以人际关系为中心的领导方式。

以任务为中心的领导方式的特点：领导者最关心的是工作任务的完成，他们实际上是把工作任务放在首位，而对人际关系不大关心，有时为了完成任务甚至不惜损害人际关系。这种领导方式通常可以带来较高的工作效率，但也会降低成员的满意度，并会影响团结。

以人际关系为中心的领导方式的特点：领导者最关心的是建立良好的人际关系，他们尊重、关心和支持下属，通过良好的人际关系去推动组织任务的完成。这种领导方式能够提高成员的满意程度，并能加强群体的团结，但对工作效率的影响不总是积极的。

（3）从领导风格的角度可以把领导方式划分为事务型领导方式和变革型领导方式。

事务型领导方式的特点：领导者对管理职能推崇备至，勤奋、谦和而且公正，重视非人格的绩效内容，如计划、日程、预算等，对组织有使命感，尽可能使工作有条不紊地进行。

变革型领导方式的特点：领导者注重变革、创新和开创新事业，领导过程是有系统、有目的、有组织地寻求变革，通过行动来实现他们的设想，以激发组织的活力。

Section 2　Styles of Leadership

The style of leadership is the behavior of a leader to influence his subordinates to complete the organization's objectives.

9.2.1　Styles of Leaders' Influence

In leadership activities, leaders use their power to influence those who are under leadership to make their psychology and behavior change in expectation. Therefore, power is the basis of the influence, and the influence is the implementation process and core of power. According to the varieties of power, power-based influence is divided into two categories：

(1) External influence. Based on the leaders' external power, their influence on followers is obsessive and cannot be defied. Psychology and behavior of the follower manifest as negative and passive obedience. This obedience has the characteristics of superficiality and temporary. Specific effect styles include：①The influence of traditional concepts. ②The influence of interests to meet. ③The influence of fear.

(2) Internal influence. Based on the leaders' internal power, it is mainly to attract followers by leaders' good quality and behavior, and make influence on employees' psychology and behavior by stimulating the inner motivation. Internal factors influence orderly and gradually without any force. Specific effect styles include：①The influence of the rational worship. ②Emotional impact.

9.2.2　Styles of Leadership

Leadership can be divided into different styles according to different angles.

(1) In terms of the use of power, leadership can be divided into three types：autocratic leadership, democratic leadership and permissive leadership.

The feature of autocratic leadership：Such kind of leaders is always arbitrary and likes to order their subordinates and make them obedient. They completely control their subordinates by rewards and punishments, which sometimes work in the short-term, however, this style cannot lay the foundation of making constant success for it cannot satisfy those people who are leaded.

The feature of democratic leadership：Leaders can not only rely on their own aptitude but also do well in taking their subordinates advices as well as encouraging them to exert their creativity and talent.

The feature of permissive leadership：Rather than fully exert their power, leaders always empower their subordinates with considerable independence and freedom, which can enable members of the team to do their own things freely, but it is easy to cause members act of their own free wills.

（2）In terms of the preference of leadership behavior, leadership can be divided into two basic types, the assignment-oriented and the relation-oriented.

The feature of assignment-oriented leadership: What leaders most care about is the accomplishment of the assignment and they always put the assignment in the first place but care little about the interpersonal relationship. Sometimes those leaders might finish their job at the sacrifice of the interpersonal relationship, which can usually bring about higher work efficiency but will undermine the satisfaction of their members and affect the team spirit.

The feature of relation-oriented leadership: What leaders most care about is how to build harmonious interpersonal relationship. They respect, care and support their subordinates and pull the accomplishment of the organizational assignments through good interpersonal relationship, which can not only enhance the team members' degree of satisfaction, but also motivate the team spirit. But the influence on work efficiency is not always positive.

（3）In terms of the use of power, leadership can be divided into both assignment-oriented leadership and transformation-oriented leadership.

The feature of assignment-oriented leadership: The leaders who are assignment-oriented are in favor of managerial functions, diligent, modest and justice. They attach great importance to performance, such as plans, schedules, expenditures, etc. And they try their best to make the work in perfect order.

The feature of transformation-oriented leadership: The leaders of transformation-oriented leadership focus on transformation, innovation and starting new enterprise. The leading process is to purchase transformation systematically, organizationally, with purpose. And they always put their assumptions into practice to motivate the vitality of organization.

【小链接】

表 9-1　三种领导方式的差异

项目	专制型	民主型	放任型
群体方针的决定	一切由领导者决定	所有方针均由群体讨论决定，领导参与协调	任由群体或个人决定，领导者不参与
群体活动的了解与透视	方法和步骤由领导者决定，以命令的方式让成员接受	在讨论中了解工作程序和最终目标，成员有选择方法的自由	提供工作上所需要的各种材料，对成员提出的问题及时给予回答
工作的分担与同伴的选择	由领导者指定工作任务及其工作伙伴	工作分担由群体决定，同伴自由选择	领导者完全不干预

（续上表）

项目	专制型	民主型	放任型
工作参与及工作评价	回避群体作业，领导者以个人善恶来表扬或批评	在精神上成为群体成员，依据客观事实来表扬或批评	除非成员要求，不经常发表评论，不主动协调
与下属的关系	严厉不可亲近，以特别身份出现，高高在上	可以亲近，且觉得可以依靠，不以特别身份出现	可以亲近，但觉得不太可能
与上下级的关系	只听从上级指示，不考虑下属的情况	关心下属，将下属的要求反映到上级	不关心下属，也不在乎上级
发生问题时	不向下属做任何说明即下命令	向下属说明情形，再加以适当指示	不向下属做任何说明，也不作指示
听取下属意见	根本不让下属发表意见	尽可能听取下属的意见	不太注意下属的意见
成员反应	缺乏主动意识，失去个性，依赖性强，消极、自卑、不满、不负责任	个性发扬，群体观念强	感到自由，但缺乏群体观念

（资料来源：杨明刚：《现代实用管理学——知识·技能·案例·实训》（第二版），上海：华东理工大学出版社 2005 年版）

第三节　有关领导的理论

一、领导特质理论

特质理论主要是通过研究领导者的各种个性特质，来预测具有怎样性格特质的人才能成为有效的领导者。早期提出这种理论的学者认为，领导者所具有的特质是天生的，是由遗传决定的。显然，这种认识是不全面的。实际上，领导者的特质是在实践中逐渐形成的，可以通过教育和培训造就。当然，不同的环境对领导者提出的要求是不同的。下面列举一些人们提出的领导者应具有的特征和品格。

日本有效领导观要求一个领导者具有 10 项品德和 10 项能力。10 项品德是：使命感、责任感、信赖感、积极性、忠诚老实、进取心、忍耐性、公平、热情和勇气。10 项能力是：思维能力、决策能力、规划能力、改造能力、洞察能力、劝说能力、对人的理解能力、解决问题能力、培养下级能力、调动积极性的能力。

美国企业界认为一个企业家应具备 10 个条件，即合作精神、决策才能、组织能力、精于授权、善于应变、敢于求新、勇于负责、敢担风险、尊重他人、品德超人。瓦伦·本尼斯研究了 90 位美国最杰出和最成功的领导者，发现他们拥有 4 种共同的能力：有令人折服的远见和目标意识；能够清晰地表达这一目标，使下属明确理解；对这一目标表现出一致性并全力投入；了解自己的实力并以此作为资本。

苏伦斯·格利纳在哈佛大学通过对 300 多人进行调查，提出了有效领导者的 10 项重要特质：①劝告、训练与培训下属；②有效地与下属沟通；③让下属人员知道对他们的期望；④建立标准的工作要求；⑤给予下属参与决策的机会；⑥了解下属人员及其能力；⑦了解组织的士气状况，并能鼓舞士气；⑧不论情况好坏，都让下属了解实情；⑨愿意改进工作方法；⑩下属工作好时，及时给予表扬。

德鲁克认为，领导的有效性是一种后天的习惯，是一系列实践的综合。20 世纪 90 年代的研究发现，领导者有 6 种特质：进取心、领导愿望、诚实与正直、自信、智慧、业务知识。

从成功学的角度来研究，成功的领导者应在以下几方面得到修炼：善于思考、明确目标、调适心态、积极行动、不断学习、发挥潜能、养成习惯、管好时间、全力以赴。

从这些研究发现，作为一名优秀领导人，必须在多个方面具有比常人更强的能力和更好的品格。这些标准可以用于领导者的选拔和考核。

【小链接】

领导的性别差异

一般来说，男性与女性都能成为有效的领导者。只是情况也许有些不同：男性领导擅长军事领域，女性领导则在教育、社会服务、政府机构等领域更容易获得成功。为什么会这样，目前还不完全清楚。

认真考虑一下，在领导作用的发挥上，男性和女性的表现有不同之处吗？存在着"男性"领导模式吗？如果有，与"女性"领导模式有什么不同？有些人认为是的，但 Carly Fiorina 不这样认为。她是美国最著名的也是最有影响力的女性高管之一，经常被下列用来形容做大买卖的男性高管的词汇——坚定、大胆、有魄力所描绘。

根据《哈佛商业评论》中的一篇文章的说法，第一位女性领导为了进入高层管理，不得不模仿男性领导。然而今天，大量的女性已经利用其独特的技能和态度进入了高层管理。在这些方面，男性似乎更逊色一些。作家 Judy Rosener 说，男性领导似乎更多依靠其职位权力、奖励和惩罚（即合法权、奖励权和惩罚权），女性领导则倾向于依靠其气质、人际交往能力、勤奋的工作和个人感召力。Rosener 通过研究发现，女性领导者鼓励参与、主张分权、信息分享以及增强他人的自信心。更多的学术研究证实，女性管理者比男性管理者更愿意采用参与型领导方式。

Admiral Louise Wilmot 退休时，是美国海军中军衔最高的女性。她的领导风格是强调团队协作和人际关系。当被问到她的风格是否源于她是女人时，她回答，一个领导者应该"保持你的个性，保持好的、有益的、你感兴趣的并与他人不同的方面。这个世界上，没有任何理由让你放弃你的灵魂、你的个性或你的人格"。

思科的 John Chambers 认为女性作为领导者蕴藏着巨大的能量。他相信，伟大的女性领导才能正等待开发，将会登上硅谷的舞台。来自哈佛的 Rosabeth Moss Kanter 支持这种看法，"在信息全球化的时代，团队协作和合作是非常重要的，女性拥有更多的这种技能以获得成功"。

（资料来源：贝特曼等著，王雪莉译：《管理学：新竞争格局》（第六版），北京：北京大学出版社 2007 年版，第 408 页）

二、领导行为理论

对领导行为的研究始于 20 世纪 40 年代，主要研究领导者实际做什么、如何做。

1. 俄亥俄州立大学的研究

从 1945 年开始，美国俄亥俄州立大学工商企业研究所发起了对领导行为的研究，由著名学者斯托格迪尔主持，利用领导者行为描述问卷（LBDQ）来识别领导行为的基本维度。通过统计分析，发现领导行为可分成关怀和定规两个方面。前者是指关心下属的感受，尊重下属的想法；后者是指明确上下级各自的角色，通过计划、沟通、日程安排、分派任务、给予指示等方式指导群体完成任务。在高度关怀（或定规）和低度关怀（或定规）之间有无数不同程度的关怀（或定规）。以关怀为纵坐标、以定规为横坐标，以高低为分界点形成的一个二维构面大致把领导行为分为四种方式：高关怀低定规、高关怀高定规、低关怀低定规、低关怀高定规。俄亥俄州立大学的研究还指出，最有效的领导者是那些在关怀和定规两方面都做得好的人。

2. 密歇根大学的研究

20 世纪 40 年代末，在著名学者利克特的带领下，密歇根大学的研究人员开始识别导致有效群体绩效的领导行为模式。通过对众多高效或低效群体的比较，他们发现领导行为有两种基本形式：生产中心和员工中心。前者是指领导者主要关心任务的完成，后者是指领导者主要关心员工的福利。利克特假设了四种管理方式，以此来研究和阐明他的领导原则，这四种领导方式是：利用—命令式、温和—命令式、商议式、集体参与式。利克特提倡员工参与管理，指出员工中心的领导者比生产中心的领导者更有效。

3. 领导行为连续统一体理论

这是由美国管理学家坦南鲍姆（R. Tannenbaum）和施密特（W. H. Schmidt）提出的，如图 9 - 1 所示：

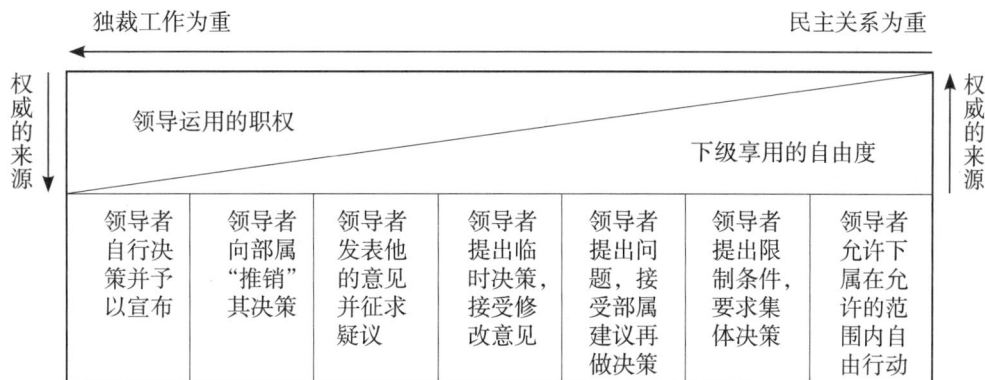

图 9 - 1　领导行为连续统一体理论示意图

这种理论认为领导并不只有独裁和民主两种极端的方式，而在这之间领导方式还可以分为七种不同的领导方式，这些方式有相应的授权程度和决策方式。

4. 管理方格理论

这是由美国管理学家布莱克（Robert R. Black）和穆顿（Jane S. Mouton）提出的，如图 9 - 2 所示：

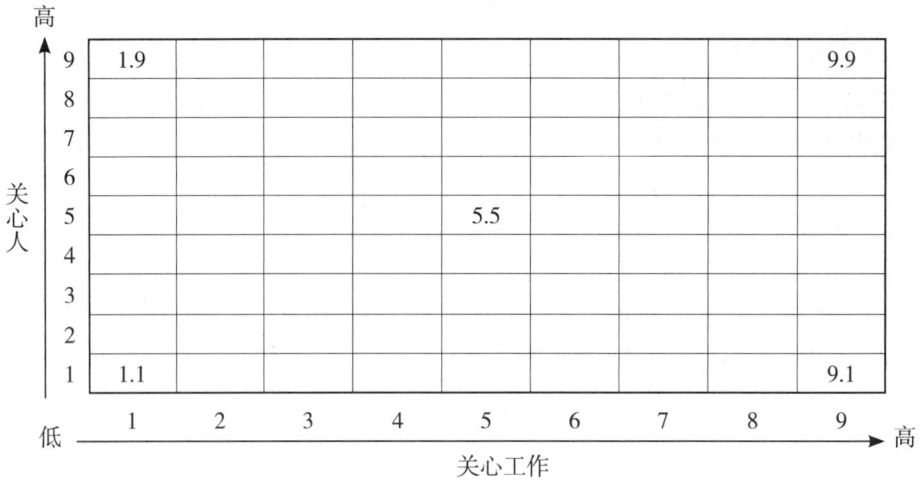

图 9－2　管理方格理论示意图

图中根据领导者对工作的关心程度和对人的关心程度可分成 9×9＝81 种领导方式，典型的有五种：

1.1 方式为"贫乏型管理"。领导者以最少的努力来完成必须做的工作和维持人际关系，对职工、生产都不关心。

9.1 方式为"任务型管理"。领导者只关心生产，不关心人；只考虑工作效率，不理会人际关系。

1.9 方式为"俱乐部型管理"。领导者极少甚至完全不关心生产而只关心人。他们尽量促成一种人人都感到轻松、友爱、快乐的环境，却不考虑如何完成企业的目标。

9.9 方式为"团队型管理"。领导者对生产和人都极为关心，他们把企业的生产需要和职工的人个利益完美地结合起来，企业内士气旺盛，大家齐心协力地完成生产任务。

5.5 方式为"中间型管理"。领导者对人与生产都有适度的关心，既有正常的效率完成生产任务，又保持一定的士气。

上述五种典型的领导行为，都仅仅是理论上的描述，也是极端的情况。在实际生活中，很难见到这么典型的范例。

三、领导权变理论

1. 菲德勒权变理论

这种理论是由美国管理学家菲德勒（F. E. Fiedler）提出的。他认为一种具体的领导方式不会到处都适用，有效的领导方式应随着被领导者的特点和环境的变化而变化。影响领导效果的权变因素有三个方面：

一是领导者与被领导者的关系（上下级关系），即领导者和其工作群体间关系的性质，如好的或差的。

二是工作任务的结构。即群体工作任务规定的明确程度，如任务是明确的、例行的，则任务结构就属于明确的，反之任务结构就是复杂的，就是不明确的。

三是领导者的职位权力。即领导者职位赋予领导者相关的权力，如权力较大，则认为职位权力较强，反之认为职位权力较弱。具体如表9－2所示。

表9－2　菲德勒权变理论示例

上下级关系	好				差			
任务结构	明确		不明确		明确		不明确	
职位权力	强	弱	强	弱	强	弱	强	弱
情境类型	1	2	3	4	5	6	7	8
领导所处的情境	有利				中间状态			不利
有效的领导方式	任务导向				关系导向			任务导向

这一理论将三种权变因素组合为八种情况，三种条件都具备或基本具备，是有利的领导情境。类型（如1、2、3）；三种条件都不具备，是不利的领导情境 类型（如8）。在有利和不利两种情况下，采用"任务导向型"的领导方式，效果较好；对处于中间状态的情境类型（如4、5、6、7），则采用"关系导向型"的领导方式，效果较好。

2. 路径—目标理论

领导者的工作是帮助下属达到他们的目标，并提供必要的指导和支持，以确保各自的目标与组织的总体目标一致。

根据路径—目标理论，领导者的行为被下属接受的程度，取决于下属是将这种行为视为获得当前满足的源泉，还是作为未来满足的手段。为此，豪斯确定了四种领导行为：指导型领导者让下属知道他对他们的期望是什么，以及他们完成工作的时间安排，并对如何完成任务给予具体指导，这种领导类型与俄亥俄州立大学的定规维度相似；支持型领导十分友善，表现出对下属需要的关怀，它与俄亥俄州立大学的关怀维度相似；参与型领导则与下属共同磋商，并在决策之前充分考虑他们的建议；成就导向型的领导设定富有挑战性的目标，并期望下属发挥出自己的最佳水平。与菲德勒的领导方式学说不同的是，豪斯认为领导者是灵活的，同一领导者可以根据不同的情景表现出任何一种领导风格。

Section 3　Theories of Leadership

9.3.1　Trait Theories

Trait theories of leadership differentiate leaders from non-leaders by focusing on personal qualities and characteristics. The scholars who raise the theory believe that the qualities of leaders are born, and are determined by the gene. Obviously, this understanding is not comprehensive. In fact, the trait of leaders is gradually formed in practice, through education and training. Of course, the standards are different for leaders in different environments. Here are examples presented by some people, indicating what characters and features leaders should have.

Japanese concept of effective leadership requires a leader with ten morals and ten capacities. The ten morals are: a sense of mission, responsibility, trust, enthusiasm, loyalty and honesty, initiative, patience, fairness, passion and courage. The ten capabilities are: thinking, decision-making, planning, transforming, insight, persuading, understanding, problem-solving, training subordinates, motivating.

Corporate of America believes an entrepreneur should have ten conditions: the spirit of cooperation, decision-making skills, organizational skills, proficient authorization, good emergency response, innovation, responsibility, risk-taking, respect for others, best character. Warren Bennis studied 90 America's most prominent and most successful leaders, and found four common superior abilities: compelling vision and sense of purpose, able to clearly express the goal to make subordinates clearly understanding, consistency and dedication to the goal, understand their strength as capital.

Suellen Galena, through investigating more than 300 people at Harvard University, puts forward ten important characteristics of the effect leaders: ① Advice, and train subordinates. ② Effectively communicate with subordinates. ③ Let staff know about their expectations. ④ Establish the standard of work requirements. ⑤ Offers opportunities for the subordinates to participate in decision-making. ⑥ Understand the subordinate personnel and ability. ⑦ Understand the state of morale in the organization, and can boost morale. ⑧ Whether the situation is good or bad, allow subordinates to understand truth. ⑨ willing to improve working methods. ⑩ When subordinates work well, praise them.

Drucker thinks that the effectiveness of leadership is a kind of acquired habit, and a series of comprehensive practice. In the 1990s, according to a study, leader has six characteristics: initiative, leadership desire, honesty and integrity, self-confidence, intelligence and business knowledge.

Studying from the angle of success, successful leaders should practice in the following aspects: be good at thinking, clear about objectives, adjustment of the state of mind, positive action, constantly learning, fulfill their potential, good habit, manage time, do best.

From these studies, as a good leader, you must have a greater capacity and better character than the common in many ways. These standards can be used in the selection and assessment of the leaders.

9.3.2 Behavioral Theories

Researchers on leaders' behavior began in the 1940s, mainly to study the leaders should do what and how to do.

1. Research of Ohio State University

Since 1945, the institute of industry and commerce of Ohio State University launched the study of leadership behavior, presided over by a famous scholar, Stodgill. Leader behavior description questionnaire (LBDQ) is used to identify the basic dimension of leadership behavior. Through statistical analysis, they found that leadership behavior can be divided into two aspects, consideration and regulation. The former refers to the concern for the feelings of subordinates and respect for the ideas of subordinates. The latter refers to their clear respective roles. By planning, communication, scheduling, assigning task, and giving instructions so the leaders can guide the group to complete the task. There are numerous different levels of care (or the regulation) between high degree of care (or the regulation) to low degree of care (or the regulation). The leadership behavior is roughly divided into four ways by a two-dimensional facet where care is the vertical axis, regulation is the horizontal axis, with high and low as the cut-off point: high care and low regulation, high care and high regulation, low regulation and low care, low care and high regulation. Ohio State University's study also noted that the most effective leaders are those who doing well in both of the two aspects.

2. Research of the University of Michigan

In the late 1940s, led by the famous scholar, Likert, researchers at University of Michigan, began to identify leadership behavior patterns lead to effective group performance. By comparing many efficient or inefficient groups, they found that the leadership behavior has two basic forms: production-centered and staff-centered. The former refers to the leaders concerned chiefly with the completion of task, and the latter mainly refers to the leaders concerned about the welfare of employees. He assumed four kinds of management methods, in order to study and clarify his leadership principles, they are: use-imperative style of leadership, moderate-imperative style of leadership, consulting style of leadership, participating style of leadership. Likert promotes employees to participate in the management, and points out that the staff-centered leaders are more effective than production-centered leaders.

3. Continuum of Leadership Behavior Theory

This is put forward by American management scientists R. Tannenbaum and W. H. Schmidt, as shown in Diagram 9 − 1:

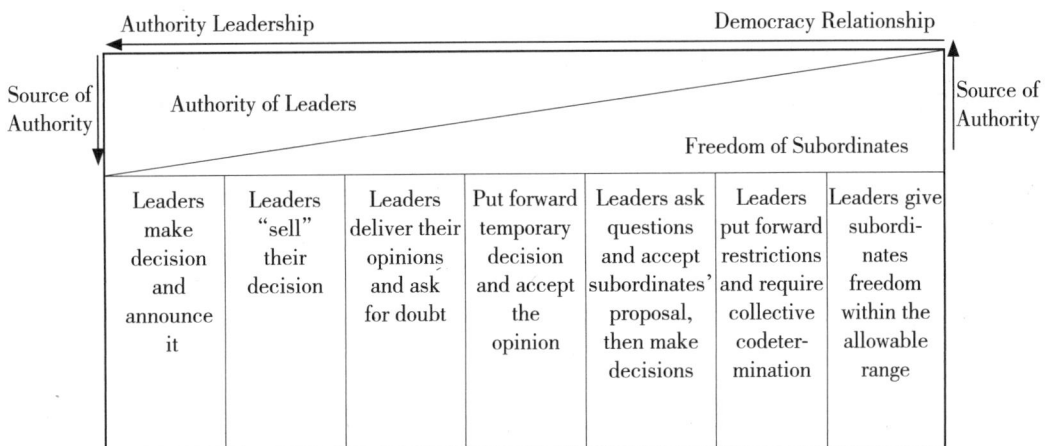

Diagram 9 − 1　Continuum of Leadership Behavior Theory

This theory supposes that leadership is not only two extreme ways of dictatorship and democracy, between them the leadership styles can also be divided into seven different styles, these approaches have corresponding authorization extent and way of decision-making.

4. The Managerial Grid Theory

This is put forward by the American management scientists Robert R. Black and Jane S. Mouton, as shown in Diagram 9 – 2：

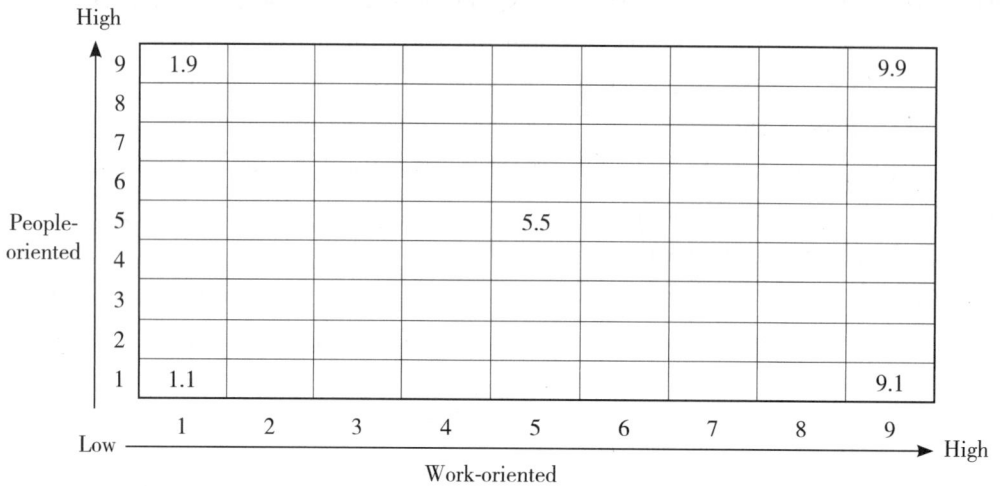

Diagram 9 – 2　The Managerial Grid Theory

The diagram according to the leader's care for work and concern for people divides leadership style into $9 \times 9 = 81$ kinds. There are five typical kinds of leadership style：

1. 1 Way is the "poor management". Leaders only make the least efforts to complete what must do, and maintain relationships, do not care about the production and workers.

9. 1 Way is the "task management". Leaders are only concerned with the production, but don't care about people, and only consider work efficiency, but ignore interpersonal relationships.

1. 9 Way is the "club management". Leaders rarely or even do not care with production and only care about people. They try to make everyone feel at ease, love, and happy, without thinking about how to fulfill the goals of the enterprise.

9. 9 Way is the "team management". Leaders are very concerned about both the production and the people. They combine the company's production needs with personal interests of the workers perfectly. With high morale, all work together to complete production tasks.

5. 5 Way is the "moderate management". Leaders have moderate concern with people and production, so as to complete production in normal efficiency and maintain certain morale.

These above five typical kinds of leadership style are all theoretical, and in extreme cases. It is rare to see in practice.

9.3.3　Contingency Theory of Leadership

1. Fiedler Model

This theory is carried out by F. E. Fiedler, an American manager. In his opinion, any specific leadership cannot be worked anywhere, and the effective behavior of leader should follow the change of the features of leaders and environment. There are three contingency factors influencing the leading effects:

Leader-member relations refer to the quality of the relationship between leaders and members, good or poor.

Task structure is exactitude of the task and rule of work in groups. If the task is specific and routine, the task structure is specific, otherwise, it is complicated and indefinite.

Position power is the power that the position gives. The stronger the power is, the stronger the position is. More details are shown in table 9 – 2:

Table 9 – 2　Fiedler Model

Leader-member Relations	Good				Poor			
Task Structure	Definite		Indefinite		Definite		Indefinite	
Position Power	Strong	Weak	Strong	Weak	Strong	Weak	Strong	Weak
Types of Situation	1	2	3	4	5	6	7	8
Situation of the Leader	Favorable		Moderate					Unfavorable
Effective Types of Leadership	Task-oriented		Relationship-oriented					Task-oriented

This theory divides the combinations of three contingency factors into eight situations. What is beneficial for leadership is completely or basically with three conditions (category 1, 2, 3). What goes against is none of three conditions (category 8). If you are faced with two situations (category 4, 5, 6, 7), you'd better choose "task-oriented". If you stand between two situations, you're better choose "relation ship-oriented".

2. Path-goal Theory

The task of leaders is to help their members achieve their goals and provide necessary guidance as well as support, ensuring their own targets are in accordance with the organizational total goal.

According to the path-goal theory, the degree of underlings' acceptance of leaders' behavior depends on whether underlings regard this behavior as the source of obtaining present satisfaction or the method of future satisfaction. For that, Hauss ensures four leadership behaviors: Leading leaders let their underlings know their forward to them and the time arrangement they finish the jobs, and give the detailed guidance on how to finish the tasks. It is similar to regulation dimensions from Ohio State University. Supporting leaders are really kind, showing their concern to their underlings' needs. It is similar to care structure from Ohio State University. Leaders of participating-oriented leadership negotiate with underlings. They fully consider underlings' suggestions before making decisions. Leaders of achievement-oriented leadership prefer to setting challenging goals and hoping their members to do their best. Different from Fiedler's leadership style, Hauss thinks leaders are flexible, which means that the same leader can show any one of leadership styles according to various places and times.

第四节　领导的素质和艺术

一、领导失败的原因

有些领导只拥有管理者的称号，却不能成为真正的领导人。这是因为他们不能被组织共同认可。领导人在领导一个群体之前，必须首先属于这个群体，应比群体中的其他成员更遵守已经为群体所接受的理念和行为标准。做不到这一点，就起不到领导的作用。

有些管理者虽然已被群体成员所接受，并被视为群体的领导，但他们还是失败了。原因在于他们完全没有发挥领导的作用，他们所做的是保护和维持组织的现状。只要组织没有要求他们发动、推动变革，他们的领导地位就不会受到威胁。

也有些领导者已被组织认可，并起到了积极的领导作用，但他们还是失败了。原因在于错误的或不合时宜的目标，他们不是没有能力，而是才智不足，缺乏管理才能。在所有失败当中，这是最难观察的原因之一，因为积极的、强有力的领导掩盖了他们自身的不足。

领导活动是领导者、被领导者和环境三方面共同影响、共同作用的过程，这一过程是否有效，直接取决于这三方面因素的契合或适应过程，也就是说这三个因素当中，任何一个因素的变化，均会导致不同的领导效率，这也正是领导艺术性之所在。因此，提高领导有效性的关键在于最大限度地促进领导者、被领导与环境之间的相互适应和相互协调。显然，领导者的素质起着根本性的作用。

二、领导者的素质

领导者的素质是指领导者的品质、性格、学识、能力、体质等特性的总和，良好的领导素质是提高领导有效性的重要条件，领导者应该具备的素质很多，概括起来可分为三大方面，即思想品德素质、知识素质和能力素质。

（1）思想品德素质。领导者的思想品质是其非职位影响力的主要来源，具体的要求包括：政治思想、道德情操、理想抱负、言行作风、心理健康。

（2）知识素质。领导者的主要工作是管理，因而要求有一个良好的知识结构，即"T"形结构，或称纵横结构。纵表示某一方面专业知识的深度，横表示某一领域相关的知识面的广度。"T"形结构就是要求领导者既有较宽的知识面，又要对某一知识领域有一定的深度了解。这种结构还必须是一种动态结构，即领导者的知识结构必须随着社会的发展和科学技术的进步不断地更新。具体来说，包括以下三个部分：

①专业知识。这要求领导者成为本部门、本单位或本行业的内行。

②管理知识。一个现代领导者，必须要懂得现代管理学的理论、原理、方法，并且要探索适用于本组织的管理制度和管理方法。

③ 相关知识。这包括与专业知识相关的知识和与管理相关的知识两个方面。

（3）能力素质。能力素质在领导者素质中占有重要地位，一个人是否能成为优秀的领导者，在很大程度上取决于他的能力。能力来源于学习、实践或经验。其关键能力有：

①洞察事物、提出构想的能力。洞察力是指用某种观点看待未来，并在一定程度上看清别人还不太清楚的事。洞察事物的本领，是领导者正确制定未来构想的前提，它直接关系到组织发展的兴衰，善于构想的人，必须是勤于思考、热衷于某一事业、善于发现机会和搜寻信息的人，也是乐于面对挑战的人。

②协调一致的能力。不管是什么领导，一项重要的任务就是将成员统一到组织的构想上来，这就要协调一致。有的领导能做到，有的领导能做好，而有的领导却做不到，也做不好。这就是领导艺术性。

③调动员工积极性的能力。能否调动员工积极性和创造性，以达成组织目标，是衡量领导者能力的重要标志。没有积极性的群体，是很难完成任务、实现目标的。

对一个领导者来说，上述三种素质是必不可少的。当然，不同层次的领导者对素质的要求是不同的，也会各有侧重。

三、领导艺术

管理是科学也是艺术，作为管理重要组织部分的领导也有其艺术性。领导艺术是建立在一定知识、经验基础之上的非规范化的、创造性的领导方法、技巧等，具有随机性、主观能动性、经验性、情感性的特征。

领导艺术的内容包括：决策艺术、用人艺术、授权艺术、激励艺术、沟通艺术、有效利用时间的艺术。

【新视角】

领导的发展趋势

领导的发展，呈现以下趋势：

一、授权型领导

传统型领导向授权型领导转变，来自两方面力量的推动：一是发生的问题需要快速决策；二是进入20世纪90年代以来，随着员工素质的提高或知识结构的变化，管理幅度显著增加。因此，事无巨细的管理是行不通了，因而管理者必须授权给他们的下级。合理授权的原则是：①明确职责；②因事择人，视能授权；③授权要留责；④授权而不放任；⑤授权要适度。

二、变革型领导

传统的领导多数是事务型领导，这些领导者通过明确决策和任务要求而指导下属，但由于环境的变化和竞争的加剧，要求组织不断地变革，以适应动荡的环境、动荡的年代，因而变革型领导逐渐取代事务型领导。变革型领导关怀着每一个下属的日常生活和发展需要，帮助下属转变观念，激励下属为实现目标而不断努力。

三、跨职能型领导

面对环境的快速变化，组织领导必须要有跨职能部门看问题的视角，因而，领导者必须能充分理解每个部门必不可少的作用，成为一个全面手。只有这样才能够做出正确的决策。

四、全球型领导

随着世界经济一体化发展速度的加快，生产的社会化已超越了国界，分工协作从企业内部地区之间发展到国与国之间，企业要从事跨国界运动，未来领导人就必须成为全球型的领导。

【阅读资料】

哪种领导类型最有效

ABC 公司是一家中等规模的汽车配件生产集团。最近，对该公司的三个重要部门经理进行了一次有关领导类型的调查。

1. 安西尔

安西尔对他本部门的产出感到自豪。他总是强调控制生产过程、出产量的必要性，坚持下属人员必须很好地解释生产指令，以得到迅速、完整、准确的反馈。当遇到小问题时，安西尔会放手交给下级去处理，当问题很严重时，他则委派几个有能力的下属人员去解决问题。通常情况下，他只是大致规定下属人员的工作方针、完成怎样的报告及完成期限。安西尔认为只有这样才能形成更好的合作，避免重复工作。

安西尔认为对下属人员采取敬而远之的态度对于一个经理来说是最好的行为方式，所谓的"亲密无间"会松懈纪律。他不主张公开谴责或表扬某个员工，相信他的每一个下属人员都有自知之明。

据安西尔说，在管理中最大的问题是下级不愿意接受责任。他讲到，他的下属人员可以有机会做许多事情，但他们并不是很努力地去做。

他表示不能理解在以前他的下属人员如何能与一个毫无能力的经理相处，他说，他的上司对他们现在的工作运转情况非常满意。

2. 鲍勃

鲍勃认为每个员工都有人权，他偏重于管理者有义务和责任去满足员工需要的观点，他说，他常为他的员工做一些小事，如给员工两张下个月举行的艺术展览的入场券。他认为，每张门票才 15 美元，但对员工和他的妻子来说却远远超过 15 美元。这种方式也是对员工过去几个月工作的肯定。鲍勃说，他每天都要到工厂去一趟，与至少 25% 的员工交谈。鲍勃不愿意为难别人，他认为安西尔的管理方式过于死板，安西尔的员工也许并不那么满意，但除了忍耐别无他法。

鲍勃说，他已经意识到在管理中有不利因素，但大都是由于生产压力造成的。他的想法是以友好、粗线条的管理方式对待员工。他承认尽管自己的部门在生产率上不如其他单位，但他相信他的雇员有高度的忠诚与士气，并坚信他们会因他的开明领导而努力工作。

3. 查里

查里说他面临的基本问题是与其他部门的职责分工不清。他认为不论是否属于他们的任务都安排在他的部门，似乎上级并不清楚这些工作应该谁做。查里承认他没有提出异议，他说这样做会使其他部门的经理反感。他们把查里看成朋友，而查里却不这样认为。查里说过去在不平等的分工会议上，他感到很窘迫，但现在适应了，其他部门的领导也不以为然了。

查里认为纪律就是为了使每个员工不停地工作，预测各种问题的发生。他认为作为一个好的管理者，没有时间像鲍勃那样握紧每一个员工的手，告诉他们正在从事一项伟大的工作。他相信如果一个经理声称为了决定将来的加薪与升职而对员工的工作进行考核，那么，员工则会更多地考虑他们自己，由此而产生很多问题。他主张，一旦给一个员工分配了工作，就让他以自己的方式去做，取消工作检查。他相信大多数员工知道自己把工作做得怎么样。

如果说存在问题，那就是他的工作范围和职责在生产过程中发生了混淆。查里的确想过，希望公司领导叫他到办公室听听他对某些工作的意见。然而，他并不能保证这样做不会引起风波而使情况有所改变。他说他正在考虑这些问题。

（资料来源：阿诺德、菲尔德曼著，邓荣霖等译：《组织行为学》，北京：中国人民大学出版社 1990 年版）

Section 4　Culture and Art of Leadership

9.4.1　The Reason for Leadership Failure

Some leaders only belong to managers, but real heads. This is because they cannot be all agreed by the organization. Before leading the group, the leader should be a member of the group first of all, and conform to the ideas and standards accepted by the members more seriously and carefully than other members. Otherwise, the leader is impossible to play a leading role.

Some managers have already been accepted by the members and seen as the heads of the groups, but they fail. The reason is that they entirely don't play their leading roles. What they do is protecting and maintaining the groups' statue. As long as the groups don't require them to have revolutions, their leading status won't be threatened.

Some leaders have been agreed by the groups and play an active role, but they fail. This results from wrong and inopportune goals. They are capable, but unwise and lack of management perspective. Among all the failures, this is one of the reasons that are most difficult to be discovered, because positive and strong leading covers up the shortages themselves.

Leadership is the period affected by three factors, leaders, members and environment. Whether the period is effective depends on the cooperation and adaptation period of three factors, that is, among three factors, the change of any factor will cause different leading efficiency. That is the art of leadership, thus the key to improving leading efficiency is to promote leaders, members and environment to adapt to and coordinate with each other to most extent. Obviously, the culture of the leaders works originally.

9.4.2　The Culture of Leadership

The culture of leadership means total characteristics of leaders' quality, character, knowledge, capability, constitution. Good culture of leadership is an important condition to improve leading efficiency. The leaders should master a lot of culture, in a word, ideological and moral quality, academic quality and capability.

(1) Ideological and moral quality. This is main factor of non-position influence, of which includes political culture, moral culture, personal perspective, personal behavior, psychological heath.

(2) Academic quality. The main responsibility of leaders is management, so it requires a large amount of knowledge, which is T model or vertical-horizontal model. Vertical one means the depth of some part of specialized knowledge. Horizontal one means the range of knowledge in one field. T model requires the leaders to be erudite and professional. What's more, it must be a developable structure, that is, it must update following the development of society and science and technology. To be specific, it includes three parts:

①Professional knowledge. It requires leaders to be experts of the department, company and industry.

②Management knowledge. A modern leader must master the theory, principle, method of modern management and explore the management system and method that are suitable for their organization.

③ Relative knowledge. It has two parts of knowledge, relative to professional and management knowledge.

(3) Capability. It is very essential in the leadership culture. The way to be an excellent leader mostly depends on his capability. It comes from study, practice and experience. The key capabilities are:

①The capability of insight and imaging. Insight means you can see future through some perspectives and know things that others don't know in some degree. The ability of insight is the premise of ensuring future's ideas correctly, concerning the vicissitude of the organization directly. The one who is good at imaging must be someone who frequently considers, loves his enterprise, hunts the opportunity acutely and searches the information, as well as faces to challenges willingly.

②The capability of coordinating. No matter what kind of leader one choose to be, one of the important tasks is to unite the members to the ideas of organization. Some leaders can do it, some do it well, however, some can't do it or do it bad. It is the art of leadership.

③The capability of encouraging. The important sign of the evaluation of the ability of leaders is encouraging the members' enthusiasm and creation to achieve the group's goals. Without a group of enthusiastic members, it's hard to finish the tasks and achieve the goals.

For a leader, capabilities in the above aspects are necessary. Surely, the requirement of culture differs from the various levels of leaders and weights.

9.4.3　The Art of Leadership

Management is a kind of science as well as a kind of art. As the leader of the key part of management in the group, it has its art. The art of leadership is the non-standardized, creative leading methods and skills established on knowledge and experience. Its features are random, subjective initiative, empirical, emotional.

The contents of the art of leadership include the art of decision-making, employment, authorization, encouragement, communication and time-efficiency.

【本章提要】

● 领导作为一种管理职能，其实质是影响别人，其目的是让被领导者服从、接受并努力去实现组织目标。

● 领导权力有以下几种表现形式：法定权、奖赏权、强制权、表率权和专长权，前三者来自组织的职位，是一种外在性权力；后两者来自领导本身的因素，是一种内在性权力。

● 领导的作用包括：指挥、激励、协调、感召、造势。领导者的任务概括起来有两项，一是实现组织或群体目标，二是满足组织或群体成员的具体需要。

● 领导方式从不同的角度可以划分为不同的类型，没有一成不变的领导方式。领导方式的选择应取决于领导者所处的环境。

● 领导是科学，更是艺术，一个优秀的领导者应当具备三方面的素质：思想品德素质、知识素质和能力素质。

【关键词】

领导（Leadership）　　领导权力（Leadership Power）　　内在影响（Internal Influence）

外在影响（External Influence）　　民主型领导方式（Democratic Leadership）

变革型领导方式（Transformation-oriented Leadership）

领导素质（The Culture of Leadership）　　领导艺术（The Art of Leadership）

【复习与思考】

1. 领导者是如何对被领导者施加影响的？

2. 领导者应完成哪些任务、做好哪些工作？

3. 领导方式主要有哪几类？其特点是什么？

4. 一个优秀的领导者应具备哪些素质？

5. 什么样的领导才能与未来组织发展相适应？

【研究与讨论】

1. 领导者与管理者有何不同？你认为领导者是天生的吗？

2. "什么是领导？5 点下班时尚未完成工作，却能让员工将工作完成后再下班，这就是领导。"这句话有无道理？

3. 如果你是一名部门经理，你会发现上级对你的要求和下级对你的要求是不同的。采取什么样的领导方式只能满足某一方的要求？采取什么样的领导方式能够同时满足双方的要求？

4. 20 世纪 20—50 年代，领导理论重点研究个人特征；20 世纪 50—60 年代重点研究领导行为；20 世纪 60—70 年代重点研究情景领导；20 世纪 70—80 年代研究重点又回到了个人特征和行为。这说明了什么？

5. 怎样才能做一个有效的领导者？

【实践演练】

1. "领导就是服务。"请联系实际和课程内容谈谈你对这句话的理解。

2. 列举出一些领导的名单进行分组讨论，你为什么认为他们是领导者？每组选出一位发言人，向全班汇报讨论结果。

3. 在现实生活中找出一位领导者，评价这位领导并列举出值得你学习的地方。

【管理模拟】

如果你是领导者：（1）如何提升你的素质和能力？
                （2）如何有效运用领导理论和领导艺术？

【本章案例】

经过一场被广泛深入报道的竞争之后，杰克·威尔茨在 1981 年成为通用电气公司的总裁。拥有化学工程博士学位的威尔茨成为通用电气第 8 位、也是最年轻的首席执行官。在很短的时间内，威尔茨对公司的各个方面做了迅速彻底的变革，改变了公司的业务组合和组织文化。他所确定的目标是使通用电气成为它参与竞争的每个市场的前两名。他以巨大的决心和勇气迎接这一挑战。

从青年时代的体育场到现在的职业生涯，威尔茨一直都是一位强有力的竞争者。他已经把通用电气的事业当作自己的全部事业。威尔茨最初在通用电气取得成功，是由于他大幅度地增加了塑料部门的销售收入和利润，使之由一个很小的部门发展成通用电气一个收入与利润来源的主要部门。从在通用电气职业生涯的早期阶段起，威尔茨就对公司僵化的官僚机制感到失望，他花费了大量时间对这个体制进行改革，试图找到新方法把工作做好。他发现公司变革成功的关键因素是激发首创的精神、赋予管理者自主权和淘汰无所事事、工作不力的管理者。

根据在通用电气若干年的经验，威尔茨已经确信，公司的管理机构官僚僵化，重叠臃肿，根本无法迅速地做出决策，更不用说有效地实施这些决策了。通过削减一些管理层次，威尔茨开始对较低的但能够最先发现问题并迅速采取最为合适的解决措施的管理层次授权。在 1981 年，通用电气的每个事业单位都拥有 9 至 11 个层次的官僚结构；到 1991 年，威尔茨已将管理层次削减了大约一半，使之降为 4 至 6 个层次。他把公司总部的职员从 1 700 人削减到 1 000 人以下，几乎所有部门都进行了裁员。从 1981 年至今，通用电气已经裁员 180 000 人，出售了价值 120 亿美元的业务。

出售这些业务并非一帆风顺。在 20 世纪 80 年代，卖掉主要的事业单位并辞退其 50% 的员工对公司员工的士气影响极大。员工们的态度开始分化。他们中的一部分赞赏威尔茨，而另一部分则对他极为憎恶。工会开组织会时公开反对威尔茨采取的措施。"通用电气得了一种病——'威尔茨病'"，电子产业工人国际联盟主席约瑟夫·艾根说："这种病源于公司的野心、狂妄自大和对员工的轻视。"

但是，威尔茨的崇拜者们坚信，威尔茨是在做一件非常了不起的大事。他们声称：威尔茨的远见卓识和他在通用电气所做的艰苦卓绝的变革，正是这个公司的当务之急。在威尔茨来到通用电气之前，通用电气的一位董事会副主席曾指出这个公司"像消化系统一样平稳和可以预测，它需要振奋"。威尔茨给通用电气公司带来了变革的激情以及如何参与未来全球化市场竞争的前景。

思考问题：

1. 杰克·威尔茨是有效的领导者吗？为什么？
2. 你认为威尔茨采取的领导方式是怎样的？
3. 参阅威尔茨写的书，评述威尔茨的领导风格与成功法则。

【本章参考文献】

［1］芮明杰：《管理学——现代的观点》（第二版），上海：上海人民出版社 2005年版。

［2］［美］F. 赫塞尔本等主编，吕一凡等译：《未来的领导》，成都：四川人民出版社1998年版。

［3］周三多：《管理学》，北京：高等教育出版社 2000 年版。

［4］［美］约瑟夫·M. 普蒂等著，丁慧平、孙先锦译：《管理学精要——亚洲篇》，北京：机械工业出版社 1999 年版。

［5］［美］安弗莎妮·纳哈雯蒂著，王新译：《领导力》，北京：机械工业出版社 2003年版。

第十章 激 励

Chapter 10　Motivation

一个良好的组织所包含的人才中，每一个人都要能提供这个团体其他成员所未拥有的特殊才能。

拿破仑·希尔

The talents in an efficient organization should provide for unique abilities，the ones that the others in the organization fail to acquire.

Napoleon Hill

有效培训的秘诀在于激励。

小克劳德·乔治

The secret of effective training is to motivate.

Claude S. George

【本章学习目标】

知识目标：

了解激励的实质和功能。

理解激励的方式和原则。

学习激励的有关理论。

技能目标：

掌握激励的过程。

能够运用激励理论。

完善激励机制。

【Learning Objectives of Chapter 10】

Objectives of Knowledge：

Understand the essence and functions of motivation.

Understand the methods and principles of motivation.

Learn some theories related to motivation.

Objectives of Skill：

Master the process of motivation.

Apply the theories of motivation.

Improve the motivation mechanism.

【小故事】

一天，北风和南风比威力，看谁能把行人身上的大衣吹掉。北风首先来一个寒风，凛冽刺骨，结果，行人把大衣裹得更紧了。南风则徐徐吹动，顿时风和日丽，行人觉得春意在身，便开始解开纽扣，继而脱掉大衣。因而南风获得了胜利。

【引例】

沃尔玛的员工激励

世界上最大的零售商沃尔玛公司，目前正面临着如何激励员工的问题。多年来，这家公司都使用一种相对宽松和直接的方式来激励员工，以保持他们的忠诚度。公司主要是通过给员工股权来激励他们，而员工的正常薪水并不高。

在沃尔玛公司历史上，股权激励制度曾经起过很大的推动作用。比如，一名员工在1970年公司股票上市时，用1 650美元买了100股，到1993年时，他拥有股票的价值就是350万美元。20世纪70年代后期到80年代这段时间里，沃尔玛的股票每年都上涨不少。公司通过利润分享计划建立了养老基金，基金中大部分的钱投资于购买公司的股票。这样，养老基金也会随着公司股票价格的上涨而有很大的激励作用。山姆·沃尔顿是公司的创立者，他本人也促使了这种忠诚度和工作动机的形成。他平易近人的处事方式和公司的良好运作，使公司拥有了零售业界最忠诚、最积极献身的员工。公司一直被员工和业界认为具有非常优越的工作环境。

然而到了20世纪90年代，情况开始发生变化。首先，虽然公司仍然利润相当高，但公司的发展减缓，收入和利润已经没有太大的增长，从而导致了沃尔玛股票价格的下跌。1993年，公司股票每股的价格是30多美元，到1995年底，就只有20美元左右了。股票的下跌大大削减了养老基金和员工个人股票的价值。结果，公司长期拥有的员工忠诚度开始下降，工作动机开始减弱。

1992年山姆·沃尔顿去世以后，公司文化也开始发生一些微妙的变化，这使问题更加严重。公司新的管理层试图保持原有的经营方式以及与员工之间的关系，但不少主管人员缺乏领导魅力，也不能坚持山姆·沃尔顿过去倡导的与员工个人接触的管理方式。另外，新来的员工当然不可能有机会见到公司的创立者山姆·沃尔顿本人，因而也无法从老一辈公司领导那里受到教育和感染。除了忠诚度和工作动机方面的问题以外，沃尔玛还面临因经济危机引发的其他问题。比如说，在避免工会组织不利于公司的集会方面，以前沃尔玛做得很好。但现在由于员工对养老金和其他激励越来越不满，工会组织各种集会并取得胜利的机会越来越多。

自1991年至1993年，整个公司只出现过三次工人集会，而1994年一年就出现过四次。等待着沃尔玛的将是什么呢？每个人都在猜测。虽然沃尔玛作为一个雇主的形象受到了负面的影响，但大多数专家从一个雇员的角度来看，仍然认为它是该行业最好的公司之一。而且，公司现在还是在赢利，管理层也坚信股票价格会再次上升。因此，他们相信员工还是会对公司满意的，也会为公司继续做贡献。但也有人认为，出现的问题已经对公司造成损害，沃尔玛将不会再度拥有它曾代表的优越工作环境的形象。

思考问题：

1．用什么激励理论能最恰当地解释沃尔玛出现的问题？

2．如果在当前的困难情况下，由你来管理沃尔玛，你将如何激励员工？

第一节　激励的实质和功能

组织的发展，需要全体成员长期的协作和努力，如何激发和调动组织成员的积极性，是管理的一个基本课题。

一、激励的含义

激励是指创造满足人们需要的条件，激发人们的动机，使之产生实现组织目标的特定行为的过程。包含四个方面的内容：

（1）激励的出发点，就是满足人们的各种需要，即物质上和精神上的需要。

（2）激励贯穿于组织员工的全过程，包括对个人需要的了解、个性的把握、行为过程的控制和行为结果的评价等。

（3）信息沟通的好坏，会直接影响激励制度的运用效果和激励的成本。

（4）激励的最终目的在于充分发挥人的能动作用，实现组织目标。

二、激励的原理

人们的行为是受动机支配的，动机又是由人的需要引起的。需要产生动机，动机驱使人们寻找目标，当人们产生了某种需要，一时又不能得到满足时，心理上会产生一种不安和紧张状态，并成为一种内在的驱动力，促使个体采取某种行动，这种内在的驱动力就称为动机。有了动机以后就需要寻找满足各种需要的目标，找到目标后，就进行需要满足的活动。需要满足后，紧张和不安会消除，但新的需要又会产生，并引发新的动机和行为，如此不停地反复下去。激励正是利用这一过程，在分析人们需要的基础上，不断激发、引导人们沿着组织所希望的方向去行动，以取得预期的成效。从这个意义上说，激励也就是对需要与动机进行持续诱导的过程。

三、激励的功能

1．激励有助于激发和调动组织成员的工作积极性

积极性是人们在完成工作任务时一种能动的、自学的心理和行为状态，这种状态可以促进人们智力和体力的充分释放，并促成一系列积极的行为后果，如提高工作效率，超额完成任务，良好的服务态度等。实验证明未受过激励的职工，其积极性只能发挥 20% ~ 30%；受过激励的职工，其积极性可发挥 80% ~ 90%。

2．激励有助于将成员的个人目标导向实现组织目标的轨道

个人目标及个人利益是人们行动的基本动力，它们与组织的目标和总体利益之间既有一有致性，又存在着许多差异。当二者发生背离时，个人目标往往会干扰组织目标的实现，激励的功能就在于以个人利益和需要的满足为基本作用力，引导成员把个人目标统一

于组织的总体目标，推动成员为完成任务做出贡献，进而促进个人目标和组织目标的共同实现。

3. 激励有助于提高组织的凝聚力，促进内部各个组成部分的协调和统一

一个组织是由若干个体、工作群体及各种非正式群体组成的有机结构，为保证组织协调运转，除了用严密的组织结构、严格的规章制度加以规范外，还需要运用激励的方法，满足成员多方面的需要，鼓舞其士气，协调其人际关系，从而增强组织的凝聚力，促进各个部门的群体、成员的密切协作。

四、激励的类型

激励可按不同的方法分类。

1. 物质激励与精神激励

这是按激励的内容划分的。物质激励作用于人的生理方面，着眼于满足人们的物质需要。精神激励作用于人的心理方面，着眼于满足人们的精神需要。物质激励的形式主要是颁发奖金和实物，精神激励则有授予称号，颁发奖状、奖章，记功，开会表扬，宣传事迹等多种具体形式。

2. 正激励与负激励

按激励的性质，可分为正激励和负激励。所谓正激励，就是当一个人的行为表现符合社会需要和组织目标时，通过表彰和奖励来保持和巩固这种行为，更加充分地调动成员的积极性。所谓负激励，就是当一个人的行为不符合社会需要或组织目标时，通过批评和惩罚来抑制这种行为并使其不再发生，同时引导组织成员的积极性向正确的方向转移。正激励和负激励都是对人的行为进行强化，所不同的是取向相反。正激励起正强化的作用，是对行为的肯定；负激励起负强化的作用，是对行为的否定。

3. 内激励和外激励

按照激励的方式，可以把激励分为内激励和外激励。内激励是通过启发诱导的方式，激发人的主动性，使他们的工作热情建立在高度自觉的基础上，充分发挥内在的潜力。外激励则是运用环境条件来鼓励或制约人们，以此来强化或削弱有关行为，提高成员的工作意愿。内激励着眼于调动人的内因，带有自觉性的特征；外激励则侧重外因，具有一定程度的强迫性。

Section 1　Essence and Functions of Motivation

The development of the organization relies on the long-term endeavor and cooperation of the staff, so how to keep the employees motivated and stimulate their working enthusiasm is a basic subject of management.

10. 1. 1　Definition of Motivation

Motivation is the process to create supporting conditions for people to fulfill their needs and to motivate them, which will lead to specific behaviors in favor of the attainment of the organizational goals. The definition of motivation contains four points:

（1）The start point of motivation is to satisfy people's various needs both materially and spiritually.

（2）Motivation should be applied to the whole process of staff management, including identifying the individual needs and personalities, controlling behavioral process and accessing the results of behavior.

（3）The efficiency of information communication has a direct impact on the cost and the result of motivation.

（4）The ultimate goal of motivation is to make full use of the human motility to fulfill the goal of the organization.

10. 1. 2　The Law of Motivation

Human behaviors are dominated by incentives which are aroused by human needs. The needs arouse corresponding motivation which will drive people to seek some targets. The intense state aroused by unsatisfied needs will become an interior drive to motivate individuals to take some actions. The inner drive is called incentive. When there is an incentive, people will search for some targets, after which they will take some actions to meet the targets and needs. If the needs have been met, the intense and unease state will elapse. When a need is satisfied, there will be a new one to be met, followed by new incentives and behaviors. It is in the circular process that motivation works. On the basic of analyzing individual needs, managers can arouse individual enthusiasm and lead them to behave as the organization needs to obtain the expected performance. In this perspective, motivation is a cyclic process to arouse individual needs and incentives.

10. 1. 3　The Functions of Motivation

1. Help Arouse and Stimulate the Enthusiasm of the Staff

Enthusiasm is a mental and physical state in which people are active and self-teaching in order to complete a task. Such state can promote people to fully develop their mental and physical potentials, leading to a series of positive behaviors, such as high efficiency, over-fulfilled tasks, good service attitudes, etc. Experiments indicate that the workers failing to be motivated, play only $20\% \sim 30\%$ of their enthusiasm and when motivated, play $80\% \sim 90\%$。

2. Help the Staff Align the Individual Goals with the Organizational Goals

Individual goals and interests are the source of energy. Sometimes individual goals and interests are consistent with organizational goals and interests, but sometimes they conflict with organizational goals and interests. When individual goals and interests conflict with organizational goals and interests, individual goals and interests will be an obstacle to organizational goals and interests. On the basis of fulfilling individual interests and needs, motivation is to unite individual goals with organizational goals, driving the staff to try their best to fulfill the tasks and facilitating the attainment of both individual and organizational goals.

3. Improve the Organizational Cohesion and Promote the Harmony and Integration of the Internal Parts

An organization is an organic structure constituted by some individuals, work groups and various kinds of informal groups. In order that the organization will operate in harmony, we should apply motivation to meeting various needs, thus arousing morale, harmonizing interpersonal relations, increasing organizational cohesion and promoting intimate cooperation of every group and individual.

10. 1. 4　Types of Motivation

Motivation can be classified by different methods:

1. Material Motivation and Spiritual Motivation

It is classified by the ways used to motivate. Material motivation has physical impact on people to fulfill individual material needs. Spiritual motivation has psychological impact on people to fulfill individual spiritual needs. Material motivation takes form of prize money and material benefits while spiritual motivation takes form of honorable title, certificate of merit, medal, recording, praise, advertisement and so on.

2. Positive Motivation and Negative Motivation

According to the property, motivation can be divided into positive motivation and negative motivation. Positive motivation is to encourage and award the behaviors which benefit the society and the organization, therefore maintaining and strengthening the behaviors. Negative motivation is to punish or criticize individuals for their inappropriate behaviors, keeping them from the inappropriate behaviors. Both positive and negative motivation can strengthen individual behaviors, but they operate in different directions. Positive motivation is an affirmation of the behaviors, strengthening the current behaviors but negative motivation is a denial of the current behaviors, trying to keep people from making the same mistake.

3. Internal Motivation and External Motivation

According to the methods, motivation can be divided into internal motivation and external motivation. Internal motivation takes form of inspiring to stimulate the individual enthusiasm and make the best of the internal potentials. External motivation will use the external conditions to constrain individual incentives, strengthening or weakening some behaviors to raise the working enthusiasm. Internal motivation focuses on the internal incentives, depending on the individual while external motivation focuses on external incentives, depending on the external forces.

第二节　激励的过程、方式和原则

一、激励的过程

需要、动机和目标作为激励的主要心理机制分别处于行为的不同阶段，三者既彼此独

立又相互依存，并按照所处阶段密切连接，顺次对行为发挥激励功能，由此构成一个完整的激励过程。（如图 10 - 1 所示）

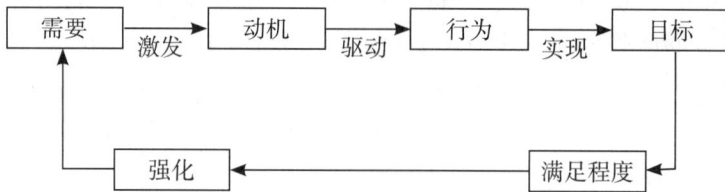

图 10 - 1　激励的过程

可见，激励实质上是以未满足的需要为基础，利用各种目标诱因激发动机，驱动和诱导行为，促进实现目标，提高需要满足程度的连续的心理和行为过程。在企业管理中，根据激励的作用原理，对过程的不同阶段施以各种诱因或条件，可以达到有效激励员工行为的目的。

二、激励的方式

激励的方式多种多样，内容也很丰富，下面介绍几种常用的激励方式：

1. 基于经济利益的激励

这也称物质激励，它是通过物质刺激来进行激励的方式。

具体有以下几种：

（1）与业绩相联系的薪酬。这是一种将薪酬与员工的工作业绩相联系来激励员工的方法，薪酬不仅是一种激励手段，也是员工价值的体现。具体有四种表现形式：

①计件工资：把员工的收入与生产效率相联系。

②销售提成：根据员工的销售量而获得相应的收入。

③利益分享：员工减少成本或提高效益的额外收入。

④利润分享：按一定的比例提取公司利润分配给员工。

用这种方式激励员工，其优点在于能使员工相信只要把业绩提高就能得到相应的报酬，从而调动他们的积极性。

（2）津贴福利计划：是物质激励的另一个重要表现形式，它通常被称为间接报酬，具体包括：①带薪休假。②社会保障基金。③养老金计划。④岗位津贴。津贴福利的优点在于能够满足员工的安全需要。

（3）员工持股计划：这是指本公司员工所认购的公司股份，在公司上市后，就可以在市场流通，或从公司的经营成果中，分享一定的红利。持股的员工，就是公司的股东，就会以主人的工作态度投入工作。

2. 基于非经济利益的激励

这也称精神激励。具体方式有以下几种：目标激励；荣誉激励；形象激励；榜样激励；感情激励；兴趣激励；培训和晋升激励；参与激励。

激励方式的内容很多，但主要包括物质激励和精神激励两个方面。但相同的方式对不同的人，效果会有差异，因此，在实施激励过程中一定要认清个体差异、职位差异，根据具体情况采用不同的激励方式。另外，各种方式的激励的混合使用，会提高激励的效果，但要注意激励的成本。

3. 工作激励

实践中经常有以下几种：工作的适应性；工作的挑战性；工作的完整性；工作的自主性；工作的扩大化；工作的丰富化；及时的工作成果反馈。

【新视角】

进入 20 世纪 90 年代以来，西方企业在多种激励理论的基础上，提出了一些新的激励计划，竭力改善员工的满意度和绩效。这些计划主要包括绩效工资、分红、员工持股、总奖金、知识工资和灵活的工作日程等。这些激励计划增强了组织对熟练员工的吸引力，最终有效降低了招聘和培训员工的成本。

三、激励的原则

1. 物质激励与精神激励相结合的原则

人既有物质需要，也有精神需要，相应地，在激励方式上就应该坚持物质激励与精神激励相结合。因为物质需要是人类最基本的需要，也是最低层次的需要，所以，物质激励是一种基本的激励形式，但其激励作用是有限的。随着生产力水平和人的素质的提高，人们的精神需求增强，就应该更加强调精神激励。换句话说，物质激励是基础，精神激励是根本，应在两者结合的基础上，从物质激励逐步过渡到以精神激励为主。在这个问题上，应该避免走极端，迷信物质激励则导致拜金主义，迷信精神激励则导致唯意志论或精神万能论，事实证明，这两种做法都是片面的、有害的。

2. 外激励与内激励相结合的原则

人的行为既受到内因的驱动，又受到外因的影响；内因的作用是根本，外因必须通过内因而起作用。这就要求领导者要善于将外激励和内激励相结合，并且以内激励为主；要着眼于激发员工的高层次需要和深层动机，使其内心深处焕发出工作的热情和动力。这种工作动力比外激励所引发的动力要深刻和持久得多。

3. 正激励与负激励相结合的原则

正激励和负激励各自针对不同的行为，而这两种行为在组织中都是常见的，所以，正激励和负激励都是必要而有效的。它们不仅作用于当事人，而且会间接地影响周围的其他人。只有将二者结合运用，才能树立正面的榜样和反面的典型，扶正祛邪，形成一种好的风气，产生无形的动力，使整个群体或组织的行为更积极、更有生气。但鉴于负激励有一定的消极作用，容易产生挫折行为，应该慎用。领导者在坚持正激励与负激励相结合的同时，应坚持以正激励为主。

4. 目标结合原则

在激励机制中，设置目标是一个关键环节。目标设置首先必须体现组织的目标要求，否则激励就会偏离正确的方向；其次，目标设置也必须能够满足员工个人的需要，否则无法达到满意的激励强度。只有将组织目标与个人目标结合好，使组织目标包含较多的个人目标，使个人目标的实现离不开为实现组织目标所做的努力，才能收到良好的激励效果。

5. 按需激励原则

激励的起点是满足员工的需要，但员工需要存在着个体差异性和动态性，因人而异，因时而异，并且只有满足最迫切需要（即主导需要）的措施，其激励强度才大。因此，领导者在进行激励时，必须进行深入的调查研究，不断了解员工需要层次和需要结构的变化趋势，然后采取有针对性的激励措施，这样才能收到实效。

6. 公正民主原则

公正是激励的一个基本原则。如果奖罚不分，不仅收不到预期的效果，甚至会适得其反，造成许多消极后果。公正就是赏罚严明并且赏罚适度。赏罚严明就是要铁面无私、不论亲疏、不分远近、一视同仁，正如韩非子所说："诚有功，则虽疏贱必赏；诚有过，则虽近爱必诛。"赏罚适度就是要从实际出发，赏与功相匹配，罚与罪相对应，既不能小功重奖，也不能大过轻罚。

公正的一个主要体现就是在物质激励上要贯彻按劳激励原则。使职工多劳多得、少劳少得。只有这样，才能破除平均主义的传统观念，激励职工勤奋劳动、积极竞争，在为组织做出贡献的同时获得更多的个人利益，也只有这样，物质激励手段才能真正起到应有的作用。

民主是公正的保证，也是激励的基本要求。在制定激励制度、奖惩方案的过程中吸收职工参与和监督，可以有力地防止不正之风，最大限度地确保公正。

Section 2　Process，Methods and Principles of Motivation

10.2.1　Process of Motivation

Needs，incentives and targets will work in different stage during a behavior process and they are the main psychological mechanisms. Although they are separate with each other in terms of time，they influence each other and depend on each other. The working process is indicated as follows. (Diagram 10 – 1)

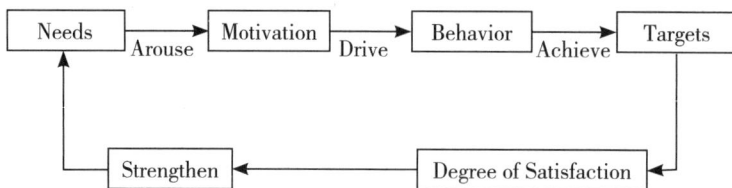

Diagram 10 – 1　The Process of Motivation

As showed above，naturally speaking，the foundation of motivation is unmet needs，which will arouse the corresponding incentives. When individuals perceive the incentives，they will adopt some behaviors to fulfill the targets. It is a continual psychological and behavioral process to raise the degree of satisfaction. Making various inducements and conditions in different stages of enterprise management according to the theory of motivation，can achieve the purpose of effective motivation on the staff.

10.2.2　Methods of Motivation

There are various methods for motivation. Below are some frequently-used methods.

1. Financial Motivation

It is also called material motivation, which is to motivate by rewarding material things. To be specific, there are some kinds of forms as following.

(1) Relating the performance to the salaries. It is the motivation method by relating the performance to salary. Salary is not only a tool of motivation, but also the reflection about the value of employees. To be specific, it has four kinds:

①Piece-rate wage: relating the income of the staff to production efficiency.

②Sales commission: relating the sales volumes to the salary.

③Benefit sharing: relating the salary to extra earnings created by reducing costs and increasing efficiency.

④Profit sharing: allocating a certain percentage of the organizational margins to the employees.

The advantage of such motivation method lies in that the employees will believe that if they improve their performance, they can get the corresponding rewards, therefore arousing their enthusiasm.

(2) Subsides and welfare program: It is an important form of material motivation, and is also called indirect reward. Specifically speaking, there are: ①Paid leave. ②Social security funds. ③Pension plans. ④Job subsides. The advantage of subsides and welfare program is the sense of security it brings to employees.

(3) Employee stock ownership plan: It is referred to the enterprise's stocks that employees buy from the enterprise. With the cooperation being listed, the stockholders can sell the stocks or gain the bonus when the firm goes well. The employees are the stockholders, so they will work heart and soul as masters.

2. Non-economic Motivation

It is also called spiritual motivation, and has the following methods: Target motivation, honor motivation, image motivation, model motivation, emotion motivation, interest motivation, training and promotion motivation, participation motivation.

Although there are various motivation methods, they can be mainly divided into material motivation and spiritual motivation. Even if we adopt the same methods of motivation, the results can be different because individuals differ from each other. In the application of motivation, much attention should be paid to individual differences and positional differences and we should adopt different ways accordingly. The combination of different ways of motivation will strengthen the effect and we should take the costs into consideration at the same time.

3. Job Motivation

It will include the following forms: the adaptability of the work, challenge of the work, the integrity of the work, job autonomy, job enlargement, job enrichment, timely job feedback.

10. 2. 3　Principles of Motivation

1. Combining Material Motivation and Spiritual Motivation

Individuals have both material needs and spiritual needs. Accordingly, we should stick to the principle of combining material motivation and spiritual motivation. Material needs are the basic needs of human beings and the lowest level ones. Although material motivation is the basic form of motivation, the function of material motivation is limited. With the development of productivity and human quality, much importance should be attached to spiritual needs and spiritual motivation. In other words, material motivation is basic while spiritual motivation is fundamental. On the basis of combining both motivations, we should shift the focus from material motivation to spiritual motivation. We should try every effort not to go to extremes. Having a blind faith in material motivation will lead to money worship, while having a blind faith in spiritual motivation will result in voluntarism and theory of the "omnipotence of the spirit". In fact, both tendencies are one-sided and harmful.

2. Combining Internal Motivation and External Motivation

Both internal motivation and external motivation can influence human behavior. Internal motivation plays a fundamental role and external motivation functions through internal incentives. It is required that the leaders should be good at combining internal motivation and external motivation while focusing on internal motivation. Moreover, the leaders should arouse higher level needs and deeper motivation of the employees, stimulate the working enthusiasm and impetus from their inner hearts. Such working impetus is more profound and lasts for a longer time.

3. Combing Positive Motivation and Negative Motivation

Positive and negative motivation have their own targeted behavior, and often they are different from the other. But both kinds of behaviors are common in the organizations, so both are necessary and effective. They will influence not only the targeted employees, but also the people around. Only if we make a combination of positive motivation and negative motivation, can we set up positive examples and negative examples, strengthening the good behaviors and weakening the bad ones. As a result, we can obtain excellent culture, which will invisibly drive the whole group and organization to work harder and more enthusiastically. Considering that negative effects will accompany negative motivation, we must be careful about the application of negative motivation, which is vulnerable to cause frustration. So the leaders should stick to the principle of combining positive motivation and negative motivation and moreover, they should recognize the dominant role positive motivation plays.

4. Combining Individual Goals and Organizational Goals

In the motivation mechanism, goal-setting is a critical step. First of all, goal-setting should embody the demand for fulfilling the organizational goals, preventing the motivation form operating in the wrong direction. Secondly, goal-setting will provide friendly conditions for individuals to meet their own needs, otherwise it will be impossible to make individuals satisfied. Only through combining individual goals and organizational goals, allowing as many individual goals to match the organizational goals and making the individual goals depend on the organizational goals, can we get the results we expect.

5. Motivating on the Basis of Needs

The starting point of motivation is to fulfill employees' needs, which are sometimes the same and sometimes different. Moreover, only if the most urgent needs (the dominant needs) have been met, can we get the expected results. So leaders must make a deep investigation in motivation, and try to learn the trend about the hierarchy of needs and the structure of needs. And then they should take the specific measures to gain the positive results.

6. The Principle of Justice and Democracy

Justice is a basic principle of motivation. If we fail to award those who should be awarded and punish those who should be punished, not only can't we get the expected results, but make things worse, inducing negative results. Justice is not just about awarding and punishing but the appropriate degree of award and punishment. A strict award and punishment system will require the managers to be selfless and treat others equally without discrimination. Just as Han Feizi said, "Award meritorious people, even the ones who I dislike and stay away from and punish the blamable people, even the ones who I love and are in an intimate relationship with me". Awarding and punishing in appropriate degree means do things from the actual situation, award matches the contribution, punishment matches the fault. We can't award heavily with little contribution, and punish slightly with great fault.

A prominent feature of justice is labor-based motivation, in which the hard-working employees get more while the lazy ones get less. Only then can we break the tradition of egalitarianism, promoting the hard work and competition. Only when we allow those who make more contributions to gain more, can we make the best of the potential functions of material motivation.

Democracy guarantees justice, and democracy is a basic need for motivation. Try to let the employee participate in and supervise the plan of the motivation system and program, reduce the inappropriate culture and maintain justice at large.

第三节　激励理论

一、需要层次论

需要层次论是美国心理学家马斯洛（A. H. Maslow）于 1943 年提出来的，该理论的内容包括三个要点：

1. 人类的需要分五个层级

（1）生存的需要。这是人类维持生存所必需的最基本的需要，包括对衣、食、住和行的满足等。

（2）安全的需要。这是有关人类免受危险和威胁的需要。

（3）社交的需要。这是感情和归属方面的需要。

（4）尊重的需要。人一旦满足了社交的需要，就会要求自尊和被别人所尊重，从而产生尊重的需要。

（5）自我实现的需要。马斯洛认为这是最高层次的需要。它指的是要实现个人理想和抱负、最大限度地发挥个人潜力并获得成就的需要。这种需要往往是通过胜利感和成就感来满足的。

2. 五种需要的递进关系

马斯洛认为，对一般人来说，这五种需要由低到高依次排成一个阶梯（如图 10-2 所示）。当低层次的需要获得相对的满足后，下一个较高层次的需要才能占据主导地位，成为驱动行为的主要动力。也就是说，任何一个人在某个时候不一定都有这五种需要，已有的需要也不是等量齐观的，但是总有一个决定他行动方向的主导需要。

图 10-2　需要层级

3. 人们的需要结构不同

马斯洛认为，由于各人动机结构发展的状况不同，这五种需要对于每一个人的优势位置也不同。任何一种需要都不会因为高层次的需要获得满足而消失，只是对行为的影响力会减轻而已，此外，当一个人的高层次需要和低层次需要都能满足时，他往往追求高层次需要，因为高层次需要能给人们更深刻的幸福和满足感。但是如果满足了高层次需要，低层次需要得不到满足时，有些人就可能牺牲高层次需要而去谋取低层次需要，还有些人可能为了实现高层次需要舍弃低层次需要。

二、双因素理论

双因素理论是美国心理学家赫茨伯格根据他在匹兹堡地区对 200 多名工程技术人员和会计人员的访问调查而提出来的。后来，赫茨伯格及其同事又对其他一些工业组织进行了多次调查，进一步验证了这一理论。

首先，赫茨伯格认为，传统的把"不满意"作为"满意"的对立面的看法是不正确的，"满意"的对立面应当是"没有满意"，"不满意"的对立面应当是"没有不满意"。他通过调查发现，使职工感到满意的因素都是属于工作本身或工作内容方面的；使职工感到不满意的因素，都是属于工作环境或工作关系方面的。他把前者叫做激励因素，后者叫做保健因素或维持因素。保健因素不能直接起激励职工的作用，但能防止职工产生不满情绪。它就像卫生保健一样，只能预防疾病，而不能提高健康水平。只有激励因素才能产生使职工满意的积极效果，才能激励职工的工作热情。下表是一些激励因素和保健因素的实例：

双因素理论

保健因素	激励因素
工资	工作本身
监督	赏识
地位	提升
安全	成长的可能性
工作环境	责任
政策与管理制度	成就
人际关系	成长

赫茨伯格同时也注意到，激励因素与保健因素也有若干重叠。例如，赏识属于激励因素，基本上起积极作用，但当没有受到赏识时，又可起消极作用，也会引起不满意。又如，工资是保健因素，但有时也能产生使职工满意的结果。

【小链接】

激励因素、保健因素还是干扰因素

20世纪90年代初，雪茄生产商专门花钱请人为从事枯燥工作的员工读故事。在纺织行业，管理者允许小猫在场地上玩耍。这些都有助于员工驱除工作烦躁感。现在，感到烦躁的员工可以佩戴随身听。员工说这能使思想放松，更快地度过难挨的工作时间。他们还认为，音乐或肥皂剧不是干扰因素，不会影响工作绩效。

一些管理者认为音乐会干扰员工的注意力和互相交流，因此禁止员工工作时听音乐。但是其他管理者却认为这是有益的。第一银行的一位主管研究了人们工作方式的发展周期，认为随身听能够提高员工的注意力和工作质量。一项对一家医学设备生产工厂装配线工人进行的研究发现，耳机对工作绩效没有影响，人们戴耳机工作会带来更高的工作满意度。

其他一些对工作产生厌倦的人则把时间用在聊天室、参加其他与工作无关的网络活动以及电脑游戏上。在一家核电厂，员工们迷上了多人联网游戏《世界末日》。信息技术管理者声称安全问题并未直接受到影响，但《世界末日》文件太大，减缓了PC机网络的运行速度。这位接受某杂志采访的管理者请求不要提及他的姓名。

有些员工在工作中做这些事情，有些是在吃午饭时，还有些是在打电话时。某公司相信它的员工在工作时访问的网址中有60%～70%与公司业务无关。很多公司对此采取了惩罚措施。卡夫食品公司安装了一个系统来防止员工访问与他们的工作无关的国际互联网网址。公司信息部门主管说："我们到这里是为了工作，不是个人娱乐。"与此同时，各地的员工们正在寻找各种手段来避免管理者的监督和控制，甚至出现了一些诸如《秘密冲浪：关于如何一边在网上遨游，一边看起来却是在忙于工作的秘诀和技巧》的文章。

一些管理者声称这些活动降低了公司的生产率，一些人认为没有影响，还有一些则认为员工每工作一段时间就需要休息一下。许多主管也做同样的事情，然而一些主管还是坚持认为一旦抓住那些在工作时间做这些事的员工就应解雇。

对此你是怎么想的？这些活动与工作设计、激励和工作满意度有何关系？如果你是一名管理者，对于这个问题你将如何制定政策？对于从事这些活动的员工你将如何处理？

（资料来源：贝特曼等著，王雪莉译：《管理学：新竞争格局》（第六版），北京：北京大学出版社 2007 年版，第 443 页）

三、期望值理论

1964 年，美国行为科学家费隆（Victor H. Vroom）在他的著作《工作与激励》一书中首先提出了期望值理论。

期望值理论的基础是，人之所以愿意从事某项工作并达成组织目标，是因为这些工作和组织目标会帮助他们达成自己的目标、满足自己某方面的需要。

该理论认为，某一活动某人的激发力量取决于他所能得到的成果的全部预期价值与他认为达到该成果的期望概率。用公式表示就是：

$$M = V \times E$$

其中：

M——激发力量。指调动一个人的积极性、激发出人的内部潜力的强度。

V——效价。指某项活动成果所能满足个人需要的价值的大小，或者说是某项活动成果的吸引力的大小，其变动范围在 -100% 至 $+100\%$ 之间。

E——期望值。指一个人根据经验所判断的某项活动导致某一成果的可能性的大小，以概率表示。

期望值理论包含着辩证的思想，具有较大的综合性和适用性。为深刻理解这一理论，需把握以下几条：

（1）对于其中的效价应理解为综合性的。它既可以是精神的，也可以是物质的；它不是指某一单项效价，而是指各种效价的总和。

（2）同一项活动和同一个激励目标对不同的人效价是不一样的；对同一个人在不同的时候，效价也是不一样的。

（3）期望概率是当事人主观判断的概率，它与个人的能力、经验以及愿意做出的努力程度有直接关系。

（4）效价和大家平均的个人期望概率相互影响。平均概率小，效价相对增大；平均概率大，效价相对减少。

期望值理论对我们实施激励有如下启示：

（1）管理者不要泛泛地抓各种激励措施，而应当抓多数组织成员认为效价最大的激励措施。

（2）设置激励目标时应尽可能加大其效价的综合值。

（3）适当控制实际概率与期望概率。期望概率既不是越大越好，也不是越小越好，而是要适当。期望概率过高，容易产生挫折；期望概率太低，又会减小激发力量。但期望概率并不完全由个人决定，它与实际概率的大小有关，而实际概率在很大程度上是由组织或者领导者决定的。实际概率应使大多数人受益，它最好大于平均的个人期望概率，让人喜出望外，而不要让人大失所望。但实际概率应当与效价相适应，效价大，实际概率可小些；效价小，实际概率可大些。

四、公平理论

公平理论又称社会比较理论，它是美国的亚当斯（J. S. Adams）于 20 世纪 60 年代首先提出来的，该理论侧重于报酬对人们工作积极性的影响。其基本观点是，当一个人做出了成绩并取得报酬以后，他不仅关心所得报酬的绝对量，而且关心自己所得报酬的相对量。因此，他要进行种种比较来确定自己所获报酬是否合理，比较的结果将直接影响今后工作的积极性。

该理论的核心是如下公平方程式：

$$O_P/I_P = O_a/I_a \text{ 或 } = O_H/I_H$$

其中：

O_P——对自己报酬的感觉。

O_a——对别人所获报酬的感觉。

O_H——对自己过去报酬的感觉。

I_P——对自己所做投入的感觉。

I_a——对别人所做投入的感觉。

I_H——对自己过去投入的感觉。

公平理论指出，每个人都会自觉或不自觉地把自己付出的投入和所获报酬相比的收支比率，同其他人在这方面的收支比率做社会比较，又同自己过去在这方面的收支比率做历史比较。如果这种比较表明收支比率相等，即上述等式成立，他便会感到自己受到了公平的待遇，因而心情舒畅，努力工作。如果收支比率不等，即上述等式不成立，则可能出现以下情况。

当 $O_P/I_P < O_a/I_a$ 时，他会感到不公平，他可能要求增加自己的报酬或减少自己今后的努力程度；或者要求组织减少比较对象的报酬、让其今后增大努力程度；或者另外找人做比较对象，以求得心理上的平衡；也可能发牢骚，消极怠工，制造矛盾甚至离职。

当 $O_P/I_P > O_a/I_a$ 时，他可能要求减少自己的报酬或在开始时自动多做些工作，但久而久之，他会重新估计自己的技术和工作情况，当终于觉得自己确实应当得到那么高的待遇时，工作状态又会回到过去的水平了。

当 $O_P/I_P < O_H/I_H$ 时，他会有不公平的感觉，并因此导致工作积极性下降。

当 $O_P/I_P > O_H/I_H$ 时，他一般不会感到不公平，而会认为就应该这样，因而不会更加积极地工作。

心理学认为，不公平会使人们的心理产生紧张和不安状态，因而影响人们的行为动机，导致工作积极性和工作效率降低，旷工率、离职率随之上升。因此，管理者应当在工作任务分配、奖金的评定以及工作成绩的评价中，力求公平合理，以保证和调动职工的积极性。不过，公平也是相对的、主观的，在客观上只能做到让多数人认为公平，让每个人都感到公平是不可能的。

五、强化理论

美国心理学家斯金纳（B. F. Skinner）提出的强化理论认为，人们为了达到某种目的，都会采取一定的行为，这种行为将作用于环境。当行为的结果对他有利时，这种行为就会重复出现；当行为的结果对他不利时，这种行为就会减少或消失。这就是环境对行为强化的结果。

根据强化的性质和目的，可将强化分为正强化和负强化两种类型。在管理上，正强化就是奖励那些组织上需要的行为，从而加强这种行为；负强化就是惩罚那些与组织不相容的行为，从而削弱这种行为。正强化的具体形式包括对成绩的认可、表扬，改善工作条件，提升、安排担任挑战工作，给予学习和成长的机会等，负强化的形式有批评、处分、降级等，甚至有时不给奖励或少给奖励也是一种负强化。

强化理论的应用原则主要有以下三条：

（1）要针对强化对象的不同需要采取不同的强化措施。

（2）小步子前进，分阶段设立目标，及时给予强化。如果目标一次定得太高，就难以发挥强化的作用，也很难充分调动强化对象的积极性。

（3）及时反馈。即要通过一定形式和途径，及时将工作结果告诉行动者。结果无论好坏，对行为都具有强化的作用。对好的结果及时反馈，能够更有力地激励行动者继续努力；对不好的结果及时反馈，可以促使行动者分析原因，及时纠正。

Section 3　Motivation Theory

10.3.1　The Hierarchy of Needs Theory

The hierarchy of needs theory is proposed by American psychologist A. H. Maslow in 1943. This theory includes three main points：

1. Five Hierarchies of Needs

（1）Physiological needs. It is the basic needs for human existence including dressing, eating, sheltering and traveling.

（2）Safety needs. Security and protection from dangers and threatens.

（3）Social needs. The needs for affection and affiliation.

（4）Esteem needs. When the social needs have been met, the needs for esteem and respect will arouse.

（5）Self-actualization needs. Maslow described the self-actualization needs as the highest level of needs. It is referred to as the needs for the realization of dreams and ambitions and to make the best of the individual potentials. A sense of success and achievements can meet such kind of needs.

2. The Progressive Order of the Five Needs

Maslow thought that the individual moves up the steps of the hierarchy (seeing Diagram 10 – 2). As one of these needs is substantially satisfied, the next needs becomes dominant and drives action. In other words, people may not have the five needs at the same time and the importance of the current needs is not the same, but there will be one needs to dominate his behaviors.

3. The Different Structure of Human Needs

Maslow believes the five needs may have different impact on different people for their structures of incentives are different. Every level of needs doesn't disappear after the fulfillment of higher needs, but the effect of this level of needs will weaken. Besides, if the higher-level needs and lower-level needs can be satisfied at the same time, people will pursue the higher-level needs, because the sense of happiness and gratification brought by the actualization of higher-level needs are profound. If the higher-level needs are able to be met while the lower-level needs are not, some will sacrifice the higher-level needs for the lower-level needs, while others will make the opposite choice.

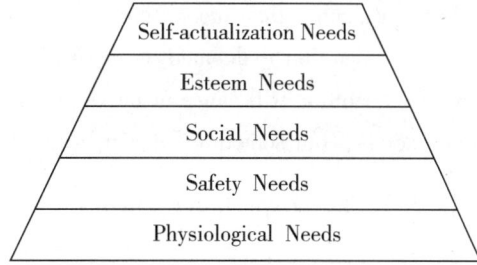

Diagram 10 – 2   The Hierarchy of Needs Theory

10. 3. 2   Two-factor Theory

The two-factor theory is proposed by the American psychologist Herzberg, who conducted a research about more than 200 engineers and accountants in Pittsburgh. After that, Herzberg and his fellows made several further investigations and confirmed the theory.

The data suggests, says Herzberg, that the opposite of satisfaction is not dissatisfaction which is traditionally believed. The opposite of satisfaction is "no dissatisfaction" while the opposite of dissatisfaction is "no dissatisfaction". The data suggests the satisfying factors come from the job and its contents and the dissatisfying factors come from the working conditions and working relations. He calls the former ones the motivating factors, and the latter ones the hygiene factors or maintaining factors. The hygiene factors can not motivate the employees directly, but they can keep the employees from dissatisfaction. It looks like the medical hygiene and heath care, which can't promote the health level but can protect human being from diseases. Only motivating factors can make employees satisfied, arousing their working enthusiasm. Below are the examples of motivating and hygiene factors.

Two-factor Theory

Hygiene Factors	Motivating Factors
wage	the work itself
supervision	recognition
status	promotion
security	the possibility of growth
the work environment	responsibility
policy and management system	achievement
interpersonal relationship	growth

Herzberg notes that motivating factors and hygiene factors overlap with each other. For example, recognition is deemed as motivating factors and plays a positive role basically, but the failure of recognition will cause negative effect, leading to dissatisfaction. Moreover, wage can be hygiene factors, but sometimes it can bring about satisfaction.

10.3.3 The Expectancy Theory

The American behavior scientist Vroom proposed the expectancy theory in his masterpiece *Jobs and Motivation* in 1964.

The foundation of expectancy theory is that people are willing to engage themselves in the jobs just because these jobs and organizational goals will help them obtain their own goals and fulfill their needs.

The theory maintains that the energy aroused by a certain activity will depend on the total expected value he hopes to get and the expected possibilities of achieving the targets that he estimates. The formula is as followed:

$$M = V \times E$$

In this formula:

M—Energy. It refers to the intensity of arousing individual initiative and internal potential.

V—Value. It refers to the value a certain activity can provide in terms of fulfilling individual needs and in other words, it is the attraction of the result of a certain behavior. It ranges from -100% to $+100\%$.

E—Expectancy. It refers to the possibilities that one activity can lead to a certain result according to one's experience. It is called probability.

Expectancy theory includes the dialectical thought and it is both comprehensive and applicable. To get a profound knowledge of the theory, one should pay attention to several points as followed:

(1) The value should be regarded as comprehensive. It is both spiritual and physical. It is not a single value, but the comprehensive value.

(2) The value may be various for the same activity and same incentives. The value may be different for the same person in different time.

(3) Expecting probability is the probability of the party's subjective judgment, which directly relates to personal ability, experience, and the degree of effort willings to make.

(4) Value and the average expectancy probability influence each other. The value will strengthen with the higher average expectancy, while the value will weaken with lower average expectancy.

The expectancy theory will give us the following enlightenment:

(1) The managers should focus on the motivation methods that will give most employees the best value rather than take all kinds of motivation methods without emphasis.

(2) Enlarge the total value when setting goals.

(3) Try to maintain the actual probability and expectancy at a proper level. The expectancy

should be proper rather than too low nor too high. If the expectancy is too high, people are vulnerable to fail. If the expectancy is too low, it will weaken the motivation. The expectancy does not depend on individual decisions totally and it has a relationship with the actual probability, which depends on the organization or the leaders. The actual probability should benefit most people and it is better to keep it higher than the average individual expectancy, thus making people delighted rather than disappointed. The actual probability should match the value. If the value is high, the actual probability may be lower. If the value is low, the actual probability could be higher.

10.3.4 Equity Theory

The equity, also called social comparison theory, was proposed by the American, J. S. Adams in the 1960s. The theory focuses on the effect of rewards on individual working enthusiasm. The basic point is that when people do the job and get some rewards, what they focus is not only the absolute rewards but also the relative rewards. So they will make all kinds of comparisons to find out whether their rewards are appropriate, the result of which will have a direct impact on the future activity.

The core of the theory is fair equation as follows:

$$O_p/I_p = O_a/I_a \text{ or } = O_H/I_H$$

In this formula:

O_p— the feeling about the outcome they get.

O_a—the feeling about the outcome others get.

O_H—the feeling about the past outcome they get.

I_p—the feeling about the input they make.

I_a—the feeling about the input others make.

I_H—the feeling about the past inputs they make.

The equity theory suggests that people will consciously or unconsciously compare their outcome-input ratio with others' outcome-input ratio, and compare their current outcome-input ratio with their past outcome-input ratio. If the ratio is the same or the equation is true, they will feel fair, so they would be happy and work hard. If the equation is not true, there will be the following conditions.

When O_p/I_p is smaller than O_a/I_a, they will feel unfair. They would ask to increase their rewards or to decrease their inputs or they will ask the organization to decrease the comparisons' rewards or increase their inputs or they will seek other comparisons to maintain a psychological balance. If not, it is possible for them to complain, take a negative attitude towards job, have conflicts and even resign.

When O_p/I_p is larger than O_a/I_a, they may ask to decrease their outcomes and start to work harder but as time goes by, they will re-evaluate their skills and work conditions. When they feel that they deserve such high salary, their work status will back to the past level.

When Ip/Ip is smaller than O/I_H, they may feel unfair and work with less positivity.

When O_p/O_p is larger than O_H/I_H they may not feel unfair but think that it is just how it is, thus they'll not work more actively.

Psychology holds that inequity may cause people intense and unease, which affect their motivation and lead to low activity and efficiency, as well as high absenteeism and separation rate. So managers should strive for fair in work allocation, bonus and work performance evaluation, to make sure workers' activity. However, equity is relative and subjective, in fact we can only make most feel fair, and it is impossible to make everyone feel fair.

10.3.5　Reinforcement Theory

The American psychologist B. F. Skinner puts forward the reinforcement theory, maintaining that people will take some actions to obtain their goals, which will influence the environment. If the results of the action benefits him, he will repeat the action. If the results do no good to his interests, he will weaken the action or even abandon the action. This is the effect of the environment on the behaviors.

Reinforcement could be classified into positive reinforcement and negative reinforcement according to the nature and the goals. In the perspective of management, the positive reinforcement is to award the behaviors needed for the organization to encourage the behaviors. The negative reinforcement is to punish the behaviors which are not allowed by the organization, thus weakening the behaviors. The specific forms of positive reinforcement are recognition of the performance, praise, improvement about the working conditions, promotion, assigning challenging jobs, providing the opportunities of learning and growth. To be specific, negative reinforcement can be criticism, punishment, demotion and sometimes no awards or reduced awards could be a kind of negative reinforcement.

There are three main application rules for reinforcement theory：

（1）Take different measures for different people.

（2）Divide the process of reinforcement into small steps and in different stages, set different goals and try to reinforce timely. If the goals are too high, we could not make the most of reinforcement and thus it is hard for us to arouse the individual enthusiasm.

（3）Timely feedback. We should try to give the feedback to the employee in certain ways and forms. Regardless of the results, it will have reinforcement effect on the behaviors. If we can feedback the good results, the employee would be encouraged to work hard as before. For the bad results, it can urge the employee to analyze the causes and make things right.

【阅读资料】

塑造组织行为的汉默尔规则

规则1，不要对所有的个体给予同样的奖励。为了使行为强化有效，奖励应基于工作绩效。对每个人都给予同样的奖励，实际上是强化了不好或中等表现，忽视了突出表现。

规则2，注意忽视强化对于员工行为产生的影响。管理者做出反应或不做出反应都会影响下属行为。没表扬一个理应表扬的员工，会挫伤其积极性。

规则3，一定要让员工清楚如何做才会得到奖励。组织应建立一套行为标准，让每个人都知道自己所做的能否得到奖励。

规则4，务必告诉员工他们错在哪里。否则员工会迷惑不解，或许认为他被愚弄了。

规则5，不要当众惩罚员工。当众指责会使员工感到屈辱，也有可能引起团队成员对管理者的不满。

规则6，要公正。没有奖励该奖励的人，或过度奖励不值得奖励的员工，都会削弱奖励的激励效果。

第四节　激励机制

一、激励机制的概念

激励机制是指在企业系统中，激励主体通过激励因素和激励手段与激励客体之间关系的总和，是激励活动的各项要素在运行中的相互联系、相互作用、相互制约及其与激励效果内在联系之间的综合机能。激励机制包括外部激励机制和内部激励机制两个方面。

1. 外部激励机制

这主要包括市场上同类人才的密集程度、行业变化、人才市场的建立和规范化、职业经理市场的建立和完善等方面的内容，同类人才越是密集，外部的竞争压力就越大，人才在企业之间流动的因素就越多，这就造成一种外部环境的激励。行业之间的各种差异造成掌握一定技能的人才，从低层待遇到高层待遇的流动，因而对人才形成一种激励。人才市场的建立和规范有利于从市场的角度对人才的价值做出评价，形成一种有效的激励机制。

2. 内部激励机制

这是指企业对员工的激励和对经营者的激励。从激励的内容上看有物质激励机制、工作设计激励机制、参与管理激励机制、组织气氛和组织文化激励机制等。我们讨论的激励机制主要是企业内部的激励机制。

二、激励机制的建立

激励机制的建立就是为实现企业目标，根据企业成员的个性需要，制定适当的行为规范和分配制度，以实现人力资源的有效配置，达到企业利益和个人利益的一致。

1. 建立有效的物质激励机制

这是最基本的激励机制，物质激励机制建立后，员工可以通过良好的工作表现，获得工资以外的奖金和各种福利，大大增强他们的工作积极性，满足他们生活的物质需要。

2. 建立多种形式相结合的激励机制

单靠物质激励达不到激励目的，尤其是在人们的物质生活水平不断提高，企业员工的需要越来越多样化时，采用单一的物质激励必将与员工的需要不相适应。企业应当考虑以物质激励为基础，多种激励相结合的激励机制。

3. 建立和完善经营者的激励机制

激励作为管理的重要手段，既需要对员工进行激励，也需要对经营者进行激励，对其恰当的激励能防止经营者背离投资人和股东的利益行使其权力，使经营者的目标与股东的目标在最大程度上保持一致。因此，要建立和完善经营者的激励机制，使经营者的得奖与经营效益挂钩。

Section 4　Motivation Mechanism

10.4.1　The Concept of Motivation Mechanism

In the perspective of the enterprises, motivation mechanism includes motivation subjects, motivation objects, motivation methods and motivation incentives. The motivation subjects apply the motivation incentives and motivation methods to the motivation objects. The four factors will influence, constrain and relate with each other and the motivation mechanism is the comprehensive functions of the four factors. Motivation mechanism includes the external motivation mechanism and internal motivation mechanism.

1. The External Motivation Mechanism

It mainly includes the intensity of talents of the same level, the industrial changes, the establishment and the standardized operation of the talent market, the establishment and improvement of professional managers. The more intense same-level talents are, the fiercer external competition is and the more mobile talents are in the firms, which will create the motivation by the external conditions. The differences in different industries will make the skilled employees flow from low-paid jobs to high-paid jobs, which is a kind of motivation. The establishment and standardized operation of talent market will benefit the assessment of talents on the basis of the market, which will form an effective motivation mechanism.

2. The Internal Motivation Mechanism

The internal motivation mechanism is set up for employees and managers. Motivation mechanism includes material motivation mechanism, job design, participation in management, organizational atmosphere and the organizational culture. We mainly refer to the internal motivation mechanism of a firm when we discuss the motivation mechanism.

10.4.2　Establishment of Motivation Mechanism

On the basis of fulfilling the organizational goals and individual needs, motivation mechanism is to make an appropriate behavioral regulations and allocation system to allocate the human resources effectively while make the organizational interest fit with the personal interest.

1. Establish the Effective Material Motivation Mechanism

It is the basic motivation mechanism. After the establishment of motivation mechanism, employees would get all kinds of welfare and benefits besides salaries, which will arouse their enthusiasm and the material needs for their lives.

2. The Motivation Mechanism Should Include All Kinds of Motivation Methods

With single material motivation method, managers may fail in attaining the goals of motivation. As the needs of employees become more and more various, the single material motivation does not fit with the needs of the employees. On the basis of material motivation, managers should employ all kinds of motivation methods.

3. Establish and Improve the Motivation Mechanism for Managers

As an important means of management, we should not only motivate the employees but also the managers. The appropriate motivation will prevent the managers from impairing the benefits of the investors and stockholders, allowing the goals of managers match the goals of stockholders at most. So we should establish and improve the motivation mechanism for managers to make the outcomes of the managers consistent with their performance.

【本章提要】

● 激励是指创造满足人们需要的条件，激发人们的动机，使之产生实现组织目标的特定行为的过程，激励与需要、动机密切相关，在管理过程中发挥重要的功能。

● 激励方式多种多样，按不同的方法分类，有物质激励与精神激励，正激励与负激励，内激励与外激励。

● 激励应当遵循以下原则：物质激励与精神激励相结合的原则；外激励与内激励相结合的原则；正激励与负激励相结合的原则；目标结合原则；按需激励原则；公正民主原则。

● 激励理论主要包括：需要层次论、双因素理论、期望值理论、公平理论、强化理论。

● 在市场经济体制下，建立一套完善的激励机制是非常重要的。

【关键词】

激励（Motivation）　　激励过程（Motivation Process）　　动机（Incentive）
需要层次论（The Hierarchy of Needs Theory）　　内激励（Internal Motivation）
外激励（External Motivation）　　双因素理论（Two-factor Theory）
期望值理论（Expectancy Theory）　　激励机制（Motivation Mechanism）

【复习与思考】

1. 什么是激励？它有哪些功能？
2. 激励有哪些类型？应遵循哪些原则？
3. 激励的方式有哪些？
4. 激励理论对我们有何启示？
5. 如何建立有效的激励机制？

【研究与讨论】

1. 有人说："金钱不是万能的，但没有金钱是万万不能的。"你是否赞成这一观点？

阐述你的理由。

　　2. 假如让你为公司设计奖励制度，你会依据哪种激励理论来设计？为什么？

　　3. 请讨论需要层次理论的现实意义。

　　4. 试分析员工持股计划的优点与不足。

【实践演练】

　　1. 调查一家公司，了解公司的激励制度及其有效性，并提出自己的建议。

　　2. 分组讨论，列出你最不愿意做的四项工作。从中选出一项工作进行讨论，提出激励的措施。然后将每组讨论的结果进行交流讨论。

　　3. 每位同学用一张纸，列出你生活中最开心和最不开心的事，然后分析使你开心或不开心的因素。

【管理模拟】

　　某企业的老板通过学习有关激励理论，受到很大启发，并着手实践。他授予下属更多的工作和责任，而且通过表扬和赏识来激励下属。结果事与愿违，下属的积极性不但没有提高，反而对老板的做法强烈不满，认为他是在利用诡计来剥削员工。

　　请你根据所学的激励理论，分析老板做法失败的原因，并提出可行的建议。

【本章案例】

林肯电气公司的激励制度

　　林肯电气公司总部设在克利夫兰，年销售额为44亿美元，拥有2 400名员工，它形成了一套独特的激励员工的方法。该公司90%的销售额来自于生产弧焊设备和辅助材料。

　　林肯电气公司的生产员工按件计酬，他们没有最低小时工资。员工为公司工作两年后，便可以分享年终奖金。该公司的奖金制度有一整套计算公式，全面考虑了公司的毛利润及员工的生产率与绩效，可以说是美国制造业中对员工最有利的奖金制度。在过去的56年中，平均奖金额是基本工资的95.5%，该公司中相当一部分员工的年收入超过10万美元。近几年经济发展迅速，员工年均收入为44 000美元左右，远远超出制造业员工年收入17 000美元的平均水平。在不景气的年头里，如1982年的经济萧条时期，林肯公司员工收入降为27 000美元，这虽然与其他公司相比还不算太坏，可与经济发展时期相比就差了一大截。

　　公司自1985年开始一直推行职业保障政策，从那时起，他们没有辞退过一名员工。当然，作为对此政策的回报，员工也相应要做到几点：在经济萧条时他们必须接受减少工作时间的决定，而且要接受工作调换的决定；有时甚至为了维持每周30小时的最低工作时间，而不得不调到一个报酬更低的岗位上。

　　林肯公司极具成本和生产率意识，如果员工生产出一个不合标准的部件，那么除非这个部件修改至符合标准，否则这件产品就不能计入该员工的工资中。严格的计件工资制度和高度竞争性的绩效评估系统，形成了一种很有压力的氛围，有些工人还因此产生了一定的焦虑感，但这种压力有利于生产率的提高。据该公司的一位管理者估计，与国内竞争对手相比，林肯公司的总体生产率是他们的两倍。自20世纪30年代经济大萧条以后，公司年年获利丰厚，没有缺过一次分红。该公司还是美国工业界中员工流动率最低的公司之一。前不久，该公司的两个分厂被《幸福》杂志评为全美十佳管理企业。

思考问题：

1. 你认为林肯公司使用了本章中讨论的何种激励理论来激励员工的工作积极性？

2. 为什么林肯公司的方法能够有效地激励员工？你认为这种激励系统可能会给管理层带来什么问题？

【本章参考文献】

［1］［美］丹尼尔·A. 雷恩著，赵睿等译：《管理思想的演变》，北京：中国社会科学出版社2000年版。

［2］周三多：《管理学》，北京：中国高等教育出版社2000年版。

［3］吴照云：《管理学》，北京：中国社会科学出版社2006年版。

［4］周健临：《管理学教程》，上海：上海财经大学出版社2001年版。

第十一章　沟　通

Chapter 11　Communication

管理的定义很简单，过去、现在、未来都是沟通。

松下幸之助

The definition of management is very simple. Its past, present and future are all communication.

Konosuke Matsushita

人际沟通始于聆听，终于回答。

威尔德

Interpersonal communication begins with listening and ends with answers it.

Weald

【本章学习目标】

知识目标：

了解沟通的作用与过程。

掌握沟通的方式和原则。

熟悉沟通的渠道。

技能目标：

实现有效沟通。

学会解决冲突的方法。

【Learning Objectives of Chapter 11】

Objectives of Knowledge：

Understand the function and process of communication.

Master the way and principles of communication.

Be familiar with the channel of communication.

Objectives of Skill：

Achieve effective communication.

Learn to resolve conflicts.

【小故事】

古时候有个山东秀才，无论说话还是写文章，总爱咬文嚼字，以此夸耀自己的高深学问。有一天晚上，他在睡梦中被屋梁上掉下来的一只蝎子蜇了一下，疼得他马上醒了过来，急忙摇头晃脑地喊道："贤妻，速燃银灯，尔夫为毒虫所袭！"

他连说了好几遍，妻子怎么也听不明白。这位秀才在黑暗中一摸，摸到一截硬硬的树枝一样的东西，正在奇怪，又被蝎子蜇了一下。这下子他疼得实在受不了，捧着手指大声叫道："老婆，快点灯，我让蝎子蜇啦！"

【引例】

制定沟通的策略

假定你是一家大型全国性公司的一个分支机构的经理，你对地区事业部经理负责。你的分支机构有 120 名员工，在他们与你之间有两个层次的管理人员——作业监督人员和部门负责人。你所有下属人员都在本分支机构的所在地工作。

案例 1

你的 1 名新任命的部门经理明显地没有达到该部门预算的目标。成本控制人员的分析报告表明，该部门在上个月，原材料和设备费、加班费、维修费和电话费等项目超支了40%。当时你没有说什么，因为这是部门经理就任的头 1 个月。但这次你感到必须采取某种行动了，因为上个月该部门的开支又超预算55%，而其他的部门并没有这样的问题。

案例 2

你刚刚从地区事业部经理的电话中听说，你们公司已被一家实力雄厚的企业收购。这项交易在 1 小时内就会向金融界宣布。事业部经理不知道具体的细节，但要求你尽快将这个消息告诉你手下的人。

案例 3

一项新的加班制度将在 1 个月内生效。过去，作业监督人员在确定加班人员时，是当面或通过电话并按工龄长短的次序征求个人意见后敲定。这样，资历较深的工人便享有加班工作的优先选择权。这种做法已被证明为慢而低效，因为过去几年内不少资深的工人已经减少了加班时间投入。而新的制度将在加班任务安排方面给各位监督人员以更大的变通性，也即要提前 1 个月征得工人们对加班的允诺。你发现部门经理和监督人员都明确赞成这项新的制度，且大多数的工人也都会喜欢，但一些资历较深的工人可能会对此有意见。

案例 4

你的上司曾在你的职位上工作过多年。这次你了解到，他越过你而直接同你的两位部门经理进行了沟通。这两位部门经理向你的上司报告了几件对你不利的事情，并由此使你受到了轻微的责备。你有些惊讶，因为尽管他们所说的是事实，但他们并没有向你的上司全面地说明情况，否则，你又会处于有利的地位，而不会受到这种待遇。你的上司两天后要来分支机构考察，你想就这一误会向他做个解释。

（资料来源：朱克强、王凤彬编著：《管理学教学案例精选》，上海：复旦大学出版社 1998 年版）

思考问题：

请针对上面描述的四种案例情形分别制定出有效的沟通方案或策略。并说明你采取这种策略的理由。

第一节　沟通的作用与过程

任何一个组织的运行，都离不开组织成员的分工与协作，而成员之间的分工与协作以及行为协调均有赖于相互之间的信息沟通。如果没有这种沟通，不但不能进行协调与合作，还会给组织运行造成障碍，甚至导致组织的失败。

一、沟通的概念

沟通就是指为了一定的目的，将信息或思想在个人、群体和组织之间进行传递、交流的过程。在现代管理中，有效的信息沟通是领导与指挥的重要手段之一。事实上，领导者或管理者日常工作的大部分内容都与沟通有关。在组织内部，有员工之间的沟通、员工与群体之间的沟通以及群体与群体之间的沟通；在组织外部，有组织与客户之间的沟通、组织与组织之间的沟通。

二、沟通的作用

从人际关系来看，沟通不仅是一个人获得他人思想、感情、见解、价值观的一种途径，同时也是一种重要的有效影响他人的工具和改变他人的手段，特别是在以人为中心的管理模式中，沟通的地位越来越重要，其作用主要表现在四个方面：

（1）收集信息。沟通过程实际上是一个信息双向交流的过程，通过沟通可以了解别人的意见、倾向、价值观、工作状态及需要等，了解各部门的人际关系、管理效率等，作为决策的依据。

（2）改善人际关系。通过沟通可以解除人们内心的紧张和不满，使人们感到舒畅、增进彼此的了解，改善相互之间的关系，减少不必要的冲突，创造一个和谐的氛围。

（3）改变人们的行为。在沟通过程中，信息接收者收到并理解了发送者的意图之后，一般来说，会做出相应的反应，表现出合作的行为，使人与人的行为相互协调。

（4）建立外部联系。沟通也是组织与外部环境建立联系、树立组织形象、发展公共关系的桥梁。

三、沟通的过程

沟通的过程是指信息的传递者通过选定的渠道把信息传给信息接收者的过程。如下图所示：

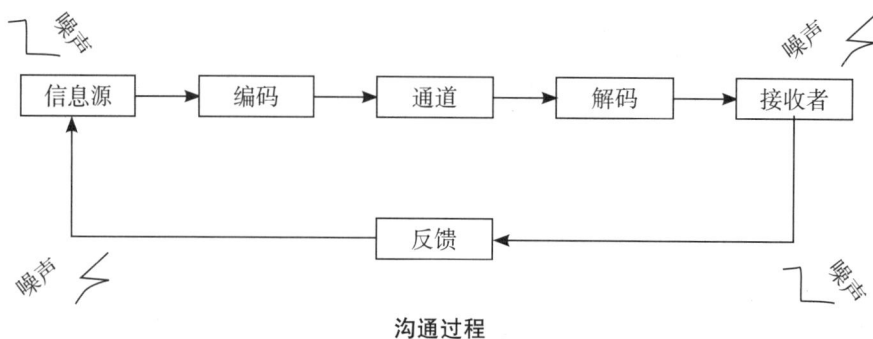

沟通过程

（1）信息源。指持有信息、意图、观念的人。信息沟通过程开始于需要沟通的主动者——信息发送者或信息源。信息发送者一定要明确所传递的信息。

（2）编码。当发送者明确传递的信息之后，还要将这些信息转变为双方都能理解的"语言或信号"，就是编码。如文字、图片、表情等。

（3）通道。指信息传递的渠道或媒介物，如电话、会议、电视等，通道视发送者的具体情况而定。

（4）解码。指信息接收者在收到信息时的思维过程，即对已编码信息的解释，要把信息中的符号译成接收者可以理解的形式。

（5）接收者。指接收并解释信息的人。沟通的接收者会受到自身的素质、知识、技能等多种因素的限制，同一信息不同的接收者会有不同的理解。

（6）反馈。接收者把接收到的信息反馈给发送者，使信息源的发送者成为接收者。通过这种反馈可以使发送者知道信息是否被接收，如果理解有误，则及时做出解释，纠正沟通内容。

Section 1　Function and Process of Communication

Any organization cannot operate without the division of labor and cooperation of members, and the division of labor and collaboration, and coordination between members depend on the information communication between each other. If there is no such kind of communication, they not only cannot coordinate and cooperate, but also cause obstacles for organization operation, and even lead to the failure of the organization.

11. 1. 1　Concept of Communication

Communication means the process that for a certain purpose, the information or ideas pass between individuals, groups and organizations. In the modern management, effective information communication is one of the important means of leadership and command. In fact, most of the leader's or manager's daily work is related to communication. Within the organization, there are communications between staff, between staff and groups, and between groups. On the outside of the organization, there are communication between organization and customers, and between organizations.

11. 1. 2　Function of Communication

From the perspective of interpersonal relationships, communication is not only a way for a person to get others' thoughts, feelings, opinions, values, but also an important tool to effectively influence people and the means of changing others, especially in the people-centered management model, the status of communication is becoming more and more important, its functions are mainly manifested in four aspects：

（1）Collect information. Communication process is a process of bidirectional communication of information, through which people can understand others' opinions, values, working status and needs, understand each department's interpersonal relationships, management efficiency, etc. , as the basis of decision-making.

(2) Improve interpersonal relationship. Through communication, people can remove the inner tension and dissatisfaction, which makes people feel happy and get to know each other so as to improve the relationship between each other, reduce unnecessary conflicts, create a harmonious atmosphere.

(3) Change people's behavior. In the process of communication, information receivers receive and understand the intentions of the sender, in general, this will be reflected in cooperative behaviors, so that makes people's behavior coordinate with others'.

(4) Establish external contact. Communication is the bridge for a group to contact with the external environment, to set up the group image and develop public relations.

11. 1. 3　Process of Communication

Communication refers to a process of information transmission through the selected channel from the sender to the receiver. As shown in below:

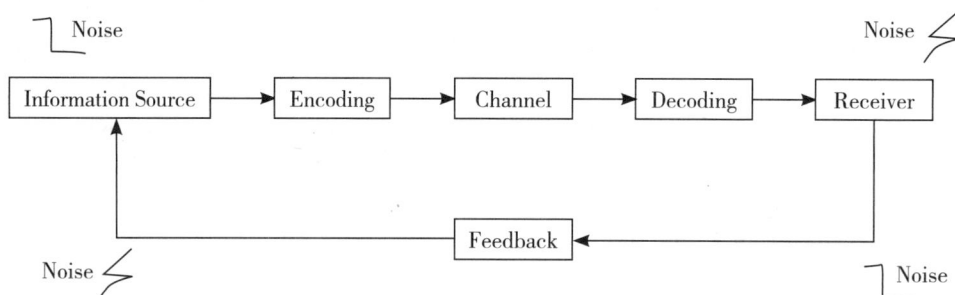

Process of Communication

(1) Information sources. It refers to those who hold information, intentions and ideas. Information communication process begins with the need to communicate of the initiative— information sender or information source. Information sender must be clear about the message.

(2) Encoding. When the sender makes sure of the message to send, he should transfer the information into "language or signal" both the sender and the receiver can understand, and this is encoding. Such as words, pictures, expression, etc.

(3) Channel. It refers to the information transmission channel or medium, such as telephone, meetings, TV. Channel is determined by the sender and the circumstances.

(4) Decoding. It refers to the thinking process of the receiver when he receives information, namely the interpretation of the encoded information, to draw the symbols in the information into the form that the receiver can understand.

(5) Receiver. It refers to the person who receives and interprets the information. Communication receiver will be affected by one's own quality, knowledge, skills, such as the limitation

of many factors. Different receiver will have different understandings of the same information.

(6) Feedback. The receiver gives feedback after he receives the information, making the sender of information become receiver. Through this feedback, the sender knows whether the information is accepted, if not, he can explain it timely or correct the content.

第二节　沟通的类别

一、沟通的分类

沟通的类别因划分的标准不同而不同。

1. 工具式沟通和感情式沟通（按照功能划分）

工具式沟通指发送者将信息、知识、想法、要求传达给接受者，目的是影响和改变接受者的行为。感情式沟通指沟通双方表达情感，获得对方精神上的同情和谅解，最终改善相互之间的人际关系。

2. 口头沟通、书面沟通、非语言沟通和电子媒介沟通（按照方法划分）

口头沟通是用口语来传递信息的方式，包括面谈、会议、讨论、演说、传闻及小道消息等。这种方式的优点是灵活快捷，不仅可以传递信息，还可传递感情和态度，使传递信息既丰富又准确。其不足是要求信息传递者具有较高的表达能力，口头传递层次太多，会逐步失真。

书面沟通是用文字来传递信息的方式，如备忘录、报告、通知、信函、文件等。其优点是便于长期保存，可以核实查询；有权威性，避免了随意性。其不足是比较呆板，也不能得到及时反馈；沟通效果受接收者文化水平的限制。

非语言沟通，主要包括动作、表情、声调、光信号等。其内涵丰富，寓意灵活，但传递距离有限，界限模糊，只能意会，不能言传。据调查，在面对面的沟通过程中，来自语言文字的信息不会超过35%，有65%的信息是通过非言语方式来传递，因而这种非言语的沟通方式越来越受到人们的重视。

电子媒介主要是传真、闭路电视、计算机网络、电子邮件等，传递速度快、信息容量大、可同时传递、廉价。随着信息和通信技术的发展，电子媒介在沟通中将扮演愈来愈重要的角色。

3. 正式沟通和非正式沟通（按照组织系统划分）

正式沟通一般是指在组织系统内依据组织明文规定的途径所进行的信息传递与交流。主要有：按正式系统发布的指示、命令、文件；组织召开的正式会议；组织内部上下级之间或同事之间因工作需要的正式接触等。

正式沟通的优点是：沟通效果好，比较严肃、约束力强、易于保密、有一定的权威性。缺点是比较刻板，沟通速度较慢，中间环节较多，信息易损耗。

非正式沟通是通过正式系统以外的途径来进行信息传递与交流，这种沟通不受组织的监督，也没有层次结构的限制，是由员工自行选择进行的，它主要是通过非正式组织和个人之间的接触来进行的。非正式沟通有如下基本特点：①渠道内的信息是不完整的、无规律的，不能作为决策的依据。②该渠道涉及较多的有关感情和情绪方面的问题，容易被人利用。③该渠道的建立与个性的相似性有关，因而容易沟通，形成合作。④信息传递速度较快。⑤是正式沟通状态的晴雨表。

非正式沟通是客观存在的，它在组织中也扮演着重要角色，管理人员应当正确对待非正式沟通。

4. 下行沟通、上行沟通和平行沟通（按照方向划分）

下行沟通是指上级将信息传递给下级，是一种自上而下的沟通。如把计划方案传达给基层群众，发布组织的相关政策。

上行沟通是指下级的意见向上级反映，即自下而上的沟通。上级应该鼓励下级反映情况，只有上行沟通顺畅，上级才能全面掌握情况，做出符合实际的决策。

平行沟通是组织中各平行部门之间的信息交流。有时也会出现斜向沟通，即处于不同层级又无隶属关系的人员之间的沟通。

5. 单向沟通和双向沟通（按照是否进行反馈划分）

单向沟通是指发送者和接收者之间的地位不变（单向传递），一方只发送信息，另一方只接受信息。双方无论在情感上还是在语言上都不需要信息反馈，如做报告、发布指令等。这种信息传递方式速度快，但准确性较差，有时还容易使接收者产生抗拒心理。

双向沟通中，发送者和接收者之间的位置不断交换，且发送者是以协商和讨论的姿态面对接收者的，信息发出以后还需及时听取反馈意见，必要时可以进行多次重复商谈，直到双方明确和满意为止：如交谈和协商。其优点是沟通信息准确性较高，接收者有反馈意见的机会，可能产生平等感和参与感，增加信心和责任感，有助于建立双方的感情。但对于发送者来说，在沟通时会受到接收者的质询、批评和挑剔，因而心理压力较大，同时信息传递速度也较慢。

二、组织中的沟通

组织内每时每刻都存在着大量的沟通信息流动，这些沟通信息不仅来自组织中个体间的人际交流，还包括组织内沟通的信息和组织间沟通的信息。组织内沟通是指组织中以工作团队为基础单位对象进行的信息交流和传递的过程；组织间沟通就是组织之间如何加强有利于各自组织目标的信息交流和传递的过程。管理者不但要具备良好的人际沟通的技能，还应当学会管理组织内的沟通和组织间的沟通。

1. 人际沟通

组织中最普遍的沟通形式就是成员间的人际沟通。在知识经济时代，组织成员是组织流程中的专有知识载体，是产生组织效率的核心资源。个体间的人际沟通在某种程度上代表了组织知识的传播和扩散。在这一意义上，组织中的人际沟通是指组织中的个体成员如何将个体目标和组织目标相联系的过程。每个企业都由数人、数十人、数百人甚至成千上万人组成，企业每天的活动也由许许多多的具体工作构成。由于个体的地位、利益和能力不同，他们对企业目标的理解、所感受的信息也不同，这就使得各个个体的目标有可能偏离企业总的目标，甚至完全背道而驰。如何保证上下一心、不折不扣地完成企业的总目标呢？这就需要相互交流意见，统一思想认识，自觉地协调各个个体的工作活动，以保证组织目标的实现。因而，人际沟通在组织中是基本的协调工作。另外，人际沟通也是由人的自利行为的客观性和多样性决定的。人际沟通对组织的重要意义，还在于组织中的人的管理。

在人际沟通过程中，各种噪声的干扰构成了对组织成员有效沟通的挑战。信息的发出失真、传输失真、接受失真和反馈失真，主要根源于人际因素、文化因素和结构因素的威胁。

2. 组织沟通

（1）团队沟通。团队沟通是指组织中以工作团队为基础单位对象进行的信息交流和传递的过程。团队是两个或两个以上的成员相互作用和协作以便完成组织预定的某项特别目标的单位。团队的概念包含三个要素。第一，需要两个或两个以上的人员，团队的规模可大可小，但一般规模都低于十五人。第二，团队人员有规律地相互接触，彼此间不打交道的人不能组成一个团队。第三，团队人员共享绩效目标。团队概念意味着一种使命感和竞争感。

重视组织中的团队工作，是指重视团队沟通的需要。团队成员在一起工作，以便完成任务，团队的沟通结构既影响团队绩效又影响员工的满意度。团队沟通对组织的意义在于，在高度竞争的全球环境中，组织应用群体或团队解决复杂问题。当团队活动复杂而且难度大时，所有成员都应该在一种分权的结构中共享信息，以便解决问题。团队需要在各个方向上自由沟通，应该鼓励团队成员彼此间讨论问题，员工的大量时间应该用于信息加工。

（2）组织间沟通。所谓的组织间沟通是组织同其利益相关者进行的有利于实现各自组织目标的信息交流和传递的过程。组织间沟通的宗旨是充分利用社会的各种资源，协调各方利益，实现组织共生的可持续发展。20 世纪 90 年代以来，组织间的沟通日益成为组织沟通中的重要一环。

Section 2　Categories of Communication

11. 2. 1　The Classification of Communication

The category of communication varies according to the division standard.

1. Instrumental Communication and Emotional Communication （According to the Functions）

Instrumental communication refers to the sender conveys information, knowledge, ideas, and orders to the receiver, whose purpose is to influence and change the behavior of the receiver. Emotional communication refers to both sides express emotion, to get each others' spiritual sympathy and understanding, eventually improve the interpersonal relationship between each other.

2. Oral Communication, Written Communication, Nonverbal Communication and Electronic Media Communication (According to the Method)

Oral communication uses spoken language to transfer information, including interviews, meetings, discussions, speeches, rumors and gossips, etc. This approach is flexible and fast, which can not only convey information, but also send affection and attitude, so as to make information abundant and accurate. Its defect is the requirement of high expression ability. Oral transmission levels are so cumbersome, which will gradually distort the information.

Written communication uses words to convey information, such as memos, reports, notifications, letters, documents, etc. Its advantages are easy for long-term preservation so as to verify the query, authoritative, to avoid the randomness. Its defects are inflexible, and cannot receive feedback in time and its communication effect is restricted by the receiver's cultural level.

Nonverbal communication mainly includes movements, facial expressions, tone of voice, light signal, etc. Its connotation is rich, flexible, but the transmission distance is limited, blurred, the meaning can only be understood, not be talked about. According to a survey, in the process of face-to-face communication, information of language and words is no more than 35%, and 65% of the information is passed through nonverbal means, thus the nonverbal communication is being more and more appreciated.

Electronic media is primarily fax, closed-circuit television, computer networks, E-mail, etc. With high delivery speed and large information capacity, it can pass information with low cost. With the development of information and communication technology, electronic media will play a more and more important role in communication.

3. Formal Communication and Informal Communication (According to the Organization System)

Formal communication generally refers to the transmission and communication of information in the organization system bases on ways organization stated. Mainly includes: instructions, commands and files issued according to the formal system; formal meetings organized by organization; formal contacts between supervisor and colleagues in the organization because of work needs, etc.

Advantages of formal communication are: Communication has good effect, it is serious and has strong binding force. It's easy for secrecy and has a certain authority. Defects are that it's relatively rigid, with slow communication speed, the intermediate links are many, information is easy to be wrong and lost.

Informal communication uses the way outside a formal system for information transmission and communication. This communication is not supervised by the organization, nor limited by the structure of hierarchy, but conducted by employees who choose it freely, mainly through informal contact between organizations and individuals. Informal communication channels have the following basic features: ①Within the channel, information is not complete, and is irregular, cannot be used as the basis for decision-making. ②The channel involved more issues concerning feelings and emotions, so it is easy to use. ③The establishment of the channel is associated with the similarity of personality, and therefore it is easy to communication and cooperation. ④Information transfers fast. ⑤It is a barometer of formal communication.

Informal communication is objective existence, and it plays an important role in the organization. Staff should correctly treat the informal communication.

4. Downward Communication, Upward Communication and Parallel Communication (According to the Direction)

Downward communication refers to the superiors pass information to subordinate levels, also named top-down communication. For example, giving work plan to grassroots, releasing the relevant policy of the organization.

Upward communication refers to subordinates report opinions to the superiors, also named bottom-up communication. The superiors should encourage the subordinates to report the situation, as long as the upward communication is smoothly processed, superiors are able to fully grasp the situation, and then make practical decisions.

Parallel communication is the information communication among the parallel departments. Sometimes it can also appear as inclined communication that is the communication between personnel at different levels who has no subordinating relationship.

5. Unilateral Communication and Bilateral Communication (According to the Feedback)

Unilateral communication refers to the communication for unchanged position between sender and receiver (one-way). One party just sends information. The other party only receives information. The two sides don't need feedback neither on emotion nor language, such as reports, instructions, etc. This way of information transmission is of high speed, but the accuracy is poor. Sometimes receivers could produce psychological resistance.

In bilateral communication, positions between sender and receiver exchange constantly, and the sender negotiates and discusses with the receiver. After sending messages, the sender still need to listen to feedback in time. When necessary, negotiations can be repeated for many times, until there are agreement and satisfaction between each other, such as conversation and negotiation. Its advantages are: The accuracy of communicating information is high, and the receiver has the opportunity to give feedback, generates equality and sense of participation, and increases confidence and sense of responsibility, which helps build the relationship between each other. But for the senders, they face the receivers' inquiry, criticism in the process of communication. So they endure psychological pressure. At the same time, the speed of information transmission is slow.

11.2.2 Communication Inside the Organization

There is a lot of communication information which flows every time in the organization. This communication information is not only from the communication among individuals in the organization, but also includes the information within the communication and the information between organizations. Communication within the organization refers to the progress of the communication and transmission of information which are conducted by work teams as basic units. Communication between organizations refers to progress the process of strengthening the benefits of the communication and transmission of their respective organizational goals. Managers should not only possess good interpersonal communication skills, but also learn to manage communication within and between organizations.

1. Interpersonal Communication

The most common form of communication is interpersonal communication among organization members. In the knowledge economy era, more and more organization members, as knowledge carrier, are becoming the core resource of producing organization efficiency. In a way, interpersonal communication among individuals represents the organization dissemination and diffusion of knowledge. In this sense, interpersonal communication refers to the process in which the personal members of the organization link individual targets with organizational target. Each enterprise consists of several, dozens, hundreds or even thousands of people, its daily activities also consist of many specific works. Because of the difference of individual status, interests and ability, their understandings of business goals, feelings of information vary as well, which may cause each individual's goal deviate or even contravene the enterprise's general goal. How to ensure the single-mindedness of individuals to faithfully complete enterprise's general goal? This would require communicating with each other, unifying ideological understanding, and coordinating each individual's work activities consciously. Therefore, interpersonal communication is the basic coordinating work in the organization. Besides, interpersonal communication is decided by the objectivity and diversity of people's self-serving behaviors. The great significance of interpersonal communication also depends on people's management.

In the process of interpersonal communication, all kinds of noise interference constitute a challenge for members to communicate effectively. The distortion of information during its delivery, transmission, reception and feedback is mainly rooted in the threats of interpersonal factors, cultural factors and structure factors.

2. Organizational Communication

(1) Team communication. Team communication refers to the process of the communication and transmission of information which are conducted by work teams as basic units. Team is the unit of two or more than two persons interacting and collaborating in order to complete the organization's predetermined and specific goal. The concept of team consists of three elements. First, two or more persons are needed. The size of the team can be either big or small, but generally less than 15 people. Second, team members should contact with each other regularly, those who fail to get along with others cannot form a team with them. Third, team members share corporate performance targets. Team concept means a strong sense of mission and competition.

Attaching great importance to team work means putting high value on the need of team communication. Members work together to complete the task, and team communication structure affects team performance and employees' satisfaction. The sense of team communication for an organization is that in the highly competitive global environment, organizations or teams should solve complex problems. When team activities are complex and difficult, all members should share information in a decentralized structure in order to solve problems. The team need to communicate freely in all directions, team members should be encouraged to discuss problems with each other. Employees should spend a lot of time in information-processing.

（2）Communication between organizations. It is the process in which organizations communicate with their stakeholders. It will benefit achieving themselves' information communication and transmission for organizational goals. Communication among organizations aims to make full use of various social resources, coordinate interests of all parties, and realize the sustainable co-development of organizations. Since the 1990s, communication among organizations has increasingly become an important part of organizational communication.

【新视角】

走动式管理对组织中各级管理者来说都是十分有效的面对面沟通方式。管理者们在工作区走动，与员工和其他管理者就存在的问题进行非正式的沟通，而不是通过正式会议与下属沟通。这种非正式沟通为管理者和下属提供了重要的信息，同时培养了积极的关系。

美国管理协会总结出沟通中应注意的十个问题：①沟通前先将概念澄清。②检讨沟通的真正目的。③考虑好沟通时的一切环境。④计划沟通内容时，应尽可能听取他人的意见。④做好必要的记录。⑤尽可能地传递有效资料。⑥有必要的反馈。⑦沟通时不仅要着眼于当前，更要着眼于未来。⑨言行一致。⑩成为一位好听众。

第三节 有效沟通

管理者进行沟通的目的就是要通过有效沟通，消除沟通过程中的障碍，从而提高沟通的效果。所谓有效沟通，就是传递和交流的信息可靠性和准确性高，表明组织对噪音的抵抗能力高。

一、有效沟通的障碍

（1）发送者方面的障碍：也称原发性障碍。一般是由于对信息含义的理解不同，表达不够清楚，编码失误等造成的。

（2）沟通过程中的障碍：媒体（介）选择与信息、信号选择不匹配而导致无法有效传递，或信息传递渠道不佳，传递技术差等。

（3）接收者方面的障碍：接收者由于本身的问题，如价值观、知识、情绪以及行为习惯等所造成的障碍。

（4）反馈过程中的障碍：反馈渠道本身的设置问题，如果不能有效运作，有可能使信息失真；传递技术和编译码存在问题等，也可能造成沟通的障碍。

以上是从沟通的过程来观察的。影响有效沟通的障碍，既有个人因素（选择和沟通技巧差异）、人际因素（沟通双方的相互信任、信息来源的可靠性等），又有结构因素（地位差别、信息传递链、团体规模和空间约束）、技术因素（语言、非语言暗示，媒介有效性和信息过量）。

二、有效沟通的基础

要想实现有效沟通，提高沟通效率，必须打下良好的沟通基础，注意以下几个问题：

（1）明确沟通的重要性，正确对待沟通。明确、清晰的信息是良好沟通的开端。

（2）创造一个相互信任、有利于沟通的小环境。信任和诚意是沟通的重要基础。

（3）培养"倾听"的艺术。倾听不仅是要听到，而且要弄懂所听到的内容和意义。积极的倾听必须专注、接受、完整。

（4）建立合理的信息传播体系，以便控制企业内部横向及纵向的信息流动，使各部门及员工都有固定的来源。

（5）缩短信息传递链，拓宽沟通渠道，保证信息的畅通无阻和完整性。

（6）提高利用非正式沟通渠道的自觉性：在强化正式沟通时，必须有意识地提高利用非正式沟通渠道的自觉性，通过非正式沟通渠道处理一些正式渠道不能办、难办的事。

（7）加强平行沟通，促进横向交流。这对组织间的沟通尤为重要。

【小链接】

管理者的沟通技巧

作为信息发送者，管理者的沟通技巧有：发送清晰而完整的信息、将信息编码成接收者易理解的传输符号、选择适当的传输媒介、选择接收者能监控的媒介、避免信息被过滤和曲解、确保信息中包含反馈机制、提供准确的信息避免谣言传播。

作为信息接收者，管理者的沟通技巧有：寻找兴趣点，注意领会要点，集中注意力，训练自己的大脑，保持头脑开放、沉着，成为好的倾听对象，移情，灵活多变。

三、沟通的方法

沟通的方法是多种多样的，但运用最广泛的是发布批示、会议制度和个别沟通。

1. 发布批示

在指导下级工作时，指示是重要的方法之一，它可使一项活动开始、变更或终止，它是使组织正常运转的必要环节。管理中使用指示方法时应考虑下列问题：

（1）一般的或具体的。这取决于管理人员对周围环境的预见能力，以及下级的影响程度。对授权持有严格观点的管理人员，倾向于具体的指示，而在实施指示周围环境不能预见的情况下，大多采用一般形式。

（2）书面的或口头的。这要根据上下级关系的持久性、信任程度以及避免指示的重复而定。如果上下级关系持久，信任程度较高，则不必采用书面指示。如果为了防止命令的重复和司法上的争执，为了对所有有关人员，宣布一项特定的任务，则书面指示就是必要的。

（3）正式的或非正式的。对每个下级准确地发布正式的或非正式的指示是一种艺术，正确采用非正式的方式启发下级，用正式的方式来命令下级。

2. 会议制度

会议制度可以为人与人之间进行思想、情感方面的交流提供场所和机会，具体作用有：

（1）会议是组织活动的主要表现形式，与会者在组织中的身份、影响、所起的作用都会在会议中有所表现，会议中的信息交流，会在人们的心理上产生影响。

（2）会议可集思广益，通过会议交流可形成共同的见解和行动。

（3）会议可使人们了解共同的目标，了解自己的工作与他人工作的关系，更好地选择自己的工作目标。

（4）通过会议可以对每个与会者产生约束力。

（5）通过会议能发现人们未注意的问题，从而加以认真地考虑和研究。

3. 个别沟通

这是指领导者用正式的或非正式的形式在组织内外同下属或同级人员个别交谈，征询谈话对象对组织中存在问题的看法，或对别人以及对自己的意见。这种形式大部分是建立在相互信任的基础上的，能够表露人们的真实思想，从而使领导者能掌握下属人员的思想动态，在认识和见解、信心等方面取得一致。管理者要积极倾听、善于运于反馈手段，以提高方法的有效性。

选择沟通方法时应考虑的因素：当管理者面临某种沟通需要时，究竟应采取哪一种沟通方法，是一个复杂的问题，没有哪一种方法绝对有效。以下四个因素可供管理者在选择沟通方法时参考：

（1）沟通问题的性质。

（2）沟通人员的特点。

（3）人际关系的协调程度。

（4）沟通渠道的性质。

总而言之，沟通方法的运用要随机制宜，因人而定。

【阅读资料】

群体会议：爱它还是恨它

许多人都痛恨会议，许多公司都被那些过多的没有实效的、有损其实的会议所拖累。但是有些会议就真的不应错过，下面就是一些喜欢它们的人描述的例子。

MaMaMedia. com 每周都要召开叫作"思想碰撞"的会议，该会议为人们提供了日常工作中创造性开发的机会。Rebecca Randall 从不缺席这些会议，因为"对我来说，这是从日常工作中解脱出来，并产生做好工作的方法的一个极佳方式。"公司在网站上为12岁以下的儿童提供娱乐性学习，而这些会议"近似于儿童通过探索、娱乐、惊奇和想象进行学习的方式"。每周的会议是由不同团队来计划和主持的。

在美国，顶尖的家居公司 Kaufman and Broad Home 公司，由营销和沟通部门员工参加的月度"五点后"会议通常在 Marketing War 房间进行，甚至有一次是在以每小时65英里的速度行驶的巴士上召开的。会议属于头脑风暴式的，其主题是关于如何将公司的品牌形象用更有趣的方式表达出来。一次会议的结果是使用 Marge 和 Homer Simpson 的家的完全复制版进行大型促销活动。会议的规范是什么都可以做。"要比 Mclauglin 集团想得更好，好主意最初听起来都是非常疯狂的，所以我们不希望人们加工他们的想法。我们的潜规则是，想什么就说出来。"

北电网络的加勒比和拉丁美洲事业部每月进行一次虚拟领导学院。利用电视会议技术，领导学院让那些地理上分散的员工了解重要的战略问题。Emma Carrasco 从不缺席，因为网络会议"让我们可以在全公司分享领导能力和专长……我们展现了北电的技术和文化……强化了一种核心的文化价值——突破技术是提高而不是消除人们之间的互动"。

摩托罗拉的运营经理 Terry Pope 从不缺席与其他三十多个管理者、工程师和技术人员每天早晨的会议。会议目的是沟通过去 24 小时产生的而且需要在未来 24 小时解决的问题。如果发现了问题，负责人会说："这就是问题，而这就是我们要避免它再次发生的做法。"他不想错过会议是因为"它解决了整个工厂和文化的节奏，是每天对问我们执行能力的演练"。

Pete Kirwan 与工程师、程序员和技术作家新进行的"火边小叙"，会议的规范是不受拘束的、坦率的和建设性的批评。"这是在友好、非正式的气氛中讨论棘手问题的好机会……企业的问题与个人和组织的问题一样，总是在变化。"他将家里的壁炉点上火，摆好椅子，会议就开始了。这看上去很傻，但它使人们放松，从而可以畅所欲言，他能从中学到东西，也帮助别人学习。

企业家 Craig Forman 从不缺席星期天晚上与家人的聚会。"这个'会议'让我们聚在一起，给我们下周工作的动力。对我们三口人来说，它都是一个休息。"他希望家庭不要在硅谷的创业文化中被抛在后面。

（资料来源：贝特曼等著，王雪莉译：《管理学：新竞争格局》（第六版），北京：北京大学出版社 2007 年版，第 482~483 页）

思考问题：

1. 你能找出上述会议主题的共同点和不同点吗？

2. 参加这些例行会议的人不想错过它，你认为原因可能是什么？

3. 这些会议对士气、凝聚力和团队有何作用？如何产生以及为什么会产生这样的作用呢？

4. 你尽量避免参加的会议是什么？为什么？你有很想参加的会议吗？

5. 作为管理者，你将召开什么样的例会？你将怎样避免人们讨厌它，并让他们不想错过它？

6. 你还需要做什么来创建一个强有力的团队？

Section 3　Effective Communication

The purpose of effective communication is to remove obstacles in the communication process through effective communication, to improve the effect of communication. The so-called effective communication is reliable, with high accuracy of information's transmission and communication, which shows organization's strong resistance to noise.

11.3.1　Obstacles to Effective Communication

(1) Obstacles of senders: It is the primary obstacle, ususlly results from different understanding of the information, unclear expression, coding errors, etc.

(2) Obstacles in the process of communication: Mismatching among media selection and information selection and signal selection, which causes the failure of transmission, or poor information transmission channel, low transmission technology, etc.

(3) Obstacles of receivers: The obstacles caused by receivers' own reasons, such as values, knowledge, emotion and behavior.

(4) Obstacles in the process of feedback: The problem of setting feedback channels, if it can't process effectively, may make information distorted. Something wrong with the transmission technology and the encoding or decoding can cause communication barriers too.

Above are observed from the communication process. Obstacles affecting the effective communication consist of personal factors (different ways of selection and communication), interpersonal factors (trust between each other and reliability of the source of information, etc.), as well as structure factors (status differences, information transmission chain, group size and space constraints), technology factors (language, nonverbal cues, media effectiveness and too much information).

11.3.2　Foundations of Effective Communication

If you want to achieve effective communication and improve the efficiency of communication, you have to build solid foundation for communication, pay attention to the following questions:

(1) Know the importance of clear communication and have a right attitude towards communication. Clearly, the clear message is the beginning of good communication.

(2) Create a mutual trust environment which is advantageous to the communication. Trust and sincerity is the base of communication.

(3) Develop the art of "listening". Listening is not only to hear, but also to understand what they hear. Active listening must be concentrated, acceptable and complete.

(4) Establish a reasonable system of information dissemination. In order to control the vertical and horizontal flow of information within the enterprise, make each department and employee has a fixed source.

(5) Shorten the information transmission chain, broaden the communication channels, ensure the unimpeded and completeness of the information.

(6) Improve the consciousness of using informal communication channels: When strengthening official communication, must consciously improve the consciousness of using informal communication channels, put the difficult tasks some formal channels can't do in the informal communication channels to deal with.

（7）Strengthen the horizontal communication, promote the horizontal communication. This communication is particularly important to organizations.

11.3.3 Methods of Communication

Methods of communication are varied, but the most widely used are giving instructions, meeting system and individual communication.

1. Giving Instructions

In guiding job of a lower level, indicator is one of the important methods, it can make an activity began, modify or discontinue, it is necessary for normal operation of the organization. When the management of indicator is used, it should consider the following questions:

（1）General or specific. It depends on the managers' ability of prediction on the surrounding environment, and the influence degree of the subordinates. For authorized management personnel who has strict views prefer specific instructions. In the case of surrounding is unforeseeable in the implementation of instruction, the most general form is adopted.

（2）Written or oral. It depends on the degree of persistence of the relationship between higher and lower, trust and avoiding repeat instructions. If lasting relationship exists between higher and lower levels, and the trust is of high degree, then there is no need to adopt written instructions. If it is to prevent the repeat orders and judicial disputes, in order to announce a specific task to all relevant persons, then the written instructions is necessary.

（3）Formal or informal. Issued accurate formal or informal instruction to lowers is an art. Correctly use informal way to inspire subordinates, and command the lower in formal way.

2. Meeting System

The meeting system can provide places and opportunities for people to communicate thoughts and emotions. Specific functions are:

（1）The meeting is the major forms of organization activities, participants' identity, influence in the organization and the role will show up in the meeting, the meeting's information communication will influence people's psychology.

（2）The meeting is brainstorming, can form common understandings and actions.

（3）The meeting can make people to understand common goals, the relationship between their work and others, and better choose their own work goals.

（4）By meeting it can have binding force on each of the participants.

（5）By meeting it can found problems people did not pay attention to, thus trace to serious consideration and research.

3. Individual Communication

It means that leaders communicate with subordinates or staff at the same level in formal or informal ways in or out of the organization and consulting interlocutors' opinions about problems existing in the organization, or others' suggestions for the leader himself. This form is based on mutual trust, which can show people's actual ideas so that the leader can grasp subordinates' ideological trend and agree on acquaintance, opinions and confidence with others. Leaders should listen actively and be good at making use of feedback so as to improve the efficiency of his measures.

The following factors should be taken in consideration when choosing communication ways: When faced up with a kind of communication need, taking which way to communicate is a complex problem, for there's no way that is absolutely effective. The following four factors are provided for leaders to consider when choosing a good of communication:

(1) Nature of problem which will be communicated.

(2) Characteristics of the communication personnel.

(3) The degree of harmony of interpersonal relationship.

(4) Nature of the communication channel.

All in all, communication methods should be used compatibly according to different persons.

【阅读资料】

沟通十戒

"沟通十戒"是指沟通中的十种不良习惯，它是由 R. C. 尼柯斯提出的。他认为，沟通过程中的不良习惯主要表现在十个方面，克服这些不良习惯，是改善沟通的重要内容。①对对方所谈的主题没有兴趣。②被对方的姿态所吸引而忽略了对方所讲的内容。③当听到与自己意见不同的地方，就过分激动，以致不愿再听下去，对其余信息也就此忽略了。④仅注意事实，而不肯注意原则和推论。⑤过分重视条理而对欠条理的人的讲话不够重视。⑥过多注意造作掩饰，而不重视真情实质。⑦分心于别的事情，心不在焉。⑧对较难的言辞不求甚解。⑨当对方的言辞带有感情时，则听力分散。⑩在听别人讲话时还思考别的问题，顾此失彼。

第四节　冲突与谈判

一、冲突产生的原因

冲突是指由于某种差异而引起的抵触、争执或争斗的对立状态。沟通是为了减低组织的管理成本，进而降低组织之间的交易成本。人与人之间、组织与组织之间在利益、观点和对信息或事件的理解上都可能存在差异，这就有可能产生冲突。冲突产生的原因大体上可归纳为三类：

（1）沟通差异。由于文化和历史背景不同、语义困难、误解及沟通过程中噪音的干扰，都可能造成人们之间意见的不一致。沟通不良是产生冲突的重要原因，但不是主要的。

（2）结构差异。由于分工造成的组织结构中垂直方向和水平方向各层次、各单位、不同岗位的分化，组织分化越细密，协调就越困难，冲突就不可避免。

（3）个体差异。由于每个人的社会背景、教育程度、修养、价值观等存在差异，合作与沟通的困难也易导致冲突的发生。

由于客观上存在冲突，因而管理冲突是非常必要的。

二、冲突的管理

管理冲突实际上包括两个方面：一是设法消除冲突产生的负面效应；二是利用和扩大冲突产生的正面效应。优秀的管理者管理冲突的方法有：

（1）谨慎地选择要处理的冲突。

（2）仔细研究冲突双方代表人。

（3）深入了解冲突产生的根源。

（4）妥善选择处理的办法，如回避、迁就、强制、妥协、合作等。

三、有效谈判

谈判是双方或多方为实现某种目标就有关条件达成协议的过程。谈判是冲突管理的重要内容，谈判是解决冲突的有效途径。谈判有两种基本方法：

（1）零和谈判。即有输有赢的谈判。

（2）双赢谈判。即双方都赢的谈判。

Section 4　Conflict and Negotiation

11. 4. 1　The Causes of Conflict

Conflict refers to the opposite state of resistance, disputes or conflicts caused by some kind of difference. Communication is to reduce the management cost of organization, and reduce the transaction cost. Different people and organizations may differ in the interests, views and understanding of the information or events, so there could be conflicts. The reason of conflicts can be generally divided into three categories:

（1）Communication differences. Different cultural and historical context and semantic difficulties, misunderstanding and noise in the process of communication, are likely to cause inconsistency between people. Poor communication is the important reason for the conflict, but it is not the main reason.

（2）Structural differences. It is caused by division of the organizational structure in the vertical direction and horizontal direction at all levels and units. The more detailed the division is, the more difficult the coordination is. Conflict is inevitable.

（3）Individual differences. Because of each person's social background, the degree of education, culture, values and other differences, the difficult of cooperation and communication may easy lead to conflict.

Because the existence of conflicts can not be avoided, conflict management is very necessary.

11.4.2　Conflict Management

Conflict management actually includes two aspects: one is trying to get rid of the negative effect produced by conflict, the other is to use and expand the positive effect of the conflict. Good methods used by excellent managers are:

(1) Carefully choose conflicts you want to deal with.

(2) Study the conflicting representatives from two parties.

(3) Understand the root which causes conflicts.

(4) Choose an appropriate choice to solve conflicts, such as avoiding, accommodating, mandatory, compromise, cooperation, etc.

11.4.3　Effective Negotiation

Negotiation is the process where two or more sides try to achieve a certain goal or agreement regarding the conditions. Negotiation is an important content of conflict management, negotiation is the effective ways to conflict resolution. Negotiation has two basic methods:

(1) Zero negotiations. There is win and lose in the negotiation.

(2) Double-won negotiations. Both sides win the negotiation.

【小链接】

关于谈判的认识

谈判有术，既是一门科学，也一门艺术。

世界是一张谈判桌，人人都是谈判者。

谈判是一种风尚、能力与智慧。

谈判就像走钢丝，充满着刺激、悬念、满足感。

谈判是实力与智慧的较量，学识与口才的较量，魅力与演技的较量。

谈判的目的不是输赢、单赢，而是双赢、多赢。

谈判能力可以通过修炼和培训来获得。

谈判的核心要义是合作的利己主义。

谈判是一种利益相关者的沟通行为。

【本章提要】

● 沟通是信息传递与理解，它在管理中起着收集信息、改善人际关系、改变人们的行为和建立外部联系的作用。

● 沟通过程就是信息发送者把要发送出去的信息，按一定的程序进行精心的编码后，使信息经过一定的通道传递给接收者，接收者在将信息解码后，将收到的信息反馈给发送者。

● 沟通有不同的类别，也各有其长处与不足。组织中的沟通包括人际沟通、团队沟通和组织间沟通。

- 有效沟通，就是传递和交流的信息可靠性和准确性高，表明组织对噪音的抵抗能力高。

- 管理者要想实现有效沟通，就必须清理沟通的障碍，建立有效沟通的基础，采用适宜的沟通方法。

- 冲突是客观存在的，与沟通的有效性有关，通过谈判也可消除或缓解冲突。

【关键词】

沟通（Communication）　　冲突（Conflict）　　谈判（Negotiation）

沟通过程（Communication Process）　　人际沟通（Interpersonal Communication）

组织沟通（Organizational Communication）　　正式沟通（Official Communication）

非正式沟通（Unofficial Communication）　　团队沟通（Team Communication）

沟通差异（Communication Difference）

【复习与思考】

1. 沟通对一个组织而言有何重要作用？
2. 沟通有哪些类型？
3. 沟通过程应包括哪些环节？
4. 沟通的障碍有哪些？如何克服？
5. 如何管理冲突？

【研究与讨论】

1. 为什么说有效沟通对管理者的成功来说十分重要？
2. 根据研究，管理人员每天花 2/3 的时间用在沟通中，其中倾听占 40%，说话占 35%，阅读占 16%，书写占 9%。你是否是一个好听众？
3. 联系实际谈谈如何才能实现有效沟通？
4. 下级在汇报工作时，有时会猜测领导的意图，投其所好，报喜不报忧。怎样才能避免这种情况发生？
5. 你认为大多数管理者对冲突的看法是什么样的？

【实践演练】

1. 访问一位企业经理，与他讨论沟通问题，请教他有效沟通的经验。
2. 选择一个你熟悉的组织，了解该组织的沟通类型、沟通障碍及沟通方法。
3. 模拟一个组织中不同角色之间的沟通。

【管理模拟】

将全班同学分成若干小组，模拟一家公司，有总经理、部门经理和员工。学习和解决以下问题：

 1．他们在沟通中有哪些障碍？

 2．如何扫清这些障碍以实现有效沟通？

 3．讨论和掌握沟通的技巧。

【本章案例】

  格雷丝·李从新加坡国立大学大学毕业后，去她父亲罗宾·李先生那里工作，他拥有一家大型百货商店。公司经过几年的发展，已经从一个小商店变成了一个规模颇大并且利润颇丰的百货商店，整个家庭都参与了公司的各种活动。

  罗宾·李亲自负责公司的日常管理。他频繁地与管理人员召开长时间的会议。他每周至少在商店走动一次，观察各层次的员工并与他们保持联系。

  他最担心的是沟通和激励，虽然他觉得在开会时，所有的管理者及职工都认真地倾听自己，他们后来的行为却使他疑惑他们到底是否理解了他的意思。他的许多政策和指导都得不到实施。看了所收集的一些反馈及交流信息，他发现一些管理人员承认自己并不知道公司的目标，但是他们相信如果某些信息沟通得当，他们会做得更好。大多数办事人员和行政人员都缺乏想象力和驱动力。他还担心公司员工的流动性，其中有一些员工还在竞争对手那里任了职。

  当女儿走进他的办公室，以特别助理身份开始工作时，他说："格雷丝，我的两个问题是沟通和激励。我知道你在大学的专业是管理，并且我也听过你谈及沟通的重要性。我在考虑你是否学到了一些知识，可以帮助我改善沟通。你对改善我们公司的生意有何建议？"

  思考问题：

 1．格雷丝会怎样回答她父亲的问题？

 2．你将如何对罗宾·李先生所面临的问题进行分析？

 3．对于改善这种形势，你有什么建议？

【本章参考文献】

 ［1］周三多：《管理学》，北京：中国高等教育出版社 2000 年版。

 ［2］［美］哈罗德·孔茨、海因茨·韦里克著，郝国华等译：《管理学》，经济科学出版社 2001 年版。

 ［3］吴照云：《管理学》，北京：中国社会科学出版社 2006 年版。

 ［4］周健临：《管理学教程》，上海：上海财经大学出版社 2001 年版。

 ［5］陈传明、周小虎编著：《管理学》，北京：清华大学出版社 2003 年版。

第十二章　控　制

Chapter 12　Control

有效的管理者应该始终督促他人，以保证应该采取的行动事实上已经在进行，保证他人应该达到的目标事实上已经达到。

罗宾斯

Effective managers should always urging others to ensure that action that should be taken has in fact already been taken, ensure the goals that others should achieve in fact has been achieved.

Robbins

正像控制开始于计划的尾声一样，决定开始于控制的尾声。

汉普顿

As control begins at the end of plan, decision starts at the end of control.

Hampton

【本章学习目标】

知识目标：

了解控制的含义和内容。

掌握管理控制的基本过程。

理解管理控制的类型、原则和要求。

熟悉管理控制的一般方法。

技能目标：

具备构建控制系统的基本能力。

具有分析管理控制系统的能力。

能够应用相关控制方法。

【Learning Objectives of Chapter 12】

Objectives of Knowledge：

Define the meaning and the content of control.

Master the process of management control.

Understand the types, principles and requirements of management control.

Be familiar with the basic methods of management control.

Objectives of Skill：

Have the ability of constructing control system.

Have the ability of analyzing management control system.

Be able to apply control methods.

【小故事】

盛水的木桶是由许多块木板箍成的，盛水量也是由这些木板共同决定的。若其中一块木板很短，则木桶的盛水量就被短板所限制。这块短板就成了这个木桶盛水量的"限制因素"（或称"短板效应"）。若要使此木桶盛水量增加，只有换掉短板或将短板加长才行。人们把这一规律总结为"木桶原理"或"木桶定律"，又称"短板理论"。

【引例】

摩托罗拉的"6 西格玛"和质量控制

20 世纪 80 年代中期，摩托罗拉在市场竞争中不断受到外国企业的冲击。这些外国企业以高质量、低成本的产品在市场上占据优势地位。摩托罗拉当时的 CEO Bob Galvin 在公司内部启动了一项提高质量的计划——"6 西格玛"计划。希腊字母 σ（西格玛）在统计学中用来表示某一过程估计的标准差或方差。"西格玛水平"越低，过程中的方差越大，差错越多。反之，差错越少。

"西格玛水平"通常用来表示某一过程中每 100 万次机会中差错的数量（DPMO）。例如，"2 西格玛水平"的过程中含有 308 537DPMO（过程没有受到很好的控制）。如图 12-1 所示，"4 西格玛水平"的过程含有 6210DPMO。而"6 西格玛"计划使摩托罗拉在产品、生产和销售上减少了大量的错误，减少了生产周期，降低了成本，从而为顾客创造了价值。

"6 西格玛"计划的显著效果是使摩托罗拉成为市场的主宰，并在 1988 年获得了鲍勃里奇国家质量奖。从此"6 西格玛"计划在各大公司得到应用，最成功的例子是通用电气、霍尼韦尔、默克和道化学。通过"6 西格玛"计划的实施，这些公司极大地降低了生产成本，提高了市场占有率，实现了更好的财务业绩。

通用电气在 2002 年为"6 西格玛"计划花了 6 亿美元，主要是用来支付 4 000 个全职员工 6 西格玛专家的薪水，并为 10 万名员工提供基础培训。但是这笔钱花得很值，公司估计已经节省了 80 亿美元，并且还可能再有 25 亿美元的节省。实际上，通用电气非常相信"6 西格玛"计划，而且将管理者 40% 的收入与"6 西格玛"活动挂钩。道化学估计"6 西格玛"计划帮助它减少了 70% 的装配错误，从而将为公司节省 15 亿美元。

美国质量协会前任仲裁、顾问 Gregory H. Waston 说："'6 西格玛'计划是过去 100 年来我们对质量认识的最大综合。"该方法并不仅适用于车间，在健康服务公司 Wellmark，过去一般要用 65 天的时间将一名医生添加到其保险计划里，"6 西格玛"活动让公司发现了问题出在哪里并加以解决，现在只要花 30 天就可以用更少的员工完成相同的工作。使用"6 西格玛"计划的医院认为这帮助它们标准化了配药的流程，减少了给患者误服药品的可能性，而且企业处理实验结果的时间也短了。

西格玛水平	DMPO	4西格玛够吗？
2σ	308 537	考虑这些4西格玛质量的日常表现：
3σ	66 807	● 每小时丢失2万个邮件或信件
4σ	6 210	● 每天有15分钟的饮用水是不令人放心的
5σ	233	● 每周发生5 000次不正确的外科手术
6σ	3.4	● 每年开出20万个错误的药方
		● 每月停电7小时

图 12 – 1　西格玛水平与 DPMO 之间的关系

（资料来源：Tom Rancour and Mike McCracken. Applying 6 Sigma Methods for Breakthrough Safety Performance, *Professional Safety*，October，2000，No. 10，pp. 29 – 32）

思考问题：

"6 西格玛"对于产品质量控制的现实意义如何？

第一节　控制的含义和内容

控制是实现战略计划的手段，在管理工作中，控制是重要的管理职能之一，也是保持组织稳定、维持组织正常运作的手段。

一、控制的概念

控制就是按既定的目标和标准，监督衡量各项活动，并发现和纠正偏差，以保证组织活动符合既定要求的过程。这一概念包含：①控制有很强的目的性，即控制是为了保证组织的活动按计划进行的。②控制是通过监督和纠偏来实现的。③控制是一个过程。

控制和计划是密不可分的，它们的关系表现为：

（1）计划为控制提供衡量的标准，控制又是实现计划的保证。

（2）计划和控制的效果均依赖于对方。计划越明确具体，控制工作就越容易进行，效果就越好。而控制越深入越准确，就越能保证计划的顺利进行。

（3）一切有效的控制方法，首先是计划方法，选择控制方法和设计控制系统时必须考虑到计划本身的特点。

（4）计划本身也需要一定的控制，控制工作本身也必须需要一定的计划。

二、管理控制的必要性

控制对一个组织来说之所以必要，其主要原因是：

（1）组织计划实现目标的需要。没有控制就很难保证组织计划的顺利执行，而计划不能执行，组织目标便无法实现，这是由外部环境和内部条件的变化决定的。只有通过管理控制，才能够为主管人员提供必要的信息，了解计划执行中的问题，采取措施，保证计划顺利进行，从而达成组织的目标。

（2）管理职能有效运行的需要。管理控制通过发现和纠正偏差的行动与计划、组织、领导三个职能紧密地结合在一起，使管理过程形成一个相对封闭的系统。在这个系统中，计划选择和确定了组织的目标、战略、政策以及实现的程序等，并通过组织工作和领导工作等职能去实现这些计划。控制则是为保证计划能够顺利实现，而对计划实施过程加以监督。同时有效的控制，也离不开计划、组织和领导。因此，管理控制存在于管理活动的全过程，它不仅可以维持其他职能的正常运转，而且有时可通过采取纠偏行动来改变其他管理职能的活动。

三、管理控制的内容

就企业组织而言，管理控制的主要内容包括以下五个方面：

（1）对员工的控制：组织的目标是由人来完成的，为了让员工都能按计划去做，就必须对员工加以控制。最常见的方法就是直接巡视，发现问题马上进行纠正。另一种方法就是对员工进行系统化的评估，对绩效好的予以奖励，维持其良好表现；对绩效差的要采取有效措施，纠正出现偏差的行为。

（2）对财务的控制：为使企业获得利润，维持企业正常运作，必须进行财务控制，主要包括审核各期的财务报表，保证一定的现金流量，保证债务负担不重，保证各项资产得到有效的利用等。

（3）对作业的控制：作业就是指从劳动力、原材料等资源到最终产品的转换过程。作业控制就是通过对作业过程的控制来评价提高作业的效率和效果，从而提高组织提供的产品和服务的质量，一般有生产控制、质量控制、库存控制。

（4）对信息的控制：随着人类步入信息社会，信息在组织中的地位越来越重要，不精确的、不完整的、不及时的信息会大大降低组织效率。因此，在现代组织中，对信息的控制最为重要，对信息控制就是要建立一个管理信息系统，为管理者提高充分可靠的信息。

（5）对组织绩效的控制：组织绩效是组织上层管理者的控制对象，组织目标的达成与否都从这里反映出来。有效实施对组织绩效的控制，关键在于科学地评价、衡量组织绩效，然而组织绩效又很难用一个指标加以衡量。因此，关键要看组织目标的取向，即要根据组织完成目标的实际情况，并按照目标所设置的标准来衡量组织绩效。

Section 1　Meaning and Contents of Control

Control is the method to achieve strategic plan and important managerial function to maintain stability and normal operation of the organization.

12. 1. 1　Meaning of Control

Controlling is the process of monitoring, comparing and correcting work performance in accordance with the established goals and standards. It means：①Control has clear purpose to ensure that activities are conducted according to the plan. ②Control is achieved by monitoring. ③Control is a process.

Control is closely associated with plan：

（1）Plan provides standard for control, control ensures the achievement of plan.

（2）The effects of plan and control depended on each other. The more specific the plan is, the more convenient the control will be. The deeper and the more accurate control is, the smoother the implementation of project is.

（3）The effective control method is firstly a plan method, choosing control method and designing control system must consider the plan itself.

（4）The plan itself also needs certain control, and control itself also needs certain plan.

12. 1. 2　Necessity of Control

The reasons why control is so important for an organization are:

（1）The requirement of achieving organization goals. If managers don't control, they have no way of knowing whether their goals and plans are being achieved and what future actions to take, which depends on the change of external environment and internal conditions. Only by control, necessary information can be sent to managers. Understanding problems in the implementation of the plan, taking actions to ensure activities are completed appropriately lead to the attainment of goals.

（2）The requirement of performing management function. Management control through the action of discovering and correcting the deviation closely unifies the functions of planning, organizing, leading together, making the management process form a relatively closed system. In this system, planning chooses and determines the goal, strategy, policy and the process of the organizations, and through the organizing and leading or other functions to achieve these plans. Control supervises the implementation process of plan in order to realize the plan smoothly. And effective control can't do without planning, organizing and leading. So management control exists in the whole process of management activities, which can not only maintain the operation of other functions, but also change activities of other functions through corrective actions.

12. 1. 3　Contents of Control

For an organization, the main content of control includes five parts:

（1）Control of personnel. Personnel are those who achieve the organization goals. To ensure that people assume their responsibility as planned, there must be control on personnel. Inspection is the most common method because problem can be corrected immediately. The other method is systematic evaluation to personnel. Giving awards to advanced workers to maintain his performance or taking effective actions to correct bad performance.

（2）Control of finance. To make the enterprise profit and maintain normal operation, financial control must be taken seriously, which includes the audit of financial reports of the periods, guarantee of cash flow, ensure the debt burden is not heavy and the effective use of assets.

（3）Control of operation. Operation is a conversion process of transforming labor, raw materials and other resources to the end products. Operation control can improve efficiency and influence through the control of the process, so as to improve the quality of products and services provided by organization, including production control, quality control and inventory control.

（4）Control of information. As human being is stepping into the information age, the information becomes more and more important to corporations. Inaccurate, incomplete and untimely information will greatly reduce the organizational efficiency. Therefore, in the modern organizations, it is significant to reinforce the information control and establish an information management system to provide reliable and abundant information.

（5）Control of organizational performance. Organizational performance is the object controlled by top managers from which the achievement of organizational goals is reflected. The key to conducting effective organizational performance control is scientific evaluation. However, it is hard to use an index to measure the performance. Therefore, the core of evaluation is the organization's mission, which is based on the real situation and the target set by the standards of organizational performance.

【新视角】

今天的管理者所要面对的一个基本问题是怎样在要求具备灵活性、革新精神和创造力的公司中实施足够的控制。……在不断变化、高度竞争的市场中，大多数公司的管理者不可能把所有的时间和精力都用来确保每个人都在做预期的工作。有人认为管理者只要雇用不错的员工、调整激励手段并且抱着最好的希望就能实现良好控制，这种想法是不现实的。现在的管理者必须鼓励员工主动改进现有的方法并创造新的方法来对客户需求做出反应，但是这些又必须以一种受控的方式进行。

第二节 控制的基本过程

控制过程分为四个阶段：即确定控制标准—衡量实际成效—分析偏差—采取管理行动。

一、确定控制标准

1. 控制标准的内容和形式

控制标准是控制目标的表现形式，是对企业中人力、物力、财力以及各种生产经营活动方式和内容等所规定的量值界限，是控制工作的依据和基础。

由于控制的目的是为了保证计划和组织目标的实现，所以控制标准的确定必须以计划和组织目标为依据。控制工作的范围很广泛，因而，为进行控制而制定的标准也有许多种，常用的主要是六种：实物量标准、价值标准、时间标准、质量标准、行为标准、无形标准。

2．控制标准的要求

（1）简明，即对标准的量值、单位、可允许的偏差范围要有明确说明；对标准的表述要通俗易懂，便于理解和接受。

（2）适用，即标准要有利于组织目标的实现，要能够反映组织活动状态。

（3）稳定，即标准要能适用于一段较长的时间，既有弹性，也在一定的原则范围内变化。

（4）可行，即标准既不能过高，也不能过低，要使绝大多数职工经过努力都可达到。

（5）可操作，即标准要便于比较、衡量、考核过程中的使用。

3．制定控制标准的方法

控制的目的是为了保证计划和组织目标的实现，但是，不能完全用计划代替标准来进行控制，而是应该制定专门的控制标准。控制标准的制定应以计划和组织目标为依据。

常用的制定控制标准的方法有：

（1）分解法，即把企业经营目标、经营计划按生产单位、管理部门，或按产品零部件，或按工艺、工序等分解为具体的计划指标，作为控制的依据。

（2）预算法，即将企业生产经营活动中需开支的各种费用，按其明细项目确定出预算额，作为各使用部门的费用支出标准。

（3）定额法，即根据技术测定、统计分析、经验估计、比例计算等方法，制定出各种实物量标准、时间标准等，作为对各生产环节和人员的控制标准。

（4）标准化法，即根据国际标准、国家标准、部颁标准和企业标准，确定有关生产经营的各种技术标准和管理标准。

二、衡量实际成效

衡量实际成效就是根据控制标准衡量、检查工作情况，并对计划执行的现状和阶段性成果进行如实反映和客观评价。

有了完备的标准体系，第二步工作就是要采集实际工作的数据，了解和掌握实际工作的概况。在衡量工作中，衡量什么，以及如何衡量，是它的核心问题。

1．衡量什么

衡量什么问题在衡量工作之前就已经得到了解决，因为管理者在确立标准时，就已经确定下来了，一般来说，管理者并不是去观测所有的活动，而是挑选一些关键的控制点，通过它们对全部活动进行控制。关键控制点一般是计划实施过程中起决定作用的点，或者是容易出偏差的点等。

2．如何衡量

具体情况，具体分析。

（1）个人观察：直接取得第一手资料，是一种非常有效的衡量方法。但个人的方法是有局限的。

（2）统计报告：它是按统计方法对实际工作的数据进行加工处理后形成的报告。它的价值取决于真实性和全面性。

（3）口头报告和书面报告：口头报告的优点是快捷方便，而且能够得到立即的反馈；

缺点是不易保存和调查；书面报告要比口头报告更加准确、全面，如会计报告、工作总结等，但在时间上会滞后一些。

（4）抽样调查：在工作量比较大而工作质量又比较平均的情况下，管理者可以通过抽样检查来衡量工作。

在衡量工作中，除了要选择衡量方法外，还要特别注意所获取信息的质量问题，如准确性、及时性、可靠性、适用性等。

衡量实际工作成效是整个控制过程的基础性工作，而获得符合要求的信息，又是衡量整个工作的关键。

三、分析偏差

在取得实际工作成效的信息后，就要将标准与实际成效进行对比，发现其偏差，并进行分析，为采取管理行动做好准备。

比较的结果无非两种：一种是存在偏差，另一种是不存在偏差。实际上偏差会有一个范围，只要不超出这个范围，就算正常。

如果工作结果出现了偏差（正偏差和负偏差），特别是存在负偏差，就要做进一步分析。一般来说，造成偏差的原因有三大类：

（1）计划操作原因：这是由于执行者自身的原因而发生的偏差。如工作不认真，能力不够不能胜任工作等。

（2）外部环境原因：当外部环境发生重大变化时也会导致计划不能实现。如国家政策变化，主要经销商、供应商的变化等，这些原因通常是不可控的。

（3）计划不合理原因：由于计划制订得不切实际，或预测有误，这也是造成偏差的原因。如市场占有率太高，达不到等。

分析衡量结果是控制过程最需要理智分析的环节，是否要进一步采取管理行动就取决于分析的结果。如果分析结果表明没有偏差或只有正偏差，那么控制人员就不必进行下一步了，控制工作也就到此完成了。

四、采取管理行动

控制过程的最后一项工作就是采取管理行为——纠正偏差。由于偏差是由控制标准与实际成效的差距产生的，因而，纠正偏差的方法也有两种，要么改进工作绩效，要么修订标准。

（1）改进工作绩效：如果比较分析的结果表明，计划是可行的，标准也是切合实际的，问题出在工作本身，那么要采取改进工作的行动，如果问题出在外部环境上，那只能采取一些补救的措施，以尽量消除不良影响，然后改变策略，变换目标，另辟蹊径。

改进工作绩效的行动可分为立即纠正行动和彻底纠正行动两类：前者是指发现问题后马上采取行动，力求以最快的速度纠正偏差，以避免造成更大的损失；后者是指发现问题后，通过对问题本质的分析，挖掘问题的根源，采取相应的措施，力求永久性地消除偏差。在实际工作中可以将两者结合起来。

（2）修订标准：如果偏差来自不切合实际的标准，如标准过高或过低，这时，就要修订标准。管理者应从控制的目的出发仔细分析，确认标准的确不符合控制的要求时，方可修订标准。标准过高会影响士气，标准过低会产生懈怠的情况。

Section 2　Basic Control Process

The process of control can be divided into four stages: determine the control standard—evaluate actual performance—analyze the variation—take managerial action.

12.2.1　Determine the Control Standard

1. The Content and Form of Control Standard

Control standard is the expression of the control target, the stipulated boundaries of the content and form of labor, material and financial resources and various production and business operation, the basis and foundation of control work.

Because the purpose of control is to ensure the completion of plans and organizational goals, so the determination of control standards must be based on planning and organizational goals. Therefore, the standards of control work also has many types, six of them are mainly used: quantity standard; value standard; time standard; quality standard; behavior standard and intangible standard.

2. The Requirements of Control Standard

(1) Concise. It should specify the standard of value, unit and the permissible deviation range. The expression of standard should be easy to understand and accept.

(2) Applicable. The standard should contribute to the achievement of organizational goals and reflect the activities.

(3) Stable. The standard can be suitable for a long time, even if it is elastic. Change is acceptable within certain scope.

(4) Feasible. The standard should not be too high or too low to complicated, which should be achieved by most staff through effort.

(5) Operational. The standard is facilitated to apply in comparison, measure and evaluation.

3. The Method of Making Control Standard

The aim of control is that the organizational goals and plan can be accomplished. However, standard can't be replaced by plan to control, but it is better to make special control standard that based on planning and organizational goals.

There are some frequently used methods of setting control standard:

(1) Decomposition method. The enterprise's operation goals, business plan are decomposed into specific subjects according to production unit, management department, or product components, or the process of operation, as the basis of control.

(2) Budget method. Determine budget as the department expense standard according to detail project of various costs that incurred under the enterprise operation activities.

（3）Quota method. Make some quantity standard and time standard as the control standard to control each production link and personnel according to the technical measurement, statistical analysis, empirical estimates and ratio calculation, etc.

（4）Standardized method. Determine the variety of technical and management standards about production and operation in reference to international standards, national standards, departmental standards and enterprise standards.

12. 2. 2　Evaluate Actual Performance

Evaluating actual performance is the inspection of present situation with control standard, and the reflection and objective evaluation of program achievements.

After having complete standard system, the second step is collecting the actual data of work, understanding an overview of actual performance. What should we evaluate and how to evaluate are the key of evaluating.

1. What to Evaluate

The answer of what to evaluate has been solved before the work of evaluating, it is determined by managers when they determine the control standard. In general, instead of observing all activities, manager control all performance through some key points that play an important role in implementation or are easy to deviant.

2. How to Evaluate

It is suitable to find a distinct way to interpret a specific issue.

（1）Personal observation. It is a very effective method to get the firsthand knowledge, but it has limitations.

（2）Statistical reports. It is the report formed by analyzing the data of actual performance. The advantage depends on its reliability and completeness.

（3）Oral reports and written reports. The advantages of oral report are its fast way to get information which allow for verbal and nonverbal feedback immediately, but the information is filtered and can't be documented. Written reports are more accurate and comprehensive than oral reports, including accounting reports and work summary. However it takes more time to prepare usually.

（4）Sample survey. Manager can apply this method when volume of work should be done and the quality is under the condition of average.

In the evaluating work, managers should not only consider which method to choose, but also pay attention to the quality of information, such as its accuracy, timeliness, reliability and suitability.

Its fundamental project of entire control process is to evaluate actual performance and to get correct information is the key of the work of evaluating.

12. 2. 3　Analyze the Variation

After getting the information of actual performance, it should be compared with control standards and find the deviations between them so as to prepare for taking managerial action.

There are two results of comparing. One is there is deviation, the other is there is no deviation. Actually, deviation has its range, as long as it isn't out of the range inside the range of variation, it is normal.

There are three reasons why the deviation happened, especially negative deviation:

(1) Scheduled action: The practitioner's own reason causes the deviation, such as work half-hearted, inadequate capacity to accomplish the job and so on.

(2) External environment: Plan cannot be implemented when external environment changed sharply, such as the change of national policy and the change of main distributors and suppliers, which are often uncontrollable.

(3) Unreasonable plan: Making unreasonable plan and wrong prediction are also the cause of deviation. Such as the market share is too high to reach.

Analysis of evaluation results is the step that needs rational analysis most in control process, which result will determine whether to take further management action. Control personnel don't have to proceed to next step if the analysis result shows that there is no deviation or only positive deviation, then, control work is finished.

12.2.4 Take Managerial Action

The last step of control is taking managerial action—correct the deviation which is caused by the gap between the standard and actual performance. So the method of correcting the deviation is correcting actual performance or revises the standard.

(1) Correct actual performance. If the comparative analysis of the results shows that the plan is feasible, standards are practical, the problem is the performance itself, then we should improve the work. If the problem lies in is external environment, the only thing we can do is to take some remedial measures. Try to eliminate the bad effect and change the strategy and goal.

The action of improving performance can be divided into immediate corrective action and thorough corrective action, the former corrects deviation at once to get performance back on track to avoid greater loss, the latter looks at how and why performance deviated before correcting the source of deviation. We can combine both actions in actual performance.

(2) Revise the standard. Deviation may be a result of an unrealistic standard—a goal that's too high or too low. In this case, the standard—not the performance—needs corrective action. Managers must analyze seriously the purpose of control and ensure that standard is only revised when it can't match the requirement of control. Only in this situation, revising a standard upward or downward is allowed. If the standard is too high to achieve, the team will fall down. On the other hand, the low standard will cause the team remiss.

第三节　控制的类型、原则和要求

一、控制的基本类型

根据控制时点的不同可将控制分为前馈控制、同期控制和反馈控制，三者的关系如图 12－2 所示。

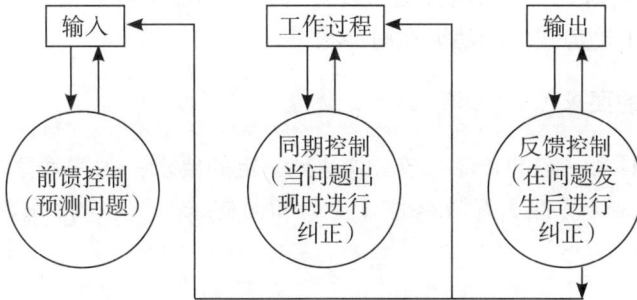

图 12－2　控制过程与控制类型

1. 前馈控制（或称事前控制）

它是在系统运行的输入阶段就进行控制，以防止问题的发生。也称为面向未来的控制。前馈控制强调建立一个控制系统，在问题发生之前就采取措施避免问题发生，而不是当问题出现时再补救。这种控制利用的不是系统的输出信息，而是系统的输入信息。

2. 同期控制（或称事中控制）

它是在系统运行之中同步进行控制，又称现场（现时）控制。它能及时发现偏差，及时采取纠正措施，将损失控制在最低程度，是一种经济有效的方法，但对控制人员的素质要求较高，因为管理者须即时完成比较、分析、纠偏等控制工作。当然，这也需要授权。

3. 反馈控制（或称事后控制）

它是在系统运行之后进行的一种控制，把注意力放在行动的结果上，并以此作为改进下次工作的依据，最大的缺陷就是滞后性，从衡量结果、比较分析，到制定并实施纠偏措施，都需要时间，而且损失已经发生。

另外，反馈控制是通过信息反馈及行动调节来保证系统的稳定性的，它要求反馈的速度必须大于控制对象的速度。否则，系统将产生振荡，处于不稳定状态。

反馈控制虽然有一些不足，但它仍然是一种常用的控制类型，因为很多事情只有在发生后才能看清结果。另外，事物往往是循环发展的，反馈控制能给后面的工作提供信息和借鉴。

二、有效控制的原则

构建有效控制的原则：

（1）反映计划要求原则——控制系统必须紧紧围绕计划进行，要根据计划的特点确定控制标准，衡量方法和纠偏措施。

（2）组织适宜性原则——控制必须适应组织结构的特点，符合组织结构的要求。

（3）控制关键点原则——控制工作不可能面面俱到，应根据具体情况选择关键点实行重点控制，以取得事半功倍的效果。

（4）例外原则——还要对超出一般情况的特殊点给予足够的重视。

（5）直接控制原则——就是控制有关管理控制人员和执行人员的素质，通过提高有关人员的工作能力和业务水平以及自觉性等，使出现偏差的概率下降，即使出现偏差也能迅速采取行动。

（6）控制趋势原则——有效的控制系统应有预警功能，能在出现某种趋势的苗头时，迅速采取措施，跟上趋势或将其消灭在萌芽状态。

三、有效控制的要求

有效控制必须具备一定的条件，或必须达到一定的要求：①准确性。②及时性。③灵活性。④通俗性。⑤经济性。⑥战略性（全局和面向未来）。⑦多重标准。⑧采取纠正行动。

Section 3 Types, Principles and Requirements of Control

12.3.1 Types of Control

According to the control point, control can be divided into feed-forward control, concurrent control and feedback control. The relationship between them is shown in Diagram 12 – 2.

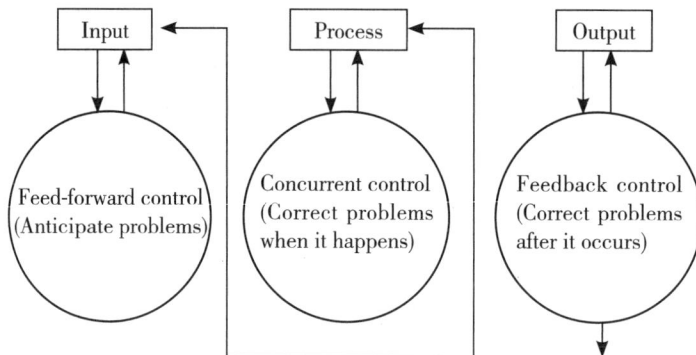

Diagram 12 – 2 Process and Types of Control

1. Feed-forward Control

It is the type of control which prevents problems from taking place before the actual activity. It is also called the control for the future. The key to feed-forward control is establishing a control system that can take managerial action before problems occur instead of remedying when problems happen, which uses input information instead of output information.

2. Concurrent Control

Concurrent control, as its name implies, takes place while an activity is in progress, and is also called on site control. The deviation can be discovered as soon as possible and action can be taken in time in order to minimize the loss. The concurrent control is the most economic and effective method which needs high quality of controller who has to compare, analyze and correct deviation timely. Of course, it needs authorization.

3. Feedback Control

The control takes place after the activity is done, focusing on the result of action so as to provide precaution for the next time. The biggest flaw is hysteresis. It will take a long time to analyze the results, conduct comparative analysis to formulate and implement corrective measures. And the loss has occurred.

In addition, feedback control is through the information feedback and action adjustment to ensure the stability of system. It requires that the speed of feedback must be higher than the speed of the controlled object. Otherwise, the system will generate oscillation, in a state of flux.

Although it has some shortcomings, it is a frequently-used approach of control, because only when many events happen that we can see the results. In addition, things tend to be in cyclic development. Feedback control can provide information and reference for the next work.

12.3.2　Principles of Effective Control

The principles of establishing effective control system：

(1) To reflect the requirement of plan—Control system must match the plan. Control standard, measurement and correction of deviation should be based on the feature of plan.

(2) To suit the organization—Control must suit the characteristic and requirement of organization structure.

(3) To control the key points—Control must base on the specific situation to get double results with half the effort.

(4) Exception—Giving enough attention to special points beyond the general situation.

(5) Direct control—Control the quality of the management and enforcement personnel, by improving the relevant personnel's work ability and professional level and consciousness, etc. to reduce the probability of errors or to take action quickly if deviation appeared.

(6) To control the trend—Control system should have early warning function which can make managers take managerial action immediately when there is a trend of deviation.

12.3.3　Requirements of Control

Effective control must be based on certain conditions, or must meet certain requirements：
①Accuracy. ②Timeliness. ③Flexibility. ④Popularity. ⑤Economy. ⑥Strategy (global and for the future). ⑦Multiple standards. ⑧Taking corrective action.

【小链接】

管理信息系统是一个以人为主导，利用计算机硬件、软件、网络通信设备以及其他办公设备，由管理者计划和设计的，用来进行信息的搜集、传输、加工、存储、更新和维护，以有效地履行管理职能的人机系统。完整的管理信息系统的逻辑结构通常由输入系统、中央处理系统（包括数据库、方法库、模型库）和输出系统三部分组成。管理信息系统是支持管理的工具和技术，又是管理系统的组成部分，该系统的建立过程通常被称为系统开发，系统开发过程包括系统分析、系统设计和系统实施三个主要阶段。

第四节　管理控制的方法

一、预算控制

在管理控制中使用最广泛的控制方法就是预算控制，它清楚地表明计划与控制的关系。预算是计划的数量表现，是组织未来某一个时期具体的、数字化的计划，也就是用财务数字和非财务数字来表明非财务的结果。预算不仅是一种计划，也是一种预测，更是一种重要的控制方法。

1. 预算的种类

（1）收支预算：收入预算，是某一时期有关收益及其来源的预算，如销售收入或其他收入。支出预算是在一定时期内支出的预算，如各种费用。

（2）实物预算：以实物为计量单位的预算，如产量、消耗量等。

（3）投资预算：指用于投资方面的预算，如固定资产的投资等。

（4）现金预算：指一定时期内现金的收支情况。

（5）综合预算：综合考虑各种因素，通过多种预算方法所进行的预算。

2. 预算可能带来的危害

预算使管理控制目标明确，但也会在一定程度上带来危害：如预算目标取代组织目标；预算过于详细，缺乏灵活性，可能会导致心理预期下降。

3. 弹性预算

弹性预算也称可变预算，其基本思想是按固定费用和变动费用分别编制预算，以确保预算的灵活性。在编制弹性预算时，应根据具体情况研究各种费用的变动程度，以确保预算的合理性和准确性，减少预算变动的频度。

4. 零基预算

其基本思想是在编制预算时，必须对每项费用都予以重新核查，要以目前的需求作为核查的基准。要求每个项目的费用要以零为基数，通过仔细分析各项开支的合理性，并在成本效益分析的基础上确定预算。它迫使管理者重新确定费用支出，促使其精打细算，量力而行。但工作量太大，有时费用估计有一定的主观性。

二、非预算控制

除了预算控制以外，管理控制还有其他一些管理控制方法。

1. 视察

这种方法的优点是：①不仅能够掌握第一手资料，还能使管理者不断保持和更新对组织的感觉，感觉到系统是否正常地运转。②可以发现人才，找到解决问题的办法。③有利于创造一种良好的组织气氛。其不足是下级可能误解上级的视察，以为是对自己的不信任或监督。但是视察是成功组织经常采用的方法。

2. 报告

报告是用来向负责实施计划的主管人员全面、系统地报告计划的进展情况，存在的问题及原因，已经采取了哪些措施，收到了什么效果，预计可能出现的问题等情况的一种方式。报告要及时、简明、突出重点。报告可根据需要可分为专项性报告和综合性报告。

3. 比率分析法

（1）财务比率分析。即计算实际的财务比率，并将其与目标值相比较，及时采取措施。

①反映盈利能力的比率：销售利润率＝净利润/销售收入；投资报酬率＝净利润/投资总额。

②反映偿债能力的比率：流动比率＝流动资产/流动负债；速动比率＝速动资产/流动负债。

③反映负债能力的比率：负债比率＝负债总额/资产总额。

④反映资金周转的比率：存货周转率＝销售成本/存货额；资产周转率＝销售收入/资产总额。

（2）经营比率分析。即计算实际的经营比率，并将其与目标值相比较，及时采取措施。

①市场占有率。

②投入产出比。

③盈亏平衡点－固定成本总额/（单位产品价格－单位产品变动成本）。

控制的方法还有许多种，如成本控制、质量控制、作业控制、生产控制、库存控制等。

三、作业控制

作业控制是为了保证各项作业计划的全面完成而进行的一系列管理工作，即衡量作业计划的实际执行情况，将其与控制标准进行比对，发现偏差并分析偏差产生的原因，采取一定的措施纠正偏差以保证作业计划的顺利实施。一般来说，作业控制主要包括成本控制、质量控制、库存控制等。

1. 成本控制

成本控制是在对系统的所有工作做了全面详细分析后，层层分解成本指标，以其作为衡量控制的标准。也就是说，通过监控成本形成的过程来控制成本，从而提高企业的竞争优势，确保组织在预定成本下获得预期目标利润。

2. 质量控制

质量控制是指管理者通过监控质量的全过程，以确保产品质量符合既定的标准。全面质量管理是目前提高质量较流行的方法之一，它是指为保证产品质量符合规定标准和满足用户使用要求，企业需要在产品设计、试制、生产制造直至使用的全过程中，进行全员参与的、事后检验和预先控制相结合的，从产品赖以形成的工作质量到最终产品的质量，控制影响质量的每一个环节，全方位抓好质量管理。全面质量管理突破了事后检验和统计抽样检验的局限性，贯穿于组织的整个作业流程。

3．库存控制

一般来说，库存是指为了满足未来需要而暂时闲置的资源，人、财、物、信息等各方面的资源都有库存问题。企业的生产要正常连续地进行，供应流不能断，需要一定的库存。但库存控制主要解决这些问题：哪些物资要有库存？合理的库存量是多少？隔多长时间检查一次库存量？何时提出补充订货？每次订多少？等等。库存控制的目标不是增加库存，而是在保证一定服务水平的基础上，不断降低库存。

四、审计控制

审计是对反映企业资金运动过程及其结果的会计记录及财务报表进行审核、鉴定，以判断其真实性和可靠性，从而为控制和决策提供依据。审计控制主要分三种类型：外部审计、内部审计和管理审计。

1．外部审计

外部审计是由外部机构（如会计师事务所）选派的审计人员对企业财务报表及其反映的财务状况进行独立的评估。为了检查财务报表及其反映的资产与负债的账面情况与企业真实情况是否相符，外部审计人员需要抽查企业的基本财务记录，验证其真实性和准确性，并分析这些记录是否符合公认的会计准则和记账程序。外部审计的优点是可以保证审计的独立性和公正性。但是，由于外来的审计人员不了解内部的组织结构、生产流程的经营特点，在对具体业务的审计过程中可能遇到困难。

处于战略的考虑，企业也可以利用公开信息对竞争对手或其他公司进行外部审计。这类审计包括：①调查其他公司，寻找并购的可能性。②对主要的供应商的信誉进行评估。③发现竞争对手的长处和短处以保持或加强企业的竞争优势。外部审计常常作为发现和调查借贷欺诈行为的反馈控制手段。

2．内部审计

内部审计是对公司本身的计划、组织、领导和控制过程进行的阶段性评估。它评估的是：公司为自己做了什么？为客户或产品和服务的接受者提供了什么？公司可以对很多因素做出评价：财务的稳定性、生产效率、销售效果、人力资源开发、盈利增长、公共关系、社会责任或其他有关组织效果的指标。审计涉及公司的过去、现在和未来。

内部审计可以由财务部门指定人员作为一项独立任务来完成。在规模较大的组织里，也可以由一个专职的内部审计小组来进行。审计的范围和深度根据公司的规模和政策的不同有所不同。既可以进行相对较窄的调查，也可以除对控制系统进行评价之外，还对公司的政策、程序、权力的使用以及管理方法的整体质量和效果等，进行广泛的、综合的分析。通过对现有的控制系统有效性的检查，内部审计人员可以提供有关改进的建议，以促使公司政策符合实际，工作程序更加合理，作业方法被正确掌握，从而实现组织的自我修正。

3．管理审计

管理审计是一种对企业所有管理工作及其绩效进行全面系统地评价和鉴定的方法。管理审计既可以由内部的有关部门进行，也可以聘请外部的专家来进行。管理审计的方法是利用公开记录的信息，从反映企业管理绩效及其影响因素的若干方面将企业与同行业其他企业或其他行业的著名企业进行比较，以判断企业经营与管理的健康程度。管理审计常常存在一些不良的现象：从事了不必要的工作；重复工作；不良的存货控制；机器设备的不经济的使用；不必要的费用和资源的浪费等。尽管如此，管理审计仍然可以对整个组织的管理绩效进行评价，为指导企业在未来改进管理系统的结构、工作程序和结果提供有用的参考。

Section 4　Methods of Management Control

12. 4. 1　Budget Control

The most popular method used in management control is budget control, which clearly shows the relationship between plan and control. Budget is the qualitative expression of plan. It is a specific, qualitative plan of the organization in future, also a result to demonstrate non-financial items using financial figures and non-financial figures. Budget is not only a project but also a prediction. More importantly, it is a way of control.

1. Types of Budgets

(1) Revenue and expenditure budget: Revenue budget is the budget about relevant revenue and its source in one period, like sales revenue or other kinds of revenue. Expenditure budget is the budget for spending in a given period, including all kinds of costs.

(2) Material budget: It is the budget based on material items, such as volume of output and consumption.

(3) Investment budget: It refers to budget for investment, such as investment for fixed asset.

(4) Cash budget: It refers to the income and expenditure of cash in a given period.

(5) Comprehensive budget: It refers to the budget which uses a lot of methods by overall consideration on all kinds of factors.

2. Possible Damages of Budget

Budget makes the target for management control more clearly, but it may bring damages to some extent. For instance, the budget target may replace the organization's mission. The budget which is too specific and lack of flexibility may also lead to psychological expectation decline.

3. Flexible Budget

It is also called variable budget. Its fundamental principal is to establish budget respectively according to fixed cost and variable cost in order to ensure the flexibility of budget. When establishing budget, we should consider the volatility of all kinds of costs to specific situations so as to ensure rationality and accuracy of budget and reduce frequency of changing the budget.

4. Zero-based Budget

It is a method with the principal that when establishing budget, we should go through every kind of cost once again according to current demand. It is required that we should take zero as the base for the cost of every item and after careful analysis of the rationality of the expense and cost-effectiveness, we make the budget. This kind of method forces the managers to reconsider the expenditure and budget strictly so that we response within our capabilities. But for the heavy workload there is a certain level of subjectivity in estimating the costs.

12.4.2 Non-budget Control

Except budget control, there are other methods for management control.

1. Inspection

The advantages are: ①It can not only help to possess first-hand information, but also assist managers to renew impression on the organization. ②It helps to discover talents and find solutions for problems. ③Last but not least, it is beneficial in creating favorable organizational culture. While its disadvantages lie in that subordinates may misunderstand the inspection from leaders with the supposition that managers distrust his subordinates. Actually, inspection is the method usually used in successful organizations.

2. Report

It is used to introduce the progress comprehensively and systematically to the supervisors who are responsible for carrying out the plans. The content includes existing problems, reasons and measures for those problems, effects we receive and problems that may happen. The report is thought to be timely, clear and focused. Reports can be divided into specific report and comprehensive report according to different requirements.

3. Ratio Analysis

（1）Financial ratio analysis is a method to compare the financial ratio from calculation with target value so as to take some measures based on the results.

①The ratio that reflects profitability: Profit margin of sales = net profit/sales income, return on investment = net profit/total investment.

②The ratio that reflects debt-paying ability: Current ratio = current asset/current debt, quick ratio = quick asset/quick debt.

③The ratio that reflects debt capacity: Ratio of liabilities = total liabilities/total asset.

④The ratio that reflects capital turnover rate: Stock turnover rate = cost of sales/price for stock, capital turnover rate = sales income/total asset.

（2）Operation Ratio Analysis. An action shall be taken when comparing the actual operation ratio with target value.

①Market share.

②Output-input ratio.

③Break-even point = Total fixed costs/(unit product price − unit product variable cost)

There are multiple methods' that can be taken to control, like cost control, quality control, operation control, production control and inventory control, etc.

12. 4. 3　Operation Control

Operation control means to conduct a series of management work in order to ensure the accomplishment of every operation plan. That is, measure the practical implementation of the project, then compare it with the control standard to find deviation and analyzes the reasons for the deviation, finally take certain measures to correct the deviation and ensure the implementation of operation plan. Generally, operation control includes cost control, quality control, inventory control, etc.

1. Cost Control

Cost control is to split the cost index after analyzing all the work in the system specifically and use it as the standard to measure the control. That is to say, by monitoring the process of cost formation to control the cost, so as to improve the competitive edge of enterprises, and ensure that the organization would gain expected profits with scheduled cost.

2. Quality Control

Quality control is the whole process of the managers' monitoring at quality, in order to ensure that the quality of products is in accordance with established standards. Total quality management is one of most popular methods to improve the quality at present. It means that the enterprise needs to control the quality of the product and every step which may influence the quality in the whole production and process. Total quality management breaks through the limitations of back testing and statistical sampling testing, throughout the whole operating process of the organization.

3. Inventory Control

In general, inventory is the resources temporarily idled which is used to meet the future needs. Inventory problems are so common in many aspects, such as personnel, finance, material, information. If the enterprise works continuously and normally, supply flow cannot be broken, it needs a certain number of inventories. But the inventory control mainly solves these problems: What material need to have inventory? What is the reasonable inventory level? How often do we check the inventory? When to put forward the added order? How much to order each time? And so on. The goal of inventory control is not to increase inventory, but decrease inventory on the basis of the guarantee of the service level.

12. 4. 4　Audit Control

Audit is to review, identity the accounting record and financial statements, which reflect the enterprise's capital movement process and results, to determine its authenticity and reliability, so as to provide the basis for the decision-making and control. Audit control could be mainly divided into three types: external audit, internal audit and management audit.

1. External Audit

External audit is an independent assessment of the financial statement and situation of the enterprise judged by auditors appointed by external agencies (e. g. , certified public accountants)

In order to check whether the financial statements and the assets and liabilities of the book conform to the enterprise's actual situation, external auditors need to spot check the basic financial records of the enterprise, to verify its authenticity and accuracy, and analyze whether these records are in accordance with accepted accounting principles and accounting procedures. External audit has the advantage that it can guarantee the independence and impartiality of the audit. However, due to the external auditors do not know the internal organizational structure and the operating characteristics of the production process, they may face some difficulties in the process of auditing.

Thinking about the strategy, the enterprise can also use public information to do external audit on competitors or other companies. This kind of audit includes: ① Investigate other companies, to find the possibility of merger. ②Investigate the main supplier of credit. ③Find the competitor's strengths and weaknesses in order to maintain or enhance the enterprise's competitive advantage. External audit is often seens as feedback control method to discover and investigate loan fraud.

2. Internal Audit

Internal audit is the periodic evaluation of company's own planning, organizing, leading and controlling process. It evaluates: What has a company done for itself? What does it provide for the customer or his receiver? Companies can make evaluation on many factors: Financial stability, production efficiency, sales effect, human resources development, profit growth, public relations, social responsibility, or other index about organizations effect. The audit involves the company's past, present and future.

Internal audit can be an independent task worked by designated personnel from financial department. In the larger organization, it can also be worked by a full-time internal audit team. The scope and depth of the audit is different according to the size and the policy of the company. It can be relatively narrow investigation, and also can be broad, comprehensive analysis. In addition to evaluating the control system, also evaluate the company's policies, procedures and the use of power and the overall quality and effect of management method, etc. Through the check of the effectiveness of the existing control system, internal auditors can provide relevant suggestions for improvement, and to promote company policies in line with the reality, working procedure is more reasonable, operation method is correctly grasped, so as to realize the self-repair.

3. Management Audit

Management audit is a kind of method to comprehensively evaluate all the management and performance of the enterprise. Management audit can be conducted by the internal departments, or outside experts. Management audit is to use the public information, compare the reflection of certain aspects of enterprise management performance and influencing factors of the enterprise and other industry or other industry's well-known enterprises, to judge the health degree of the enterprise operation and management. Management audit often has some bad phenomenon: the unnecessary work, duplication of effort, poor inventory control, not uneconomic usage of the machine, unnecessary cost and waste of resources, etc. Even so, the management audit can evaluate the management performance of the entire organization, and provide a useful reference to guide enterprises to improve the structure of management system, working procedures and the results in the future.

【阅读资料】

管理控制与一般控制的比较

管理学中所讲的控制一般是指管理控制，它与一般意义的控制既有联系又有区别。管理控制是管理工作的一个过程，一般控制是指控制论中所有的控制，它研究的对象是控制体系。两者之间的关系如下：

1. 相同点

（1）都是信息反馈过程。管理控制的实质也是信息反馈，通过信息反馈，发现管理活动中的不足之处，促进系统进行不断的调节和改革，使其逐渐趋于稳定、完善，直至达到优化状态。

（2）管理控制也有两个前提条件，即计划指标在管理控制中转化为控制标准；有相应的监督控制机构和人员，根据内外部环境变化进行调整，保持系统处于稳定状态。

（3）控制也包含三个基本步骤，即拟定标准、衡量成效、纠正偏差。

2. 不同点

（1）一般控制实质上是一个简单的信息反馈，它的纠正措施往往是即刻就可付诸实施的，而且，若在自动控制系统中，一旦给定程序，衡量成效和纠正偏差往往都是自动进行的，而管理控制就要复杂得多。管理者要衡量实际成效，并将之与标准相比较，找出偏差，分析原因，并随之做出必要的纠正。因此，管理者必须为此花费一定的人力、物力和财力，拟订并实施计划，才有可能纠正偏差，达到预期的成效。

（2）一般控制中的反馈信息是简单的信息，包括能量的机械传递、电子脉冲、神经冲动、化学反应、书面或口头的消息，以及能够借以传递消息的任何其他手段。管理控制中的信息是根据管理过程和管理技术组织起来的，在生产经营活动中产生，并且经过了分析整理后的信息流或信息集，它们所包含的信息种类繁多，数量巨大。这种管理信息（包括管理控制中的信息）和管理系统结合在一起，就形成了一个复杂的系统——管理信息系统，成为决策、科学管理和严格执行计划的有力工具。

（3）一般控制的目的是设法使系统运行产生的偏差不超出允许范围，使系统活动维持在某一平衡点上，即维持现状。管理控制的目的不仅是要按照原定计划，维持组织正常活动，实现既定目标，而且还要力求创新，提出和实现新的目标。管理活动的过程通过信息反馈，形成了一个闭合回路系统。管理控制一方面要像一般控制那样，使组织活动维持在一个平衡点上，另一方面还要使组织活动在原有平衡点的基础上有所创新。

【本章提要】

• 控制就是监督组织的各项活动，以保证按计划进行的过程。控制与计划密不可分，控制的内容很多，归纳起来主要是对员工、财务、作业、信息和组织绩效五个方面的控制。

- 完整的控制过程可分为四个步骤，即确定控制标准、衡量实际成效、分析偏差、采取管理行动。
- 根据控制时点的不同，控制可分为前馈控制、同期控制和反馈控制。
- 构建一个有效的控制系统，应遵循一定的原则，符合一定的要求。
- 预算控制是管理控制中一种常用的方法，视察、报告、比率分析法等非预算控制，以及作业控制，审计控制，在实践中也被广泛地采用。

【关键词】

控制（Control）　控制标准（Control Standard）　前馈控制（Feed-forward Control）
同期控制（Concurrent Control）　反馈控制（Feedback Control）
预算控制（Budget Control）　弹性预算（Flexible Budget）
控制关键点（Key Points of Control）　审计控制（Audit Control）

【复习与思考】

1. 什么是控制？计划与控制有何关系？
2. 管理控制的内容有哪些？
3. 管理控制的基本过程是怎样的？
4. 试比较三种控制类型的差异。
5. 有效控制系统的原则、要求有哪些？

【研究与讨论】

1. 有人说"计划是事前的事，控制是事后的事"，这种说法对不对？为什么？
2. 对控制信息的要求，及时与可靠是有矛盾的。在无法兼顾的情况下，应该优先考虑哪一项？
3. 在控制过程中，衡量什么比如何衡量更加关键。这是为什么？
4. 要想使控制工作更加有效，应该怎么做？

【实践演练】

1. 分别举出前馈控制、同期控制和反馈控制的 2 个例子。
2. 运用所学的控制原理，设计一个控制系统，用来衡量和评价你在学习方面的情况。
3. 运用所学知识对一个小组织的控制系统进行分析，提出改进意见。

【管理模拟】

模拟一家超市的管理者，探讨并找出最容易失控的关键点，应采取何种方法加强控制？

【本章案例】

麦当劳公司以经营快餐闻名遐迩。1955年，克罗克在美国创办了第一家麦当劳餐厅，其菜单上的品种不多，但食品质量高，价格低廉，供应迅速，环境优美。连锁店迅速发展到每个州，至1983年，国内分店已超过6 000家。1967年，麦当劳在加拿大办了首家国外分店，以后国外业务发展很快。到1985年，国外销售额约占它的销售总额的1/5。在40多个国家里，每天都有1 800多万人光顾麦当劳。

麦当劳金色的拱门允诺：每个餐厅的菜单基本不同，而且"质量超群，服务优良，清洁卫生，货真价实"。它的产品、加工和烹制程序乃至厨房布置，都是标准化的，严格控制的。它撤销了在法国的第一批特许经营权，因为他们尽管盈利可观，但未能达到快速服务和清洁方面的标准。

麦当劳的各分店都由当地人所有和经营管理。鉴于在快餐饮食业中维持产品质量和服务水平是其经营成功的关键，因此，麦当劳公司在采取特许连锁经营这种战略开辟分店和实现地域扩张的同时，特别注意对各连锁店的管理控制。如果管理控制不当，使顾客吃到不对味的汉堡包或受到不友善的接待，其后果就不仅是这家分店将失去这批顾客及其周遭人光顾的问题，还会影响其他分店的生意，乃至损害整个公司的信誉。为此，麦当劳公司制定了一套全面、周密的控制办法。

麦当劳公司主要是通过授予特许权的方式来可办连锁分店。其考虑之一，就是使购买特许经营权的人在成为分店经理人员的同时也成为该分店的所有者，从而在直接分享利润的激励机制中把分店经营得更出色。特许经营使麦当劳公司在独特激励机制中形成了对其扩展中的业务的强有力控制。麦当劳公司在出售其特许经营权时非常慎重，总是通过各方面调查了解后挑选那些具有卓越经营管理才能的人作为店主，而且事后如发现其不符合要求则撤回这一授权。

麦当劳公司通过详细的程序、规则和条例规定，使分布在世界各地的所有麦当劳分店的经营者和员工们都遵循一种标准化、规范化的作业。麦当劳公司对制作汉堡包、炸土豆条、招待顾客和清理餐桌等工作都事先进行翔实的动作研究，确定各项工作开展的最好方式，然后再编成书面的规定，用以指导各分店管理人员和一般员工的行为。公司在芝加哥开办了专门的培训中心——汉堡包大学，要求所有的特许经营者在开业之前都接受为期一个月的强化培训。回去之后，他们还被要求对所有的工作人员进行培训，确保公司的规章条例得到准确的理解和贯彻执行。

为了确保所有特许经营分店都能按统一的要求开展活动，麦当劳公司总部的管理人员还经常走访、巡视世界各地的经营店，进行直接的监督和控制。例如，有一次巡视中发现某家分店自行主张，在店里摆放电视机和其他物品以吸引顾客，这种做法因与麦当劳的风格不一致，立即得到了纠正。除了直接控制外，麦当劳公司还定期对各分店的经营业绩进行考评。为此，分店要及时提供有关营业额和经营成本、利润等方面的信息，这样总部管理人员就能把握各分店经营的动态和出现的问题，以便商讨和采取改进的对策。

麦当劳公司的另一个控制手段，是在所有经营分店中塑造公司独特的组织文化，这就是大家熟知的"质量超群，服务优良，清洁卫生，货真价实"口号所体现的文化价值观。

麦当劳公司的共享价值观建设，不仅在世界各地的分店，在上上下下的员工中进行，而且将公司的一个主要利益团体——顾客也包括进这支建设队伍中。麦当劳的顾客虽然被要求自我服务，但公司特别重视满足顾客的要求，如为他们的孩子们开设游戏场所、提供快乐餐和组织生日聚会等，以形成家庭式的氛围，这样既吸引了孩子们，也增加了成年人对公司的忠诚度。

思考问题：

1. 麦当劳提出的"质量超群，服务优良，清洁卫生，货真价实"口号是如何反映它的公司文化的？以这种方式来概括一个组织或公司的文化，具有哪些特色或不足？

2. 麦当劳公司所创设的管理控制系统具有哪些基本构成要素？该控制系统是如何促进麦当劳公司全球扩张战略的实现的？

【本章参考文献】

［1］周三多：《管理学》，北京：中国高等教育出版社 2000 年版。

［2］［美］哈罗德·孔茨、海因茨·韦里克著，郝国华等译：《管理学》（第九版），北京：经济科学出版社 1993 年版。

［3］吴照云：《管理学》，北京：中国社会科学出版社 2006 年版。

［4］杨明刚：《现代实用管理学——知识·技能·案例·实训》，上海：华东理工大学出版社 2005 年版。

［5］陈传明、周小虎：《管理学》，北京：清华大学出版社 2003 年版。

第十三章 创 新

Chapter 13　Innovation

创新是一个民族进步的灵魂，是国家兴旺发达的不竭动力。

江泽民

Innovation is the soul of a nation's progress and the inexhaustible force of a country's prosperity.

Jiang Zemin

一个组织缺少创新因素，就会失去活力。

多丽丝·舍佩尔

Lacking innovation, an organization will lose vitality.

Doris Schopper

【本章学习目标】

知识目标：

理解创新的特点和作用。

掌握创新的原则和程序。

熟悉创新的主体与内容。

技能目标：

学会创新的方法。

具备创新的精神。

【Learning Objectives of Chapter 13】

Objectives of Knowledge：

Understand the characteristics and functions of innovation.

Master the principles and procedures of innovation.

Be familiar with the subjects and contents of innovation.

Objectives of Skill：

Master innovative approaches.

Possess the spirit of innovation.

【小故事】

到了月底，建筑公司总经理忽然收到一份购买两只小白鼠的账单，不由地感到奇怪。他仔细一问，原来这两只小白鼠是他的一位主管买的。他把那个主管叫到办公室，问他买两只小白鼠做什么。

那主管解释说："上星期我们公司去修的那所房子，要安装新电线。我们要把电线穿过一根10米长，但直径只有2.5厘米的管道，管道砌在砖石里，并且有4个弯。我们当时谁也想不出怎么让电线穿过去。最后我想了一个主意。我到商店买来两只小白鼠，一公一母。然后我把一根线绑在公鼠身上，并把它放到管子的一端。另一名工作人员则把那只母鼠放到管子的另一端逗它吱吱叫。公鼠听到母鼠的叫声，便沿着管子跑去救它。公鼠沿着管子跑，身后的那根线也被拖着跑。我把电线拴在线上，公鼠就拉着线和电线跑过了整个管道。"

总经理听完以后点点头，很快升了这位主管的职位。

【引例】

迪斯尼：创新管理

如果你要寻找美国企业中的佼佼者，佛罗里达州的迪斯尼世界（也称迪斯尼乐园）无疑是有史以来最出色的。在忙碌的夏季，一天中最少也有10多万人光临迪斯尼世界，乐园每年接待大约2 400万名来自世界各地的旅游者，总收入约7.5亿美金。到底是什么吸引了这么多游客，并达到如此高的收入呢？一句话，就是乐园注册商标"米老鼠"具有不可抗拒的魔力。如何能够维持这一处装扮出来的景色长盛不衰呢？人们见到的是一个巨大的舞台，但是要使这个舞台真正活跃起来却需要表演，迪斯尼公司优于他人之处就是创新文化管理、创新知识管理。

1. 创新文化管理

迪斯尼公司首先为自己的企业价值进行了准确、清晰的定位，即表演公司，为游客观众提供最高满意度的娱乐和消遣。如何实施公司这一定位呢？必须依靠员工。公司最终提供给顾客的产品和服务，必须要由员工实施。所以迪斯尼强调，将企业价值灌输给工作人员。这种灌输从招聘环节就已经开始了，同时也体现在员工的训练中，就连整个游乐园的设计也充分显示了这一管理思想。迪斯尼的目标就是：不惜一切来确保其1.9万名工作人员中的每一个人都明白自己角色的信条和重要性，而这些信条又恰好是企业的价值所在。

迪斯尼公司中没有人事部门，招聘工作由演员中心负责，每位新受雇的人员都必须先在瓦尔特·迪斯尼大学中接受传统方式的培训。迪斯尼公司精心安排训练的每一个细节，目的是要使其工作人员明了，迪斯尼世界首先是一个表演企业。

每天的训练总是以赞扬式的回顾开始，当训练人在班上讲述米老鼠、白雪公主等这些奇妙的形象时，他是在向新来的人敞开瓦尔特·迪斯尼有关这座梦幻王国的想象，训练人营造一种气氛，似乎瓦尔特本人就在房间里，正欢迎新的工作人员来到他的领地，其目的是使这些新的工作人员感到自己是这位乐园奠基人的合作者，和他共同来创造世界上最美妙的地方。一家大公司向其工作人员灌输本身的价值，恐怕再没有比迪斯尼乐园更好的了。

员工们首先需要学习的是，要对游客友好、客气、彬彬有礼、有求必应。要让他们觉得来到迪斯尼世界所花费的美金是值得的，然后才是学习如何生动活泼地表演。培训本身也是一种演出，或者严格一点说是一种彩排，是由训练人员口传身授的。让每一个人明确他在表演中扮演的角色，在传统的培训方式完成之后，新的工作人员进入乐园实习三天。

员工们必须牢记，从来到大街的那一时刻起，就登上了舞台，就得时时面带笑容，要记住自己所扮演的人物要说的话，记住当人们在市政大厅门前时要给他们讲些什么，记住自己要帮他消磨时间，这些都是头等重要的大事。对迪斯尼的人员来说，列队通过大街是最长和最苦的差事，但他们的步伐、姿势整齐一致，对游客来说也是一种款待。乐园强调，不在演员名单上的人，绝不允许偷看一个除掉面具的角色，那种头戴面具的印象必须永远保持，这些演员接到指示在任何情况下都不准破坏角色的形象。

迪斯尼被称为完美画面里的活动，因为它的全部准备工作实际是在舞台之下——地下乐园的隧道网络（乐园之下的地面一层）。设置在这条地下隧道中的是一个控制灯光的计算机中心，一家为工作人员设立的咖啡店和一处藏衣室。每天一早提供给演员的是干干净净的戏服，由于众多的节目和大量的库存，这里是世界上最大的藏衣室。在这谢绝一切游人的地下隧道之中，工作人员可以吸烟、进餐、喝水和化妆，一般地说也可以自如地行动，然而他们一旦被送出隧道，穿过僻静角落中不显眼的门洞进入上面的魔幻王国，他们就来到舞台之上，进行人们预期的表演。

收获是显而易见的，这一魔幻王国很快就成了一个童话世界。时间流逝，但这里仍盛况空前，人们被这里的魔幻气氛所吸引不断涌来，而一旦步入园内就会忘乎所以，仿佛真的回到了童年时代。

迪斯尼体现了这样一种思想，就是企业文化管理的贯彻比企业文化的定位更为重要，也更为复杂。

2. 创新知识管理

迪斯尼不会枯竭的灵感源泉，实质上是让创新形成一种知识固定化的业务模式，别人看来天才造化般的神奇作品，在迪斯尼却成为例行性生产作业流程的结果。迪斯尼，用一个旧的方法——系统化，完成了一个令无数人绞尽脑汁的任务——持续推陈出新。

事实上，在早期推出米老鼠、唐老鸭、古飞狗等家喻户晓的卡通形象后，迪斯尼在连续创造数十年的辉煌战绩之际，如何持续创新便成为制约企业发展的真正瓶颈。但直至今日，我们还会发现，在迪斯尼动画工厂，几乎每天都有新的创意产生，每年都有新的动画大片推出。这些新作品是如此全面地汲取原有作品的优势与人所称道之处，同时融入了创作者天才的创作灵感与智慧。迪斯尼作品，始终能给我们以耳目一新、赏心悦目的感觉。

迪斯尼如何做到了这一点？其原因就在于，迪斯尼公司内部早已创建了一套"创新知识管理流程"，使创新不再简单体现为毫无依据、凭空想象的过程。在整个作品的创作过程中，每一个参与编写剧本、动画设计、采编剪辑、录制合成等工作的人员，都能够在本人负责的环节上借鉴所有整合提炼好的知识资源，并在一定的业务规则指导下，有条不紊地输出智慧。这使得企业的创新动力不再仅仅依赖于个人的魅力与智慧，而是靠组织整体的协同运作。规范化的业务流程与业务规则看似"腐朽"，却成为迪斯尼不断创新的源泉。

（资料来源：杨明刚：《现代实用管理学——知识·技能·案例·实训》，上海：华东理工大学出版社 2005 年版）

思考问题：

1. 迪斯尼主要在哪些方面进行了创新？
2. 这些创新对迪斯尼公司有哪些促进？

第一节　创新概述

一、创新的含义与特征

1. 创新的含义

创新是一种思想及在这种思想指导下的实践，是一种原则及在这种原则指导下的具体活动。美国的经济学家熊彼特在其《经济发展理论》一书中首次提出了创新的概念。他认为，创新是对"生产要素的重新组合"，具体来说，包括以下五个方面：①生产一种新产品，也就是消费者还不熟悉的产品，或是已有产品的一种新用途和新特征。②采用一种新的生产方法，也就是在有关的制造部门中未曾采用的方法。这种方法不一定非要建立在科学新发现的基础上，它可以是以新的商业方式来处理某种产品。③开辟一个新的市场，就是使产品进入以前不曾进入的市场，不管这个市场以前是否存在过。④获得一种原材料或半成品的新的供给来源，不管这种来源是已经存在的还是第一次创造出来的。⑤实现一种新的企业组织形式，如建立一种垄断地位或打破一种垄断地位。

之后，许多研究者也对创新进行了定义。有代表性的定义有以下几种：①创新是一种开发新事物的过程。这一过程从发现潜在的需要开始，经历新事物的技术可行性研究阶段，到新事物的广泛应用为止。创新之所以被描述为一个创新性过程，是因为它产生了某种新的事物。②创新是运用知识或相关信息创造和引进某种有用的新事物的过程。③创新是对一个组织或相关环境的新变化的接受。④创新是指新事物本身，具体说来就是指被相关使用部门认定的任何一种新的思想、新的实践或新的制造物。⑤创新是新思想转化为具体行动的过程。

由此可见，创新概念所包含的范围很广，涉及许多方面。比如，有的东西之所以被称作创新，是因为它提高了工作效率或巩固了企业的竞争地位；有的是因为它改善了人们的生活质量；有的是因为它对经济有根本性的提高。但值得注意的是，创新并不一定是全新的东西，旧的东西以新的形式出现或以新的方式结合也是创新。我们说，创新是生产要素的重新组合，其目的是获取潜在的利润。管理创新是管理者根据内外环境的变化而采用某种新的、更有效的资源整合与协调方式来促进管理系统效率和效益目标实现的过程。

2. 创新的特征

（1）创新的不确定性。

①市场的不确定性。市场的不确定性主要是指不易预测市场未来需求的变化。外界因素如经济环境、消费者的偏好都会对市场产生影响。当出现根本性创新时，市场方向无从确定，也就无法确定需求。市场不确定性的来源，还可能是不知道如何将潜在的需要融入

创新产品中去，以及未来产品如何变化以反映用户的需要。当存在创新竞争时，市场的不确定性还指创新企业能否在市场竞争中战胜对手。

②技术的不确定性。技术的不确定性主要指不确定如何用技术来体现、表达市场中消费者需要的特征；能否设计并制造出可以满足市场需要的产品和工艺。有不少产品构思要么无法制造，要么制造成本太高，因此这种构思和产品都没有什么商业价值。新技术与现有技术系统之间的不一致性也是一个重要的不确定来源。

③战略的不确定性。战略的不确定性主要是针对重大技术创新和重大投资项目而言的。它指一种技术创新的出现使已有投资与技能过时的不确定性，即难以判断它对创新竞争基础和性质的影响程度，以及面临新技术潜在的重大变化时企业如何进行组织适应与投资决策。

（2）创新的保护性与破坏性。

不同创新对企业产生的影响的范围、程度和性质是不同的。两个极端的情况是：保护性的创新和破坏性的创新。保护性的创新，会提高企业现有技术能力的价值和可应用性。破坏性的创新则使企业现有的技能和资产遭到毁坏，新的产品或工艺技术会使企业现有的资源、技能和知识只能勉强满足市场的需要，或者根本无法满足市场要求，从而降低现有能力的价值，在极端情况下，会使现有能力完全过时。

（3）创新的必然性和偶然性。

必然性是由管理的不可复制性产生的。管理的不可复制性客观上要求管理创新，从泰罗制管理到丰田生产方式，再到现代流行的 CIMS、虚拟系统、电子商务、网络营销等，可以说任何一种新的管理模式、方法的产生都和时代发展、科技进步密切相关。在很多情况下，创新是在大量的实验、调研、严谨思考的背景下产生的。然而，另一种创新方式对管理人员来说也是丝毫不能忽视的，那就是偶然性创新。就像牛顿从苹果落地而发现万有引力定律一样，一些偶然的事件也可以引发创新。

（4）创新的被排斥性。

创新活动常常受到来自各方面的排斥、压力和抵制。习惯于原有生活方式和思维方式的人们往往不欢迎任何改动和变革。形象地说，创新恐惧症已成为现代组织——企业、学校、政府的一种通病。因为在原有状况下，没有麻烦，没有威胁，也没有紧迫感，一切都显得平平稳稳。所以一项新产品的创新就其本质而言，是一场推进创新力量和排斥、抵制创新力量之间的激烈斗争，管理者所面临的挑战就是如何在这些力量中间保持平衡。需要注意的是：我们应该对华而不实的或仅仅是象征意义的新产品，以及与新产品战略目标不相一致的新产品持抵制态度，这种抵制不应受到阻挠。

（5）创新的复杂性。

创新过程就像一条链条，只要增加上游的基础研究的投入就可以直接增加下游的新技术、新产品的产出。但在实际经济活动中，创新有许多的起因和知识来源，可以在研究、开发、市场化和扩散等任何阶段发生。创新是诸多因素之间一系列复杂的、相互渗透并且共同作用的结果，创新不是一个独立的事件，而是由许多小事组成的一个螺旋式上升的轨迹，是一个复杂的系统过程。

（6）创新的时效性。

从企业角度来看，创新一般总是从产品创新开始的。一种新的市场需求总是表现为产品需求，因而，在创新初期，企业的创新活动主要是产品创新。一旦新产品被市场接受，企业将把注意力集中在过程创新上，其目的是降低生产成本、改进品质、提高生产效率。当产品创新和过程创新进行到一定程度时，企业的创新注意力又会逐渐转移到市场营销创新上，目的是提高产品的市场占有率。在这些创新的不同时间段，还会伴随着必要的组织创新。当新产品投放市场一定时间后又会被更新的产品所代替，这种替代也使得创新具有时效性。新产品被更新的产品所替代的原因可能有两方面：一是消费者的偏好发生了变化；二是生产技术得到了更新。正是因为创新具有时效性，所以在进行创新决策时，要考虑三个问题：消费者对创新产品需求的持续时间，该产品被其他产品替代的可能性以及创新所处的时期。

（7）创新的动态性。

事物是发展变化的，不仅组织的内外部环境不断发生变化，而且组织的创新能力也要不断积累、不断提高，决定创新能力的创新要素也都要进行动态调整。从企业间的竞争来看，随着企业创新能力的扩散，企业竞争优势将会消失，这就要不断推动新的一轮又一轮的创新，以便不断确立企业的竞争优势。因此，创新绝不是静止的，而是动态的。不同时期组织的创新内容、方式、水平是不同的。从企业发展的总趋势看，前一时期低水平的创新，总是要被后一个时期高水平的创新所替代。创新活动的不断开发和创新水平的不断提高，正是推动企业发展的不竭动力。

二、创新的作用

1. 创新可以提高企业竞争实力

创新可以将企业的竞争劣势转化为竞争优势，将不利因素转化为有利因素。例如，洗衣机的载物洗涤容量一般为5公斤，而且还呈增大趋势。海尔公司凭着灵敏的市场触角，巧妙地在产品的细微之处大胆创新，与消费潮流背道而驰，思维逆转，推出2公斤装的"小小神童"洗衣机。海尔的"只有淡季的思想，没有淡季的产品"的创新理念，使海尔随时保持创新思维，建立了一整套技术创新制度和相应的科研管理模式，最终赢得了市场。

2. 创新为企业的长期持续发展提供动力

企业要想持续发展，必须进行创新，不进行创新，其发展就会缺乏推动力。早在1994年，著名的经济学家克鲁格曼就提出了"虚拟的亚洲经济"的观点。他认为亚洲（除日本外）经济的增长只是依靠资金和劳动力的大量投入，而不是依靠科技进步，因此这一地区的经济高速增长是不可能持续很久的。这一预言不幸被言中。1997年爆发的东南亚金融危机波及整个亚洲，导致这些国家的经济增长放缓，甚至出现负增长。

与此相反，美国自里根时代以来，便重视和强调创新的作用，从而出现了目前自第二次世界大战以来最长时间的持续的经济增长，特别是1997年的亚洲金融危机以及1998年的俄罗斯和拉美的金融风暴，导致了大多数发达与不发达国家经济的倒退，而美国经济却始终稳定有力地增长。这正好说明了光靠资金和劳动力的大量投入来推动经济增长是不可持续的，必须把重点转移到知识创新上来。

3. 自主创新是取得进步的根本

对任何企业而言，创新都是根本。一个企业要取得先进的知识有两个途径：一是引进；二是创新。引进当然不失为一种快捷的方法，这种方法曾经是一些发展中国家和企业实现赶超的根本途径，但事实上，这样永远也无法真正赶超发达国家和先进企业，因为你并未掌握和拥有真正的技术核心。因此，要真正强大起来，必须走自主创新之路，这对于我国尤其重要。

Section 1 Overview of Innovation

13. 1. 1 Meanings and Characteristics of Innovation

1. Meanings of Innovation

Innovation is a kind of ideology and a practice under the guidance of this ideology, and is a kind of principle and a specific activity under the guidance of it. Joseph Alois Schumpeter, an American economist, puts forward the concept of innovation for the first time in his book *The Theory of Economic Development*. In his consideration, innovation is a recombination of production factors, which includes the following five aspects：①Produce a new product, that is, the product that consumers are not familiar with yet or a new use and new feature of the existing products. ②Use a new production method, which is a method that is never used by the department before. The establishment of this method is not necessarily on the basis of scientific discoveries, it can rather be a new way of business to handle some kind of products. ③Exploit a new market, which makes products enter a market never entered before, whether the market exists or not before. ④Gain a new source of supply of raw material or semi-manufactured goods, whether it has already existed or is created for the first time. ⑤Bring about a new form of enterprise organization, like establishing a monopoly or breaking a monopoly.

After that, many researchers also define innovation. There are some typical definitions：①Innovation is a process of the development of new things. This process begins with the discovery of potential needs, through the research of the new things' technical feasibility stage, and ends up with these new things being widely used. Innovation is described as an innovative process because it produce some new things. ②Innovation is the process of using knowledge or information related to create and introduce some new things that are useful. ③Innovation is to accept new changes of an organization or related environment. ④Innovation is new things itself, specifically, it is any kind of new ideas, new practices or new products identified by related user department. ⑤Innovation is the process of new ideas turning into specific actions.

This shows that the range of the concept of innovation is very wide, it involves many aspects. For instance, something is called innovation, because it improves work efficiency or consolidates enterprise's competition position; because it improves people's living quality; because it fundamentally improves the economy. But it is worth noting that innovation is not necessarily something entirely new, something old appears in new forms or combines in new ways can also called innovation. So we say that innovation is a recombination of production factors, the purpose of it is to obtain the potential profit. Management innovation is the process that managers on the basis of changes of internal and external environment, use some new and more efficient resources integration and coordination modes to facilitate the achievement of efficiency of management system and target.

2. Characteristics of Innovation

(1) The uncertainty of innovation.

①The uncertainty of market. The uncertainty of market refers mainly to the difficulty of predicting changes of market's demand in the future. External factors, such as economic environment, preference of consumers will have impact on market changes. When fundamental innovation appears, we cannot determine the market orientation, so demand become indeterminate. The source of market uncertainty also can be the ignorance of how to integrate the potential needs into innovative products, and how to update products to reflect the needs of consumers in the future. When there is innovation competition, the market uncertainty also refers to whether innovative enterprises can beat the marketing competition.

② The uncertainty of technology. The uncertainty of technology mainly refers to the uncertainty of how to use technology to embody and express the characteristics of consumers' need in the market, of whether the design and products can meet the market needs. There are many product speculations, products according to these are either unable to manufactured or may have high costs, hence this kind of speculations and products has no commercial value. The inconsistency between the new technology and the existing technology system is an important source of uncertainty as well.

③The uncertainty of strategy. The uncertainty of strategy mainly refers to major technical innovation and major investment projects. It refers to the uncertainty that the emergence of a technological innovation makes the existing investments and technology out of date, that is, it's hard for people to judge the extent of influence of the basis and nature of innovation, and when face potential significant changes of new technology how enterprises get on organizational adaptation and investment decision.

(2) The protective and destructive of innovation.

Different innovations have influences of different scopes, degrees and nature on the enterprise. Two extreme situations are: protective innovation and disruptive innovation. Protective innovation can improve value and applicability of the existing technical ability of enterprise. Disruptive innovation damages the existing skills and assets of enterprise, a new product or process technology can make the enterprise's existing resources, skills and knowledge hardly meet the needs of the market, or cannot meet the market demand, thereby reducing the value of existing capabilities, in extreme cases, it can make the existing ability completely out of date.

（3）The necessity and contingency of innovation.

Necessity is produced by the unduplicatedness of management. The unduplicatedness of management is necessary for management innovation, from the management of "Taylor theory" to the Toyota production system, and then to the modern popular CIMS, virtual system, e-commerce, Internet marketing, etc. We can say that any kind of new management mode and the produce of new method is closely related to era development and scientific and technological progress. In many cases, innovation is taken place on the background of a large number of experiments, research, and hard thinking. However, another way of innovation that managers cannot be ignored, is accidental innovation. As Newton from apple falling to the ground found the law of universal gravitation, some accidental events can also lead to innovation.

（4）The rejection of innovation.

Innovation often has pressure of rejection from all sides. Accustomed to the original life style and thinking mode, people often do not welcome any change and reform. Figuratively speaking, fear of innovation has become a common fault for a modern organization, enterprises, schools, and government. Because in the original condition, there is no trouble, no threats, no sense of urgency, everything appears balance. Therefore, a new product innovation in terms of its essence is the fierce struggle between innovation strength and resistance force, and the challenge faced by managers is how to keep the balance among these forces. Need to be aware that we should resist new product which is gaudy, or just has symbolic meaning, and which is not consistent with the strategic target. This kind of resistance should not be obstructed.

（5）The complexity of innovation.

Innovation process is like a chain, as long as upstream increase investment in basic research the output of new technologies and new products of downstream will increase. But in actual economic activities, innovation has many causes and knowledge source, it can take place at any stage in the research, development, market, etc. Innovation is the result of joint action of a series of complex, mutual penetrating factors. Innovation is not an isolated event, but is made up of many small spiral paths, is a complex system process.

（6）The timeliness of innovation.

From the perspective of enterprise, innovation always starts from product innovation. A new market demand is always characterized by product demand. Therefore, in the early stage of innovation, enterprises' innovation activities are mainly product innovation. Once the new product is accepted by the market, enterprises will focus on process innovation, its purpose is to reduce production cost, improve quality and production efficiency. When the product innovation and process innovation reach a certain extent, the innovation attention of the enterprise will gradually shift to the marketing innovation, its purpose is to improve the product's market share. In the different period of innovation, there is indispensable organizational innovation as well. When a new product launches in the market after a certain period of time, it will be replaced by newer products, this alternative makes innovation have timeliness. The cause of the new products is replaced by a newer product may have two aspects: one is consumer's preferences have changed, the other is the production technology of products is updated. It is because the innovation has timeliness, when making decisions on innovation we have to consider three questions: the duration of the consumers' demand for innovative products, the possibility that product is replaced by other products and the period that innovation is in.

（7）The dynamic of innovation.

Things is developing and changing, not only the organization's internal and external environment change constantlly, but also the innovation ability of organization which should be accumulated and improved constanty and the innovation elements which decides the innovation capability adjust dynamically. From the perspective of competition between enterprises, with the spread of the enterprises' innovation ability, the enterprises' competitive advantage will disappear, this is about to push new rounds of innovation, in order to establish the competitive advantage of enterprises continuously. Therefore, innovation is not static, but dynamic. Contents and way of organization innovation in different periods are different. Look from the general trend of enterprise development, the low level of innovation is always replaced by a high level of innovation later. The development of innovation and improvement of innovation's level are the driving force to promote the development of enterprises.

13.1.2　Functions of innovation

1. Innovation Improves the Competitiveness of Enterprise

Innovation can help companies transfer competitive disadvantage into competitive advantage, as well as transfer the unfavorable factor into favorable factor. For example, on the general market, washing capacity of the washing machine is generally 5kg with the trend of increasing. However Haier produced its new products against the main trend, realizing its innovation in some unnoticed places, launching new 2kg mini washing machines. With the concept of "no off-season products but thoughts", Haier kept its innovation and wined the market by setting up a whole series of technical innovation system and relative management model.

2. Innovation Provides Enterprise with Sustainable Developing Motivation

Innovation is a must for enterprises who want to keep sustainable development. Without innovation, enterprises lack their inner motivation for development. Early in 1994, famous economist Paul Krugman proposed the view of "virtual Asian economy", holding that the high speed of economic growth of this area which depends much on input of capital and labor instead of technology could not last for long. It turned out to be the Southeast Asian financial crisis happened in 1997, which slowed down the economic growth and worse still, led to negative growth in these countries.

On the contrast, since the Reagan administration, innovation had been laid emphasis on, which led to the longest lasted economic growth of the United States since the World War Ⅱ. The United States kept a steady and powerful growth especially during the period of Asian financial crisis in 1997 and financial turmoil of Russian and Latin American in 1998, while most developed and undeveloped countries went through economic recession. It reflects that economic growth can only be supported by knowledge innovation instead of input of capital and labor.

3. Self-innovation Is Fundamental for Progress

Innovation is of fundamental importance. There are only two accesses for an enterprise to get advanced knowledge: introduction and innovation. Of course introduction is a quick way, which used to be a basic way of development for some developing countries and enterprises. In fact, they can never surpass those developed countries and advanced enterprises only because they have no core techniques. Therefore, independent innovation is a must for our enterprises to really become stronger and more powerful.

第二节 创新过程与主体

一、创新的原则

为了推动创新并保证创新活动的顺利进行，需要正确处理各方面的关系，遵循一定的原则。创新的主要原则有以下几点：

1. 创新与维持相协调的原则

创新活动与维持活动既有区别，又相互联系、相辅相成。维持是创新的基础，创新是维持的发展；维持是为了实现创新的成果，创新则为维持提供了更高的起点；维持使企业保持稳定性，创新使企业具有适应性。维持和创新都是企业生存和发展所不可缺少的。然而创新与维持有时也相互矛盾、相互冲突。正确处理二者的关系，寻求创新和维持的动态平衡和最优组合，是管理者的职责，也是创新应遵循的原则。例如，研究开发新产品，要受原有产品技术水平、人员素质、管理水平以及资金积累的制约；新产品处在研究开发甚至开始生产和投入市场阶段，原有产品的生产也同时进行，这就需要正确处理新产品开发和原有产品生产之间的关系，从而满足创新与维持相协调的原则的要求。在企业中，创新与维持的平衡和组合更复杂，如创新目标、规模、顺序的选择要适当，新技术的引入和改进创新要紧密结合，创新组织与其他组织之间要相互配合等。

2. 开拓与稳健相结合的原则

开拓是创新的本质要求。所谓开拓就是要不断地向新的领域、新的高度进发。没有开拓进取，就没有创新。然而，组织中不思进取、安于现状的现象往往普遍存在，创新活动也经常受到来自各方面甚至是高层管理人员的非议、排斥、压力和抵制，不少人担心创新会付出更大的代价，担心会改变熟悉的工作方式，担心会失去既得的利益等。这些现象成为企业创新的最大障碍。因此，管理者应以极大的热情鼓励、支持和组织创新活动，要创造促进创新的企业氛围，重塑企业文化，激发员工人人奋发向上、开拓进取的精神。

组织创新总是建立在现实的基础之上，任何成功的创新都是科学的，不容半点虚假。开拓精神还必须同求实态度相结合。求实稳健并非安于现状、墨守成规，而是面向社会、面向市场，从实际出发，量力而行，这是创新成功和稳步发展的重要保证。脱离实际的变革，不可避免地会出现盲目性、随意性和反复性。大量事实表明，创新者不是专注于冒险而是专注于机会，通过将感性认识上升为理性认识，在系统分析创新机会来源的基础上，找准机会并加以利用。一旦创新展开，就必须脚踏实地地采取各种措施，经过持续的努力，确保创新的成功。

3. 统一性和灵活性相结合的原则

有组织的创新，必须有统一明确的目标、相互协调的行动、优势集中的兵力。没有统一明确的目标，创新活动将失去方向，形成盲目乱干；没有相互协调的行动，创新人员就不能团结合作，容易各自为政、相互封锁；没有优势兵力的集中，创新力量分散，则不仅会拖延时间，痛失良机，甚至会导致失败。但是，创新本身又具有偶然性或机遇性，并不都在可以预料的计划之内。另外，多数创新者往往是"骑在丰富想象力上获得冒险成功的人"，他们酷爱做自己幻想的事。因此，创新的组织应具有灵活性，要放松对员工的控制，使计划具有弹性。如允许创新者自己确定题目，允许使用部分工作时间去探索新的设想，提供一定的创新尝试所需要的资金、物质条件和试验场所，允许创新者自己选择合作伙伴等，这样既有利于充分调动创新者的积极性，又有利于及时捕获创新机会。

4. 奖励创新、允许失败的原则

创新的创造性、风险性、效益性，决定了组织应对创新者的劳动及其成果进行公正评价和合理奖励。对所有的创新建议，都要实施正向的激励政策，对创新成果确有重大价值并得以采用的，要在物质上给予重奖，在职称、职务上予以破格晋升，使奖励与创新的风险和贡献相一致。同时，创新者的创新动机有一种对个人成就感的追求和自我实现的满足，创新的精神奖励不仅是必要的，甚至是更为重要的。因此，不仅要对创新成果进行精神的、物质的奖励，而且要在创新的全过程中给予创新者更多的理解、尊重和支持，给予创新者放手施展抱负和才能的条件和权利。

创新是不断探索尝试，经常受挫失败，又努力改进提高的过程。在创新过程中，一帆风顺是极为罕见的事情，允许失败则是对创新者积极性、创造性的保护和支持。对于失败，创新者不应悲观失望、半途而废，管理者不应冷眼相看、横加指责。创新的组织管理者对待失败要宽容，要热情主动地帮助创新者总结和吸取教训，鼓励创新者坚持不懈，继续进行大胆探索和试验，直到取得成功。

二、创新的过程

要有效地组织创新工作，就必须研究和揭示新的规律。创新有无规律？对这个问题的答案目前颇有争议。美国是创新活动比较活跃的国家，对创新活动也有比较深的理解，所以 3M 公司的一位常务副总裁在一次演讲中甚至这样开头："大家必须以一个坚定不移的信念作为出发点，这就是：创新是一个杂乱无章的过程。"

应该说，杂乱无章是创新的本质的说法可以为人们所接受。因为创新是对旧事物的否定，是对新事物的探索。对旧事物的否定，必定要突破原先的制度，破坏原先的秩序，必须不遵守原先的章法；对新事物的探索，意味着要在不断的尝试中去寻找新的秩序、新的方法，在取得最终成果之前，要经历无数次的反复、无数次的失败。因此，它看上去必然是杂乱的。但这种杂乱是相对于旧制度、旧秩序而言的，就创新的总体来说，它们必然遵循一定的步骤、程序和规律。

总结众多成功企业的经验，成功的创新要经历：寻找机会—提出构想—迅速行动—坚持不懈这四个阶段。

1. 寻找机会

创新是对原有秩序的破坏。原有秩序之所以要打破，是因为其内部存在着或出现了某种不协调的现象。这些不协调对系统的发展造成了某种不利的影响。创新活动正是从发现和利用旧秩序内部的冲突开始的，可以说冲突为创新提供了契机。

旧秩序中的不协调既存在于企业的内部，又可产生于企业的外部。就外部而言，有可能成为创新契机的变化主要有：

（1）技术的变化。技术变化可能影响相关资源的获取、生产设备及产品的技术水平。

（2）人口的变化。人口的变化可能影响劳动力市场的供给和产品销售市场的需求。

（3）宏观经济环境的变化。迅速增长的经济背景可能给企业带来不断扩大的市场，而整个国民经济的萧条则可能降低企业产品需求者的购买能力。

（4）文化与价值观念的转变。文化与价值观念的转变可能改变消费者的消费偏好或劳动者对工作及报酬的态度。

就内部来说，引发创新的不协调现象主要有：

（1）生产经营中的瓶颈。生产经营中的瓶颈可能影响劳动生产率的提高和劳动积极性的发挥，因而始终困扰着管理人员。这种不协调环节的产生原因，既可能是某种材料的质地不够理想，且始终找不到替代品，也可能是某种工艺加工方法的不完善，或是某种分配政策的不合理。

（2）意外的成功和失败。如派生产品的利润贡献不声不响地、出人意料地超过了主营产品；老产品经过精心整顿、改进后，结构更加合理，性能更加完善，质量更加优异，但并未得到预期数量的订单等。这些出乎意料的成功和失败，往往可以把企业从原先的思维模式中解放出来，从而成为创新的一个重要源泉。

2. 提出构想

敏锐地观察到了不协调的现象以后，还要透过现象研究原因，并据此分析和预测不协调的未来变化趋势，估计它们可能带来的积极或消极的后果，并在此基础上，努力利用各种方法，消除不协调现象，使企业在更高层次上实现平衡的创新构想。

3. 迅速行动

创新成功的秘密主要在于迅速行动。提出的构想可能还不很完善，甚至可能很不完善，但这种并非十全十美的设想必须立即付诸实施才有意义。"没有行动的思想会自生自灭"，这句话对于创新思想的实践尤为重要。一味追求完美，以减少受讥讽、被攻击的机会，就可能坐失良机，把创新的机会白白地送给自己的竞争对手。例如，20世纪70年代，施乐公司为了把产品做得十全十美，在罗彻斯特建造了一座供工商管理硕士（MBA）使用的29层高楼。这些MBA们在大楼里对第一件可能开发的产品设计了拥有数百个变量的模型，编写了一份又一份的市场调查报告。然而，当这些人继续不着边际地分析时，当产品研制工作被搞得越来越复杂时，竞争者已抢走了施乐公司50%以上的市场。所以创新的构想只有在不断的尝试中才能逐渐完善，企业只有迅速地行动才能有效地利用不协调提供的机会。

4．坚持不懈

构想经过尝试才能成熟，而尝试是有风险的，不可能一击即中。创新过程是不断尝试、不断失败、不断提高的过程。因此，创新者在开始行动以后，为取得最终的成功，必须坚定不移地继续下去，决不能半途而废，否则便会前功尽弃。

三、创新的主体

1．全体员工是创新活动的源泉

管理创新活动的源泉在于全体员工的积极性、智慧和创造力的发挥，因此，管理者要创造出鼓励创新的氛围，依靠全体员工开展管理创新活动。这样才能不断涌现新的创意，使管理创新活动的推行更容易得到支持。当然，作为个人的员工很难成为管理创新的主体，因为其操作性质属于操作层，且受到上司多方面的控制，虽有创意也很难在工作中进行实践。但作为群体的员工却往往能成为管理创新的主体，这是因为群体中可以包容大量的创意，当这些创意得到企业家认可并付诸实施时，这些员工们就成了真正的管理创新主体，他们在每天的工作过程中就可以进行亲身实践。比如，日本企业通过成立各种小组，全员性地参与管理创新，如合理化建议制度、零缺点运动、质量管理小组、创造发明委员会等。它创造出的许多广为流传的管理创新成果，像著名的全面质量管理、即时生产体制等，为企业创造了大量的财富。

2．管理者是管理创新的中坚力量

许多管理者是在专业分工的条件下对自己职责范围内的事务、人员、资源进行管理的。这些管理领域如人事、财务、生产、营销等都存在着大量的创新空间，因此，这些管理者如果提出创意并加以有效实施的话，就能成为管理创新的主体。当然，这一阶层的管理者受到上级和自身权限的约束，其创意往往需要得到上级的认可才能转变为创新活动。如果在企业家的鼓励下，一个企业中许多管理人员都在进行管理创新，那么这种企业必定是充满活力的。例如在福特"让工薪阶层都有一部福特车"的创新思维的指导下，生产部门的管理人员会同技术人员经过艰苦努力，不断修改创意，设计实施方案，最后终于推出了"生产流水线"这一生产流程方面的重大创新，极大地扩张了生产规模，降低了产品成本，成为自工业革命以来足以同其他重大科技发明创造相提并论的一项管理创新。

3．管理专家和研究机构是管理创新的辅助力量

在复杂、多变和激烈的竞争环境中求生存，单凭企业家和几个管理人员的知识、智慧、经验是不够的，还需要借助一些专门的管理专家、参谋机构的理论和智慧，依靠他们来分析收集信息，制订创新方案，并帮助企业家付诸实施。这种利用"外脑"的方式对管理创新是非常重要的。据资料表明，国外一些企业的重大创新成果很多是由专家组成的"智囊团"和研究机构做出来的。因此，管理创新也要充分发挥这部分力量的作用。

4．创新型企业家是管理创新的关键

企业家在整个企业发展中拥有特殊地位和管理支配力，他们或亲自提出创意付诸实施，或对管理创新活动产生重大影响。因此企业家是管理创新成败的关键人物。企业要想不断创新，首先必须有锐意进取的创新型企业家。

企业家应始终寻求变化，对变化做出及时反应，并把变化作为创新机会予以利用。企

业家的创新精神要求他们必须具备一定的心智特征和能力结构。

（1）创新型企业家的心智特征。

心智特征是指由过去的经历、素养、价值观等形成的基本固定的思维方式和行为习惯。作为管理创新主体的企业家应具备下面一些心智特征：

①善于学习，具有广博的知识。这是产生对某一问题的超越常人的看法或认识的基础。因为新的知识和信息是对过去知识体系的一种冲击和发展，可以使人们从过去无法解决的问题中得到新的启迪，也是保证管理创新的主体具备较高的思维起点的关键。

②善于思考，具有系统的思维方式。这是一种发散式的思维，同平常人的线性思维方式不同。创新型企业家通常采取一种系统的全方位思维方式，即从具体到综合，从局部到全局，从现象到原因的思考方式，对问题的相关方面都考虑到。许多管理上的创意都是这样产生的。

③勇于进取的价值取向。只有具备强烈的事业心、高度的责任感、永不满足的价值观，他们对创新的追求才能永无止境，不断攀登管理的高峰。

④健全的心理素质。这是确保企业家创新活动成果的重要心理特征。它包括自知与自信、理智的情绪、坚强的意志、雄伟的胆略、宽容的心态、对挫折的忍耐、敢于冒险等多项素质。

⑤优秀的品质。使命感、信赖感、责任感、诚实、公平、勇气、热情等，都是创新型企业家应具备的优良品质。

（2）创新型企业家的能力结构。

作为管理创新主体的企业家必须具备一定的能力才可能完成管理创新的过程。这些能力可分为三个层次：核心能力、必要能力和增效能力。核心能力突出地表现为创新能力；必要能力包括转换和应变能力；增效能力则表现为组织协调能力。

①创新能力。创新能力表现在企业家善于敏锐地观察旧事物的缺陷，准确地捕捉新事物的萌芽，提出大胆新颖的推测和创意，继而进行周密的论证，拿出可行方案并付诸实施。它基于个人的创新意识，是管理创新主体最重要的能力，不具备这种能力管理创新就无从谈起。

②转化能力。转化能力是指管理创新主体将创意转化为可操作的具体方案的能力。转化能力表现为企业家要善于在转化过程中运用综合、移植、改造、重组、创新等技法，来保证好的创意能够转化为可实施的方案。

③应变能力。管理创新本身就是应变的产物，应变是主观思维的一种"快速反应能力"，是创新能力的基础。应变能力表现为能审时度势，能在复杂的变化中辨明方向，产生应对的创意和策略。

④组织协调能力。管理创新需要投入相当多的资源，需要一定的周期，而且可能面临来自各方面的阻力。只有管理创新主体具备较强的组织协调能力，才能够有效地安排所投入的资源，在改变原来的管理模式，推行新的管理程式时，使企业依然有效运转；才能使创新行为得到合作各方的支持，从而提高管理创新成功的可能性。

Section 2   Process and Subjects of Innovation

13. 2. 1   Principles of Innovation

In order to promote innovation and ensure the smooth progress of innovation activities, relationship between various aspects need to be correctly handled, following certain principles. The main principles of innovation are as follow:

1. The Principle of Innovation Coordinates with Maintenance

Innovation and maintenance of activities have both distinctions and interactions. Maintenance is the foundation of innovation. Innovation is the development of maintenance. Maintenance is to realize the innovation achievement. Innovation provides a higher starting point for maintenance. Maintenance keeps enterprises' stability. Innovation makes enterprises possess applicability. Both maintenance and innovation are essential for an enterprise to survive and develop. However, sometimes these two aspects can be conflicted. Handling the relationship between the two aspects correctly and seeking for dynamic equilibrium and optical combination of the two is the responsibility of managers, and is the principle that innovation should follow as well. For example, the study to develop new products is restricted by the original product technology level, personnel quality, management level and the restriction of capital accumulation. When new products are in the phase of research and development or are even started to produce and launched in market, the original production should be produced at the same time, it's need to correctly handle the relationship between the new product development and the production of original product, which satisfies the requirement of innovation and the principle of coordination. In the enterprise, the balance and combination of innovation and maintenance are more complex, such as the choice of innovation goals, scale, the order should be appropriate, the introduction of new technology and the improvement of innovation should closely integrate, innovation organizations and other organizations should cooperate with each other and so on.

2. The Principle of Combining Pioneering and Robustness

Pioneering is the essential requirement of innovation. The so-called pioneering is to move forward to new horizons, new heights. Without marching ahead, there is no innovation. The phenomenon that the organization is satisfied with the status quo exists generally, innovation is also often suffered rejection, pressure and resistance from various aspects, even from top managers, many people worry about innovation will pay a greater price, fear of changing the familiar ways of working, fear of losing vested interests, etc. These phenomena become the biggest obstacle to enterprise innovation. Therefore, managers should encourage, support and organize activities of innovation with great enthusiasm, in order to create an atmosphere of promoting innovation, reshape the corporate culture, motivate employees strive forward and forge ahead.

Organization innovation is always based on the reality. Any successful innovation is scientific. Pioneering spirit also must be combined with the realistic attitude. Being realistic is not being content with the status quo, but market oriented, face to the needs of society, this is the important guarantee of success and steady development of innovation. Divorced from the actual change, there will inevitably be blindness, randomness and repeat. A large number of facts show that innovators focus on opportunities rather than risks, through improving the perceptual knowledge to rational knowledge, on the basis of analyzing the sources of innovation opportunities, get the opportunities and take advantage of them. Once innovation is started, it must be grounded to take various measures, through continuous efforts, to ensure the success of innovation.

3. The Principle of Combining Uniformity and Flexibility

Organization innovation must have a unified and clear objective, coordinated action, and the centralized force. Innovation will lose direction without unified and clear objectives. Without coordinated action, workers cannot unite and cooperate with each other. No centralized force results in waste of time, loss of opportunity, and even failure. However, the innovation itself is unexpectedly incidental or opportunistic. In addition, most of the innovators often take adventures on their way to success based on their rich imagination, who love to do things on their own fantasies. Therefore, innovative organization should have the flexibility to loosen control on staff to make flexible plans. Such as allowing them to determine the topic of innovation, allowing the use of part of the working time to explore new ideas, providing financial, material conditions and laboratory place they need, as well as their preferred innovation partner, which helps to fully mobilize innovators' enthusiasm, also is conducive to the timely capture of opportunities for innovation.

4. The Principle of Rewarding Innovation and Accepting Failure

Creativity, risk and profitability of the innovation decide that organizations should fairly evaluate and reasonably reward the work and results of innovators. All of innovative proposals should be implemented with positive incentives, among which those with great value and can be applied, should be given a big reward and be exceptional promoted on the job title and duties, making contribution of the risks consist with rewards of innovation. Meanwhile, the innovative motivation contains a quest for personal fulfillment and self-realization, which means that the spiritual award is not only necessary, but even more important. Therefore, more understanding, respect and support to the innovators during the whole process of innovation, as well as rights and conditions for them to realize their ambitions and talents, are of more importance.

Innovation is a continuing process of exploration, attempts, failures and improvements. In the innovation process, smooth sailing is extremely rare, during which the tolerance of failures is protection and support of innovators' enthusiasm and creativity. For failure, innovators should not despair, while managers should not be cynical. Innovative organizational managers should be tolerant about failure, being enthusiastically initiative to help innovators summarize the lessons learned, encourage innovators to persevere and continue to boldly explore and experiment until succeed.

13. 2. 2　Process of Innovation

It is a must to make research on new pattern of innovation for effectively organizing new job. It still remains a debate whether innovation has its own pattern. The United States is an active innovation nation, who has a deep understanding of innovation activities. So it is not surprising that one of the vice presidents of 3M Company started his speech with appealing his staff with a fierce thought that innovation is a disorganized process.

This saying can be accepted because innovation is a deny of old things, which break through the original system and order, disobeying the former rules, and exploring new ones, which means trying to look for new order and approach. Before its success, countless reversal and failures cannot be avoided, and this is why innovation is disorganized. However, it is disorganized when compared to old system and order, but follows certain steps, programs and patterns in the whole process of innovation.

From the successful experience, four necessary stages of innovation are: looking for opportunities—proposing idea—quick actions—perseverance.

1. Looking for Opportunities

Innovation is the destruction of the existing order. The reason why the original order needs to be broken is that its existence of the phenomenon that job seekers are uncoordinated, which causes some adverse effects to the development of the system. Innovation begins from discovery and usage of internal conflict of the old order. We can say the conflict provids an opportunity for innovation.

The conflicts of old order exist in the internal enterprise, and also produce in the external business. Externally, changes that are likely to be a major opportunity for innovation include:

(1) Changes in technology. Technological changes may affect access to resources, technical level of production equipment and products.

(2) Changes in the population. Population changes may affect the supply and demand of the labor market and the product selling market.

(3) Changes in the macroeconomic environment. Rapidly growing economic background could expand the enterprise, and the entire national economy depression may reduce the purchasing power of the demanders.

(4) Changes in culture and values. Changes in culture and values may change consumers' preferences or attitudes toward work and workers' compensation.

Internally, phenomenon that triggers innovation disharmony includes:

(1) Dilemma of production and management. Dilemma in the production and management may affect the increase in labor productivity and workers' initiation, which places challenges for managers. The reason for this dilemma of production can be the texture of certain material is less than ideal, with no alternatives, or some imperfect craft processing methods, as well as some kind of irrational allocation policy.

(2) Unexpected success and failure. For example, profit contribution of derived products

unexpectedly exceeds that of main products; with carefully consolidation, products with the improved and more reasonable structure, having more perfect performance and more excellent quality cannot get the expected number of orders, etc. The unexpected success and failure can often liberate the enterprise from the original mode of thinking, thus become an important source of innovation.

2. Proposing Ideas

After keenly observation of the imbalance, we should focus more on the causes behind the phenomenon and analyze and predict future trends of the uncoordinated things, estimating the positive or negative consequences they could bring, and basing on which, use a variety of methods to eliminate the lack of coordination, and enable enterprises to achieve balanced innovative ideas at a higher level.

3. Quick Actions

The secret of success lies in quick action. The idea proposed may not be perfect, or even far from perfect, but it is not a perfect idea being put into practice immediately that makes sense. "Thinking with no action will fend for themselves." This sentence is particularly important for the practice of innovative ideas. Blind pursuit of perfection, to reduce the chance of being attacked, could be a loss of opportunity. For example, in the 1970s, in order to design a perfect product, Xerox built a 29-story building for Masters of Business Administration (MBA) in Rochester. These MBAs in the building may have designed hundreds of variable models, written mountainous report of market survey on their first product. However, white these people continued to analyze irrelevantly, making the product development work more complex, Xerox's competitors have already snatched up more than 50% of the market. So the idea of innovation gradually improves in the constant attempts. Companies that act quickly can effectively seize the opportunity provided by uncoordinated things.

4. Perseverance

Conception become feasible after practice, but it is risky to attempt, impossible to hit in a very much short time. Innovation process is a constant process of attempts, failures, and improvements. Therefore, after taking actions, in order to achieve ultimate success, innovators must firmly persist, not to give up halfway, otherwise it will come to naught.

13. 2. 3　Main Subjects of Innovation

1. Staffs Are the Origins of Innovation

Management innovation origins from the enthusiasm, wisdom and creativity of the staffs. So managers should carry out management innovation activities and create an atmosphere that encourages innovation depending on their staffs, through which it can inspire more new ideas and the innovation can get more support. However, individual is hard to be the subject of innovation due to his operating feature and is controlled by his boss, which narrows his creativity to implement. But groups of staffs can make it since they do have abundant ideas. When one of them is accepted and implemented, they can be the real main body of innovation during their daily work. For instance, Japanese enterprises form different groups, participating in management innovations like rationalization of the proposed system, zero defects movement, quality management team, creating invention commission, which creates a lot of widely spread management innovations like total quality management and instant production system, making a huge profit for enterprises.

2. Managers Are the Backbone of Management Innovation

Many managers manage their affairs, staffs and resources under professional distribution. There is a lot of space for innovation in fields like HR, finance, producing and marketing. Therefore, if new ideas come up in the management system and are effectively implemented, they can be the main body of the innovation. But middle managers are also restricted by their boss and their own authority. Their ideas only turn into innovations with the approval of their boss. An enterprise must be energetic when its managers are making innovation exploration with the encouragement from entrepreneurs. Under the guidance of "making every working class own their Ford", staffs from management and technical department worked hard and continuously improved their ideas, designed and implemented their plan, and finally launched a major innovation of "production line", which greatly expanded the scale of production, reduced product costs and became one of the greatest management innovation since the Industrial Revolution compared with other major scientific and technological inventions.

3. Management Experts and Research Institution Are the Assistant Power of Management Innovation

It is obviously not enough to survive in today's complex, instable and fierce competition only through knowledge, wisdom and experience of several countable entrepreneurs and managers. Some specialized management experts, advisors can also help gathering information and analyze, develop and implement innovative solutions, by which external means make sense to the innovation of an enterprise. It is indicated that some of major innovations of some foreign companies are carried out buy some expertise group and research institution. So it is important to make full use of this part of power when conducting management innovation.

4. Innovative Entrepreneurs Are the Key to Management Innovation

Due to the special position and dominance of the entrepreneurs in the development process of the enterprise, they propose and implement their ideas or make a great impact on innovations. So they are the key to management innovation. Progressive innovative entrepreneurs are must for enterprise innovations.

Entrepreneurs always look for changes, make timely reactions, and regard changes as opportunities. The innovative spirit of entrepreneurs requires them of certain mental characteristics and ability structure.

(1) Mental characteristics of innovative entrepreneurs.

Mental characteristics refer to the basic features of a fixed thinking and behavior through past experiences, qualities and values. Innovative entrepreneurs, as a main body of management innovation, should have mental characteristics as below:

①Good at learning, with extensive knowledge. This is the foundation of perception or understanding beyond the ordinary. Because new knowledge and information is a breakthrough and development of past knowledge systems that can make people get new inspiration from the unsolved problems, which is also the key to ensure the subject of management innovation with a higher starting point.

②Good at thinking, with a systematic way of thinking. This is a divergent thinking, different from the linear thinking of ordinary people. Innovative entrepreneurs usually have to take a systematic comprehensive way of thinking, which is a way of thinking from concrete to comprehensive, from local to global, from phenomenon to reason, with all relevant aspects of the problem taken into account. Many creative management ideas are produced in this way.

③Progressive enterprising values. Only with a strong sense of professionalism, high sense of responsibility, insatiable values, never they end their pursuit of innovation, constantly reaching their management milestones.

④Improved psychological quality. This is an important psychological characteristic to ensure the outcome of entrepreneurial innovation. It includes insight and self-confidence, emotional intellect, strong will, magnificent courage, tolerant attitude, tolerance for frustration, adventurous and many other qualities.

⑤Excellent quality. Sense of mission, sense of trust, responsibility, honesty, fairness, courage, passion, etc., are the qualities innovative entrepreneurs should have.

(2) Ability structure of innovative entrepreneurs.

An entrepreneur must have a certain ability to complete the process of management innovation. These capabilities can be divided into three levels: core competencies, the necessary capabilities and efficiency ability. Core competencies manifest as innovation, the necessary capabilities include conversion capacity and resilience, while efficiency ability reflects on coordinating and organizing skills.

①Innovation. Good performance in the entrepreneurial innovation is reflected on keenly observing defects on matters, accurately capturing the burgeoning new things, speculating and making bold new ideas, and then carrying out and implementing a detailed discussed and feasible proposal. It is based on the individual's sense of innovation, and is the most important ability of management innovation, without which no manage innovation is possible.

②Conversion capacity. Conversion capacity refers to transforming the ideas of management innovation into specific and feasible projects. Conversion capacity requires that entrepreneurs should be adept at integration, migration, transformation, restructuring, innovation and other techniques in the transformation process, to ensure that ideas can be transformed into implementary programs.

③Resilience. Management innovation itself is the product of resilience, which is a rapid reaction capability in subjective thinking and is the basis for innovation ability. One with the ability of resilience can assess the situation and distinguish direction in the complex changes, then generating ideas and strategies.

④Organizing and coordinating skills. Management innovation needs to invest considerable resources, which requires a certain period, and might face resistance from all sides. Only with strong organizing and coordinating skills, can the subjects be able to efficiently schedule the resources invested, ensuring that enterprises remain under effective operation when changing the original management and implement new management programs, making innovative behavior be cooperated and supported by all parties, thereby increasing the likelihood of success of management innovation.

第三节　创新的内容与方法

一、创新的内容

系统在运行中的创新要涉及许多方面。在此，我们主要以社会经济生活中大量存在的企业系统来介绍创新的内容。

1. 观念创新

管理观念又称为管理理念，它是指管理者或管理组织在一定的哲学思想支配下，由现实条件决定的经营管理的感性知识和理性知识构成的综合体。一定的管理观念必定受到一定社会的政治、经济、文化的影响，是企业战略目标的导向、价值原则，同时管理的观念又必定折射在管理的各项活动中。20 世纪 80 年代以来，经济发达国家的优秀企业家提出了许多新的管理观念，如知识增值观念、知识管理观念、全球经济一体化观念、战略管理观念、持续学习观念等。在我国，企业的经营观念存在着经营不明确、理念不当、缺乏时代创新等问题，因此，应该尽快适应现代社会的需要，结合自身条件，构建自己独特的经营管理理念。

2. 目标创新

我们知道，知识经济时代的到来导致了企业经营目标的重新定位。为什么？原因很简单：一是企业管理观念的革命，要求企业经营目标重新定位；二是企业内部结构的变化，促使企业必须重视非股东主体的利益；三是企业与社会的联系日益密切、深入，社会的网络化程度大大提高，企业正是这个网络中重要的连接点。因此，企业经营的社会性越来越突出，从而要求企业高度重视自己的社会责任，全面调整自己的经营目标。众所周知，美国曾经推崇利润最大化，赢利能力曾经是评价美国企业好坏成败的唯一标准，可是就在美国，今天评价企业的标准已经发生了巨大的变化。适应知识经济时代的多元目标相互协调的企业经营目标观念被广为接受。例如，在全世界享有盛誉的美国《财富》杂志最近评选最优秀企业时，采用了创新精神、总体管理质量、财务的合理性程度、巧妙地适应公司财产的效率以及公司做全球业务的效率等多项指标。从这些带有导向性的指标中我们看到，企业对员工、社会和用户的责任等指标在整个指标体系中占了相当分量。所以，在新的经济背景下，我国企业要生存，目标就必须调整为："通过满足社会需要来获得利润。"

3. 技术创新

技术创新是企业创新的主要内容，企业中出现的大量创新活动都是有关技术方面的。技术水平高低是反映企业经营实力的一个重要标志，企业要在激烈的市场竞争中处于主动地位，就必须不断地进行技术创新。由于一定的技术都是通过一定的物质载体和利用这些载体的方法来实现的，因此企业的技术创新主要表现在要素创新、要素组合方法的创新和产品创新三个方面。

一是要素创新。企业的生产过程是一定的劳动者利用一定的劳动手段作用于劳动对象，使之发生物理、化学形式或性质变化的过程。参与这个过程的要素包括材料、设备以及企业员工三类。材料是构成产品的物质基础，材料的费用在产成品中占很大的比重，材料的性能在很大程度上影响产品的质量。设备创新对于减少原材料、能源消耗，对于提高劳动生产率、改善劳动条件、改进产品质量有十分重要的意义。企业的人事创新，既包括根据企业的技术进步的要求，不断地从外部取得合格的新的人力资源，也包括注重企业内部现有人力的继续教育，提高人的素质，以适应技术进步后的生产与管理的要求。

二是要素组合方法的创新。利用一定的方式将不同的生产要素加以组合，这是形成产品的先决条件。要素的组合包括生产工艺和生产过程两个方面。工艺创新既要根据新设备的要求，改变原材料、半成品的加工方法，又要求在不改变现有设备的前提下不断研究和改进操作技术和生产方法，以求实现对现有设备的更充分的利用和对现有材料的更合理的加工。工艺创新与设备创新是相互促进的，设备的更新要求对工艺方法做相应的调整，而工艺方法的不断完善又必然促进设备的改造和更新。企业应不断地研究和采用更合理的空间分布和时间组合方式，协调好人机配合，提高劳动生产率，缩短生产周期，从而在不增加要素投入的情况下，提高要素的利用效率。历史上，福特汽车公司将泰罗的科学管理原理与汽车生产实际相结合而产生的流水线生产方式是一个典型的生产组织创新。

三是产品创新。产品创新包括品种和结构的创新。品种创新要求企业根据市场需要的变化，根据消费者偏好的转移及时地调整企业的生产方向和生产结构，不断开发出用户欢迎的产品；结构创新在于不改变原有品种的基本性能，对现有产品结构进行改进，使其生产成本更低，性能更完善，使用更安全，更具市场竞争力。产品创新是企业技术创新的核心内容。它既受制于技术创新的其他方面，又影响其他技术创新效果的发挥；新的产品和产品的新结构，往往要求企业利用新机器设备和新工艺方法；而新机器设备、新工艺的运用又为产品的创新提供了更优越的物质条件。

4. 制度创新

制度是组织运行方式、管理规范等方面的一系列的原则规定，制度创新从社会经济角度来分析企业系统中各成员间的正式关系的调整和变革。企业具有完善的制度创新机制，能保证技术创新和管理创新的有效进行。如果旧的、落后的企业制度不进行创新，就会成为严重制约企业创新和发展的桎梏。企业制度主要包括产权制度、组织制度和管理制度三个方面的内容。企业制度创新就是通过调整和优化企业所有者、经营者和劳动者三者的关系，使各个方面的权利和利益得到充分的体现；不断调整企业的组织结构和修正、完善企业内部的各项规章制度，使企业内部各种要素合理配置，并发挥最大限度的效能。

5. 结构创新

在工业化社会的时代，市场环境相对稳定，企业为了实现规模经济效益，降低成本，纷纷以正规化、集权化为目标。但随着企业规模的不断发展，组织复杂化程度越来越高，信息社会的到来，使环境不稳定因素越来越多，竞争越来越激烈。当管理者意识到传统的组织结构不适应现代环境的多变性时便会实施创新。一个有效的企业应当是能随着环境的变化而不断调整自己的结构，使之适应新的环境的企业。根据已有的认识，现代企业组织正不断朝着灵活性、有机性方向发展。

6. 环境创新

环境是企业经营的土壤，同时也制约着企业的经营。环境创新不是指企业为适应外界变化而调整内部结构或活动，而是指通过企业积极的创新活动去改造环境，去引导环境朝着有利于企业经营的方向变化。例如，通过企业的公关活动，影响社区政府政策的制定；通过企业的技术创新，影响社会技术进步的方向。就企业而言，市场创新是环境创新的主要内容。市场创新是指通过企业的活动去引导消费，创造需求。人们一般认为新产品的开发是企业创造市场需求的主要途径。其实，市场创新的更多内容是通过企业的营销活动来进行的，即在产品的材料、结构、性能不变的前提下，或通过市场的地理转移，或通过揭示产品的物理使用价值，来寻找新用户，通过广告宣传等促销工作，来赋予产品一定的心理使用价值，影响人们的某种消费行为，诱导、强化消费者的购买动机，增加产品的销售量。

7. 文化创新

现代管理发展到文化管理阶段，可以说已达到顶峰。企业文化通过员工价值观与企业间直观的高度统一，通过企业独特的管理制度体系和行为规范的建立，使得管理效率有了较大提高。创新不仅是现代企业文化的一个重要支柱，而且还是社会文化中的一个重要部分。如果文化创新已成为企业文化的根本特征，那么，创新价值观就能得到企业全体员工的认同，行为规范就会得以建立和完善，企业创新动力机制就会高效运转。

【小链接】

3M 公司的创新文化规则

● 设置创新目标：根据公司规定，年销售的 25%～30% 必须来自五年或五年以内的新产品。

● 投入研发：3M 公司用于研发的费用几乎是美国公司平均数的两倍，研发的目的是将引入新产品的时间缩短一半。

● 鼓励内企业家精神：鼓励倡导者试验新想法，他们有机会去管理他们的产品，就如同运作自己的公司一样。3M 公司允许他们用 15% 的时间去从事与公司当前项目无关但个人感兴趣的研究。

● 支持，不要阻碍：事业部保持较小的规模并允许在很大程度上独立运作，他们具有固定的途径去获取信息和技术资源。有好创意的研究人员被给予 5 万美元的奖励，用以将他们的灵感开发成新产品。

● 关注消费者：3M 对质量的定义是去证明产品是按客户的需求而不是某些专断的标准生产的。

● 允许失败：3M 人知道如果他们的想法失败了，他们仍然会被鼓励去从事其他的创新。管理层知道员工会犯错误，也知道有害的批评会扼杀创造性。

(资料来源；贝特曼等著，王雪莉译：《管理学：新竞争格局》（第六版），北京：北京大学出版社 2007 年版，第 579 页)

二、创新的策略

1. 首创型创新策略

首创型创新，是创新度最高的一种创新活动。其基本特征在于首创。例如，率先推出全新的产品，率先开辟新的市场销售渠道，率先采用新的广告媒介，率先改变销售价格等，所有这些行为都可称为首创型创新。首创型创新具有十分重要的意义，因为没有首创，就不会有改创型创新或仿创型创新。每一项重大的首创型创新，都会先后在不同的地区引起一系列相应的改创型创新和仿创型创新活动，从而具有广泛而深远的创新效应。对于一般企业来说，进行首创型创新，可以开辟新的市场领域，提高企业的市场竞争力，获得高额利润。对于处于市场领先地位的企业来说，要想保持自己的市场领先地位，也必须不断地进行首创型创新。

一般来说，首创型创新活动风险较大，成本较高，相应的利润也较高。市场需求的复杂性和市场环境的多变性以及生产、技术、市场等方面的不确定性，给首创型创新活动带来较大的不确定性和风险。

2. 改创型创新策略

改创型创新的目标是对已有的首创进行改造和再创造，在现有首创的基础上，充分利用自己的实力和创新调价，对他人首创进行再创新，从而提高首创的市场适应性，推动新市场的不断发展。这是一种具有中等创新度的创新活动。改创型创新战略，是介于首创战略与仿创战略之间的一种创新战略。改创者不必率先创新，而只需对首创者所创造的物品进行改良或改造，因此，改创者所承担的创新成本和风险比较小，而所获的创新收益却不一定比首创者少。当然，改造也是一种创造，也具有一定的风险。首创是重要的，改创也是重要的。如果没有首创，便没有改创的前提和基础；然而，如果没有改创，许多首创便没有市场发展前景。例如，飞机、汽车、计算机等首创产品，如果没有后来的不断改进和再创新，也就不会有今天这样的市场大发展。

3. 仿创型创新策略

仿创型创新是创新度最低的一种创新活动，其基本特征在于模仿性。模仿者既不必率先创造全新的新市场，甚至也不必对首创进行改造。仿创者既可模仿首创者，又可以模仿改创者，其创新之处表现为自己原有市场的变化和发展。一些缺乏首创能力和改创能力的中小企业，往往采用模仿战略进行仿创型创新。

一般来说，仿创者所承担的市场风险和市场开发成本都比较小。虽然仿创者不能取得市场领先地位，却可以通过自己某些独占的市场发展条件来获得较大的收益和优势。例如，仿创者可以采取率先紧跟首创者的策略，从而取得时间优势；或者采用市场割据策略、低成本策略，从而获得价格优势。仿创有利于推动创新的扩散，因而也具有十分重要的意义。任何一个首创或改创企业，无论它拥有多大的实力，也无法在一个比较短的时间内占领所有的市场。因此，一旦首创或改创获得成功，一大批仿创者出现就成为必然。

总之，在制定创新战略时，不同的企业应该选择一个适当的创新度，进行适度创新。所谓适度创新，就是既要适应市场需求的发展状况，又要适应本企业的创新条件。只有这样，创新者才能充分利用和发挥本企业的创新优势，尽量减少或避免创新的风险，提高创新的效果，促进企业的发展。

三、创新的方法

1. 头脑风暴法

它是美国创造工程学家 A. F. 奥斯本在 1939 年发明的一种创新方法。这种方法是通过一种别开生面的小组畅谈会，在较短的时间内充分发挥群体的创造力，从而获得较多的创新设想。当一个与会者提出一个新的设想时，这种设想就会激发小组内其他成员的联想。当人们卷入"头脑风暴"之后，各种各样的构想就像燃放鞭炮一样，点燃一个，引爆一串。这种方法的规则有：

（1）不允许对别人的意见进行批评或反驳，任何人不做判断性结论。

（2）鼓励每个人独立思考，广开思路，提出的改进设想越多越好，越新越好。允许相互之间的矛盾。

（3）集中注意力，针对目标，不私下交谈，不干扰别人的思维活动。

（4）可以补充和发表相同的意见，使某种意见更具说服力。

（5）参加会议的人员不分上下级，平等相待。

（6）不允许以集体意见来阻碍个人的创造性设想。

（7）参加会议的人数不超过 10 人，时间限制在 20 分钟到 1 小时。

这种方法的目的在于创造一种自由开放的思考环境，诱发创造性思维的共振和连锁反应，以产生更多的创造性思维。讨论 1 小时能产生数十个乃至几百个创造性设想，适用于问题较单纯、目标较明确的决策。

这种方法在运用中又发展出"反头脑风暴法"，做法与头脑风暴法相反，对一种方案不提肯定意见，而是专门挑毛病、找矛盾。它与头脑风暴法一反一正，可以互相补充。

2. 综摄法

这种方法是美国人哥顿在 1952 年发明的一种开发潜在创造力的方法。他是以一致的东西为媒介，把毫不关联、互不相同的知识要素结合起来创造出新的设想，也就是吸取各种产品和知识精髓，综合在一起创造出新的产品或知识，故名综摄法。这样可以帮助人们发挥潜在创造力，打开未知世界的窗口。

综摄法有两个基本原则：

（1）异质同化，即"变陌生为熟悉"。这实际上是综摄法的准备阶段。是指对待不熟悉的事物要用熟悉的事物、方法、原理和已有的知识去分析对待它，从而提出新设想。

（2）同质异化，即"变熟悉为陌生"。这是综摄法的核心。是指对熟悉的事物、方法、原理和知识，用不熟悉的态度去观察分析，从而启发出新的创造性设想。

3. 逆向思考法

这种方法是顺向思考的对立面。逆向思维是一种反常规、反传统的思维。顺向思维的常规型、传统型，往往导致人们形成思维定式，是一种从众心理的反映，因而往往使人们形成一种思维"框框"，阻碍着人们创造力的发挥。这时如果转换一下思路，用逆向法来考虑，就可能突破这些"框框"，取得出乎意料的成功。

逆向思考法由于是反常规、反传统的，因而它具有与一般思考不同的特点：

（1）突破性。这种方法的成果往往冲破传统观念和常规，常带有质变或部分质变的性质，因而往往能取得突破性的成就。

（2）新奇性。由于思维的逆向性，改革的幅度较大，因而必然是新奇、新颖的。

（3）普遍性。逆向思考法适用范围很广，几乎适用于一切领域。

（4）实效性。

【新视角】

创新思维的特征

创新思维与程序性的一般逻辑思维不同，它的主要特征是创新思维在思路的选择上，在思考的技巧上，在思维的结论上，都具有独到之处。在前人和现有的思想基础之上有新的发现、新的突破，从而具有一定范围内的首创性和开拓性。创新思维并不十分看重别人的经验和方法，不完全遵循现有的程序，它在方式、方法、程序、途径等各方面都是没有限制的，因而可以自由想象，可以多方位地试探解决问题的方法。它与任何固守某一思路并陷入僵化的思维完全不同。创新思维作为一种开创性的、灵活多样的思维活动，就像审美判断和艺术创造一样，往往因人而异、因时而异、因问题和对象而异，不存在普遍适用规范化的方法和程序，因而也是不可效仿和模拟的。新思维所要解决的是管理中出现的史无前例的问题，认识的是内外环境中的全新的变化情况，所以是一种探索。

4. 检核表法

这种方法几乎适用于任何类型与场合的创造活动，因此又被称为"创造方法之母"。它用一张一览表对需要解决的问题逐项进行核对，从各个角度诱发多种创造性设想，以促进创造发明、革新或解决工作中的问题。实践证明，这是一种能够大量开发创造性设想的方法。

检核表法是一种多渠道的思考方法，包括以下一些创造技法：迁移法、引入法、改变法、添加法、替代法、缩减法、扩大法、组合法和颠倒法。它启发人们缜密地、多渠道地思考问题和解决问题，并广泛运用于创造、发明、革新和企业管理上。它的关键是一个"变"字，而不把视线凝固在某一点或某一方向上。

5. 类比创新法

类比就是在两个事物之间进行比较，这两个事物可以是同类的，也可以是不同类的，甚至差别很大。通过比较，找出两个事物的类似之处，然后再据此推出它们在其他方面的类似之处，因此，类比创新法是一种富有创造性的发明方法，它有利于发挥人的想象力，从异中求同，从同中求异，产生新的知识，得到创新性成果。类比方法很多，有拟人类比法、直接类比法、象征类比法、因果类比法、对称类比法、综合类比法等。

6. 信息交合法

它通过若干类信息在一定方向上的扩展与交合，来激发创造性思维，提出创新性设想。信息是思维的原材料，大脑是信息的加工厂。通过不同信息的撞击、重组、叠加、综合、扩散、转换，可以诱发创新性设想。要正确运用信息交合法，必须注意抓好以下三个环节：

（1）搜集信息。不少企业已设立专门机构来搜集信息。网络化已成为当今企业搜集信息的发展趋势。如日本三菱公司，在全世界设置了115个海外办事处，约900名日本人和2 000多名当地职员从事信息搜集工作。搜集信息的重点放在新的信息上，只有新的信息才能反映科技、经济活动中的最新动态、最新成果，这些往往对企业有着直接的利害关系。

（2）拣选信息。包含核对信息、整理信息、积累信息等内容。

（3）运用信息。搜集、拣选信息的目的都是为了运用信息。运用信息，一要快，快才能抓住时机；二要交合，即这个信息与那个信息进行交合，这个领域的信息与那个领域的信息进行交合，把信息和所要实现的目标联系起来思考，以创造性地实现目标。信息交合可通过本体交合、功能拓展、杂交、立体动态四个方式进行交合。

总之，信息交合法就像一个魔方，通过各种信息的引入和各个层次的交换会引出许多系列的信息组合，为创新对象提供了千万种可能性。

7. 模仿创新法

人类的创造发明大多是由模仿开始的，然后再进入独创。勤于思考就能通过模仿做出创造发明，当今有许多物品模仿了生物的一些特征，形成了仿生学。模仿不仅被用于工程技术、艺术，而且也被用于管理方面。

Section 3　Contents and Methods of Innovation

13. 3. 1　Contents of Innovation

System innovation involves many aspects in the operating process. Here, we introduce innovative contents mainly through the cases of enterprise systems existing in social and economic life.

1. Concept Innovation

Management concept refers to the complex consisting of managerial perceptional and rational knowledge determined by realistic conditions, which is established by managers or management organizations under the guidance of a certain philosophy. Certain management concept is affected by social politics, economics and cultures, and is the guidance and value principle of the strategy targets of an enterprise, which is also reflected in different management activities. Since the 1980s, outstanding entrepreneurs from developed countries raised many new management concepts, such as knowledge of value-added ideas, knowledge management concepts, the concept of global economic integration, strategic management concepts, the concept of continuous learning, etc. In China, problems in business concept include unclear corporate business, improper ideas, lack of innovation and other issues. Therefore, enterprises should form their own business concept with their different conditions to meet the demand of modern society.

2. Target Innovation

As we all know, the arrival of knowledge economic era forces enterprises to relocation. The reasons are obvious. The first is the revolution of management concept requires the enterprise to relocation. The second is the changes of internal structure make the enterprises lay more emphasis on the benefits of non-shareholders. The third one comes from the closer relations between the enterprise and the society. As social networking is more and more popularized, enterprise is becoming more and more important connecting spot of this networking. Thus the sociability of enterprises is much clearer, which requires enterprises to focus more on their social responsibility and adjust their management target. The United States has most emphasis maximizing profits, profitability once became the only evaluation of the quality of the success of the American enterprise. But nowadays things have changed a lot. Concept of coordination among multiple targets which suits knowledge economic era is now widely accepted. When the famous *Fortune* Magazine named the world's most prestigious outstanding enterprises, it uses a number of global business indexes including innovative spirit, the overall quality of management, financial rationality extent, cleverly adapted to the efficiency of the company's property as well as the efficiency of the company. From these indicators with specific orientation, we see index involving corporate employees, the community, the responsibility of the user account for a considerable amount in the whole index system. So under the new economic context, the target of our enterprises need to be adjusted to "earn profit from meeting the needs of our society", in order to manage to survive.

3. Technology Innovation

Technology innovation is the major content of an enterprise, a lot of which is about technology. The level of technology is an important symbol of the power of an enterprise. One has to continue its technology innovation to keep a subjective position in the market competition. Certain technology is performed through some materials and methods of using these materials, therefore, technical innovation is mainly about 3 aspects: element innovation, element combination innovation and product innovation.

Element innovation: The production process is about certain workers acting on certain labor object through some means of labor, causing physical and chemical changes. The elements of this process include material, facilities and staffs. Material is the basis of a product, the fees of which cover a main part of the total expanse, and the performance of which affects the quality of the products to some extent. While facilities innovation is of significance to reduce the consumption of material and energy, as well as improve the productivity, labor condition and quality. Human resource innovation requires not only the improvement of techniques and sustainable access to new qualified staff, but also the education of internal human resources to meet the demands of producing and management after technology upgrade.

Element combination innovation：Making a combination of different elements is the premise of producing a product, which includes producing crafts and producing process. The crafts innovation changes the machining of raw material and semi-finished products. It also requires to research and improve manufacturing techniques and methods to make a more reasonable and efficient process under the circumstance of maintaining the existing facilities. The two kinds of innovation are improved by each other. The upgrade of facilities requires adjustment of crafts, while the improvement of which then leads to another innovation of the facilities. So, an enterprise should do research and adopt a more rational distribution of space and time combination, machine with good coordination, improve labor productivity, to shorten the production cycle and raise the efficiency, without input of elements added. In history, that Ford Motor Company combined Taylor's scientific management principles with the reality of automobile production which results assembly line of production mode is a typical production organizational innovation.

Product innovation：It includes innovation of variety and structure. According to changes in market demand and the shift in consumer's preferences, variety innovation requires enterprise to adjust the direction and production structure of enterprises to continuously develop products according to the shift of user's preference. Structure innovation does not change the basic properties of the original species, but improve the structure of existing products to lower production costs, better performance, making it safer and more competitive. Product innovation is the core of technology innovation, which is affected by other aspects but at the same time affects the other innovative consequence. New products and new product structure, often requires companies to take advantage of new equipment and new technology methods, and the use of new equipment, new technology, then offer innovative products superior material conditions.

4. System Innovation

System is a series of principles including organizations operating mode, management practices and other aspects. System innovation analyzes adjustments and revolutions of official relations among members of enterprise system from the angle of social economics. Completed system innovative mechanism ensures technology and management innovation. On the other hand, old-fashioned system without creation will hinder enterprise from innovation and development. Enterprise system includes property rights system, organization and management systems. System innovation is actually a revolution. By adjusting and optimizing the relationship between business owners, managers and workers, make the rights and interests of the various aspects to be fully reflected. Constantly adjust and revise the organizational structure of enterprises, improve their internal rules and regulations, so that enterprises can rationally allocate various elements inside and maximize its performance.

5. Structure Innovation

In the time of industrialized society, the market environment is relatively stable. In order to realize the economy efficiency of scale and lower the costs, enterprises add standardization and centralization into goals. With the continuous development of enterprise scale, increasingly high degree of organization complexity, the arrival of the information society makes the environment more and more instable and competitive. Managers who have realized that traditional organizational structure no longer suited to modern environmental variability will implement innovation. An effective enterprise should be able to change with the environment and constantly adjust their structure to adapt to the new environment of the enterprise. According to the understanding of modern business, organizations are constantly developing in a flexible and organic direction.

6. Environment Innovation

Environment is the basis of enterprise business, which also affects enterprise business a lot. Instead of an internal structural adjustment or activities, environmental innovation refers to innovative activities by enterprises actively transform the environment to boost environment in favor of business. For example, corporate public relations activities affect government policy of the community, or technology innovation of enterprises affects the direction of social and technological progress. As for the enterprises, marketing innovation comes from the first when talking to the environment innovation. Marketing innovation refers to the function of guiding consumption and creating demands. It is generally thought that the development of new product is a major passage to create demands. But actually, more marketing innovation is performed by marketing activities, which means by geographic market shift, or by revealing the physical use value of products, to find new users, through advertising and other promotional work, to give the product a certain psychological use value to make an impact on consumption behavior, to induce and strengthen consumers' purchase motivation as well as increase sales of the product.

7. Culture Innovation

Modern management can be regarded to be at its peak when it develops to the stage of cultural management. The culture of an enterprise integrates the value of staffs and the firm, which is established by unique management system and behavior rule of an enterprise, resulting in a great improvement of management efficiency. Innovation is not only an important part of modern culture, but also has its position in broader social cultural fields. If cultural innovation becomes the basic feature of an enterprise culture, then the innovative value can soon be agreed and accepted by most of the staffs, so that the behavior standard can be established and improved, and the innovative mechanism can work more efficiently.

13.3.2 Strategies of Innovation

1. Original Innovation

Original innovation is the most innovative creation, the basic characteristic of which is its originality, such as promoting a new product, expanding new marketing channel, using new advertisement media, firstly changing the selling price. Original innovation is of significance because it is the root of reformed and imitated innovation. Every great original innovation has its wide and deep effectiveness causing the occurrence of a series of reformed and imitated innovation in different areas sooner or later. For an enterprise, original innovation means to open a new market area, to strengthen its competitive edge and earn high profits. It also suits to those marketing leaders as they have to conduct original innovation to keep their leading position.

Generally speaking, original innovation is faced with high risks and costs, but also high profits. It is also uncertain and risky due to complexity and instability of market environment and uncertainty of producing, technology and market.

2. Reformed Innovation

Reformed innovation is to construct and reconstruct the existing innovations. Enterprises make full use of its capability and adjustment to conduct and recreate original innovations from others to improve the adaptability of the products and thus push the new market further develops. It is a moderate innovation between original innovation and imitated innovation. Innovator does not need to make original innovation, only need to reform the original innovative products. So the reformer takes a smaller risk and a lower cost, but gets profit no less than original innovation. Both original and reformed innovation makes sense as the original innovation is the premise and the basis while the reformed innovation develops the potential of the market. Original innovations like planes, autos, personal computers won't have today's booming without continuous reform and recreation.

3. Imitated Innovation

Imitated innovation is the least innovative creation, the basic characteristic of which is its imitation. Imitators don't create new market nor reform the original innovations. They can imitate both the original and reformed innovators, but whose innovation is shown in the changes and development of the original market. For middle or small enterprises that lack originality or reform ability, imitated strategy is frequently used.

Generally, imitators take least risks and costs. Though they have no chance to come to the leading position of the market, but they can get huge profits and generate advantages through occupying certain developing conditions alone. Like following strategy—to seize the advantage of timing, or incised marketing, low cost strategy to have the price benefit. Imitated innovation does contribute to the expansion of innovation. No original or reformed innovative enterprises can conquer every specific market in a short time. Therefore, the appearance of imitator is a natural trend after the success of an original or reformed innovation.

To sum up, different enterprises should have their appropriate innovation according to their degree of innovation when making their strategies, adapting to the developing condition of the market, as well as the innovative condition of the enterprise. Only in this way can the innovators make full use of the advantage of innovation, lower or avoid the risk of innovation, improve the effectiveness and promote the development of the enterprise.

13. 3. 3　Methods of Innovation

1. Brainstorming

It is an innovative approach invented by the United States project scientist A. F. Osborne in

1939. This approach is to fully develop a creative community to obtain more innovative ideas in a short period of time through a special conference. When a participant proposes a new idea, this idea will inspire other members' more relative ideas. So when a group of members begin brainstorming, many ideas come out continuously, just like firecrackers, one burned, all cracked! The rules of brainstorming include:

(1) Criticizing or refuting to opinions of others are not allowed, do not make any judgmental conclusions.

(2) Encouraging everyone to think independently, open his mind and broaden his vision. The more, the newer, and the better. Contradiction between them is allowed.

(3) Focus on, aiming at target, no personal conversation, do not interfere with other people's thinking activity.

(4) Complementing and expressing the same views are allowed, which makes an opinion more convincing.

(5) Participants in the meeting are regarded equally.

(6) Collective views to hinder individual creative ideas is not allowed.

(7) The number of people attending the meeting is no more than 10 people, the time is limited between 20 minutes to 1 hour.

The purpose of this approach is to create an environment of free thinking, inducing creative thinking resonance and chain reaction, to produce more creative thinking. Discussion in one hour can produce dozens or even hundreds of creative visualization, which apply in the relatively simple, clearly objective decisions.

This approach also develops another anti-brainstorming in its application, in which people do not mention a positive opinion, but specifically look for flaws and contradictions in a specific proposal, which complement with each other with the former brainstorming approach.

2. Synectics

This method is the way to develop the potential innovation when American Gordon invented it in 1952. He combined different knowledge elements without associations, using integrated things as media, to create a new vision, which is the essence of products and knowledge combined together to create new products or knowledge, and also where the name synectics comes from. This approach can help people play the potential of creativity, open the window of the unknown world.

Synectics has two basic principles:

(1) Heterogeneous assimilation, which means to make the strange familiar. This is actually the preparation stage of synectics, which refers to use familiar things, methods, principles and existing knowledge to analyze the unfamiliar things, so as to come up with new ideas.

(2) Homogeneity of alienation, which means to change the familiar unfamiliar. This is the core of synectics, which refers to perceive and analyze the familiar things, methods, principles and knowledge with unfamiliar attitude, thereby inspire new creative ideas.

3. Reverse Thinking

This approach is the opposite of forward thinking, which is actually an anti-conventional thinking. The conventional and traditional way of forward thinking, often leads people to form mind set, reflected a conformity, and therefore tend to trap people in a thinking "frame", hindering people's creative thoughts. Then if one tries to convert his idea, considering an inverse method, it is possible to break these "boxes" to obtain unexpected success.

Because it is anti-conventional, anti-traditional, reverse thinking method, has different characteristics compared with general thinking:

(1) Breakthrough. The outcome of this approach is often to break through the traditional concepts and practices, with a nature of qualitative change or part of qualitative change, which can often achieve a breakthrough.

(2) Novelty. Because of the reverse of magnitude, reform thinking must be novel and original.

(3) Universality. Reverse thinking can be applied broadly, which is suitable for almost all fields.

(4) Effectiveness.

4. Checklist

This method is suitable for almost any type of creative activities and occasions, it is also known as the "mother of innovative approach". It is to list all the problems need to be solved and check them one by one, inducing a variety of creative vision from every angle, in order to promote inventions, innovations or solutions for working problems. Practice has proved that this is a way to develop a large number of creative imaging.

Checklist is a way of thinking multi-channel, including the creation of the following techniques: migration act method, introduction method, change method, add method, alternative method, reduction method, expanding method, combination method and reverse method. It inspires people to think and solve problems in a careful and multi-channel way, and is widely used in the creation, invention, innovation and enterprise management. The key of this method is keep changing, instead of focusing the sight on a certain direction or a certain point.

5. Analogy Innovation

Analogy is to compare between two things, which may be the same, or may be of different type, or even with a large difference. By comparison, we can identify their similarities, and then figure out other similarities according to the found one. So the analogy innovative method is a process full of creativity, which is conducive to play people's imagination, seek the same from the different, seek the different from the same, and generate new knowledge, get innovative results. There are many analogies, such as personified analogy, direct analogy, symbolic analogy, causal analogy, symmetric analogy, integrated analog, etc.

6. Information Intersection

Information intersection stimulates creative thinking and puts forward innovative ideas through several types of information expanding and intersecting in a certain direction. Information is the raw material of thinking, while the brain is the processing plant of information. By striking, reorganizing, overlaying, comprehending, diffusing, conversing different information, innovative ideas can be induced. To properly take advantage of information intersection, we must pay attention to grasp the following three aspects:

(1) Gather information. Many companies have set up a special agency to gather information. Networking has become the development trend of companies to gather information. Like Japan's Mitsubishi Corporation, it sets 115 overseas offices worldwide, where about 900 Japanese and 2,000 local staffs are engaged in information gathering. The focus of information gathering lies in gathering new information, because only new information reflects latest developments and results in technological, economic activities, which often has a direct stake with the enterprise.

(2) Sort information. It includes a process of cross-checking information, organizing information, accumulating information and so on.

(3) Use information. Collecting and sorting information are aimed at using the information. The key of using information includes being fast which means quickly seizing the opportunity and interaction, which means one information interacts with the other, or one field of information interacts with another one. Then we begin our thinking by combining the information collected with the preset target, in order to achieve our goals. Information intercourse can be achieved by four ways of intercourse including the body intercourse, the function expansion, hybridization, and three-dimensional dynamic way.

In short, the information intercourse is just like a magic cube. By exchanging information at all levels, it will lead to a lot of information combinations, providing millions of possibilities of innovative object.

7. Imitation Innovation

Most human inventions start from imitation, and then the original creation. Through hard thinking, we can make inventions through imitation. There are many items mimicking some of the characteristics of organisms, resulting in the formation of bionics. Imitation is not only used for engineering, arts, but also management.

【阅读资料】

创新之"过"

多数知识型或科技型企业都将创新视为企业的灵魂，视为企业发展的不竭动力。但是经过对众多企业的调研发现，创新不足是问题，盲目创新也是问题。事实上，创新对企业发展具有正反两方面的作用。创新需要管理，盲目的创新、过分的创新，可能意味着自杀。

尽管很多公司成天谈论开发革命性新产品的必要性，但真正的突破几乎总是来自充满活力的年轻初创企业。这里的主要原因很好理解，建立新市场所需要的技巧是冒险、试验和有点鲁莽的热情，这与运作成熟企业所需的技巧不同。

这样说并非否认创新是企业发展的动力和赢得竞争优势的重要手段，但企业创新不同于大学等专门科研机构的创新。专门科研机构创新的目的在于发现新知识或新技术，其制约因素主要在于由人、财、物构成的科研能力的大小。企业创新有着特殊的制约因素，那就是市场需求，包括客户需求和竞争需求。高绩效的企业创新来自市场需求导向，失去市场需求导向的创新是盲目的创新。多数拥有创新声誉的企业巨擘都深谙创新之道，但它们最好的点子往往是借鉴而来的。

过快创新

过快创新是单纯追求技术推出速度而脱离市场节奏的一类创新。不给创新成果一个相对稳定的应用过程，总是在快速不断地推陈出新，更新换代，虽然满足了技术人员的创造欲望，但会造成创新的不经济。日本的汽车企业在20世纪80年代，就品尝过汽车换型过快（平均3~4年）、研发投入过多的教训。尽管赢得了局部竞争的胜利，但让企业背上了较重的财务包袱。相比而言，英特尔公司有节奏地推出新产品的策略，就是对创新进行有效管理的成功案例。从286到586，又从奔腾到奔4，表面看来是按照摩尔定律进行的技术创新、产品换代，实际上是对市场节奏的巧妙把握，对游戏规则的灵活掌握。企业应该以市场为导向而不能以技术为导向。创新是为客户服务的，而不是给客户找麻烦的。

不仅是技术，管理创新也会有过快的问题。深圳华为公司提出的"先僵化，再优化，后固化"的思路，就是为了尽量避免管理学习过程中过快创新可能带来的问题。

过早创新

企业存在的理由是满足客户需要，但更高调和更激进的企业往往提出要"创造客户需求"。尽管俗话说"买的不如卖的精"，但是这种假定自己比客户聪明的想法亦有问题。比如，由于过去超前的技术或产品创新是为少数超前客户服务的，它可能导致短期内无法形成有效的、有规模的市场，美国铱星系统公司的失败即是典型案例。跟不上客户需求是问题，超越了客户需求同样是问题，正所谓"领先一步是先进，领先三步是先烈"。

过早创新产生的理由之一往往是强调所谓的长远目标或长期战略，而忽视了企业近期的生存需要，于是当欣赏新技术所描绘的美好愿景的人数过少时，创新可能会演变成"找死"的盲动主义。企业创新必须注意短期市场和长期市场的协调，"明天是美好的，但别在黎明前死去"，活着才是硬道理。

企业创新必须以客户需求为导向。北京中关村流行的一句话说得很好，"卖出去才是硬道理"。当企业陷入不得不批评竞争对手产品技术落后，不久就会被淘汰，而客户却不大以为然的时候，就得反思企业是否偏离了客户需求导向。

以技术优势而自豪的高科技企业更容易滑向技术导向。北大方正激光照排产品的成功就是因为竞争对手过分得意于产品在某些特殊功能上的技术优势，比如能够排版微积分、苯环等，错误地将目标客户集中在了特定出版社等狭窄领域，从而给北大方正留出了报社等广阔的市场空间。背离客户需求的创新是盲目创新，脱离有效客户需求的创新同样是盲目创新。

深圳华为企业可以说是非常崇尚技术创新的企业，但它为自己确定的宏观商业模式是"产品发展的路标是客户需求导向，企业管理的目标是流程化组织建设"，再次确认了走客户需求导向不走技术导向的成长之路。

过度创新

过快和过早创新主要是从技术和产品角度看的，掉进这两个陷阱可能是因为竞争所致，与企业过强的技术导向有密切关系，但过度创新则与技术因素无关。

过度创新指的是企业在组织或管理变革方面过于激烈的、疾风骤雨式的创新。由于创新或变革对原有组织或管理系统造成过大冲击，使组织失去了起码的稳定性和连续性，这是很多企业创新或变革失败的主要原因之一。企业规模越大，其管理结构、流程以及人际关系就越复杂，适宜搞改良，不适宜闹革命；适宜循序渐进，不适宜大的震动。华为总裁任正非形象地将这种创新叫"文火慢慢烤"，联想柳传志先生则将它比喻为"绕大弯"。

管理进步的标志之一就是流程化，流程化可以减少和避免随意性。在某种意义上，小企业怕超速扩张，大企业怕随意变革。

避免过度创新有一些原则可循。比如，衔接有序原则：防止变革过程中出现决策和责任真空，在新组织完全建立前，旧的决策模式不完全消失，保障业务变革有序进行；继承发扬原则：反对"一朝天子一朝臣"，反对新干部上台否认前人的管理，反对随意地破坏原有文化或管理的合理的内核以及与周边已形成的习惯性协调；评估论证原则：稳定发展时期不能提倡管理上的大胆探索，任何管理改进，都要以全局为目标来进行评估，任何变革都必须经相关委员会充分论证后批准。

企业要保持持续的创新，还需要建立创新的激励和保障机制。为创新分配充足的资源是必要条件，同时不能忽视对创新成果的正确考评。比如，创新成果必须是为企业创造效益的，而不是为科研人员晋升职称的，创新成果必须是不断积累成文档的，而不能只是储存于员工头脑中。

总之，创新是实现企业持续成长的一种手段，而不是目的。因此，创新本身没有对错，但创新的结果可能是吃到馅饼，也可能是掉进陷阱。有研究表明，中小企业的特殊优势在于新产品、新技术的创新能力，大企业的特殊优势不是创新能力而是对各种资源的吸收和整合能力。所以，对于志在做大、做强、做久的企业来讲，创新重要，如何管理创新、避免创新陷阱更为重要。

【本章提要】

● 创新是生产要素的重新组合，其目的是获取潜在的利润。管理创新是管理者根据内外环境的变化而采用某种新的、更有效的资源整合与协调方式来促进管理系统效率和效益目标实现的过程。

● 创新是一个复杂的过程，一般经历寻找机会—提出构想—迅速行动—坚持不懈这四个阶段。企业家、管理人员、员工都是创新的主体。

● 系统在运行中的创新要涉及许多方面，包括观念创新、目标创新、技术创新、制度创新、结构创新、环境创新、文化创新。

● 创新活动是一个充满创意和风险的过程，既要适应市场需求的发展状况，适应本企业的创新条件，又需要运用适当的策略和方法。

【关键词】

创新（Innovation）　　　　　　　　　适度创新（Appropriate Innovation）

技术创新（Technology Innovation）　　管理创新（Management Innovation）

头脑风暴法（Brain Storming）　　　　综摄法（Synectics）

检核表法（Checklist Method）

【复习与思考】

1. 全面理解创新的含义和特征。

2. 创新的作用和原则有哪些？

3. 创新的主体包括什么？

4. 管理创新的主要内容有哪些？

5. 创新的策略与方法有哪些？

【研究与讨论】

1. 创新对一个民族和企业的意义如何？

2. 维持与创新的关系是什么？

3. 创新型企业家应具备怎样的素质和能力？

【实践演练】

1. 10 人一组，运用头脑风暴法提出一些改进学习方法的新点子。

2. 调查一家管理创新工作富有成效的企业，总结其经验，并写出调查报告。

3. 辩论：思维创新是管理创新的前提。

【管理模拟】

1. 实地或网上调查一家企业管理创新成功或失败的例子，深入剖析其原因，写出调查报告。

2. 组建一家点子公司，为其他企业提供创新的建议。

【本章案例】

海尔：创造新动力

创新是企业文化的灵魂，是保持企业持续发展的动力。多年来，海尔不满足于自己的成就，不断地打破已有的成功经验，追求创新，重塑自我，从五个方面建立了自己独有的创新文化。

一、战略创新：寻找企业的出路

海尔人认为，"没有思路就没有出路"。在这一观念指导下，创造了对海尔最有利而又富有远见的发展战略。

（1）实施品牌战略。1984—1991年海尔首先实行"要么不干，要干就争第一"的品牌战略，以高质量确立了中国家电第一品牌的地位，使"海尔，中国造"享誉全球。

（2）实施多元化经营战略。1992—1998年海尔开始实施多元化战略，将海尔产品由冰箱扩展到冰柜、洗衣机和空调。在进一步扩大"白色家电"生产规模的同时将产品扩展到以电视为代表的"黑色家电"和以电脑为代表的"灰色家电"领域。

（3）实施资本经营战略。在品牌战略过程中海尔成功地进行了资本运作。利用海尔的文化盘活有形资产，利用海尔的品牌进行低成本扩张，使海尔先后兼并18个企业（从800亩海尔工业园到青岛、莱阳，进一步南下湖北、安徽、贵州、广东等地）无一失败，共盘活包括5亿元亏损在内的18亿元资产，现在海尔的产品已由1984年的一个冰箱型号发展到拥有门类齐全的家电类69大类，10 800多个规格品种的产品群。

（4）实施国际化战略。1998年，海尔在自有品牌家电占国内市场30%并已预见入世在即的时候，开始实施国际化战略。其规划是1/3国内生产国内销售，1/3国内生产国外销售，1/3国外生产国外销售，充分利用全球市场资源，完成由"海尔的国际化到国际化的海尔"的跨越。

在实施过程中，海尔落实战略部署的三步棋：一是海尔坚持"先难后易"的战略部署，即先用品牌开拓国外市场，凭质量敲开世界家电市场的大门，打"知名度"，然后按照"先有市场，后建工厂"的原则开办海外工厂，二是海尔采取"三融一创"即融资、融智、融文化的办法，利用当地的资源和资本，用海尔的文化创出本土化的世界品牌。1999年4月，海尔用这个办法成功地在美国南卡州建起了占地600亩的美国海尔工业园，让美国人有史以来第一次接受了中国式的企业管理和文化。三是海尔又用两三年的时间，在全球主要经济区建起了有竞争力的贸易网络、设计网络、制造网络、营销与服务网络。到目前为止，海尔在全球已有贸易中心56个，设计中心15个（其中海外8个），工业园7个（包括生产3种以上的产品，占地600亩以上），工厂46个（其中海外10个），服务网点11 976个，营销网点53 000个（其中海外38 000个）。

二、管理创新：确保战略创新的成功

海尔的管理创新是从实际出发，由低要求向高要求推进。

（1）在创业伊始，海尔曾制定了"管理13条"，其中有一条是不准随地大小便，可见当时管理基础之差。

（2）经过加强管理有了初步成效之后，海尔创造了"日事日毕，日清日高"的管理法。这个方法获得当时国家级企业管理现代化成果一等奖。这项管理方法要求每个职工在完成好当天的工作外，还必须以每天提高1%的观念，在原有的基础上提高质量或增加数量，或者降低成本，改进工艺，革新技术。现在"日清日高"变成了每个员工的岗位职责，成为全公司的行为准则。每个班组都张贴有每日、每周、每月的进展情况，每个员工的奉献以"岗位明星""改进明星""革新明星""创新明星"等称号公布于众，并给予物质奖励。

（3）用领导文化推动群众文化。海尔公司的领导从首席职行官、总裁到各事业部部长都必须坚持每周六的上午齐集于"海尔大学"共同分析新形势，研究新问题，从观念、战略到策略、方法，从科学技术到管理制度，互助互学，提高领导素质和管理能力。

（4）海尔从 1999 年开始，创造了模拟市场对企业内部进行管理的方法，即"下一个工序是上一个工序的用户"的"海尔内部市场链"管理体系。这个方法获得国家现代企业管理成果特等奖，被收进了瑞士国际管理学院案例库。

这套管理系统是以海尔文化的"日清日高"为基础，以订单信息为中心，带动物流和资金流运行，以达到"三个零"（质量零缺陷、服务零距离、零运营成本）为目标的业务流程。它激励员工创造并完成有价值的订单，使员工人人对用户负责，"绝不对市场说不"，实现了企业管理的创新飞跃。

三、技术创新：企业实力的坚强后盾

（1）在指导思想上坚持"市场的难题就是技术开发的课题"的原则。开发的成果要接受市场的检验。

（2）在创新的定位上要坚持国际化，盯住全球行业先进水平进行创新。作为保证条件，他们建立了国际化信息网络、国际化科技开发网络和国际认证中心。经海尔认证的产品，现在可以直接进入 48 个国家和地区。

（3）在创新宣传上还要坚持超前性，保持观念、技术、产品结构调整的三个超前。海尔由白色家电向黑色、灰色家电的拓展就是在看到数字技术、网络技术将使家电、电子、电讯"三电一体"为企业带来新的竞争平台和商机的情况下，对产品结构不断进行的超前调整。

（4）在创新策略上，着眼于利用全球科技资源。除了在国内建立一批有独立经营能力的高科技开发公司外，还在东京、里昂、洛杉矶、阿姆斯特丹等 6 个国外城市建立了海外开发设计分部，并与一些世界著名大跨国公司建立了技术联盟，2000 年海尔研发投入资金占集团销售收入的 6%。目前，海尔平均每个工作日开发 1.2 个新产品，完成和申报 2.3 个专利项目。

四、组织创新：一切行动的根基

（1）实行事业部制。在 20 世纪 80 年代，海尔同其他企业一样实行的是纵向一体化的"工厂制"。集团成立后，从多元化经营和规模扩大的需要出发，实施"事业部制"，集团由总部、事业本部、事业部、分厂四个层次组成，分别承担战略决策与投资中心、专业化发展中心、利润中心和成本中心职能，海尔称其为"联合舰队"体制。

（2）重视物流、资金流与商流。这一体制能调动事业本部的积极性，分散风险，但各事业本部采购服务自成系统，资源利用率不高，所以海尔又成立了物流、资金流、商流（分国内商流、国外商流）四个本部，统一调配全球的供应资源和全球的用户资源。尤其是商流本部成立后，建立了科学有序的客户管理系统。1 万多个销售网点遍布全国城乡，30 多个电话中心 24 小时运行。只要用户打一个电话或浏览一下海尔网站，就可得到产品开发、制造、售前、售中、售后、回访六个环节情况的回答和完善的服务。2000 年 4 月，海尔还成立了海尔电子商务有限公司，截至 2001 年 4 月，海尔网上交易额已达到 105 亿元。

五、观念创新：一切创新之源

（1）充分理解和认识"观念创新是一切创新之源"。海尔的每一步发展、每一个成绩都是从观念创新开始的。他们认为要做成人们认为不可能做成的事，首先必须创新观念。当市场饱和、产品供大于求时，海尔提出了"创造需求、创造市场""只有淡季的思想，没有淡季的市场"的市场观念，为了使自己的产品在市场竞争中永远领先，海尔提出了"必须在别人否定你的新产品之前自己否定自己"的创新产品观念。为了取得用户的信任，海尔提出"用户永远是对的""为用户服务真诚到永远"的服务观念。为开拓国际市场，海尔提出了"无内不稳，无外不强"的发展观念。为了给每个员工创造显示品德和才华的空间，海尔提出了"人人是人才，赛马不相马"的人才观念。当取得一定成绩，有了知名度后，为了防止盲目骄傲，海尔又提出了"永远战战兢兢，永远如履薄冰"的生存观念。

（2）观念创新要有个震撼作用的大举动。海尔的观念创新是从 1984 年开始的。当时张瑞敏接到群众来信，反映海尔冰箱质量有缺陷，调查发现库内还有 76 台质量有缺陷的冰箱。当时对人们来讲冰箱是非常昂贵的东西，一台冰箱的价格相当于职工两年的工资，因此很多人希望把冰箱处理给大家。但张瑞敏认为要彻底改变旧的质量观念，就宣布谁制造的就由谁把冰箱砸掉，同时宣布"这个是我的责任，扣我的工资，以后谁出问题就扣谁的工资"。这一砸，惊醒了海尔人，使海尔人树立了"有缺陷的产品就是废品""用户满意的产品才是合格的产品"的质量观。

六、五大创新之间的关系

海尔的创新是系统的、全面的、无时无刻不在进行的。

五个创新的关系是：战略创新是方向，管理创新是基础，技术创新是手段，组织创新是保证，观念创新是先导。

海尔就是靠这些创新机制的协调、聚合使企业从总体上把握消费、快速反应、创造市场的能力不断增强，使海尔获得丰厚的回报，并迅速强大起来。

思考问题：

1. 海尔连续高速增长，其成功得益于什么？

2. 海尔五大创新的内容主要体现在哪些方面？其五大创新关系又是怎样的？

【本章参考文献】

［1］周三多：《管理学》，北京：中国高等教育出版社 2000 年版。

［2］杨明刚：《现代实用管理学——知识·技能·案例·实训》，上海：华东理工大学出版社 2005 年版。

［3］侯先荣、吴奕湖：《企业创新管理理论与实践》，北京：电子工业出版社 2003 年版。

［4］周健临：《管理学教程》，上海：上海财经大学出版社 2001 年版。

［5］陈传明、周小虎：《管理学》，北京：清华大学出版社 2003 年版。